READER'S DIGEST
BOOK OF
Amazing Facts

READER'S DIGEST
BOOK OF
Amazing
Facts

A Children's Guide
to the World

PUBLISHED BY
THE READER'S DIGEST ASSOCIATION LIMITED
LONDON NEW YORK SYDNEY MONTREAL

Reader's Digest Book of Amazing Facts

Edited and designed by Toucan Books Limited,
Fourth Floor, 32-38 Saffron Hill, London EC1N 8FH
Written by David Burnie, Linda Gamlin,
Douglas Palmer, Alex Martin, Tim Healey,
Robin Hosie, Mary Emma Baxter, Michael Wright
Edited by Robert Sackville West,
Helen Douglas-Cooper, Andrew Kerr-Jarrett,
David Scott-Macnab, Jane MacAndrew
Designed by Bradbury and Williams
Picture research by Christine Vincent
Consultants David Burnie, Kate Petty,
Peter Nixon, Lynda Nixon

For Reader's Digest

Editors   Henrietta Heald, Sarah Bloxham,
Caroline Boucher, Alastair Holmes
Production Controllers   Kathy Brown, Jane Holyer

Reader's Digest General Books

Editorial Director   Cortina Butler
Art Director   Nick Clark
Executive Editor   Julian Browne
Style Editor   Ron Pankhurst

ISBN 0 276 42434 4

Contents

How to use this book

T he book is divided into five sections and a Fact File. Within the sections, each double-page spread deals with a different subject. Subjects are covered in question and answer form to give you easy access to information.

Fact File
This quick-reference section provides answers to the basic Who What When Where questions.

Main heading
This always appears on the left-hand page.

Page number

Cross references
These lead you into a series of related topics, where you can discover more about the subject.

Introduction
This leads you into the subject covered on the spread.

Question
Questions and headings act as springboards into the subject. You can use them to dip into different topics, find the bits of knowledge you need, or learn all about something that interests you.

Answer
The clear, detailed answers present information in easy-to-read chunks, packed with facts and figures.

Picture description
Captions explain the photographs and diagrams.

Photograph
Stunning photographs bring subjects to life.

That's Amazing
Fact boxes provide unusual facts that will surprise or even astound you.

---

200 **Bridges, dams and tunnels**

🌐 Cars and bicycles p.182 · The age of the train p.184 · Houses and buildings p.198 · Fact File p.316

R oads, railways, bridges, canals, dams, tunnels and harbours are complicated to build. They have to stand up to enormous stresses, both from extreme weather conditions and heavy use. The structures, and the materials used, must be strong and last for many years. The person in charge of designing them is a civil engineer, whose calculations have to be very accurate, as many people's lives and large sums of money depend on them.

Direct line Railway tracks have to be as straight, level and stable as possible. The rails are laid on wooden or concrete 'sleepers' which sit on a thick bed of crushed rock or stones.

How are bridges built across wide rivers?
All bridges rest on large pillars known as piers. Sometimes these piers have to be built in a river. As building underwater is impractical, a dry area has to be created. To do this in shallow water, interlocking sheets of steel are driven into the riverbed to form a waterproof circle. The water is then pumped out of the enclosure, and a pier is built inside on foundations resting on rock below the riverbed. In deeper water, a giant concrete tube is used instead.

How are tunnels made?
First, geologists (experts in rocks and how they are formed) carry out a survey to find out what kinds of rock or soil lie in the area of the tunnel. Then the best route is chosen. Tunnels through soft rock like chalk are excavated by laser-guided drilling machines. If the rock is hard, it is blasted out with explosives. Supports are put up as quickly as possible to prevent the roof from collapsing. Temporary railways or roads are built inside the tunnels to remove the broken rock and to carry workers in and out.

High dam The Hoover Dam on the Colorado River is the highest dam in the United States.

Load bearing
Bridges carry so much weight that they have to be built on solid rock or on concrete rafts to spread the load widely. A series of short spans, forming a viaduct, can also spread the load.

Why don't dams burst?
Engineers design dams to suit the size and site of the river. Dams across wide rivers are known as embankment dams; they are made of soil, clay, stone and cement. Dams in narrow river gorges have thick concrete walls, built in a curve or supported by buttresses to give them extra strength. All dams have deep foundations to prevent water from flowing under them, and to anchor them against the weight of the water. Another safety feature is the spillway, which channels water from heavy rains around the sides of the dam.

THAT'S AMAZING
LONGEST BRIDGES
The world's longest bridge is the Pontchartrain Causeway in Louisiana, USA, finished in 1969. It is 38 km (24 miles) long and is supported by 9000 concrete piers. The longest suspension bridge in the world is the 1991 m (6532 ft) Akashi-Kaikyo Bridge in Japan, completed in 1998.

Section title and symbol
These appear in the top right-hand corner. They help you find the section you want quickly.

Section symbols
Each section of the book has its own symbol.

 PLANET EARTH

 THE LIVING WORLD

 THE HUMAN BODY

 SCIENCE AND TECHNOLOGY

 THE HUMAN WORLD

 FACT FILE

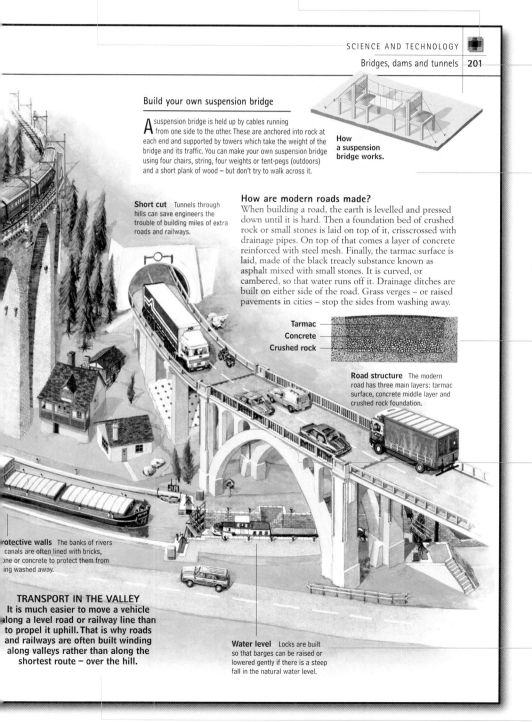

SCIENCE AND TECHNOLOGY

Bridges, dams and tunnels | 201

Build your own suspension bridge

A suspension bridge is held up by cables running from one side to the other. These are anchored into rock at each end and supported by towers which take the weight of the bridge and its traffic. You can make your own suspension bridge using four chairs, string, four weights or tent-pegs (outdoors) and a short plank of wood – but don't try to walk across it.

How a suspension bridge works.

Short cut Tunnels through hills can save engineers the trouble of building miles of extra roads and railways.

How are modern roads made?
When building a road, the earth is levelled and pressed down until it is hard. Then a foundation bed of crushed rock or small stones is laid on top of it, crisscrossed with drainage pipes. On top of that comes a layer of concrete reinforced with steel mesh. Finally, the tarmac surface is laid, made of the black treacly substance known as asphalt mixed with small stones. It is curved, or cambered, so that water runs off it. Drainage ditches are built on either side of the road. Grass verges – or raised pavements in cities – stop the sides from washing away.

Tarmac
Concrete
Crushed rock

Road structure The modern road has three main layers: tarmac surface, concrete middle layer and crushed rock foundation.

Protective walls The banks of rivers and canals are often lined with bricks, stone or concrete to protect them from being washed away.

TRANSPORT IN THE VALLEY
It is much easier to move a vehicle along a level road or railway line than to propel it uphill. That is why roads and railways are often built winding along valleys rather than along the shortest route – over the hill.

Water level Locks are built so that barges can be raised or lowered gently if there is a steep fall in the natural water level.

Main heading
This is repeated on the right-hand page to help you find the subject you are looking for.

Feature box
This provides additional facts, intriguing stories, or ideas for things to do yourself.

Diagram
Diagrams, tables, charts and maps provide extra information and help explain complicated subjects.

The big picture
A large, detailed picture illustrates the main subject.

Labels
These point out the important parts of the picture.

The big picture story
This tells you what the main picture is about.

Planet Earth

🌐 Our star, the Sun p.14 · The birth of the planets p.16 · Force and motion p.150 · Fact File p.264

If you look into the night sky, what you see is the Universe – or at least part of it. The groups of stars, known as galaxies, the planets and their moons, the floating lumps of rock, called asteroids, even the cold empty spaces between them, were formed as many as 15 billion years ago in a sudden flash known as the 'Big Bang'.

How did the Universe begin?

Around 15 billion years ago, all the matter from which our Universe is made was packed into a superhot, superdense fireball less than 1 cm (½in) wide. This fireball flew apart in a violent explosion known as the 'Big Bang', and within a millionth of a second, it had grown to some 16 billion km (10 billion miles) across. It continued to expand, but as it did so it cooled – just as steam rising from a kettle cools as it expands.

Atoms, the building blocks of our Universe, began to form. Over the course of the next few billion years, the force of gravity drew matter together into clumps to form galaxies and stars.

Looking into the past

Like everything else, light takes time to travel across space. Light from the Moon takes just over a second to reach us, and light from the Sun about eight minutes. When you look into the sky, then, you are not seeing the present but the past – a wave of light that may have set out several thousand years ago. Our ability to look into the past is limited by our eyesight. But with modern telescopes, which can pick up not only light waves but also X-rays and radio waves, we can see even farther back – more than 10 billion years. In 1964, two American scientists detected a microwave 'hiss' coming from all directions of the sky. They realised that this hiss must be radiation released in the Big Bang still echoing throughout the Universe.

A microwave map of the sky, compiled from data gathered by satellite, glows with light created when the Universe began.

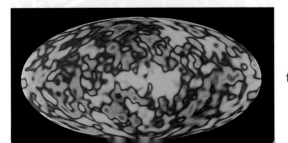

Big Bang During the Big Bang, the fireball flies apart, expanding rapidly and then cooling to form the first atoms – the simplest ones within three minutes, more complex ones taking 500 000 years.

Star birth In the first billion years or so, clouds of atoms of hydrogen and helium gas thicken into the beginnings of galaxies and stars.

Universe now Today, clusters of stars form different-shaped galaxies and groups of galaxies. The heat of the Big Bang has dwindled to a faint background radiation.

HOW IT ALL BEGAN
The story of the Universe is a remarkable one. It all began 15 billion years ago with a flash and a bang – called the Big Bang. A fireball blew apart, cooled and then clumped together as galaxies and stars, including – eventually – our own, the Sun.

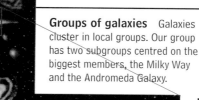

Groups of galaxies Galaxies cluster in local groups. Our group has two subgroups centred on the biggest members, the Milky Way and the Andromeda Galaxy.

Milky Way The Milky Way is a spiral, rather like a Catherine wheel, burning with the light of more than 200 billion stars. Our Sun lies about two-thirds of the way out from the centre.

Sun Our Sun, the central star of the Solar System, is a luminous ball of burning gas. Its massive gravity guides the nine planets, including the Earth, around the sky.

Earth in space The Earth is the third closest planet to the Sun. It is unique in the Solar System in having vast oceans of liquid water and an oxygen-rich atmosphere.

Our place in space

Less than 500 years ago, people thought that the Earth was the centre of the Universe. It is only within the last few hundred years that we have learnt that the Earth is just one of nine planets revolving around the Sun.

What's more, our Sun is just one of more than 200 billion stars in our galaxy, the Milky Way; and the Milky Way is one of countless billions of unknown galaxies within the Universe.

Will the Universe ever come to an end?

At present, the Universe is still expanding – as it has done ever since the Big Bang. Whether it will continue to do so is one of the big unanswered questions of astronomy – the science of the stars. There are two main theories about what will happen. The Big Chill idea suggests that the expansion will continue for ever with the galaxies, stars and planets growing ever farther apart, darker and colder; eventually even the stars will go out. Alternatively, some astronomers believe that the force of gravity in the Universe is such that the galaxies will eventually begin to fall back on each other and that the Universe will collapse, in a superhot moment known as the Big Crunch.

THAT'S AMAZING

EXPANDING SPACE

The farther away a galaxy is, the faster it moves. This revelation led to the discovery that the Universe is expanding. It was made in 1929 by American Edwin Hubble. The Hubble Space Telescope is named after him.

Our star, the Sun

🔄 The making of the Universe p.12 · The birth of the planets p.16 · Fact File p.268

The Sun, a glowing globe of hot gas thousands of times bigger than the Earth, lies at the heart of our Solar System. Yet it is a pretty ordinary star. It is just one among 200 billion in our galaxy alone. Scientists estimate that it is about halfway through its life, having formed – along with the Earth and the other planets – around 5 billion years ago. Although it is 1 392 000 km (865 000 miles) wide, it is middle-weight in star terms and of only medium brightness.

1 Five billion years ago
A spinning cloud of dust and gas collapsed under its own weight. As it did so, the centre began to heat up.

Birthplace of stars
Pillars of gas and dust, called nebula, contain the raw material for new stars.

Why is the Sun yellow?

The colour of a star depends on how hot it is – and this, in turn, depends on its size and age. Our Sun is a star of medium size and brightness, with a surface temperature of about 5500°C (10 000°F), which makes it look yellow. As it gets older and uses up more of its energy, the surface temperature will drop to about 4000°C (7200°F) and it will look red. When it has exhausted almost all of its energy, the Sun will collapse and heat up briefly in a white flare.

2 A star is born As the cloud continued to spin, it flattened into a disc. At the centre of the spinning disc (our future Solar System) lay the embryo star, our future Sun, which began to glow as it continued heating up.

3 Full ignition When the temperature at the centre of the embryo star reached about 15 million°C (27 million°F), nuclear reactions began turning hydrogen into helium, causing it to radiate heat and light.

Colour code Very hot stars look bluish-white (left); cooler ones look yellow; and cold ones look red.

What makes the Sun shine?

Light from the Sun radiates through the entire Solar System. This light is generated in the core of the Sun, where temperatures reach around 15 million°C (27 million°F), as hydrogen gas is converted into another gas, called helium, in a series of thermonuclear explosions, billions of times more powerful than the biggest nuclear bombs: a mere pinhead of these gases would be hot enough to ignite everything for 100 km (60 miles) around. The hot gases churn slowly towards the Sun's surface, where the burning solar gas shines for millions of miles into space.

4 Our Sun today
Energy generated in the core of the Sun radiates to the surface in great churning currents. At the surface, the temperature is more than 5500°C (10 000°F), and billions of tons of hot gas flare into space.

6 Star death The Sun will eventually collapse, squeezing the last particles of fuel so tightly that it will reheat and glow bright white. At this stage, a star is known as a white dwarf.

MAKING THE SUN

The Universe is made up of countless clouds of gas and dust. Around 5 billion years ago, one of these swirling clouds formed a middling-sized star – our Sun. The energy released by its burning gas provides the light and warmth necessary for life on Earth.

The star dust inside us all

When our Sun was formed 5 billion years ago, temperatures reached 15 million°C. In a chain of nuclear reactions, atoms of carbon released enormous amounts of energy, creating the building blocks of life. The carbon, hydrogen, nitrogen and oxygen from which our own bodies are made were created billions of years ago. Similar elements can be identified in the fragments of meteorites that have crash-landed on Earth and which are our closest records of conditions in the early Solar System.

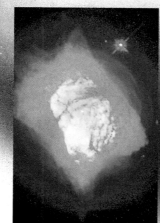

Approaching the end
A white dwarf forms in the centre of a collapsing star.

A piece of meteorite that fell to Earth on Christmas Eve, 1965.

Will the Sun last for ever?

Stars last a long time, but not for ever. Our Sun probably reached its peak brightness about 800 million years ago, and should continue to glow with the same intensity for another 1.5 billion years before beginning to fade. Its decline will be a slow process. First, in about 4 billion years, it will grow into a huge red giant star, swallowing the Earth and the inner planets. Then it will collapse into a white dwarf star before cooling and becoming extinct.

5 Tomorrow's Sun? When the Sun has burnt up the fuel at its centre, it will start to expand rapidly and cool down, and it will become a red giant.

THAT'S AMAZING

BLACK HOLES

Massive stars, ten to a hundred times bigger than our Sun, have a life story different from the one illustrated here. They eventually explode, creating a supernova. All the matter from which they are made may collapse back on itself under gravity. Not even light can escape from the collapsing star. It becomes a 'black hole' invisible to even the most powerful telescope.

🌐 Our star, the Sun p.14 · Man on the Moon p.18 ·
Spinning Earth p.22 · Fact File p.268

The nine planets, including Earth, that form our Solar System are accompanied through space by 63 moons, dozens of comets, and hundreds of thousands of lumps of rock that never grew into planets. All of them are held together and guided on their journeys by the Sun, which weighs almost 1000 times as much as the rest of the Solar System put together.

Early Solar System.

Specks of dust collide.

Blobs of gas and dust shrink and solidify.

THE MAKING OF THE EARTH

After Mercury and Venus, Earth is the third planet from the Sun. This is how geologists think the Earth has developed over the past 4.6 billion years. The whole planet and a close-up of the surface are shown for each stage.

Where did the planets come from?

Five or six billion years ago, a disc-shaped cloud of dust and gas in our Milky Way galaxy began to collapse inwards towards the centre – forming the Sun. One theory suggests that specks of dust in the gas cloud around the Sun kept bumping and clumping into each other until they formed the planets.

Another theory claims that the gas cloud broke up into large blobs, which got smaller and harder, forming the planets.

Formation of the planets
The planets are all different. Some probably formed mainly from colliding specks of dust, and others from collapsing blobs of gas and dust.

Beginnings
Particles of dust and rock collided and clumped together to form the beginnings of the Earth (right).

4.6-4.2 billion years ago
Meteorites crashed into the Earth's liquid surface (below). The heat from these collisions caused the rock in the growing planet to melt. Heavier metals, such as iron, sank towards the core, while lighter materials rose to the surface.

4.2-3.8 billion years ago As the Earth began to cool, its surface congealed to form a crust over the semiliquid layers beneath (left). Heat in the Earth's centre created huge volcanoes that poured out lava onto the surface (below left). Meteorites continued to bombard the planet.

Science fact or fiction?

Mars has often been thought to be inhabited by alien beings. In 1894 the American amateur astronomer Percival Lowell mapped networks of 500 'canals', joined by 'oases', over the surface of the planet. He thought that they must have been dug by Martians to water their dry and dusty landscape.

From the close observation of the space probe Viking 1 in 1976, we know that there are 'canal-like' structures on the surface of Mars, like the huge 4500 km (2800 mile) long 'Mariner Valley'. We also know that these 'canals' formed naturally (like our own river valleys). The 'oases' are in fact huge volcanoes. One, called Olympus Mons, is the largest yet discovered in the Solar System at 25 km (15 miles) high.

An alien meets an astronaut in a 1940s illustration.

Is there life on other planets?

Scientists reckon that the chances of life somewhere else in the Universe are high enough to spend hundreds of millions of dollars searching for it, but they are more doubtful about extraterrestrial life in our own Solar System. Life depends on two-dozen chemical elements, of which carbon, hydrogen, oxygen, nitrogen, sulphur and phosphorus are the most important. For life to continue, light and warmth are needed. Mars has the right chemical ingredients and may once have had the right conditions. A 4.5 billion-year-old meteorite from Mars, found in Antarctica, contains what some scientists think is a fossilised microbe that may have lived on the 'Red Planet'.

Conditions now, including subzero temperatures, are not suitable for life on Mars. They may, however, be kinder on Europa, one of Jupiter's moons. Satellites have photographed ancient river valleys on Europa, and there may still be water below its ice cover.

Water moon? Cracks crisscross the ice floes forming the surface of Europa. There may be water beneath.

3.8–2.5 billion years ago The hot gases and water vapour that spewed from the Earth's volcanoes cooled and condensed into clouds – the Earth's first atmosphere (left). There were thunderstorms and torrential rains. Water – in the form of rivers, lakes and oceans – appeared for the first time (below left). Primitive bacteria – the first signs of life – appeared.

How was the Earth formed?

Scientists believe that the Earth formed from dust particles that clumped together to form lumps, which collided and formed larger lumps and clusters, gradually building into a planet. Temperatures rose to more than 5000°C (9000°F) – enough to melt the early Earth into a churning cauldron. As the Earth started to cool, the surface formed a rocky crust. But deep inside the Earth, temperatures are still 4500°C (8100°F) and the rocks are molten – rising to the surface most spectacularly when a volcano erupts.

2.5 billion–600 million years ago The crust split into mobile plates that began to resemble the continents (left and below).

THAT'S AMAZING

TIGHT SQUEEZE

In space, people grow larger – by up to 5 cm (2 in) – because there is no gravity to pull their body parts downwards. This increase in size can cause problems. On one Shuttle mission, the astronauts found they had grown so much that they could hardly squeeze into a tight-fitting chair that they were supposed to sit in for an important experiment.

Man on the Moon

🌑 Comets, meteors and asteroids p.20 ·
Travelling in space p.192 · Fact File p.270

The Earth has only one moon orbiting around it. Our Moon is a dry and dusty place, pockmarked with craters. Once, there may have been life there, but no traces have yet been found. The only way that the Moon might support life in the future is if it comes from Earth: a manned lunar space station would provide a useful launch site for exploring our Solar System and beyond. But life could only be sustained if there is water on the Moon.

How was the Moon formed?

The Earth and the Moon are locked together in their joint orbit of the Sun; and they are made from rock of the same age – about 4.5 billion years old. They are so similar that it is likely the Moon was originally part of the Earth, but was torn from it when the Earth collided with another planet. The Earth's surface was torn apart in the collision, and gas, molten lava and rocks from the Earth's interior were thrown into space. These cooled and condensed into a single ball with a hard crust orbiting the Earth as our Moon.

THAT'S AMAZING

ASTRONAUT ATHLETICS

The Moon's gravity is only a sixth as strong as that of the Earth. This means that, on the Moon, the world high-jump champion could leap nearly 15 m (48 ft), and the long-jump record would be about 54 m (180 ft). But having to wear a spacesuit might limit an astronaut athlete's performance.

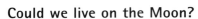

Rocks orbit Earth   **Moon orbits Earth**

Space crash To rip rock the size of the Moon from the Earth, the object that crashed into the Earth must have been the size of the planet Mars.

Object crashes into Earth

Could we live on the Moon?

The Moon has no atmosphere to protect it from the Sun's rays. It is baked during the day and frozen at night, as the day's warmth escapes into space. To survive on the Moon, humans need spacesuits for insulation and air. Food and water have to be brought from Earth. It is possible that water in the form of ice is already present at the Moon's poles. If it could be melted, algae and bacteria brought from Earth could then be grown as food.

MOON BASE

In March 1998, instruments on board the American lunar probe Prospector detected hydrogen at the Moon's poles, which indicates that there may be up to 300 million tonnes of water frozen into the Moon's surface. If this is the case, then a permanent space station on the Moon could become possible, making the exploration of deep space easier. The station would use solar panels for collecting light energy from the Sun and providing power and heat. Because of the Moon's low gravity, spacecraft taking off from the Moon towards distant parts of the Solar System would require less energy and fuel.

Deliveries A cargo lander delivers equipment and supplies.

Other moons

All the planets in the Solar System, except Mercury and Venus, have at least one moon, and Saturn has 18 or more. The smallest of Saturn's moons, Pan, is only 20 km (12 miles) in diameter, and the biggest, Titan, is 5150 km (3200 miles), which makes it larger than the planet Mercury. It also has an atmosphere with a pressure ten times greater than the Earth's. This atmosphere protects Titan from bombardment by meteorites. The Cassini spacecraft, launched in 1997, will reach Saturn in 2004 and send a probe to sample Titan's surface.

Saturn's largest moon is Titan.

Living quarters Astronauts live and work in lunar habitation modules. Each module has its own solar panels and satellite communications dish.

Moon. No wind disturbs the footprints.

In 1966, the unmanned Soviet space probe Luna 9 landed on the Moon. But it was not until three years later that the first human set foot there. On July 20, 1969, Neil Armstrong of the Apollo 11 mission landed in an area of the Moon called the Sea of Tranquillity. Armstrong descended from the lunar module, claiming 'one small step for man, one giant leap for mankind'. Thousands of samples of Moon rock and soil were collected, and hundreds of photographs taken, before Apollo 11's three-man crew returned safely to Earth. In all, only 12 people have so far set foot on the Moon.

Arrival and departure Astronauts arrive in lunar landing vehicles.

Keeping in touch Astronauts communicate with Earth via satellite.

Power Solar panels produce power for heat and for running equipment.

Comets, meteors and asteroids

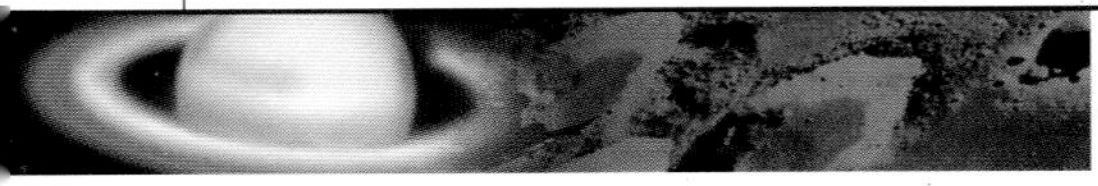

The birth of the planets p.16 · The Earth's atmosphere p.28 · Dinosaurs p.74 · Fact File p.267

In 1962 two American policemen in the little town of Manitowoc on the shores of Lake Michigan found a 9 kg (20 lb) chunk of red-hot metal embedded in the street. It was the remains of the Russian satellite, Sputnik 4. Quite apart from the man-made junk from old spacecraft, there are also various natural objects – mostly lumps of rock and metal – that approach the Earth from outer space from time to time. Most are spectacular but harmless, burning a blazing trail through the sky, but others threaten the continued existence of life on Earth.

IMPACT EARTH
The Earth is constantly bombarded by debris from space. Most is small enough to burn up as it enters the Earth's protective atmosphere. But from time to time, larger objects get through. Some explode before they reach the Earth's surface. Others collide with the Earth and puncture its crust.

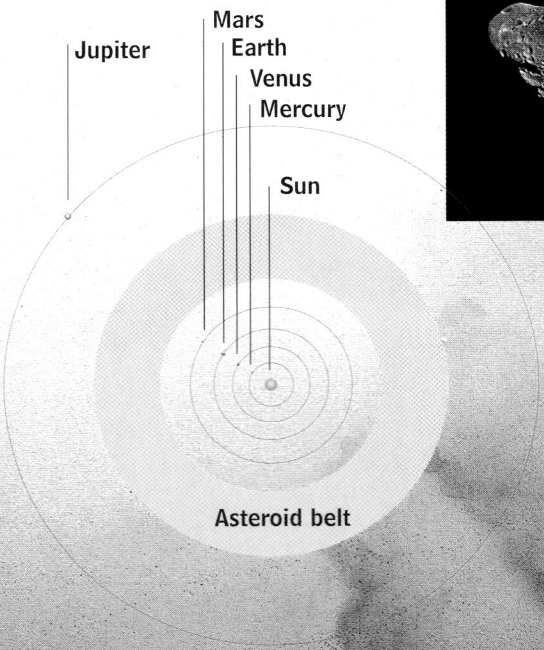

Jupiter
Mars
Earth
Venus
Mercury
Sun
Asteroid belt

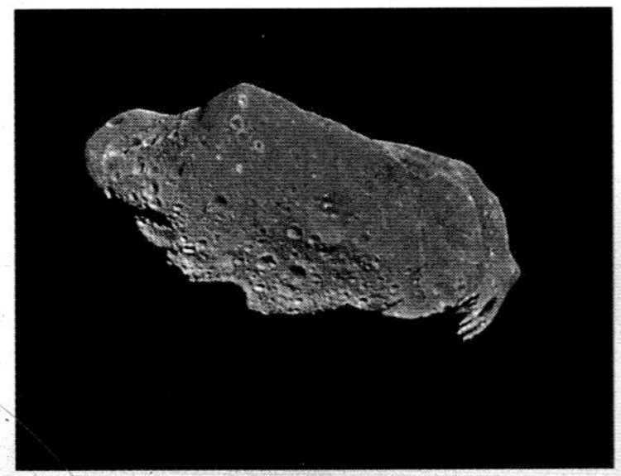

Space rock On its way to Jupiter, the space probe Galileo photographed a stony asteroid called Ida, which is 58 km (36 miles) long and 21 km (13 miles) wide.

What are asteroids?

Tens of thousands of rocks, ranging in size from 1.6 km (1 mile) to 1000 km (600 miles) across, are flying about the Solar System. They are called asteroids, and are mostly found in a belt which lies far beyond the Earth, between the orbits of Mars and Jupiter. The Earth (along with the three other inner planets of the Solar System, Mercury, Venus and Mars) is struck by an asteroid every 200 000 years – or so scientists believe. Our Moon, which does not have an atmosphere to protect it from flying objects, is marked with thousands of impact craters.

3 **Shock effects** Shock waves from the explosion travel outwards from the centre of the blast. They flatten trees and any other structures. The shock waves also trigger earthquakes and set off fires.

1 High speed from space A comet speeds through the Earth's atmosphere at up to 20 km/second (12 miles/ sec), causing the atmosphere to heat up quickly.

What happens when a meteorite hits the Earth?

About 50 tons of meteorites enter the Earth's atmosphere every day – mostly dust-sized particles, but sometimes rocks several metres wide. Most of this material is burnt up as it hurtles through the atmosphere at speeds of between 32 and 95 km/second (20-60 miles/sec): the blaze can be seen from the Earth as 'shooting' or 'falling' stars. Around 500 meteorites a year are big enough – more than a centimetre or so wide – to survive the passage through the atmosphere and do hit the Earth. At Meteor Crater in Arizona, United States, a hole 1.2 km (¾ mile) wide and 170 m (600 ft) deep was blasted out by one such meteorite about 20 000 years ago.

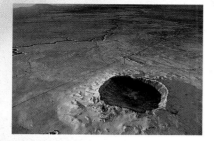

Impact zone Meteor Crater, Arizona, is the result of bombardment from space.

Comet's path A comet with a fiery tail passes through the Earth's orbit.

How often do comets come near the Earth?

Comets are like dirty snowballs – lumps of rock, ice and gas – that travel around the Solar System, guided in their orbit by the gravity of the Sun. They reappear in the night sky at regular intervals – at anything between every six years for some and every 2000 years for others, depending on the size of their orbits. Some comets shine spectacularly as they approach the Sun and ice burns off as gas vapour, forming a blazing tail up to 300 million km (200 million miles) long. Halley's comet, which reappears every 76 years, was first spotted in 239 BC; it was first illustrated in the Bayeux tapestry, which commemorated the Norman invasion of England; and was photographed most recently, on March 13, 1986, by the space probe Giotto.

2 Explosion in the sky The comet explodes 9 km (6 miles) above the Earth's surface. The heat vaporises rocks, which rain back down on Earth.

THAT'S AMAZING

DIAMOND WALL

The stone walls of the old church in Nordlingen in Germany contain millions of tiny diamonds – the size of specks of dust. These were formed from molten rock, blasted from the Earth's surface when a meteorite crashed onto it 35 million years ago.

The end of the dinosaurs?

About 65 million years ago, something strange happened to the Earth. A 'missile' 10 km (6 miles) wide – thought to be an asteroid from outer space – hit the Yucatan peninsula in Mexico. It dug a crater 12 km (7 miles) deep and 100 km (60 miles) wide. The force of the impact blasted molten droplets of rock across the Americas and set off huge firestorms. Tidal waves 1 km (½ mile) high crashed along the shores, and a dust cloud blotted out the Sun. The dinosaurs may have died out as a result.

The meteor blast reverberated over a wide area.

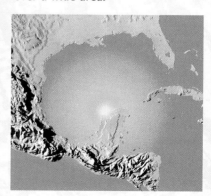

🌐 The birth of the planets p.16 · Man on the Moon p.18 · Around the coast p.38 · Fact File p.266

All the planets in the Solar System spin as they orbit the Sun, but each does so at a different speed. The Earth takes 24 hours to complete a full spin, and it is this that gives us day and night. While a place faces towards the Sun, it has daylight; while it faces away from the Sun, it has night. The planets also take different lengths of time to orbit the Sun: the Earth, for example, takes 365 days – an Earth year. While the Earth orbits the Sun, the Moon orbits the Earth, taking 29 days – a lunar month – to complete a circuit.

THE FOUR SEASONS
The Earth's axis tilts at an angle of 23.5°. This tilt, combined with Earth's orbit, gives hot summers and cold winters, and two seasons of change, spring and autumn.

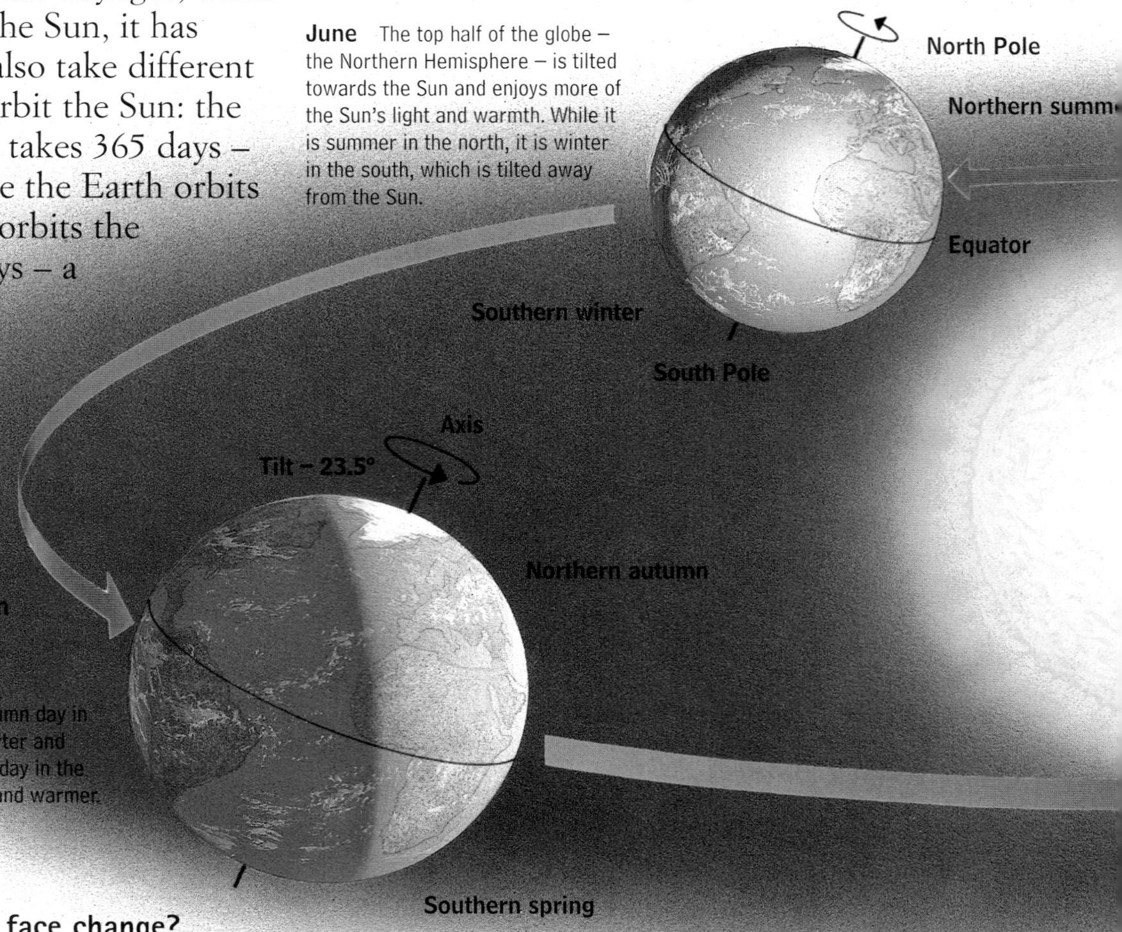

June The top half of the globe – the Northern Hemisphere – is tilted towards the Sun and enjoys more of the Sun's light and warmth. While it is summer in the north, it is winter in the south, which is tilted away from the Sun.

North Pole

Northern summer

Equator

Southern winter

South Pole

Axis

Tilt – 23.5°

Northern autumn

Orbit around Sun

September The autumn day in the north is getting shorter and cooler, while the spring day in the south is getting longer and warmer.

Southern spring

Why does the Moon's face change?
When we look into the sky, the thing that appears to change most from night to night is the Moon. But the Moon itself does not change shape. What we see is the Sun's light reflected off the Moon (the Moon generates no light of its own), and this reflection changes as the Earth and the Moon move around the Sun. At the beginning of the lunar month – the new Moon – the lit side of the Moon faces away from Earth, so we see nothing. The portion of the Moon that we can see grows, or waxes, first into a thin sliver or crescent, then into a round full Moon; then it grows smaller, or wanes, in a reversal of the process.

Waxing and waning As the Moon orbits the Earth, the portion of its lit side that can be seen from Earth changes. The black boxes show what we see of the Moon at each stage in its orbit.

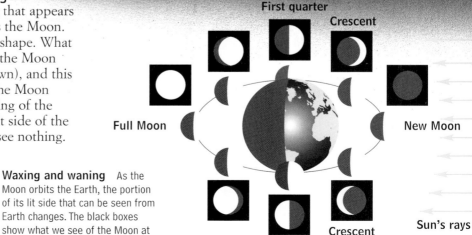

First quarter

Crescent

Full Moon

New Moon

Crescent

Last quarter

Sun's rays

What is an eclipse?

On rare occasions the Sun, the Moon and the Earth are in line with each other. The Moon blocks the light from the Sun, casting a shadow 160 km (100 miles) wide on the Earth. The affected area is plunged into darkness in what is known as a solar eclipse. Because the Earth and the Moon are on the move, solar eclipses last for only 7½ minutes.

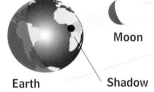

Moon

Earth

Shadow

Sun

Solar eclipse When the Earth, the Moon and the Sun are in line, the Moon casts a shadow over part of the Earth's surface.

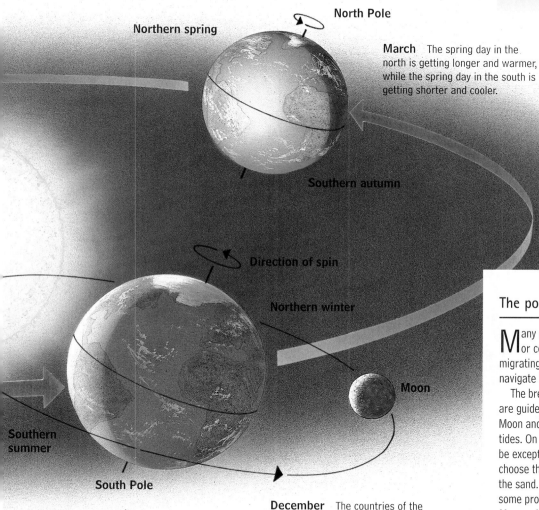

North Pole

Northern spring

March The spring day in the north is getting longer and warmer, while the spring day in the south is getting shorter and cooler.

Southern autumn

Orbit around Sun

Direction of spin

Northern winter

Moon

Southern summer

South Pole

December The countries of the Northern Hemisphere are tilted away from the Sun and get the least light and warmth. While it is winter in the north, it is summer in the south, which is now tilted towards the Sun.

The power of the Moon

Many animals use the Moon as a clock or compass. Night-flying birds, such as migrating thrushes, time their journeys to navigate by moonlight.

The breeding habits of many sea creatures are guided by the Moon. This is because the Moon and Sun cause the movement of the tides. On May and June nights the tides can be exceptionally high, and horseshoe crabs choose this time to lay their eggs in nests in the sand. High tides give the buried eggs some protection from predators.

Horseshoe crabs laying eggs.

Why does daylength change through the year?

Earth's tilt is responsible for changing daylength as well as the changing seasons. In summer, when the North Pole tilts towards the Sun, it is light there 24 hours a day. Everywhere else in the Northern Hemisphere has a relatively long day and short night. In winter, the position is reversed. The North Pole tilts away from the Sun and the Northern Hemisphere has a relatively short number of daylight hours. The same situation occurs in the Southern Hemisphere.

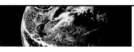

🌐 The birth of the planets p.16 · Volcanoes and earthquakes p.26 ·
Mountains and mountain ranges p.32 · Fact File p.278, 284

The centre of the Earth is very hot. This heat produces enough energy to keep the ground under your feet constantly moving as the major land masses, or continents, are carried slowly along on a lower layer of semi-liquid rock. This movement causes the continents to be pulled apart in some places, creating new oceans. In other places, they collide and create mountain ranges.

Deep heat Temperatures in South Africa's 3 km (2 mile) deep goldmines reach 49°C (120°F).

A SHIFTING WORLD

Scientists have discovered that around 250 million years ago all of today's main continents were joined together. Animals alive at that time, such as the dinosaurs, were able to move freely across this huge single landmass. By 200 million years ago, it was starting to break up.

250 million years ago
North and South America, Europe, Asia, Australia and the Antarctic formed one big continent called Pangaea. The rest of the Earth was covered by an ocean called Panthalassa.

135 million years ago
Africa and South America began to split apart as the South Atlantic opened up. The North Atlantic formed between North America and Europe.

Continental collision Below the continents are layers of rock. When continents collide, they eventually fuse together.

Mid-ocean ridge
Under the oceans, molten rock wells up between neighbouring plates and forms new crust.

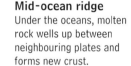

What is the Earth made of?

The Earth has an outer layer of solid rock called the crust (5-60 km/3-37 miles thick); a middle layer of hot, semiliquid rock called the mantle (2900 km/1800 miles thick); and a very hot liquid centre, the core (3470 km/2160 miles in radius). Inside the Earth, the temperature increases rapidly towards the centre, where it is nearly as hot as on the surface of the Sun.

The solid crust is broken into pieces, called plates, which float on the mantle. Some plates are covered by oceans, others by the continents. The plates fit together like a jigsaw, and the places where they meet are called plate boundaries. In some places, two plates push together and one slides over the top of the other. Along some boundaries under the ocean, the plates are moving apart.

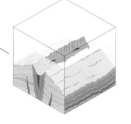

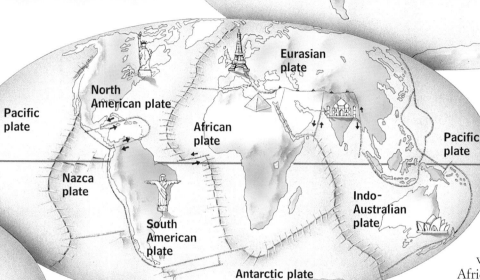

Today Movement continues along the plate boundaries.

Future world Over the next 50 million years, Africa will collide with Europe. Australia will move north. The Atlantic and Indian oceans will expand and the Pacific will shrink.

Will the continents join up again?

As long as there is heat within the Earth, the continents will continue to move. At the moment, the widening Indian Ocean is driving Africa towards Europe. This is slowly closing the Mediterranean. It is also causing volcanic eruptions and earthquakes in countries around the Mediterranean, such as Italy, Greece and Turkey. As Africa drifts away from Asia, the Red Sea is getting wider, and will gradually form a new ocean.

How do the continents move?

All over the Earth, oceans are growing bigger due to a process called seafloor spreading, which happens along the mid-ocean ridges. Heat from deep within the Earth travels outwards, creating movement in the semiliquid rock, called magma. When magma reaches the crust under the oceans, which is much thinner than the crust under the continents, it pushes against the rocks at the surface and stretches them until they crack apart.

Hot liquid rock wells up through these cracks in the ocean floor, then cools, forming new rock. The new rock cracks apart as more liquid rock pours out. So the ocean grows wider, and the continents on either side are carried farther apart. America is moving away from Europe at a rate of 5 cm (2 in) a year.

Floating apart

The movement of the continents over millions of years has had a dramatic effect on the animals that live on them. The remains of extinct animals that lived on Pangaea 250 million years ago are now widely scattered over different continents. For example, fossil remains of a reptile called *Mesosaurus* have been found buried in the ancient seabed of South America and Africa, on either side of the Atlantic. Originally, when the two continents were close together, *Mesosaurus* lived in shallow seas between them. When the Atlantic Ocean opened up, it split the *Mesosaurus* population into two groups, on either side of the deep ocean divide.

A *Mesosaurus* fossil found in South Africa.

Spinning Earth p.22 · Inside the Earth p.24 · Mountains and mountain ranges p.32 · Fact File p.276, 284

Volcanoes and earthquakes are reminders of the power locked up deep inside the Earth. Heat from the Earth's core circulates through the semiliquid layer of rock called the mantle, making it move about. This movement pushes and pulls at the solid crust, causing earthquakes and forcing lava out through weak spots in the Earth's surface.

What makes earthquakes happen?

Earthquakes happen along the boundaries of the plates that make up the Earth's crust. In some places, two plates slide past each other. In other places, plates are being pulled apart. But rocks in the Earth's crust cannot bend or stretch much, and there comes a point when they snap. The break sends shock waves through the surrounding rock in all directions, and this is felt at the surface as an earthquake.

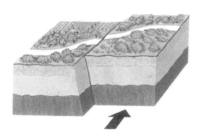

Sliding by The line along which rocks break apart and move during an earthquake is called a fault line.

Can we prevent earthquakes?

Although we know where the main earthquake zones are, it is impossible to prevent an earthquake happening. Because many people live near active earthquake zones – for example, over 3 million Americans live near the San Andreas fault zone in California – it is becoming increasingly important to predict these events.

Scientists use special instruments to measure rock movement deep underground in the hope that they will be able to tell when danger levels are reached. Local people can then move to safety.

Devastating force
Earthquakes release immense power, destroying very stong structures. An earthquake in Kobe, Japan, in 1995 toppled this elevated highway.

THAT'S AMAZING!

NEAR MISS

Volcanoes blast dust and magma high into the atmosphere. In June, 1991, the jet engines of a Japanese aeroplane were stopped by invisible particles from the eruption of Mount Pinatubo in the Philippines. The aeroplane fell several thousand metres before the pilots could start the engines again.

Roman remains

In AD 79, the Roman cities of Pompeii and Herculaneum in Italy were completely destroyed when nearby Vesuvius erupted. The inhabitants tried to escape, but were choked to death by the fast-travelling gas cloud and buried under hot ash. In the 18th century, the remains of the two cities were rediscovered, and they have since been excavated. By pouring cement into spaces in the hardened ash, archaeologists have produced casts of the bodies of men, women, children, their pets and farm animals. We can see how they died trying to protect themselves.

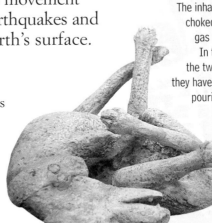

The concrete cast of a chained dog that was buried by ash at Pompeii.

Fiery fountain Red-hot magma forces its way up the centre of a volcano. Pressure builds up until the magma bursts out at the top.

Why do volcanoes erupt?

Pressure inside the Earth squeezes magma, a mixture of liquid rock and gas, up through weak spots in the Earth's crust. Near the surface, the rapid expansion of gas bubbles in the magma causes it to foam and pour out of the volcano as lava. Lava cools and hardens to form volcanic rock. This builds up in layers each time a volcano erupts.

Although lava can be very destructive, it flows slowly, so people usually have time to get out of its way. But if the pressure inside a volcano builds up rapidly, it can explode, like a shaken-up fizzy drink. In 1991, 300 m (1000 ft) of rock was blasted from the top of Mount Pinatubo in the Philippines, and the cloud of rock and dust rose 40 km (25 miles) through the atmosphere. Killer clouds of hot ash and poisonous gas can pour down the slopes of explosive volcanoes at speeds of up to 200 km/h (125 mph).

Early in the morning, people in the Caribbean port of St Pierre are not aware there is anything unusual about Mont Pelée.

At 8 am, a 200°C (392°F) cloud of poisonous gas and burning ash blasts from the volcano and pours down its slopes.

Within minutes, the town's buildings and ships in the harbour are on fire and people are overcome by the gas.

MONT PELEE
On August 8, 1902, the Caribbean island volcano of Mont Pelée erupted unexpectedly. Within minutes, it rained down gas, ash and rocks on the nearby port of St Pierre. The only survivor among the 29 000 people who lived there was a prisoner in the town jail.

The Earth's atmosphere

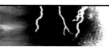

🌐 Weather and climate p.30 ·
Fphere Fact File p.266

The air around us is actually part of the Earth's atmosphere. It is made of layers of gases and water vapour that surround the whole planet. The atmosphere is over 2400 km (1500 miles) thick and is held in place by the Earth's gravity. It contains oxygen, which living things depend on. It traps warmth and moisture close to the Earth's surface, and it prevents damaging rays and small pieces of rock from outer space reaching our planet.

Why do we need an atmosphere?

Without the atmosphere, all the water on the Earth would evaporate, and living things would not be able to exist. Temperatures on Earth would vary between extremes of hot and cold. We would be bombarded by harmful rays from the Sun, such as ultraviolet light, which can cause sunburn and cancer. The Earth is not the only planet to have an atmosphere, but only the Earth's atmosphere can support living things. For example, the atmosphere of Venus is made of carbon dioxide and the surface temperature is around 475°C (887°F).

Invisible protector
The layers of the atmosphere surround our whole planet and are essential to life.

EARTH'S SHIELD
The atmosphere has five layers. Three-quarters of the gas in the atmosphere is found in the lowest 16 km (10 miles). The lower levels are made up mostly of light gases, such as nitrogen and oxygen, which sustain life. The upper levels contain hydrogen and helium, which do not support life.

THAT'S AMAZING

A WEIGHT ON MY MIND
We think air is weightless, but actually we each have a column of air pressing down on the top of our heads with a force of 1 kg per sq cm (15 lb per sq in) at sea level. This force is the equivalent of having 40 bags of sugar on our heads. Fortunately, our bodies are designed to withstand this pressure.

Weather satellite
Orbits at 700-1500 km (420-900 miles).

Space Shuttle
Passes through all layers.

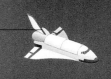

Meteor showers
Meteors burning up in the atmosphere create streaks of light.

48-85 km (30-55 miles)
This layer is known as the mesosphere. With no clouds, dust or ozone layer for protection, the temperature at this level falls from 0°C (32°F) to −90°C (−130°F) and winds reach 3000 km/h (2000 mph).

11-48 km (7-30 miles)
This layer is called the stratosphere. It contains less oxygen than the layer below, but it includes the ozone layer, which protects us from harmful ultraviolet light from the Sun.

Concorde Reaches 18 km (11 miles).

Volcanoes Ash clouds from volcanoes have reached 12 km (8 miles) high.

0-11 km (0-7miles)
This layer is called the troposphere. Living things can exist in this layer, where there is enough oxygen to breathe and warmth for survival. Air movement in this layer causes activity that we know as the weather.

Clouds Cirrus clouds are the highest. They form up to 15 km (9 miles) above the Earth's surface.

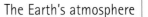
Communications satellite Reaches 36 000 km (22 000 miles)

Space

700-2400 km (435-1500 miles)
This layer is known as the exosphere. The outer edge of the atmosphere changes from a mixture of the gases helium and hydrogen to hydrogen.

Hubble Space Telescope
Reached 512 km (318 miles) in 1990.

85-700 km (55-435 miles)
This layer is known as the thermosphere. Radiation from the Sun breaks up some of the gas molecules, causing the temperature to rise to over 2000°C (3600°F).

Aurora
Particles from the Sun collide with gas molecules in the atmosphere, causing flickering light effects in the sky above the Poles.

Heat from the Sun

Heat trapped near the Earth

Heating up More carbon dioxide in the atmosphere traps more heat.

Heat given off by Earth

What is global warming?
Some of the gases in our atmosphere, particularly carbon dioxide, trap heat given off by the Earth. We are releasing increasing amounts of man-made carbon dioxide from factory chimneys and car exhausts, so the atmosphere is trapping more heat than in the past and average temperatures around the world are rising by about 1°C every 25 years – an effect called global warming. If it continues, eventually the polar ice caps will melt and raise sea levels.

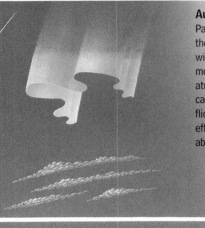

Light show The aurora effect over the North Pole is known as the aurora borealis or Northern Lights.

Why does the sky change colour?
Light rays from the Sun are made up of violet, indigo, blue, green, yellow, orange and red rays. When these rays pass through the atmosphere, they are scattered in different directions. During daytime, water droplets and gas molecules scatter blue light rays, making the sky look blue. In the evening, the atmosphere can be full of dust particles. These scatter the red light rays, creating red sunsets.

Flying high
A manned balloon reached 35 km (22 miles) in 1961. An unmanned balloon reached 52 km (32 miles) in 1972.

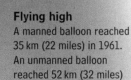

Hole in the ozone

In 1985, scientists discovered a hole in the protective ozone layer over Antarctica. The 'hole' is caused by a temporary loss of ozone from the stratosphere. This is happening every year and the hole is getting bigger. It means that more harmful ultraviolet light from the Sun can get through our atmospheric shield. The loss of ozone is blamed on the release into the atmosphere of man-made chemicals called CFCs, or chlorofluorocarbons. These were used in refrigerators and aerosol cans, but they are now banned.

The grey, red and blue area in the centre shows the ozone hole over Antarctica in 1996.

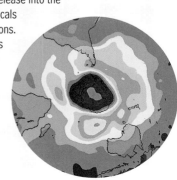

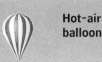

Hot-air balloon

Aeroplanes
747 jumbo jets can reach 11 km (7 miles). DC9s reach 8 km (5 miles).

Highest mountain
Mount Everest is 8846 m (29 002 ft) high.

Weather and climate

🌐 Spinning Earth p.22 · The Earth's atmosphere p.28 · Fact File p.280, 284

The North Pole has a very different climate from the Equator, but both have stormy weather from time to time. Climate is the name we give to the typical weather pattern in one place, which does not change much. Weather, on the other hand, is caused by activity in the Earth's atmosphere. Air is always on the move; it heats up and cools down; and can become water-laden or dry. In many places, the weather is always changing, even from hour to hour and over a few miles.

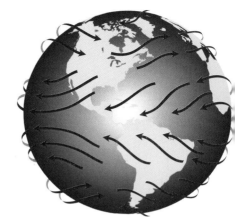

Afloat in the garden In Indonesia, the annual monsoon rains can cause heavy flooding.

Climate rules

A place's climate is controlled by its distance from the Equator. The Sun is at its hottest at the Equator, while it gives little warmth at the Poles. This affects not only the amount of heat a place receives, but also how much rainfall there is. Climate influences all aspects of people's lives, from the clothes they wear to the way they build their houses.

Why does the wind blow?

When air passes over ground warmed by the Sun, it is heated and becomes lighter. Because the air is lighter, it rises, leaving an area with less air pressure – called a low-pressure area. Air is sucked into this area from surrounding areas, where the air pressure is higher. This movement of the air is what we call the wind. The bigger the difference in pressure between the low and high-pressure areas, the stronger the wind.

World wind patterns Cool, high-pressure winds blow towards the low-pressure area at the Equator. Some winds are drawn towards the Poles.

RAINED OFF

Warm and cold air follow each other, but do not mix easily. Where warm and cold air meet, the boundary is called a front. When warm air follows behind cold, the boundary is called a warm front. When cold air follows warm, the boundary is called a cold front. Fronts bring rain. Some fronts move quickly, so even a fine day can be interrupted by a storm.

Warm front

Cold front

Sunny start It's a fine day with wispy, high clouds and a slight breeze as a warm front approaches.

Warm front Warm air at ground level begins rising gradually. Clouds build up and the breeze gets stronger.

Gentle rain When the gently rising air at the warm front reaches a high altitude, it cools and drops its moisture as light rain. A cold front moves in behind the warm front.

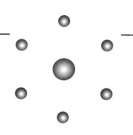

Rain Water droplets in a cloud link up until they are big and heavy enough to fall to the ground as rain.

Snow In freezing temperatures, moisture droplets in the clouds freeze to form snowflakes.

Hail Water droplets sometimes freeze to form hailstones.

THAT'S AMAZING

THUNDER AND LIGHTNING

Electricity builds up in storm clouds. When a cloud cannot hold any more electricity, it is discharged in an enormous spark called lightning. A single flash of lightning can generate a current of 500 000 amps, similar in strength to the output of a large power station. A flash of lightning heats the air around it very quickly, causing the air to expand very fast. The sudden expansion causes the rumbling noise we hear as thunder.

What are clouds made of?

The way clouds form is similar to the way steam is produced when water boils. Warm air can hold moisture in the form of water vapour. When warm air rises and cools, any water vapour in the air turns into small water droplets (less than 0.05 mm or 1/64 in wide). If the air temperature is below freezing, the moisture forms ice crystals. The droplets or crystals form clouds. They are easily blown about in the wind, so the shape of a cloud constantly changes. The water droplets fall as rain or hail, ice crystals as snow.

Will there be another Ice Age?

During the last Ice Age, 18 000 years ago, ice sheets covered much of Europe and North America. So much water was locked up in these ice caps that the sea level was lower, and people walked from Asia to America across a land bridge.

There have been at least six major ice ages in the history of the Earth. The Earth's climate has always followed an overall pattern of warming and cooling, so there will probably be another ice age, although we do not know when.

Northern ice cap in the last Ice Age.

Cold front Cold air pushes in under the warm air, making the warm air rise steeply. This air cools rapidly producing heavy rain, and sometimes thunder and lightning.

Heavy rain and hail Air currents inside the clouds carry droplets up and down, and some freeze at higher levels, forming hail. The cold front slowly moves away.

Storm over The air clears. Sunlight shining through distant rain forms a rainbow. The clouds are fewer and higher. Another warm front approaches.

Mountains and mountain ranges

● Inside the Earth p.24 · Volcanoes and earthquakes p.26 · Rocks and minerals p.48 · Fact File p.276

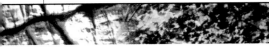

The mountains we can see today are made of hard rock that has been crumpled, broken and pushed about as if it was soft. The rocks that make up continents have often travelled thousands of kilometres before being crushed together and pushed upwards to form mountain ranges. Mountains are many thousands of metres high, and several changes in temperature, weather and vegetation occur between the bottom and the top. Mountains are also found under the ocean, in places where the ocean bed is so deep that there is no sign of them at the surface.

Carved landscape
At the Grand Canyon, in the USA, the Colorado River has cut deep into the rock at the Earth's surface, and erosion has created fantastical shapes.

Mountain building

When continents collide, the rocks along their edges are pushed together and squashed down in layers. As the continents press together, these layers are pushed into huge folds that form mountain ranges. The folds are pushed upwards as the continents continue to move. The rock surface is worn away in places by wind and water. Water freezes and expands in cracks in the rock, causing pieces to break off. This process is called erosion and it slowly carves out the individual mountains in a range.

What are mountains made of?

On land, mountains are mainly formed from layers of sediment – particles of sand and mud deposited by ancient oceans and rivers. The layers have been squashed down and hardened into rock. Often, thick piles of sandstone, mudstone and limestone can be seen in steep mountainsides. Limestone is a chalky mud formed on the seabed and is often full of fossil shells. Deep in the roots of mountains, heat and pressure can be so great that the rock melts. If this molten rock, or magma, cools slowly at depth, it hardens into granite.

Mountains under the oceans are made of piles of hardened lava that pours out from cracks and volcanoes on the ocean floor.

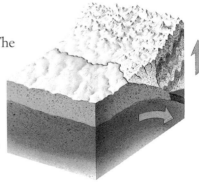

Fully grown
As the two landmasses came together, the layers of rock were forced higher and higher. Some rock that began on the ocean floor ended up near the top. Erosion began to shape the individual peaks.

Himalayas in the making As India began pushing against Asia, layers of rock crumpled into huge folds. These folds were pushed upwards, forming the beginnings of the mountain range. Volcanoes poured out lava.

India on the move
Around 40 million years ago, India was moving north towards Asia at a speed of 10 cm (4 in) a year, squeezing the ocean floor between them.

THAT'S AMAZING

OXYGEN SHORTAGE

To survive high on mountains, people have to cope with less oxygen in the air. Climbers take an oxygen supply. No one could reach the top of Mount Everest, the highest mountain in the world, until 1953, when Edmund Hillary and Tenzing Norgay used breathing equipment invented during the Second World War.

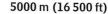

Floating mountains

The weight of rock in a mountain is so great that if it were not supported by something, it would soon sink down into the surface of the Earth. Around 80 km (50 miles) below the roots of mountains, rocks are dense, hot and flexible. Mountains themselves are made from lighter, more brittle rocks that 'float' on the heavier rocks below. Only the topmost part of a mountain is buoyed up above the Earth's surface.

Mountains extend deeper into the Earth's surface than lower-lying land.

LIFE ON A MOUNTAIN

The Andes Mountains of South America rise from hot, wet tropics at sea level to bare rock and ice above 6000 m (20 000 ft). Life changes from banana plantations grown in the rain forest, maize and potatoes on the high grasslands, to scrubby grasses where tough, thick-coated llamas, tended by their herders, are the only large animals to survive.

Future mountains

Because the continents are constantly on the move, they will continue to press into one another in the future. And wherever continents collide, mountain ranges are pushed up. When Australia eventually crashes into southern Asia, and Africa into southern Europe, new mountain ranges will be formed as the rocks between them are crumpled and jammed together.

5000 m (16 500 ft)
A freezing climate of snow and ice. Some red algae, mosses and lichen are all that can survive.

4600 m (15 000 ft)
A cold desert climate. The ground is often frozen, with barren rocks and tufts of hardy rock plants living in the crevices between them.

4000 m (13 000 ft)
A cold, dry, alpine climate. Llamas and alpacas graze on patchy grasses. This zone has low oxygen levels.

3000 m (10 000 ft)
Forest gives way to grasses, shrubs and giant leafy plants, some as big as trees.

1200 m (4000 ft)
A cooler climate produces temperate forest. Native food plants such as potatoes and maize are grown.

Sea level A hot, humid climate. The lower slopes are covered in tropical forest teeming with wildlife, except where people have cleared the forest for farming and homes.

🌐 Mountains and mountain ranges p.32 · Around the coast p.38 · Fact File p.276

As rainwater hits the ground, gravity pulls it downhill towards the sea. At first, the water flows in tiny trickles, but the trickles soon join up to form streams, and streams join up to form rivers. By the time a river nears the coast, it may be many miles wide. Lakes form where water from streams or underground springs collects in craters or hollows on the Earth's surface, or sometimes where a river changes its course.

Long drop Waterfalls form where a river tumbles over a sharp edge of extra-hard rock. At the bottom of the fall, the water carves out a deep pool.

Slowing down Away from mountains, as a river reaches less steep ground, it slows down. The water in the middle of the river moves faster than the water near the banks.

Muddy river China's Yellow River picks up sediment in the mountains where it rises.

Why are rivers different colours?

Some rivers are crystal clear, but most are not. This is because they carry sediment (tiny particles of rock and soil) and substances dissolved out of the soil as rainwater seeped through it. Sediment can make a river look brown, green, or even yellow. China's Huang Ho or Yellow River carries more sediment than any other river in the world.

How long does water take to reach the sea?

This depends on how far it has to travel, on the type of terrain it is travelling through, and whether it is travelling underground or on the surface. Some large rivers flow more than 40 km (25 miles) a day. Water that is seeping through the ground may move just a few metres each year.

A spring In places where the rock or soil is permanently saturated water emerges at the surface, and flows away if it can.

Wandering about When a river reaches level ground, it often flows through a series of bends, called meanders. Rivers shift the mud along their banks, building up some bends and digging away at others, which gradually changes the shape and position of the meanders.

THAT'S AMAZING
MYSTERY WATERS
Scientists have recently discovered lakes far beneath the Antarctic ice cap. These lakes have been cut off from the outside world ever since the ice cap first formed millions of years ago. It is possible they contain living animals that exist nowhere else on Earth.

CARVING A LANDSCAPE
Water always follows the steepest an quickest path downhill that it can fin When it is moving fast, it picks up litt pieces of grit. These scrape against th ground as they are carried along by th water. Over many thousands of years, t constant scraping cuts into rock like a producing deep valleys and gorges.

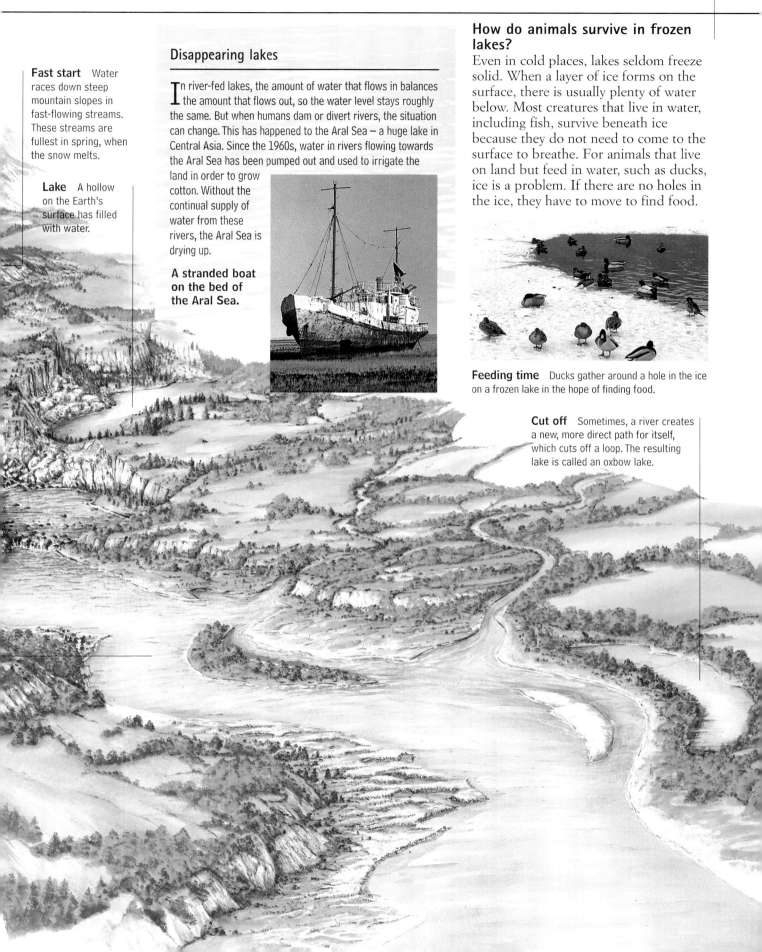

Fast start Water races down steep mountain slopes in fast-flowing streams. These streams are fullest in spring, when the snow melts.

Lake A hollow on the Earth's surface has filled with water.

Disappearing lakes

In river-fed lakes, the amount of water that flows in balances the amount that flows out, so the water level stays roughly the same. But when humans dam or divert rivers, the situation can change. This has happened to the Aral Sea – a huge lake in Central Asia. Since the 1960s, water in rivers flowing towards the Aral Sea has been pumped out and used to irrigate the land in order to grow cotton. Without the continual supply of water from these rivers, the Aral Sea is drying up.

A stranded boat on the bed of the Aral Sea.

How do animals survive in frozen lakes?

Even in cold places, lakes seldom freeze solid. When a layer of ice forms on the surface, there is usually plenty of water below. Most creatures that live in water, including fish, survive beneath ice because they do not need to come to the surface to breathe. For animals that live on land but feed in water, such as ducks, ice is a problem. If there are no holes in the ice, they have to move to find food.

Feeding time Ducks gather around a hole in the ice on a frozen lake in the hope of finding food.

Cut off Sometimes, a river creates a new, more direct path for itself, which cuts off a loop. The resulting lake is called an oxbow lake.

Oceans and seas

➡ The Earth's atmosphere p.28 · Weather and climate p.30 · Around the coast p.38 · Fact File p.278, 284

Oceans cover almost three-quarters of the Earth. Near coasts they are often quite shallow, but in some places they can be over 10 km (6 miles) deep – more than enough to submerge a mountain the height of Mount Everest. If you threw a coin into water this deep, it would take more than an hour to reach the bottom. The surface and the seabed teem with life, but in between is an emptier world.

Why is seawater salty?

If you have ever swallowed seawater while swimming, you'll know that it is too salty to drink. This salt comes from rocks in the Earth's crust that have been dissolved by rain seeping through the ground. Most of the salt is the kind we use on our food. If all the seawater evaporated and the salt was left behind, it would form a layer 55 m (180 ft) deep.

If we could walk on the seabed, what would it be like?

In many places you would disappear, because you would sink into a deep layer of soft and slimy ooze. This ooze forms from the skeletons of tiny plants and animals that drift down to the seabed after they die. The ooze forms at an amazingly slow rate – just a few millimetres a century – but it has been building up for so long that in some places it is several metres deep.

Surface life Creatures such as whales stay near the surface.

Gulper eel

Why aren't deep-sea animals squashed by the water above?

If you squeeze an air-filled ball, you will be able to squash it out of shape. You will find a solid ball far more difficult to squeeze. Deep-sea animals use the same principle to avoid being crushed by the water around them. Their bodies contain little or no air, so the water pressure leaves them unharmed.

Angler fish

THE ABYSSAL ZONE

The abyssal zone is thousands of metres beneath the surface. It is always dark and cold. Strange fish hunt each other in the darkness. Most have giant mouths to scoop up potential food, and some have lures that light up to attract prey. Other animals sift through the ooze on the ocean floor, feeding on particles of food that have drifted down from above.

Ancient life Fossils of plankton that lived in the sea 570 million years ago.

NAUTILE

A submersible is used to explore the ocean floor

Tripod fish

THAT'S AMAZING

WALKING ACROSS OCEANS

During the last Ice Age, about 18 000 years ago, the sea level was over 100 m (330 ft) lower than today because a huge amount of the Earth's water was ice. People could walk across what is now the seabed from mainland Europe to Britain and from Asia to Alaska.

Brittle stars

Sea spider

Sea cucumber

LIFE ON THE SHELF

The continental shelf is a shallow part of the sea that stretches out from the coast. Here, the water is often warmer than deep in the ocean, and daylight can reach the seabed. The continental shelf is home to thousands of different kinds of animals, including most of the fish we eat. Seaweeds live in shallow water, where the light is brightest. They form underwater gardens that are nurseries for young fish.

Ocean currents

Currents steadily move water around all the world's oceans. Surface currents, which are warm because the water is heated by the Sun, are caused by the wind. Where surface currents are diverted north and south by the continents, they form huge loops. Deep-water currents transport cold water from the Poles. These deep-water currents move slowly. On average, it takes water about 275 years to travel across the floor of the Atlantic, and over 500 years to travel across the floor of the Pacific.

Warm (red) and cold (blue) currents.

Eel grass

Kelp

Lobster

Dogfish

Crab

Whelks

Plaice

Sand eels

Cod

🌐 **Man on the Moon p.18 · Spinning Earth p.22 · Oceans and seas p.36 · Force and motion p.150 · Fact File p.278, 280, 284**

Coastlines change as the tide rises and falls and the sea pounds away at the land. Coasts teem with life, but the nonstop battering means that plants and animals have to be tough to survive. Many shore animals are protected by hard shells, and seaweeds have rubbery stalks that are difficult to break. On sandy shores, most animals live buried beneath the surface, safe from the push and pull of the waves.

What makes the tides?

Tides are produced by the gravity of the Moon and Sun. This force tugs at the oceans as the Earth spins around, pulling the water in one direction, then another. The Moon is much closer to Earth than the Sun is, so even though it is quite small, its gravity has the bigger effect. When the Sun and Moon are in line, their combined gravitational pull causes high spring tides.

Spring tide
At the new and full Moon, the Sun and Moon are in line. The blue area around the Earth illustrates the tidal bulge.

Neap tide
During the Moon's first and third quarters, the pull of the Moon and Sun are at right angles to each other.

EBB AND FLOW

The shore between the high and low-tide marks is called the 'intertidal zone'. Plants and animals living here have to survive both under water and in air. Barnacles and limpets fastened to the rocks show where the intertidal zone begins.

Land beneath the sea

In some parts of the world, new land has been made by pushing back the sea. People have been doing this in the Netherlands for over 500 years, and now more than a quarter of the country is below sea level. In this man-made landscape, high banks called dykes keep the sea at bay.

In Hong Kong in the 1990s, enough land has been reclaimed from the sea to build a large new international airport.

The runways at Hong Kong airport are built on reclaimed land.

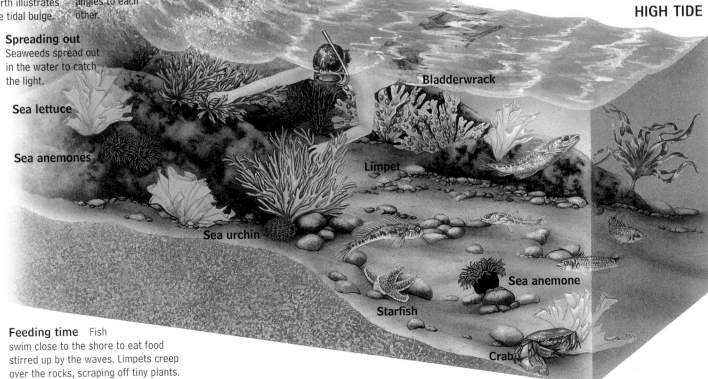

HIGH TIDE

Spreading out
Seaweeds spread out in the water to catch the light.

Sea lettuce

Sea anemones

Sea urchin

Bladderwrack

Limpet

Starfish

Sea anemone

Crab

Feeding time Fish swim close to the shore to eat food stirred up by the waves. Limpets creep over the rocks, scraping off tiny plants.

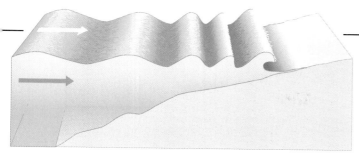

Deep water Waves are far apart.

Inshore The seabed rises and waves become bunched together.

Where do waves come from?

Waves are normally made by the wind as it blows across the surface of the open sea. In deep water, waves are shallow and wide apart. As waves approach the coast, they become higher and closer together because the seabed rises and interrupts their progress. Eventually, a wave becomes top-heavy and topples over, forming a breaker that crashes against the shore. A tidal wave, called a tsunami, is a giant wave that is triggered by an underwater earthquake or a volcanic eruption. Tsunamis can race across the oceans at over 650 km/h (400 mph). When they reach the shore, they can be more than 30 m (100 ft) high – big enough to smash trees and buildings and to carry boats far inland.

How do coral reefs form?

Coral reefs are made by tiny animals called coral polyps. The polyps have soft bodies and protect themselves by building hard cases from a chalky substance dissolved in water. They attach their cases to those of older polyps and the cases pile up to form reefs. Coral reefs are the biggest structures made by living things. The world's largest reef – the Great Barrier Reef off eastern Australia – covers over 200 000 km² (80 000 sq miles). It has taken more than 8000 years to form. Corals cannot survive in temperatures below 20°C (68°F).

Coral reef
Most corals grow only a few inches each year.

LOW TIDE

Sun protection
Seaweeds lie across the rocks. A jelly-like coating helps protect them from water loss, but also makes them slippery.

Lying low Many small animals, such as periwinkles and tiny crabs, hide in the seaweed, where they are sheltered from the Sun.

Sea anemones

Starfish

Sea urchin

THAT'S AMAZING

REACHING INTO SPACE

If all the world's coastlines – including every small inlet and island – were joined together and stretched out straight, they would form a line long enough to reach the Moon.

Clinging on
Limpets clamp their shells to the rock, trapping moisture underneath and protecting themselves from predators.

Grasslands

⮕ Surviving extremes p.92 · Ecology: connecting the living world p.100 · Wildlife conservation p.102 · Fact File p.280

G rasslands form where the climate is too dry for forests but where there is enough rain to prevent the land turning into a desert. Africa's grasslands, which are also known as savannah, are the most extensive in the world and are home to the largest herds of animals found anywhere on Earth.

Weaver birds These birds make their nests from stems of grass.

How does grass grow?

Most plants grow by stretching out the tips of their stems. Grass plants are different, because their stems grow from near the ground. This means that they can survive being nibbled, chewed, and trampled by elephants, whereas most other plants would die. Grass plants have another useful trick: they can spread sideways, which helps them to cover large areas of open ground and increases their chances of survival.

ALTERNATING SEASONS

In the grasslands of Africa, most of the rain falls during a few months each year. During the long dry season, the grass slowly shrivels and turns brown. Rivers dry up and animals have to visit waterholes to drink. When the rain arrives, the grass quickly comes back to life. Animals can get water from rivers and streams as well as waterholes, and spread out across the plains.

Danger time During the dry season, lions and other hunters lie in wait near waterholes. Elephants and buffalo are too big to be eaten, but antelope risk being attacked while they drink.

DRY SEASON

Vultures

Lions

Elephants

Buffalo

Termite mound

Gazelles

Fire!

Towards the end of the dry season, grasslands often catch fire. The fires are usually started by lightning, and they quickly spread across the parched and dusty plains. These fires look dangerous, but they are not as disastrous as they seem. The flames burn off the dead grass, but they soon move on and the grass plants quickly recover.

Birds chase insects forced into the open by a bushfire.

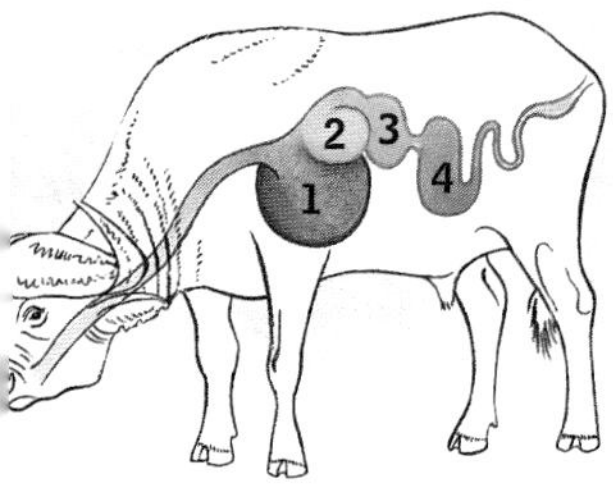

Serial stomachs Grass-eaters have a series of stomachs to break down tough grasses.

Why can't we eat grass?
Grass contains cellulose, a tough substance that humans cannot digest. Many mammals that eat grass have a four-chambered stomach. One of the chambers contains microbes (minute living organisms) that break down the grass so that it can be digested.

Why do grassland animals live in herds?
Grassland sometimes has scattered clumps of trees, but apart from these, there are few places where animals can hide. By herding together, grassland animals improve their chances of avoiding attack. While some members of a herd feed, others watch out for signs of danger.

Herd of springbok Some graze while others keep watch.

WET SEASON

Food for all After the rain, the grass can grow over 1.5 m (5 ft) high. At this time of year, grassland animals are much harder to see.

Giraffe

Zebra

Buffalo

THAT'S AMAZING

HIDDEN ROOTS
A single grass plant can have over 100 km (60 miles) of roots. The roots make up a dense mat close to the surface, which helps to keep the grassland soil in place. If the grass plants are removed, the soil quickly dries out and is easily blown away.

🌐 Tree life p.70 · Migration: great animal journeys p.94 · Ecology: connecting the living world p.100 · Fact File p.280

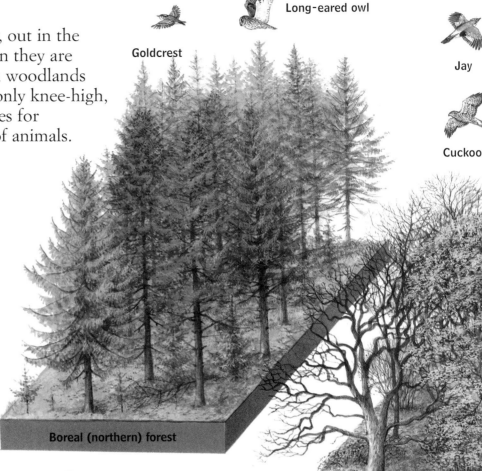

Long-eared owl

Goldcrest

Jay

Cuckoo

Trees can grow singly, out in the open, but more often they are crowded together in woodlands and forests. While some are only knee-high, others provide high-rise homes for hundreds of different kinds of animals.

FOUR TYPES OF FOREST

Climate has a major effect on the world's forests. In tropical regions near the Equator the climate is warm and wet. Trees grow all year round, resulting in tropical rain forests. Farther from the Equator, the weather changes with the seasons: parts of the year are too dry in monsoon regions, and too cold in temperate regions, for trees to grow. At these times the trees rest, and many shed their leaves. In northern regions, trees are tough enough to survive many months at subzero temperatures.

Why are forests important?

Forests are home to many different animals, but they are also valuable in other ways. Tree roots help to bind the soil together and stop it being washed away when it rains. Their leaves take in carbon dioxide and give off oxygen, keeping the atmosphere fit to breathe. In mountains, forests also act as living crash barriers against avalanches.

Boreal (northern) forest

Fly agaric toadstool · Red squirrel · Roe deer

Boreal (northern) forest   Nearly all the trees in this kind of forest are conifers (fir trees). They grow for just a few weeks each year, and they have tough leaves that can survive frost, wind and snow.

Temperate forest

Primrose · Fallow deer · Badger

Temperate forest   In temperate regions, broadleaved trees lose their leaves in autumn, and grow a new set in spring.

How many kinds of trees grow in forests?

This depends on where the forest is, because more tree species live in warm places than in cold ones. An area of tropical rain forest the size of a football pitch may contain over 200 different kinds of tree, but in an area of northern forest 1000 times bigger, the total may be as low as six different sorts.

Forest log-pile   Logs of different shapes, sizes and colours show the range of tree species in a forest.

THAT'S AMAZING

TREE GIANTS

The tallest trees alive today are California redwoods, which grow in northern California. Some reach 110 m (360 ft) high. In Australia in the 19th century, mountain ash trees, or giant gums, reached over 150 m (500 ft).

Trees of stone

In some parts of the world, such as Arizona, prehistoric forests have become 'petrified' – they have been turned into fossils made of stone. After millions of years buried underground, these fossil treetrunks are revealed when wind and rain eat away at the surrounding rock.

Fossil forest, Arizona

Why do so many types of animals and birds live in tropical rain forests?

There is a huge amount of food for animals in tropical rain forests, so many different species can survive side by side. Rain forests have existed for a long time, and animals living in them have developed many varied ways of life.

Rain-forest inhabitant The three-toed sloth spends most of its time in treetops and feeds on leaves.

Black vulture

Malabar pied hornbill

Macaw

Monsoon forest

Tropical rain forest

rchid   Cobra   Nilgai

Monsoon forest In this kind of tropical forest, trees lose their leaves during the long dry season. During the drought, many animals live on seeds.

Passionflower   Mosaic frog   Jaguar

Tropical rain forest
Rain forest is the tallest and lushest kind of forest. Trees can be over 75 m (250 ft) high. They have large evergreen leaves, and they produce a year-round supply of food for forest animals.

⊙ Surviving extremes p.92 · Ecology: connecting the living world p.100 · Fact File p.276, 280

Saguaro woodpecker

Deserts cover nearly one-third of the land on Earth. In some, the daytime temperature can climb to over 48°C (120°F), and it is so dry that hardly any living things survive. Others can be cold; the daytime temperature in winter in the Gobi Desert can drop to –20°C (–4°F). And most have a few bursts of heavy rain each year.

Why are deserts so dry?
Most large deserts are in the subtropics, north and south of the area around the Equator. The air contains little moisture, so it rarely rains. Some deserts, such as the Gobi Desert in Asia, are thousands of miles from the sea, so moist air never reaches them. Others are close to high mountains, and by the time air has crossed the mountains, most of its moisture has fallen as rain.

Gobi Desert   The ground is so dry that cracks open up.

DESERTS BY DAY AND NIGHT
In North America's Sonoran Desert, daytime temperatures can reach over 40°C (104°F), but nights are cooler – around 22°C (72°F) in summer and 4°C (39°F) in winter. Many animals hide during the day and emerge only after dark. This desert is home to many kinds of cactus, including the biggest of them all, the saguaro, which can grow over 15 m (50 ft) high.

Hummingbirds

Saguaro

Day shift   During the day, roadrunners hunt for lizards and snakes. Hummingbirds visit saguaro flowers to drink their sugary nectar.

Lizard

Roadrunner
This bird hunts on the ground, sprinting round cacti and rocks.

Prickly pear

Kangaroo rat

DESERT BY DAY

Bats

CENTURIES OF DROUGHT

In the Atacama Desert on the west coast of South America, there are places where it has probably not rained for at least 400 years. People who live there drink water brought in by tanker or piped in from the Andes Mountains.

Waiting for rain

Some plants and animals have an unusual way of surviving long droughts: they come to life only after rain. Within days of a storm, flowers suddenly burst into bloom, and the ground is alive with small animals that must hurry to reproduce. These animals include tiny tadpole shrimps, which breed in puddles left after sudden storms.

Poppies bloom in the Mojave Desert.

What is an oasis?

Even in the driest deserts, there is water deep underground. This water comes from rain that fell long ago, often far away. An oasis is a place where the ground is low enough for this water to reach the surface. Oases are important places for desert animals, and also for people who travel or live in deserts.

Water An oasis in the Namibian Desert.

How long can desert animals go without drinking?

At the hottest time of year, camels can survive for over a week without water. When they do find water, they can drink up to 50 litres (11 gallons) at one go, even if the water is salty. Some desert animals, such as kangaroo rats, never drink at all. They get all the water they need from their food.

Night shift Coyotes, rattlesnakes and burrowing owls hunt once the Sun has set. While the hummingbirds are roosting, saguaro flowers are visited by bats.

Burrowing owl These birds often nest in holes that other animals have dug.

Coyote

Rattlesnake These snakes can sense their prey in complete darkness.

DESERT BY NIGHT

Kangaroo rat

🔄 Surviving extremes p.92 · Migration: great animal journeys p.94 · Fact File p.280

The North and South Poles are by far the coldest places on Earth, with temperatures that drop to −80°C (−112°F). Biting winds blow for much of the year, and winter brings many months of darkness around the clock. Despite these severe conditions, the Arctic in the north and the Antarctic in the south are full of life. Most of this life is based in the sea, which is warmer than the air.

What is at the Poles?

Explorers first reached the North Pole in 1909, and the South Pole in 1911. Today, the North Pole is still uninhabited, and is simply a point on the drifting sea ice that covers the Arctic Ocean. The South Pole is quite different, because the ice is thicker and covers rock. There is a permanent research station at the South Pole. Here, scientists investigate the Earth's atmosphere and weather.

Cold work Scientists live for several months at the research station at the South Pole.

THAT'S AMAZING

FROZEN WATER STORE

Antarctica is covered by about 25 million km³ (6 million cu miles) of ice. If all this ice melted, sea levels around the world would rise by about 50 m (165 ft).

Where do icebergs come from?

Icebergs are not made from frozen seawater. They are produced by glaciers (rivers of frozen freshwater that move very slowly across land). At the coast, glaciers flow into the sea and break up. Giant icebergs can be over 600 m (2000 ft) deep and many kilometres across, but even small ones can be dangerous to ships. Icebergs float low in the water, and only one-sixth shows above the surface.

ARCTIC AND ANTARCTIC LIFE

If you parachuted down near one of the Poles, you would be able to tell where you were by looking at the animals. Polar bears and walruses live only in the Arctic, while penguins and leopard seals live only in the Antarctic. The Arctic tern, a bird, is one of the few creatures that is found near both Poles.

Waiting game During the winter, polar bears catch seals by grabbing them as they surface to breathe through holes in the ice. Bears rarely hunt seals in summer because they cannot catch them in open water after the sea ice has melted.

Cleaning up Arctic foxes often eat food that polar bears have left.

Keeping warm Walruses have a thick layer of blubber to protect them from the cold. Males and females have tusks.

ARCTIC LIFE

3000 m
2000 m
1000 m
0 m

South Pole

Ice-covered continent If you could look at a slice of
Antarctica, you would see thick ice on top of the rock.

How deep is polar ice?
The ice over the South Pole is about 2700 m (8800 ft) thick.
In other parts of Antarctica, the ice is even thicker. This ice
lies over solid rock, and it has built up over several million
years. The ice over the North Pole is thinner – even in
midwinter it is only 5 m (15 ft) thick. This is
because the ice is floating on the sea.

**White-
capped
albatross**

Life around the clock

Polar animals can feed around the clock
in midsummer, because the Sun never
sets at this time of the year at either the
North or South Poles. This nonstop daylight
is useful for some creatures, but for snowy
owls it can disrupt their routine. These
Arctic birds usually hunt by night, but in
midsummer they have to feed by day.

**The snowy owl's white feathers
help to camouflage it in daytime.**

Home of the reindeer A herd of reindeer in
Alaska.

Where do
reindeer live?
Reindeer, wolves
and lemmings all
live on the
tundra, a cold,
treeless landscape
that circles the Arctic Ocean. During winter the tundra is
bleak and harsh, and animals struggle to survive. Reindeer
scrape away the snow to find food, but lemmings stay
beneath the snow, feeding in tunnels that spread out
across the ground. As soon as the snow starts to
melt in spring, plants flower, migrating
birds arrive, and there is plenty of food.

Snow petrel

Cold start
The emperor penguin
is one of the few
birds that breeds on
solid ice.

Hidden hazard
Leopard seals lurk close to
the ice, and catch
penguins as they feed.

ANTARCTIC LIFE

➲ Inside the Earth p.24 · Mountains and mountain ranges p.32 · Gems and precious metals p.50 · Fact File p.312

G o wherever you like on Earth, you will be standing on a layer of solid rock between 12 and 60 km (8 to 37 miles) deep. Although rock seems firmly fixed in place, the tremendous heat of the Earth's interior keeps it slowly moving. Over millions of years, new rock is built up and then gradually worn away, and this has formed all the different features, such as mountain peaks, gorges and valleys, that we see on the surface.

What is rock?

Rock is the solid material that forms the surface of the Earth on land and under the sea. In some places, particularly near volcanoes, rock can be quite young, having formed a few thousand or only a few hundred years ago. In most places rock is very old. The oldest rocks discovered so far are in north-west Canada. They date back nearly 4 billion years, to a time when the Earth's crust had only recently formed.

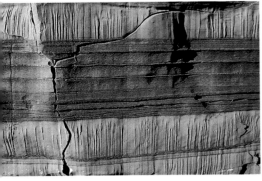

Ancient rockface   These rocks, in Western Australia, are 3 billion years old.

THAT'S AMAZING!

FLOATING ROCKS

The lightest rock, called pumice, is produced by volcanoes. Pumice is full of gas-filled spaces, and some is so light that it floats on water. In 1883, a volcano called Krakatoa erupted and produced so much floating pumice that boats had trouble getting through it.

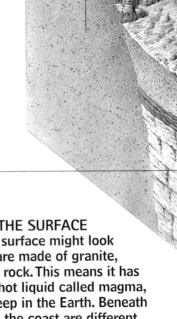

Tough stuff   Granite takes thousands of years to wear away.

Porous rock
Limestone is a type of sedimentary rock that is often made from the shells of tiny animals. Unlike granite, it is porous, which means that water can seep through it.

SEEING BENEATH THE SURFACE

A slice of the Earth's surface might look like this. The hills are made of granite, which is an igneous rock. This means it has been formed from a hot liquid called magma, which comes from deep in the Earth. Beneath the low ground and the coast are different rocks, arranged in layers. These are called sedimentary rocks because they are made from sediment – particles of soil and eroded rock that have been washed down from higher ground. As layers of sediment pile up, the lower layers are squashed down to form rock.

Glued grains
Sandstone is a type of sedimentary rock made from grains of sand that have become cemented together.

History in rock

When water seeps through limestone, it slowly dissolves the rock. After thousands of years, this process results in a cave. When water drips through the ceiling of a cave, it leaves behind tiny deposits of minerals dissolved out of the rock, and these gradually grow down to form columns, called stalactites. Where water drips onto the cave floor, columns called stalagmites grow up.

Sometimes stalactites and stalagmites meet, forming pillars.

Why are some rocks harder than others?

The hardness of a rock depends partly on what minerals it contains. Some minerals are very hard, but a few are quite soft. You can test a mineral's hardness by seeing what will scratch it. For example, a steel nail will scratch calcite but not quartz. No natural substance can scratch a diamond because it is the hardest mineral of all.

Scale of hardness The five minerals on the right are arranged in order of hardness, starting with the softest – gypsum. Below each mineral is an object that matches it in hardness.

Gypsum   **Calcite**   **Fluorite**   **Quartz**   **Apatite**

Fingernail   **Bronze coin**   **Iron nail**   **Steel knife**   **Glass**

Are minerals the same as rocks?

Minerals are the chemical ingredients that make up rocks. Minerals often form crystals, and sometimes one type is found on its own. More often, different minerals are mixed together, forming rock. Granite is made up of three different minerals – quartz, feldspar and mica.

Mineral mixture
Mineral crystals glint in the light. Can you see them in this piece of granite?

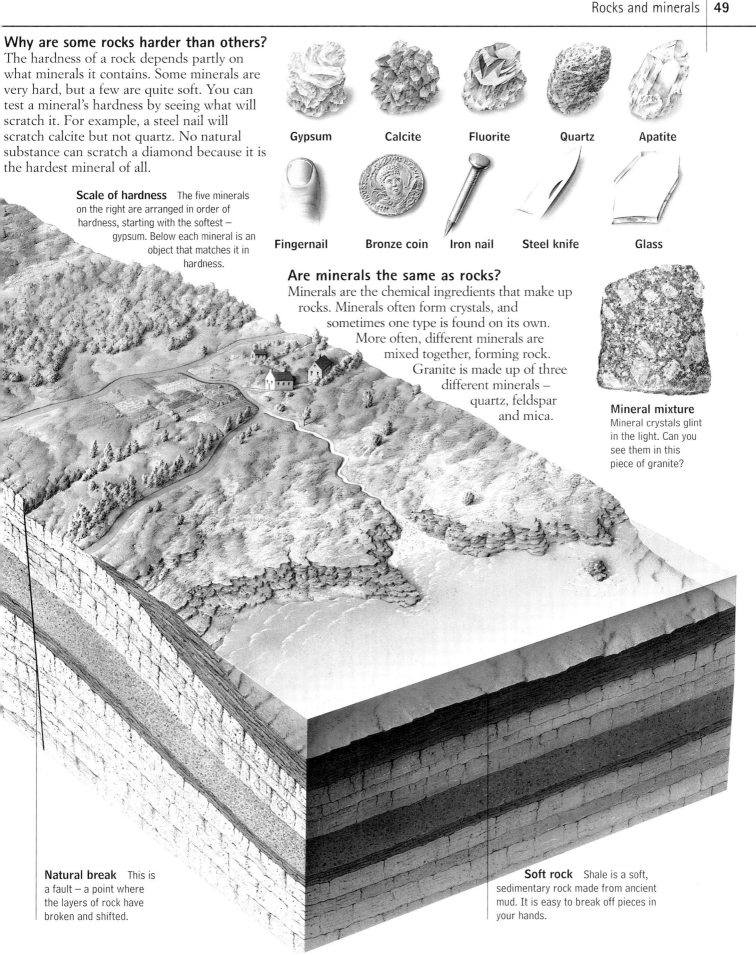

Natural break This is a fault – a point where the layers of rock have broken and shifted.

Soft rock Shale is a soft, sedimentary rock made from ancient mud. It is easy to break off pieces in your hands.

Inside the Earth p.24 · Rocks and minerals p.48 · Fact File p.312

Gems are formed by mineral crystals, and these crystals come in different shapes and colours. Most gems are extra-hard and can be cut and polished to produce gemstones. Precious metals sometimes turn up as pure lumps, called nuggets. More often, they are found in the form of an ore, that is, mixed in with other minerals. Some gems and metals have special uses in industry and electronics, but many are valuable because they are beautiful and rare.

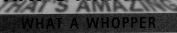

THAT'S AMAZING
WHAT A WHOPPER
The biggest nugget of pure gold ever discovered was found in Australia in 1869. It weighed about 70 kg (154 lb), and was nicknamed the 'Welcome Stranger'. At today's prices, it would be worth about £425 000.

Emerald This beautiful gemstone gets its green colour from tiny traces of a metal called chromium.

How do you cut a diamond?
Diamond is the hardest substance on Earth, so the only thing that can cut it is a diamond-bladed saw. The person cutting a rough diamond marks where the blade should go, so that as little as possible is wasted. Each piece is cut into a shape that has lots of flat faces, called facets, arranged at precise angles to each other to reflect light in all directions.

Long process This is the procedure for cutting over 50 facets. They give a diamond its sparkle.

North America Precious metals, including gold, silver and platinum.

Colombia The best emeralds and the largest single diamond crystal.

Brazil The biggest aquamarine crystal ever found, and the largest emerald.

What is so special about precious metals?
Precious metals are unusual in several ways. Platinum is useful as a catalyst – a substance that speeds up chemical reactions. Gold and silver are about ten times better than steel at conducting heat. They are also good at conducting electricity, and are used in electronics. Gold is quite soft, so it can be hammered very thin, and never rusts or tarnishes.

Gold frame Gold is available in thin sheets, called gold leaf. Here, it has been used to decorate a carved wooden picture frame.

Aquamarine Crystals of this mineral develop in cavities inside blocks of granite.

Agate This is an unusual form of the mineral called quartz. It is made of tiny crystals laid down in coloured bands.

Zircon Although not particularly rare, this crystal is hard and can be cut to make brilliant gems.

Amethyst This is a kind of quartz. It is stained with tiny amounts of iron.

Gold Soft and easy to shape, gold has been highly prized for thousands of years.

Jasper This hard gemstone can be red, brown or yellow.

Crystal quartz Quartz is common, but big crystals are quite hard to find.

NATURAL TREASURES
These are some of the world's most valuable gems and precious metals. The gems are shown in their raw state, and as cut stones. Some look like glassy crystals, others like solid, coloured rock.

Rose quartz This kind of quartz gets its colour from a metal called titanium.

Russia The Ural Mountains are a source of large emeralds and diamonds.

Fluorite This glassy crystal occurs in a variety of colours.

The Klondike Goldrush

In 1896, gold was discovered in the Klondike region of the Yukon Territory, Canada. It started one of the world's biggest 'goldrushes', as people – known as prospectors – poured into the area to find gold for themselves. The goldfields could only be reached by a hazardous journey through high mountains, at a time when the region had no surfaced roads. The Klondike Goldrush lasted for about five years before the gold ran out.

Prospectors in the Klondike.

Myanmar (Burma) The largest and best-quality rubies.

Sri Lanka Some of the world's biggest sapphires.

South Africa The deepest gold mines in the world.

Australia The largest cut sapphire; the largest-ever gold nuggets.

Ruby This gem contains aluminium, a metal that is common in the Earth's crust. Perfect examples are extremely rare.

Malachite This gem gets its green colour from a metal called copper.

Citrine This is a rare brownish or yellow form of quartz.

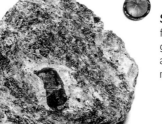

Sapphire Among the five most valuable gemstones, sapphires are similar in chemical make-up to rubies.

Fluorspar Compared to other gems, these crystals are common. They can be purple, green or even yellow.

Why are some gems so rare?
Rare gems form in unusual underground conditions that do not occur in many places. Once these gems have formed, they can be difficult to find. For example, diamonds are made of carbon, which is one of the commonest elements on Earth. But carbon turns into diamond only when it is squeezed and heated deep in the Earth's crust. Before a diamond can be found, it has to be carried up to the surface by moving rock – something that does not happen often.

Silver This sometimes forms nuggets, but it is also produced from ores.

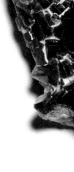

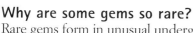

Fossil fuels

🌐 Inside the Earth p.24 · Oceans and seas p.36 · Fossil trails p.60 · Fact File p.282

In prehistoric times, people learned how to burn wood to keep themselves warm. Less than 3000 years ago, people discovered that coal, oil and natural gas also burn, and that they give off a lot more heat than wood. Since then, these three fuels have become an essential part of daily life. We use them for heat and light, and for powering all kinds of machines. They are known as 'fossil fuels' because they formed from the buried remains of living things.

How is coal formed?

If you look at a piece of coal through a magnifying glass, you may be able to spot pieces of fossilised wood and bark, and even the outlines of leaves. These show that coal is made from plants – mostly large tree ferns – and that it formed long ago. The plants grew in huge swampy forests in warm parts of the world. As they died, their remains piled up on the ground, but the stagnant swamp water stopped them rotting away. Instead, they were buried under mud and silt until they lay deep underground. Over millions of years, pressure underground squeezed the remains of the trees, turning them into the black, shiny rock we call coal.

Fern fossil Fossilised fern leaves from plants that grew in prehistoric times can be seen preserved in this piece of coal.

How do we know where to find oil?

Oil is found in scattered areas, known as oilfields. To discover where these are, geologists first look for places where layers of sedimentary rock – usually sandstone, limestone and shale – have folded, as pockets of oil and gas can be trapped in the folds. They do this by measuring variations in gravity and in the Earth's magnetic field. Then they set off small explosions and listen for echoes from underground. If these tests are positive, a test well is drilled to find out if oil and gas are there.

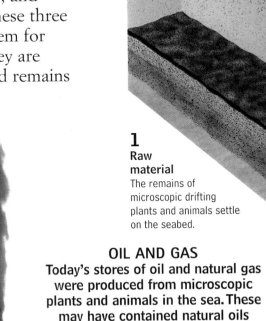

1
Raw material
The remains of microscopic drifting plants and animals settle on the seabed.

OIL AND GAS

Today's stores of oil and natural gas were produced from microscopic plants and animals in the sea. These may have contained natural oils when alive. When they died, their remains settled on the seabed and became buried by sediment. Once buried, the pressure of the sea and sediment pressing down from above slowly turned them into fossil fuels.

Finding oil Scientists prepare to carry out geological tests. When oil is found, underground pressure can force up a powerful jet (left).

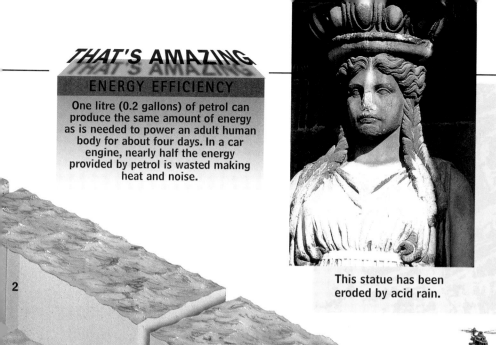

THAT'S AMAZING

THAT'S AMAZING

ENERGY EFFICIENCY

One litre (0.2 gallons) of petrol can produce the same amount of energy as is needed to power an adult human body for about four days. In a car engine, nearly half the energy provided by petrol is wasted making heat and noise.

This statue has been eroded by acid rain.

Fossil fuels and air pollution

When oil and coal are burned, they release gases into the air. Some of these gases are poisonous, which is why smoky air can make you cough and choke. One of these gases is called sulphur dioxide. It can combine with moisture in the clouds to form acid rain. This rain damages buildings and trees. Fossil fuels also give off a gas called carbon dioxide. Increased carbon dioxide in the Earth's atmosphere is causing global warming.

2
Conversion into oil and gas
Warmth from the Earth's interior, combined with pressure from the sediment above, converts the rotting remains of animals and plants into oil droplets and minute bubbles of gas.

3 Coming within reach
Over millions of years, the layers of rock buckle and bend. Oil droplets and gas bubbles squeeze upwards through the rock until they reach dense rock at the Earth's surface.

When will fossil fuels run out?
The Earth has huge reserves of coal – probably enough to last at least another 500 years. But coal is not an ideal fuel: it produces lots of smoke when it burns, and it is not much good for powering cars or planes. There is still plenty of natural gas, but the world's oil reserves could begin to run out within the next 50 years. This is one of the reasons why scientists are developing renewable energy sources using heat from the Sun and wind power.

4
Extracting oil
Oil rigs drill down to the rock layers where oil droplets and gas bubbles have become trapped. Pressure underground forces oil and gas up the drill pipe to the surface.

The Living World 2

The birth of the planets p.16 · The Earth's atmosphere p.28 · Satellites in space p.180 · Fact File p.268, 274

If you could go back 4 billion years in time, you would find the Earth a very strange place. You would not be able to breathe because the air would be filled with poisonous gases, and you would not be able to eat because there would be no food, and no living things. There would be nothing flying in the sky and nothing swimming in the water. Most of the ground would be bare rock. But in the sea, somewhere, the beginnings of life would be stirring.

How did life on Earth begin?

We can never know for sure, but scientists are certain that it cannot have happened all at once. Instead, they believe that it developed very gradually, through a series of chemical reactions. Scientists test this idea by re-creating the conditions of the early Earth in laboratory experiments. In one experiment, they put a small amount of water in a glass container, to imitate the sea. Next, they remove all the air above the water, and replace it with the gases they think were in the atmosphere 4 billion years ago. After this, they seal the container, and pass electric sparks through the gases, to imitate lightning flashing through the air. When they open the glass container, they find that the water contains some of the complex chemicals that make up living things. Experiments like these suggest that life could have started quite by accident, most probably in the sea.

IN THE BEGINNING

There were more volcanoes on Earth 4 billion years ago than there are now. And they erupted more often because the centre of the Earth was much hotter. The volcanoes pushed gases into the air, such as methane, hydrogen and ammonia. Some of these were crucial to the formation of life.

THAT'S AMAZING

OXYGEN AVOIDERS

Some prehistoric bacteria from the start of life have descendants that we can study. These bacteria cannot tolerate oxygen, because it was not part of Earth's ancient atmosphere. They live in the black mud at the bottom of marshes, or in other places without oxygen. They make food by chemical reactions, and do not rely on sunlight like other living things.

Oxygen changes everything

The earliest living things were bacteria, which grew by using chemicals in the sea. When the chemicals started to run out, it became harder for life to survive. Some living things, called cyanobacteria, found a new way of growing, called photosynthesis. Photosynthesis works by using the energy in sunlight, and it produces oxygen as a waste product. As this new gas began to build up, the Earth's atmosphere changed, creating the kind of air we breathe today.

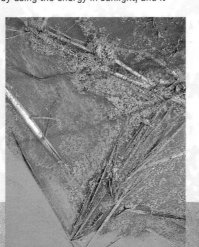

Cyanobacteria growing in the Darling River, Australia.

Why does the Earth have life?

Several things about planet Earth make it uniquely suited to life. The main one is abundant water. No other planet that we know of has the huge oceans we have, nor the many lakes and rivers. Water is a very important ingredient of all living things because it has many properties that no other substance has. All the important reactions that occur inside our cells require water, and all the organs in our bodies, such as the heart and lungs and liver, rely on being surrounded by water. Without water, life as we know it could not go on. Could there be a completely different kind of life form that is not based on water? Scientists have tried to imagine such life forms, but it is hard to see what could take the place of water.

Is there life in outer space?

Despite listening very carefully for radio signals, scientists have not found any signs of life in space. But many of them think it likely that life has developed elsewhere. How many other planets might be inhabited? To answer this difficult question, an astronomer called Frank Drake devised the equation that is shown below. When all the different parts of the equation are filled in, it gives an idea of how many civilisations might exist in our galaxy. Astronomers' estimates vary from several billion to just one.

R^*	f_p	n_e	f_l	f_i	f_c	f_L
How many stars are formed in the Milky Way?	What per cent of these stars form planets?	What per cent of the planets are suitable for life?	On what per cent of these has life evolved?	What per cent of these planets have intelligent life?	What per cent of these can communicate?	How long can a communicating civilisation last?
Around ten a year	%	%	%	%	%	100 years– 1 billion years

Drake's equation

Why not make your own estimate of the total number (N) of communicating civilisations in our galaxy?

$$N = R^* \times f_p \times n_e \times f_l \times f_i \times f_c \times f_L$$

=

The story of evolution

🔄 Fossil trails p.60 · Microscopic life p.62 ·
Genes and heredity p.132 · Fact File p.274, 286

Every living thing on Earth is descended from one common ancestor that lived long ago. We know this because, although living things have different genes, they have all inherited the same genetic code to make those genes work. That ancestor was probably a creature similar to a bacterium. But how could a bacterium produce descendants as different as sharks, daisies, cucumbers and camels? Living things slowly change, or evolve. Over millions of years, tiny differences have built up to produce completely new species.

Horse ancestor
Hyracotherium had feet with four toes.

Anchytherium

Hypohippus

Merychippus

Hyracotherium

Mesohippus

Pliohippus

THE EVOLUTION OF THE HORSE

Horses belong to a family of animals 50 million years old. The earliest ancestor of the horse, called *Hyracotherium*, was the size of a dog, and had four-toed feet. Its descendants grew bigger, and evolved longer legs with fewer toes. Today's horses have just one toe or hoof on each foot.

From tadpole to frog

The ancestors of frogs were fish that could pull themselves around using strong, fleshy front fins. About 300 million years ago, these fish gradually started to crawl out onto dry land. Today, frogs still re-enact this part of their past, because they start life as tadpoles, which swim around by lashing their tails. After a few weeks tadpoles start to lose their tails. They grow legs and take up life on land.

Tadpoles, like the ones shown on the left, are born with tails and no legs.

Why do animals evolve?

Evolution has produced all the creatures found on Earth. The evidence for this comes from fossils, and from comparing the structure and chemistry of living creatures. But what makes evolution happen? Scientists believe that the answer is something called 'natural selection'. All animals and plants produce more young than can possibly survive. Some die, while others go on to produce young of their own. In general, the ones that are best suited to their environment survive, while the weakest die out.

Because the best adapted survive and are most likely to pass on their genes to the next generation, the species gradually becomes more and more suited to its environment.

The same but different
The Cape pangolin, or scaly anteater (top), from Zimbabwe and the armadillo (above) from Florida both feed on ants, and both have developed protective plating and long snouts for rooting.

Why does a pangolin look like an armadillo?

Sometimes, animals that live in the same way and eat much the same food evolve to look like each other, even though they are not closely related. The armadillo's main diet is ants and termites, which it digs out of the ground with powerful claws. It has a long snout for nosing around in the ground after insects, and thick plates of bone protecting its skin from the ants' painful stings. This bony armour also gives it protection from predators out on the open plains where the ant nests are found. Armadillos live only in the Americas, but in Africa there are animals called pangolins that look remarkably similar. They, too, live out on the plains and feed mainly on termites and ants. The pangolins and armadillos are not related, but because they live the same kind of life, they have evolved along similar lines. This is called 'convergent evolution'.

Hipparion

Equus

Gone for ever The dodo was hunted to extinction in the late 17th century.

Onager
Equus hemionus

Zebra
Equus burchelli

Przewalski's wild horse
Equus caballus

Today Horses now have feet with just one toe.

Why do some animals become extinct?

Some creatures die out, or become extinct, while others flourish. This is part of the process of evolution. Successful species move into new areas, or start eating new food, or adapt to a change in climate, and so evolve into new forms. The extinctions make space for new species to emerge. Human activities such as forest clearance, building and road-making, which are not part of a natural process, are now also causing extinctions – too quickly for evolution to fill the gaps. We are now losing thousands of species every day, and they are not being replaced.

🌐 Rocks and minerals p.48 · Fossil fuels p.52 ·
Prehistoric animals p.72 · Dinosaurs p.74 · Fact File p.274

No one has ever seen a tyrannosaurus, or any other dinosaur, but we know a lot about them. Almost all our knowledge about prehistoric animals comes from fossils, which are rock-like 'models' of the bones of animals. The bones themselves were buried in layers of mud or sand, millions of years ago, and then slowly turned to rock themselves by a natural chemical process. Very rarely, softer parts of the body such as skin, feathers and fur also become fossilised, giving many useful clues about life in the past.

HOW FOSSILS FORM
If a dinosaur dies beside a lake and falls into the shallow water, it has a very good chance of slowly turning into a fossil. The dinosaur's body is slowly covered by muddy sediment. Its skin and flesh start to rot away, leaving just the bare bones. But once the bones are completely covered up, they do not break down any more. Instead, they are slowly fossilised, or turned into rock.

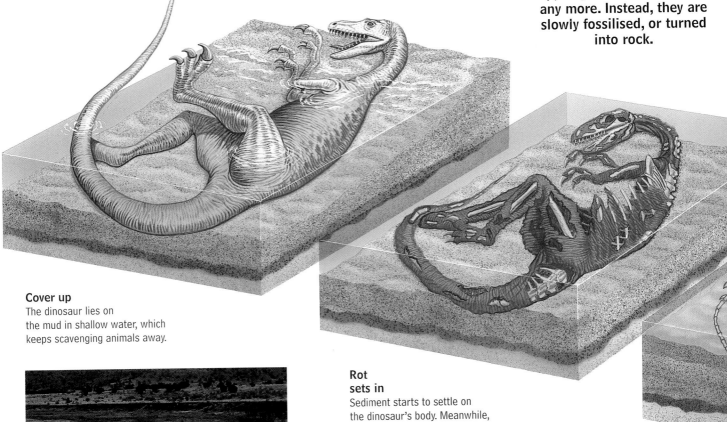

Cover up
The dinosaur lies on the mud in shallow water, which keeps scavenging animals away.

Rot sets in
Sediment starts to settle on the dinosaur's body. Meanwhile, bacteria attack the body's soft parts, making them rot away.

What are the best places to find fossils?
Fossils are found in rocks such as chalk, limestone, sandstone and shale. These were formed long ago by sediments building up on the seabed or at the bottoms of lakes. They are called 'sedimentary rocks'. Rocks formed by volcanic action, such as granite and basalt, do not contain fossils. You can find fossils where sedimentary rocks are being cut away by erosion, such as in sea cliffs or river gorges.

Follow the footprints
Erosion by running water has revealed fossilised dinosaur footprints in Colorado, USA.

Fossils within fossils

Sometimes, a fossil animal is found with another fossil animal inside it. The larger animal may have been pregnant with young at the time it died, in which case the animal inside is an unborn baby animal. In other cases, the animal inside was eaten by the larger animal just before the larger animal died, and became fossilised with it.

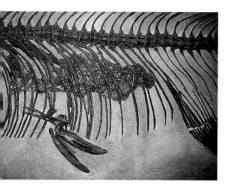

The remains of a fish inside another fossilised creature.

Do dead animals always turn into fossils?

When animals die, the bones are usually chewed by other, scavenging animals, scattered by the rain and wind, or bleached and broken down to dust by the Sun. For this reason, the bones of most animals do not turn into fossils, but disappear forever. Of all the animals that have ever lived, no more than one in a million has survived as a fossil. Fossils form only when a dead animal is buried quickly by sediments, before there is a chance for the bones to be destroyed. When this happens, the bones are locked up in the sediment as it slowly turns to rock. The bones themselves also turn to rock in the process, but they keep their shape. Millions of years later, erosion strips away the layers of rock and exposes the fossil.

What is coal?

Coal is just old wood, twigs and leaves. It began as forests, which grew in swampy land more than 300 million years ago. When the trees died they fell into the swamp water, which prevented them from breaking down properly. They turned into peat, a soft brown substance. The huge pressure of rock layers building up above turned the peat into coal.

Prehistoric plants Animals are not the only things that can turn into fossils. Coal sometimes contains the fossilised bark and leaves of giant ferns and clubmosses – trees that grew in swampy forests more than 300 million years ago.

Dead and buried After hundreds of years, the bones are safely buried beneath the surface. Water seeps into the bones, leaving behind minerals that help to turn the bones into fossils.

Finished fossil As the sediment piles up, pressure grows. After thousands of years, this turns the sediment and fossils into rock.

THAT'S AMAZING

TRACKS THROUGH TIME

Animal footprints can be preserved in the rocks, and so can insect trails or even the traces left on the seabed by worms and jellyfish. However, these small, delicate structures can only be preserved in rock that originally comes from mud or sand.

Microscopic life

How life began p.56 · Immune system p.136 ·
Microscopes and telescopes p.166 · Fact File p.286

A huge part of the living world is too small to be seen except under a microscope, which magnifies everything tens or even thousands of times. Some of these microscopic creatures are harmful to us, causing diseases or making food rot. Others are useful, such as the yeasts that help us make bread, and the bacteria that make yoghurt and cheese.

Chlamydomonas This tiny organism lives near the surface of lakes and ponds. Like plants, it needs sunlight to survive.

Vorticella Each vorticella consists of a single cell with a cup on a long stalk. Tiny beating hairs (cilia) drive food particles into the centre of the 'cup', where they are absorbed.

What's living on you?

In the wild, most animals have fleas, lice and other small parasites living on their bodies. The same was true of our ancestors. A large, warm-blooded creature such as a human being is like a walking restaurant to smaller forms of life, and the meals are all free. Today, we use soap and water to get rid of these small parasites from our bodies and our clothes, and if all else fails we use chemicals to kill them. But there are many microscopic creatures sharing our lives that we do not even know about. Most of them do us no harm at all. Some are even beneficial, such as the bacteria which live on our skins and in our intestines.

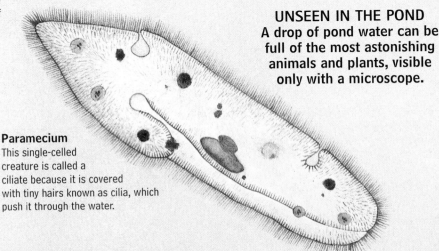

Paramecium
This single-celled creature is called a ciliate because it is covered with tiny hairs known as cilia, which push it through the water.

UNSEEN IN THE POND
A drop of pond water can be full of the most astonishing animals and plants, visible only with a microscope.

What tiny creatures share your home?

If you think your house just belongs to you and your family, think again. As well as flies, spiders and woodlice, there are many microscopic animals and plants living with you. No matter how clean your house is, the carpets, armchairs and mattresses are probably full of tiny animals called house dust mites. These feed on the flakes of skin that you shed every day. Before the mites get to them, these bits of skin provide food for microscopic moulds, and the mites eat the moulds along with the skin. As long as you are not allergic to moulds or dust mites, neither will do you any harm.

Invisible occupant
This dust mite, a tiny relative of spiders, is magnified around 375 times. It collects food with microscopic pincers, and usually feeds at night.

Unwelcome guest A human head louse, magnified around 30 times, clings to a strand of hair.

Euglena Euglena moves around by beating a hair-like growth called a flagellum. It lives like a plant, by harnessing energy from sunshine.

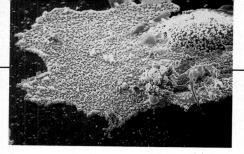

Small but effective
The yellow spheres are flu viruses inside a human cell (above).

Deadly bite Malaria is caused by single-celled parasites that are carried by mosquitoes (1). When an infected mosquito bites a person, some of the parasites get into the blood (2), feed inside red blood cells, and attack the liver.

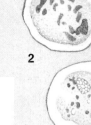

1

2

Rotifers Rotifers (left) are related to roundworms (nematodes), even though they look nothing like worms. There are 2000 different species, mostly living in ponds or on wet mosses in woodlands.

What is the smallest living thing?

The smallest living things are viruses. They are like car engines without any wheels or bodywork attached: they have no way of moving around and no cell wall, unlike other living things. Viruses do not even have any way of reproducing themselves. In order to produce more viruses, they have to invade other cells and take them over. This is why viruses cause diseases. When you catch a cold, the cells in your nose have been taken over by viruses so that they can reproduce themselves.

The microscopic world that feeds the whales

Blue whales feed on very small animals called krill, using their huge sieve-like mouths to catch thousands at a time. The krill feed on microscopic animals and

Krill are tiny, shrimp-like creatures.

plants called plankton that float in the upper layers of the ocean. So blue whales, which are the largest living creatures in the world, are directly dependent on some of the smallest creatures for their food.

Cyclops Cyclops are microscopic relatives of crabs and shrimps. They get their name from the fact that they have only one eye, like the Cyclops of Greek legend. The two little bags attached to either side of this animal's tail contain eggs, showing that it is female.

Daphnia
Daphnia (above) are related to crabs and shrimps. They can just be seen with the naked eye, but you need a microscope to see their structure. They are transparent, so you can watch their stomach digesting food, and all the other internal organs. They swim by beating their brush-like antennae.

THAT'S AMAZING

HOW TO LIVE ON LEAVES

Animals such as deer and horses have bacteria in their digestive systems that allow them to digest grass and leaves. Our ancestors once had these bacteria too, and attached to your intestine is an 'appendix'. This empty pocket is all that remains of the large structure which once held leaf-digesting bacteria.

Heliozoans
Heliozoans (right) have spiky skeletons. They live mainly in ponds and lakes. The spikes are made of silica – the same substance that makes glass.

Fungi: mushrooms and toadstools

🔄 Forests p.42 · Microscopic life p.62 ·
Fact File p.286, 291

People often think that living things are either plants or animals. But there are many other kinds of life. Some are tiny creatures such as bacteria. Others, called fungi, can look like plants, but grow by absorbing food instead of by using sunlight. Fungi spread by scattering spores – dust-like particles much simpler than seeds.

Why does bread go mouldy?
Bread is an ideal food for many fungi. Their spores are everywhere in the air, and as soon as you take out a loaf of bread, some mould spores fall on it. Long before you see any furry mould on the bread, moulds are growing but, in small amounts, they do us no harm.

Bread mould   The brown dots contain spores, which are constantly being released and germinate into new mould.

Attacks by fungi
In Australia, koalas can become infected with different kinds of fungi. One of the fungi is associated with certain types of eucalyptus tree – the trees that koalas live in and feed on. The fungi are not passed from one koala to another, and most healthy koalas are not killed by them. Koalas are not the only victims of fungi. A fungus carried around by beetles, for example, caused the Dutch elm disease that wiped out many of Britain's elm trees in the 1970s.

FOREST FUNGI
Forests are good places to find fungi, because many fungi feed on wood or on fallen leaves. Some, like the red-and-white fly agaric, are useful to trees because they help them to collect nutrients from the soil. Others, like the honey fungus, are much less welcome because they attack living wood.

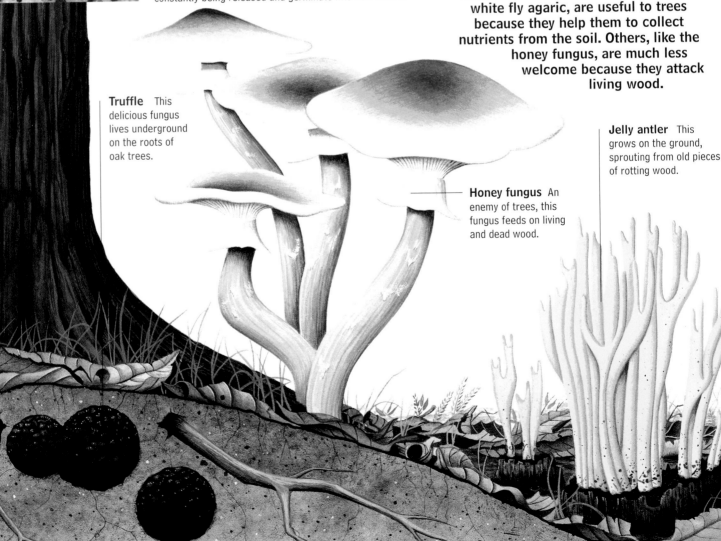

Truffle   This delicious fungus lives underground on the roots of oak trees.

Honey fungus   An enemy of trees, this fungus feeds on living and dead wood.

Jelly antler   This grows on the ground, sprouting from old pieces of rotting wood.

Are toadstools poisonous?

Some toadstools are very poisonous. You would only have to touch them and lick your fingers for them to make you ill. People have died from eating just a few of them. In 1534, Pope Clement was killed by the death cap toadstool, the world's most poisonous fungus. There are many delicious wild fungi, but you need to be an expert to distinguish them from the poisonous ones.

Danger: keep clear! The death cap (below) grows in woodland in Europe and North America. Some edible fungi look quite like it.

Living gravestones
If you see a cluster of honey fungi (above) near a tree, you can be sure that the tree is either dead or about to die.

The mouse's whiskers

Most fungi release spores into the air. These fly about and, if they settle in the right place, grow into new fungi. One fungus is much more cunning about spreading its spores. It grows on mouse droppings, and produces spores with long, upright threads attached. These stand up in the air and catch on the whiskers of passing mice, where they stick fast and are carried off. Later the mouse washes its face and swallows the spores, which travel right through its stomach and intestines. When the mouse next leaves droppings, the spores are there, ready to start growing.

Spores carried in mouse droppings.

Oyster fungus This edible fungus grows on dead or dying trees.

Fly agaric
Beautiful but highly poisonous, this brilliantly coloured fungus usually lives close to birch or spruce trees.

Red cage fungus
This fungus is about the size of a golf ball. The inside of the 'cage' contains slimy spores that are spread by flies.

THAT'S AMAZING
FUNGAL GIANTS

One of the largest toadstools ever found was an example of an edible kind called *Polyporus frondosus*. It weighed 33 kg (72 lb). Fungi on living trees can grow even larger. One in the United States measured 142 cm (56 in) across and weighed at least 140 kg (300 lb).

Lemon disc This fungus feeds on dead wood, growing in dense clusters on old fallen branches.

➡ Tree life p.70 · Genes and heredity p.132 ·
Cooking, food and drink p.230 · Fact File p.287, 290

Look at trees and other plants, and what colour do you see? The answer, almost always, is various shades of green. That green colour is produced by a chemical called chlorophyll, which is found on the leaves of plants. Chlorophyll is one of the most important substances on Earth, because it absorbs energy from sunlight, and enables plants to grow. Without it, plants could not survive, and animals would have nothing to eat.

How do plants feed?

Unlike animals, plants do not need to find food. Instead, they make food 'out of thin air' with the help of chlorophyll. The chlorophyll in a plant's leaves absorbs energy from sunshine. The plant then uses this energy to combine water with carbon dioxide, making a sugary food substance called glucose. This process is called photosynthesis. Plants use glucose to grow. They also use it to form sweet-tasting fruits, and to make nectar, a syrupy liquid that attracts insects to flowers. Any spare sugar is stored in the plant's seeds or roots.

Light is essential for plants, because they cannot make glucose without it. This is why they grow towards the light. If a plant is shut up in a dark place, it turns pale because its chlorophyll breaks down, and eventually it dies.

Sugar from the Sun
Plants make glucose in their leaves, using energy from the Sun.

Glucose

Energy from Sun

Water from roots

Carbon dioxide from air

Oxygen released into air

Insect-eating plants

Some plants that grow in poor soil get the nutrients they need by trapping and digesting passing insects. Most produce an attractive scent or glistening drops that look like nectar to lure insects to their doom. Sticky glue or a pool of liquid keeps an insect in the trap while the plant closes and begins to digest it.

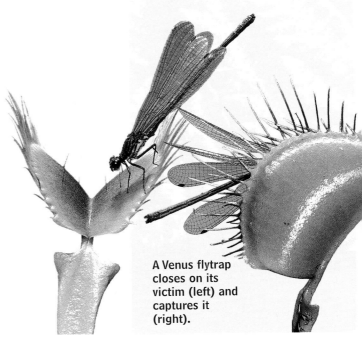

A Venus flytrap closes on its victim (left) and captures it (right).

How do plants drink?

Although plants can absorb a little water through their leaves, they get most of the water they need by drawing it up from the ground through their roots. The roots are in close contact with the particles of soil around them. Tiny rootlets connected to the roots extend into the soil, and these draw in moisture. If you pull up a plant, you can see the delicate white roots, but you cannot see the microscopic rootlets that absorb water. If a plant is pulled up, the rootlets are broken. As soon as they stop working, the plant starts to wilt.

Above and below
The branches and stems of a plant that you can see above the ground are sometimes less extensive than the roots below the ground.

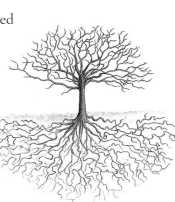

All life depends on plants

Almost every living thing depends on plants for its food supply. Even the leopard and lion, which only eat meat, are actually feeding on plants, because that is what feeds their prey. In the same way, if you drink milk you are really consuming grass: without grass, there would be no cows to give us milk. The grass turns the Sun's energy into food, the cow turns that energy into milk, and you use that energy to kick a football around, or dance or do homework. Even reading this book uses up some of that energy! The link from grass to cows to humans, or from grass to antelope to lions, is called a food chain.

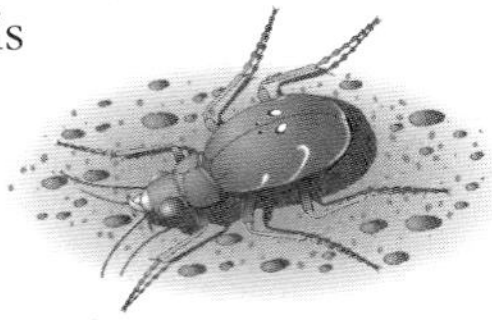

Hawk catches swallow

Hawk carcass eaten by maggots

Swallow eats beetle

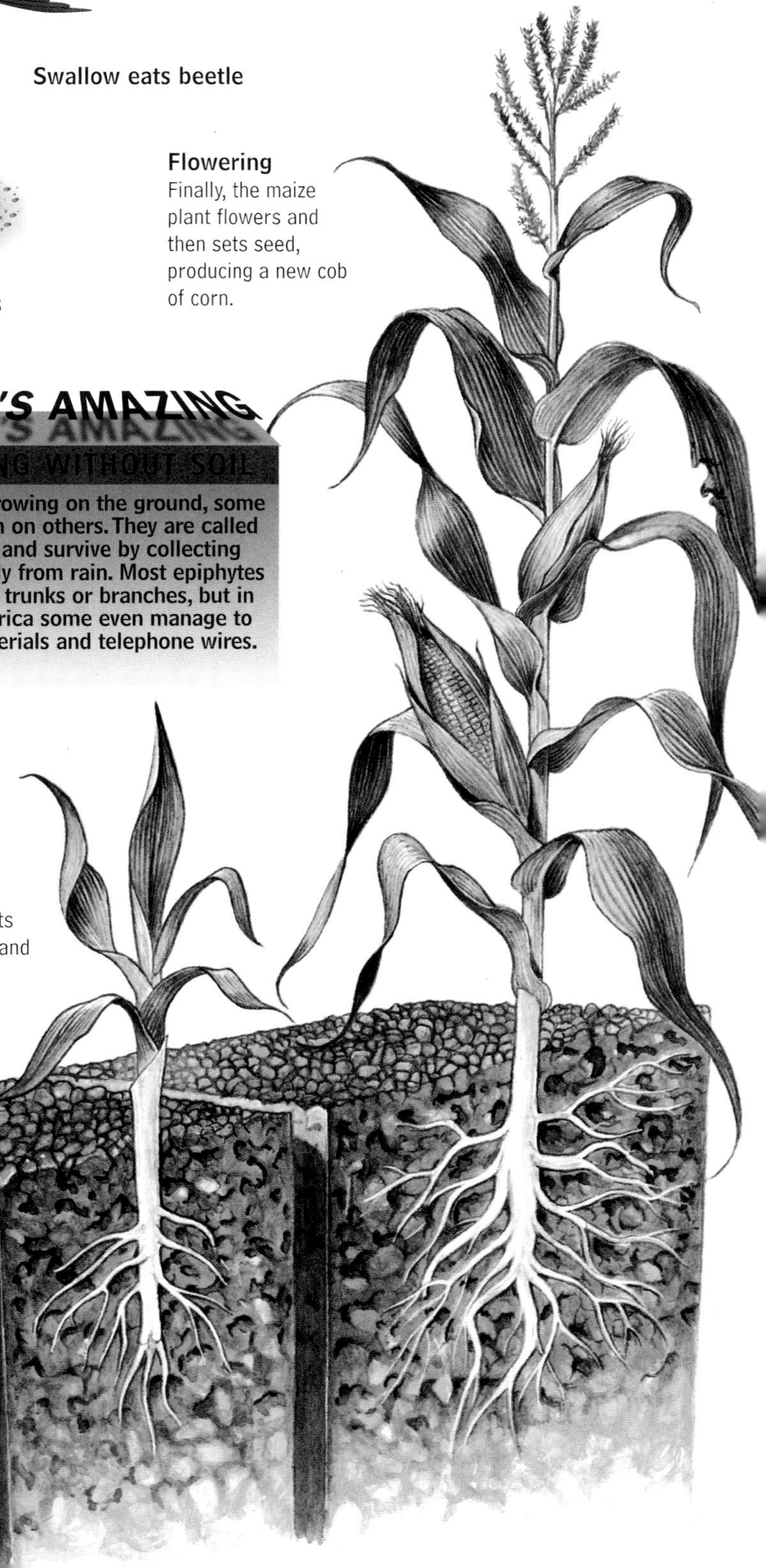

Flowering Finally, the maize plant flowers and then sets seed, producing a new cob of corn.

Pass on energy At each stage of a food chain, the energy the leaf made from the Sun is passed on.

Beetle eats small bug

Aphid eats leaf

Bug eats aphid

THAT'S AMAZING

GROWING WITHOUT SOIL

Instead of growing on the ground, some plants perch on others. They are called epiphytes and survive by collecting water directly from rain. Most epiphytes live on tree trunks or branches, but in South America some even manage to live on TV aerials and telephone wires.

FROM SEED

Most plants – like the maize plants we eat as 'sweetcorn' – start life as seeds. However tiny, they contain all the genetic 'instructions' needed to make a new plant. A seed starts to grow in moist soil. At first, the plant lives on a store of food packed inside the seed. After a few days, it grows its first leaves and starts to make its own food by collecting the energy in sunshine. Eventually the plant flowers, and grows seeds of its own.

Growth More roots grow below ground, and more leaves above ground.

Lightwards The shoot grows up, while the roots grow down.

Germination The seed absorbs moisture from the soil and starts to grow.

How plants reproduce

Fungi: mushrooms and toadstools p.64 · How plants live p.66 · Fact File p.287, 290

Plants have to reproduce, just as animals do. First of all, most develop flowers which are then fertilised or pollinated, to produce seeds. The seeds ripen, and are scattered far and wide, eventually growing into new plants. Ferns and mosses reproduce in a different way. They do not have flowers. Instead of making seeds, they make microscopic spores which drift through the air.

How are flowers pollinated?

Flowers contain male parts which produce a fine dust called pollen, and female parts which produce seeds when they receive pollen from another flower. Some plants rely on the wind to spread their pollen, but most use animals. Insects, birds and bats visit flowers to feed on their sugary nectar. As they travel from bloom to bloom, they carry pollen with them, pollinating or fertilising the flowers they visit.

Busy bee In a day a honeybee pollinates thousands of flowers.

Fern spores Most ferns make their spores in tiny pads on the undersides of their leaves. When their spores are ripe, the pads split open, and the spores drift away on the wind.

Seeds on the move

Seeds need to move away from the plant they came from, so that they can grow in a clear space with plenty of light. Some seeds travel on the wind: dandelion seeds, for instance, use 'parachutes' to travel, while sycamore seeds use 'propellers'. Other seeds have tiny hooks which attach to the fur of a passing animal (or to our trousers and sweaters) and get carried about in that way. Coconut seeds are covered with thick fibres, so that the seed floats, and they are carried by the sea from one island to another. The liquid inside a coconut gives the young coconut plant some fresh water, which it needs when it lands on a sandy beach and starts to grow.

Sycamore

Burdock

Dandelion

Coconut

Do seeds die when birds eat them?

When birds eat many small fruits, they also eat the seeds inside them. They digest the fruit, but the seeds usually survive and come out in the bird's droppings. The seeds can germinate and grow, with the droppings providing the fertiliser they need for a good start in life.

Spreading seed Birds often drop seeds when they perch on walls.

How do plants grow from cuttings?

When a storm breaks branches from willow trees growing by a river, these fall in the water, float downstream, and can get stuck in the bank. The broken-off branches may make roots in the mud and grow into new trees. Many plants can grow in this way, and gardeners use the process to 'take cuttings' from plants.

Taking a cutting Gardeners cut off a small stem or twig and push it into a pot of soil. The cutting develops roots and grows into a new plant.

THE RACE TO REPRODUCE

On a forest floor in early summer, plants are busily reproducing – in a variety of ways. Wild strawberries develop flowers and grow 'mini-plants' on long stalks called runners. Ferns and mosses make spores on the undersides of their leaves, or in special containers called capsules. They are not as colourful as flowers, but they are still easy to see.

Moss life cycle Mosses spread by shedding spores. Before spores can be made, a tiny male cell has to swim over the surface of the moss to fertilise a female cell.

Spores spreading in air

Capsule releases spores

Male cell

Female cell

Adult moss plant with spore capsule

Adult moss plant

Strawberry runner This young plant will soon take up life on its own.

🌐 Forests p.42 · How plants live p.66 ·
Ecology: connecting the living world p.100 · Fact File p.287, 290

A tree is just like any other plant, except that it can grow very tall. To keep upright, it needs a thick, strong central stem, called the trunk. Water from the roots travels up the trunk to the leaves. Sugar made in the leaves moves down the trunk to the roots, where it is stored until needed. So the tree trunk is rather like a vertical motorway, connecting the leaves with the roots.

THE OAK TREE'S STORY
If you see a large, gnarled oak tree still alive today, it could be as much as 800 years old. It may have begun to grow in the Middle Ages, and was already a large tree when Columbus sailed to the Americas.

1500s After 300 years, the oak is a sturdy young tree.

1200s A small sapling sprouts from an acorn.

Why do some trees lose their leaves?
Some trees lose their leaves in winter, and grow a whole new set of leaves the next spring. This is their way of getting through the winter – 'going into hibernation' just as some animals do. When the tree loses its leaves, it is closing down its operations and waiting until the worst weather is over. One advantage of doing this is that the tree produces leaves in the spring that are fresh and efficient at making food. They do not have to be especially strong, because even if insects damage them, they will be thrown away at the end of summer and replaced next year. Trees that keep their leaves through the winter have to make tougher leaves.

Autumn colour
Leaves turn a range of yellows, golds and reds as they die in autumn.

The tree house

Thousands of different animals can live in a single tree. There will be insects feeding on the leaves or on nectar from the flowers, boring into the wood, and laying eggs. Birds such as nuthatches, tree creepers and woodpeckers will come to feed on the insects. Squirrels, pine martens and voles will feed in the tree, while deer will come in search of fruit such as acorns.

A red squirrel feeds in a pine tree.

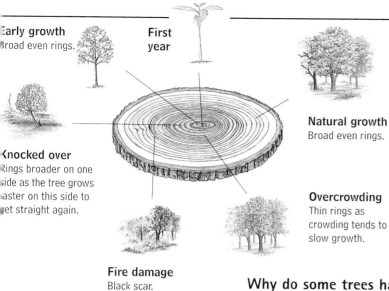

Early growth Broad even rings.

First year

Knocked over Rings broader on one side as the tree grows faster on this side to get straight again.

Natural growth Broad even rings.

Overcrowding Thin rings as crowding tends to slow growth.

Fire damage Black scar.

How can you tell a tree's age?

When a tree has been cut down, you can count the rings in the cross-section of the trunk. Each ring marks one year of growth. The light part of the ring is the fast growth that occurs in the spring, while the dark part of the ring is the slower summer growth. The rings also reveal what the weather was like at the time. Fat rings show a good year, with plenty of rainfall and sunshine producing rapid growth. Thin rings show a bad year, when growth was slow. Scientists can tell the age of trees without cutting them down. They use a tube-like instrument with a sharp end to bore into the trunk from the side, and pull out a long, thin sample of wood that shows all the rings.

Why do some trees have needles?

Coniferous trees, such as pines and spruces, have needles instead of leaves. One advantage of needles is that they are hard, and difficult for insects to chew. They are also useful for keeping in moisture, so the pine trees grow well in hot, dry places such as Greece or California. And where there is heavy snow in winter, the snow slides off without harming them.

Pine needles Most conifers are evergreen. Their tough leaves last for several years.

Late 1900s The oak is still alive today, while the world around it has changed beyond recognition.

1800s When the first railway lines were built in the 19th century, the oak was already an old tree.

THAT'S AMAZING

LIVING THE LONGEST

The oldest trees in the world are the bristlecone pines found in the Rocky Mountains of the USA. These trees have a further claim to fame: they are also the oldest living things on Earth. Some are thought to be as much as 6000 years old.

⟳ The story of evolution p.58 · Fossil trails p.60 · Dinosaurs p.74 ·
Origins of the human race p.206 · Fact file p.274

There were many animals alive in the past that are no longer living today. They are called prehistoric animals because they died out before history began: before people invented writing. This means there are no descriptions of these animals for us to read. But we have a good idea of what they looked like, because many of their bones have been preserved as fossils.

MAN AND TIGER
This is a scene that may have taken place on the plains of Africa about 2 million years ago. A sabre-tooth tiger is attacking a prehistoric relative of mankind called a robust australopithecine. We know that such attacks took place, because australopithecine skulls have been found with the telltale bite marks of sabre-tooth tigers on the top of the head.

What were the first animals to live on land?
Life first evolved in the sea, and it was many millions of years before any animals moved onto the land. The first to venture out of the water were probably small animals such as insects. They found rich forests in which to feed. Soon they were followed by fish that had strong fins to pull themselves around on dry land. In time, the strong fins of these fish developed into legs, as they evolved into amphibians: ancestors of the salamanders, newts and frogs that are still alive today.

Australopithecine These human-like animals are among our direct ancestors. Australopithecines walked on two legs. They probably used sticks to hunt animals and to dig for water, but they did not know how to make tools out of stone.

Ancient link The salamander is a descendant of prehistoric amphibians.

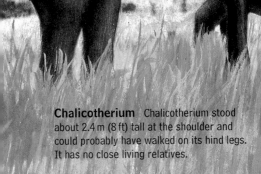

Chalicotherium Chalicotherium stood about 2.4 m (8 ft) tall at the shoulder and could probably have walked on its hind legs. It has no close living relatives.

Skeletons and fossils

An expert can tell a great deal about an animal by looking at its fossilised bones. The teeth show what it ate; the size of the bones show how large it was, and its shape shows whether it ran fast, or hopped slowly, or burrowed in the ground, or swam in the water. What is more, the details of the skull and other bones show if it was related to any animals that are still around today. All this information allows us to draw pictures of animals that no one has ever seen alive. There is one thing that fossils cannot tell us: what colour the animals were, and whether they had spots or stripes.

The skull of a sabre-toothed tiger.

Sabre-toothed tiger
Huge stabbing front teeth made these predators dangerous. There were many species of these big cats, living at different times in different parts of the world. The last ones died out about 11 000 years ago.

Did anything fly before the birds?

Insects were the first animals to fly, but a hundred million years ago flying reptiles known as pterosaurs were the kings of the air. Today, there are no reptiles left that can truly fly, although some snakes and lizards can glide through the air. The pterosaurs were true fliers. Some were no bigger than sparrows; others had a wingspan of 10 m (30 ft). On land they were clumsy and shuffled along with their wings sticking out. These flying reptiles, living at the time of the dinosaurs, died out as birds evolved and took over the skies.

Early fliers
Pterosaurs had big, bat-like wings and large heads.

Whale trail This animal, *Pakicetus*, is an extinct relative of today's whales.

Did whales once have legs?

Whales are mammals, which means that they evolved from ancestors that once lived on land. Their ancestors were probably plant-eating animals called condylarths, which have long been extinct. The oldest known fossils of whales belong to animals that lived about 50 million years ago. They had short, stubby limbs, rather like those of otters, which they eventually lost as they evolved into streamlined swimming animals that never left the sea.

Elephants Alongside prehistoric animals lived elephants that were very similar to those alive today.

Pelorovis Pelorovis was a gigantic cow-like animal with huge horns.

THAT'S AMAZING

GOING EXTINCT

Since life first began, about 99 per cent of all the species that have ever existed have become extinct. New species have evolved to take their place. On average, each species lasts for several hundred thousand years.

⟳ The story of evolution p.58 · Fossil trails p.60 · Prehistoric animals p.72 · Fact File p.274

The dinosaurs were a large group of reptiles that lived between about 200 million years ago and 65 million years ago. There were a great many different kinds of dinosaur, which is one of the things that makes them so interesting. Some grew very large; others were no bigger than chickens. They included harmless plant-eaters, which often fed in herds, but also some of the biggest, fastest and most dangerous meat-eating animals ever to have walked the Earth.

Did anything eat Tyrannosaurus rex?

Like lions and tigers today, *Tyrannosaurus rex* was a 'top predator'. This means that it preyed on many other animals, but was never killed and eaten itself. But the eggs and young of *Tyrannosaurus rex* may have been eaten by smaller predatory dinosaurs and other animals.

A STING IN THE TAIL

Ankylosaurs were plant-eating dinosaurs with a powerful means of defence against meat-eaters such as *Tyrannosaurus rex*. As well as large, bony spines on its back, and armour plating, the ankylosaur had a heavy club of solid bone at the end of its tail, which could be used as a weapon.

Giant tooth The tooth of *Tyrannosaurus rex* (shown life-size) had a serrated edge for tearing flesh.

How big were the dinosaurs?

The largest of the land-living dinosaurs were the brachiosaurs, which lived about 160 million years ago in North America and Africa. The largest of these dinosaurs stood about 14 m (46 ft) tall, and measured 22 m (72 ft) from nose to tail. Its weight has been estimated at over 30 tonnes. Other brachiosaurs were not so tall, but more heavily built, and probably weighed about 50 tonnes.

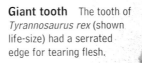

THAT'S AMAZING

MYSTERY NOSE

Brachiosaurus's nostrils were in a very strange place – on the very top of its head. At one time, scientists thought that it used them like a snorkel, to breathe underwater. It is now thought more likely that they were used for making sounds.

Tallest The long-necked *Brachiosaurus* stood about 14 m (46 ft) high with its head up – higher than any other land animal.

Least brainy *Stegosaurus* could be up to 10 m (33 ft) long, but its brain weighed only about 60 g (2 oz).

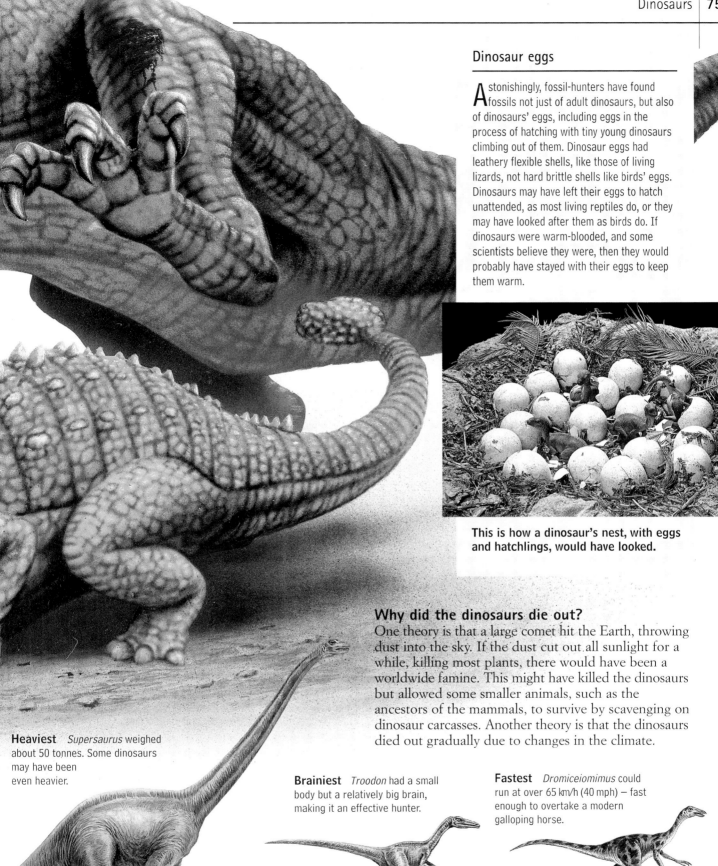

Dinosaur eggs

Astonishingly, fossil-hunters have found fossils not just of adult dinosaurs, but also of dinosaurs' eggs, including eggs in the process of hatching with tiny young dinosaurs climbing out of them. Dinosaur eggs had leathery flexible shells, like those of living lizards, not hard brittle shells like birds' eggs. Dinosaurs may have left their eggs to hatch unattended, as most living reptiles do, or they may have looked after them as birds do. If dinosaurs were warm-blooded, and some scientists believe they were, then they would probably have stayed with their eggs to keep them warm.

This is how a dinosaur's nest, with eggs and hatchlings, would have looked.

Why did the dinosaurs die out?

One theory is that a large comet hit the Earth, throwing dust into the sky. If the dust cut out all sunlight for a while, killing most plants, there would have been a worldwide famine. This might have killed the dinosaurs but allowed some smaller animals, such as the ancestors of the mammals, to survive by scavenging on dinosaur carcasses. Another theory is that the dinosaurs died out gradually due to changes in the climate.

Heaviest *Supersaurus* weighed about 50 tonnes. Some dinosaurs may have been even heavier.

Brainiest *Troodon* had a small body but a relatively big brain, making it an effective hunter.

Fastest *Dromiceiomimus* could run at over 65 km/h (40 mph) – fast enough to overtake a modern galloping horse.

⟳ **The story of evolution p.58 · Animals in flight p.78 ·**
Fact File p.288, 292-302

H ow often do you trip over when running about? Probably quite often, because moving on two legs is not easy. Some other animals move like us, but many more use four legs, six legs, or none at all. Humans have been walking for about 5 million years, but animals have been running, jumping, slithering and swimming much longer. Over hundreds of millions of years, they have evolved amazingly varied ways of moving – on land, through water and in the air.

Dingo

Emu

Marsupial mouse

Why do some animals hop and others run?

Hopping is a good idea if the ground is hot, because both feet come off the ground for a moment, and into the air where they can cool down. That is probably why hopping first evolved in animals such as kangaroos and hopping mice, which live in hot, dry places. But once hopping is perfected, it is also a fast way of getting around. Hopping can also confuse a predator in close pursuit. A hopper can suddenly change direction, leaving the predator going the wrong way.

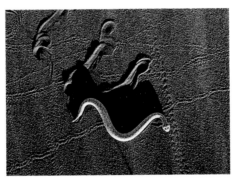

Wriggling along A viper slithers forwards and sideways across the desert sand.

Fast hoppers A red kangaroo's top speed is about 65 km/h (40 mph).

How do animals without legs move over the ground?

If you lie face down, with your arms by your side and legs together, you may be surprised how far you get by wriggling. Snakes evolved from lizard-like animals with four legs by learning to wriggle. By moving like this, they can slither through vegetation, go down burrows after mice or bury themselves in sand.

Burrowing under The marsupial mole has powerful front feet for tunnelling through the earth. Its armoured nose pushes the loose soil aside.

THAT'S AMAZING
BREATHTAKING BOUNCE
Grasshoppers jump with the help of a substance that works like elastic, flicking them into the air. Some can manage an 8 m (26 ft) 'long jump' – equivalent to a human jumping nearly 200 m (650 ft).

Marsupial mole

Inch worms

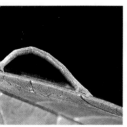

Looper caterpillar

Looper caterpillars are also called 'inch worms' because they seem to measure the leaves and twigs as they move along them. They have a set of legs at the front of the body, and a set at the back. To move forwards, a looper caterpillar brings its back legs forwards and grips the leaf just behind its front legs, making a loop with its body. Then it holds on with the back legs, lets go with the front, and straightens its body. It repeats this process many times.

How do animals move in water?

Most animals swim by moving their body from side to side – something humans cannot do. A very flexible spine is needed, and powerful muscles in just the right places. Fish and whales have large, paddle-like tails that they use to push against the water. But even snakes, with no 'paddle', can swim well simply by swinging from side to side. Few animals use their limbs to swim, as humans do, but frogs are an exception. They kick with their legs like someone swimming breaststroke.

Jet power Cuttlefish swim by squirting water backwards through a nozzle. The force of the jet pushes them in the opposite direction.

ANIMALS ON THE MOVE

These animals from Australia all move in different ways. Kangaroos, emus and the frilled lizard all race along on two legs, but dingoes, marsupial mice and rabbit-eared bandicoots use four. Snakes slither across the ground or through water by curving their bodies; fish swim by using fins.

Sticky feet Geckos have special pads on their toes, which allow them to cling to smooth surfaces. The bell frog also clings, using its sucker-like toes.

aroo

Gecko

Rabbit-eared bandicoot

Frilled lizard

Spotted water snake

Murray cod

Animals in flight

⬅ The story of evolution p.58 · Prehistoric animals p.72 · How aeroplanes work p.190 · Fact File p.288, 292–302

The first animals to fly were insects, much like modern dragonflies. They took to the air over 300 million years ago. The Earth then was covered with dense forests, and flying probably made it easier for these insects to reach distant sources of food. Because there were no other flying animals at that time, they had no predators. Some grew to enormous sizes, with wingspans of 70 cm (28 in). With these tasty morsels flapping about, it was not long before larger animals evolved the power of flight. The ancestors of birds and bats quickly wiped out the giant dragonflies, which were easy prey. Smaller, faster-flying insects evolved to replace them.

BY DAY AND BY NIGHT
Day-flying animals need to see what is around them – otherwise flight could end with a crash. They have good vision. Those that fly at night navigate differently. Bats have a system called echo-location, which is similar to radar, for homing in on moths and other prey.

How do animals learn to fly?
Puffins nest in burrows in cliffs beside the sea. The adult puffins feed their chicks until they are very fat, and then leave them. The puffin chick stays in its burrow without food, but after a week it becomes hungry and then it leaves, too. Emerging at night, the chick flies out over the waves, never having flown before but knowing exactly what to do. The skills of flying are inherited and instinctive: the young bird has the knowledge in its brain, even before it hatches. Other species of birds may watch their parents, but they also rely on instinct to fly.

Natural fliers Young puffins know how to fly without being taught by their parents.

Fast flight
Compared to most moths, hawkmoths are powerful fliers.

When did birds first fly?
One of the most exciting fossils ever found is *Archaeopteryx*, a 'missing link' between the dinosaurs and the birds. *Archaeopteryx* has feathers like a bird, but teeth and a long, bony tail like a reptile – birds' tails are just made of feathers. Its wings show clearly how birds' wings evolved from the front limbs of small, fast-running dinosaurs. Because the bones of *Archaeopteryx* were quite heavy, unlike the hollow bones of birds, it seems unlikely that it could fly well. Scientists believe that it glided or flapped clumsily from one tree to another. *Archaeopteryx* lived about 150 million years ago, and its immediate descendants were probably the first true flying birds.

Keel

Bird A bird has powerful flight muscles anchored to a bony flap on its chest. The flap is called a keel.

Archaeopteryx Unlike birds, *Archaeopteryx* was flat-chested – it did not have a keel.

How do animals fly?

Animals fly in a completely different way from aeroplanes. Planes have fixed wings that create lift when air flows past them, and they move forwards by pushing air very fast through a jet engine or around a propeller. The wings of animals do both these jobs at once. When the wings flap downwards, they push the bird or bat or insect forwards, as well as keeping it aloft and stabilising its flight.

Four wings Ladybirds have two pairs of wings. The hind-wings do most of the work.

Smooth shape A swallow's body is streamlined to help it fly at speed.

THAT'S AMAZING

RIDERS ON THE WIND

Spiders do not have wings, but they often travel by air when they are young. They do this with the help of the silk that they make. To take off, a baby spider waits for a windy day. It climbs to the top of a plant, and lets out a long silk line. The line floats away in the breeze, carrying the spider with it.

Do flying squirrels really fly?

If a bird or a bat takes off from a tree, it can either drop towards the ground or climb into the air. But a flying squirrel can only go in one direction: down. This is because flying squirrels are not true fliers – they glide on flaps of skin that stretch between their arms and legs. To take off, a flying squirrel gives a sudden kick. Once it is airborne, its furry flaps open out, and it travels up to 50 m (165 ft) through the air, dropping all the time. The squirrel uses its tail like a rudder, making sure that it lands safely on another tree trunk. Some snakes, too, are able to glide by flattening their bodies till they are wide and ribbon-like.

A flying squirrel glides towards a tree trunk.

Bat flight A bat's wings are made of skin, stretched over very long finger bones.

Hunters and hunted p.82 · Animal defences p.84 · Animal behaviour p.90 · Fact File p.288, 292-302

Animals need senses to find out what is happening in the world around them: to help them find their way around, to keep out of danger and, most important of all, to track down food. Animals often have much keener senses than we do, and some can detect things that we cannot. Sharks can sense fish by 'feeling' the electricity around their bodies, while some snakes can 'see' the warmth that comes from their prey.

Different ways of seeing

Each of your eyes has a single lens, so it produces a single picture of what it sees. Insect eyes are built in a different way. They are divided into lots of compartments, which work like separate eyes side by side. Each compartment sees just a small part of the view around an insect's head, but the insect's brain adds together the pictures from all the compartments to build up an all-round image. Some insects have only a few dozen compartments in each eye, but dragonflies have over 20 000. Their eyes are so big they fill up most of their heads.

Insect eye
A cutaway diagram of the inside of an insect's eye. The part sticking out is a compartment magnified hundreds of times.

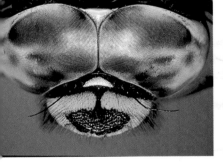

Dragonfly eye The 20 000 compartments in a dragonfly's eye send signals to the insect's brain, which then constructs a mosaic view of the world.

DEADLY GAZE
Many spiders snare their food in webs, but the jumping spider catches insects by leaping on them. It has superb eyesight – thanks to its eight eyes, which help it to pounce with pinpoint accuracy. Two of its eyes face forwards, like miniature headlamps. The remaining six look sideways.

Unusual ears

Imagine listening to your favourite sounds with your ears around your waist or even halfway down your legs. For grasshoppers and crickets it is a normal fact of life. These insects – and many other animals – use sound to communicate. Each species has its own call, and males use their calls during the breeding season to attract mates and warn away rivals. Mammals are the only animals with ears that stick out. In other animals, ears are often harder to spot. Lizards and birds have small ear openings behind their eyes, although in birds these are hidden by feathers.

This cricket has long antennae (feelers) and ears hidden away on its legs.

How do animals find their way in the dark?

For us, moving about in the dark is not easy. But for animals that are active at night, darkness presents no problems. Cats and owls have extra good eyesight that works in dim light, while many smaller hunters find their way by touch or by smell. Bats sense their surroundings by using bursts of high-pitched sound. They use echoes from flying insects to locate their invisible food.

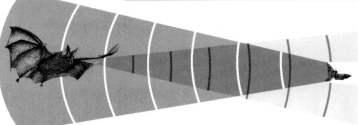

Night sight Bats home in on flying insects by sending out a beam of sound. They listen for any echoes that bounce back in midair.

Sideways-facing eye

Main eye

Sensitive hairs

THAT'S AMAZING

MEGA EYES

The giant squid has the biggest eyes of any animal. They can measure about 40 cm (16 in) across, which is about 1 1/2 times wider than a football. Giant squid live so deep that they have never been seen alive, but they probably use their eyes to see the flickering light made by their prey.

Sniffer moth Male moths have feathery antennae like these. The females' antennae are smaller, because they do not need such a good sense of smell.

Sitting target Flies are experts at spotting movement, which is why they are so hard to swat. However, they are not nearly so good at noticing things that keep perfectly still. Jumping spiders make use of this by 'freezing' as they get ready for a jump.

Which animal has the best sense of smell?

Polar bears and albatrosses can smell food up to 30 km (18 miles) away, but they can do this only when the food is rotting, and very smelly indeed. The real best-smellers in the animal world are moths, because they can sense smells in much tinier amounts. Male moths often track down females by scent alone. Using their sensitive feathery antennae, they pick up faint traces of a female's scent, and then work their way upwind towards her. Some male moths can do this when the female is 10 km (6 miles) away.

🌐 Animals in flight p.78 · Ecology: connecting the living world p.100 · Origins of the human race p.206 · Fact File p.288, 292–302

Animals that catch other animals for food are called predators. These hunters use a wide variety of clever tricks to capture their prey, such as camouflage, stalking and pouncing. Some animals hunt in packs, but many search for food on their own. Although it may seem cruel, hunting is an important part of the cycle of nature.

THAT'S AMAZING

HUNTING WITH BUBBLES

Humpback whales sometimes trap shoals of fish by blowing a 'net' of bubbles around them. The fish swim away from the bubbles, so that they are packed together in the middle of the net. The whale then charges upwards into the shoal, swallowing huge mouthfuls of fish.

Why do wolves hunt in packs?

Wolves live in groups of up to 20 animals and work together to hunt large prey such as deer, caribou and wild horses. The pack will choose young, old or sick animals that tire easily. The wolves take it in turns to chase their victim, and then they all encircle it for the kill.

THE AFRICAN EAGLE GOES FISHING

Most eagles live on mammals, such as hares and rabbits, but the African fish eagle hunts over lakes and rivers, where it catches unsuspecting fish. It uses dead trees as lookout posts, and if it spots a telltale ripple it immediately takes off. After climbing into the sky, the eagle swoops down over the water, catching the fish in its needle-sharp claws, called talons.

In for the kill When the eagle is within inches of the water's surface it snatches its prey, often using just one of its feet to hold the catch. Rough scales on the soles of its feet help the bird to grip the slippery fish. Once it has landed back on its perch, the bird uses its hooked beak to pull the fish's flesh from its bones.

Hunters' feast
Members of a wolf pack share a freshly killed deer.

How does a crocodile catch fast-moving prey?

A crocodile lies motionless in the water like a harmless log. Only its eyes and nostrils stick up above the water as it watches for large mammals and birds coming to drink. If any animal comes too close to the edge, the crocodile quickly grabs it in its powerful jaws and drags it under the water until it drowns. The crocodile then twists about in the water to pull the animal to pieces before devouring it.

Feeding frenzy
A Nile crocodile lunges at the legs of a wildebeest to drag it into the water.

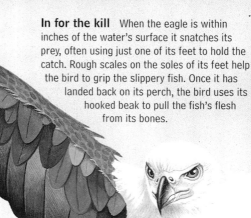

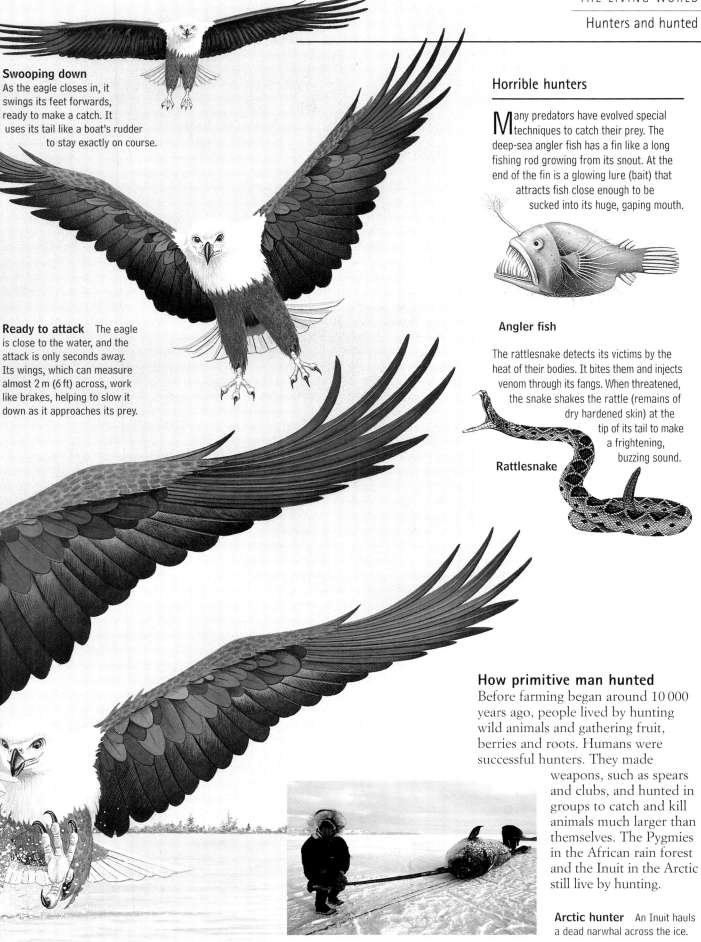

Swooping down
As the eagle closes in, it swings its feet forwards, ready to make a catch. It uses its tail like a boat's rudder to stay exactly on course.

Ready to attack The eagle is close to the water, and the attack is only seconds away. Its wings, which can measure almost 2 m (6 ft) across, work like brakes, helping to slow it down as it approaches its prey.

Horrible hunters

Many predators have evolved special techniques to catch their prey. The deep-sea angler fish has a fin like a long fishing rod growing from its snout. At the end of the fin is a glowing lure (bait) that attracts fish close enough to be sucked into its huge, gaping mouth.

Angler fish

The rattlesnake detects its victims by the heat of their bodies. It bites them and injects venom through its fangs. When threatened, the snake shakes the rattle (remains of dry hardened skin) at the tip of its tail to make a frightening, buzzing sound.

Rattlesnake

How primitive man hunted
Before farming began around 10 000 years ago, people lived by hunting wild animals and gathering fruit, berries and roots. Humans were successful hunters. They made weapons, such as spears and clubs, and hunted in groups to catch and kill animals much larger than themselves. The Pygmies in the African rain forest and the Inuit in the Arctic still live by hunting.

Arctic hunter An Inuit hauls a dead narwhal across the ice.

🌐 **Hunters and hunted p.82 · Camouflage and mimicry p.86 ·**
Fact File p.288, 292-302

For animals, the world is a dangerous place. Every time they venture out to find food, they risk becoming a meal for another animal. To survive, they rely on their defences. Some animals specialise in making a quick getaway, while others use armour or weapons to make themselves difficult to attack. Lizards have one of the strangest defence tactics of all: they shed their tails as they run away.

What are antlers and horns used for?

Antlers and horns are grown by plant-eating animals, such as deer, antelope and rhinos. Antlers are solid and are made of bone. Horns are hollow, and are made of the same substance as hooves and fingernails. Antlers and horns are mainly used during courtship for fighting rivals, but they are useful at other times, too. Musk oxen form a circle around their calves to fend off wolves with their horns.

Row of horns   Standing shoulder to shoulder, musk oxen are difficult for wolves to attack.

How do stings work?

A sting works by injecting poison into an animal's skin. Wasps usually make a quick jab with their stings and then pull them out, but honeybees often leave their stings behind. Bees' stings have backward-pointing spines, which make them difficult to remove once they have been implanted in the skin. The deadliest stingers are scorpions: they kill several thousand people every year.

Stinging action   A bee holds tight with its legs and forces its sting through the skin. Once it has lost its sting, it dies.

CREATING A DIVERSION

If a lizard is suddenly cornered by an enemy, it will often shed its tail. This may seem like a drastic thing to do, but it can save the lizard's life. The tail wriggles about on the ground, distracting the predator while the lizard makes its escape. Over the following few months, the lizard's tail slowly grows back.

Ready to run   Here, a lizard is being attacked by a snake. As the snake moves in, the lizard tenses special muscles at the base of its tail, ready to make the tail drop off.

How does a porcupine fend off its enemies?

Porcupines are covered in long spines, or quills, that have sharp points. They cannot fire their quills through the air – as people sometimes think – but they can use them to teach their enemies a painful lesson. If a porcupine is threatened with attack, it makes its quills stand on end, pointing backwards. It then rattles its quills and stamps its feet to show that it is dangerous. If this does not work, the porcupine suddenly reverses into its enemy, making the quills stick in the enemy's skin.

Prickly porcupine   This African porcupine is fending off an attacker. As long as it keeps its back to the attacker, the porcupine has a good chance of causing serious injury to its enemy and surviving.

THAT'S AMAZING

BACKFIRING BEETLES

The bombardier beetle is the world's only explosive insect. If it is threatened, it mixes two chemicals together in a chamber at the back of its body. The chemicals instantly explode, and a jet of hot stinging gas shoots through a nozzle towards the beetle's enemy.

Deadly meals

In Central and South America, tiny frogs use deadly poisons to protect themselves from attack. They store the poisons in their bodies, and they have brilliant colours to show other animals that they are dangerous to eat. American Indians used these frogs to make poison-tipped arrows. One species of frog contains enough poison to kill 1000 people. Arrow-poison frogs are so dangerous that they have few natural enemies.

Arrow-poison frog, Costa Rica.

Tail away   As the snake moves in, the tail muscles suddenly tighten, and the end of the tail drops off. The muscles seal off the tail's blood supply, so that the stump hardly bleeds.

Saved by a tail   Several weeks later, the lizard has begun to grow a new tail. Eventually, the new tail will be as big as the old one, although it will often be a different colour.

Camouflage and mimicry

Oceans and seas p.36 · Polar regions p.46 · Hunters and hunted p.82 · Animal defences p.84 · Fact File p.286-304

One way of escaping predators is to run fast; another is to be covered in prickles, or to appear dangerous. But many animals survive by camouflage: matching the world around them so that they are not seen. As long as they keep still when predators pass by, they may go unnoticed. Some predators, too, are camouflaged so they can lie silently in wait for their prey.

HOW MANY ANIMALS CAN YOU SPOT?

The picture on these two pages shows ten different animals that use camouflage. All are experts at keeping still, because a single move would quickly give them away. See how many you can identify, and then check your answers at the bottom of the page opposite.

How do chameleons change colour?

Chameleons can match the colour and pattern of almost any leafy background using chemical colours, or pigments, which are stored in their skin. The chameleon's outer skin is basically yellow, but the creature can change this to green or brown by moving specks of dark pigment up into the yellow layer. Each part of the skin is controlled by its own nerves, so different parts can be different colours.

Hidden hunter Chameleons use camouflage to hunt insects in trees.

THAT'S AMAZING

QUICK COLOUR CHANGE

Chameleons can change colour completely in less than two minutes. Cuttlefish, which live in the sea and are related to octopuses, are even faster. They take less than one second to change their colour.

How does white fur help polar bears?

Polar bears, like other bears, are hunters. While most bears are brown or black, polar bears have white fur to match the ice and snow of the Arctic lands where they live. White fur helps the polar bear to creep up on prey, such as seals, unnoticed. Many other Arctic animals, both hunters and prey, have white fur (or feathers) in winter but brown fur in summer, for better camouflage when the snow melts.

Polar predator   Only a polar bear's nose and eyes show up against the snow.

Lookalikes   Hoverflies look like wasps, but are harmless.

Why do hoverflies look like wasps?

Birds are careful not to attack wasps because they have learned that wasps sting. Hoverflies are small flies, related to bluebottles and house flies. They have no sting to defend themselves, but birds leave them alone because hoverflies are striped black and yellow like wasps. This kind of defence is called mimicry and is quite common, especially among insects and snakes.

Weedy wonders

In the Atlantic Ocean is an area full of floating seaweed called the Sargasso Sea. Many camouflaged creatures live among the seaweeds of the Sargasso, but one of the strangest is the Sargassum fish. This odd-looking fish matches the colour and patterns of the seaweed perfectly. To improve its camouflage further there are long straggly outgrowths all over its body. These give it a shape that is very unlike a fish, making it almost impossible to see.

Sargassum fish

Answers   How many camouflaged animals did you manage to spot? Which was the hardest?

Bird-dropping spider   Leaf insect   Brimstone butterfly   Leaf-tailed gecko

Vine snake   Nightjar   Spider

Thorn bugs   Horned frog   Stick insect

🔵 Rivers and lakes p.34 · Oceans and seas p.36 · Animal behaviour p.90 ·
Surviving extremes p.92 · Fact File p.288, 292–302

Some animals spend their whole lives on the move, and never have a place that can be called their home. Others build homes so that they can protect their young or hide away from danger. Animals use many different types of building material, including wood, leaves, mud and even their own saliva (spit). Unlike us, they do not need any plans, and they do not have to learn how to build. Instead, they simply follow their instincts.

How do birds build their nests?

Birds that feed on the ground – such as pheasants and ostriches – are the least impressive builders. Many of them simply scratch a hollow in the earth or sand. Birds that nest in trees are much more expert. Most of them make small cup-shaped nests from twigs which they often line with moss or mud. Some – like the weaver birds – build nests with roofs and private entrances. The smallest tree-nests are made by hummingbirds, and are about the size of a thimble. The biggest are made by bald eagles, which live in North America. The largest bald eagle's nest ever recorded was in Florida, and measured nearly 3 m (10 ft) across and 6 m (19 ½ ft) deep. It is estimated to have weighed more than 3 tonnes.

Tying the knot A weaver bird begins its nest (above) by tying a strip of grass to a branch (left).

INSIDE A WASPS' NEST

Many wasps build their nests from paper. They make this by chewing up tiny fibres of wood into a soft paste, which they spread out in sheets. The inside of a wasps' nest is made up of six-sided compartments called cells, which house the eggs and larvae (newly hatched insects). The outside walls help to keep the nest warm.

Why do beavers make dams?

People sometimes think that beavers make dams to catch fish, but they actually feed on wood, and build dams to protect their homes. A beaver's home is called a lodge. It looks like a giant pile of sticks, and it is surrounded by water. The lodge's entrances are hidden well below water level, so that the beavers can come and go without being seen.

Beavers use their dams to control the water level around the lodge. Some of their dams are over 250 m (820 ft) long, making beavers by far the best engineers in the whole animal world.

Building materials Worker wasps scrape wood fibres from fence posts and tree trunks.

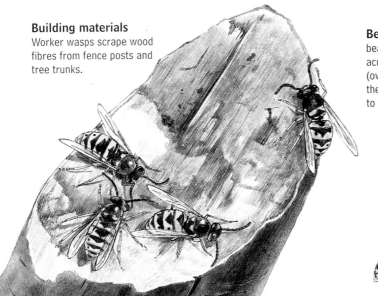

Beaver lodge A beaver hauls willows across a spillway (overflow channel) in the dam on the way to its lodge.

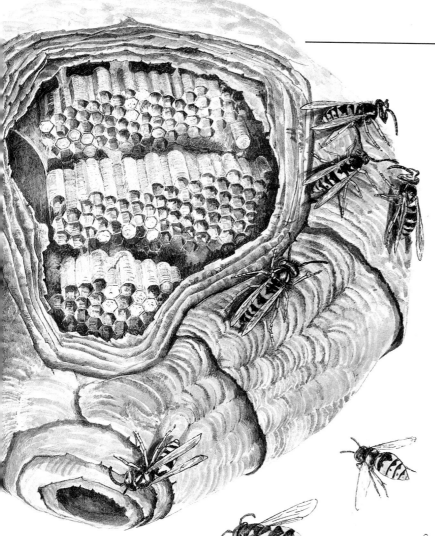

Tent-making bats

During daylight hours, most bats hide away in dark places, such as hollow trees and attics. In Central and South America, some bats behave in a very different way. These bats make daytime hideouts out of giant leaves. To do this, they hang underneath a leaf and gnaw part of the way through the rib that holds it up. The end of the leaf flops down, hiding the bats from prying eyes.

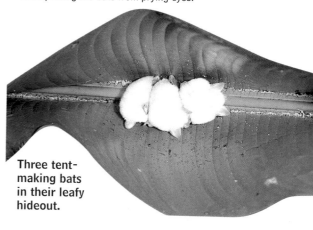

Three tent-making bats in their leafy hideout.

Making space   The cells inside a wasps' nest are arranged in layers, like floors in a house. Throughout the summer, the wasps keep adding more 'floors', and they rebuild the walls to make more room. The entrance is at the bottom of the nest. This keeps warm air inside.

THAT'S AMAZING

THE NESTS WE EAT

The world's most valuable nests are made by birds called cave swiftlets, which live in South-east Asia. These birds build their nests entirely from saliva, which turns white and rubbery when it dries. For centuries, empty nests have been used to make bird's nest soup – a famous Chinese delicacy. The best nests are worth over £750 for 1 kg (2.2 lb).

How often do animals move home?

Many animals build a home once a year, so they have somewhere to raise their young. But some make a new home every evening, and move on when the next day dawns. The biggest of these daily movers are gorillas. They make platform-shaped nests on the ground or in trees – a job that usually takes less than five minutes. In the sea, parrotfish protect themselves in a different way. As the sun begins to set, they make slimy 'sleeping bags' from mucus produced by glands in the skin, and settle down to sleep inside. At dawn, they eat up their overnight homes and swim off to feed.

Pacific parrotfish   This parrotfish is sleeping next to its favourite food – living coral.

Animal behaviour

🌐 The story of evolution p.58 · Animal homes p.88 · Growth and development p.98 · Fact File p.288, 292–302

For wild animals, there is no such thing as good or bad behaviour – all that matters is doing the right thing at the right time. Most animals start life with a lot of their behaviour built in. For example, they know how to react to danger, how to find food, and how to communicate. But animal behaviour is not always like this. Some animals – particularly mammals – learn new kinds of behaviour as they grow up.

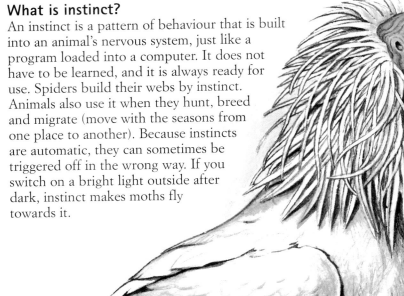

Unsure shot Egyptian vultures crack open eggs entirely by instinct. They do not understand how stones break eggs, and they often throw stones onto the ground, instead of onto the egg.

What is instinct?

An instinct is a pattern of behaviour that is built into an animal's nervous system, just like a program loaded into a computer. It does not have to be learned, and it is always ready for use. Spiders build their webs by instinct. Animals also use it when they hunt, breed and migrate (move with the seasons from one place to another). Because instincts are automatic, they can sometimes be triggered off in the wrong way. If you switch on a bright light outside after dark, instinct makes moths fly towards it.

Spider's web Spiders instinctively know what shape their webs should be. Each species – in this case, the female garden spider – builds its own kind.

THAT'S AMAZING

THE SONG OF THE WHALES

Humpbacked whales have the longest, most complicated songs in the world. Each song can last over 30 minutes, and can be heard by other whales up to 160 km (100 miles) away. No one knows what these eerie songs mean.

Why do birds sing?

Unlike humans, birds do not sing just for fun. Male birds sing to attract females, and to keep rival males away. Birds are born with the instinct to sing, but at first they are not very good at it. They get better by listening to older birds, and they can pick up a 'local accent' as they learn. Bird songs often contain lots of notes packed closely together – the notes follow each other so quickly that we can hear only the overall sound of the song.

Big sound
Male wrens are tiny, but they have amazingly loud voices. They sing from the tops of trees and fenceposts, so that their songs can be heard all around.

Why do animals fight?

In nature, animals often have to fight off their enemies, but they sometimes fight among themselves. This happens most often during the breeding season, when males fight for the chance to mate. In most species, these fights rarely cause any harm, but in elephant seals they can end in serious injuries.

Bloody fight   Bull elephant seals often draw blood. The oldest males are usually covered with scars.

The world's brainiest animals

It is easy to measure an animal's brain, but much more difficult to decide if it is 'brainy'. Many animals can use stones or twigs to get at food, but only the brainiest animals can shape tools for particular tasks. We are the world experts at doing this, but chimps come second on the list. They use leaves as scoops to collect water, and they snap off twigs and peel away the bark to make 'fishing sticks' for collecting antlike insects called termites. Young chimps learn this kind of behaviour by watching and copying adults.

A young chimp uses a tool to collect termites.

CRACKING OPEN A MEAL

For an Egyptian vulture, an ostrich egg is a giant meal. But how can a bird with a small beak break through the egg's thick shell? The answer is that it uses a special type of behaviour. It picks up stones in its beak, and then flings them downwards at the egg. With luck, the eggshell starts to crack, and the vulture gets its meal.

⬅ Deserts p.44 · Polar regions p.46 · Animal homes p.88 ·
Animal behaviour p.90 · Fact File p.280, 288, 292–304

Can you imagine spending the night on a mountain without a sleeping bag? Or walking across the Sahara Desert without water? You would not survive, but there are plenty of animals that do. It is all a question of having the right features, or 'adaptations': thick fur for the mountain top, and a tough skin that keeps in moisture for the desert. Animals have less obvious adaptations as well – in severe heat or intense cold, special behaviour often helps them to survive.

Animal antifreeze

Some mammals and birds survive the sub-zero temperatures of the Poles by raising their body temperature. Other creatures, such as fish, survive instead by using a built-in antifreeze, which prevents their blood and the liquid in their body cells from freezing. Without this antifreeze, ice crystals would form inside their bodies and they would quickly die.

Arctic fox Thanks to their amazingly thick fur, Arctic foxes can survive temperatures as low as −50°C (−58°F).

How do animals survive the cold?

When there is snow on the ground, many small animals survive by burrowing underneath it. They may have a set of runways and grassy feeding spots on the ground below, which you cannot see. They have a thick coat of fur, and in many cases a thicker coat grows at the beginning of winter for extra warmth. Breathing very cold air can damage the lungs. Some animals have special channels in their nostrils which warm up the incoming air by taking heat from the outgoing air.

In salty seawater, ice fish survive temperatures of −1.5°C (29°F).

DRY SEASON

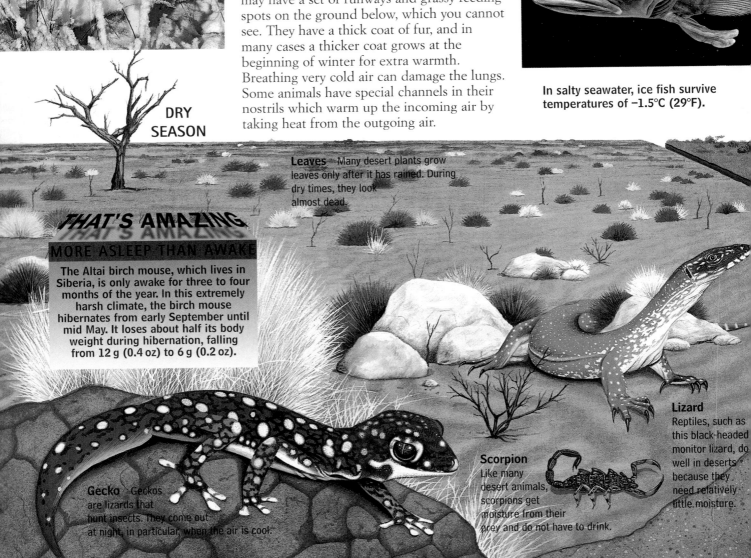

Leaves Many desert plants grow leaves only after it has rained. During dry times, they look almost dead.

THAT'S AMAZING

MORE ASLEEP THAN AWAKE

The Altai birch mouse, which lives in Siberia, is only awake for three to four months of the year. In this extremely harsh climate, the birch mouse hibernates from early September until mid May. It loses about half its body weight during hibernation, falling from 12 g (0.4 oz) to 6 g (0.2 oz).

Gecko Geckos are lizards that hunt insects. They come out at night, in particular when the air is cool.

Scorpion Like many desert animals, scorpions get moisture from their prey and do not have to drink.

Lizard Reptiles, such as this black-headed monitor lizard, do well in deserts because they need relatively little moisture.

Heavy drinker A camel can drink up to 50 litres (11 gallons) of water at a time. Its hump contains a store of energy-rich fat.

How do animals survive in the desert?

There are two big problems in the desert: keeping cool and saving water. Camels survive by using their fur like a sunshade, and by drinking huge amounts of water whenever they get the chance. Other desert animals hide from the heat during daylight hours. Desert frogs and toads have a different survival technique: they spend most of their lives underground, inside a coat of mucus which stops them drying out. When it rains, they dig their way to the surface to mate and lay eggs.

Why do animals hibernate?

If there is not enough food to survive the winter, it makes sense for an animal to sleep through it, or hibernate. During hibernation, an animal's breathing and heart rate slow right down, and its body temperature falls to just above the temperature of the surroundings. By going into this 'half-alive' state, the animal saves energy. It can survive right through the winter on the food it ate in the late summer and autumn. If the temperature outside gets so cold that the animal is in danger of freezing, a special mechanism in the brain wakes it, so that it can become active and warm itself up.

Dormouse This hibernating dormouse is in such a deep sleep that it will not wake even if picked up.

SURVIVING THE DESERT

Even in deserts, storms sometimes soak the ground. Buried seeds germinate, the desert is carpeted with flowers, and animals race to breed. The good times are short-lived: the ground soon dries out.

WET SEASON

Germination Plants grow from seeds that stay dormant for many years. They grow, flower and set seed themselves all in the space of a few weeks.

At rest Kangaroos rest during the hottest part of the day, like many desert animals.

Dry season frog A thin coat of transparent mucus stops this frog drying out during many months underground.

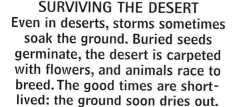

Wet season frog Rainwater dissolves the frog's jacket of mucus, and it scrabbles its way to the surface.

⬤ Animal senses p.80 · Animal behaviour p.90 ·
Animal reproduction p.96 · Fact File p.288, 292–304

E very spring, millions of salmon swim up rivers to breed. At the same time, billions of birds head north across land and sea, and clouds of butterflies stir from their winter sleep, getting ready to follow the northward trail. These animals are all migrants – species that make long journeys at particular times each year. By migrating, they get the best of two very different habitats.

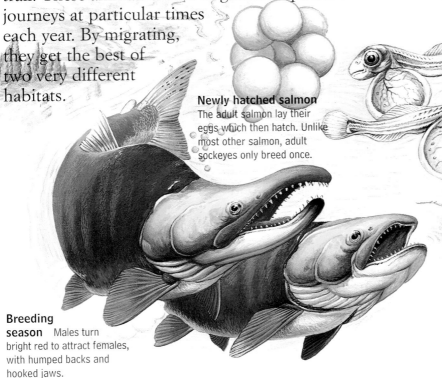

Newly hatched salmon
The adult salmon lay their eggs which then hatch. Unlike most other salmon, adult sockeyes only breed once.

Breeding season Males turn bright red to attract females, with humped backs and hooked jaws.

Young salmon Young salmon spend 1-3 years in fresh water before they migrate downriver and out to sea.

JOURNEY FROM THE SEA
Sockeye salmon live in the northern Pacific Ocean, but they start life in fresh water. In late spring in order to breed, the adults make their way back to the streams where they hatched, leaping rapids and dodging bears.

The great eel mystery

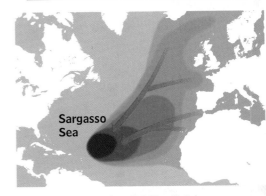

Sargasso Sea

The eel's 5000 km (3000 mile) journey.

F or centuries, European eels had mystified fishermen, because young eels could never be found. In the early 1900s, scientists discovered that eels lay their eggs far from Europe, in the warm waters of the Sargasso Sea. Once they have hatched, the young eels – which are only about 7 cm (3 in) long – make their way across the North Atlantic, before taking up life in Europe's rivers.

Which animals migrate farthest?
Birds are the greatest long-distance migrants, and the Arctic tern is the greatest of all. Every year, it flies from the Southern Ocean to the far north – a return journey of about 40 000 km (25 000 miles). Another sea bird, the short-tailed shearwater, follows a figure-of-eight course around the Pacific Ocean, travelling 33 000 km (20 500 miles) in three months. No animals journey this far overland, but some travel great distances in the sea. Turtles and tuna fish migrate thousands of kilometres to their breeding grounds, and so do many whales. The grey whale travels along the coastline of North America, from Mexico to the Arctic Circle. During its lifetime, it migrates about 800 000 km (500 000 miles) – which is as far as to the Moon and back.

Reindeer (caribou) 2000 km

Monarch butterfly 7000 km

Bluefin tuna 20 000 km

Loggerhead turtle 20 000 km

Grey whale 16 000 km

Night flight Migrating geese flit across the night sky in Canada.

Bear threat In Alaska, brown bears gather around rapids in order to catch the adult salmon as they swim upriver.

How do migrating animals find their way?

Unlike human travellers, animals do not have maps. Instead, they navigate by using many different clues. Salmon find their way back to their breeding grounds by tasting the water where rivers meet the sea. If the taste is right, they head upstream. Whales often go along the coast, as do birds, which can follow rivers and mountain ranges as well. Birds use other navigational aids, including the Sun and stars as a compass. They can even check their position by sensing the direction of the Earth's magnetic field (Earth is like a magnet with Poles at north and south).

THAT'S AMAZING

HOMING INSTINCTS

In the 1950s, a Manx shearwater was taken from an island off the coast of Wales, and sent by plane to Boston, USA. After being released, the bird managed to find its way back across the Atlantic Ocean in just 12 1/2 days.

How do migrating animals know when to start?

For migrating animals, setting off at the right time is just as important as ending up at the right place. Their timing is amazingly precise: cuckoos, for example, nearly always arrive in Britain during the second or third week of April. To do this, they use an inbuilt 'body clock', which keeps time by the changing length of the days. Other animals – such as spiny lobsters and wildebeest – set off when the temperature or weather changes.

Bird attack Herons attack the young salmon on their journey out to sea.

Right on time Wildebeest move out onto open grassland in Africa when the rainy season begins, and when the grass starts to grow.

Dangerous journey Adult salmon swim up to 2500 km (1550 miles) to reach the rivers where they hatched.

Animal reproduction

⤶ Migration: great animal journeys p.94 ·
Growth and development p.98 · Fact File p.288, 292–304

If you have ever kept mice, guinea pigs or even stick insects, you will know that animals are very good at reproducing. They have to be, because after eating, reproduction is the most important task in any animal's life. Most animals have young every year, and their families vary in size from just one to a million or more. A smaller number of animals breed only once – after that they die.

Why do animals have to mate?

Before most animals can reproduce, male sperm cells and female egg cells have to join together. This is called fertilisation. It works well in water, but does not work on land, because the cells would soon dry out and die. To get around this problem, most land animals mate: the male puts his sperm cells directly into the female's body, and fertilisation takes place inside her.

Insect mates   These two ladybirds are mating. Once mating is over, the female will lay her eggs.

BORN ON A BEACH
Turtles spend almost all of their lives at sea, but once a year the females come ashore to lay their eggs. They haul their heavy bodies up sandy beaches, and dig a nest hole with their back flippers. Once they have laid their eggs, they cover up the nest, and head back out to sea. By the time the baby turtles hatch – ten weeks later – their mother is far away.

Insect birth   Female aphids can reproduce without mating. In summer, they give birth up to five times a day.

Do animals always have two parents?

Some animals can produce families without needing a mate. These animals are mostly very small, like amoeba, but they also include some kinds of sea anemones, aphids and fish. These single parents have unusual families, because their babies are like a giant collection of identical twins. All of them are exactly the same.

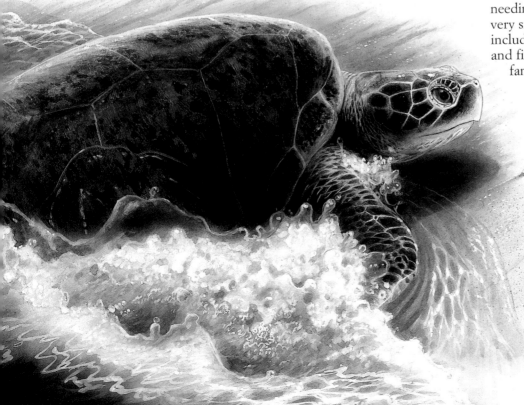

1 Coming ashore   Turtles usually come ashore on dark, moonless nights. They have to clamber above the high-tide mark before they can begin to dig their nests.

THAT'S AMAZING

EGGS BY THE MILLION
A female cod can lay up to 5 million eggs a year. If all these survived to adulthood (instead of a tiny per cent), there would be enough cod within ten years to fill the world's oceans.

2 Time to lay

After digging her nest hole, the turtle lays about 100 eggs. The eggs drop into the hole, but they do not break because their shells are soft and leathery.

Odd eggs

Birds all begin life in an egg – but so do many other animals as well. Some eggs are round, but others are oval and some are shaped like sausages. A few are laid on stalks to stop other animals from reaching them. Can you guess which animals laid the eggs below? Here are the answers, written back to front: 1 nohtyp; 2 ylfrettub; 3 gniwecal; 4 hsifgod; 5 supotco; 6 drib. How many did you get right?

1

2

3

4

5

6

Do all animals look after their young?

In the animal world, parents behave in different ways. Birds and mammals have small families, and they look after their young carefully. Some fish and frogs are careful parents and so are scorpions and crocodiles, but most other animals leave their young to fend for themselves. These animals often have thousands or even millions of young, many of which die early.

Infant care A female scorpion carries her newly hatched young.

3 Dash to the sea

The baby turtles dig their way to the surface and then scuttle towards the sea.

Growth and development

🌐 Animal reproduction p.96 ·
Fact File p.288, 292-304

As living things get older, they get bigger, and they also change shape. In mammals, these shape changes are usually quite small, so it is not too hard to guess what a young mammal will look like when it is fully grown. But in other animals – such as ladybirds, crabs and frogs – the shape changes are much more dramatic, making the young and the adults look completely different. This kind of development is called metamorphosis.

1 Eggs Ladybirds lay eggs on leaves.

2 Hatching The young ladybird eats its way out of the egg.

3 Larva The larva crawls about on stubby legs, feeding on aphids.

Why do animals change shape?
When animals are young, they concentrate on feeding and growing. When they are adult, they concentrate on reproducing. By changing shape, they make sure that they are equipped for these different tasks. If you watch caterpillars growing up, you can see how this double life works. Caterpillars spend most of each day feeding, but when they turn into butterflies, feeding takes up much less of their time. Their bodies are now developed enough for reproduction, and they travel far and wide looking for a mate. Because butterflies have wings, it is easy for them to reach good places to lay their eggs.

A LADYBIRD GROWS UP
Like other beetles, a ladybird suddenly changes shape as it grows up. It starts life as a wingless grub, called a larva. Next comes a resting stage, when the larva turns into a pupa (or chrysalis). Two weeks later, a brand-new adult ladybird emerges, with working wings.

4 Pupa After several weeks the larva turns into a pupa (chrysalis). The chrysalis has a hard 'skin' that protects the insect while it is changing shape.

Growing up in a pouch

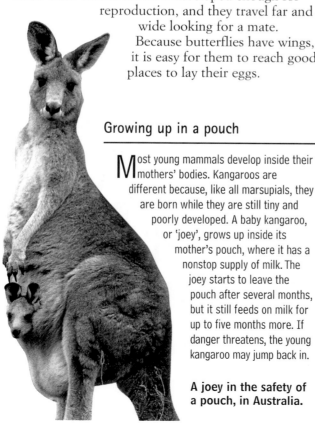

Most young mammals develop inside their mothers' bodies. Kangaroos are different because, like all marsupials, they are born while they are still tiny and poorly developed. A baby kangaroo, or 'joey', grows up inside its mother's pouch, where it has a nonstop supply of milk. The joey starts to leave the pouch after several months, but it still feeds on milk for up to five months more. If danger threatens, the young kangaroo may jump back in.

A joey in the safety of a pouch, in Australia.

How does an animal's body start to form?
Most animals start life as a single cell. Soon after fertilisation has taken place, the original cell divides many times, until thousands or millions of new cells are formed. These cells move into different positions, and they start to work in different ways. Some of them make skin or bones, while others make muscles and nerves. Eventually the new animal is complete.

Baby bird The herring gull chick has than three weeks to develop from a sin

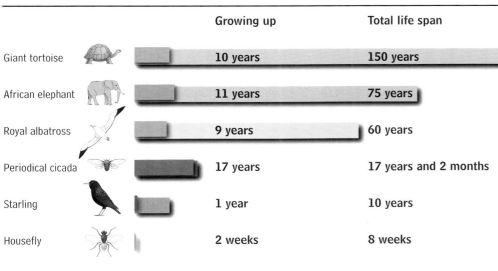

	Growing up	Total life span
Giant tortoise	10 years	150 years
African elephant	11 years	75 years
Royal albatross	9 years	60 years
Periodical cicada	17 years	17 years and 2 months
Starling	1 year	10 years
Housefly	2 weeks	8 weeks

Age range Different animals take different lengths of time to grow into, and then live as, adults.

How long do animals take to grow up?

The answer depends partly on an animal's size, and also on the way it lives. Small animals usually grow up more quickly than big ones. A housefly, for example, can develop from an egg to an adult in just two weeks, as long as the weather is warm. Compared to the housefly, most birds and mammals take a long time to grow up, but they also live much longer too. The prize for the longest 'childhood' probably goes to a North American insect called the periodical cicada. It takes 17 years to become adult, and then dies two months later.

THAT'S AMAZING

FOREVER YOUNG

The tiger salamander, a lizard-like creature from North America, can breed without ever growing up. It starts life in water, and normally changes shape before taking up life on land. Sometimes tiger salamanders stay in water all their lives, breeding but never turning into land-living adults.

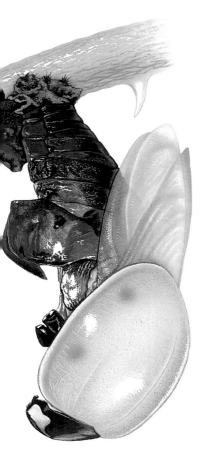

5 Adult The adult ladybird breaks open the case of the pupa.

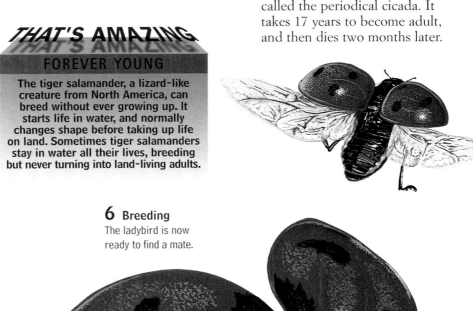

6 Breeding The ladybird is now ready to find a mate.

Ecology: connecting the living world

➡ Fungi: mushrooms and toadstools p.64 · How plants live p.66 ·
Hunters and hunted p.82 · Fact File p.280, 288–304

On Earth, nothing can live entirely on its own. Living things are all connected to each other in complicated ways. Plants collect energy from the Sun, animals feed on plants, and some animals eat each other. When plants and animals die, their remains do not pile up. Instead, fungi and bacteria break them down, so that they can be recycled and re-used. Ecology is the science that investigates all these different connections, and the way they work.

FILL–IT–YOURSELF FOOD WEB
A food web shows how food is passed from one living thing to another. In this picture, the animal at the tip of each arrow eats whatever is at the base. There are question marks where three animals are missing. By deciding what a grasshopper, a buzzard and a mole eat, see if you can work out where each of them goes.
(Answers at foot of page.)

What is the biosphere?
The biosphere is all the parts of the world where living things can be found. It includes the land and the sea, and also the lower part of the atmosphere. Scientists have recently discovered that the biosphere also reaches far beneath our feet, because some bacteria live in rocks hundreds of metres below the Earth's surface.

Life underground Even in the dry valleys of Antarctica, life exists beneath the surface of the rocks.

Do living things help one other?
In nature, living things always look after themselves. However, it sometimes pays them to team up with other forms of life. Flowering plants provide insects with sugary nectar. In return, insects help plants by spreading pollen from flower to flower, in a partnership called symbiosis.

Bird and beast Oxpeckers help rhinos by eating the ticks that feed on their blood.

Fox

Question 1

Deer

Beetle

Oak leaves and acorns

Answers
1 = mole
2 = grasshopper
3 = buzzard

Grasshopper

Missing links Here are the three animals missing from the picture. Where should they go?

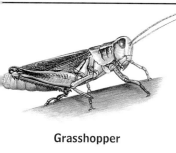

Buzzard

Mole

Weasel

Rabbit

Starling

Question 3

Question 2

Introducing species

In nature, each species lives in a particular part of the world. It is used to the other species around it, because they share a long history of living in the same place. When humans carry plants or animals from one part of the world to another, we sometimes upset this natural balance. 'Introduced' species can damage local wildlife, spreading rapidly and using up food or space that other species need. A South American water-fern called *Salvinia* screens out sunlight so that local waterplants cannot grow. It has been spread to many warm parts of the world. In Africa, it grows so quickly on some lakes that boats get trapped and have to be abandoned.

A hippo wallows in water-ferns.

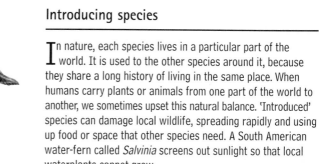

THAT'S AMAZING

GREAT SURVIVOR

The house sparrow, originally from around the Mediterranean, is a very successful species. It has survived on scraps of food in coal mines, and has even been seen 80 floors up in New York's Empire State Building.

Do hunters ever run out of prey?

Hunting animals are often faster than their prey, but they never manage to catch them all. If they did, they would have no more food. Hunting is not an easy way of life. Each chase takes a lot of time and effort, and sometimes fewer than one in ten ends with a successful kill.

In pursuit Canadian lynxes are fast, but they have to work hard to catch Arctic hares.

Wildlife conservation

⬅ Forests p.42 · The story of evolution p.58 ·
Ecology: connecting the living world p.100 · Fact File p.304

In today's world, wild places are hard to find. Roads, houses, farms and factories are spreading. We use more water and wood than people did 50 years ago, and we produce more waste. All this means that life is getting harder for Earth's natural inhabitants. Without conservation, many of them could die out.

EYE IN THE SKY
Before endangered species can be protected, scientists have to find out where they live and how much space they need. For birds like the harpy eagle, one way to do this is to use radio transmitters. The transmitters are attached to the eagle's nestlings, and they beam signals up to a satellite. The signals pinpoint the young birds once they have left the nest and can then monitor their lives and needs.

What is the most endangered animal in the world?
Birds have been badly affected by changes in their habitats, and one in ten species is now facing serious problems. Among the rarest birds of all is the kakapo from New Zealand – the only parrot that cannot fly. At present there are only about 55 kakapos left. They live on three small offshore islands.

Parrot in peril   A kakapo on Maud Island, off the coast of New Zealand, flaps its stubby wings.

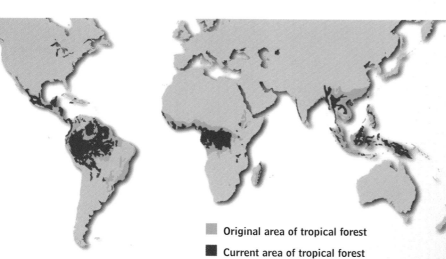

■ Original area of tropical forest
■ Current area of tropical forest

Why does it matter if forests are cut down?
Tropical forests are home to more animals than any other habitat on land. When forests are cut down, most of these animals have nowhere else to go. Half of the world's tropical forests have already disappeared, and most of the remaining forests are now divided up into small pieces, which do not hold much wildlife. The only large areas left are in the Amazon Basin of South America and Central Africa.

Visiting the nest   Scientists use a crossbow to fire a line over a branch. This line is used to pull a rope up the tree. The scientist then climbs up the rope.

Harpy eagle at home
Harpy eagles live in the rain forests of Central and South America. They build their nests in giant trees, sometimes over 70 m (230 ft) above the ground.

Keeping in touch A transmitter is attached to the nestling's back, using a harness. The scientist has to work quickly, because adult eagles will attack if they return and find an intruder.

THAT'S AMAZING

SAVED FROM EXTINCTION

In 1951, there were only 33 Hawaiian geese left alive. A handful of the birds were caught, and sent to reserves where they were encouraged to breed. Today, there are around 3000 Hawaiian geese, and the species is safe.

Can animals be saved by keeping them in zoos?

Zoos help to protect species that are in danger of becoming extinct. Sometimes they can encourage animals to breed, so that their numbers start to recover. But zoos cannot protect species forever; that can be done only by helping them to survive in the wild. The most effective way of saving animals, and the plants they eat, is by preserving their habitats – their homes in the natural world.

Bengal tiger   In the 21st century, the only tigers left may be those that live in zoos.

Border patrol

Most rare animals are now protected by law. Despite this, some are still hunted, and others are caught and sold as pets. Wildlife investigators help to track down people involved in the illegal wildlife trade. Customs officials also join in. They search people's luggage for live animals, and also for animal products such as rhino horn, tortoiseshell and ivory. These are sometimes smuggled across borders and sold.

A wildlife investigator with contraband spotted cat and crocodile skins in Brazil.

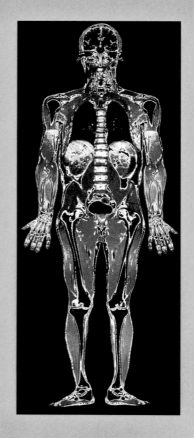
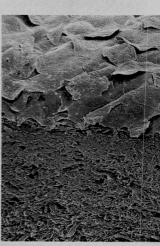
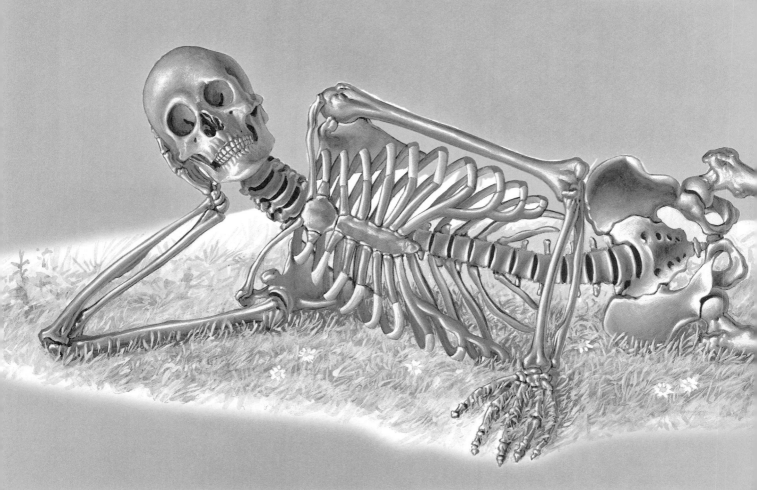

The Human Body

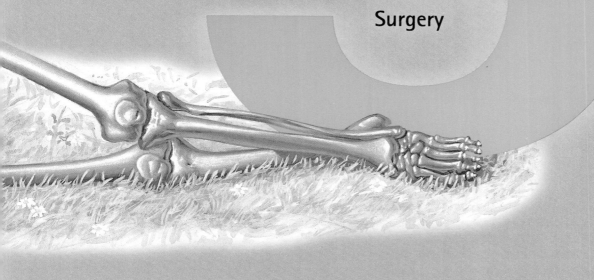

Bones and skeletons

Muscles and movement p.108 · Growing up p.134 · Medical treatment p.142 · Fact File p.306

Bones support your body, and make up about one-fifth of your total weight. Without them, you would not be able to move, to eat, or even to breathe. Bones change as you grow up, and they also get thicker and stronger if they have to do a lot of extra work or carry extra weight. Together, they make a flexible framework for your body. Some bones have a Latin name as well as an English name.

BONES ON SHOW
The human skeleton is made up of bones of many shapes and sizes. About one-tenth of all the bones in your body form your skull, while more than half are crammed into your hands and feet. Some bones, such as the shoulder blades, are thin and flat, but most of the bigger bones are long and hollow.

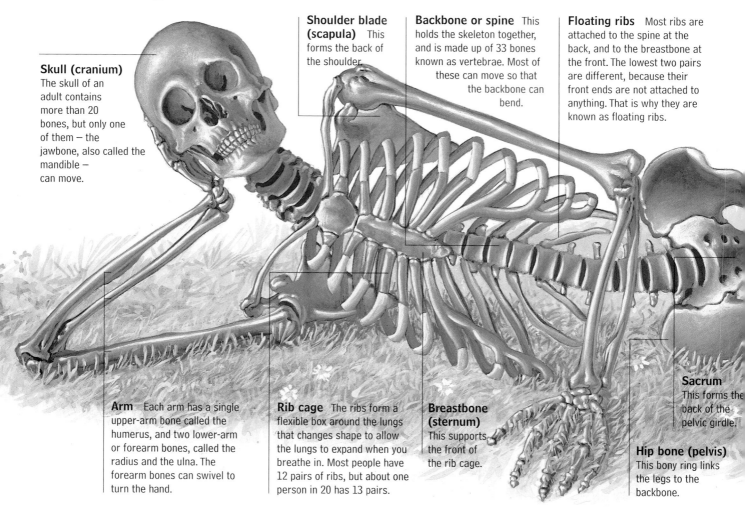

Skull (cranium) The skull of an adult contains more than 20 bones, but only one of them – the jawbone, also called the mandible – can move.

Shoulder blade (scapula) This forms the back of the shoulder.

Backbone or spine This holds the skeleton together, and is made up of 33 bones known as vertebrae. Most of these can move so that the backbone can bend.

Floating ribs Most ribs are attached to the spine at the back, and to the breastbone at the front. The lowest two pairs are different, because their front ends are not attached to anything. That is why they are known as floating ribs.

Arm Each arm has a single upper-arm bone called the humerus, and two lower-arm or forearm bones, called the radius and the ulna. The forearm bones can swivel to turn the hand.

Rib cage The ribs form a flexible box around the lungs that changes shape to allow the lungs to expand when you breathe in. Most people have 12 pairs of ribs, but about one person in 20 has 13 pairs.

Breastbone (sternum) This supports the front of the rib cage.

Sacrum This forms the back of the pelvic girdle.

Hip bone (pelvis) This bony ring links the legs to the backbone.

What are bones made of?
Nearly two-thirds of a bone's weight is made up by crystals of a mineral called calcium phosphate. The other third is made up by fibres of a substance called collagen. The crystals and fibres are produced by bone cells, which are scattered throughout the bone. Tiny channels running through the bone allow blood to reach the bone cells.

Inside a bone This is part of a section through a bone, magnified around 100 times. The rings are made of mineral crystals. Fibres and bone cells live in the small gaps between the rings. The mineral crystals give a bone its strength, while the fibres help it to bend without breaking.

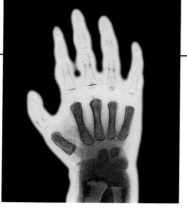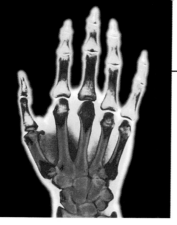

Bony fingers These two X-rays show the hand of a 3-year-old (left) and of a 13-year-old (right). In the 3-year-old, many bones have not yet formed.

How many bones are there in my body?

It depends how old you are. At birth, a lot of the skeleton is made of a rubbery substance called cartilage. As you grow older, most of this turns to bone. Then some bones start to join up. For example, two bones that form your forehead grow together soon after birth. In your mid-teens, five bones near the base of your spine start to form a single bone called the sacrum. By your mid-twenties, you will have about 206 bones.

Thigh bone (femur) Like all bones, the thigh bone contains marrow, a jelly-like substance that makes blood cells.

THAT'S AMAZING

RENEWABLE BONES

Many bones are constantly producing new bone tissue to make up for the wear and tear they receive. For example, the cells at the lower end of the thigh bone, where it joins the knee, are replaced every four months.

Joints

Joints are the places where bones are connected. In the joints that enable different parts of your body to move — for example, your shoulders, elbows, hips and knees — the bones are tipped with smooth cartilage. This is made slippery by an oily fluid so that the bones can slide over each other. In other joints, particularly ones in your skull, neighbouring bones are firmly locked together. This ensures that these parts of the skeleton stay in exactly the right position.

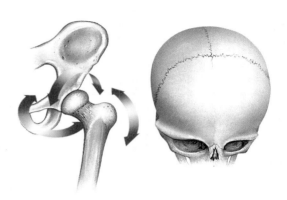

The hip joint is shaped so that the thighbone can swivel in many different directions. In the skull, zigzag joints keep bones locked together so they cannot move. This protects the brain.

Kneecap (patella) This small bone protects the knee against injury. It is held in place by tough cords called tendons.

Foot Each of your feet contains 26 bones — one fewer than each hand.

Large and small In an adult, the thigh bone (left) can weigh over 200 000 times as much as the stirrup bone (below) hidden away in the inner ear.

Which are the largest and smallest bones?

The biggest bone in the human body is the thigh bone, or femur. In an average man, it is about 45 cm (18 in) long. The ends of a thigh bone contain lots of small spaces filled with marrow cells, which help to save weight. Without these spaces, moving about would be hard work because the bone would be very heavy. The smallest bone is the stirrup, inside the ear. It is just 5 mm ($1/5$ in) long and helps to carry sounds into the inner part of the ear. There are three bones in each ear, and they are so small that they would all fit inside a matchbox.

Muscles and movement

⏩ Bones and skeletons p.106 · Brain and nervous system p.116 · Fact file p.306

Our muscles are bundles of fibres that alternately shorten and relax to make parts of the body move. They make up more than half your body's weight. Muscles enable you to walk, run, breathe and blink, and they keep your body in position when you sit or stand. Some muscles, such as the biceps in your arms, work only when you want them to. Others, such as your heart, never stop working.

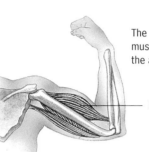

The biceps muscle bends the arm.

Biceps

Muscle pairs
In order to move an arm or a leg and then return it to its original position, many muscles are arranged in pairs.

Triceps

The triceps muscle straightens the arm.

How do muscles work?
Muscles are made up of millions of cells called muscle fibres, which contain overlapping chemical threads. When a muscle receives signals from the nervous system, the threads slide closer together, making the whole muscle shorten or contract. This moves the part of the body to which the muscle is attached.

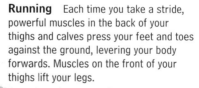

Inside a muscle

Muscle sheath

Bundle of fibres

Muscle fibre

Chemical threads

Running Each time you take a stride, powerful muscles in the back of your thighs and calves press your feet and toes against the ground, levering your body forwards. Muscles on the front of your thighs lift your legs.

Closing up
When bright light shines in your eyes, muscles inside your eyes automatically make your pupils smaller to reduce the amount of light getting in.

Can we control all our muscles?
You can control nearly all of your skeletal muscles – the ones attached to your bones. You can control some of the muscles that work other parts of your body, such as the ones you use to swallow, and those you use to make faces. You also have muscles, such as those in your eyes and digestive system, that work without your telling them to.

THAT'S AMAZING

MINIATURE MUSCLE
The smallest skeletal muscle in the human body is the stapedius, which is inside the ear. This tiny muscle is only about 1 mm (1/32 in) long. It steadies a tiny bone called the stirrup or stapes. This protects your ear from being damaged by loud noises.

WORKING TOGETHER

When you make complicated movements, such as running and jumping, you use many different muscles at the same time. Leg muscles push you along, arm muscles help you to stay balanced, and muscles in your back hold your body upright. Continual repetition of a movement develops your ability to make all these muscles work together.

In the air Muscles in your shoulder and upper arm raise and bend your arms to help you stay balanced when your body is off the ground. Muscles in your thighs raise your legs and keep them bent.

Making faces

You have more than 40 different muscles in your face. You use them all the time when you are awake, and sometimes when you are asleep. They help you to speak, eat and blink, and they also enable you to alter your expression. For humans, facial expressions are very important, because they allow us to show other people how we are feeling. Babies know how to smile and laugh, but we learn many other expressions as we grow up. Try making faces at a friend, and see how many different feelings you can communicate without using words.

Try making faces to express your feelings.

What makes muscles ache?

Muscles need energy to work. They get it by using oxygen to break down a chemical fuel called glucose, a form of sugar, which is delivered to them by the blood. If a muscle is working hard, it starts to run short of oxygen and it cannot break down glucose in the normal way. Instead, glucose is turned into lactic acid. The acid builds up inside the muscle and makes it ache. If the muscle is allowed to rest, the acid is broken down and the ache disappears.

Landing Thigh muscles hold your legs steady, with knees and ankles bent, ready to take the force of the impact with the ground. At the same time, muscles on the front of your body tighten up, keeping your stomach and intestines in place as you suddenly come to a halt.

Tired out Athletes push themselves very hard during competition and their leg muscles take time to stop aching.

Blood and circulation

Immune system p.136 · Medical diagnosis p.140 · Surgery p.144 · Fact File p.306, 322

Blood is pumped to every part of your body by your heart. In an adult, up to 5 litres (8 pints) hurtle through arteries and veins, completing a double loop around the body in less than one minute. During this endless high-speed journey, blood delivers oxygen, collects waste, and supplies the substances that all your body's cells need to survive. Blood also helps the body to fight diseases, and it spreads warmth from one part of the body to another.

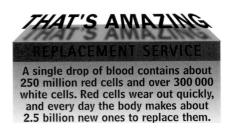

THAT'S AMAZING

REPLACEMENT SERVICE

A single drop of blood contains about 250 million red cells and over 300 000 white cells. Red cells wear out quickly, and every day the body makes about 2.5 billion new ones to replace them.

What is blood made of?

Blood is a complicated mixture of liquids, chemicals and cells. If you could separate out the ingredients in a single drop of blood, you would find that just over half of it is made of a liquid called plasma. Plasma consists mainly of water, but it also contains many dissolved chemicals. One of these is glucose, the substance that your body uses to make energy. The rest of the drop of blood would consist of millions of cells so tiny that they can only be seen under a microscope. Most of these cells are the red blood cells, which carry oxygen. Scattered among them are transparent cells called white cells, which are involved in fighting disease. Red blood cells are shaped like tiny coins. White blood cells are bigger, and many can move about by changing shape.

Assorted cells
An electron micrograph shows the coin-shaped red cells and the larger, more spherical white cells, magnified about 2000 times.

WHERE DOES BLOOD GO?

Blood travels around your body in a network of pipes called blood vessels. The blood vessels that carry blood away from the heart are called arteries; the ones that carry it back again are called veins. Arteries and veins are connected to each other by more than 80 000 km (50 000 miles) of capillaries, tiny vessels much thinner than a hair. Arteries expand every time your heart beats. In places such as the wrist, this creates a 'pulse' you can feel.

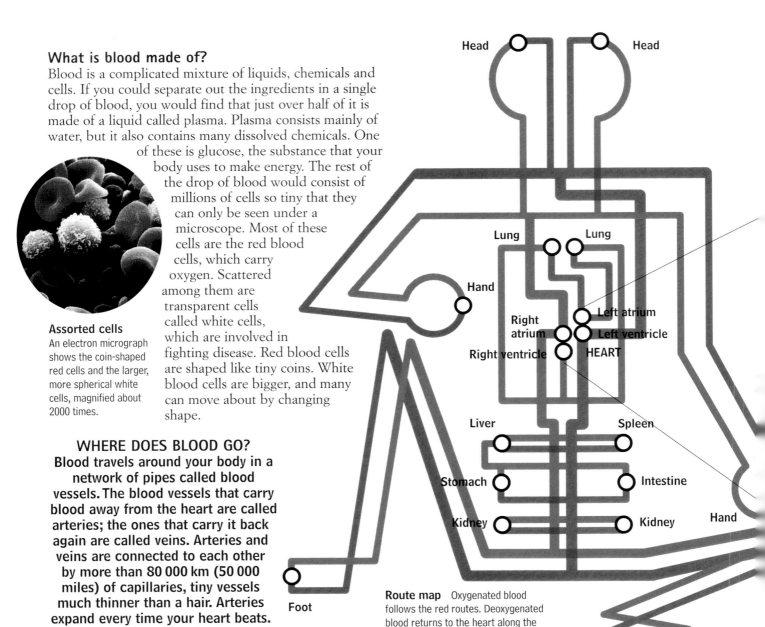

Route map Oxygenated blood follows the red routes. Deoxygenated blood returns to the heart along the violet routes so that it can be re-charged with oxygen.

Why is blood red?

Blood gets its colour from a red chemical called haemoglobin, which is stored in red blood cells. When blood flows through the lungs, the haemoglobin collects oxygen and carries it to other parts of the body. Haemoglobin that is carrying oxygen is bright red, but after it has released its oxygen into the body's cells as it flows past them, it becomes much darker. As a result, the blood flowing in your arteries is brighter red than the blood flowing in your veins.

Blood sample
This sample has been separated into liquid plasma and dark red blood cells.

Inside the heart
This shows the front view of the heart, looking towards the chest.

Why do scabs form?

If blood was like water, it would drain away through cuts and grazes. Instead, small leaks are quickly plugged, bringing bleeding to a halt. This happens because blood contains a chemical called fibrinogen. When a blood vessel is cut, the fibrinogen turns into another chemical, called fibrin, which creates a maze of sticky strands. Blood cells get trapped in the strands, making a solid plug called a clot. Once a clot has formed, the skin underneath starts to heal. Eventually, the clot dries out to form a scab, which later falls off. By this time, the injury has been fully repaired.

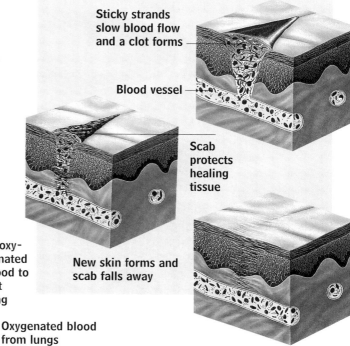

Sticky strands slow blood flow and a clot forms

Blood vessel

Scab protects healing tissue

New skin forms and scab falls away

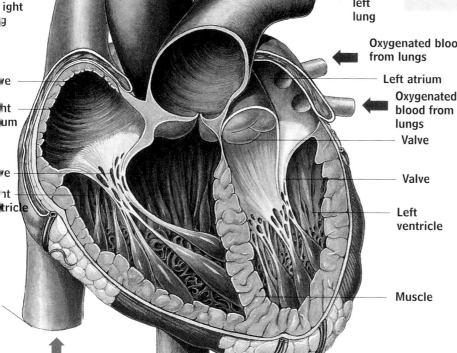

Oxygenated blood from head and arms

ygenated blood from and arms

Aorta

Deoxy-genated blood to left lung

oxygen-d blood ight g

Oxygenated blood from lungs

ve

Left atrium

ht um

Oxygenated blood from lungs

Valve

ve

Valve

ht tricle

Left ventricle

Muscle

Deoxygenated blood from lower body

Oxygenated blood to lower body

How does the heart work?

Your heart is made of muscle, and has two chambers, called the atrium and the ventricle, on each side. About 100 000 times a day, the heart fills with blood and then contracts to pump the blood out again. This contraction is called a heartbeat. Deoxygenated blood from your body flows into the right side of your heart, and is pumped to the lungs, where it takes in oxygen. The oxygenated blood returns to the left side, which pumps the blood out through a large artery called the aorta and around your body. Each side of your heart has two valves. These are flaps that stop blood flowing backwards after each beat.

Lungs and breathing

🔵 Muscles and movement p.108 · Blood and circulation p.110 ·
Medical diagnosis p.140 · Surgery p.144 · Fact File p.306

Humans need oxygen to survive. Each time you take a breath, air rushes into your lungs and oxygen passes from the air into your blood. To get enough oxygen into your body, your lungs need a very large surface area in contact with the air. If your lungs could be unpacked and laid out flat, they could wrap up your body at least 25 times.

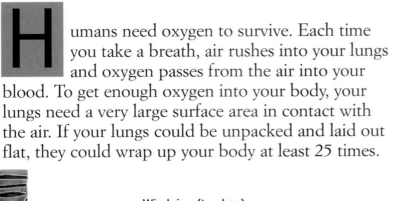

Diaphragm At the base of your chest is a sheet of muscle called the diaphragm.

Breathing in
When you take a deep breath, your diaphragm contracts and flattens and your ribs lift up and outward, to make your chest and lungs expand. This draws air down your windpipe into your lungs.

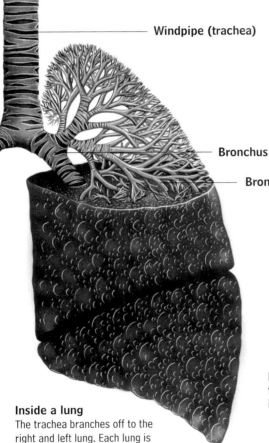

Windpipe (trachea)

Bronchus

Bronchiole

Inside a lung
The trachea branches off to the right and left lung. Each lung is made up of a mass of subdividing airways.

What do lungs look like?
Lungs are like air-filled sponges. Air flows into the lungs through a tube called the windpipe. This tube divides into many smaller tubes called bronchi, and these subdivide again into even smaller tubes called bronchioles. Each bronchiole ends in a cluster of tiny air pockets called alveoli, which are buried deep inside the lungs.

Blood flowing into lung

Blood flowing out of lung

Bronchiole

Air pocket

Inside an air pocket

How do lungs work?
When you breathe in, air flows through the bronchi and bronchioles in your lungs, and comes to a halt in millions of air pockets, known as alveoli. These pockets are surrounded by blood vessels that are so tiny they can be seen only under a microscope. The blood vessels are so thin that gases can pass straight through them. As blood flows around the air pockets, oxygen passes into the blood, while carbon dioxide waste in the blood passes into the pockets to be breathed out.

Air pockets The air pockets stretch open when you breathe in. They shrink when you breathe out, but a slippery inner lining prevents them from sticking shut.

THAT'S AMAZING
BIG BREATHERS
People take, on average, more than half a billion breaths during a lifetime. Each person's lungs move about 250 000 m³ (8 million cu ft) of air – a quantity that would fill the biggest airship ever built.

Gasping for air At rest, a 10-year-old takes in about 0.25 litre (15 cu in) of air with each breath. If you take deep breaths, you will take in seven times more air than this. If you work hard you will force more air out of your lungs and take in ten times more air.

| 0.25 litre (15 cu in) | 1.75 litres (105 cu in) | 2.5 litres (150 cu in) |

BREATHING IN AND BREATHING OUT
Lungs do not have any muscles, so they cannot move air on their own. Instead, muscles in the chest make the lungs expand, or blow up like a balloon, as air is sucked in. Most of the work of breathing is done by muscles that raise the ribs, but if you breathe out hard – for example when blowing a trumpet – you use muscles on the front of your belly as well. This pushes your insides upwards, squeezing the air out of your lungs more forcefully.

Why do you get out of breath?
The amount of oxygen you need depends on how hard your body is working. If you are resting you need only a small amount. If you are running or playing football, you use up oxygen more quickly producing enough energy. An area in your brain automatically adjusts your breathing rate to make sure you get the oxygen you need, by breathing faster and more deeply.

Breathing out
Normally, breathing out is easy because your ribs gently squeeze the air out of your lungs. To play a trumpet, you need to push air out using your diaphragm and muscles in your belly.

Sneezes and hiccups

Breathing normally happens so smoothly that we hardly notice it. But sometimes it is interrupted by a cough, a sneeze, or by hiccups. Hiccups happen when your diaphragm contracts suddenly and air rushes into your lungs. Your vocal cords – membranes lying across your trachea that you use to talk – close, making a loud squeak. Coughs and sneezes clear out dust and other particles that get trapped in your airways and the lining of your nose. Colds cause coughs and sneezes for a few days; smoking can give people a cough for years because some of the smoke gets stuck in the lungs.

Drops of moisture, dust and germs shoot into the air when you sneeze.

Skin, hair and nails

🌐 Brain and nervous system p.116 · Taste, smell, touch and balance p.120 · People of the world p.220 · Fact File p.308

Skin grows in step with the rest of your body, and although it constantly wears away, it is also replacing itself all the time. Like hair and nails, skin helps to protect your body from the outside world. It can do this because its surface is made of dead cells. These are very tough, and they form a barrier that shields the living cells underneath. Like the surface of skin, most of each hair is also made of dead cells.

UNDER THE SURFACE
Each part of your body has a different type of skin. For example, the skin on the back of your arm is covered with lots of hairs, although they may be too small for you to see. The skin on the palms of your hands and the inside of your fingers has no hair at all, but it does have lots of tiny ridges and invisible openings called sweat glands.

What is skin made of?
Skin is made of cells arranged in three main layers. The deepest layer, called the dermis, contains living cells, blood vessels, and nerve endings that sense pressure, heat, cold and pain. Above this is a thin layer, called the epidermis, that produces new cells all the time. The new cells die as they are slowly pushed towards the surface, where they form a protective outer layer. Then they fall away in small flakes.

Skin ridges These ridges are found only on fingers and toes, and on the palms of your hands and soles of your feet. They help to give you a good grip. The skin underneath them is extra thick for added protection.

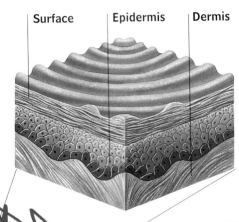

Surface · Epidermis · Dermis

Flaking away The surface of skin, magnified about 200 times, with flakes of dead cells forming.

Same but different
Some people have more of a particular skin pigment than others. Apart from this, everyone's skin is the same.

Fingernails
Nails protect your fingertips (and toenails your toes), and also help you to pick things up. They are made from keratin – the same substance that makes hair. On average, a fingernail grows at a rate of about 1 mm ($1/32$ in) per week – four times faster than a toenail.

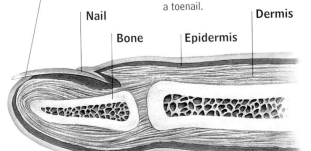

Nail · Bone · Epidermis · Dermis

Why are people different colours?
Skin gets its colour from chemicals called pigments present in skin cells. One pigment, called melanin, makes skin brown or black. Another, called carotene, gives skin a yellow colour. Pigments help to protect skin against damage by strong sunshine. People with pale skin have very little pigment and may easily get sunburned. If your skin is like this, it is important to stay covered up in strong sunshine, or to use sunblock.

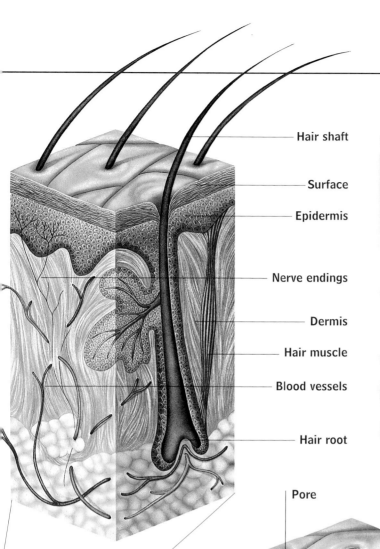

Hair shaft

Surface

Epidermis

Nerve endings

Dermis

Hair muscle

Blood vessels

Hair root

Hair Hair protects your head and eyes from the sun. On other parts of your body, it helps you feel things brushing against your skin. And it helps to keep you warm. Most of a hair is made of dead cells.

Sweat glands Sweat is a watery fluid that helps to keep you cool. It is made by coiled glands that open onto the surface of your skin. The palms of your hands have more sweat glands than anywhere else – up to 500 per cm² of skin (3250 per sq in).

Pore

Sweat gland

Fingerprints

Whenever you touch anything smooth, your fingers leave marks. These marks are called fingerprints. Fingerprints are made of sweat and body oils, and they are exact copies of the tiny ridges that cover your fingertips. Identical twins have matching fingerprints, but everybody else has their own unique pattern, which will resemble one of the basic patterns shown below. Fingerprints are often used to identify people present at the scene of a crime. To find fingerprints, police scientists dust the objects at a crime scene with a fine powder. This sticks to the sweat and oil that the fingers have left behind, making the marks show up. The police then see if the marks match up with the fingerprints of any of their suspects.

Arch   Loop   Whorl   Composite

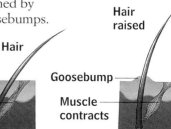

THAT'S AMAZING

NATURAL WASTAGE

Every year, the average person sheds 4 kg (9 lb) of dead skin flakes, up to 30 000 hairs, and about 5 cm (2 in) of fingernail clippings.

Can hair really stand on end?

If you are cold or frightened, your hair may feel as if it is standing on end. A tiny muscle pulls on the root of each hair, levering it into a more upright position. As each hair moves, it pushes against the skin, making a 'goosebump'. Long ago humans had lots of body hair, and warm air would have been trapped in the little pits formed by goosebumps.

Goosebumps
A hair is pulled upright, forming a goosebump.

Hair

Hair raised

Goosebump

Muscle relaxed

Muscle contracts

Brain and nervous system

Muscles and movement p.108 · Sound and vision p.118 ·
Taste, smell, touch and balance p.120 · Fact File p.306

Every second, whether you are awake or fast asleep, your brain is busy processing information. It receives millions of signals from all parts of the body, and it sends out signals that control the way your body works. These signals travel along nerves – bundles of cells that conduct tiny bursts of electricity. The brain itself contains more than 1000 billion nerve cells, and when they are busy these cells generate enough electrical energy to power a lightbulb.

Seeing the world
Several areas of your brain are involved in interpreting signals from the optic nerves in your eyes.

How do nerves work?

Most nerve cells have a long thread, called an axon, which works partly like a battery and partly like a wire. When the nerve is resting, the axon is charged with electricity – just like the terminals of a battery. When the nerve is triggered into action, the charge suddenly changes, creating a signal that flashes down the axon. The nerves that the signals pass along to tell muscles to contract are called 'motor' nerves. The nerves that carry messages from sense organs to your brain are called 'sensory' nerves. Signals travel along nerves at about 360 km/h (225 mph) – fast enough to travel from your brain to your toes in less than $1/50$ of a second.

Motor nerve
In adults, some nerve cells are over 1 m (3 ft) long.

Spinal cord

Axon

Muscle

Tuning in
The area that deals with interpreting sounds, called the auditory area, receives signals from nerves in your ears.

THAT'S AMAZING
LOST FOREVER
Unlike other cells in your body, the cells in your brain cannot be replaced when they get worn out. As a result, the number of cells in your brain steadily decreases as you get older.

Fine control
Whenever you make complicated movements, for example when using a keyboard, the part called the premotor area helps to control your muscles.

How do we remember things?

Scientists are still not certain how the brain remembers things, but they have produced a likely explanation. They know that each cell in the brain is connected to thousands of other cells via connection points called synapses. They think that the brain stores new information by forming new sets of connections between cells; it is as if the cells in the brain are constantly being rewired. At first, information is stored in your short-term memory. The information is then transferred into your long-term memory, which can store it for days, months or even years.

Thinking and understanding
The front of the brain is where thinking takes place. The ability to think makes us aware that we exist. The two sides work in slightly different ways. In most people, the **right side** deals with shapes and feelings.

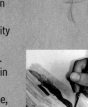

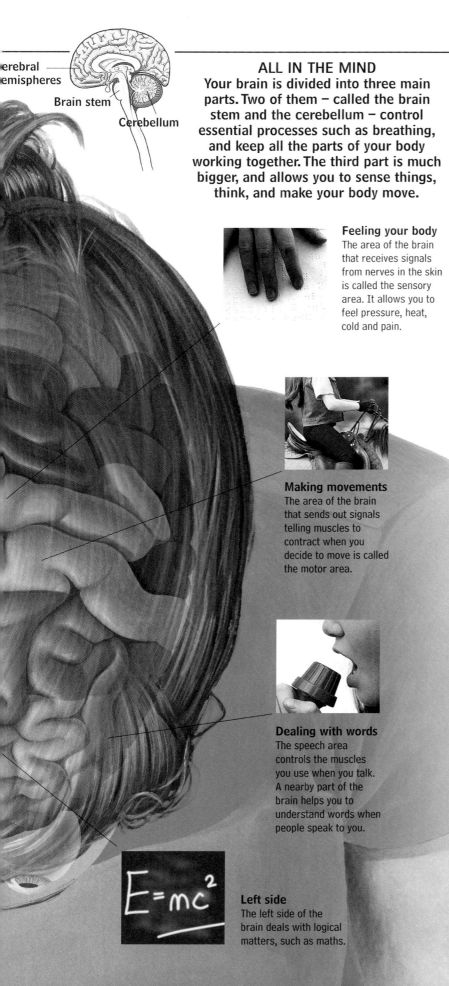

Cerebral hemispheres

Brain stem

Cerebellum

ALL IN THE MIND

Your brain is divided into three main parts. Two of them – called the brain stem and the cerebellum – control essential processes such as breathing, and keep all the parts of your body working together. The third part is much bigger, and allows you to sense things, think, and make your body move.

Feeling your body
The area of the brain that receives signals from nerves in the skin is called the sensory area. It allows you to feel pressure, heat, cold and pain.

Making movements
The area of the brain that sends out signals telling muscles to contract when you decide to move is called the motor area.

Dealing with words
The speech area controls the muscles you use when you talk. A nearby part of the brain helps you to understand words when people speak to you.

$E = mc^2$

Left side
The left side of the brain deals with logical matters, such as maths.

Reflexes

If you touch something very hot, your hand pulls away almost instantly, without waiting for your brain to tell it to. This is an example of a reflex – a rapid reaction that helps to protect you from injury. A message flashes from your hand to your spinal cord – the bundle of nerve cells running down your spine that link the brain with all parts of your body. The message is then passed straight to motor nerves, which make your arm muscles contract.

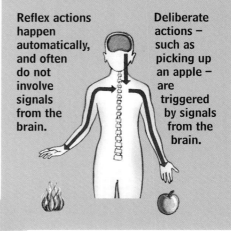

Reflex actions happen automatically, and often do not involve signals from the brain.

Deliberate actions – such as picking up an apple – are triggered by signals from the brain.

Sensitive parts

All over your body, you have nerve endings that give you information about the things you touch. Instead of being spread out, they are concentrated in places where the sense of touch is most useful. In the picture below, the parts of the body that have the most nerve endings are drawn enlarged. The most sensitive parts are the mouth and fingertips, while the least sensitive are the backs of the arms and legs. You can prove this by closing your eyes, and asking a friend to touch your skin gently in sensitive and less sensitive areas with a pencil or paintbrush.

The gentle touch
Extra-sensitive hands and fingertips help us to adjust our grip when we pick things up.

🌐 Brain and nervous system p.116 ·
Taste, smell, touch and balance p.120 · Fact File p.306

Humans rely on vision and hearing more than any other senses. Our eyes can adjust to a huge variety of light levels, from brilliant sunshine to almost total darkness, and they can tell the difference between millions of shades of colour. Our ears can pick up the faintest whisper, but they can also cope with the roar of a jet engine 10 billion times as loud. Eyes and ears work by producing nerve signals, which are then sent to the brain. Colour vision is so complicated that one-quarter of the brain is devoted to collecting information from the eyes and making sense of what we see.

Colour vision

Look at the picture below and see if you can make out a number. If you cannot, you may have what is called a colour deficiency – an inherited condition that makes it difficult to tell some colours apart. Colour deficiency, sometimes called 'colour blindness', is common in boys and men, but affects very few girls and women. True colour blindness, when a person has no colour vision at all, is extremely rare.

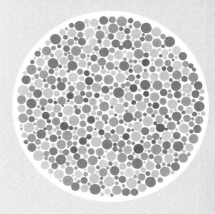

How do our eyes work?

Light enters your eye through a transparent outer covering called the cornea, and then through a hole called the pupil. Just behind the pupil, it passes through a lens. The lens focuses the light onto a curved screen called the retina at the back of the eye. The retina contains millions of nerve cells that sense light according to its brightness and colour. Signals from these cells travel along the optic nerve to your brain, and the brain analyses these signals to piece together whatever you are looking at. The image on the retina is upside down, but the brain reassembles it the right way up.

THAT'S AMAZING
RESTLESS EYES

The cells in your retina can work only if your eyes keep moving and the pattern of light falling on the cells constantly changes. Even when your eyes seem to be perfectly still, they make tiny flickering movements about 50 times every second. Without these flickers, you would be unable to see.

How do we see in the dark?

If you step into a darkened room on a sunny day, your eyes adjust to the change. The irises, which control the size of the pupils and therefore how much light enters, open wide to let in as much light as possible. Even so, it may be difficult to see much. If you wait for five minutes, you will then see better. This happens because your eyes have two types of nerve cells, called rods and cones. Cones can sense colour, but need bright light to work effectively. Rods cannot sense colour, but are good at working in dim light. When you step into a darkened room, the rods gradually take over from the cones, giving you a clear but grey view of your surroundings.

Why do our ears go 'pop'?

Behind each of your eardrums is a small air-filled chamber. The pressure inside it has to be kept the same as the pressure outside, or there would be a risk that your eardrums might burst. If you suddenly change altitude – for example, during takeoff in an aeroplane – the pressure inside and outside your ear becomes unequal. The balance is restored when air flows through the Eustachian tube, a narrow passage that connects the ear chamber with your throat. As the pressure equalises, you hear a sudden pop.

SIGHT AND SOUND
Having two eyes, each giving a slightly different view of the world, enables you to judge distances when you look at things. And having two ears lets you listen in 'stereo', so you can judge where a sound is coming from.

Now you see it, now you don't

Seeing is a two-stage process. Your eyes collect light and turn it into nerve signals, and your brain then has to sort through the signals to make sense of what you see. Your brain is very good at doing this, but sometimes it gets it wrong. The pictures here are designed to trick your brain into drawing the wrong conclusions from what you are looking at. Pictures like these are known as optical illusions.

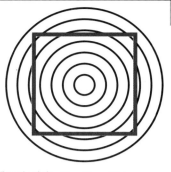

Visual trick The sides of this square look curved, but they are straight. You can check this with a ruler.

Shifting images Do you see the cube from above or below? And do you see a vase or two facial profiles? Stare at each image for a few moments and it will suddenly change.

All muddled up
The artist has deliberately jumbled up things that are near with those that are farther away.

How do our ears work?

The outer part of your ear gathers waves of sound and channels them through the ear canal deep inside your head. Here, the sound waves strike your eardrum and make it vibrate – up to 40 000 times a second for the highest sounds we can hear. Three tiny bones – the anvil, hammer and stirrup – then transmit these vibrations to a spiral chamber called the cochlea, where the movement is sensed by nerves. These send signals to your brain via the auditory nerve.

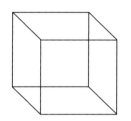

Cornea
Pupil
Iris
Lens
tic nerve

tina

Semicircular canals
Stirrup (stapes)
Anvil (incus)
Hammer (malleus)
Eardrum

Ear canal
Eustachian tube to throat
Cochlea

Taste, smell, touch and balance

🌐 Brain and nervous system p.116 ·
Sound and vision p.118 · Fact File p.306

If you ask most people how many senses they have, they will probably answer five: vision, hearing, taste, smell and touch. Together, these different senses tell you almost everything you need to know about your surroundings, and about the things you eat and drink. In fact, you also have a sixth sense, called balance, which enables you to perform one of the most amazing feats in the living world – standing and moving about on two legs.

Staying upright
A very good sense of balance stops acrobats toppling over. Without a sense of balance, people would find it impossible to stand upright, even on the ground.

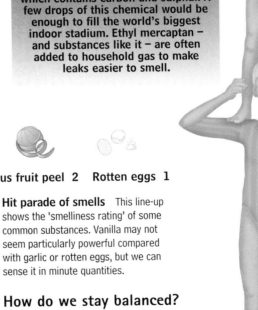

Why do some things smell while others don't?

Your sense of smell works by detecting chemicals in the air. Most of these chemicals are 'volatile', which means that they easily evaporate. Living things make lots of these chemicals, which is why the natural world is full of smells. Some of these chemicals are used in perfumes, and others help to flavour our food. Non-living materials, such as metals or rocks, contain very few volatile chemicals, or none at all, so they rarely smell. Soil, on the other hand, often does smell. This is because it contains living things.

THAT'S AMAZING

MAKING A STINK

The smelliest substance in the world is a chemical called ethyl mercaptan, which contains carbon and sulphur. A few drops of this chemical would be enough to fill the world's biggest indoor stadium. Ethyl mercaptan – and substances like it – are often added to household gas to make leaks easier to smell.

Vanilla 30 000   **Garlic oil 300**   **Rose oil 50**   **Almond essence 25**   Citrus fruit peel 2   Rotten eggs 1

Hit parade of smells   This line-up shows the 'smelliness rating' of some common substances. Vanilla may not seem particularly powerful compared with garlic or rotten eggs, but we can sense it in minute quantities.

Hot and cold

Most of our senses quickly get used to a new stimulus, and we stop noticing it. You can prove this by pouring three containers of water – one cold, one lukewarm, and the other hand-hot. Put the fingers of one hand in the cold container and the fingers of the other hand in the hand-hot container, and leave them there for three minutes. Then move them to the middle container, one hand at a time. The fingers of each hand will have got used to either hot or cold, so the lukewarm water will seem cold to the fingers from the hot container, and hot to the fingers from the cold container.

How do we stay balanced?

Your sense of balance tells you which way up you are, and lets you know whether your body is moving or still. These tasks are carried out in small, fluid-filled chambers, called semicircular canals, next to the innermost part of each ear. Nerve endings in these chambers sense the pull of gravity, and can tell if your head is moving. Balance can also be affected by what you see. For example, most people have no difficulty standing on a chair. But if the chair is put on top of a table, balancing becomes more difficult. This is because your brain is distracted by height. Acrobats have to train themselves to overcome this effect.

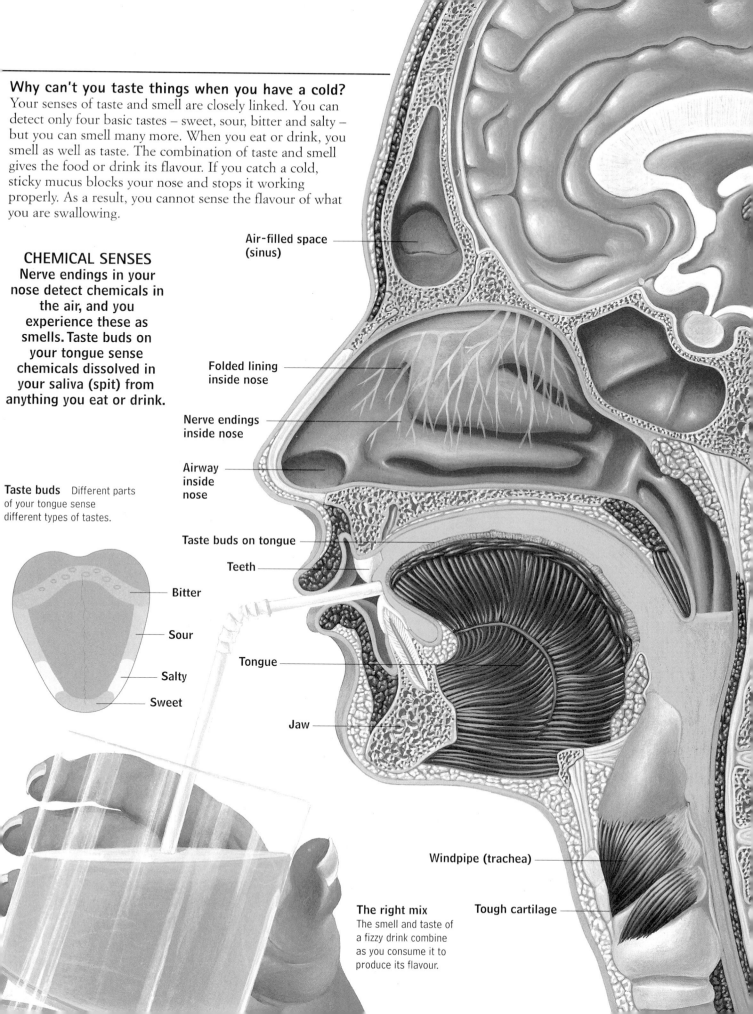

Why can't you taste things when you have a cold?

Your senses of taste and smell are closely linked. You can detect only four basic tastes – sweet, sour, bitter and salty – but you can smell many more. When you eat or drink, you smell as well as taste. The combination of taste and smell gives the food or drink its flavour. If you catch a cold, sticky mucus blocks your nose and stops it working properly. As a result, you cannot sense the flavour of what you are swallowing.

CHEMICAL SENSES

Nerve endings in your nose detect chemicals in the air, and you experience these as smells. Taste buds on your tongue sense chemicals dissolved in your saliva (spit) from anything you eat or drink.

Taste buds Different parts of your tongue sense different types of tastes.

- Bitter
- Sour
- Salty
- Sweet

Air-filled space (sinus)

Folded lining inside nose

Nerve endings inside nose

Airway inside nose

Taste buds on tongue

Teeth

Tongue

Jaw

Windpipe (trachea)

The right mix
The smell and taste of a fizzy drink combine as you consume it to produce its flavour.

Tough cartilage

⊙ Food and nutrition p.138 ·
Fact File p.308

The toughest parts of your body are not your bones, but your teeth. Each tooth is covered with a substance called enamel, and is so strong that it can cut or crush the toughest kinds of food. There is a price to pay for this toughness: unlike bones, teeth cannot repair themselves, and it pays to take care of them.

OPEN WIDE

We have different types of teeth so that we can bite and chew food. Teeth vary in shape, but are all built in the same way, and are held in place by roots. The top of each tooth, called the crown, is made of two layers of hard material, called enamel and dentine. The inside is soft. The soft part, called the pulp cavity, contains living cells. It has its own blood supply and nerves.

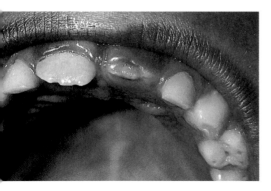

Toothy grin This 8-year-old has a mixture of milk teeth (at the sides and back) and adult teeth (at the front). Milk teeth have small roots, so adult teeth can push them out as they grow.

Why do our first teeth fall out?

Unlike most other parts of the body, teeth cannot grow larger once they have formed. Adult teeth would be far too big to fit into a young child's jaws, so we all have a set of smaller 'milk teeth' during our early years.

What is a 'wisdom tooth'?

Wisdom teeth are the last adult teeth to appear, right at the back of the jaw. There are usually four of these teeth, and in most people they appear between the ages of 17 and 21. Sometimes wisdom teeth have to be removed because there is not enough room for them behind the other teeth.

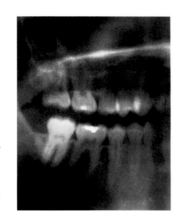

Final appearance This X-ray picture shows an upper and lower wisdom tooth emerging at the back of a person's jaw.

Molars These flat-topped teeth are shaped for chewing. They are near the back of the mouth, where the jaw is strongest.

Premolars These teeth are used for crushing and chewing. Unlike molars, they have two raised edges.

Hidden away Milk teeth have short roots. In adult teeth, a tooth's roots are often much bigger than its crown.

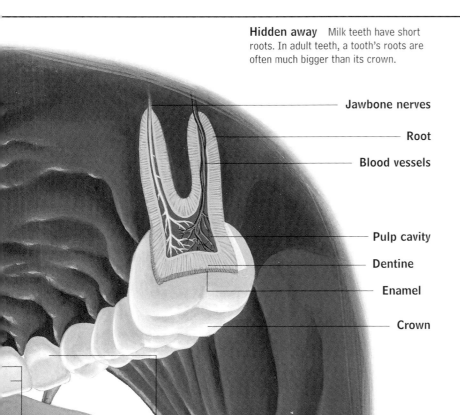

Jawbone nerves

Root

Blood vessels

Pulp cavity

Dentine

Enamel

Crown

Check out your teeth

Your teeth are as individual as your fingerprints. Dentists keep track of them by making a checklist called a dental formula, which shows how many of each type you have. With the help of a torch and a mirror, you can do this for yourself. Starting at the front, see if you can find your incisors, canines, premolars and molars. Children have 20 milk teeth (8 incisors, 4 canines and 8 molars). Adults usually have 32 permanent teeth (8 incisors, 4 canines, 8 premolars and 12 molars).

Why do we have to clean our teeth?

Even the cleanest mouth harbours millions of bacteria. Some of them stick onto the surface of teeth, where they feed on sugars in your food. If these bacteria are not cleaned away by brushing, they can dissolve the surface of your teeth and start to attack the soft part inside. Dentists can protect teeth by covering them with a plastic sealant, but brushing is still the best way to keep teeth healthy.

THAT'S AMAZING!
NEVER-ENDING TEETH
It is not unusual for people to have extra teeth. In rare cases, people have been known to grow a complete extra set during their lifetime, in addition to their milk and adult teeth. The biggest number of sets ever recorded is four.

Fighting decay A dentist checks for signs of decay. A decayed tooth will need a filling.

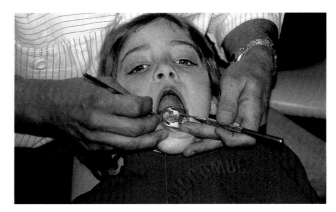

Incisors Chisel-shaped edges make these teeth good at biting and slicing.

Canines These teeth help to grip food. They have one sharp point.

➲ **Getting rid of waste** p.126 · **Food and nutrition** p.138 · **Fact File** p.308

During your life, you will probably spend more than 50 000 hours eating. This may sound a long time, but you will spend far longer digesting food. In the process of digestion, food travels along a hollow tube that runs through your body. Nutrients that the body can use are broken down and absorbed. The rest travels on, and is eventually disposed of as waste.

What makes us feel hungry?

You feel hungry when the amount of sugar in your blood drops below a certain level. A part of the brain called the hypothalamus sends signals to your stomach, telling it to prepare for the next meal. Your stomach may begin to make rumbling noises, and the sight and smell of food will make you feel even hungrier.

Hypothalamus This sends a message to the stomach.

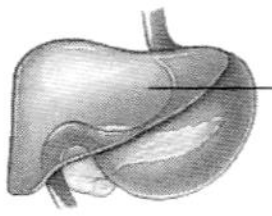

Liver This releases sugar into the bloodstream.

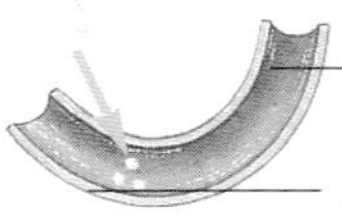

Low blood sugar

High blood sugar

Feeling hungry You become hungry when the level of sugar in your blood falls. Your liver releases more sugar into your blood, but it cannot keep doing this for long so you will continue to feel hungry until you have had something to eat.

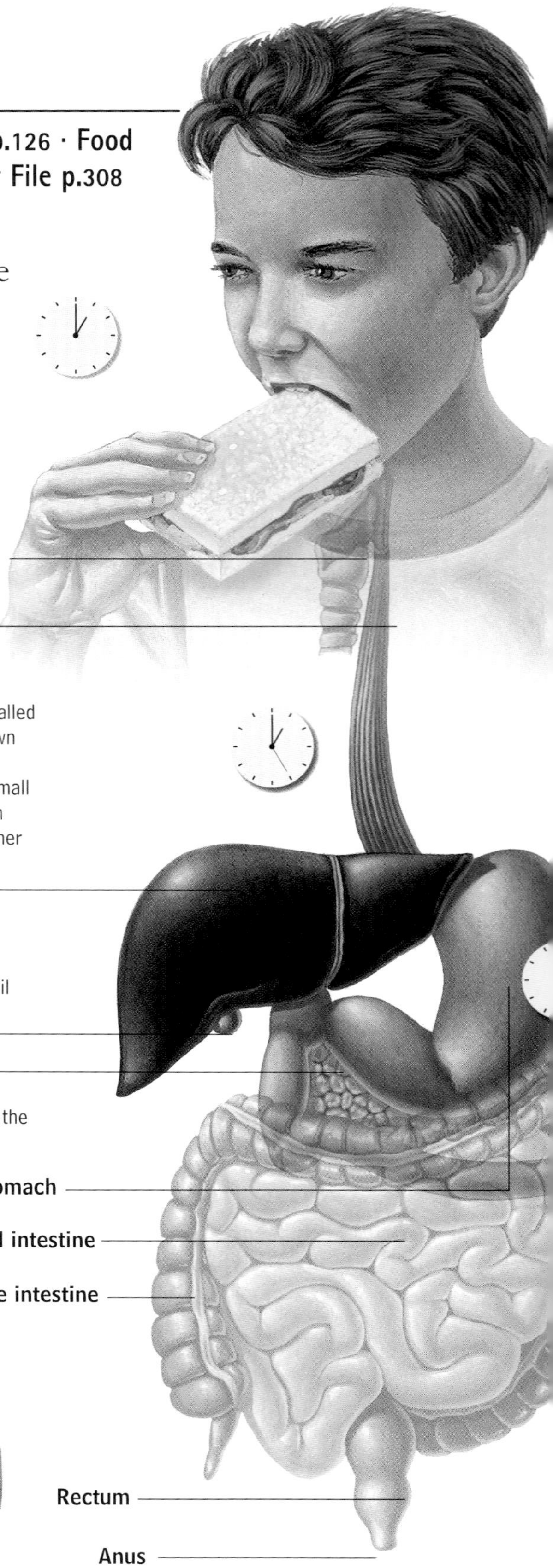

Trachea (windpipe)

Oesophagus

Liver This makes a liquid called bile, which helps to break down fats in food. It also receives digested nutrients from the small intestine, and processes them before sending them on to other parts of the body.

Gall bladder This stores bile produced by the liver until it is needed.

Pancreas This produces chemicals that help to digest the proteins in food.

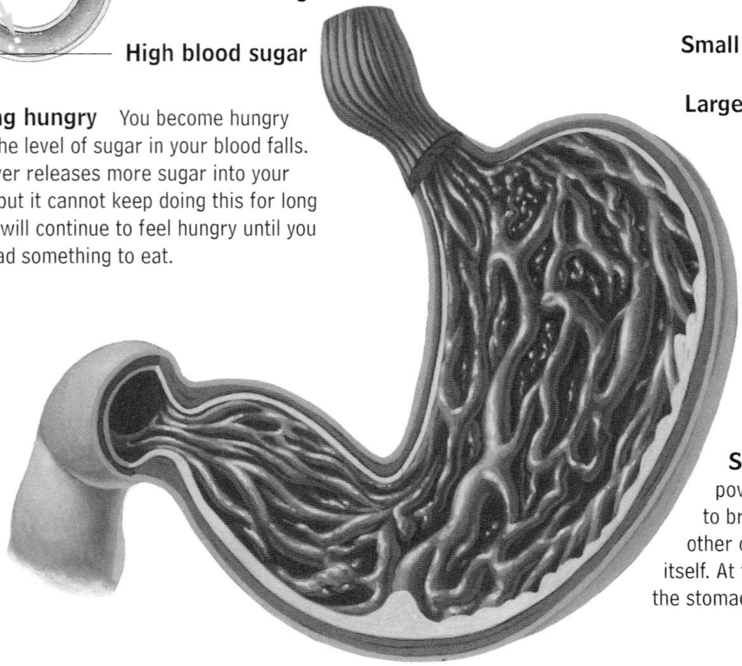

Stomach

Small intestine

Large intestine

Rectum

Anus

Stomach Cells lining the stomach produce a powerful acid called hydrochloric acid that helps to break down food. Sticky mucus produced by other cells stops the acid digesting the stomach itself. At the lower end, a ring of muscle keeps food in the stomach until it is ready to move on.

What happens when food 'goes down the wrong way'?

When you swallow, a flap called the epiglottis closes off your trachea (windpipe). Sometimes it does not close quickly enough, and food goes down the wrong tube. This makes you cough, which dislodges the food from your windpipe and sends it back up.

Oesophagus

When you swallow, this part of the digestive system squeezes the chewed food from your mouth down to your stomach.

JOURNEY THROUGH THE BODY

Food moves through your body inside your alimentary canal. This tube goes from the mouth through several sections to the anus, and in adults is up to 9 m (30 ft) long. Each section is constructed to carry out particular tasks. Organs attached to the alimentary canal, such as the gall bladder and the pancreas, also play a part in digestion.

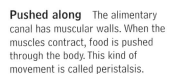

Pushed along The alimentary canal has muscular walls. When the muscles contract, food is pushed through the body. This kind of movement is called peristalsis.

Why do we burp and fart?

When you swallow food, you cannot help swallowing air as well. When you belch or burp, this air escapes. When food is digested in your intestines, it often produces gas as a waste product. These gases make food rumble and squeak as it works its way through your digestive system. Farting releases this gas.

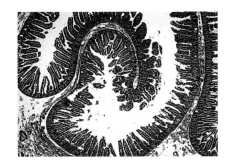

Forest of fingers The lining of the small intestine is covered with millions of finger-like projections, called villi and microvilli. These absorb nutrients, which pass into the bloodstream.

Small intestine
This long tube completes the process of digestion and absorbs useful nutrients.

Looking inside

Until the 19th century, people had little idea how digestion worked. In 1822, US army surgeon William Beaumont treated a 19-year-old man who had been shot in the stomach. The patient recovered, but the hole in his stomach remained open. This provided Beaumont with a living laboratory. He withdrew gastric juices through the hole and analysed them. Between tests, the patient worked as a handyman.

Beaumont takes a sample of gastric juices.

THAT'S AMAZING

SLOW FOOD

An adult's small intestine is nearly 6 m (20 ft) long, much longer than the large intestine, but it is only about 2.5 cm (1 in) wide. Travelling at top speed, food normally moves through it at about 2 m (6 ft) an hour – slower than a snail's pace.

24 hours later

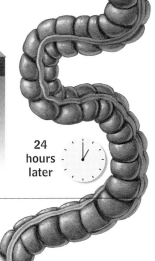

Large intestine This absorbs water from the waste left behind after food has been digested.

Anus Muscles normally keep the anus closed, but they open it when waste is ready to leave.

Rectum This is the last part of the intestines. Waste is stored here until it is ready to leave your body.

Getting rid of waste

🔄 Blood and circulation p.110 · Digestion p.124 · Fact File p.308

All living things – including humans – regularly get rid of waste. This waste is produced as a result of the chemical processes that keep our bodies working properly, and it consists of water and chemicals that our bodies cannot use. The process of getting rid of waste is called excretion, and it keeps the body's chemistry in balance. Without it, we would quickly become ill.

YOUR BODY'S WATER BALANCE
Your body ensures that the amount of water you consume every day equals the amount of water that you get rid of. You take in water in food and drink. You dispose of it through your skin (in sweat) and lungs (in your breath), and in urine (pee) and faeces (poo). The hotter the weather, the faster you lose water and the more you need to drink.

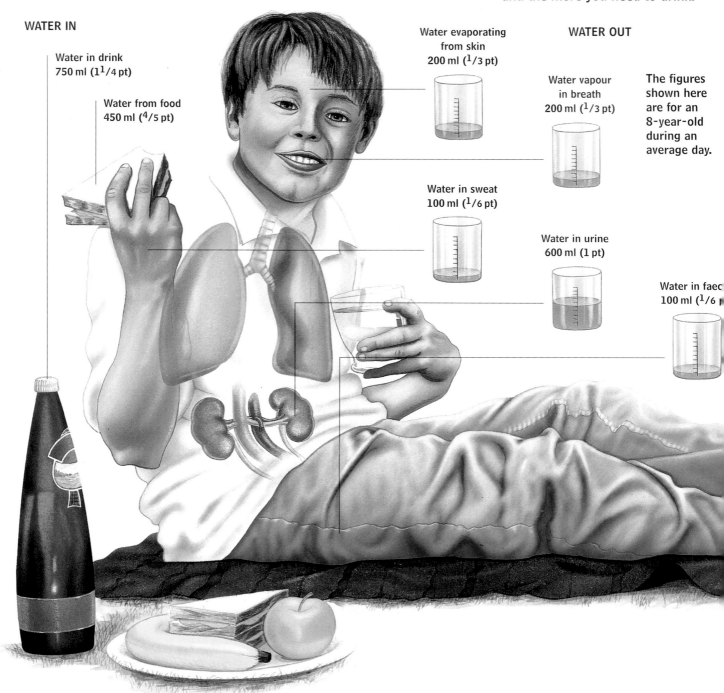

WATER IN

Water in drink
750 ml (1$^{1}/_{4}$ pt)

Water from food
450 ml ($^{4}/_{5}$ pt)

Water evaporating
from skin
200 ml ($^{1}/_{3}$ pt)

WATER OUT

Water vapour
in breath
200 ml ($^{1}/_{3}$ pt)

The figures
shown here
are for an
8-year-old
during an
average day.

Water in sweat
100 ml ($^{1}/_{6}$ pt)

Water in urine
600 ml (1 pt)

Water in faec
100 ml ($^{1}/_{6}$ p

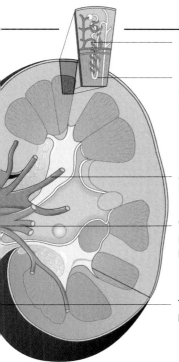

- Blood vessels inside kidney
- Microscopic tubes that collect waste
- Artery carrying blood to kidney
- Vein carrying blood away from kidney
- Tube leading to bladder

What do kidneys do?

Kidneys filter your blood, removing chemical waste that the blood has collected from the cells in your body. You have two kidneys, and more than a million microscopic tubes are packed into the outer layers of each. As blood flows through the kidneys, the waste trickles into the tubes, making urine. The urine flows from the kidneys into an expandable bag called the bladder. When your bladder is stretched, nerve endings there send a message to tell your brain that it is time to empty it.

Waste removal The kidneys clean the blood as it passes through them.

A familiar feeling If a telling-off makes you anxious, you may feel you want to pee.

Why does feeling nervous make you want to pee?

If something makes you anxious or frightened, your body prepares to cope with danger. Hormones and nerves make your heart beat faster, and make your muscles tense. One of these muscles is in the lining of your bladder. When it tenses up, it makes you feel that you need to go to the toilet, even though your bladder may not be full.

Artificial kidneys

Fifty years ago, people with diseased kidneys soon died, but today they can survive with the help of a special type of machine, called a 'dialysis unit', which does the work of the kidneys. The patient is connected to the machine via two tubes. One tube is connected to one of the patient's arteries and one to a vein, so that the patient's blood flows through the machine and back into their body again. The machine filters out the waste products that are not being removed by the patient's kidneys. The person normally has to use the machine two or three times a week, for several hours a day. Another way of helping people with kidney problems is to replace one of their kidneys with one from another member of their family. This is not as dangerous as it sounds, because people can live quite healthily with just one kidney.

A young girl undergoes dialysis.

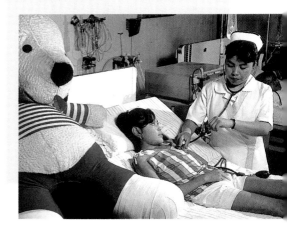

Why do we sweat?

Your body works properly only if it stays at exactly the right temperature, 37°C (98.6°F). If the weather is hot, or if you do something energetic like running, or if you are ill, you start to get hotter. As soon as this happens, your body sets about cooling things down. Sweating is one of the ways it does this. When sweat evaporates, it absorbs heat from the surface of your skin. This cools the blood circulating beneath the surface.

Hot work Sweat droplets, magnified 20 times, emerging on the skin surface after an hour's exercise.

THAT'S AMAZING!

SUPER-FILTERS

The two kidneys filter the whole bloodstream about once every 25 minutes. In an adult, this means that they filter over 500 000 litres (100 000 gallons) of blood a year – all through tiny tubes that are thinner than a hair.

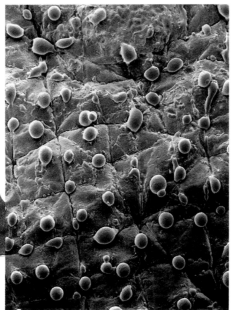

Hormones

⊙ **Blood and circulation** p.110 · **Reproduction** p.130 · **Immune system** p.136 · **Fact File** p.308

Hormones are chemicals produced inside the body that help to regulate the way different parts of the body work. Your body produces over 20 different hormones, and each one has a particular job to do. Many hormones work like an accelerator, speeding up the rate at which your body works. Hormones are made in tiny amounts, but they have important and long-lasting effects. A sudden shock or scare, for example, triggers a powerful hormone called adrenalin into action.

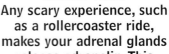

SCARY RIDE
Any scary experience, such as a rollercoaster ride, makes your adrenal glands release adrenalin. This hormone primes your body for emergency action by preparing it to work harder and faster.

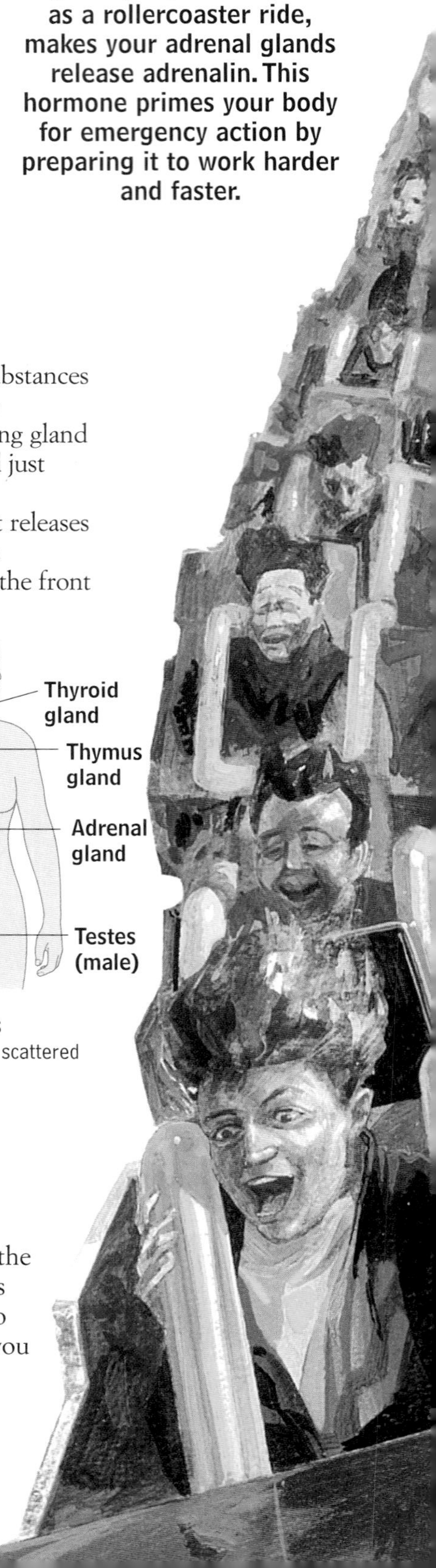

Where are hormones made?

Each type of hormone is made by a different gland. Glands are clusters of cells that produce a variety of substances needed by the body. Glands release hormones into the bloodstream. The most important hormone-producing gland is the pituitary gland, a pea-sized organ situated just beneath your brain. The pituitary gland is the headquarters of the hormone system because it releases the hormones that make other glands produce hormones of their own. The thyroid gland, at the front of your neck, helps to control growth. The thymus gland, which is in your chest, helps the body produce cells that fight disease. Beneath your ribs is your pancreas, which controls the amount of sugar in the blood. Above your kidneys are your adrenal glands, which make adrenalin. Hormones are also produced by your reproductive glands – ovaries in a girl and testes in a boy.

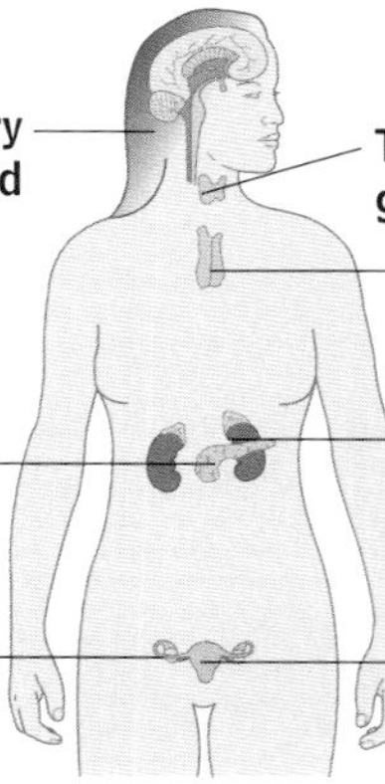

Pituitary gland

Thyroid gland

Thymus gland

Adrenal gland

Pancreas

Ovaries (female)

Testes (male)

Production points
Hormonal glands are scattered all over the body.

How do hormones work?

Seconds after being released, a hormone is carried around the body by the blood. When it reaches its target, it adjusts the way the cells there work. For example, a hormone called glucagon produced by the pancreas has a special effect on liver cells. It makes the liver cells release glucose (a form of sugar) into the blood, which helps to stimulate your body if you are running short of energy.

Walking tall If a person's thyroid gland produces too much growth hormone, and it goes untreated, he will grow into a giant.

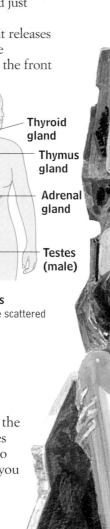

Working in pairs

Many hormones work in pairs and have the opposite effect to each other. By working together, they keep conditions inside your body properly balanced. One of the most important things that has to be balanced is the amount of sugar in your blood. Two hormones, called glucagon and insulin, make sure that the sugar level stays just right. If the blood sugar level starts to fall, glucagon steps it up. When the sugar level is too high, it triggers the release of more insulin, which lowers the level again. As a result, the sugar level settles down at the correct point.

Racing heart
Your heart beats faster, speeding up circulation so that oxygen can be transported around the body more quickly.

When blood sugar is low, glucagon increases it

When blood sugar is high, insulin reduces it

Low sugar level

High sugar level

Correct sugar level

Deep breaths   Your lungs breathe more deeply, bringing extra oxygen into your blood.

Digestion   Your digestion slows down, diverting extra blood to your muscles so that they can work harder.

Tense muscles   Adrenalin primes your muscles for action, making them work more powerfully than usual.

Pale skin   Blood is diverted away from the skin, making it look pale.

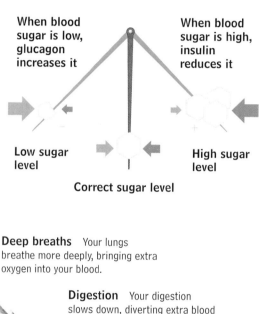

Sex hormones

Most hormones are at work from the moment you are born. Sex hormones are different, because they start to work later on. They gradually prepare the body for reproduction, and give it an adult shape. These changes start at the age of about 12 or 13, and they take about five years to complete. This stage of life is called puberty. Men have one main sex hormone, called testosterone, but women have two, called oestrogen and progesterone. Female sex hormones prepare a woman's body for pregnancy.

Changing times   Hormones are responsible for the physical changes that everyone goes through in their teens.

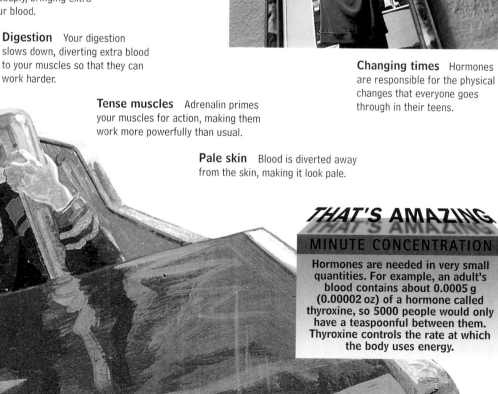

THAT'S AMAZING

MINUTE CONCENTRATION

Hormones are needed in very small quantities. For example, an adult's blood contains about 0.0005 g (0.00002 oz) of a hormone called thyroxine, so 5000 people would only have a teaspoonful between them. Thyroxine controls the rate at which the body uses energy.

Reproduction

Hormones p.128 · Genes and heredity p.132 · Fact File p.306

Everyone begins life as a single cell. These cells are called eggs, and each woman has a store of them inside her body. In order to develop, an egg cell has to join up with a sperm cell from a man. This process is called fertilisation and it takes place inside the woman's body. Once an egg has been fertilised, it starts to grow into a new human being. Nine months later, that new person is ready to be born.

Reproductive organs
Male reproductive organs produce sperm cells. Female reproductive organs produce egg cells.

— Penis

— Testis

— Ovary

— Womb (uterus)

— Vagina

8 weeks
The embryo is 3 cm (1¹/₄ in) long. Its bones are starting to form.

5 weeks
The major organs are forming, and the arms and legs are short and stubby. During this stage, the developing baby is called an embryo.

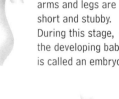

3 days After fertilisation, the egg has changed into a hollow ball of cells. It fastens itself to the lining of the womb.

Where do eggs and sperms come from?

Eggs are made in a woman's ovaries. Each woman has two ovaries. Each ovary is connected to the womb, also called the uterus, by a short tube, and eggs move down these tubes to be fertilised. Sperms are produced by ball-shaped organs called testes, which are held in a special pouch outside a man's body. They reach a woman's eggs by travelling out through the penis. This happens during the act of sexual intercourse between a man and a woman.

When girls are born, their ovaries already contain a lifetime's supply of eggs. The eggs start to ripen when a girl is about 13, and one is released every month. A boy's sperm cells do not start to develop until he is about 11 or 12 years old.

EARLY DEVELOPMENT

A baby develops inside its mother's womb, or uterus. The baby is attached to the lining of the womb, and floats inside a transparent bag filled with liquid. As the baby grows, the womb and the bag grow with it. When the baby is ready to be born, muscles in the uterus push it through the mother's birth canal, or vagina, and into the outside world.

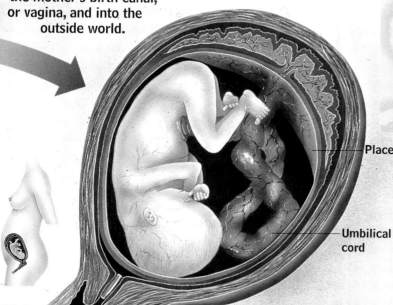

Placenta

Umbilical cord

4 months All the organs are fully formed. The embryo is now called a foetus. It is about 12 cm (5 in) long.

9 months By the end of the ninth month, the foetus lies with its head towards the birth canal, ready to be born.

Test-tube babies

Reproduction does not always go according to plan. Sometimes a woman's eggs cannot be fertilised inside her body, so she cannot become pregnant. In some cases, doctors can remove a woman's eggs and fertilise them in a test tube using her partner's sperms. The fertilised eggs are then put back into the woman's womb. Any that attach themselves to the womb will then develop in the normal way.

An egg cell (centre) is injected with sperms.

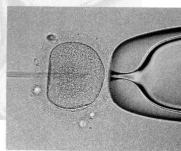

How does a baby feed while it is inside its mother?

During its time in the womb, a baby does not need to eat or breathe. Instead, it gets food and oxygen from its mother through a spongy pad called the placenta. One side of the placenta is fastened to the lining of the womb, and the other is connected to the baby by the umbilical cord. Nutrients and oxygen flow from the mother's blood through the placenta, along the cord and into the baby's body.

After a baby is born, the umbilical cord is cut and tied, leaving a 'tummy button'.

Lifeline The umbilical cord often twists as the baby moves around in the womb, but it is designed so that this does not matter.

Why do people sometimes have twins?

Twins usually come about when a woman releases two eggs at the same time, and both are fertilised. Twins like these are born close together, but they grow up to be as different as ordinary brothers and sisters. Twins who look alike, called identical twins, are produced when a single fertilised egg splits into two.

THAT'S AMAZING

POPULATION EXPLOSION

Each year, the average man produces about 50 billion sperm cells – enough to replace the entire human population of the Earth around eight times over.

Genes and heredity

🔄 Reproduction p.130 · Growing up p.134 ·
Fact File p.306, 323

A lmost every feature of your body – from the colour of your eyes to the shape of your fingernails – is controlled by chemical instructions called genes. Genes contain the information needed to build every part of your body, and they are stored inside every one of your body's cells. Parents' genes are passed on to their children.

THAT'S AMAZING

INVISIBLE INSTRUCTIONS

If all the DNA in one of your cells was stretched out in a line, it would be about 2 m (6½ ft) long. However, it would be so thin that you would not be able to see it with the naked eye.

What do genes look like?

Genes are carried on microscopic strands of a chemical called DNA. These strands are like spiral ladders, with millions of rungs spelling out instructions in a chemical code. To make the DNA strands more manageable, they are wound up into X-shaped packages called chromosomes. Most of the cells in your body contain 23 pairs of chromosomes, one set from your father and one set from your mother.

Looking at DNA If you could unwind the DNA in a chromosome, this is what you would see. DNA is a very special substance because it can copy itself when cells divide.

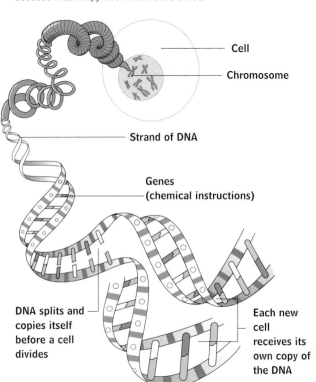

— Cell

— Chromosome

— Strand of DNA

Genes
(chemical instructions)

DNA splits and copies itself before a cell divides

Each new cell receives its own copy of the DNA

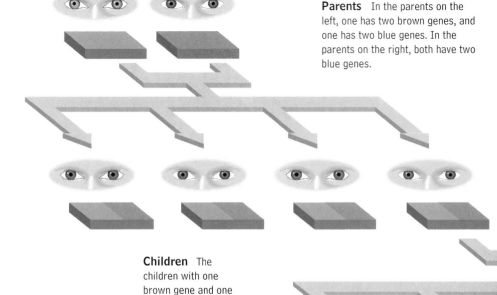

Parents In the parents on the left, one has two brown genes, and one has two blue genes. In the parents on the right, both have two blue genes.

Children The children with one brown gene and one blue gene (above) have brown eyes because the brown gene masks the blue one. The children with two blue genes (above right) have blue eyes.

How do genes work?

Genes work by telling cells how to make proteins, the material from which all living matter is built. There are thousands of types of protein, and each has a specific function. For example, one gene instructs eye cells to make a protein that produces a pigment called melanin. If you have this gene, specks of melanin build up in your eyes, making them brown.

Following instructions A single gene produces melanin molecules, making eyes look brown.

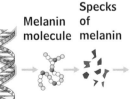

DNA carrying eye-colour gene

Melanin molecule

Specks of melanin

Melanin gives brown eyes their colour

PASSING ON GENES

Everyone has two copies of the eye-colour gene – one from each parent. The 'brown' gene always produces brown eyes, even if it is partnered by a 'blue' gene. The 'blue' gene produces blue eyes only if it is partnered by another 'blue' gene – otherwise it is 'masked'. This means that although the 'blue' gene is present, it is not operative. A masked gene can be handed on to the next generation.

Human Genome Project

The human body is built and controlled by about 100 000 different genes. In the late 1980s, scientists all over the world began the task of identifying every single human gene and finding out what each one does. This mammoth task, called the Human Genome Project, is like interpreting a giant encyclopedia written entirely in code. By the time the project is finished, early in the 21st century, people suffering from inherited diseases will stand a better chance of being cured.

These test tubes contain human cells that are being studied as part of the project.

Grandchildren Two of the grandchildren have two blue genes, so have blue eyes (far left). The other two have brown eyes (left) because they have one brown gene and one blue gene.

Great-grandchildren One of the four great-grandchildren has two blue genes, and blue eyes, even though both parents had brown eyes (right).

Boy or girl?

Right at the beginning of your life – long before your body started to take shape – the genes you were given controlled whether you would be a boy or a girl. The genes responsible for this are found on two special chromosomes, called X and Y. Unfertilised egg cells always contain one X chromosome. Sperm cells contain either an X or a Y chromosome. When an egg has been fertilised by a sperm, it has either two X chromosomes, or an X and a Y. X eggs always develop into girls, while XY eggs produce boys.

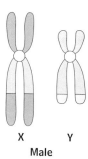

X   X
Female

X   Y
Male

Sex chromosomes An egg cell develops into a boy only if it receives a Y gene. If it has two X genes, it develops into a girl.

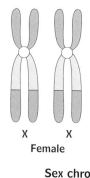

Growing up

Bones and skeletons p.106 · Hormones p.128 · Food and nutrition p.138

Compared with other animals – even ones as big as elephants and whales – humans take a long time to grow up. An elephant is fully grown by the time it is 15, but we keep growing until we are at least 18. Throughout childhood and our teenage years, our bodies get bigger, and they also change shape. This long period of development gets us ready for adult life, and also gives us time to learn about the world around us.

Why can't we live forever?

After the age of about 40, people's bodies start to show signs of age. Their hair slowly loses its colour, and in men it often starts to fall out. The skin develops lines and wrinkles, muscles begin to shrink and joints become less flexible. Scientists are beginning to understand the causes of ageing, but at the moment there is little that can be done to slow it down.

This woman is over 90 years old.

THAT'S AMAZING!

GRAND OLD AGE

The oldest man mentioned in the Bible was called Methuselah. He was said to have died at the age of 969. The oldest person in modern history was a French woman called Jeanne Calment, who died in 1997 at the age of 122. When she was 100, she was riding a bike.

What is 'puberty'?

Puberty is the period in life when the body's reproductive system gets ready to work. During puberty, girls and boys develop in different ways. Girls develop body hair, and their breasts grow larger. Boys start to grow hair on their bodies and faces, and their voices break.

All change   Puberty starts around the age of 12 or 13. Most changes happen during the early teens.

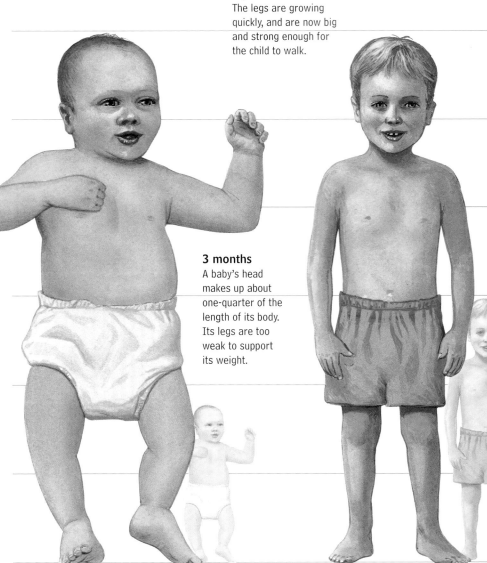

2 years
The legs are growing quickly, and are now big and strong enough for the child to walk.

3 months
A baby's head makes up about one-quarter of the length of its body. Its legs are too weak to support its weight.

Do boys grow faster than girls?

No, but they grow for longer. Girls usually start a burst of growth at about the age of 10, and they reach their adult height by about 16. Boys begin their burst of growth at about 12, but many do not reach their adult height until they are 19 or 20. At its fastest, growth in boys and girls can reach more than 8 cm (3 in) a year.

STAGES OF GROWTH

As you grow up, people will be quick to notice that you are getting taller, but they may not see that you are also changing shape. In the illustrations below, a child has been drawn the same size as a 20-year-old, making these changes easy to follow. For example, a baby's head is large in proportion to its body. The head does not grow as fast as the rest of the body, so it seems smaller in proportion to height as a person grows up.

Puzzling it out A very young child develops her learning skills through games and puzzles.

Why do we have to go to school?

Animals are guided in much of what they do by instinct (knowledge they are born with), although many also need to learn particular skills, such as how to hunt for prey, from their parents. Humans have instincts too, but we also need a great deal of knowledge and understanding about the world we live in. Through learning and practice, we gradually acquire the knowledge and skills that we will need throughout our adult and working lives, and which will also benefit the community we live in.

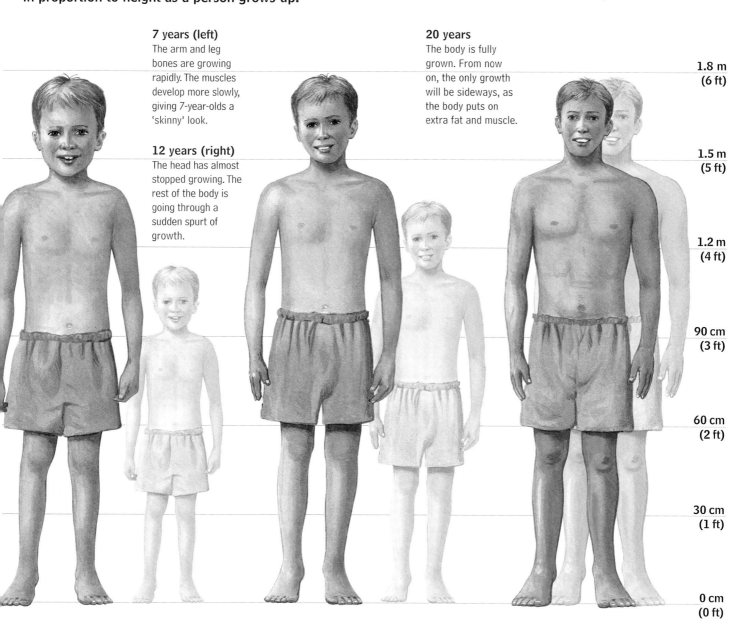

7 years (left)
The arm and leg bones are growing rapidly. The muscles develop more slowly, giving 7-year-olds a 'skinny' look.

12 years (right)
The head has almost stopped growing. The rest of the body is going through a sudden spurt of growth.

20 years
The body is fully grown. From now on, the only growth will be sideways, as the body puts on extra fat and muscle.

1.8 m (6 ft)

1.5 m (5 ft)

1.2 m (4 ft)

90 cm (3 ft)

60 cm (2 ft)

30 cm (1 ft)

0 cm (0 ft)

Hormones p.128 · Medical diagnosis p.140 · Medical treatment p.142 · Fact File p.310, 322

The average person has more than 500 000 billion bacteria living on the surface of their body – a far greater number than they have cells. Most bacteria do no harm. But if bacteria and other microbes get inside the body, they can trigger disease. To stop this happening, the body is armed with a self-defence system, called the immune system, which recognises and destroys dangerous invaders.

Where is the immune system?

Most immune-system cells are made in bone marrow. Some of them circulate in the blood, but others collect in the spleen, and in bean-shaped swellings called lymph nodes. Lymph nodes form part of the lymphatic system – a network of tubes that drain surplus fluid from body tissues and empty it into the blood. As fluid travels through the lymphatic system, the lymph nodes filter out any foreign cells.

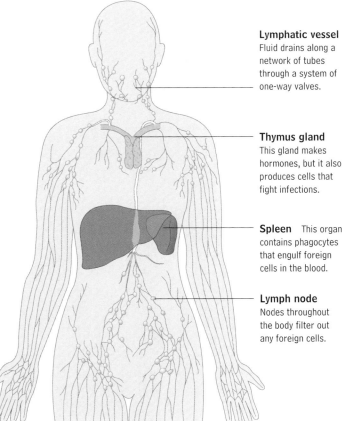

Lymphatic vessel
Fluid drains along a network of tubes through a system of one-way valves.

Thymus gland
This gland makes hormones, but it also produces cells that fight infections.

Spleen This organ contains phagocytes that engulf foreign cells in the blood.

Lymph node
Nodes throughout the body filter out any foreign cells.

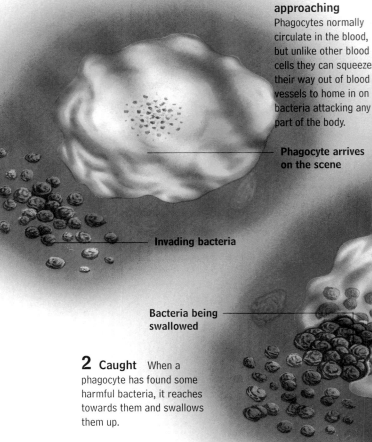

1 Enemy approaching
Phagocytes normally circulate in the blood, but unlike other blood cells they can squeeze their way out of blood vessels to home in on bacteria attacking any part of the body.

Phagocyte arrives on the scene

Invading bacteria

Bacteria being swallowed

2 Caught When a phagocyte has found some harmful bacteria, it reaches towards them and swallows them up.

ATTACKING INVADERS

If bacteria get inside your body – for example through a cut – the immune system has two ways of dealing with them. The first involves white blood cells called phagocytes, which attack all kinds of invaders. The second way consists of chemicals called antibodies that circulate in the blood. Each type of antibody locks onto a particular type of invader, putting it out of action.

Why do we catch some diseases only once?

The first time an invading germ appears, the immune system may take several days to produce antibodies, which build up slowly through cell division. This gives the disease time to take hold. Once your immune system fights off a disease, memory cells learn to recognise the germs that caused it. If the same germs reappear, even years later, the memory cells quickly produce antibodies to kill them.

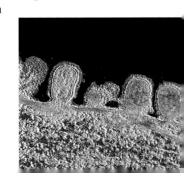

Viruses Flu viruses (orange) in an infected cell. You can catch flu more than once because the virus keeps changing.

Allergies

If you are allergic to something, it means that your immune system attacks that substance, even though the substance is harmless. Allergies are triggered by many things, but the most common ones involve plant pollens, medical drugs and substances in food. Most allergies produce a mild reaction, although they can still make people feel unwell. A few can make people dangerously ill. People who are severely allergic – for example, to nuts – have to be careful about what they eat or touch to avoid triggering their allergy by accident.

Microscopic pollen grains cause hay fever – an allergy that affects about 1 person in 10.

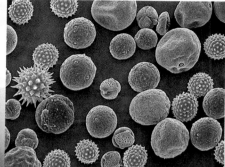

Why do you get a temperature when you are ill?

A high temperature of 38.5°C (101°F) and above is a sign that your body is fighting back. It happens because immune-system cells reset your brain's 'thermostat', making your body heat up. At this higher temperature, the immune system can make antibodies more quickly, while bacteria find it harder to reproduce. Once the infection is under control, your temperature begins to fall. During most diseases, the rise in temperature is quite small.

The flu On the first day, your temperature rises as the immune system fights the flu viruses. Fever sets in and you begin to sweat. On the second day, your temperature returns to normal – 37°C (98.6°F).

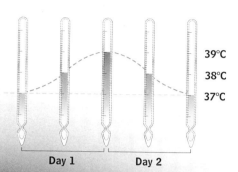

39°C
38°C
37°C

Day 1   Day 2

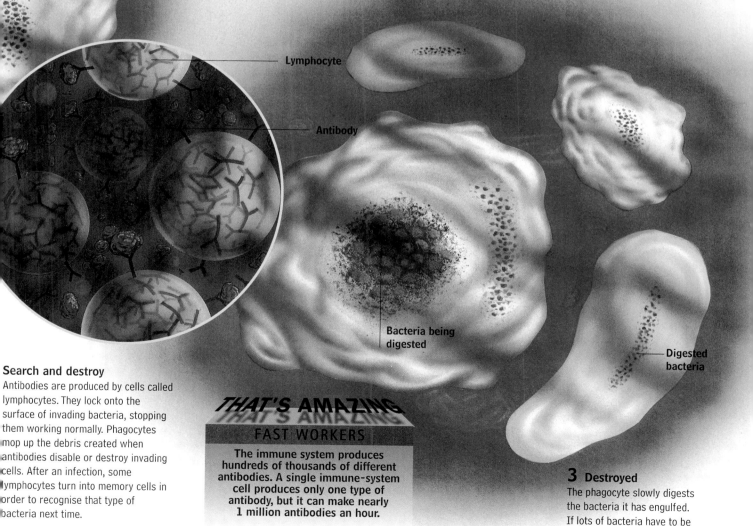

Lymphocyte

Antibody

Bacteria being digested

Digested bacteria

Search and destroy

Antibodies are produced by cells called lymphocytes. They lock onto the surface of invading bacteria, stopping them working normally. Phagocytes mop up the debris created when antibodies disable or destroy invading cells. After an infection, some lymphocytes turn into memory cells in order to recognise that type of bacteria next time.

THAT'S AMAZING

FAST WORKERS

The immune system produces hundreds of thousands of different antibodies. A single immune-system cell produces only one type of antibody, but it can make nearly 1 million antibodies an hour.

3 Destroyed

The phagocyte slowly digests the bacteria it has engulfed. If lots of bacteria have to be destroyed, millions of phagocytes arrive to help.

Food technology p.194 · Cooking, food and drink p.230 · Fact File p.308

Food is the fuel that makes your body work. Unlike the fuel that drives machines, it contains many different substances. Some give us energy; others provide the raw materials used for growth, and for replacing cells that have become worn out. The combination of food that you eat is called your diet. If your diet is well balanced, it means that you get all the substances you need in the right amounts.

What's in food?

The useful substances in food are called nutrients. We need three nutrients in large amounts: carbohydrates, which provide us with energy; fats, which provide energy; and proteins, which the body uses for growth and for replacing and repairing cells. We need other nutrients, called vitamins and minerals, in much smaller amounts. Minerals help form bones and teeth and regulate body processes. Food also contains water and dietary fibre. Fibre is made up of the tough or hard parts of fruit, seeds and vegetables, such as skins and husks, and it helps the digestive system to work.

Protein	23%
Carbohydrate	Trace
Fat	7%
Fibre	None
Water	70%

Fish   Fish contains lots of protein, very little carbohydrate, and a moderate amount of fat. It is also a good source of minerals.

Protein	10%
Carbohydrate	48%
Fat	3%
Fibre	9%
Water	30%

Bread   Bread is high in carbohydrate. Wholegrain bread also has lots of dietary fibre from the ground-up husks of grain.

Protein	Trace
Carbohydrate	9%
Fat	Trace
Fibre	2%
Water	89%

Fruit   Oranges contain lots of Vitamin C. They contain almost no protein or fat, but have some energy-rich carbohydrates.

A WEEK'S FOOD

In the pictures below, you can see how much food four different people need to eat every week. The food shown makes up a balanced diet because it contains the right mixture of different nutrients. The amount of food a person needs depends partly on their age, and partly on how active they are. The energy in food is usually measured in units called kilocalories.
One kilocalorie is enough energy to keep an ordinary lightbulb alight for about a minute.

10-year-old boy   A 10-year-old needs about 1300 kilocalories of energy a day. At this age, the body is growing quickly, so lots of protein is essential.

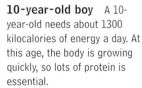

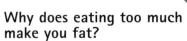

Why does eating too much make you fat?

Your digestive system absorbs all the food that you eat. If you eat more than you need, your body stores the surplus as fat – like someone putting spare money in the bank. It is useful to have some body fat, as it provides an extra source of energy. Too much body fat can cause health problems, such as heart disease. Today, more people are overweight than ever before. This is mainly because food is easily available, and because fewer people take regular exercise than in the past.

THAT'S AMAZING

LARGE APPETITE

During your lifetime, you will probably eat about 40 tonnes of food – equal to the weight of seven elephants. The energy this contains could drive a car about 125 000 km (80 000 miles).

What do vitamins do?

Vitamins are substances that help the body's chemistry to work. Our bodies cannot make vitamins, so we have to get them from our food. There are 13 vitamins altogether. Two of the most important are Vitamin C, which keeps cells healthy, and Vitamin D, which helps form teeth and bones.

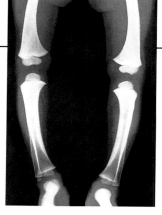

Vitamin deficiency   Curved leg bones are one side-effect of not having enough Vitamin D.

That looks good!

Good food smells nice, but it has to look appetising, too. You can prove this to yourself by dyeing your food an unusual colour. No natural food is blue, so ask your parents to add some blue food dye to rice or vegetables when they make a meal. Does the strange colour affect the way you enjoy your food?

Strange-coloured food can be offputting.

16-year-old girl
Teenagers need up to 3000 kilocalories of energy a day; sometimes more if they play lots of sports.

19-year-old woman   By the late teens, the body has almost stopped growing, and needs less energy. This 19-year-old needs about 1600 kilocalories a day.

25-year-old man
A person doing heavy outdoor work uses up lots of energy, and needs about 4200 kilocalories of energy a day.

Medical diagnosis

Blood and circulation p.110 · Immune system p.136 · Medical treatment p.142 · Fact File p.310, 321, 322

You don't have to be a doctor to know if you have caught a cold. But not all health problems are so easy to identify because diseases and accidents can affect the body in different ways. In these cases, a doctor has to examine you and carry out tests. Some of these tests are simple; others involve machines that see inside the body. Then the doctor can make a diagnosis, that is, identify what is wrong, and decide on the best treatment.

What does a doctor hear through a stethoscope?

Doctors use stethoscopes to listen to the sounds made by the heart, blood rushing through arteries, and air moving in and out of the lungs. Unusual sounds can help the doctor pinpoint medical problems. For example, when the heart beats, it makes two particular sounds a split-second apart. These sounds are produced by valves that close to stop blood in the heart flowing the wrong way. If a person's heart is making other sounds, it may indicate that their heart valves are not working properly. If someone's lungs make wheezing sounds when they breathe, this often shows that they have a lung infection.

Heart sounds This chart illustrates the sound of a single heartbeat. The first sound is made after the heart has filled with blood. The second is made when it empties.

Seeing inside the body

Doctors can see what is happening inside the body by using X-rays, magnetic fields, or even sound waves. X-rays travel straight through the soft parts of the body, but are blocked by hard substances such as bone. This helps doctors to pinpoint breaks. A different type of X-ray picture is made by a CT (computerised tomography) scanner. This machine takes X-ray pictures from many directions. The pictures are then added together by a computer to produce a 3D image. Another type of scanning machine, called an MRI (Magnetic Resonance Imaging) scanner, shows all types of tissue, not just bones. A different type of picture again is produced by bombarding the body with high-pitched sound waves, which bounce back off all parts of the body to produce a picture of what is inside. As ultrasound is very safe, it is often used to 'see' babies inside their mother's womb.

This image, made by an MRI scanner, gives a detailed picture of bones and soft tissue.

Spotting the culprit Bacteria can be identified by the shape and colour of their colonies, which can be seen under a microscope.

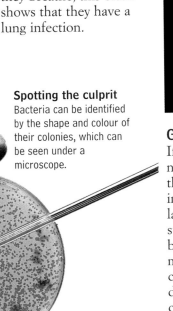

Growing germs

If a doctor thinks you might have an infection, he or she needs to identify the cause of the problem. A doctor does this by taking a sample – often of your blood, or from the inside of your mouth or throat. The sample is sent away to a laboratory, where it is wiped across a dish containing sterilised jelly. The dish is kept in a warm place, and any bacteria that are present in the sample start to grow. Bacteria multiply quickly, and within a few days they form groups called colonies, and then they can be identified. Once the doctor knows what type of bacteria are present, he or she can select the best form of treatment.

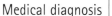

THAT'S AMAZING

REVEALING PICTURES

One of the first diagnostic X-rays to be taken, in 1896, was of a child who had swallowed a tiny model bicycle. The X-ray showed that the bicycle had stuck in the child's throat.

A HIDDEN INJURY

After an accident this boy seems unhurt, but a doctor examines his eyes and notices that one of his pupils does not react to bright light. The doctor recognises this as a warning sign of a head injury, and the boy is rushed to hospital. A CT scan confirms the doctor's suspicions – blood has built up under the boy's skull. An operation is carried out to drain the blood, and he quickly recovers. Without prompt diagnosis at the roadside and in hospital, he would probably not have survived.

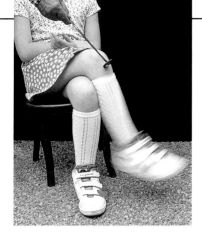

Why do doctors sometimes tap your knees?

This test checks your reflexes. A tap against your knee stretches a tendon there, and the tendon pulls on a muscle in your thigh. If your reflexes are working, the thigh muscle reacts by contracting, which makes your leg give a kick. If your leg does not kick, there may be something wrong with your nervous system.

Knee jerk   A tap on the knee should make your leg kick.

● Immune system p.136 · Medical diagnosis p.140 · Surgery p.144 · Fact File p.310, 320, 322, 323

Once a doctor has made a diagnosis of an illness or injury, he or she can decide what kind of treatment is needed to deal with the problem. Many illnesses can be dealt with by a course of drugs, while cuts and broken bones are treated by helping the body to repair itself. If an illness or injury is too severe to be cured in this way, you may need to have an operation.

THAT'S AMAZING

MOULDY MEDICINE

Antibiotics are made by moulds and other minute organisms. Many are found in soil, but one of the most useful, called cephalosporin, was first discovered in fungi that were growing in water mixed with sewage.

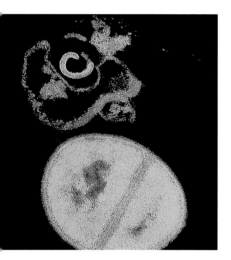

Destroyed A single bacterium cell begins to divide. Above it are the remains of a second bacterium cell, which has burst due to the action of antibiotics.

What are antibiotics?

An antibiotic is a drug that kills bacteria without killing the body's cells as well. The first antibiotic to be used, called penicillin, was discovered in 1928. Most antibiotics work by stopping bacteria building up their cell walls, so that the bacteria collapse and eventually die. Some antibiotics are effective against a small range of bacteria. Others, including penicillin, kill many different kinds. Antibiotics cannot kill viruses, which is why they cannot cure a cold or flu.

Complementary medicine

Most kinds of medical treatment deal with illnesses by targeting specific parts of the body. Complementary medicine is different, because it considers the overall health of the patient and assists the body's natural processes. There are many kinds of complementary treatment. Some techniques – such as acupuncture, which uses needles to relieve pain and assist healing – have been used in the Far East for hundreds of years. Others, such as osteopathy and chiropractic, which both involve making sure that bones and joints are in the correct position, are quite new.

Acupuncture treatment.

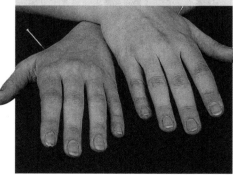

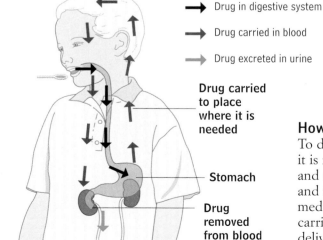

→ Drug in digestive system

→ Drug carried in blood

→ Drug excreted in urine

Drug carried to place where it is needed

Stomach

Drug removed from blood by kidneys

Bladder

How do drugs reach the right target?

To do its job, a drug has to reach the parts of the body where it is needed. Many drugs that reduce pain, called painkillers, and antibiotics can travel through the lining of the stomach and into the blood, so they can be taken in the form of pills or medicine. Once the drugs are in the bloodstream, they are carried to the place where they are needed. This method of delivering drugs is easy, but it works quite slowly. If a drug is injected directly into the area where it is needed, it works much more quickly. Injections are also more precise. For example, a dentist can use them to deaden the pain around a particular tooth, leaving the rest of the patient wide awake.

Greenstick fracture
This kind of fracture is common in children. It happens when one of the forearm bones splinters without actually breaking in two.

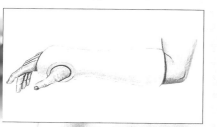

Repaired arm
Cells around the fracture produce new bone. Plaster protects the arm until the damage is repaired.

How does immunisation work?

Immunisation (also known as vaccination) is a way of preventing the spread of infectious diseases. It works by triggering the immune system, so that it can stop particular infections taking hold. To do this, the body has to be given something that makes the immune system react, without actually allowing the disease to start. The most common way of doing this involves injecting bacteria or viruses that have been treated to make them harmless. Once the treated bacteria or viruses are in the blood, the immune system learns to recognise them, and it can then fight off the harmful forms as well. Thanks to immunisation, many diseases are much rarer than they were. One killer disease – smallpox – has been wiped out through a world-wide vaccination programme.

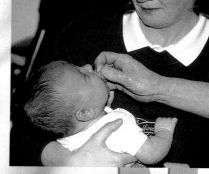

Early immunisation This baby is being immunised against polio. Polio vaccine works when it is swallowed.

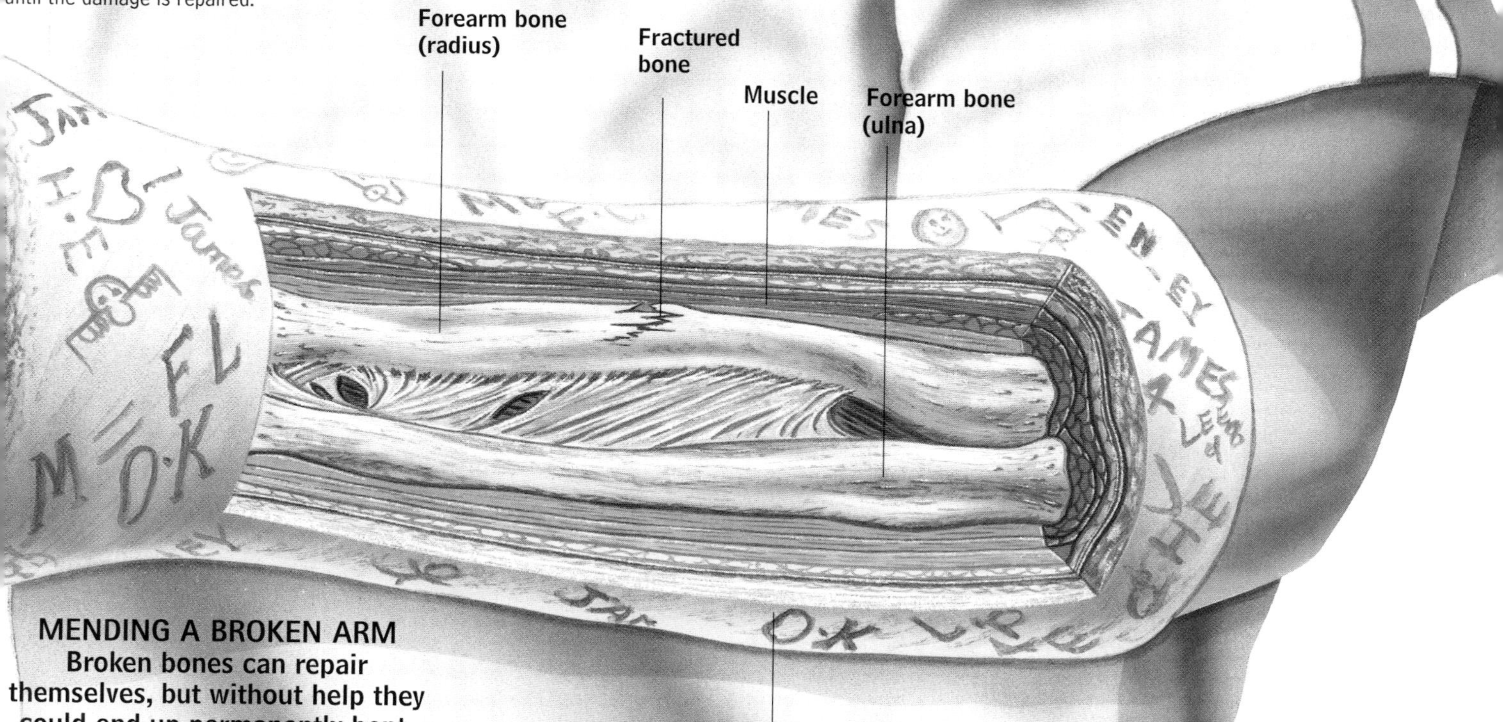

Forearm bone (radius)

Fractured bone

Muscle

Forearm bone (ulna)

Plaster keeps broken bone in position

MENDING A BROKEN ARM
Broken bones can repair themselves, but without help they could end up permanently bent. A plaster cast holds the broken ends in the right position while they grow back together.

● **Blood and circulation p.110 · Medical diagnosis p.140 · Fact File p.310, 321**

During an operation, a surgeon cuts open a person's body in order to remove or repair a damaged or diseased part of their insides. Thanks to modern equipment, such as lasers and surgical microscopes, surgeons can repair skin, bones and blood vessels, and even things such as nerve endings that are too small to be seen with the naked eye. If a part of the body, such as a hip joint, is not working correctly, surgeons can sometimes replace it with an artificial part.

Keyhole surgery

Modern instruments allow surgeons to operate on patients through holes not much bigger than a keyhole. One instrument, called an endoscope, is a thin tube fitted with an

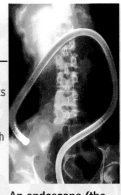

An endoscope (the pink tube) winds through a patient's intestines.

eyepiece, lenses and its own little light, and it allows the surgeon to see inside a patient's body. An endoscope can be fitted with tiny scissors and tweezers, which the surgeon can use to carry out operations.

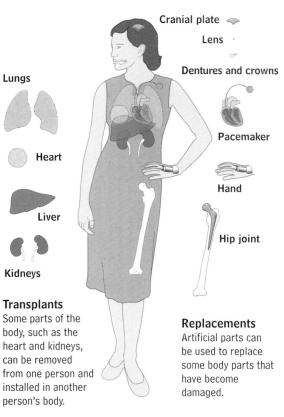

Cranial plate

Lens

Dentures and crowns

Lungs

Pacemaker

Heart

Hand

Liver

Hip joint

Kidneys

Transplants
Some parts of the body, such as the heart and kidneys, can be removed from one person and installed in another person's body.

Replacements
Artificial parts can be used to replace some body parts that have become damaged.

Which parts of the body can be replaced?

The list of artificial replacement body parts is growing. It includes hip joints, knee joints and heart valves, as well as teeth and the lenses in the eyes. Replacement parts have to work for years without needing any maintenance. An artificial heart valve, for example, has to open and close several million times without ever getting stuck.

Instrument trolley All the instruments needed for the operation are laid out ready for use.

Light source The light on the surgeon's headset is connected to this machine.

Can any organ be transplanted ?

A transplant operation involves connecting the blood vessels and nerves in the organ being transplanted to those in the patient's body. The more nerves and blood vessels there are, and the smaller they are, the harder they are to connect. Hearts are not the most difficult organs to transplant, because their arteries are large. Livers are more complicated because they have lots of blood vessels that can be difficult for a surgeon to reach.

How do surgeons stop people bleeding when they operate on them?

Surgeons prevent bleeding by fastening clamps to any cut arteries or veins. Before the operation is over, the cut ends are sewn together again so that blood can flow once more. Very small blood vessels are often cauterised – sealed with a burst of heat. If a patient does bleed during an operation, they can be given extra blood, called a blood transfusion, to make up for the blood they have lost.

Surgeon The surgeon wears special glasses focused for his own working distance, and has a light attached to his headset.

Theatre nurse The nurse knows which instrument the surgeon will need next and has it ready for him.

Anaesthetist. The anaesthetist gives the anaesthetic drug that keeps the patient asleep and free of pain, and checks the patient's breathing and heart rate.

THAT'S AMAZING

SPEEDY WORKER

Before the invention of anaesthetics, surgeons tried to work very fast. In the early 1800s, one French surgeon could cut off a person's leg in 15 seconds.

Perfusionist The perfusionist monitors the heart/lung machine, which oxygenates and pumps the patient's blood during a heart operation.

Anaesthetic trolley

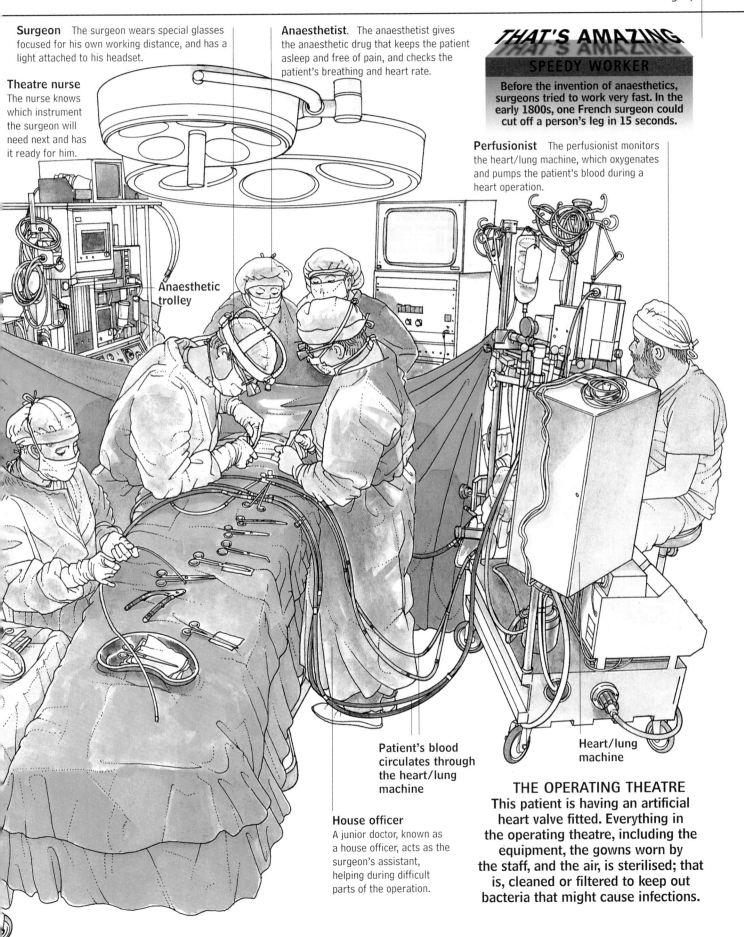

Patient's blood circulates through the heart/lung machine

Heart/lung machine

House officer A junior doctor, known as a house officer, acts as the surgeon's assistant, helping during difficult parts of the operation.

THE OPERATING THEATRE

This patient is having an artificial heart valve fitted. Everything in the operating theatre, including the equipment, the gowns worn by the staff, and the air, is sterilised; that is, cleaned or filtered to keep out bacteria that might cause infections.

Science and Technology

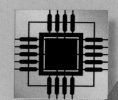

Inside the Earth p.24 · Force and motion p.150 · Energy and heat p.152 · Fact File p.312

Everything around us – including our own bodies – is made of specks of matter called atoms. There are many different kinds of atoms, but all of them are extremely small. They are so tiny that even something as small as a sugar cube contains about half a billion billion of them, packed closely together. If the atoms in just one sugar cube were shared out among the entire human population of the world, we would each have about 100 million of them.

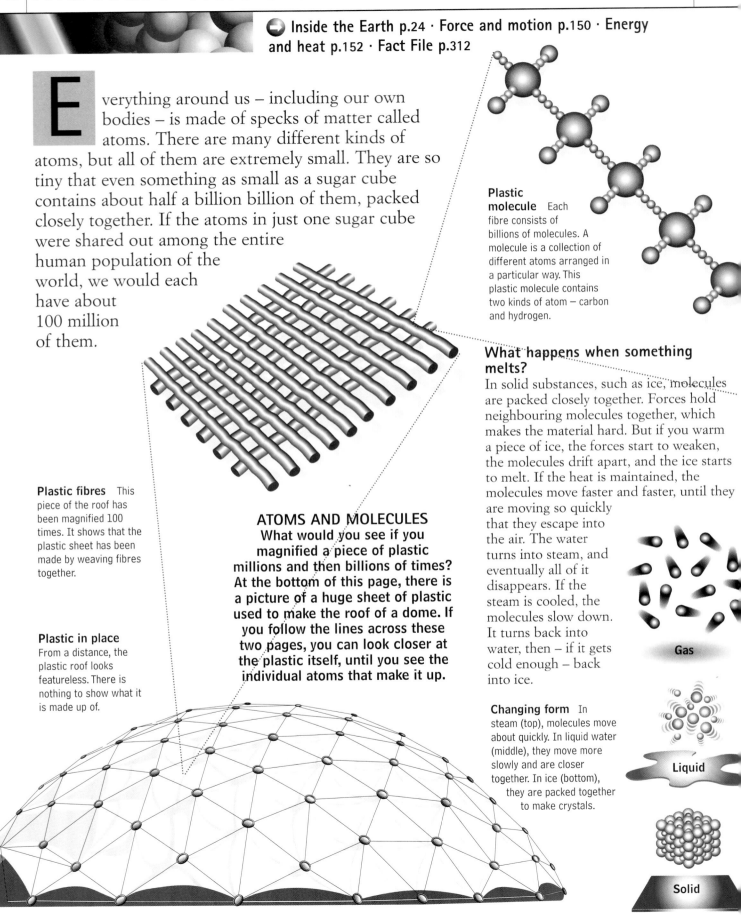

Plastic molecule Each fibre consists of billions of molecules. A molecule is a collection of different atoms arranged in a particular way. This plastic molecule contains two kinds of atom – carbon and hydrogen.

Plastic fibres This piece of the roof has been magnified 100 times. It shows that the plastic sheet has been made by weaving fibres together.

Plastic in place From a distance, the plastic roof looks featureless. There is nothing to show what it is made up of.

ATOMS AND MOLECULES

What would you see if you magnified a piece of plastic millions and then billions of times? At the bottom of this page, there is a picture of a huge sheet of plastic used to make the roof of a dome. If you follow the lines across these two pages, you can look closer at the plastic itself, until you see the individual atoms that make it up.

What happens when something melts?

In solid substances, such as ice, molecules are packed closely together. Forces hold neighbouring molecules together, which makes the material hard. But if you warm a piece of ice, the forces start to weaken, the molecules drift apart, and the ice starts to melt. If the heat is maintained, the molecules move faster and faster, until they are moving so quickly that they escape into the air. The water turns into steam, and eventually all of it disappears. If the steam is cooled, the molecules slow down. It turns back into water, then – if it gets cold enough – back into ice.

Changing form In steam (top), molecules move about quickly. In liquid water (middle), they move more slowly and are closer together. In ice (bottom), they are packed together to make crystals.

Gas

Liquid

Solid

Why are some things heavier than others?

It is easy to pick up a big block of polystyrene foam, but hard to pick up even a brick-sized lump of lead. The reason for this is that an object's weight depends partly on what kind of atoms it contains, and partly on how closely they are packed together. Polystyrene foam has light atoms, spaced well apart. Lead has very heavy atoms, tightly packed together. Compared to polystyrene, it is very dense: 1 m³ (35 cu ft) of polystyrene foam weighs about 5 kg (11 lb), while 1 m³ of lead weighs about 11 tonnes – over 2000 times as much.

Copper, a reddish metal, is one of the few elements that is sometimes found in a pure form, rather than being mixed with other elements in a compound.

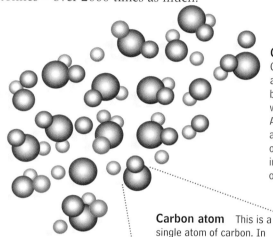

Getting together
Carbon atoms are good at making molecules, because they can link up with lots of other atoms. As well as plastics, they are found in thousands of other substances — including most of the ones in living things.

Carbon atom   This is a single atom of carbon. In the middle, it has a nucleus made of six protons and six neutrons. Six tiny particles called electrons spin around them.

Atoms and elements

Most substances contain a mixture of different atoms. Elements are different, because they contain one type of atom and nothing else. Most elements are metals; but some are gases, such as oxygen, and others are nonmetals, such as sulphur. Elements generally combine with other elements, making chemical compounds, such as water, sugar and salt. Altogether, 92 elements exist naturally on Earth, but scientists have made about 17 additional elements in laboratories.

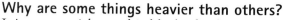

THAT'S AMAZING

MELTING METALS

Mercury is the only metal that is liquid at room temperature, but another metal – called gallium – also has a very low melting point. If you left a lump of gallium on a sunny windowsill, it would melt and run onto the floor.

What's inside an atom?

Scientists used to believe that atoms were the smallest things in the Universe. They thought that because atoms could not be split up into anything smaller. But things are not nearly as simple as this: atoms contain other particles that are much smaller than they are. Particles called protons and neutrons make up the centre, or nucleus, of each atom. Around them are electrons – particles that hurtle around the nucleus like planets orbiting the Sun. The smallest atoms, belonging to hydrogen, contain only one proton and one electron. The biggest, belonging to metals like uranium, contain over 200 protons and neutrons, and over 90 electrons.

Force and motion

➡ The birth of the planets p.16 ·
Muscles and movement p.108

Forces are at work all around us. They provide the push that gets things moving, but also include friction, the force that slows them down. They can make a jumbo jet hurtle down a runway and into the skies, or pull a snowflake towards the ground. Forces can also make things change direction, and they can stretch, squash and bend them out of shape. We cannot see forces themselves, but we can see and feel what they do.

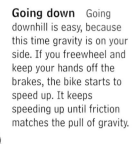

Going down Going downhill is easy, because this time gravity is on your side. If you freewheel and keep your hands off the brakes, the bike starts to speed up. It keeps speeding up until friction matches the pull of gravity.

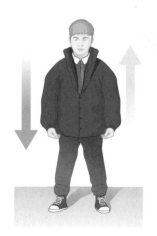

Going up When you go uphill, you have to counteract the downward force of gravity. The bike starts to slow down unless you put in extra work to match the downward pull.

Matching forces When you are standing still, you and the Earth pull at each other with equal and opposite forces.

How does gravity work?
We know what gravity feels like, but it is still a mysterious force. Everything in the Universe – even your own body – attracts other objects towards it. When you stand on the ground, the Earth attracts your body and your body attracts the Earth. Because the Earth is so huge, its gravitational pull keeps you on the ground.

PEDAL POWER
Riding a bicycle is a perfect way to find out about forces. When you are moving at a steady speed, the force produced by your legs exactly balances friction – the force that tries to slow you down. You can never get rid of friction, but you can reduce it by keeping the bike oiled and your head down so that you lessen the friction caused by the air you push out of the way.

Staying on course
Once something is on the move, it will keep moving in a straight line. This is why passengers are thrown forwards when a car brakes. It is also why water stays in a bucket if you whirl it around in a circle: while the bucket 'turns a corner', the water tries to continue straight on.

Strapped in Seat belts bring people to a safe halt if a car stops suddenly.

THAT'S AMAZING
HOW TO LOSE WEIGHT
Because the Earth is not exactly round, the force of gravity varies slightly from place to place. If you weighed 30 kg (66 lb) at the North Pole, you would find that you weighed only 29.85 kg (65.8 lb) at the Equator.

Sliding along

A bobsleigh team in training in Japan.

When an object slides past another, friction slows it down. You can test this with two sheets of sandpaper. If you try to slide their sanded sides over each other, you will find that friction makes it hard work. If you turn the sheets over, the smooth sides make the job easier. With slippery surfaces – such as ice or snow – there is so little friction that things slide along very fast. This helps skiers and bobsleighers to reach speeds of over 200 km/h (125 mph).

On the level On flat ground, gravity has no overall effect. To keep going at a steady speed, all you have to do is match the force of friction. Some of the friction is produced by the moving parts of the bike. The rest of it is produced by the air you push out of the way. If you go really fast, 'air resistance' gets very large.

Superhuman strength

The human body is good at some tasks, but not so good at others. However, with the help of pulleys, levers, ramps and gears, we can do things that seem impossible – like lifting a car off the ground. Devices like car jacks all work by reducing the force you need to do a job, while increasing the amount of movement you have to carry out.

On tow Pulling a truck needs more force than most people can produce.

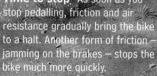

Time to stop As soon as you stop pedalling, friction and air resistance gradually bring the bike to a halt. Another form of friction – jamming on the brakes – stops the bike much more quickly.

➤ Matter: what the world is made of p.148 · Light: visible energy p.15
Sound p.156 · Electricity and magnetism p.158 · Fact File p.312

Energy makes things happen. Without it, the entire Universe would be cold and dark, and nothing would be able to move. There are many kinds of energy, including heat, light, sound and electricity. Each time we use energy, it changes from one form into others. For example, when you turn on a light, electrical energy is changed into light and heat; and when you flick the pages of this book, chemical energy from the food you eat is changed into movement.

DEMOLITION JOB
One way to demolish a tower block is to knock it down bit by bit. A much speedier way is to use explosives to release a burst of energy, bringing the building crashing to the ground. On these two pages, you can see how potential energy turns into other kinds of energy, and the dramatic results of the changes.

What happens when things get hot?
Heat is one of the most important forms of energy. When something warms up, the atoms inside it start to move more quickly, and they also spread farther apart. The hotter something is, the faster its atoms move. When atoms become really hot, they start to give out light. First they glow dull red, but if they get even hotter they turn bright red, yellow, white, and finally blue. Heat is a bit like water, because it always flows 'downhill'. That is, it moves from warm things to cool things, but never the other way round. Things feel hot when some of their heat energy travels into your skin, and they feel cold when heat energy flows from you into them.

Energy from the Earth
Plants need sunshine to grow, and animals need plants for food. If the Sun went out tomorrow, plants and animals would soon die, but some bacteria would still survive because they get their energy from chemicals inside the Earth. They live in hot springs and deep-sea vents (holes in the Earth's crust), where water brings the chemicals to the surface.

Feeding off the mineral-rich hot springs in Yellowstone National Park, USA, bacteria and algae create beautiful colour effects.

Counting down . . .
Potential energy is stored energy. Before the bang, there is potential energy in the explosives, and in the tower block, because it contains heavy materials perched high above the ground.

Temperature	
400 000 000°C	Hottest temperature ever achieved in a laboratory
14 000 000°C	Centre of the Sun
30 000°C	Inside a lightning bolt
5500°C	Surface temperature of Sun
5000°C	Hottest flame
1535°C	Iron melts
184°C	Paper catches fire
100°C	Water boils
37°C	Body temperature
0°C	Water freezes
−89°C	Lowest temperature ever recorded on Earth
−200°C	Air becomes liquid
−273.16°C	Absolute zero

How hot or cold can things become?
There is no limit to how hot things can become, but if something becomes extremely cold, its atoms stop moving. It cannot get any colder. Scientists have come close to reaching this temperature, called absolute zero, at −273.16°C (−459.69°F). Near absolute zero, matter starts to behave in strange ways. Some gases turn into metals, and some metals become 'superconductors'. This means that electricity can flow through them forever, without needing any energy from outside.

Going, going . . . When the explosion takes place, the explosives' potential energy is changed into heat, movement and sound. The tower block's potential energy also changes into movement and sound, as thousands of tons of concrete and steel come crashing down.

Gone! When the dust settles after the explosion, the potential energy in the explosives and the tower block has been changed. Most of it has been converted into different kinds of energy, which have escaped into the air.

A waste of energy As a workman digs a hole with a pneumatic drill, energy escapes in the form of noise and heat; this energy cannot be used.

What happens to energy after it is used?

No matter how many times energy is changed, it can never be destroyed. But whenever it changes, some of it always escapes. For example, a car engine turns much of the potential energy in petrol into movement. But it also turns some of it into noise and heat, and this escapes as the car moves along. No matter how well machines are designed, they always waste some of the energy that they release.

THAT'S AMAZING

ENERGY IN A RAINDROP

The amount of energy in a falling raindrop is about 175 thousand billion times less than the amount of energy of a cruising jumbo jet. But added together at any one time, the energy in all the raindrops falling on Earth is much greater than the energy of all the planes in the air.

🌐 Our star, the Sun p.14 · Sound and vision p.118 ·
Energy and heat p.152 · Radio communications p.164 · Fact File p.264

Light is the only kind of energy that we can see. It moves about a million times faster than sound, and it can travel through empty space. Some things – like the Sun – make light, but most of the things we see do not. Instead, they reflect some of the light that falls on them. Light normally travels in straight lines, but it can be made to change course, and it can be split up into different colours.

THAT'S AMAZING

LIGHT YOU CANNOT SEE

If a beam of light shone past your nose in completely empty outer space, you would not be able to see it. The reason for this is that you can see light only when it shines into your eyes. On Earth, you can see beams from the side because dust and air scatter some of the light your way.

Why can't you see around corners?

You can hear around corners because sound spreads in all directions, but you cannot see around them because light nearly always travels in straight lines. One way of getting around this is to use a mirror. This reflects the light around the corner, so you can see what – or who – is hiding behind it.

Mirror vision   A periscope uses two mirrors to make light bend around corners.

What is light made of?

Light is pure energy. You cannot touch it or pick it up, but whenever it shines into your eyes, you can see that it is there. Light energy travels in pulses called waves, and the distance between the waves decides its colour. In blue light, for example, the waves are about 0.0005 mm (0.00002 in) apart – roughly 200 times narrower than a human hair. Light belongs to a whole family of waves that includes X-rays, microwaves and radio waves.

Night sight   These soldiers were photographed, using a device that amplifies (enlarges) waves of light.

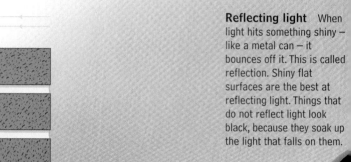

Reflecting light   When light hits something shiny – like a metal can – it bounces off it. This is called reflection. Shiny flat surfaces are the best at reflecting light. Things that do not reflect light look black, because they soak up the light that falls on them.

Making shadows   Transparent objects let light shine through them. Opaque ones – like a book – block the light and cast a shadow. Because light travels in straight lines, the shadow is the same shape as the book.

Making colours   A beam of sunlight contains all the colours of the rainbow. When it shines onto something with lots of narrow lines – like a CD – the different colours are separated, so that they can be seen. This is called diffraction. Some birds and butterflies get their colours in this way.

HOME LIGHT SHOW

Scientists investigate light with complicated pieces of equipment, but you can make a start with the everyday objects shown here. If you put them on a tabletop on a sunny day, you will be able to see how light can be reflected and bent, how it can be broken up into different colours and how it casts shadows.

Bending light   When light travels from one substance to another – for example, from air into glass, or from glass into water – it changes direction. This is called refraction. It explains why a drinking straw in a glass looks bent.

What makes a rainbow?

Rainbows appear when the Sun is shining and there is rain in the air. The falling drops split the Sun's light into seven different colours, and reflect it towards your eyes. The rainbow you see is always a 'private' one: even if someone is standing close to you, they see a rainbow made by a different set of raindrops. No matter how hard you try, you can never see a rainbow from the side or from behind, and you can never get to the rainbow's end. If you move, the rainbow moves, too.

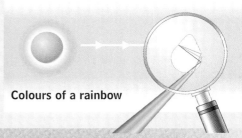

Colours of a rainbow

Starlight   Light from stars can take millions of years to reach us.

How fast does light travel?

Nothing moves faster than light – 299 792 km (186 287 miles) a second. It travels from the Sun to the Earth in around eight minutes, and it can cross the average room in about one hundred-millionth of a second. When light shines through transparent matter such as glass, it slows down by up to a third, but even then, it is still faster than anything else.

Focusing light   Lenses are designed to bend light in a particular way. The lenses in glasses help to bend light so that it makes an image on the back of the eye. Instead of being fuzzy, the image is sharp or 'focused'.

Sound: making waves

Animal senses p.80 · Sound and vision p.118 · Light: visible energy p.154 · The magic of music p.246

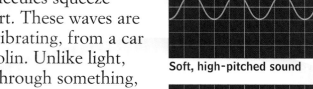

Sound is caused by waves of pressure that spread out through the air, making the air molecules squeeze together and then push apart. These waves are started by anything that is vibrating, from a car engine to the strings of a violin. Unlike light, sound always has to travel through something, so if you were floating in empty space, you would hear nothing but total silence.

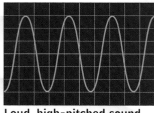

Soft, high-pitched sound

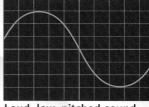

Soft, low-pitched sound

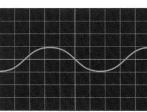

Loud, high-pitched sound

Loud, low-pitched sound

What's in a wave? Closely spaced waves (left) produce a high-pitched sound; widely spaced waves a deeper one (right). The sound is soft if the waves are shallow (top row), and loud if they are deep (bottom row).

How loud do sounds get?

Scientists normally measure the loudness of a sound by using units called decibels (dB). The softest sound that the human ear can hear has a decibel rating of about 4, while the loudest ones that it can cope with have a rating of over 150. The decibel scale works logarithmically. This means that if two sounds differ by 10 decibels, one of them is 10 times as loud as the other.

Rocket liftoff
150-190 dB

Jet takeoff
120-140 dB

Motorbike
70-90 dB

Orchestra
50-70 dB

Whispering
20-30 dB

Rustling leaves
10 dB

What is the difference between a note and a noise?

People often disagree about what makes good music, but it is easy to tell a note from a noise. A noise consists of a complicated jumble of different sound waves, while a musical note has just a few waves, all regularly spaced apart. In a pure note, the waves are exactly the same distance from each other.

Sound in the air Sound travels through the air at about 330 m (1082 ft) a second. It moves slightly faster on a warm day than on a cold one.

Underwater sound Sound travels nearly four times faster in water than it does in air. This means that a fish will hear the boat before a person standing nearby it on land.

THAT'S AMAZING

THAT'S AMAZING

HEARING FAINT SOUNDS

You may not be able to hear a pin drop, but your ears can pick up some amazingly faint sounds. The faintest sound that most people can hear is about 10 billion times quieter than the sound of a live pop concert.

SOUND ON THE MOVE

On these two pages you can see sound waves on the move. When sound comes from aboard a slow-moving boat, the sound waves spread out evenly through the air. They also travel through the water, where they move even more quickly than in air. When the sound comes from a plane, the pattern of sound waves is quite different. This is because the plane moves much more quickly, 'catching up' the sound waves that it makes.

Chasing sound   Most passenger jets move at about two-thirds of the speed of sound. At this speed, a plane keeps catching up the sound waves in front of it, and races away from the ones it leaves behind. These trailing waves make a low-pitched rumble as the plane flies away.

Fading out   As the sound waves travel outwards, their energy is slowly soaked up by the air. Eventually, they become too weak to be heard. This is why it is hard to make yourself heard a long way off – even if you shout.

How does an echo work?

Sound waves can bounce off solid objects, just as light waves can bounce off mirrors. But because sound travels much more slowly than light, it can take several seconds to reach our ears. When it arrives, we hear it as an echo. Bats and dolphins use high-pitched echoes to find their food. Echoes are also used in sonar – a way of detecting submarines and mapping the seabed.

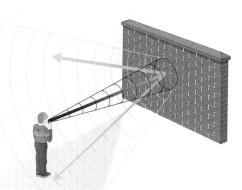

Calling back   If you shout at a wall, the sound will bounce back as an echo. To produce a good echo, the wall needs to be big and at least 25 m (80 ft) away.

Overtaking sound

If a plane flies faster than the speed of sound, air begins to pile up in front of it. When this air slips out of the way, it suddenly expands, making a loud noise called a sonic boom. At one time, scientists thought it would be dangerous for planes to fly 'supersonically', but now planes like Concorde break the sound barrier every day. They usually do it over the sea, so the deafening sonic boom is not heard on land.

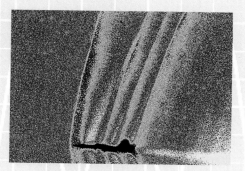

Shock waves around a supersonic jet appear as red and green lines.

Electricity and magnetism

● Matter p.148 · Generating energy
p.196 · Fact File p.312

I f you ever hear your clothes crackle when you take them off, you will have made your own electricity. Electricity is a form of energy, carried by tiny particles of matter. When these particles are on the move, their energy can do lots of useful things. Closely linked with electricity is magnetism. This is an invisible force that makes things attract or repel each other, and can be strong enough to lift cars off the ground.

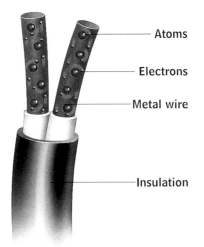

Atoms

Electrons

Metal wire

Insulation

How does electricity move through a wire?

Electric currents are carried by particles called electrons, which are part of atoms. When a current flows through a wire, electrons are jolted from atom to atom, carrying energy with them. Unlike static electricity, electric currents can only move through conductors, such as electric wires, and they always travel in a circuit. Conductors are metals and similar substances which have electrons that are easily dislodged.

How do batteries store electricity?

Unlike heat, electricity cannot be stored until it is needed. Instead, it has to be made. Batteries make electricity by using chemical reactions. In a battery, the reaction creates a charge at its negative terminal, so that it is ready to produce a current. As soon as you switch on, the battery drives electrons around the circuit. It can keep the electrons moving until its supply of chemicals is used up, and it goes flat.

THAT'S AMAZING

HARMLESS SHOCKS!

Static electricity builds up in houses, cars and clothes, and can sometimes give you a shock. These shocks can measure up to 50 000 volts, but they involve few electrons and are not nearly as dangerous as ones from a household electricity supply.

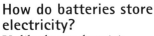

Current lights up bulb

Switch completes circuit

Terminal

Battery

Current flows through wire

Terminal

How the Van de Graaff generator works

Charging up The Van de Graaff generator makes static electricity by creating charged particles called ions. These are atoms that have extra electrons, which give them a negative charge. The negative ions are created on needles in the base of the generator, and are carried to the top by a rubber belt. They are collected by another set of needles, and transferred to a metal dome, which takes on their negative charge.

Lift off When the girl touches the dome, the negative ions spread into her body, to the tips of her hair. Each hair becomes negative, which means that it repels every other hair, and they all stand on end.

Charged dome

Charged particles travel up belt

Moving belt

How do magnets work?

In an ordinary piece of iron, the electrons spin in different directions. But in an iron magnet, they all spin in the same direction. This creates a magnetic field – an invisible region where magnetic forces are at work. Put some iron filings on a piece of thin card, and a magnet underneath. If you tap the card, the filings line up in the direction of the field.

Magnetic field
Magnets have two poles. The magnetic field spreads around the magnet from one pole to the other.

Electromagnets

Some magnets work all the time, but electromagnets produce magnetism only when they are supplied with an electric current. This is useful, because it means that they can be switched off when not needed. Electromagnets operate doorbells, microphones and loudspeakers, and they are inside telephones, computer disc drives and televisions. They are also used for lifting heavy metal objects – like wrecked cars.

An electromagnet at work

Telephone and fax

⊙ Sound recording p.162 · Radio communications p.164 ·
Satellites in space p.180 · Fact File p.322

Telephones are one of the most useful communication tools ever invented. They work by turning the sounds of the human voice into electrical signals, which can be sent along cables, and turned back into sound at the other end. Mobile phones do the same using radio waves, while faxes send a stream of electrical signals, to be decoded by another fax machine.

Why must you not use a mobile phone on an aeroplane or in a hospital?

Mobile phones are small radio transmitters. They create an electrical field when they are used, and this can disturb sensitive equipment nearby, such as an aeroplane's navigation and control systems. Hospital equipment – heart monitors and kidney dialysis machines, for example – can also be affected. Since they send and receive signals even in 'standby' mode, mobile phones should always be switched off completely in aircraft and hospitals.

How does a fax work?

A fax machine scans a page by dividing it into thousands of tiny squares and checking whether each square is black or white. It then sends a stream of yes/no signals that follow the pattern of black/white squares on the original, which the receiving fax then prints out. A fax does not recognise text, but sees it as a pattern of black marks.

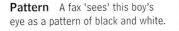

Pattern A fax 'sees' this boy's eye as a pattern of black and white.

International A telephone call can be sent overseas, either by satellite, or by an undersea cable.

International exchange

Trunk exchange

Connection The route followed by this girl's call is shown as a solid line; other phone lines are dotted.

Local exchange

MAKING A TELEPHONE CALL

When you dial the phone number of a friend in another town, your call goes first to your local telephone exchange. The exchange passes it on to the nearest trunk (long-distance) exchange, which sends it to the trunk exchange closest to your friend's town. This directs the call to a local exchange, which sends it straight to your friend's home. This all happens almost instantly: as your finger lifts off the last number dialled, your friend's phone is already ringing. International calls go straight from your nearest trunk exchange to an international exchange. This sends the call to its destination by undersea cable or by satellite.

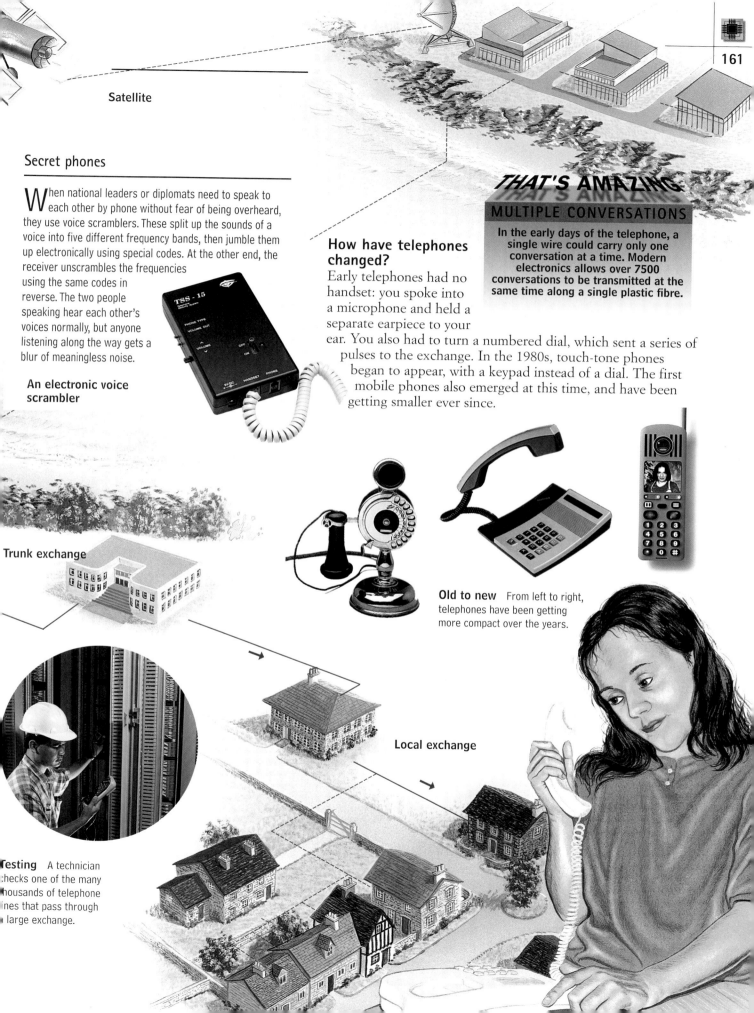

Satellite

Secret phones

When national leaders or diplomats need to speak to each other by phone without fear of being overheard, they use voice scramblers. These split up the sounds of a voice into five different frequency bands, then jumble them up electronically using special codes. At the other end, the receiver unscrambles the frequencies using the same codes in reverse. The two people speaking hear each other's voices normally, but anyone listening along the way gets a blur of meaningless noise.

An electronic voice scrambler

TSS - 15

That's Amazing

MULTIPLE CONVERSATIONS

In the early days of the telephone, a single wire could carry only one conversation at a time. Modern electronics allows over 7500 conversations to be transmitted at the same time along a single plastic fibre.

How have telephones changed?

Early telephones had no handset: you spoke into a microphone and held a separate earpiece to your ear. You also had to turn a numbered dial, which sent a series of pulses to the exchange. In the 1980s, touch-tone phones began to appear, with a keypad instead of a dial. The first mobile phones also emerged at this time, and have been getting smaller ever since.

Trunk exchange

Old to new From left to right, telephones have been getting more compact over the years.

Local exchange

Testing A technician checks one of the many thousands of telephone lines that pass through a large exchange.

Sound recording

Sound p.156 · Electricity and magnetism p.158 · Laser light p.176 · The mass media p.254 · Fact File p.382

Microphones pick up sound and turn it into electrical signals. These can be recorded using one of two systems: analogue or digital. Analogue systems record sounds in the form of a constantly changing electrical signal. Digital systems convert that signal into strings of pulses, which can be stored in a computer, on tape or on CD.

How are sounds stored on tape?

Recording tape is covered by millions of tiny metal particles. The tape passes across the record/playback head, which contains an electric magnet (or two for stereo sound). Electric signals from the microphone alter the head's magnetism, which produces changing magnetic patterns in the tape's metal particles. In playing back a tape, the head 'reads' the magnetic patterns on the tape, and converts them into electric signals, which are sent to loudspeakers.

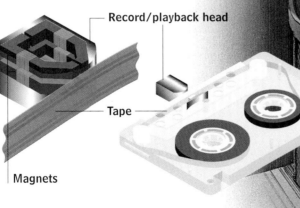

Record/playback head

Tape

Magnets

Why are some microphones covered in fur?

High-quality recordings, especially outdoors, can easily be spoiled by wind blowing into the microphone, making a loud, unpleasant 'brushing' sound. Even indoors, microphones can pick up small unwanted noises as people move about. A protective covering of sponge or nylon fur will filter out most of these unwanted sounds.

Sound engineer

In the open Fur protects sensitive microphones from unwanted noises.

Changing discs The Italian opera singer Enrico Caruso (far left), who died in 1921, recorded his voice on gramophone discs (records). In the 1960s, the Beatles (centre) sold their music on vinyl singles and LPs. By the late 1990s, most artists, like the Spice Girls, were using digital technology to make CDs.

Changing technology

In 1877, the American inventor Thomas Edison made the first successful recording of a human voice, using a needle that cut a groove of varying depth around a cylinder covered with metal foil. In 1887, Emil Berliner invented the gramophone, with the recording needle cutting a groove of varying width in a flat disc. Long-playing records (LPs) appeared in 1948. They got their name because they had a playing time of 30 minutes instead of only 4½ minutes with the old gramophone discs. Compact Discs (CDs), which use digital recordings, appeared in 1983. Read by a laser beam, CDs give the best sound yet.

Producer

Second engineer

THAT'S AMAZING

SOUND THROUGH LIGHT

The soundtrack on movies is made by using a beam of light, which gets stronger or weaker depending on the signal sent to it from the microphone. This makes a pattern on a side of the film. The sound is played back by shining light through this pattern onto a light-sensitive cell in the projector.

Recording the songsters of the oceans

Perhaps the most surprising 'performers' in sound recording have been whales. Like dolphins and porpoises, whales make many different sounds. Some are used for creating echoes, which allow the whales to 'see' in the dark depths of the oceans. Other sounds are more mysterious, especially the long, haunting moans of humpback whales, which have been called 'whale songs'. These have been recorded using special underwater microphones, called hydrophones. Many commercial recordings of whale songs have been sold to people who find that the songs help them to relax.

Humpback whales in the sea off Australia.

RECORDING STUDIO

A recording studio consists of two rooms. One is soundproofed with double doors, and has soft coverings on the walls and floor to cut out echoes. This is where the performers make their music. The other room is the control room, with the recording equipment operated by sound engineers. The engineers make sure that the recording levels are correctly set and that everything is working properly. A producer monitors the quality of the performance.

➡ The Earth's atmosphere p.28 · Sound p.156 · Satellites in space p.180 · The mass media p.254 · Fact File p.322, 377

In 1901, Guglielmo Marconi made history with a brief radio transmission in code across the Atlantic Ocean. Within decades, radios had become part of everyday life. Most of us listen to the radio for entertainment, but it is also a vital tool for airline pilots, ambulance and fire crews, the police and armed forces, and even spacecraft. Today, the airwaves are buzzing with radio communications, 24 hours a day, throughout the world.

THAT'S AMAZING

WAVE RACING

Radio waves travel at the speed of light – 299 792 km (186 287 miles) a second. Sound waves travel far more slowly, at around 330 m (1080 ft) a second through air. So music broadcast from a concert hall in London would reach a radio listener in Edinburgh sooner than it would reach someone at the back of the hall.

What are radio waves?

Radio waves are a form of energy. They belong to a large family of electromagnetic waves that are all around us, including light, radar, X-rays, ultraviolet rays and microwaves. They are called waves because they behave like waves in water, with alternating peaks (high points) and troughs (low points). Electromagnetic waves travel through air and space; some – like X-rays – can pass through solid objects as well. Radio waves are not this powerful; the farther they go, the fainter they become. Even so, they can reach around the world, or deep into space.

RADIO BROADCASTING

A microphone turns sound into electrical signals. These are combined with radio waves, and sent out by transmitters to nearby radio receivers or repeater stations in distant parts of the country. The signals can also be beamed up to a satellite for onward transmission to distant countries; or they can be angled up towards the ionosphere – a part of the atmosphere about 60-1000 km (40-600 miles) above the Earth's surface – and be 'bounced' around the globe.

Speech Most radio broadcasts consist of music or speech.

Secret The military and emergency services have their own transmitters.

Radio tower A radio station broadcasts different signals locally and around the world from its transmitters.

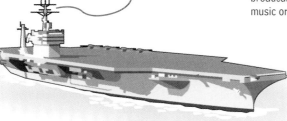

Out to sea Ships rely on their radios to receive instructions, and weather reports from shore - in this case on long wave - and to exchange information. Navy ships use special frequencies, and may even 'scramble' their messages, using codes that are known only to them and their headquarters.

Reserved frequencies

Police and emergency services use special 'reserved' radio frequencies which no one else is allowed to use.

Local radio A car radio receives signals - in this case, medium wave - from a local transmitter.

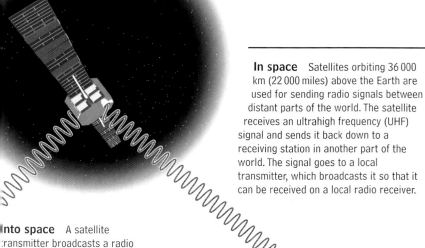

In space Satellites orbiting 36 000 km (22 000 miles) above the Earth are used for sending radio signals between distant parts of the world. The satellite receives an ultrahigh frequency (UHF) signal and sends it back down to a receiving station in another part of the world. The signal goes to a local transmitter, which broadcasts it so that it can be received on a local radio receiver.

Into space A satellite transmitter broadcasts a radio signal to a satellite in space, which sends it on to a receiving station on a distant continent.

What do the different channels on a radio receiver mean?

Radio signals are broadcast on four main wave bands: short wave, medium wave, long wave and VHF, which stands for Very High Frequency. As the names suggest, short wave indicates a signal that has a short distance between one wave and the next, while long wave is the opposite. Each wave band has its own strengths and weaknesses. Long waves, for example, travel well through water, and so are used by submarines; short waves can be bounced off the atmosphere to reach the far corners of the Earth; VHF loses power quickly, but carries a lot of information, and so can be used for high-quality stereo broadcasts. VHF is also known as FM – meaning Frequency Modulation – a technical term that refers to the way the signal is sent.

Ionosphere

Local transmitter

Bouncing waves Short-wave signals go around the world by bouncing off the ionosphere and the ground.

Satellite receiving station

Radios for entertainment Home radios have existed since the 1920s, with an ever-increasing number of stations providing news, music and entertainment. A short-wave radio, such as that shown right, can pick up broadcasts from thousands of miles away. The woman on the beach (left) is listening to a radio tuned to medium wave.

Local receiver

🔄 The making of the Universe p.12 · The birth of the planets p.16 ·
Light: visible energy p.154 · Fact File p.273, 375

Our knowledge of the world we live in, and the universe that surrounds us, owes a great deal to microscopes and telescopes. The first microscope, for magnifying small things, was made in about 1590 by Zacharias Janssen, a Dutch spectacle maker. Soon afterwards, in 1609, the Italian scientist Galileo Galilei built one of the first telescopes for magnifying very distant things. Galileo used his telescope to study the Sun, Moon, planets and stars.

What is the smallest thing we can see?

With the naked eye, we can see objects as small as a particle of dust, but without any detail. Traditional, or optical, microscopes can magnify about 1000 times. By comparison, the electron microscope, invented in 1932, can magnify around 50 000 times. Instead of light, it uses a beam of electrons to scan an object and create an image. The most powerful microscope ever made – the atomic force microscope in Switzerland – allows us to look at atoms just one ten-millionth of a millimetre across.

Eyepiece The eyepiece, which can be changed, gets its name because it is closest to your eye.

Objective lens The objective lenses get their name from being closest to the object being looked at. They are mounted on a swivelling base, which you turn to select the particular lens you need.

Path of light

Specimen

Mirror

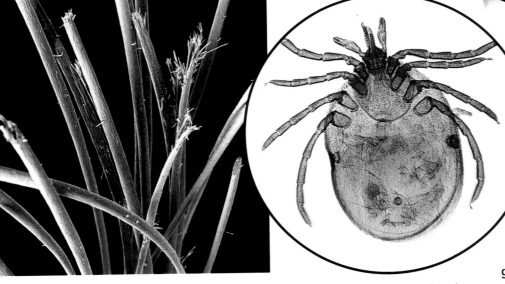

Damaged hair These are not broken twigs, but strands of human hair with 'split ends'. The image was produced by an electron microscope.

Blood-sucker If you looked through an optical microscope, this is what the underside of a tick would look like.

Crime under the microscope

Forensic scientists get valuable help from clues left unknowingly at the scene of a crime: a hair, a drop of blood, fibres from a piece of clothing, a scrape of paint from a hit-and-run car crash. By examining these under a microscope, and analysing them chemically, a forensic scientist can often match the clues with samples taken from a suspect.

MAKING THE SMALL LOOK BIG

An optical microscope uses a mirror in its base to shine light through a specimen sandwiched between two glass slides. It uses two sets of lenses, separated by a tube, to make the specimen appear bigger than it really is. At the top is an 'eyepiece', which has a magnifying power of between six and ten. At the bottom are three 'objective lenses', which usually magnify 10 times, 40 times and 100 times. To work out how much you are magnifying, multiply the power of your eyepiece by the power of your selected objective lens.

Not keeping an eye on the Sun

No one should ever try looking at the Sun directly, let alone through a telescope or binoculars. The concentrated heat and brightness of the Sun's rays will quickly cause permanent damage to the human eye. When astronomers want to study the Sun they wear special, tinted lenses, or reflect the Sun's image onto a surface where it can be safely looked at. In Arizona, in the USA, the McMath-Pierce solar telescope has been specially built for studying the Sun. This telescope gets so hot that it needs cooling pipes to keep its temperature down. It is also so big – 152 m (500 ft) in length – that much of it is underground. A series of mirrors reflect the magnified image of the Sun onto a table in an underground observation room.

The McMath-Pierce solar telescope.

How far can we see into space?

Galileo's telescope made things look 32 times bigger than they are. This allowed him to see four of the moons of Jupiter. Today, the Hubble Space Telescope orbiting the Earth is capable of magnifying things 4 billion times – making it 125 million times more powerful than Galileo's telescope. This allows us to see galaxies that are 10 billion light years away. (A single light year is equivalent to 9461 billion km – 5880 billion miles – which is the distance that light travels in space in the course of one year.)

Space Galileo studied the Moon (below), while the Hubble telescope looks deep into space (right).

THAT'S AMAZING

THE HUBBLE'S TINY FLAW

The Hubble Space Telescope uses a giant mirror in place of an objective lens. When the telescope was launched in 1990, part of the mirror was found to have an error of just 0.002 mm (0.00008 in), which blurred its vision. In 1993, astronauts fitted four tiny mirrors to fix the problem.

STUDYING THE HEAVENS

The simplest telescope is a refracting telescope; it refracts light, or bends it, down a long tube. At one end is the 'objective lens', which is pointed at the object you want to study; at the other end is a smaller 'eyepiece' lens, which you look into to see the magnified image. The bigger the objective lens, the more light it will let in, which helps to make the final image brighter and clearer.

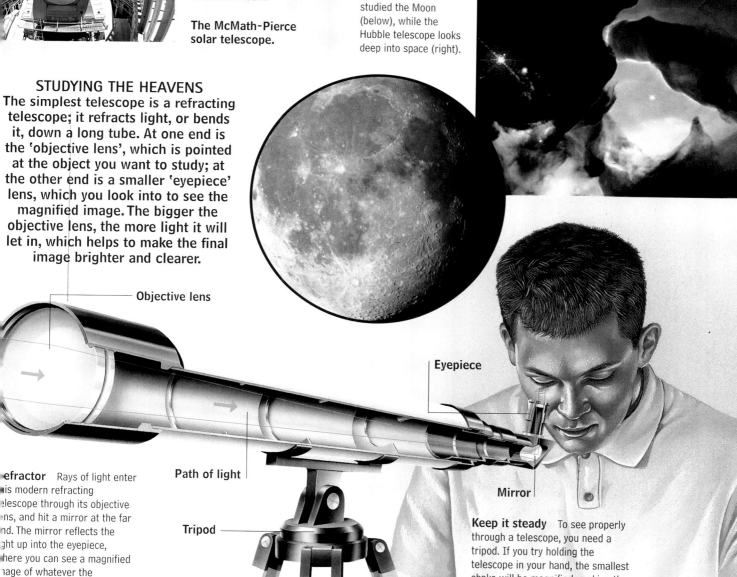

Objective lens

Eyepiece

Mirror

Path of light

Tripod

Refractor Rays of light enter this modern refracting telescope through its objective lens, and hit a mirror at the far end. The mirror reflects the light up into the eyepiece, where you can see a magnified image of whatever the telescope is pointed towards.

Keep it steady To see properly through a telescope, you need a tripod. If you try holding the telescope in your hand, the smallest shake will be magnified, making the image impossible to study.

Photography

Light: visible energy p.154 · Television and video p.170 ·
Printing and publishing p.178

A camera works very much like your eye. Rays of light come in through a small hole at the front, pass through the darkness inside and form a picture at the back. What makes a camera different is that it uses film, or a small computer, to capture the pictures that are formed in this way. During the 20th century, photography advanced from using heavy glass plates to lightweight film, and finally to digital cameras which use no film at all.

How is a picture formed on film?

A film is a clear strip of plastic coated with special chemicals, which change their appearance when exposed to light. Silver salts register variations in light and dark. To produce colour, there are also three layers of dyes. Each is sensitive to either blue, green or red. Various combinations of these three colours can be used to reproduce all the other colours in the world around us.

Dyes Three layers of dyes produce colour in film. Each layer is transparent, so you can see other layers through it.

TAKING A PHOTOGRAPH

If you take a photograph of a bird with an automatic camera, the camera senses how far away the bird is, and focuses the lens to that distance. It also senses how bright the light is, and adjusts itself accordingly. A small shutter behind the lens then opens for a fraction of a second, allowing light from outside to reach the film, which is stretched across the back of the camera. That light will carry an image of the bird, and will 'burn' this into the chemicals that cover the film. To see that image, you must process the film.

In focus An invisible beam hits the boy and bounces back to tell the camera how far away he is. It can then focus on him.

Lens movement

How do cameras focus automatically?

Automatic focusing works by scanning objects in front of the lens with an invisible beam. Some cameras send out a beam of infrared light, while others use ultrasound – sound waves that can't be heard. If the beam hits an object, it will bounce back at the camera, telling it how far away that object is. The camera then adjusts its lens, so that the object will be in focus when the picture is taken

Exposure and aperture

Modern automatic cameras make photography easier than ever before. They make calculations and adjustments that you would otherwise have to make yourself. All cameras need to control the amount of light falling onto the film. This is done in two ways – by adjusting the speed of the shutter (how quickly it opens and shuts again), and by altering the size of the opening (or aperture) through which the light passes. A dull day needs a slow shutter-speed and a big aperture; bright sunshine needs a high shutter-speed and a small aperture. On an old-fashioned manual camera, you would have to measure the light, and make these settings yourself. An automatic camera does it for you, and even gives you extra light from its flash when necessary.

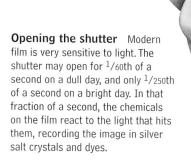

Shutter release

Information display

Flash

Film canister

Lens

Image falling onto film

Opening the shutter   Modern film is very sensitive to light. The shutter may open for $1/60$th of a second on a dull day, and only $1/250$th of a second on a bright day. In that fraction of a second, the chemicals on the film react to the light that hits them, recording the image in silver salt crystals and dyes.

What happens when a film is processed?

To see the pictures you have taken, you must have your film processed in chemicals. These reveal the image burned into the film's silver crystals, together with the colours in its dyes. With most films, however, the image you see is a negative one: shadows appear light, and bright areas look dark. The colours also look strange. This is because everything has been reversed. The final image will emerge only when the film is printed onto paper. At that point, the negative is reversed, producing a positive image.

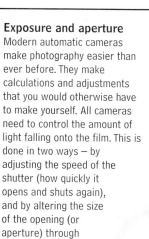

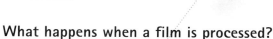

1. Snapping
An upside-down image of a girl with an umbrella is burned onto the film.

2. Processing
At first the image is invisible, but processing brings out the colours in the film's dyes.

3. Negative
The colours and tones are reversed; they will appear correctly when the image is printed.

Digital cameras

In place of film, the back of a digital camera contains a plate, which is covered with thousands of tiny light-sensitive electric cells called CCDs – charge-coupled devices. Like the dyes in film, each CCD is sensitive to only one colour – red, blue or green. Light passing through the camera lens activates the CCDs, which give out electrical signals. The overall pattern of these signals creates the whole picture, which is stored in the camera's memory in the form of a digital computer code. This can be transferred to a home computer, and stored on CD.

With a computer, you can take a digital image and change it in any way that you want.

Television and video

⊙ Sound recording p.162 · Radio communications p.164 ·
Photography p.168 · The mass media p.254 · Fact File p.322

Television works by turning light, colour and sound into electrical signals. These signals are sent out on radio waves or by underground cables to people's homes, where TV sets turn the signals back into pictures and sound. Video recorders collect the electrical signals and store them on magnetic tape. Cable and satellite TV provide special channels that people pay to watch.

FROM TV CAMERA TO TV SCREEN

As you look around you, two things create the images you see with your eyes: different colours, and different levels of brightness. A TV camera works on the same principle. It registers different colours and different degrees of brightness, and converts these into complex electrical signals. A separate audio signal for sound is also created and combined with the picture signal in such a way that it can be recovered at a later stage. A TV set converts these electrical signals back into pictures and sound.

How do TV newsreaders know what to say?

Newsreaders always know exactly what to say, yet they never look down at any notes; nor have they memorised the news. The words spoken by newsreaders appear on a special screen, called a teleprompt screen, which is attached to the front of the camera filming them. This allows newsreaders to read out the news while looking straight at the camera.

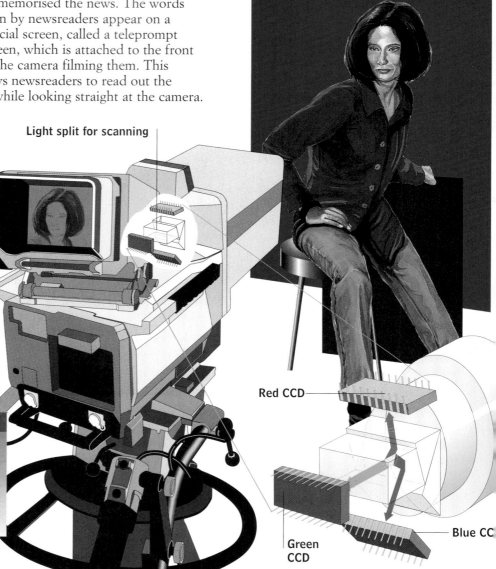

Light split for scanning

Teleprompt A newsreader can control the speed with which text moves over the teleprompt screen that he or she is reading from.

Camera The cameraman watches a small black-and-white screen to check what is being filmed. Black-and-white is used because it is easier to focus. Inside the camera, light is split into three colours – red, green and blue. Each colour is scanned separately by its own CCD, or charge-coupled device, to create its own electrical signal.

Red CCD

Green CCD

Blue CC[D]

THAT'S AMAZING

BREAKING UP A PICTURE

Like a movie camera, a TV camera takes a series of rapid still images – 25 of them every second. Unlike a movie image, however, each TV image is split into 625 horizontal lines. With high-definition TV, the image is split into 1125 horizontal lines, making the images much clearer and crisper.

Inside a TV set

A TV set contains a cathode-ray tube, which acts like a TV camera in reverse. It has three electron beams — red, green and blue. These pass through a grille, and activate tiny coloured stripes on the screen, making them glow to re-create the original picture.

Grille **Stripes on screen**

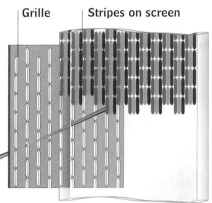

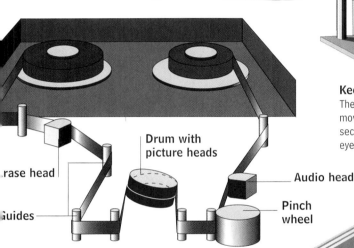

Drum with picture heads

Erase head

Audio head

Guides

Pinch wheel

Inside a video recorder

Video tape is drawn from one spool to another. From left, it goes past an erase head and a series of guides. It then goes around the drum of the picture heads and past a large pinch wheel, which keeps it tight. Finally it passes in front of the audio head.

Keeping the picture moving

The electron beams in a cathode ray tube move across the entire screen 50 times every second. This is much too fast for the human eye to follow, so it sees continuous action rather than a sequence of still pictures.

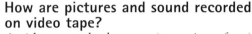

Tracks
On a video tape, the picture track is recorded diagonally; sound and control tracks run along the edges of the tape.

How are pictures and sound recorded on video tape?

A video recorder has two (sometimes four) picture heads on a large drum, which is set at an angle to the tape. The drum spins as the tape passes across it, and the signals are recorded in diagonal (sloping) tracks on the tape. An audio head records the sound signals along one edge of the tape, together with a control signal – which matches pictures and sound – along the other edge of the tape.

TV screens for the future

Television sets have traditionally been bulky items; and the bigger the screen, the bigger the back of the tube has been. However, modern screens are becoming much more compact. Flat cathode-ray tubes, which use tiny components, represent one line of development. Some are so flat that they seem hardly to jut out from the wall at all. Another development is found in flat LCD (Liquid Crystal Display) screens, like the ones in portable computers or portable game machines. These screens are being made so small that they can be worn on a person's arm, like a wristwatch.

New TVs can be much bigger and yet thinner than ever before.

What is digital TV?

Digital TV converts pictures and sounds into a coded stream of numbers rather than varying electrical signals.

These numbers are transmitted by radio waves, cable and satellite in the same way as old-style television, but need a special receiver or decoder to convert them back into sound and pictures. One of the advantages of digital TV is that it allows many more channels than before.

In focus Digital TV (below) is much clearer than old-style TV.

➡ Working robots p.174 · Printing and publishing p.178 ·
The information revolution p.202 · Fact File p.323

E lectronic devices – including computers, portable stereos, calculators, microwave cookers and digital watches – are all around us, making modern life more convenient. In spite of their many differences, these devices all rely on the same invention – the integrated circuit, also known as the microchip – which can calculate, process, send, receive and store information faster, more cheaply and more accurately than any other machine ever made.

What are microchips?

A microchip is a collection of thousands of electrical circuits, all of them tiny and laid out on wafers of silicon about the size of a fingernail. Information enters as pulses of electric current. These chase along the pathways of the circuit, picking up other pieces of information, changing it, working on it, keeping some bits and rejecting others, and producing a new set of information at the other end.

How do computers store pictures?

A computer 'sees' a picture like any other piece of information – as a complex series of codes. It breaks the picture down into thousands of tiny squares, called pixels, each with its own colour and its own code number. A computer cannot mix colours like a painter, so it creates patterns of different coloured pixels. Because these are too small to be seen by the human eye, they merge into each other to form a much bigger range of colours on the screen.

Tiny mite Surrounded by its electrical connectors, the microchip on this panel is the size of a human fingernail.

Magnified pixels
Pictures on a computer screen consist of many thousands of tiny coloured squares, called pixels.

To the screen

To the Internet

Birds of the World

To the printer

Outputs A computer has three main outputs: it displays visual infomation on its screen; it can send documents to a printer; and it communicates with the internet using a modem, which is connected to a telephone line.

HOW A COMPUTER WORKS

Computers are digital machines; this means that they store and process all information – words, music, pictures, sounds – as long strings of numbers, or codes. Computer programs, also known as software, tell a computer how to process its information by breaking down every task into a series of simple steps. These are carried out at amazing speeds. Some home computers can deal with 400 million codes per second; bigger machines are considerably faster than this.

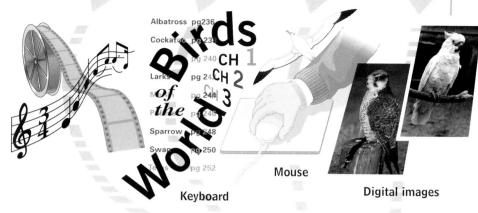

Audiovisual

Keyboard

Mouse

Digital images

Inputs Computers can receive information and instructions from several sources: audiovisual material occurs in any program that combines words, pictures and sounds; you type in words with a keyboard; you move things about with a mouse; you use a scanner to turn a picture into a digital image. All this information is reduced to sequences of numbers – or codes – which enter the computer as strings of long and short electrical pulses.

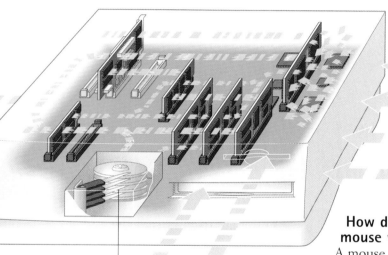

Hard disk

Floppy disk

CD

Storing information Computers store their information on different types of disks. A hard disk is mounted inside the computer. A floppy disk can transfer information from one computer to another. Some computers can also store information on CDs.

How does a computer mouse work?

A mouse has a trackball inside it, which is connected to two rollers: one for north-south movement (Y), the other for east-west (X). As the rollers move, the computer counts how many times they turn, which enables it to calculate how far the mouse has moved in any direction. It automatically sends the pointer to the correct position on the screen.

Mouse

Y roller

X roller

Electronic eye

Some tennis players can serve a ball at 200 km/h (120 mph), which is too fast for the eye to follow clearly. In professional matches, linesmen and umpires rely on an 'electronic eye' to tell them if a serve has crossed a line or not. The system sends an infrared beam along the service line, about 15 mm (1/2 in) above the ground. If the serve crosses the beam, a microchip activates a warning bleeper and a red light in the linesman's box.

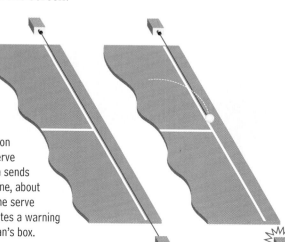

Working robots

➲ Computers and electronics p.172 · The Industrial Revolution p.216 · The history of warfare p.218 · Fact File p.363

R obots are machines that can be programmed to work for us, often in a humanlike way. They are used in factories, power stations, hospitals and schools; in transportation, firefighting and war; and in space and undersea exploration. Through laser guidance and video cameras, pressure pads and other sensors, they take in information and then make the responses they have been programmed to make. They cannot think for themselves.

AT WORK IN THE FACTORY

Most factory robots are 'robot arms', which perform the same sequence of actions hundreds of times each day. In a car factory, different robot arms do different tasks as the cars come past on the assembly line. They weld, paint, and fit windows, seats and doors.

Do robots make good workers?

Robots work best in factories, where they carry out the same tasks thousands of times each week. As robots never get ill or bored, and do not need holidays, they are cheap to run. But they need expert computer programming. They are hydraulically powered, which means that liquid flows along pipes inside them, applying pressure in different places as directed by the computer. In this way, the robots mimic the movements of human arms and hands – reaching, bending, gripping, pulling.

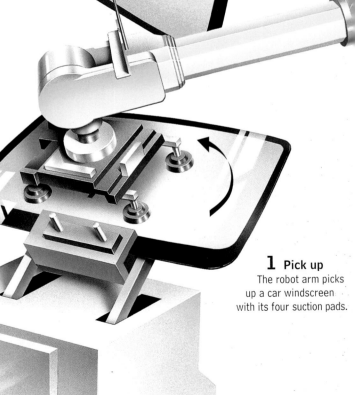

2 Fixing the clip The robot arm 'hands' the windscreen to a machine that fixes a plastic clip to one rim.

1 Pick up The robot arm picks up a car windscreen with its four suction pads.

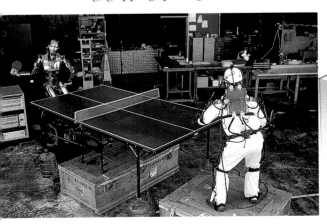

Ping vs Pong A robot table-tennis player, attached to a computer, mimics the actions of a human player, also attached to the computer.

Robots at war

Weapons that can be programmed to find a target are known as 'smart weapons'. They were first seen in action during the Gulf War in 1990. Journalists in Baghdad watched amazed as a missile flew down a street towards their hotel, turned right in front of it and sped off to blow up a military target somewhere else in the city. The age of 'war by robot' had dawned. Pilotless fighter planes, flown by computers using cameras and radar as 'eyes', are already possible, although not yet tried in war.

A 'Tomahawk' cruise missile in action.

Film of future?
Robot policeman in the film *Robocop*.

Could robots take over the world?

It is an idea you often see in films. An experiment goes wrong. An evil dictator creates an army of indestructible robots. A 'cyborg' – or human brain in an artificial body – runs out of control . . . But could it actually happen? Some aspects of the technology are almost there. We know how to clone animals, build artificial limbs that connect with the nervous system and programme computers to learn by their mistakes. In theory, genetic engineers could start trying to build intelligent 'superhumans', but in reality we are a long way from creating such creatures. And if a cyborg were made, it would almost certainly be used – as most robots are – for improving life on Earth rather than destroying it.

Are there any robots in my home?

Modern homes are full of automated machines which are, in fact, simple robots. They are programmed to do a series of specific tasks, and include washing machines, dishwashers, ovens with timers, automatic garden sprinklers, central heating and hot water systems, burglar alarms, telephone-answering machines, clock radios and video recorders.

Machine make-up
Schoolchildren using a robot that applies make-up.

3 Repeat performance The robot arm moves on and stacks the windscreen on a wooden rack, or pallet. The clip prevents the windscreen from scratching the stacked windscreens on either side. The robot arm then repeats the process.

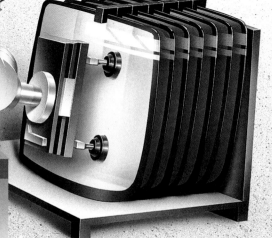

THAT'S AMAZING

WASUBOT THE PIANIST

A robot concert pianist, 'Wasubot', was built in Japan in 1986. Wasubot could read piano music and play it perfectly. It could also keep time with an orchestra, responding to sudden changes of rhythm by the conductor.

Laser light

➡ Matter: what the world is made of p.148 · Light: making waves p.154 · The information revolution p.202

Lasers are devices that produce very concentrated beams of light and heat. The first laser was built in 1960 at Malibu in California by the American physicist Theodore H. Maiman. Since then lasers have been used in many different ways – for cutting, drilling, welding, operating on the human body, measuring, mapping, recording and playing music, and sending information at the speed of light around the world.

THE WORLD OF LASERS

Lasers create beautiful light shows, but what makes them really useful is their ability to pack large amounts of information into a tiny space. They can record a symphony or a dictionary onto a CD. Laser light can also be sent through glass threads called optical fibres, transmitting information down telephone lines in fast pulses of light.

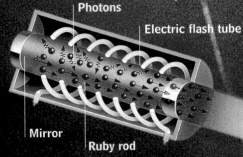

Photons

Electric flash tube

Concentrated light beam

Mirror

Ruby rod

How a laser works Atoms in the tube emit photons – and a powerful laser beam.

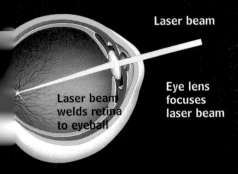

Laser beam

Eye lens focuses laser beam

Laser beam welds retina to eyeball

Eye surgery The concentrated beam of a laser offers surgeons a tool of great precision. A detached retina can be reattached to the eyeball, defects in eyesight can be corrected, and broken blood vessels mended.

How do doctors and surgeons use lasers?

Lasers are used to carry out the most delicate forms of surgery, where normal instruments will not work – in removing birthmarks, for instance, or making tiny incisions in the cornea of the eye. For surgery deep inside the body, a laser beam is focused along a slender optical fibre. The laser can burn up a cancer or clean up the walls of clogged arteries without damaging the surrounding tissue. The heat also seals up any blood vessels it touches, so there is no bleeding or stitching up to be done afterwards.

How do lasers work?

The word 'laser' stands for Light Amplification by Stimulated Emission of Radiation. Light produced by laser is different from normal daylight, which is made up of the colours of the rainbow. Laser light consists of a powerful beam of pure light. Inside the laser is a tube of material – a crystal of ruby, or a mixture of helium and neon gas. The atoms in the material are stimulated by an electrical charge to give off 'packets' of light, known as photons, which are of a single colour. This light bounces back and forth between mirrors at each end of the tube, building up more and more energy. When all this energy comes out of one end of the tube, it forms a sharp, thin beam of concentrated light.

THAT'S AMAZING
BAR CODE WONDERS

There is a laser in every supermarket checkout. When it reads the bar code on a packet, the checkout's computer converts the bar code numbers into the name and price of the product, which it then adds to your bill. The computer also tells the supermarket managers how much of every product has been sold each day, so that more supplies can be ordered.

Laser light shows

Pop groups use multicoloured laser lights to create stunning visual effects during their concerts. Laser beams are so powerful that they can also be projected onto clouds in spectacular outdoor displays at night.

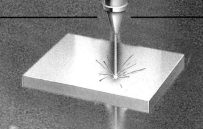

Laser drilling

Lasers produce a tiny point of intense heat which can cut or drill holes through the hardest substances on Earth, including stainless steel and precious stones such as diamonds.

Music CD

Compact discs are made by lasers burning a spiral of tiny holes or 'pits' into the surface of a disc. Every sound makes a unique pattern of pits. A CD player has a low-powered laser beam inside it which shines onto the pattern as the disc turns. The reflected light is converted back into sound.

Are lasers ever dangerous?

For science-fiction heroes, laser guns are the ideal weapon. In reality, they do not exist – not yet, at least. Military scientists are working on 'Directed Energy Weapons', super high-power lasers capable of destroying an enemy missile thousands of kilometres away by burning a hole in its fuel tanks or disabling its guidance system. In everyday life, lasers can be dangerous. Even a laser torch, which produces a bright, thin beam of light, causes damage if shined into someone's eyes.

Security cards

These can be read by a security machine at your place of work, or a bank, allowing you entry to restricted buildings, access to computer files or the money in your account.

Laser-guided weapons

Laser beams are used to guide modern weapons to their targets. Some tanks and missiles also carry LADAR, or laser radar, which tells them how far they are from the target.

Laser measuring

Lasers produce the nearest thing in the world to a perfect straight line. This can be used to guide machines for drilling tunnels and pipelines, or to bounce a light beam off a reflector in order to calculate the exact distance between two points on Earth. This is useful in map-making and in measuring movements in the Earth's surface. Lasers are also used to check the measurements of very fine wires and tools and to check the quality of optical instruments.

Optical fibres

Optical fibres are replacing metal wires for carrying long-distance telephone calls, computer data and cable TV programmes. They carry much more information, with far less interference, than wires.

A laser beam bounces back to a Geodolite, calculating distances to within a millimetre.

Printing and publishing

🔵 Photography p.168 · The written word p.210 ·
The mass media p.254 · Fact File p.345, 352, 376

The book you are reading now is one of thousands of identical copies. Before the invention of printing, every book was unique, as it was written out by hand. This made books rare and expensive, and most people did not know how to read. There are many forms of printing, which produce all the printed things we see around us – from bubble gum wrappers to encyclopedias.

How are newspapers and magazines printed?

Newspapers are printed on very large, high-speed 'web offset' presses so that they can be ready as quickly as possible. Enormous rolls of paper, up to 8 km (5 miles) long, unfurl at 600 m (2000 ft) per minute, passing between cylinders that print both sides at once. The same machines print, cut, fold and stack the newspapers at a rate of 90 000 copies an hour. A similar process is used for magazines, brochures and books when they are printed in large quantities. A normal web offset press can print the equivalent of 25 000 sheets per hour.

On press A modern newspaper printing press in action in North Carolina U.S.A.

Making words easy to read

Every printed letter has been designed with the aim of making the words easy to read (for a book or brochure) or making them jump off the page (for an advertisement or headline). The art of making printed words look good is called typography and the letter designs are known as 'typefaces' or 'fonts'. This paragraph is in a typeface known as Garamond after Claude Garamond, who was a French type designer in the 16th century.

Types Typefaces, left to right: Univers Bold, Caslon Open Face, Cochin Italic, Garamond 3.

New York

Rome

London

Paris

PRINTING IN COLOUR

Before pictures are printed they are broken up into thousands of tiny dots. You can see these dots clearly if you examine a printed picture with a magnifying glass. In colour printing, four coloured inks are applied, one after the other, to the sheet of paper. By combining these four in varying amounts, any colour can be produced.

NE

How do laser printers work?

In laser printing, the words and pictures to be printed are projected onto a revolving cylinder which has been electrically charged. This leaves an image on the cylinder where the dark bits of the image keep their electrical charge. The charged parts of the cylinder pick up a black dust called 'toner' which is baked onto the paper. The paper emerges from the machine with the words and pictures printed on it. The quality of laser printing is better than photocopying because the laser gives it greater precision.

The first presses

The first European printer was Johann Gutenberg, who lived in Germany from about 1395 to 1468. A brilliant craftsman, he invented oil-based printer's ink, a machine for printing books (inspired by the presses used to squeeze the juice out of grapes and the oil out of olives), and a way of making metal letters (type) in large quantities. The Gutenberg Bible is the earliest printed European book. The process Gutenberg invented was used for the next 500 years, but Gutenberg did not make much profit out of it. He lost the rights to it when he was sued by the man who lent him money to work on his invention.

An illuminated page from the Gutenberg Bible.

Colour printing The coloured pictures you see printed in this book and on most posters and advertisements are built up in stages. Four coloured inks are used: (1) yellow, (2) magenta (red), (3) cyan (blue-green) and (4) black. These colours combine to give a four-colour image.

THAT'S AMAZING

BOOKS IN MINIATURE

Miniature books have existed since the 16th century. Some were so tiny that you needed the magnifying glass tucked into the cover in order to read them. The world's smallest book – an edition of *Old King Cole* published in 1985 – is just 1 mm square.

The birth of the planets p.16 · Man on the Moon p.18 ·
Spinning Earth p.22 · Travelling in space p.192 · Fact File p.264, 270-3

Rockets launch satellites into orbit around the Earth. Some are in low orbit, just hundreds of kilometres above the Earth's surface. You can see them on clear nights, crossing the sky like moving stars. Satellites have cameras with which they can scan large areas of the Earth's surface, and receivers, amplifiers and transmitters that take their power from solar panels. These convert the Sun's heat into electricity. Some satellites orbit the Earth tens of thousands of kilometres above the Equator, keeping pace with the Earth as it spins. They are called 'geostationary' satellites because they stay above the same place on Earth; they make very effective communications satellites.

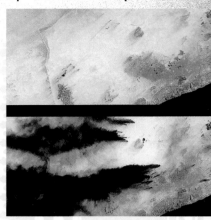

Satellite pictures of blazing oil wells in Kuwait during the Gulf War.

Spy satellites

High-powered cameras on satellites can provide amazingly detailed pictures of what is going on down below. These give valuable military and intelligence information. Some spy satellites orbit as low as 160 km (100 miles) above Earth, and can read the headlines on a newspaper. In 1987 a group of hostages being held in Lebanon were located by a spy satellite. Its cameras spotted them as they were being moved, and its radio receivers picked up walkie-talkie conversations among their guards.

How do satellites help us to forecast the weather?

Satellite pictures show where there are clouds, which way they are moving and how fast. The patterns made by the clouds are important. A hurricane, for instance, makes a huge spiral pattern. Using satellite photographs, forecasters can track the path of a hurricane, which means that they can warn people in danger from it. The first weather satellite, called Tiros 1, was launched on April 1, 1960. Before that, forecasters had to rely on information from balloons floating high in the sky, and on reports from stations around the world and ships at sea. Satellites give them much more detailed information.

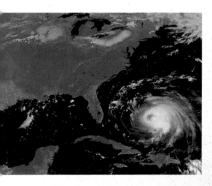

Hurricane Bonnie A satellite image of a hurricane swirling towards the coast of America.

Navstar With a radio aerial and the right computer, you can pick up signals from a navigation satellite – to help you find your way when lost.

SATELLITES OF MANY KINDS
There are two main uses for satellites: observation and communication.
Observation satellites take pictures from space and transmit them down to Earth. Communications satellites pick up radio waves from one place in the world and send them to another.

THAT'S AMAZING
HIGH-SPEED SOUND
It takes three communications satellites to send a signal right around the Earth. Radio waves travel at the speed of light – 299 792 km (186 287 miles) per second – so it takes less than a second for your voice in a telephone call to go from Britain to Australia.

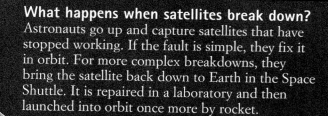

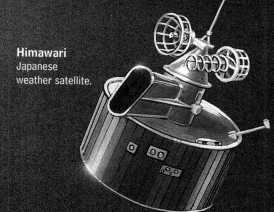

What happens when satellites break down?

Astronauts go up and capture satellites that have stopped working. If the fault is simple, they fix it in orbit. For more complex breakdowns, they bring the satellite back down to Earth in the Space Shuttle. It is repaired in a laboratory and then launched into orbit once more by rocket.

Molniya Russian communications satellite.

Jumpseat Spy satellite, for tracking military targets.

Intelsat 7 This is a comsat (communications satellite) which receives and sends thousands of telephone calls, faxes, TV pictures with sound, items of computer data and telexes. Comsats help people to communicate across the world, but also within countries. Indonesia's first satellite, Palapa 1, connected by radio, TV and telephone 200 million people living on more than 6000 islands.

Himawari Japanese weather satellite.

Landsat The US space agency NASA launched the first Landsat satellite in 1972. Landsats are observation satellites and the photos they beam back to Earth are used for accurate map-making and the study of the world's oceans, forests and rivers. They can help to keep track of forest fires, oil spills and other ecological disasters.

How does satellite TV work?

Stations broadcasting satellite TV have big, powerful transmitting dishes which send their programmes out in the form of radio waves. A communications satellite in orbit 36 000 km (22 000 miles) above the Equator picks up the signals, amplifies them and then transmits them to people's homes through receiver dishes. Journalists, too, use satellites to send news reports home from foreign countries. Sometimes, when they are in remote places, they carry special mini-transmitters with them in their backpacks, which can be operated anywhere in the world.

IRAS The telescope on IRAS views things in space that cannot be seen from Earth.

Cars and bicycles

⬤ Fossil fuels p.52 · The age of the train p.184 ·
Fact File p.282, 314, 321-2

Before bicycles and cars were invented most people never travelled more than a few miles from the place where they were born. Bicycle technology made cars possible, and car technology made planes possible. Together they have made us see the world with new eyes, giving us the freedom to go almost anywhere on Earth cheaply, safely and easily.

A CAVALCADE OF CHANGE

The first cars were little more than open carriages. Higher speeds led to problems with wind and dust, so the windscreen was added. In the 1920s electric lights became standard. Windscreen wipers, electric indicators and heaters blowing hot air from the engine appeared in the 1930s. Together with a solid roof and tyres that kept their grip on wet roads, these features made cars suitable for all weathers.

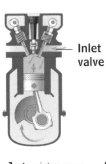

Inlet valve

Piston

Crankshaft

1. As piston goes down, fuel is sucked into cylinder.

2. On the up, piston compresses fuel, which ignites.

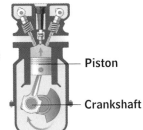

Exhaust valve

3. As fuel explodes, piston is pushed down.

4. On the way up, piston forces gas through exhaust valve.

1900 The first cars, in the last years of the 19th century, were based on horse-drawn carriages. They had buttoned leather seats, and the bodywork was wooden, hand-made by coach-builders.

1920s The Austin Swallow saloon car was based on the Austin 7, Britain's first popular car.

GP 7171

How does a car engine work?

Most cars are powered by an 'internal combustion engine'. A spray of petrol and air is drawn into each of the four cylinders (1), and compressed and ignited (2). The explosion drives down a piston (3), which turns a crankshaft connected to the car's wheels. Burnt gas is then forced through the exhaust valve (4).

Crankshaft

Piston

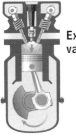

Piston power Each piston in an engine goes through the four-stage cycle above, timed so that each can fire in its turn. Here they are shown, left to right, at stages 1, 2, 4 and 3.

Future car Japan's Honda 'Dream' solar car races across Australia.

What will cars be like in 20 years' time?

The cars of the future will need to be more environmentally friendly. Electric motors are one solution: milk floats and some city buses already use them. Solar-powered cars are another possibility. So are HPVs, or Human Powered Vehicles, which use bicycle pedals, chains and gears to power small personal cars.

When were bicycles invented?

Ernest Michaux's *vélocipède,* produced in Paris in 1861, was an early version of the bicycle, known as 'the boneshaker' for its bumpy ride on wood and iron wheels. James Starley's 'penny farthing' (1870) was lighter and introduced a simple gear as well as spoked wheels. Harry J. Lawson's 'safety bicycle' (1876) brought in the chain and rear drive. Two key improvements were John Dunlop's pneumatic (air-filled) rubber tyres (1888), and gears developed by the British firm of Sturmey-Archer (1901-6). Today, materials like carbon-fibre and designs that reduce air resistance are making bikes lighter and faster than ever.

Cycle story   From the penny farthing (top) to the modern racing bike (below).

1950s   A comfortable, gas-guzzling American Cadillac Coupé de Ville.

Breaking the sound barrier

On October 13, 1997, in the Black Rock Desert in Nevada, USA, a 35-year-old RAF pilot, Andy Green, became the first person to travel faster than the speed of sound on land. Green's car, Thrust SSC, powered by two Rolls-Royce jet engines, reached a speed of 1224.95 km/h (761.18 mph). Because of a technicality, however, this feat did not count as a record. Two days later, Green tried again, and this time it was official. He set the first-ever supersonic (faster than sound) world land-speed record, hurtling across the desert at 1227.985 km/h (763.035 mph).

Thrust, the world's fastest car.

THAT'S AMAZING

TOP-SPEED CYCLING
The world speed record for cycling is 268.83 km/h (166.94 mph), set by the 50-year-old Dutch cyclist Fred Rompelberg in 1995. He was cycling in the slipstream (the stream of air behind a moving object) of a car.

1990s   Like the Ford Ka, many cars of today are small, agile and kinder to the environment. In the past 30 years, designers have made cars safer, more reliable and cheaper to build and run.

● Electricity and magnetism p.158 · Cars and bicycles p.182 ·
The Industrial Revolution p.216 · Fact File p.314, 321, 377

Trains were the first form of mechanised transport – until then our ancestors had to rely on animals such as horses and oxen to pull carts and carriages or carry loads. Thanks to the steam locomotive, invented in the early 19th century, it became possible to carry huge cargoes of heavy goods like coal and iron more quickly and cheaply than ever before. Passenger transport quickly followed.

Fireproof door

Double-glazed window

Headlight and tail lamps

Warning horn

Aerodynamically shaped nose

Which was the first train?

Trains were developed between 1800 and 1830 in England, mainly for carrying coal and iron. The steam locomotive was invented by the Cornish engineer Richard Trevithick in 1803. The first steam passenger train was built by another English engineer, George Stephenson, in 1825. It carried 450 passengers the 13 km (8 miles) from Stockton to Darlington in Yorkshire, England, at 24 km/h (15 mph).

Steam train Richard Trevithick's railroad on display in London.

How do trains work?

Electric trains pick up electricity from overhead wires or a third rail. This drives a motor that turns the wheels. Diesel locomotives are also driven by electric motors, but they use diesel-fuelled engines to generate their own electricity. In the old steam engine, a coal fire boils water, producing steam which pushes a piston up and down a cylinder. The piston is linked to the driving wheels by a connecting rod. Coal and water are carried behind the locomotive in a tender.

Signalling safety

Collisions between trains are prevented by keeping them in separate sections of track. Signals tell train-drivers when they must stop and when it is safe to go forward. The first signals were given by hand. Semaphore signals were first used in 1841, but gave way to coloured lights, similar to traffic lights, in the 1960s. When a train enters a section of track, an electrical circuit automatically changes the signal ahead and behind to red so that no other trains can enter that section. Once the train has passed and the section of track is clear, the signal changes to yellow (for caution), then green. Today's computerised signals can automatically slow down an approaching train without the driver doing anything. This allows driverless trains like the Docklands Light Railway in London to operate safely.

Stop The red 'stop' signal tells the driver not to enter the next section.

All clear A green l allows the train to en the next section.

FROM ROCKET TO EUROSTAR

George Stephenson's *Rocket,* built in 1829, broke speed records for a passenger train. It travelled at 46 km/h (36 mph). The Eurostar linked London to Brussels and Paris via the Channel Tunnel in 1994, travelling at 300 km/h (185 mph) on high-speed track.

Air outlet screens

Driver's control console

Tomorrow's trains

Imagine a train that floats above its track without touching it, whooshing along at an almost noiseless 500 km/h (310 mph). Various countries, including Japan and Germany, are experimenting with just such a train – the Maglev (magnetic levitation) train. Magnetic fields from electrical coils along the track alternately repel and attract similar coils in the train, making it speed forward without wheels and with very little friction. For normal railways, researchers are concentrating on producing trains that are faster, quieter, more comfortable, and cheaper to run.

Windscreen wipers

On-board computer

Inside out

The view from the driver's cab in a Eurostar train. The driver sits in the centre of the cab, rather than on the left or right. This gives the driver a better view.

Main controller (lever)

Travel in the future? A Maglev train speeds between Berlin and Hamburg in Germany.

Warning Two yellow lights warn the driver to be prepared to stop.

Caution One yellow light cautions the driver to stop at the next signal.

Stop The red 'stop' signal tells the driver not to enter the next section.

All clear A green light allows the train to enter the next section.

Oceans and seas p.36 · Exploring the world p.212 · Fact File p.314, 318, 349, 356

The ocean that covers two-thirds of the Earth's surface can be dangerous and unpredictable. Seagoing craft have to be strongly built to survive the high winds and enormous waves that can suddenly spring up anywhere in the world. Whatever the size, from sailing dinghies to aircraft carriers, safety, seaworthiness and good navigation – finding your way across the ocean – must come first.

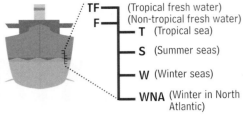

TF	(Tropical fresh water)
F	(Non-tropical fresh water)
T	(Tropical sea)
S	(Summer seas)
W	(Winter seas)
WNA	(Winter in North Atlantic)

Safe level   A loaded ship settles in the water – the heavier the load, the lower it sinks. For safety, a ship should not sink lower than the line marked on its hull. Called the Plimsoll line, the maximum safe loading varies for sea or fresh water, winter or summer, in tropical or northern waters.

Why do metal ships float?
Anything that is lighter than water will float. Most metals are heavier than water, but if you make a hollow metal container, the air inside it means that the whole thing is lighter than the same volume of water, so it floats. Try putting a metal tray or a cake tin in a basin of water. What happens? It floats. See how much weight it can carry before it sinks.

Tea clipper
Among the fastest sailing ships ever built, the square-rigged clippers flourished in the 1860s when they carried new crops of tea from China to London. It was a trip of more than 8000 km (5000 miles) and took about 100 days.

OCEAN GOERS
For thousands of years, the only way people could make long-distance sea voyages was in ships powered by oars or the wind. After 1870, sailing ships were used less and less, as steamships gradually replaced them.

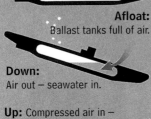

Afloat: Ballast tanks full of air.

Down: Air out – seawater in.

Up: Compressed air in – seawater out.

How do submarines go up and down?
A submarine has special tanks known as ballast tanks. It dives by flooding these with seawater and tilting downwards. To surface, compressed air is blown into the ballast tanks and the water is pushed out, lightening the submarine. To help them move up or down, modern submarines have fins on their sides which can be tilted or angled like rudders.

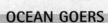

On the bridge Navigation equipment guides a ship through Antarctica.

Cruise ship

A cross between a luxury hotel and a floating holiday camp, today's cruise ship has a gym, tennis court, swimming pools, theatre, restaurants, bars, hairdressers and shops, as well as a special children's area with cinema, video arcade, whirlpool and waterfall. Specially designed six-bladed propellers and quiet motors on rubber mountings reduce vibrations and keep engine noise to a minimum.

How do ships' captains know where they are?

The science of ocean navigation is very ancient. Before the compass was invented in about AD 1100, ships used to sail along coasts, using simple charts as well as the Sun and stars to guide them. Later, astrolabes, sextants and accurate clocks were developed: all of these instruments helped navigators to calculate a ship's position. Today's ships use high-tech navigation systems linked with satellites to do the same job. Submarine captains, who cannot pick up satellite signals under water, rely on older methods of navigation. Using computers and maps of ocean currents, they work out exactly how far the vessel has travelled and in what direction.

THAT'S AMAZING

A WEEK'S SHOPPING

Groceries for a week on a cruise ship include 9000 kg (19 800 lb) of potatoes; 1850 kg (4080 lb) of fish; 12 500 kg (27 600 lb) of frozen meat; 14 000 kg (31 000 lb) of fruit and vegetables; 5250 litres (9240 pints) of milk; 16 500 bottles of beer.

Mini subs

Submersibles are small diving machines launched from a mother ship. They usually have a crew of two or three people, though some are remote controlled. They are used for exploring underwater ruins and wrecks, for making repairs to oil rigs and undersea cables, and in other forms of research. They are heavily reinforced to stand up to the huge pressure under the sea – the pressure is 400 times greater 4000 m (13 000 ft) down than it is at sea level. A submersible is usually equipped with spotlights, video cameras, robot arms, and air and ballast tanks for diving and surfacing like a submarine.

A submersible visits the wreck of the *Titanic*.

Submarine

Second World War submarines like this German U-boat used diesel engines on the surface and battery-powered electric motors – which do not use up precious air – when under water. They had to surface every few hours to recharge their batteries and take in fresh air. Today's nuclear-powered submarines can spend several weeks under water and up to two years at sea without refuelling.

Chinese junk

For many years until the 19th century, junks were the biggest, safest and most efficient ships in the world. Box-like partitions inside the hull of a junk give it strength. Sails are made of a coarsely woven fabric, and are kept flat with strips of bamboo. They can be easily opened and closed by pulling on ropes, just like blinds.

Balloons and airships

➡ Matter p.148 · How aeroplanes work p.190 ·
Fact File p.315, 320

If you have ever watched smoke curl up into the sky, you will know why balloons float. Hot air rises. If you fill a bag with enough hot air, the bag will rise, too. Hang a basket underneath for passengers, and you have a hot-air balloon. This is how the first balloon flights were made in 1783. Just as hot air floats upwards, so do light gases like hydrogen and helium. Many modern balloons comprise a mini-balloon, or sphere, filled with helium for extra buoyancy.

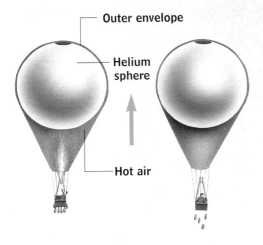

Hotting up The pilot turns on the burners (far left), heating the air in the outer envelope, and causing the balloon to rise.

Lightening the load The pilot throws ballast overboard (left); the balloon rises.

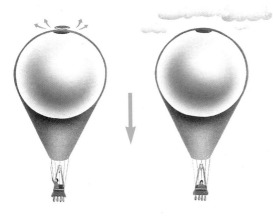

Gas release The pilot opens the valve at the top of the helium sphere (far left), releasing the gas and causing the balloon to descend.

Weather control Clouds in the sky above force the balloon to descend (left).

UP AND AWAY

Both hot-air balloons and airships have made a comeback in recent years, with strong synthetic materials and safe designs. A modern hot-air balloon has an 'envelope' of tough nylon, with stainless-steel cables to support the burners and the basket or capsule. The air in the envelope is heated, in this case, by burning liquid propane gas, which is carried in cylinders at the corners of the capsule. About 1 litre (1 3/4 pints) gas is used for every minute of flight.

Looking out The hole in the top of the passenger capsule is covered with a dome of clear plastic, so that the pilots can look up to the underside of the balloon.

Balloon party Hot-air balloons race at a balloon festival in Colorado, USA.

How do you control a hot-air balloon?

When the air in the envelope is heated by the burners, the balloon rises. As the air in the envelope cools, the balloon sinks. A quick blast of flame about once a minute keeps the balloon level. This is the only control the balloonist has. There is no steering, and the balloon is blown along by the wind, which varies in speed and direction. This is one reason why people who try to fly around the world in balloons get into difficulties.

Why doesn't the flame burn the balloon?

The gas burner shoots a big jet of flame – 3-4 m (10-13 ft) long – under the balloon, the lower section of which is made of fireproof fabric. The opening in the balloon is wide enough, and the balloon tall enough, for the flame not to touch the envelope. A temperature sensor in the top of the envelope warns the pilot if there is any danger of a fire.

The Hindenburg – Titanic of the sky

Airships were used for bombing and observation in the First World War. From 1910 Zeppelin airships, pioneered by the German inventor Count Ferdinand von Zeppelin, carried paying passengers. The *Hindenburg* was an airship – a luxury passenger liner that sailed through the sky. At 245 m (804 ft) long, it was three times the size of a jumbo jet, with double cabins for its 72 passengers, a dining room, lounge and bar complete with grand piano. There was even a promenade deck, where passengers on the three-day journey from Germany to America could go for a stroll. The *Hindenburg* was powered by four 1100 horsepower engines, giving it a maximum speed of 135 km/h (84 mph). It caught fire as it was landing at Lakehurst, New Jersey, on May 6, 1937, killing 36 people. After that, people lost confidence in airships for a very long time.

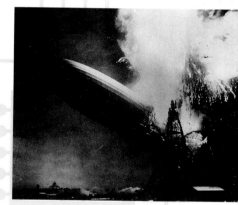

The German airship *Hindenburg* bursts into flames in 1937.

Burning up
There are three sets of burners on the capsule. Two sets are for high altitude, and one is for below 610 m (2000 ft).

Control panel
The pilots check the control panel in the balloon's capsule.

How do airships fly?

The first airship, filled with hydrogen and powered by a steam engine, was made in 1852. Modern airships are filled with helium gas. They fly at about 160 km/h (100 mph), using two propellers driven by engines. The pilot steers with rudders. Airships also have fins with flaps, called elevators, which the pilot can tilt up or down. The propellers can be tilted to allow the airship to take off and land vertically. To land the pilot needs help from a ground crew who secure the ship with cables.

Fuel tanks There are six fuel tanks on the capsule, carrying propane gas. Each tank can be released into the sea when empty.

World first The world's first commercial airline, started in 1909-10, was based on a fleet of Zeppelin airships.

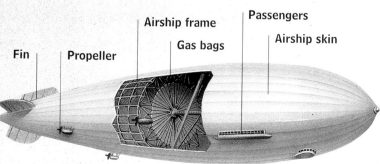

Fin   Propeller   Airship frame   Gas bags   Passengers   Airship skin

➥ Balloons and airships p.188 · Travelling in space p.192 ·
Fact File p.315, 322, 377

The earliest aeroplanes were simple constructions of wood, cloth, wire and glue which could barely carry a person more than a few miles. Today aeroplanes are huge, complicated machines that can carry hundreds of people halfway round the Earth without stopping. They can even take off, fly and land by themselves, and have become much faster, safer and more comfortable.

Why doesn't an aeroplane fall out of the sky?

The secret of flying lies in a force called 'lift'. To get lift, you need a forward speed of around 80 km/h (50 mph) for a light aircraft, 160-240 km/h (100-150 mph) for a heavier plane. You also need wings of the right shape. Most plane wings have a 'half tear-drop' shape – they are curved above and flatter below, tapering towards the back. This shape makes the air flow much faster over the top than underneath. The pressure of fast-flowing air above the wing is less than that of the slower-moving air beneath it, and this pulls the wing upwards as it moves through the air. Pilots can get more lift by increasing their speed and raising the flaps, or elevators, on the tailplane which raises the nose of the plane slightly.

Lift Air passes under the wing slightly slower, creating higher pressure and lift.

TAKEOFF AND FLYING
After checking engines and controls, the pilot asks for clearance to leave. Ground control explains which runway to use and how to get there. Throughout the flight, the pilot keeps in close radio contact with the ground.

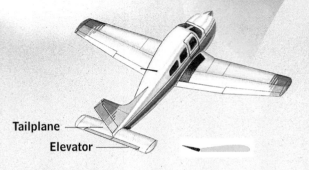

Tailplane
Elevator

2 Takeoff With the engine at full power, the plane accelerates along the runway. The pilot raises the elevators on the tail, which brings the nose of the plane up. In a few seconds, the plane is at flying speed and lifts into the air.

1 Preparing for takeoff
The pilot taxis the plane slowly to the runway and waits for clearance to take off.

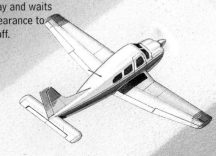

How does a helicopter work?

A helicopter's main rotor blades are, in fact, long thin wings. By spinning very quickly through the air, they create lift just like wings on an ordinary aircraft do. The pilot can change the angle or pitch of the blades to make more lift or less lift. In this way he is able to make the helicopter go up or down, or hover in midair. Helicopters also have a tail rotor which holds the helicopter steady. Without this, the helicopter would just spin round and round in the opposite direction to the main rotor.

Forwards
The pilot can tilt the main rotor so that the blades in front are set flat, and the ones behind are set steeply. This lifts the tail and pulls the helicopter forwards.

Up
The blades are set at a steep pitch or angle, giving plenty of lift.

Down
The blades are set almost flat, giving very little lift.

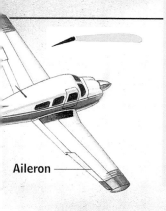

Aileron

The first powered flight

After balloonists, the first people to fly did so in gliders, aircraft without engines. They included a German, Otto Lilienthal, and a Frenchman, Octave Chanute, in the 1890s. In 1900 two American bicycle makers from Dayton, Ohio, made a wind tunnel and used it to study how glider wings work. They were the Wright brothers, Wilbur and Orville, who then built their own plane, the *Flyer*. They also built an engine for it, and invented a propeller for flying. On December 17, 1903, they made four flights in the *Flyer* – the longest lasting 50 seconds and covering 260 m (852 ft). The age of aviation had begun.

Otto Lilienthal's glider.

3 Banking To turn right, the pilot 'banks' the aircraft slightly to the right. He lowers the aileron, or flap, on the left wing and raises the aileron on the right wing. This brings the left wing up, the right wing down. He also turns the rudder on the tail to the right.

What happens on the flight deck?

The pilot and co-pilot of a passenger aircraft spend most of their time watching the plane's instruments to check that everything is going smoothly. Because big aeroplanes nowadays are computerised, the pilots no longer need to keep their hands on the controls. The whole flight is followed closely by radar and radio contact from the ground. All pilots have to make a flight plan, which they give to the air-traffic controllers before leaving. This tells the controllers where the plane is going, so that they can keep that part of the sky clear from other planes.

4 The final approach
The pilot cuts the engine speed, which puts the aeroplane into a downward glide. When clearance is given from air-traffic control, the pilot makes the final approach to the runway, using a radio beam for guidance.

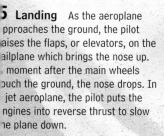

5 Landing As the aeroplane approaches the ground, the pilot raises the flaps, or elevators, on the tailplane which brings the nose up. A moment after the main wheels touch the ground, the nose drops. In a jet aeroplane, the pilot puts the engines into reverse thrust to slow the plane down.

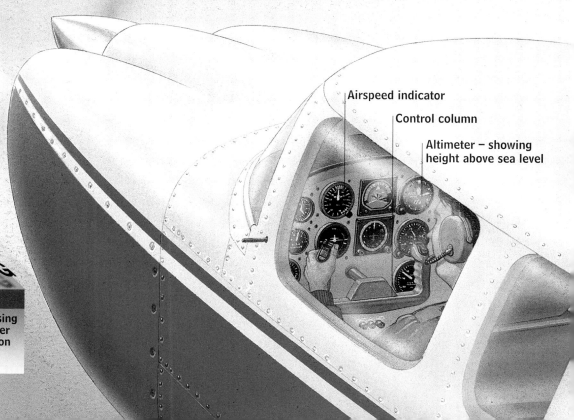

Airspeed indicator

Control column

Altimeter – showing height above sea level

THAT'S AMAZING

DEEP BREATHING

In 15 minutes, from takeoff to cruising height, each engine on a passenger jet sucks in as much air as a person breathes in 20 years.

The birth of the planets p.16 · Man on the Moon p.18 ·
Satellites in space p.180 · Fact File p.270-3, 323, 362, 369

Scientists launch spacecraft to find out more about the planets and what they are made of and about the Universe as a whole. Some craft travel around the Earth or go to the planets. Others explore deep space, taking photographs and gathering information. Some have crews who live in space for weeks or even months.

How does a spacecraft get into space?

When a spacecraft is launched, the huge engines burn fuel to make hot gases. These gases are fired out of the bottom of the spacecraft, creating a force that pushes the spacecraft upwards. This force is stronger than Earth's gravity – the force that pulls things towards the ground. If a spacecraft can get far enough away from Earth, it can go into orbit or venture into outer space.

3 Losing the main fuel tank The Shuttle flies upside down, carrying its main fuel tank piggyback. Once the tank is empty, it is blasted away and burns up in Earth's atmosphere.

2 Losing the boosters In four seconds or so, the booster rockets run out of fuel and break away from the Shuttle. They parachute into the sea and are recovered and re-used.

Why do people float in space?

In space, there is no gravity. People become weightless and float freely, with no sense of what is up and what is down. Astronauts train for this by putting on their spacesuits and practising their tasks submerged under water in a tank. This gives them some idea of how it will feel to float in space.

Helping hand The Shuttle's mechanical arm is used to move loads around.

Working inside the Shuttle
Because there is no gravity in space to hold things to the floor, everything floats around, including tools, sleeping-bags and even food, unless they are fixed down inside the spacecraft.

1 Shuttle liftoff The Shuttle's main engines and booster rockets shoot white-hot flames towards the launch pad, pushing the spacecraft into the air.

FLIGHT OF THE SHUTTLE
Unlike the rockets that went to the Moon, the Space Shuttle is a re-useable spacecraft. Only its main fuel tank needs replacing after each mission. The Shuttle has been used to deliver and mend satellites, to research the effect on humans of living in space, and to ferry crew members to and from the space station Mir.

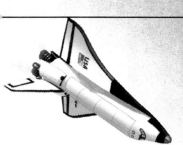

4 Into orbit Carrying the crew, equipment and any payload (cargo), the main part of the Shuttle, called the Orbiter, is now far enough from Earth to go into orbit.

THAT'S AMAZING

SPACE FOR EXPANSION

In space, people grow larger – by up to 5 cm (2 in). This is because there is no gravity to pull their body parts downwards. The increase in size can cause problems. On one Shuttle mission, the astronauts found they had grown so much that they could hardly squeeze into a tight-fitting chair that they were supposed to sit in for an important experiment.

Star gazer The Hubble Space Telescope has been orbiting the Earth since April 1990. It enables us to study distant galaxies.

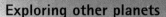

Cargo bay The cargo bay is where scientific equipment is kept. The doors open during orbit so that satellites can be launched. They can also be opened to let the Shuttle cool down.

Packed lunch The astronaut is eating from covered food containers so that his meal does not float away.

Exploring other planets

Since people first stepped on the Moon in 1969, scientists have wanted to explore the rest of the Solar System. So far, they have only sent probes (spacecraft without astronauts) to Mars, Venus and Saturn. The probes have sent back images of the planets and their moons, and analysed the chemicals that make up the planets. Scientists hope to send people to other planets one day, maybe to form research colonies.

Looking for life on Mars

No one knows if there has ever been life on Mars, although a lump of rock from the planet made the headlines in August 1996 because scientists thought it might contain the fossil of a simple life form. On July 4, 1997, the United States landed a spacecraft on Mars containing the first Mars rover. The six-wheeled rover, Sojourner, crawled down one of the spacecraft's ramps, and sent back television pictures of the surface of Mars. It also analysed the chemicals that make up the Martian rocks, soil and atmosphere.

Space probe Remote-controlled by engineers on Earth, Sojourner took over 16 000 images of Mars and made 15 chemical analyses.

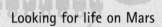

Space toilet Using the toilet in space is like sitting on an upturned vacuum cleaner. Everything sucked down it is dried out, and the extracted water recycled.

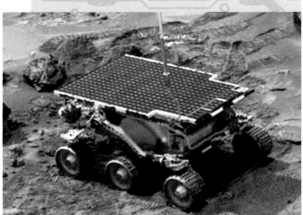

Food technology

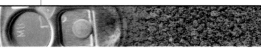

Food and nutrition p.138 · Travelling in space p.192 · Cooking, food and drink p.230 · Farms and farming p.234 · Fact File p.308

All food goes 'off' unless something is done to preserve it. For thousands of years people have known that you can keep fruits by drying them; fish and meat by smoking, pickling or salting them; and milk by turning it into yoghurt or cheese. In the past 200 years scientists have found out why these methods work. They have also discovered what substances our bodies need to stay healthy. New preserving techniques have been invented, such as canning, refrigerating, freeze-drying and irradiating – when food is exposed to radiation in order to kill off bacteria.

Why do bubbles appear when you open fizzy drinks?

Drinks are usually made fizzy by pumping CO_2 (carbon dioxide gas) into them. CO_2 dissolves easily in water, especially when it is under pressure in a bottle or can. The gas stays dissolved in the drink until someone opens the container. Then there is a hiss as the pressure is released and the gas comes out in the form of bubbles. As the drink warms up, more CO_2 is released. In champagne, fermenting yeast and sugar produce CO_2 inside the bottle. When the cork pops off, the gas bubbles up just as it does from a fizzy drink in a can.

PRESERVING THE PIZZA

Pizza is a traditional dish from Naples in Italy that has become one of the most popular foods in the world. Several forms of food technology, some ancient, some modern, go into the making and preserving of it.

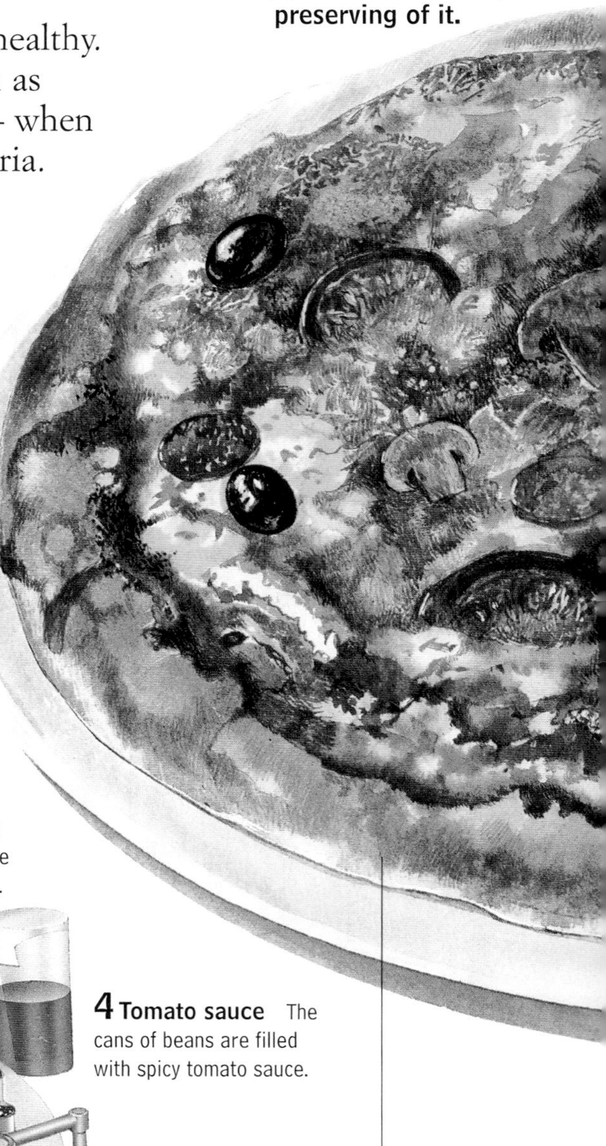

BEAN CANNING

Have you ever wondered how cans of baked beans are produced? This picture shows all the stages, from raw beans to finished article.

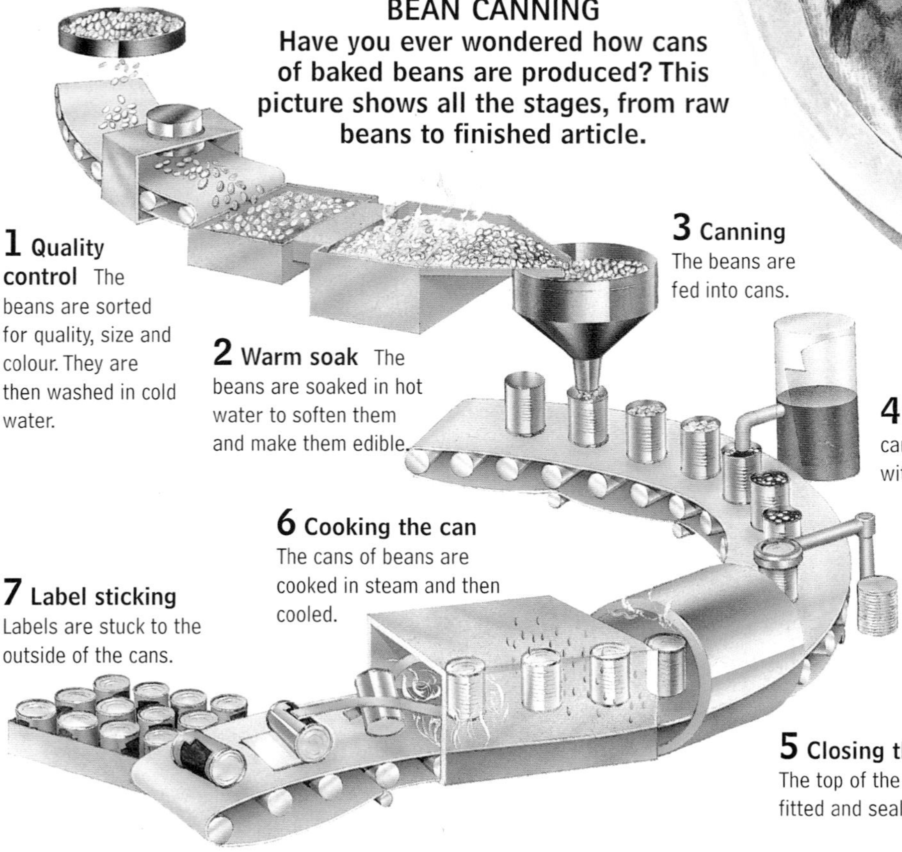

1 Quality control The beans are sorted for quality, size and colour. They are then washed in cold water.

2 Warm soak The beans are soaked in hot water to soften them and make them edible.

3 Canning The beans are fed into cans.

4 Tomato sauce The cans of beans are filled with spicy tomato sauce.

5 Closing the can The top of the can is fitted and sealed.

6 Cooking the can The cans of beans are cooked in steam and then cooled.

7 Label sticking Labels are stuck to the outside of the cans.

Pizza base The base of the pizza is a kind of bread dough – flour, water, oil and yeast mixed and left to rise. The flour is made from wheat germs ground between rollers or stones. The oil – a preservative as well as a food – is pressed from olives.

Dried herbs Thyme and oregano are scattered on the pizza to give it a pleasant flavour. Drying is an ancient form of preserving which takes away the water that bacteria and moulds need in order to live.

Ship's biscuit from a 19th-century polar expedition.

Salami Meat is preserved by drying and salting. Salt is one of the best preservatives, as nothing can live in it.

Explorer's food

People going on expeditions to dangerous or faraway places have to take specially prepared food with them. In the old days, sailing ships on long-distance voyages carried live chickens and sheep to make sure that the crew and any passengers had a good supply of fresh meat. They also carried hard-baked ship's biscuits which lasted for months without spoiling. Nowadays, astronauts take freeze-dried food. This process works by freezing food very quickly in a vacuum, then quickly heating it. Any liquid in the food was first turned into ice during the freezing, and then escapes as steam when the food is heated. The steam is sucked out by vacuum pumps. Experts claim that freeze-dried food loses little of its taste or nutritional value. At the same time, it is much lighter and less bulky for packing.

A range of freeze-dried astronauts' food.

How do they get runny caramel into chocolate bars?

You would think this was impossible – since surely the caramel would run out before the chocolate had set around it. The secret lies in a substance called invertase. This is an enzyme (a kind of chemical) that breaks down sugar into substances called fructose and glucose which dissolve more easily than sugar. To make a caramel chocolate bar, a thick sugary syrup is made. Invertase is added as the syrup cools and becomes a stiff paste. The paste is shaped and covered in melted chocolate. When the chocolate has cooled and hardened, it is warmed to 30°C (86°F). This does not melt the chocolate, but makes the invertase start breaking down the sugar and turning the thick caramel paste inside runny.

Cheese This is made by letting certain kinds of 'friendly' bacteria breed in milk. These, together with salt, prevent it from going off. Pizzas are made with mozzarella, a soft cheese that takes just a few days to make. Sometimes they also have a hard cheese such as Parmesan sprinkled on top. Hard cheeses take months or even years to mature.

THAT'S AMAZING

FRESH AFTER 120 YEARS

Tinned foods date from the Napoleonic Wars in the early years of the 19th century. In 1938 British scientists opened some tins of roast veal and carrots that had been supplied to the Royal Navy in 1818. The food was in perfect condition, although not particularly tasty!

New foods

Many new foods are gimmicks – novelty sweets, snacks and breakfast cereals. They have simple ingredients, like sugar, flour and fat which are highly processed and do not give the body much that it needs to stay healthy. Other new foods are more useful, and may help to solve one of the world's greatest problems – hunger in the poorest countries. Some new foods are created by 'genetic engineering' – changing the character of plants like wheat, rice and corn, so that they give better crops.

Generating energy

Fossil fuels p.52 · Energy and heat p.152 ·
Electricity and magnetism p.158 · Fact File p.282

Life runs on electricity. Through every light bulb, computer, radio and TV runs the same invisible energy. As we use more electricity, we have to find new ways of making it without harming the environment. This means using the energy to be found in nature – heat from the Sun and the Earth, the power of waves, rivers and wind to generate electricity.

Where does most electricity come from?

To create electricity, you need a generator and turbines. Inside the generator, where the electricity is made, a coil of wire spins at high speed between the two poles of a magnet. Turbines spin the coil. In most power stations, the turbines are fan-like machines with blades that turn when hot gases, or steam, are passed through them at high pressure. Steam is made by heating water using gas, coal, oil or nuclear energy. Around three-quarters of the world's electricity is made like this.

Power house   Inside the turbine generator room at a power station in Alaska.

Other ways to make electricity

Electricity can be made using any source of heat or movement, including the Sun, waves and tides. Some power stations, known as geothermal power stations, use the natural heat of rocks below the Earth's surface to make steam to drive the generator's turbines. One is The Geysers power station in California, which supplies most of the electricity for San Francisco. In France there is a power station, the River Rance barrage, that harnesses the force of flowing tides. Built in 1967, it was the world's first tidal power station. Wave-powered generators are being developed but these are not yet efficient enough to be widely used.

A geothermal power station, New Zealand.

FROM THE POWER STATION TO YOUR HOME

Electricity is generated in power stations and then sent all over a region or country through a network of cables called a grid. It is measured in volts. In modern power stations like the one below, burning natural gases drive a gas turbine generator. Nothing is wasted, since the hot exhaust gases are then used to turn water into steam in a boiler. The steam drives yet another generator producing electricity.

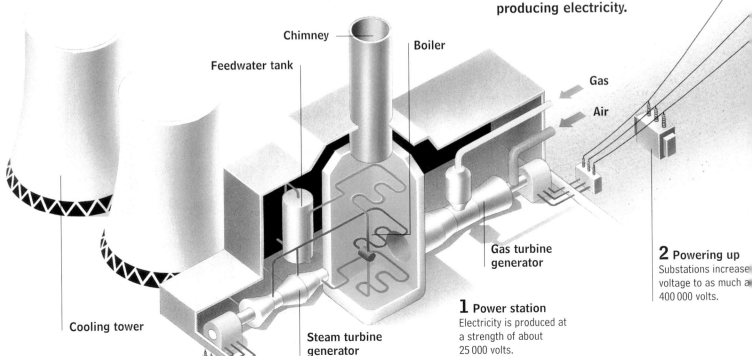

Chimney

Boiler

Feedwater tank

Gas

Air

Gas turbine generator

2 Powering up
Substations increase voltage to as much a 400 000 volts.

Cooling tower

Steam turbine generator

1 Power station
Electricity is produced at a strength of about 25 000 volts.

Wind turbine The whirling 'egg-whisk' wind turbine devised by Georges Darreius.

How do we get electricity from the wind?

Wind turbines catch the power of moving air. The wind spins a rotor shaped like the blades of an aeroplane propeller, and this drives a shaft connected to a generator. The rotor has a rudder at the back which turns the rotor to face into the wind. The Darreius wind turbine, invented by a Frenchman called Georges Darreius in 1927, uses two curved blades attached at the top and the bottom to a vertical shaft. It can catch the wind from any direction. Wind turbines are usually placed on high ground, where the wind blows faster. Less than 1 per cent of the world's electricity is currently generated by wind power, or by other alternative sources, but this will probably grow.

5 In the home
Local power lines take the electricity to more substations where the voltage is lowered for home use.

4 End users
Substations 'step down' the voltage to between 11 000 and 33 000 volts for use in factories.

3 Cross country Pylons or underground cables carry the high-voltage lines across the region or country.

Control room

Electrical room

Turbine

Water

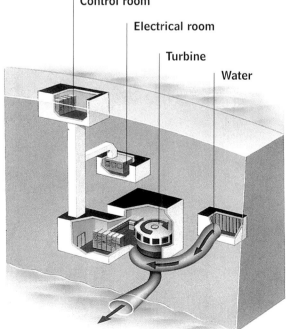

Hydroelectric power station Water from the dam spins a turbine. This, in turn, drives a generator which creates electricity.

s a dam make y?

river has enormous energy sands of tons of water on the move. A dam that energy and converts tricity. As the water rushes ough pipes in the dam, it ines that turn the coils in tors. About a quarter of s electricity is generated by s is known as Hydroelectric HEP. The advantage of at it does not pollute the nt, although when a dam an flood large areas of force people to move.

THAT'S AMAZING

EELY ELECTRICITY

The electric eel produces a 650 volt charge from the muscles and nerves in its tail. This charge stuns its prey. It is nearly three times as powerful as the electricity in our homes.

🌐 Bridges, dams and tunnels p.200 · Home life p.228 ·
Architectural styles p.238 · Fact File p.316

From simple wooden huts to dizzying skyscrapers, human beings have invented all kinds of buildings. Like animals, we build safe places where we can eat, sleep and bring up our families. We also make special buildings for work and leisure, such as offices, schools and museums. Some of the world's greatest buildings are monuments – like the Taj Mahal in India, which is an emperor's expression of love for his dead wife.

THAT'S AMAZING

HOME COMFORTS

The home of the computer software tycoon Bill Gates cost over $53 million. It has 24 bathrooms, 6 kitchens, a sports complex, a swimming pool with underwater music, and a private cinema with its own popcorn machine.

How are buildings protected against earthquakes?

Wood-framed buildings can bend and shake without falling down. Specially reinforced concrete buildings constructed around steel frames are also flexible enough and strong enough to stand up to most earthquakes. Stone and brick (masonry) buildings suffer most because they are heavy and have no way of bending. In earthquake zones, masonry buildings are avoided and steel frames preferred.

Built to last An earthquake-resistant, wood-framed building is under construction in Kobe, Japan – the site of a devastating earthquake in 1995.

Why don't skyscrapers topple over?

Foundations are very important. Skyscrapers stand on huge reinforced concrete rafts, which are supported by piles that go deep underground to rest on solid rock. Skyscrapers are also built on a framework of steel girders – the walls, floors, windows and ceilings are all fixed to this framework. Strong winds are a threat to skyscrapers. All tall buildings move in the wind, and some have rolling weights inside them to counterbalance the wind and stop the building from swaying too much.

Ground work Engineers work on the foundations of the Commerzbank.

Higher and higher and higher

Since 1996 the world's highest building has been the Petronas Twin Towers in Malaysia. At 452 m (1483 ft) the two towers are nearly 9 m (30 ft) higher than the previous record-holder, the Sears Tower in Chicago. It is the first time that the world's highest building has not been in North America. In 2001 the Petronas Towers are due, in their turn, to be outstripped – by a 460 m (1509 ft) World Financial Centre in Shanghai, China.

Petronas Twin Towers

What will homes be like in the future?

Buildings in the future will have to be less damaging to the environment and to people's health than they are today. That means using as little energy and as many natural, recycled and non-toxic materials as possible: solar energy for heating and hot water, efficient insulation to keep buildings warm in winter and cool in summer, low-energy lightbulbs, the use of sunlight instead of electricity for daytime lighting, and building materials like straw, paper and tiles made with recycled glass. Already companies are producing wood-like planks and boards for

Green home A turf roof shelters a home in the north of England.

shelves and cupboards that are made from pressed wheatstalks, glue and recycled junk mail!

EUROPE'S TALLEST
The headquarters building for Commerzbank in Frankfurt is now, at 259 m (850 ft), the tallest building in Europe. Over 2500 people work there. The illustration (below) shows it being built in 1996, with the building works in close-up (right).

Building site
Small cranes at the top of the building manoeuvre the giant steel frames into position, as the building grows at the rate of two storeys a week. Sections such as window frames are made beforehand (prefabricated) to save time on site. At the foot of the skyscraper are the underground piles on which the building rests. At the top of a skyscraper there are TV aerials, satellite dishes, air-conditioning intakes and a roof terrace.

🌐 Cars and bicycles p.182 · The age of the train p.184 · Houses and buildings p.198 · Fact File p.316

Roads, railways, bridges, canals, dams, tunnels and harbours are complicated to build. They have to stand up to enormous stresses, both from extreme weather conditions and heavy use. The structures, and the materials used, must be strong and last for many years. The person in charge of designing them is a civil engineer, whose calculations have to be very accurate, as many people's lives and large sums of money depend on them.

Direct line   Railway tracks have to be as straight, level and stable as possible. The rails are laid on wooden or concrete 'sleepers' which sit on a thick bed of crushed rock or stones.

How are bridges built across wide rivers?

All bridges rest on large pillars known as piers. Sometimes these piers have to be built in a river. As building underwater is impractical, a dry area has to be created. To do this in shallow water, interlocking sheets of steel are driven into the riverbed to form a waterproof circle. The water is then pumped out of the enclosure, and a pier is built inside on foundations resting on rock below the riverbed. In deeper water, a giant concrete tube is used instead.

How are tunnels made?

First, geologists (experts in rocks and how they are formed) carry out a survey to find out what kinds of rock or soil lie in the area of the tunnel. Then the best route is chosen. Tunnels through soft rock like chalk are excavated by laser-guided drilling machines. If the rock is hard, it is blasted out with explosives. Supports are put up as quickly as possible to prevent the roof from collapsing. Temporary railways or roads are built inside the tunnels to remove the broken rock and to carry workers in and out.

Load bearing
Bridges carry so much weight that they have to be built on solid rock or on concrete rafts to spread the load widely. A series of short spans, forming a viaduct, can also spread the load.

High dam   The Hoover Dam on the Colorado River is the highest dam in the United States.

Why don't dams burst?

Engineers design dams to suit the size and site of the river. Dams across wide rivers are known as embankment dams; they are made of soil, clay, stone and cement. Dams in narrow river gorges have thick concrete walls, built in a curve or supported by buttresses to give them extra strength. All dams have deep foundations to prevent water from flowing under them, and to anchor them against the weight of the water. Another safety feature is the spillway, which channels water from heavy rains around the sides of the dam.

THAT'S AMAZING

LONGEST BRIDGES

The world's longest bridge is the Pontchartrain Causeway in Louisiana, USA, finished in 1969. It is 38 km (24 miles) long and is supported by 9000 concrete piers. The longest suspension bridge in the world is the 1991 m (6532 ft) Akashi-Kaikyo Bridge in Japan, completed in 1998.

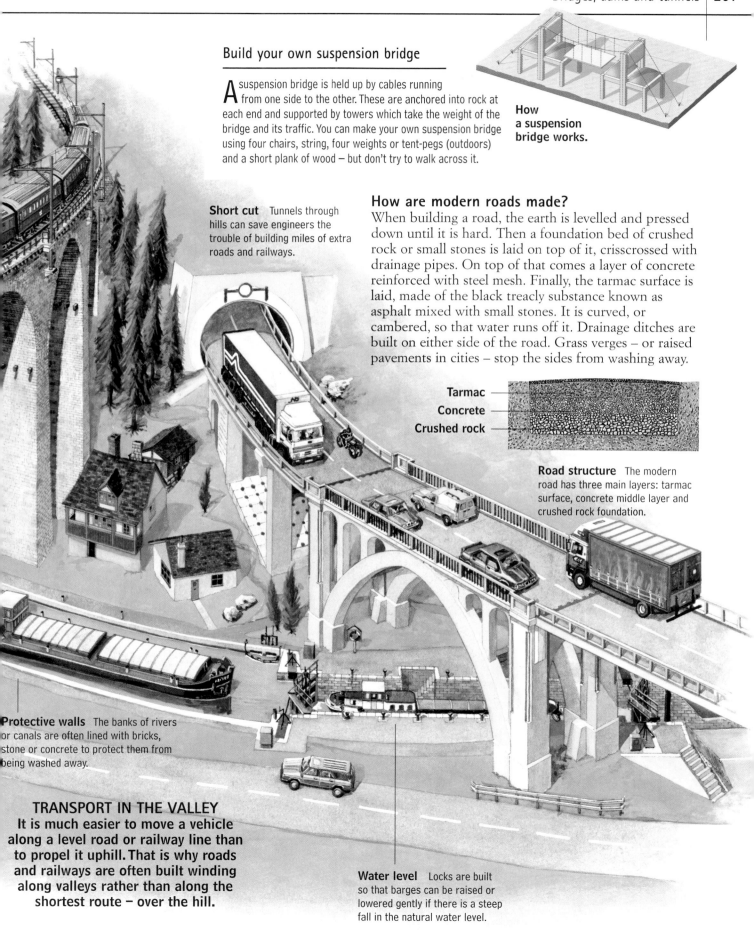

Build your own suspension bridge

A suspension bridge is held up by cables running from one side to the other. These are anchored into rock at each end and supported by towers which take the weight of the bridge and its traffic. You can make your own suspension bridge using four chairs, string, four weights or tent-pegs (outdoors) and a short plank of wood – but don't try to walk across it.

How a suspension bridge works.

Short cut Tunnels through hills can save engineers the trouble of building miles of extra roads and railways.

How are modern roads made?

When building a road, the earth is levelled and pressed down until it is hard. Then a foundation bed of crushed rock or small stones is laid on top of it, crisscrossed with drainage pipes. On top of that comes a layer of concrete reinforced with steel mesh. Finally, the tarmac surface is laid, made of the black treacly substance known as asphalt mixed with small stones. It is curved, or cambered, so that water runs off it. Drainage ditches are built on either side of the road. Grass verges – or raised pavements in cities – stop the sides from washing away.

Tarmac
Concrete
Crushed rock

Road structure The modern road has three main layers: tarmac surface, concrete middle layer and crushed rock foundation.

Protective walls The banks of rivers or canals are often lined with bricks, stone or concrete to protect them from being washed away.

TRANSPORT IN THE VALLEY
It is much easier to move a vehicle along a level road or railway line than to propel it uphill. That is why roads and railways are often built winding along valleys rather than along the shortest route – over the hill.

Water level Locks are built so that barges can be raised or lowered gently if there is a steep fall in the natural water level.

⊙ **Computers and electronics p.172 · The written word p.210 · The mass media p.254 · Fact File p.318-23, 344-63**

There have been at least three 'information revolutions' before our time. The first was the invention of writing 5000 years ago. The second was the invention of printing, first in China some time before the 8th century AD, then in Europe in the 15th century. The third revolution, the electronic revolution, began in 1837 when the electric telegraph was invented. Later came radio, telephone, sound recording, television and computers. Today's technologies, including the wonders of the Internet, mean that people can do things with information that few could have imagined even 20 years ago.

THAT'S AMAZING
LOST IN CYBERSPACE
Cyberspace is where all of the information available on the world's computers exists. How big is cyberspace? It is estimated that the amount of information now available in cyberspace is about two and a half times the total amount of written information created since the first words were written 5000 years ago in the Middle East.

What is the Internet?
When several computers are connected, they form a network. The people using them can share information, ask and answer questions, send notes, play games or buy and sell things. The Internet is a giant version of this – an International Network – with computers all over the world connected by telephone and satellite. To link up to the Internet, you need a computer, a modem (which connects your computer to a phone line), and an Internet Service Provider (ISP), which is a company with computers connected permanently to other computers.

Smileys
People who enjoy playing with computers have invented a series of symbols to show how they are feeling when they send an email or chat on the Internet. These are sometimes called 'emoticons' (emotional icons) or just 'smileys'. Turn them sideways to see how they work. This one **:-(** means 'sad'. This one **:-D** means 'laughing'. What do you think these ones mean **:-)** and **:-o** and **;-)** and **$-)**? The answers are on the opposite page.

GLOBAL CHAT
You can use the Internet to exchange messages with friends. You can also get information on thousands of topics via the World Wide Web – a system for publishing information on the Internet. You get into the Web using a 'browser' (such as Netscape or Microsoft Explorer), and you search it for information using a 'search engine' (such as Yahoo or HotBot).

From France A girl in Paris sends a picture of herself beside the Eiffel Tower to an email pal in the Caribbean and to another in New York.

Caribbean contact A young boy in St Lucia in the Caribbean receives an email on a laptop.

What is a website?

A website is a kind of electronic magazine published on the Internet. Each website has an address, known as a URL (Uniform Resource Locator), so that you can find it easily among the millions that exist on the World Wide Web. Reader's Digest has a number of websites, including http://www.readersdigest.com and http://www.readersdigest.co.uk. Most websites cost nothing to visit, apart from the cost of the phone call connecting your computer to the Internet. Many have pictures and links to other sites on similar subjects. Anyone with a computer connected to the Internet can create their own website, using a simple set of instructions known as HTML (HyperText Markup Language).

Home page Why not search for the Reader's Digest website on the World Wide Web?

Networking in New York A boy in New York accesses the same picture from his email pal in France on his handheld computer.

Protocol This is the system used to send Web pages around the Internet.

Host name This is the name of the company or owner of the website.

File path This takes you to other documents deeper in the host's site.

http://www.readersdigest.com/index.asp

Exploring a website To visit a website on the World Wide Web, you key the address, or URL. The address has two main parts: the protocol and the host name. A third part, the file path, will appear automatically as you explore.

How does email work?

The 'e' in email stands for electronic. Electronic mail is a form of postal system in which everything – writing a letter, as well as addressing, sending and reading it – is done electronically. Email letters are sent from one person's computer to another, via an electronic 'mailbox' kept on the Internet Service Provider's computer. It takes just a few seconds to deliver down the phone; it is much cheaper than ordinary mail and it can be sent or picked up at any time, anywhere in the world – even on an aeroplane.

Answers to smileys **:-)** = happy **:-o** = shocked **;-)** = winking **$-)** = greedy

The Human World

5

The story of evolution p.58 · Prehistoric animals p.72 · Hunters and h▢
p.82 · People of the world p.220 · Fact File p.274, 344

Human beings are animals, our closest relations being the apes. The remarkable skills developed by our early ancestors set them apart from their fellow creatures. They lived and hunted in organised groups, made tools and weapons, and could make and use fire. All this took time. Over millions of years, different species evolved before the emergence of our species, *Homo sapiens* (Thinking Person), some 300 000 years ago. Modern humans, *Homo sapiens sapiens*, began emerging around 100 000 years ago.

Cooking Meat was probably first dropped in a fire accidentally, and turned out more tender cooked than raw.

Are humans really related to the apes?

Scientists classify us among the primates, a group of mammals with five fingers and toes, and fingernails and toenails instead of claws. Primates first emerged on Earth about 65 million years ago. Because of the similarities in bones, teeth and body tissue, archaeologists believe that our closest relatives among the primates are the apes, such as the gorilla and the chimpanzee (our closest relative of all). Over time, humans developed larger brains than other primates and started walking upright. This development left their hands free for using tools. The first human-like creatures emerged in Africa around 4.8 million years ago. Scientists call them the australopithecines (southern apes).

Skinning People used stone tools to scrape the skin off pieces of meat.

Relative Chimpanzees can hold a stone and use it to crack open nuts.

HUNTING, SKINNING AND COOKING
From around 200 000 to 30 000 years ago, Europe and the Near East were occupied by a type of early *Homo sapiens* called the Neanderthals. They hunted by throwing spears at their prey and then chasing the injured animal until it was exhausted.

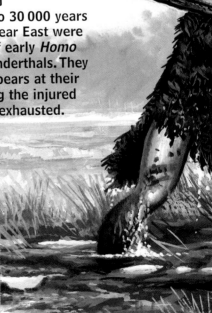

Where did the first people live?

Because the earliest fossilised remains of human-like creatures have come from sites in Africa, scientists assume that humans first emerged there. Remains have been found in eastern Africa, especially in the Rift Valley, which runs from Ethiopia down to Mozambique. A species called *Homo habilis* appeared there around 2.3 million years ago. They lived in organised social groups, making crude tools and probably communicating with basic speech. A later species, *Homo erectus,* spread from Africa across Asia and Europe. These people used fire, which would have kept them warm in northern climates.

THAT'S AMAZING

TELLTALE RELICS

'Lucy' is the name given to the skeleton of an australopithecine found in Ethiopia in 1974. She was about 1 m (3 ft) tall. Lucy lived 3 million years ago, and the shape of her skeleton suggests that she walked upright. At Laetoli in Tanzania, archaeologists have found fossilised footprints of creatures that walked on two legs, dating back 3.5 million years.

egypto- Proconsul Australopithecines *Homo*   *Homo*   *Homo sapiens*   *Homo*
ithecus   *habilis* *erectus* *neanderthal-* *sapiens*
                                                            ensis   *sapiens*

Brainy types
Increasing
brain size was
matched by
larger skulls.

What did humans look like millions of years ago?

Humans evolved from small-brained, monkey-like creatures,
through several gradual stages, into modern humans. The
australopithecines were the first to walk upright. They had a
powerful jaw, a low forehead and a brain about one-third
the size of ours. *Homo habilis* (Handy Person), who
lived 2.3 million years ago, had a larger brain. *Homo
erectus* (Upright Person), who lived 1.9 million
years ago, had a large   brain and a smaller jaw.

Prehistoric toolkit

Although some animals and birds use
tools to find food, humans are the only
creatures that use tools to make other
tools. *Homo habilis* collected stones and
used other stones to reshape them into
simple implements for cutting or scraping.
By the time of *Homo sapiens*, tools were
more sophisticated. As well as
stones, people used bones,
antlers and wood to
make carefully
crafted
arrowheads, axes
and harpoons.

**Neanderthal
tools were
made from
pieces of
stone (above).**

**Flint dagger from
3600 years ago.**

Hunting
A group of
Neanderthal hunters
attack an injured
woolly rhinoceros
with spears and
large stones.

The rise of civilisation

🔵 Origins of the human race p.206 · Farms and farming p.234 · Craft skills p.242 · Fact File p.344, 351

Groups of prehistoric hunters gradually learned how to sow crops such as barley and maize and to herd animals, and revolutionary changes in human society began to take place. People started living in settled villages and towns in order to tend their fields all year round. In the fertile river valleys of Egypt and Mesopotamia, these communities gradually grew into large, highly organised societies. The first great cities emerged, and government and trade developed.

Mayan pyramid The Pyramid of the Magician at Uxmal in northern Mexico. Mayan pyramids had a long flight of steps leading to a temple at the top.

Why did people build pyramids?

As building skills developed, people created monumental architecture to celebrate their gods and kings. The pyramid shape may have been chosen because it was a very stable structure for a large building. One of the earliest known pyramids is at Ur in Mesopotamia. It is a temple pyramid built around 4000 years ago. The pyramids in ancient Egypt were built to house the tombs of kings and to ease their journey into the afterlife. The burial chamber would be filled with treasure and located in the heart of a huge, solid pyramid to deter tomb-robbers. Other civilisations that built temple pyramids were the Mayans (4th-9th centuries) and the Aztecs (14th-15th centuries) in Central America.

RAISING A PYRAMID
Egypt's largest pyramid, the Great Pyramid at Giza, was built in the 26th century BC to house the tomb of a king, or pharaoh, called Khufu. It stands 146 m (480 ft) high, and is made from 2.3 million massive stone blocks, each weighing, on average, 2.5 tonnes.

Ramps Teams of workers hauled the stone blocks on sledges up mud-brick ramps, using ropes made from twisted papyrus – a reed that grows beside the Nile. The ramps were dismantled after the pyramid was completed.

Workshops Stone blo[cks] were cut to shape ready [for] hauling into place.

Minoan plumbing Fresh water was supplied to the Minoan palace of Knossos on Crete through terracotta pipes.

What was daily life like in ancient times?

The Minoan civilisation on Crete was the first civilisation in Greece and flourished around 2000 BC. Fine palaces were built; some even had plumbing. In early civilisations, there was often a big contrast between the lives of the rich and the poor. Noble families in ancient Rome lived in spacious villas with marble floors and furniture made of bronze, ivory or wood. The poor people of Rome lived in crowded slum buildings five or six storeys high and existed on bread or porridge.

Civilised living
A Roman glass jug and bowl.

Finished pyramid When all the stone blocks had been laid, the whole pyramid was covered with polished limestone slabs.

How did people get about?

Wheels changed from solid to spoked. Many Roman roads were straight.

Wheeled vehicles were first used in Mesopotamia around 3200 BC. Ox-carts with solid wooden wheels carried merchants' wine jars and grain sacks. Around 2000 BC, lighter, spoked wheels were invented for war chariots and speedier vehicles appeared. The Romans built straight roads so that the army could get about quickly. The roads made travel easier and could take heavy wagons.

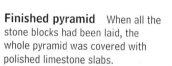

Temple

Workforce Modern scholars believe that it took 4000-5000 labourers several years to build the Great Pyramid. The workforce was probably made up of farmers, who worked on the pyramid when they could not farm due to the annual flood.

How did farming change things?

Crop-growing produced more food than hunting and gathering had done and not everyone was needed to work the land. Town craftsmen such as potters and jewellers emerged, and developed specialist skills. Architects evolved the techniques needed for building palaces and temples. People worked together on large projects, such as digging irrigation channels to bring water to dry areas of land.

THAT'S AMAZING

THE FIRST CITY

The Bible tells how Joshua and the Israelites brought down the walls of the city of Jericho with a blast of trumpets. Archaeologists have shown that Jericho really existed – and may have been the world's first city. It grew up in a farming area of the Middle East, and by 8000 BC it had massive stone walls. So when Joshua captured it in about 1400 BC, Jericho was several thousand years old.

🌐 Printing and publishing p.178 · The languages we speak p.222 · The world of literature p.244 · Fact File p.318, 344-5, 352, 376

P ineapple ... sword ... newspaper ... explosion – written words cause images to appear in the mind as if by magic. The invention of writing was one of the most important events in history, because it allowed information of every kind to be recorded and stored. And with the invention of printing in Europe in the 15th century, the number of books in circulation quickly increased. This led to the spread of knowledge and greater use of written languages.

Who invented writing?

Writing began around 3500 BC among the people of Mesopotamia, where priests and merchants wanted to keep records of harvests or areas of land sold. To begin with, picture-symbols were used. These were simplified representations of objects or people, such as 'sun', 'ox' or 'king'. Gradually, these pictures, known as pictograms, became simpler still, so that the writer could use wedge-shaped marks to represent each object and action. The marks were made with reed-tips on wet clay tablets, which then dried and hardened. This early script is known as 'cuneiform' (from the Latin *cuneus* meaning 'wedge').

WRITING TO PRINTING

In the 1440s, a German goldsmith named Johann Gutenberg invented a printing press made from a converted wine press. He spent several years perfecting it. The machine held lines of movable type made up of individual metal letters. Ink was dabbed onto the metal letters by hand, and the press applied the pressure needed to transfer the inked text onto a sheet of paper.

Early pictogram for 'cow' **Simplified pictogram** **Wedge-shaped marks replace pictogram** **Simplified symbol**

Early writing
In Mesopotamia, simple picture-symbols gradually evolved into wedge-shaped marks (left). The Egyptians based their writing, called hieroglyphics (above), on drawings.

Symbol for 'cow' is simplified again

Type style Gutenberg shaped his letters in so-called Gothic style, to look like the ornate pen-writing of the day.

Writing implement
The Mesopotamians cut reed-tips to a triangular shape for making wedge-shaped symbols. The unshaped ends were used for round symbols.

Does all writing run from left to right?

Different writing systems developed around the world, and there were no common rules about the direction in which words or symbols should run. In traditional Chinese, the words are set out in columns rather than lines. This is probably because the earliest Chinese writing was done on strips of bamboo, which were arranged top to bottom. The Western custom of writing from left to right down the page became fixed by the ancient Greeks only around 1000 BC. Arabic script runs from right to left, so Arab newspaper readers begin on what would be the back page of a Western paper.

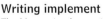

Top to bottom
Chinese writing runs in columns that are read from top to bottom and right to left across the page.

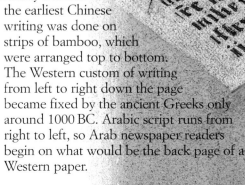

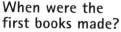

When were the first books made?

Egyptian scribes wrote on papery scrolls made from strips of papyrus, a reedy plant that grew by the Nile. True paper was a Chinese invention of around AD 100, and was made originally from a variety of materials, including pulped tree bark, hemp, old rags and fishing nets. Ancient China also gave the world the first surviving printed book, a Buddhist scripture printed from woodblocks in AD 868. In Europe, most books were copied by hand until the 1440s, and were rare and expensive. By 1500, thanks to Gutenburg's invention, cheap books were being printed in their thousands all across Europe.

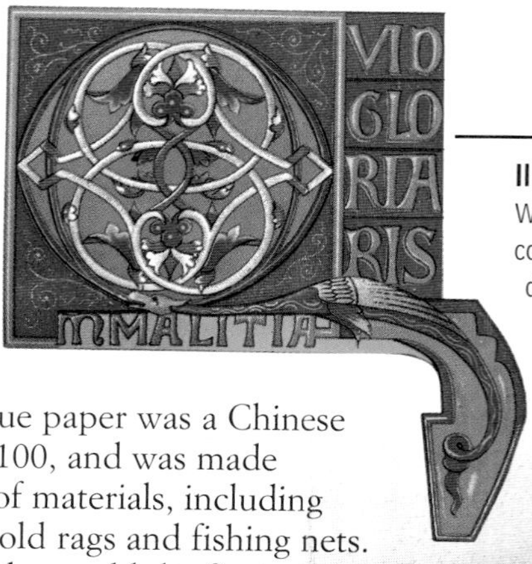

Illuminated letter
When medieval monks copied books by hand, they decorated the pages with beautiful letters and patterns.

Printing The printer prepared the press for printing a page of type.

Dabbers Leather pads were used for inking the type.

Typesetting
A person known as a compositor set up lines of metal letters in a special stick called a composition stick.

The story of the alphabet

A breakthrough in the story of writing occurred with the emergence of an alphabet in the Middle East around 1700 BC. In this system, each letter represents a single sound in the spoken language, rather than a whole object or idea.

The Phoenicians (who wrote from right to left) used a sound-based alphabet, and around 1000 BC their system was adopted by the ancient Greeks. The Greeks, however, reversed the shape of Phoenician letters and wrote from left to right. Greek letters may have been used by the Etruscans, who lived in central Italy before the Romans. Greek letters were borrowed by the Romans, who slightly reshaped them to create the alphabet we use today (the word alphabet comes from the first two Greek letters, *alpha* and *beta*).

Phoenician

Early Greek

Etruscan

Roman

Ships and seafaring p.186 · The movement of people p.214 ·
Fact File p.319, 353, 369

There were Arab and Chinese travellers during the Middle Ages, but it was from Europe, especially, that the great explorers came. From the mid 15th century onwards, an age of exploration dawned as European voyagers sailed the world's oceans in search of riches and new lands with which to trade.

Why did people go exploring?

No single reason can be given for the sudden urge in 15th and 16th centuries Europe to explore the planet. But it happened at a time when scientists were making discoveries about the world and its place in the Universe. Explorers were also lured by rumours of wealth in far-off lands. Missionary zeal was another reason: Spaniards led many of the early voyages, and they took priests to convert the people they found to Christianity.

Map-making
A 16th-century map of America based on European exploration.

How did early explorers find their way?

The magnetic compass was used for navigation from around the 11th century. The 15th-century compass consisted of a wooden box containing a magnetic needle balanced on a point, allowing it to pivot freely and find magnetic north. Arab navigators had invented a device called a cross-staff, which was lined up with the midday Sun, or a star, in order to work out its height above the horizon. This showed how far north or south a ship was. These instruments helped sailors find their way across the oceans.

THAT'S AMAZING
LOST TRIBE

In October 1993, the newspapers announced the discovery of a tribe of Stone-Age people, called the Liawep, in the jungles of Papua New Guinea. Dressed in leaves, they hunted wild pigs with bows and arrows and had never seen white people before.

Finding the way A ship's compass is shown above. The sextant (left) was invented in the 18th century for plotting a ship's position from the Sun and stars.

THE SANTA MARIA

Christopher Columbus made his first voyage to America in the *Santa Maria*, together with two smaller vessels, the *Pinta* and the *Nina*. They left the Canary Islands on September 6, 1492, and arrived in the Bahamas 33 days later.

Captain's cabin

The *Santa Maria*
Not much is known about Columbus's flagship, but it was probably a three-masted rig like this.

Tiller

Provisions All space below decks was taken up by stores and provisions – fresh water, wine, food, firewood, spare canvas and ropes, and powder and ammunition for the cannons.

Water The expedition had to carry all the fresh water they would need.

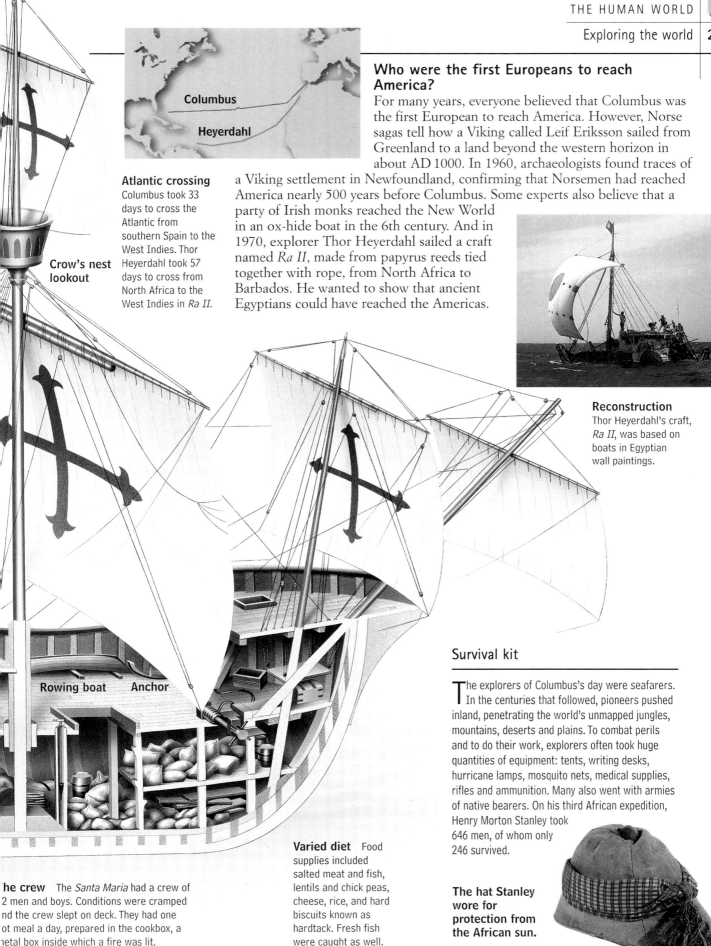

Columbus

Heyerdahl

Who were the first Europeans to reach America?

For many years, everyone believed that Columbus was the first European to reach America. However, Norse sagas tell how a Viking called Leif Eriksson sailed from Greenland to a land beyond the western horizon in about AD 1000. In 1960, archaeologists found traces of a Viking settlement in Newfoundland, confirming that Norsemen had reached America nearly 500 years before Columbus. Some experts also believe that a party of Irish monks reached the New World in an ox-hide boat in the 6th century. And in 1970, explorer Thor Heyerdahl sailed a craft named *Ra II*, made from papyrus reeds tied together with rope, from North Africa to Barbados. He wanted to show that ancient Egyptians could have reached the Americas.

Atlantic crossing
Columbus took 33 days to cross the Atlantic from southern Spain to the West Indies. Thor Heyerdahl took 57 days to cross from North Africa to the West Indies in *Ra II*.

Crow's nest lookout

Reconstruction
Thor Heyerdahl's craft, *Ra II*, was based on boats in Egyptian wall paintings.

Rowing boat   **Anchor**

Survival kit

The explorers of Columbus's day were seafarers. In the centuries that followed, pioneers pushed inland, penetrating the world's unmapped jungles, mountains, deserts and plains. To combat perils and to do their work, explorers often took huge quantities of equipment: tents, writing desks, hurricane lamps, mosquito nets, medical supplies, rifles and ammunition. Many also went with armies of native bearers. On his third African expedition, Henry Morton Stanley took 646 men, of whom only 246 survived.

The hat Stanley wore for protection from the African sun.

he crew   The *Santa Maria* had a crew of 2 men and boys. Conditions were cramped nd the crew slept on deck. They had one ot meal a day, prepared in the cookbox, a etal box inside which a fire was lit.

Varied diet   Food supplies included salted meat and fish, lentils and chick peas, cheese, rice, and hard biscuits known as hardtack. Fresh fish were caught as well.

🌐 Exploring the world p.212 · People of the world p.220 ·
Fact File p.349, 357

Far from home
The Vikings reached America around AD 1000. They settled for a short time and traded with the Native Americans.

P eople have been on the move since before historical records began, whether fleeing from their enemies or looking for new land to settle. Around 1600 BC a great famine in Canaan drove the Israelites to Egypt. Later, Vikings in longboats and Polynesians in canoes voyaged thousands of miles across the oceans. Humans, it seems, are natural wanderers.

How did humans spread across the Earth?

A narrow sea channel known as the Bering Strait divides Asia from North America. During the last Ice Age, the sea level was lower than it is today and the two continents were connected by dry land. Prehistoric people from Asia crossed this land bridge and spread down into the Americas, becoming the first Native Americans. Then, around 10 000 years ago, the sea flooded the Bering Strait and left the Indians stranded. It is thought that the first Aborigines reached Australia from South-east Asia in prehistoric times. New Zealand and other Pacific islands were settled by seafaring Polynesian islanders in more recent times.

Migration route
People crossed from Asia to North America.

Greenland

North America

VIKING EXPANSION
Most people think of the Vikings as seaborne raiders whose longships brought terror to European shores. They also made epic voyages to Iceland, Greenland and North America, and travelled south into Russia, and east to Constantinople. They were looking for new lands to settle and people to trade with.

The Slave Trade

Some mass movements of people have been forced. Between the 16th and 19th centuries, European traders shipped up to 20 million Africans across the Atlantic to America to work as slaves on sugar, tobacco and cotton plantations. Captives seized in the African interior were tethered together from neck to neck, force-marched to the coast and packed aboard slave ships. There, chained and starving, they were crammed below decks in layers as close, one trader admitted, 'as spoons fitting together'.

Slave caravan Slave traders in Africa bring in their captives, tethered together so they cannot escape.

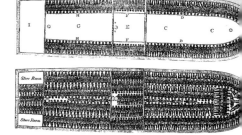

Cramped conditions
Black slaves were transported below decks. As many as 20-30 per cent of the slaves died during these voyages.

Raiders

Viking raids on Britain began in AD 793 with an attack on the Lindisfarne monastery.

An Italian family arrive in America in the early 1900s.

Why did America attract so many immigrants?

Between 1840 and 1914, 28 million people sailed to America to begin life afresh. Most were from Europe, and the first intakes came chiefly from two countries: from Ireland following repeated potato blights, and from Germany following a series of crop failures. Later tides of immigrants, including Italians, Greeks, Swedes, Poles, Slovaks, Russians and Jews also arrived. Some people came to farm the open prairies, or to find jobs in America's expanding industries. Others were fleeing injustice and persecution at home and seeking freedom in American democracy.

THAT'S AMAZING

NEW NATIONS

In Roman times, England and France were occupied by Celtic tribes. In the 5th century, the Franks from Germany invaded Gaul and created a Frankish kingdom – the original France. A tribe called the Angles crossed the English Channel to conquer what became known as Angle-land, or England.

Iceland

Norway   Sweden   Finland

Russia

Ireland

Denmark

Britain

Traders Norse merchants travelled along the rivers Dnieper and Volga into the heart of Russia, where they lived by trading with the local people.

France

Homemakers

Vikings built settlements abroad. Place-names in Britain ending in -*by*, -*thorpe* and -*beck* indicate a Viking presence.

Spain

Turkey

Exports

Viking traders' wares included furs, horn, walrus tusks and slaves.

The Industrial Revolution

● Cars and bicycles p.182 · The age of the train p.184 · Fact File p.320, 355, 376

In Britain, from the early 1700s, new inventions began to transform the way goods were produced. People used machines more and more to do work once done by hand. Factories were built, and were often sited near coalfields, which provided the fuel to feed the newly invented steam engines that powered the machines. Manufacturing towns grew up, connected at first by canals and later by railways.

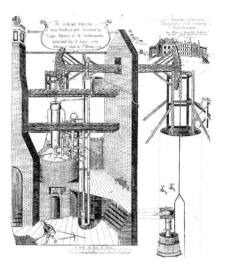

Steam Newcomen's steam engine pumped water out of flooded mines.

Why and where did the Industrial Revolution happen?

The invention of steam-driven machinery was a key reason for the Industrial Revolution. In 1712, an Englishman called Thomas Newcomen invented a steam-powered engine for pumping water. In 1775, James Watt from Glasgow made the steam engine more efficient, so it could power other machines.

Industrial development began in Britain, partly because the creation of the Bank of England in 1694 had helped businessmen to borrow money and open factories. Britain also had large supplies of iron for making goods and machinery. The Industrial Revolution spread through western Europe and the United States.

What was bad about it?

Industrialisation brought problems. Families who had once worked side by side in the fields were broken up. Factory workers were made to work long hours with hazardous fumes or dangerous machinery. In the coal mines there were accidents from roof falls and gas explosions. Smoke and soot from new coal-powered industries filled the air of factory towns.

Slums People moved to the cities in search of work, causing overcrowding and poverty.

New technology This cast-iron cooker was the latest in labour-saving devices in 1912.

How did life change for the better?

The Industrial Revolution brought many benefits. Advances were made in iron production, leading to the cheap manufacture of everything from iron bridges to iron frying-pans, and to the machines and engines used in textile mills and railway travel. Bumper harvests were achieved with new farm machinery, and transport by railways and steamships meant that food could be imported from other countries, giving people a more varied diet.

WORKING IN THE MILL
In the early 19th century, many mill-workers were women or children, because they had small, nimble fingers for working the threads and were cheaper to employ than men. They were forced to toil 12-16 hours a day.

Workers on the assembly line in an early **Ford** car factory.

Mass production

Factory output speeded up considerably when manufacturers adopted mass-production methods. The motor magnate Henry Ford pioneered this system in the United States. Instead of using skilled craftsmen to make a car from start to finish, he employed teams of workers to put together standardised parts. Each worker did the same one or two simple jobs on every car as the vehicles came past on a moving assembly line. The Model T Ford was launched in 1908, and 15 million were made in the next 19 years. Mass production meant that the 'Tin Lizzie', as the Model T was called, became cheap enough for ordinary families to afford. There was little variety in design, though. Ford said that the customer could have any colour so long as it was black!

Overseer Some overseers used whips or straps to punish workers who arrived late or neglected their machines.

Quality check A worker checks the weave of the cloth.

Young workers Younger children collected up cotton that fell between the looms, and sometimes tended the machines.

Machine operators Teenagers and adults operated the looms.

The history of warfare

➲ Working robots p.174 · Satellites in space p.180 · Ships and seafaring p.186 · Fact File p.344–363

Stone Age men hunted with flint axes and clubs, which they sometimes used for fighting each other, too. The development of metalworking led to finer weapons with sharper cutting edges. Ancient Mesopotamian soldiers wielded bronze swords and spears, and tougher, more damaging weapons made of iron appeared around 1000 BC. Wars tend to be won by the side that has the more advanced weapons.

Battering ram
This was made from a large tree trunk. It was mounted on wheels and operated by several men. The structure was covered with animal hides to give protection from arrows.

Early invention
Assyrian cavalry in the 9th century BC.

When did people first ride horses in battle?

Horses were first tamed around 2000 BC by nomads on the Asian steppes. Long afterwards, these warrior horsemen struck terror into neighbouring civilisations, and their riding skills were copied by their enemies. Egyptian pharaohs went into battle in horse-drawn chariots, and the Roman army included cavalry. The invention of stirrups around AD 400 allowed cavalrymen to carry lances and swords. By the Middle Ages, mounted knights fought in heavy chainmail, plate armour and visored helmets.

When was gunpowder invented?

Gunpowder is made by mixing saltpetre (potassium nitrate) with sulphur and powdered charcoal. A formula was published in AD 1044 in the Chinese *Complete Compendium of Military Classics*. In the 12th century, the Arabs used gunpowder to fire arrows from guns. Cannon, in which gunpowder is used to fire a cannonball, were in use in Europe from 1326.

Early flamethrower
Byzantine forces use a weapon called 'Greek fire' in a 13th-century illustration.

SIEGE MENTALITY

In medieval times, towns and castles were built with heavily fortified stone walls, towers, and walls within walls, to make them easier to defend, but attackers found all kinds of ways to breach the walls.

Fighters and bombers

Aircraft were first used in the First World War to spot enemy artillery positions. Fighter planes were invented soon afterwards, followed later in the war by the first bombers. During the Second World War, mass bombing of cities caused them to blaze like huge bonfires. In 1945, a single atom bomb dropped by the Allies on the Japanese city of Hiroshima killed or injured 130 000 people. Modern bombers and fighters are fitted with computers that navigate at supersonic speeds and calculate the positions of targets while on the move.

A stealth bomber can evade detection by radar.

Screens   Archers fired from behind movable wooden screens.

Scaling tower
These towers on wheels could be drawn up to the castle. The hinged drawbridge allowed attackers to storm the walls.

THAT'S AMAZING

OWN GOAL

Underwater warfare began in the 19th century. The first effective submarine attack was made in 1864, during the American Civil War, when the Confederates' *H.L. Hunley* fired a ram torpedo and sank an enemy ship. Unfortunately, the explosion blew up the submarine, too.

Catapult
A catapult being prepared for firing the walls. Some large stones at catapults could hurl stones weighing up to 90 kg (200 lb) over distances up to 275 m (300 yd).

Secret weapon
The British Mark V tank first went into action during the First World War.

Machine-age war

The machine gun, invented in 1884 by an American engineer called Hiram Maxim, eventually ended the supremacy of cavalry on the battlefield as horsemen were mown down in droves. During the First World War, the tank – an armour-plated gun turret mounted on caterpillar tracks – made its first appearance. The name 'tank' was a codeword invented by British officials, who wanted to keep their new weapon a secret. They hoped people would think they were talking about a water tank.

Genes and heredity p.132 · Origins of the human race p.206 · The movement of people p.214 · Fact File p.324–363

As the first humans spread across the world during prehistoric times, some settled at the margins of deserts, others at the edge of the frozen Arctic, and others still in the green depths of tropical rain forests. Over a long time, the climate, the amount of sunlight, the type of food available and many other factors affected the physical appearance of these isolated groups of people, and gave them distinct characteristics.

When did the races appear?

Modern humans, *Homo sapiens*, emerged about 100 000 years ago and spread through Europe, Africa and Asia. Among skeletons from this period, different human traits have been recognised. So a separation into races must have begun at a still earlier date, though no one can say exactly when they diverged. Genetic studies show that all people come from one common human stock, and that differences relate only to things such as skin colour, hair type and facial features.

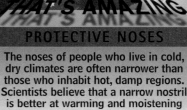

MELTING POT
There are five main racial groups in the world. Although each group originated in a particular area, they soon spread across the world.

THAT'S AMAZING

PROTECTIVE NOSES

The noses of people who live in cold, dry climates are often narrower than those who inhabit hot, damp regions. Scientists believe that a narrow nostril is better at warming and moistening chilly air as it enters the body, and so lessens the risk of harm to the lungs.

Inuits have a fold of skin covering the upper eyelid.

In the frozen north

The Inuit are a Mongoloid people of the Arctic regions. Their traditional life revolved around fishing and hunting seal and walrus among the ice floes, and over thousands of years they adapted physically to their surroundings. Their eyes are particularly narrow because their upper eyelids have developed a special fold of skin to protect their eyes from glare from the snow. A thick layer of flesh on their bodies provides insulation from the cold.

Why are some people white and some black?

As early humans spread around the world, groups settled in different climate zones. In hot, tropical areas, a high level of the dark skin pigment melanin protects the skin from strong sunshine, so people with plenty of melanin survived there better than people with pale skin. In cooler, cloudy climates, where the Sun is weaker, it is an advantage for skin to absorb more sunshine, which provides Vitamin D, so skin with less melanin is better.

Skin colour The melanin-producing cells are in the lower layers of the skin, and are very active. Melanin spreads through the upper layers, giving a darker colour.

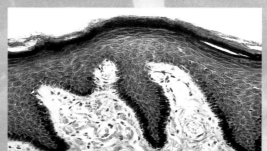

Why are some peoples taller than others?

Height has little to do with race. Heredity – the way in which characteristics are passed from parents to children – helps to determine how tall people grow, and operates within a small group much as it does in a family. Diet plays a part, too. Studies of certain groups have shown that children raised on a high-protein diet with plenty of meat and milk outgrow parents raised on a low-protein diet.

Tall and taller The Masai people of Africa are tall and slim, the ideal build for radiating heat and keeping cool in a hot climate.

Mongoloid This grouping is focused on east Asia and the Inuits of the Arctic region. Straight black hair and a flat, high-cheekboned face are characteristic.

Caucasoid This group originally lived in Europe, North Africa and the Near East. Skin colour is varied, ranging from the very pale complexion of Scandinavians to the dark brown of Berbers from North Africa and Indians.

Australoid This group includes the Aborigines, dark-skinned hunters and gatherers who inhabited Australia before the Europeans arrived.

Negroid This group's original area of settlement is Africa south of the Sahara. Features include heavy skin pigmentation, a broad nose and frizzy, dark hair.

Khoisanoid This group comprises the Bushmen and Hottentot people of South Africa. They are lighter skinned and more lightly built than their Negroid neighbours.

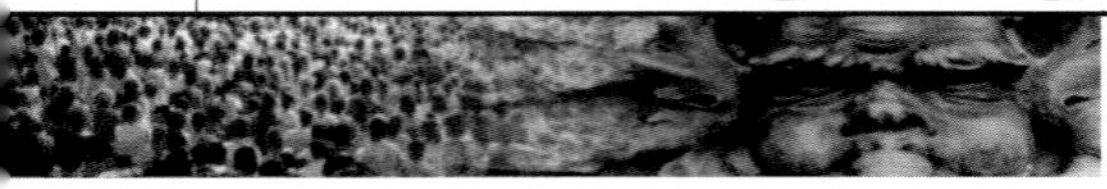

The written word p.210 · People of the world p.220 · Fact File p.324–343, 388

Animals communicate with each other through a range of about 30 vocal signals, but human language is vastly more complex. An adult human knows hundreds of thousands of words, and can arrange and rearrange those words in countless numbers of sentences. Language has played a key role in the evolution of human ideas and technology – nothing comparable exists among animals.

MANY LANGUAGES

The six official languages of the United Nations are English, French, Spanish, Russian, Chinese and Arabic. When an official makes a speech at the United Nations, translators whisper its equivalent into the headphones of ambassadors from other countries.

How did I learn my language?

Children learn to speak by imitating adults and older children. The first words that children use are simple words of recognition, such as 'mama' and 'dada'. Before they are one year old, children are capable of single-word statements such as 'there' or 'gone'. Before children are two, they have started to link words together to form basic sentences such as 'Want Mummy' or 'Teddy gone'. Next, children feel their way into more complex grammar, often making mistakes. For example, a two-year-old might say, 'Mama isn't boy, he a girl'. Children usually acquire all the essential language skills by the age of five. The learning process is much the same among all people, whether French or Chinese, English or Peruvian.

First words
In the first stages of learning to talk a baby watches its mother and listens intently to the sounds she makes as she speaks.

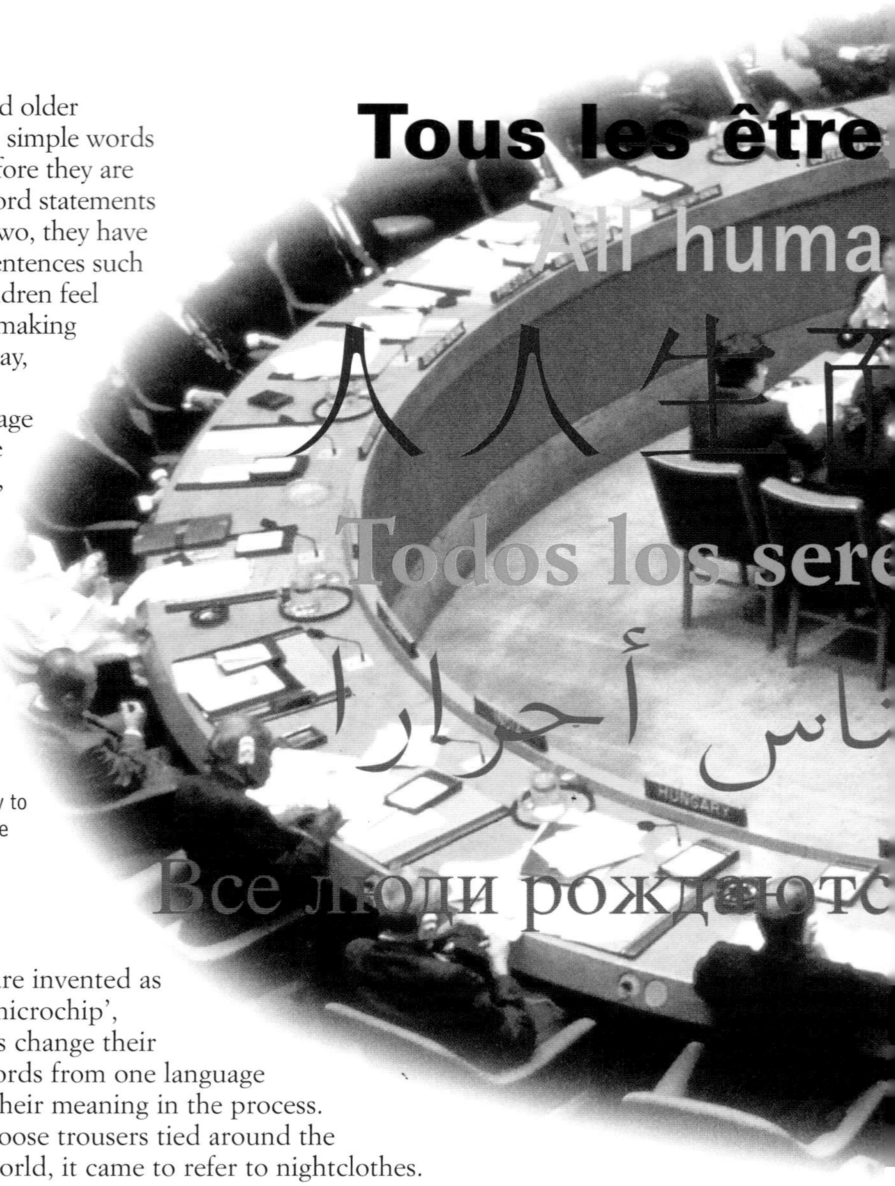

Do languages change?

Languages never stay the same; new words are invented as needed. Computer technology introduced 'microchip', 'download' and 'floppy disk'. Existing words change their meaning: 'silly' once meant blessed. Also, words from one language enter other languages, sometimes changing their meaning in the process. 'Pyjamas' was originally a Persian word for loose trousers tied around the waist. Imported into the English-speaking world, it came to refer to nightclothes.

Tous les être

All huma

人人生而

Todos los sere

أحرارا

ناس

Все люди рождают

pyjamas download micr

THAT'S AMAZING

THE MANY AND THE FEW

Chinese is the world's most spoken language. It is spoken by about 1 billion people. Sammarinese, the version of Italian used in the small republic of San Marino in Europe, is spoken by about 40 000 people. In Australia, there are around 200 different Aborigine languages, some of which are spoken by as few as six people each.

Why are there so many languages?

There are about 5000 languages in use today. They probably all descended from a handful of parent languages. As people migrated and became separated, different language 'families' developed. Chinese belongs to the Sino-Tibetan family of languages spoken in East Asia. French, Spanish and Italian, which all share Latin as their parent language, belong to the Indo-European family of languages.

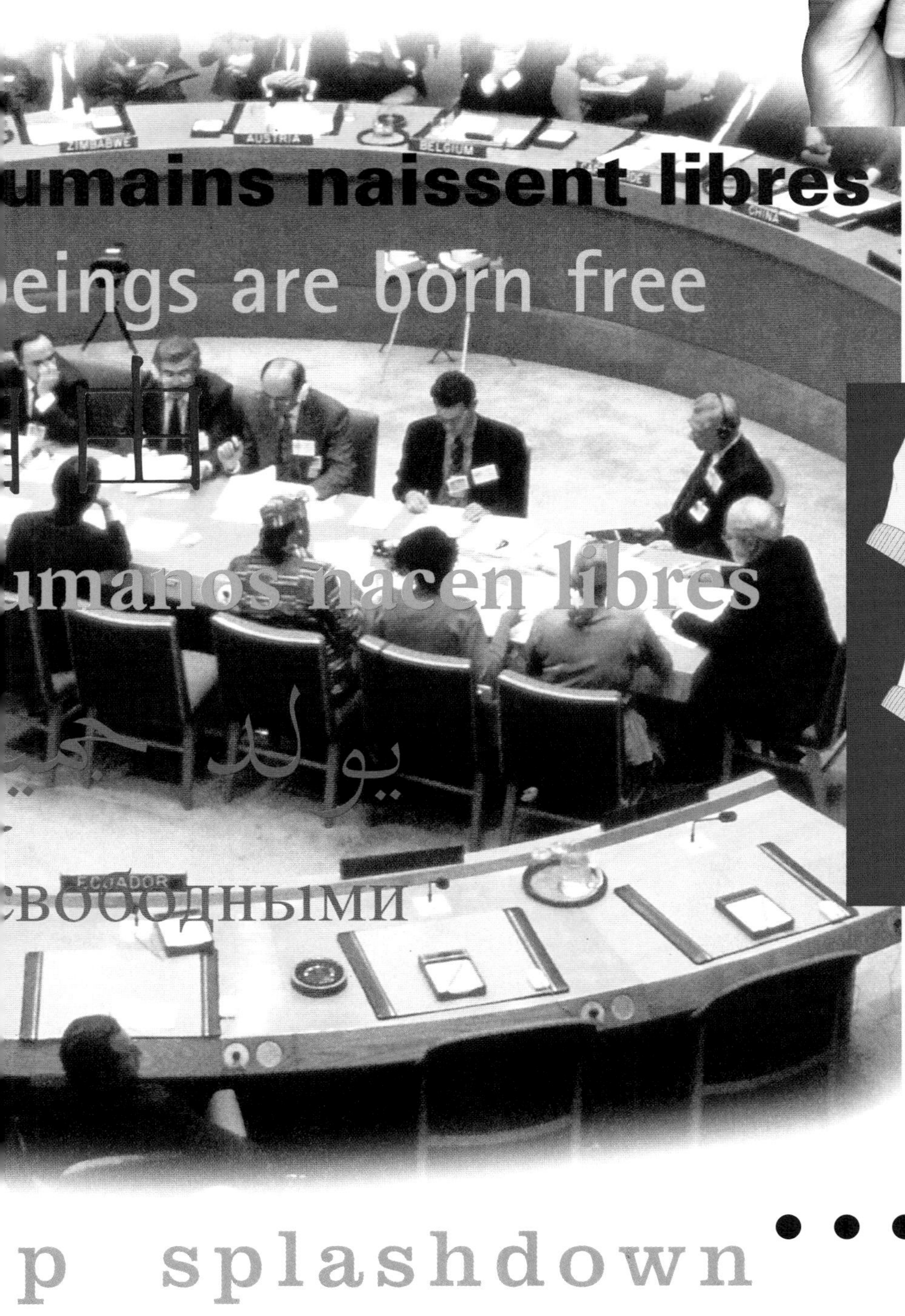

Sign language

Signs, codes and symbols provide non-verbal ways of communicating messages and ideas. A cross is a sign representing the Christian faith. The patterns and colours on a flag symbolise a nation. In the Second World War, people used the 'V' sign to signal their hopes of victory over Nazi Germany. Sometimes people use their bodies to send a message; for example, bowing indicates respect. For sending longer messages, visual and written codes can be used instead of written language. A system called semaphore, based on flags to represent letters, is used by ships and for railway signalling. Morse code uses dots and dashes. People sometimes invent secret codes. A simple version consists of replacing each letter with the next letter of the alphabet. So 'message' becomes 'nfttbhf'.

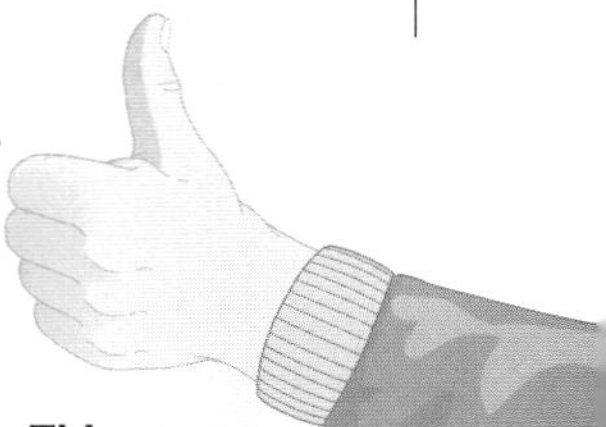

Things are looking good.

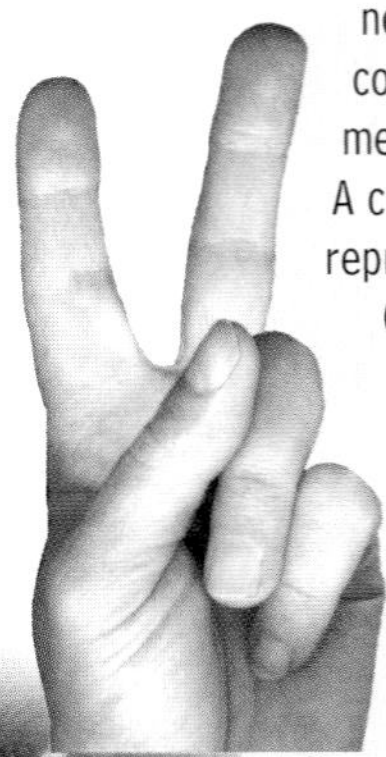

V for victory.

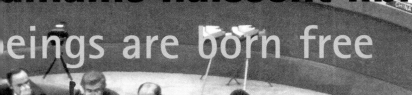

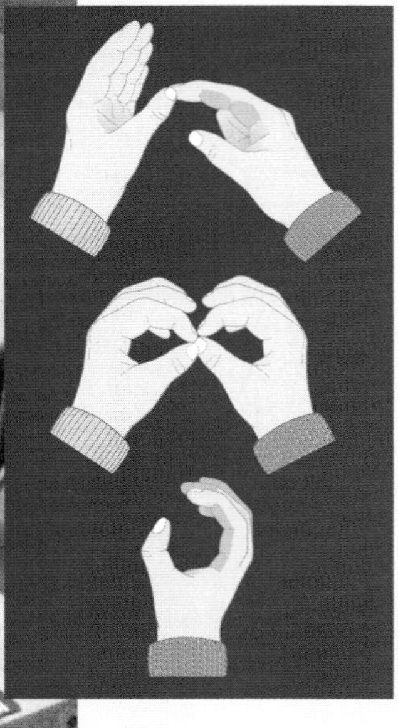

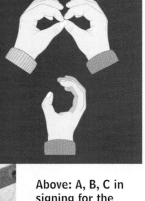

Above: A, B, C in signing for the deaf. Right: Signals from the International Code of Flags (for ships). Below: SOS in Morse Code.

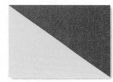

Man overboard

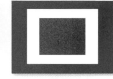

Send a doctor

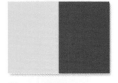

Stop at once

• • • — — — • • •

The rise of civilisation p.208 · Myths, legends and folk beliefs p.226 · Fact File p.344-50, 373-4

For many people the word 'religion' conjures up images of gods, angels and spirits. But the power of the world's many religions lies in the way that they seek to answer the great questions of human existence. How should we live our lives? Does our existence have any meaning or purpose? What happens after death? In a world full of uncertainty, religion can offer the reassurance of age-old ceremonies and beliefs.

Ceremony At their coming-of-age, Buddhist children dress as princes or princesses and go through a ceremony for becoming a monk.

CHILDREN OF RELIGION
The members of a religion share beliefs about a god, or gods, and follow similar ways of worship, ceremonies and teachings. The five major living religions in the world today are Christianity, Judaism, Islam, Buddhism and Hinduism.

Could God be a woman?
In the Jewish and Christian religions, the Almighty is referred to as 'He', but other religions have worhipped goddesses. Carved statuettes have survived from prehistoric times, suggesting that the worship of a single Earth Mother was widespread. The ancient Egyptians, Greeks and Romans, and the Vikings, worshipped goddesses as well as gods. Some religions, including Buddhism, do not refer to God at all, but speak of divine enlightenment, which is neither male nor female.

Cat goddess A statue of the ancient Egyptian goddess Bastet, who was worshipped in the form of a cat.

Rites of passage

For human beings, whatever their religion, there are certain key events in life, such as birth, marriage and death. Ritual ceremonies such as christenings, weddings and funerals mark the significance of these events, and connect a person to society and tradition. These ceremonies are called 'rites of passage' because they mark a person's passing from one stage of life to another.

An Indian family at a baby-naming ceremony.

Shared belief At Christmas, Christian children often perform a Nativity Play, which tells the story of the birth of Jesus.

THAT'S AMAZING
LOFTY EXAMPLE
Hermits live in remote places in order to concentrate on worship. An extreme example was the Christian monk Simeon Stylites (c.390-459). He spent 40 years living on top of a high column, setting a fashion for Christian 'stylites', or column-dwellers.

Does every religion have a holy book?

All of the world's main religions have their sacred texts containing early accounts of the founders' visions and teachings. The basic Hindu scriptures, the Vedas, contain hymns and prayers. They were written in Sanskrit, an ancient language of India, around 1500 BC. There are many Buddhist scriptures recording the teachings of the Buddha. The Old Testament, revered by Jews and Christians, covers 4000 years of Jewish history. Muslims follow the Koran, which records the revelations of the prophet Muhammad, founder of the Islamic faith.

Sacred text   The scrolls of the Torah contain the Jewish law and teachings.

What happens when someone dies?

Most religions teach that humans have a soul that continues to exist after death. Hindu and Buddhist traditions teach that the soul may be reincarnated in another human or an animal body, according to that person's behaviour on Earth. In Christian teachings, there is a place of bliss called Heaven and one of suffering called Hell. Some people believe that a person's spirit dies with their body.

Buddhist underworld   After death, Buddhists account for their misdeeds before reincarnation.

Daily life   Muslim schoolchildren study the Koran, the holy book of Islam. Most Hindu homes have a shrine where daily acts of worship are performed (bottom).

Preparation for life
A Jewish boy dressed for his *bar mitzvah*, the ceremony that marks the move from childhood to adulthood.

Ancient myths and legends are more than playful inventions. Myths and folk tales, which usually involved gods or supernatural forces, expressed people's beliefs and fears and their sense of right and wrong. Legends often incorporated ancient memories of real heroes from the past and offered people models of courage.

JASON AND THE ARGONAUTS
An ancient Greek legend concerns Jason and his companions, the Argonauts. Jason had to fetch the magical Golden Fleece from Colchis on the Black Sea in order to claim his throne, which his uncle Pelias had stolen from him.

1 Ship-building Jason and his companions built a 50-oared boat, the *Argo*, for their journey.

2 Aerial attack While sailing along the southern coast of the Black Sea, the Argonauts were attacked by a flock of birds that dropped bronze feathers on them.

3 Magic seeds When he arrived in Colchis, Jason was set the task of ploughing a field using fire-breathing bulls and then sowing it with serpents' teeth. The teeth turned into armed men, and he provoked them into fighting each other.

Modern myths

In 1920, members of a British expedition attempting to climb Mount Everest thought they saw tall, dark figures high above them in the snow. It was then that reporters started writing about the Abominable Snowman, or yeti, a monster said to frequent the Himalayas.

Another legendary yeti-like creature, known as Bigfoot, is said to inhabit the mountains of the west coast of North America. There have been several claimed sightings, and in 1967, Roger Patterson claimed he had film of Bigfoot. Many experts believed the film was genuine.

In Scotland in 1933, a newspaper reported the sighting of a gigantic creature 'rolling and plunging for fully a minute' in the waters of Loch Ness. It was christened the Loch Ness Monster.

These sightings may have had natural explanations. But we still need elements of mythology in our lives.

A shot of the yeti-like Bigfoot, filmed by Roger Patterson.

Was there really a Great Flood?

Of all the world's myths, the most widespread is that of a Great Flood. The story of an angry God destroying much of mankind in a deluge is told in the Biblical story of Noah, and in the earlier Epic of Gilgamesh of the Sumerians in Mesopotamia. Flood stories were also told among the Aztecs of South America and the Vikings of Scandinavia. All the stories feature a hero who avoids disaster by building some sort of ark. But how do we explain the similarities in these tales? Some people believe that deluge myths go back to the end of the last Ice Age, around 10 000 BC, when melting ice caps caused worldwide flooding. Perhaps heroic survival tales were prompted everywhere by the catastrophe.

Two by two A 10th-century manuscript illustrates Noah's Ark packed with animals.

4

Testing the legend Modern adventurer Tim Severin believed that the legend of the Argonauts was founded on a real voyage of exploration in the Black Sea. He built a Greek-style galley and retraced the route people believe the *Argo* took from Greece, across the Aegean Sea, and along the southern coast of the Black Sea.

6 Revenge Medea told Pelias that she could make people young again. She demonstrated on a ram, killing it and then substituting a young, live sheep in its place. Pelias was taken in, and allowed himself to be killed by Medea's assistants.

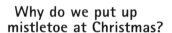

THAT'S AMAZING

VAMPIRES

Folk tales of vampires may have been inspired by a rare disease called *Erythropoietic Protoporphyria*. When patients' skin is exposed to light it bleeds, so medieval doctors used to shut them up in daytime and let them out only at night. They also encouraged patients to drink blood to replace the lost liquid. It is easy to imagine how a noble sufferer, fed on blood in his castle, might become the subject of sinister rumours.

6

4 The Golden Fleece
Jason grabbed the Fleece while his lover, the sorceress Medea, distracted the serpent that guarded it.

5 Siren song As the heroes sailed home, evil bird-women called sirens tried to lure them to their doom. Orpheus played his lyre to drown out the sirens' song.

5

Animals in mythology

Our ancestors lived close to nature, and animals often appear in their stories. Hanuman, a monkey god, is important in Hindu mythology, which tells how he and an army of monkeys once bridged the strait between India and Ceylon using boulders brought down from the Himalayas. Animals often represent natural cunning. Such is the case of Brer Rabbit, a wily character from African American folklore who appears in the *Uncle Remus* stories. More fearful are the creatures who were part human and part animal. The Minotaur of Greek mythology had a man's body and bull's head and slaughtered young men and maidens in his labyrinth. Mermaids, part woman and part fish, lured sailors to their deaths with beautiful singing.

Animal myth In the Hindu text *Ramayana*, Hanuman and the monkey army helped Prince Rama regain his kingdom.

Why do we put up mistletoe at Christmas?

Many modern customs are remnants of ancient folk belief. The tradition of hanging evergreens in the home at Christmas goes back to pagan times, when people brought branches indoors to provide refuge from the cold for woodland spirits. To the Druids, mistletoe was an especially sacred plant that could ward off evil – hence the custom of kissing under the mistletoe. Many modern customs, such as the giving of eggs at Easter, are remnants of ancient folk belief. Easter takes its name from Eostre, a Nordic goddess whose festival was held in the spring, and eggs were pagan symbols of rebirth.

⬤ Houses and buildings p.198 · Architectural styles p.238 · Fact File p.322, 344-363

Though prehistoric peoples often lived in caves, they also made tents from animal skins stretched over a frame made from wood or animal bones. Building in brick and stone came later, as did the idea of dividing the home into separate rooms. The modern home took shape as the result of a succession of inventions, such as the chimney, glass-paned window and electric light.

LIVING ROOMS THROUGH THE AGES

Primitive dwellings around the world had one dark, smoky room with a central cooking fire. In European homes, brick-built chimneys and glazed windows arrived towards the end of the Middle Ages, letting in more light and air. Living space was shared, and privacy was limited. Eventually, separate living rooms, kitchens and dining rooms appeared.

20 000 BC People in eastern Europe used mammoth bones to make their tents. People cooked, made tools, prepared animal hides and slept in the one living space, which would have been filled with smoke and the smells of old food, animal fur and damp clothing.

How was a tepee constructed?

Nomadic hunters and herdsmen need movable homes. The tepee (from the Dakota word *tipi*, a dwelling) was used by the tribes of the Great Plains in North America. It was made from buffalo hides stretched over a dozen or more long poles. It had a skin curtain hanging across the entrance hole, which faced the rising Sun. Ventilation flaps at the top could be adjusted with long poles to let out smoke from the brushwood fire. The flaps would be closed in cold or wet weather to keep the occupants warm and dry. The family's possessions were hung on the tepee walls.

When people moved to a new site, they took down the tepee and packed up the buffalo skin. The long poles were attached to packhorses and trailed behind them, forming a platform (or *travois*) on which household goods could be transported.

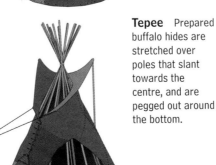

Tepee Prepared buffalo hides are stretched over poles that slant towards the centre, and are pegged out around the bottom.

Early 15th century Houses had one main room, called the hall. Family and servants all lived and ate here. Some of the household probably slept here, too, as there was little idea of privacy. A central fire was used for cooking and heating. Shuttered windows let in light and air.

THAT'S AMAZING
PAPER WALLS

Traditional Japanese houses have internal walls made of paper, with sliding screens instead of doors. The wood-framed buildings are not designed to last for more than about 40 years – but they can be rebuilt quickly in the event of earthquakes.

Alpine houses Broad, gently sloping roofs carry the weight of heavy snow.

Why are some roofs sloping and some flat?

The design of houses around the world is influenced by the local climate. In places where there is rain and snow, houses have sloping roofs to allow water to drain off quickly. In hot countries, stifling heat is the problem, and houses often have thick walls to keep out the heat and flat roofs. A flat rooftop can provide an open-air living room. People can also cook out on the roof and avoid making the house hot and smoky, or sleep under the stars on hot nights.

Family homes and clan dwellings

Many modern family homes are compact, built to accommodate father, mother and children. But in past times, a single dwelling often sheltered many more people. In a Viking longhouse, for example, several families might have been crowded together under one roof, along with their thralls (slaves) and livestock, too. Longhouse life still goes on in some tribal societies, where people live in clans rather than individual families. Borneo longhouses might house up to 50 families, including grandparents and great grandparents.

A Roman oil lamp.

Light and warmth

A simple lamp is easy to make. All that is needed is a container of some sort to hold fuel and a wick. The fuel-soaked wick is lit and feeds the flame, which provides light. In ancient times, oil or melted animal fat provided the fuel, and the wick might have been no more than a piece of twisted dried moss. Prehistoric people living in caves at Lascaux in France used stone lamps some 12 000 years ago. Similar lamps were still employed by the Inuit of Alaska in the 20th century. Adapting the principle, the Romans made candles using a wick surrounded by solid beeswax and tallow (refined animal fat). Gas lighting first appeared in 1799 in France, when a combined gas lamp and heating apparatus was patented. The first electric light bulb, the invention of a Scottish schoolmaster called James Bowman Lindsay, appeared in 1835. Electric fires appeared later that century. Today, many homes are warmed by gas, electric or oil-fuelled central heating.

In 1800, improved chimney flues made coal-fired stoves possible.

18th century Houses were divided into separate rooms for different activities, which gave people more privacy. Chimneys allowed individual rooms to be heated by fires set into the walls, and large glass windows let in light.

Late 20th century Today many people live in small households, and modern homes are more compact. Central heating has done away with the need for open fireplaces.

Food and nutrition p.138 · Food technology p.194 · Farms and farming p.234 · Fact File p.308, 344-363

Food provides living creatures with the material to build and repair body cells and the energy to fuel daily life. To stay healthy, the human body needs a balanced mixture of nutrients: proteins, vitamins, carbohydrates, fats and some minerals. Fibre, or roughage, is also important as an aid to digestion. This is why a healthy meal should contain varied elements, such as meat, fish or pulses; rice or potatoes; fresh vegetables and fruits.

CHECKOUT FOOD HISTORY
Every supermarket foodstuff has its own story. Some of the foods we eat have been cultivated for thousands of years, and come from all over the world. They were originally spread from continent to continent by early explorers and travellers.

Cucumber Cucumbers were grown in Mesopotamia as early as 2100 BC.

Frozen peas The first frozen peas were sold by Clarence Birdseye in the 1930s.

Tinned baked beans The Pittsburgh firm of H.J. Heinz first began marketing tins of baked beans in tomato sauce in 1901.

Tomatoes Explorers brought tomatoes back to Europe from Central America, probably Mexico, in the early 16th century.

Potatoes Potatoes may have been grown in South America in prehistoric times. They were brought back to Europe in the 16th century.

Coffee Coffee was first cultivated and drunk in southern Arabia in the 15th century.

Chocolate Chocolate is made from cocoa beans. The cocoa plant was grown in South America more than 3000 years ago, and people made a drink from it. Eating chocolate was developed in England in 1847 by Fry & Sons.

Cola The original cola drink was invented in 1886.

Sugar Sugar was being used in India by 3000 BC. By the 8th century AD it was being grown in southern Europe. Columbus took sugar to America on his second voyage, in 1493.

Tea This was the favourite drink of ancient China.

GARDEN PEAS

DAIRY MILK CHOCOLATE

SUGAR

COLA

80 TEA BAGS

BAKED BEANS

COFFEE

NEXT CUSTOMER

Poor people ate with their fingers.

Ways of eating

t medieval banquets, tables were set with knives and spoons. There were no forks or plates. People put their food on thick slices of bread, known as trenchers. A medieval book on table manners advised that the guest should not pick his teeth with his knife, nor wipe his mouth on the tablecloth. Forks were first used at the French court in 1589. But the poor went on eating with their fingers until the Industrial Revolution brought cheap cutlery into the home. Ways of eating vary around the world. The Chinese use chopsticks made of wood, bone or ivory. In China they are called *kwai-tse* – the quick ones – and important rules of etiquette surround their use. To lay them across the bowl signals that a guest wishes to leave the table. They are not used during a time of mourning.

The Chinese use chopsticks.

Dainty eating
A knife and fork made in 1698.

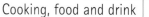

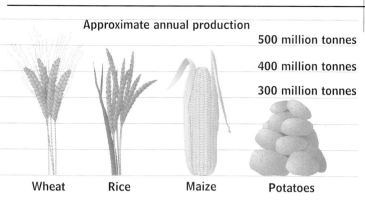

Approximate annual production

500 million tonnes

400 million tonnes

300 million tonnes

Wheat | Rice | Maize | Potatoes

What is the world's favourite food?

Rice is the most important food crop. It is the principal food of over half the world's population. Wheat and maize are other cereals grown on a large scale. Wheat flour is used in a range of foods, from bread and pastry to breakfast cereals and pasta. All cereals are rich in energy-giving starch, as are potatoes, once native to the Andes but now cultivated all over the world. Many favourite dishes, such as spaghetti bolognese and tandoori chicken with rice, combine a bulky starch base with a booster of proteins and vitamins.

THAT'S AMAZING
VEGETABLE POWER

Spinach is nutritious, but there is no truth in the idea that it is strength-building. The mistake goes back to the 1920s, when a decimal point was misplaced in a food chart, so that spinach seemed to contain ten times as much iron as other vegetables. In fact, it has much the same.

Why do we cook food?

The process of heating food can kill some of the bacteria that cause food poisoning, and can make it easier to digest. In prehistory, humans learnt to cook over fire. Early people also discovered that smoking, drying or pickling food with salt or vinegar could prevent it from 'going off'. These processes also created new flavours.

Could we live on pills?

Astronauts in space are given food pills, or sachets of food that can be squeezed into the mouth. Such examples have shown that we can live on pills and sachets. But most people still prefer to prepare and eat food in a more elaborate form. This is partly because the flavours, colours and textures of natural food are pleasurable. Also, meals shared with other people bind together families and communities, and are a central part in many religious festivals and ceremonial events.

Eating together
A festive meal brings a community together.

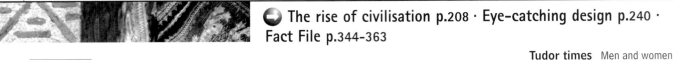

The rise of civilisation p.208 · Eye-catching design p.240 ·
Fact File p.344-363

1530

Tudor times Men and women wore exaggerated shapes and elaborately decorated fabrics.

1580

1660

S tone Age tribes learnt to sew skins together using needles made from bone. The first farmers discovered how to extract linen thread from the flax plant, and how to spin wool from their sheep, weaving it into fabric for clothing. By ancient Egyptian times, noblemen and women possessed fine pleated tunics and dresses, as well as elaborate hairstyles, jewellery and cosmetics.

Why wear clothes?

The answer might seem simple: to keep warm. But there are other reasons for wearing clothes, such as modesty and display. Clothing is used to attract the attention of the opposite sex. In primitive societies, magic provides another motive: leopard skins and sharks' teeth charms supposedly give the wearer the strength of those creatures. Some clothes are worn to show a person's position in society, whether a medieval monarch's crown or a traffic-warden's uniform.

Tribal leader The traditional headdress worn by Native Americans showed their position in the tribe.

1750

18th century
Men wore knee breeches and women voluminous dresses. By 1810, styles had become straighter and simpler.

1810

Victorian times
Women wore large hooped petticoats called crinolines to make their skirts stand out. **1850**

Why do fashions change?

In 1380, a writer complained: 'To be a good tailor yesterday is no good today. Cut and fashions change too quickly.' Styles change because fashionable people want to stand out in a crowd. As soon as everyone copies an outfit, it ceases to cause a stir and designers have to think up something new. Other factors influence changes. Hemlines rose in the Second World War because fabrics were in short supply. They rose again with the 'miniskirt' in the 1960s, when it was acceptable for women to show almost the whole length of their legs.

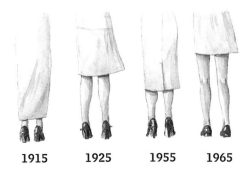

1915 **1925** **1955** **1965**

THROUGH THE AGES
In the past, kings, queens and courtiers set the fashions, which were often more complex and ornate than ordinary people could hope to match. The 20th-century trend is towards more casual and relaxed styles.

1066

1450

Medieval times
People wore fabrics dyed rich colours. The men had pointed shoes.

Why use make-up?
Cosmetics are used to cleanse the skin, to hide spots and blemishes, and to draw attention to attractive features, such as the eyes and the mouth. In ancient times, cosmetics also had magical significance. The Egyptians used a black eye paint called *kohl*, not only to make their eyes more beautiful but also to ward off danger. Ideas of beauty have changed. In 16th-century Europe, pale skin was thought attractive and women whitened their faces with a poisonous powder made from lead. In the 20th century, a suntan became fashionable.

Ancient cosmetics
This Egyptian make-up box contains jars and bowls for ointments and for mixing up cosmetics.

The story of trousers

The idea that men should wear trousers is relatively new. In the civilisations of ancient Egypt, Greece and Rome, men wore loose-fitting tunics and togas well suited to the warm climate of southern Europe and the Middle East. Trousers originated among the tribes of the chilly Asian steppe. During the Dark Ages, when these tribesmen overran much of Europe, trousers became more widespread. In later centuries, fashion-conscious noblemen preferred to wear knee breeches. At the start of the 19th century, long trousers were associated with the ordinary people of Paris who overthrew the nobles during the French Revolution. As a result, trousers came to be seen as modern, democratic garments.

Jeans began as work clothes, then became fashionable.

1920

1950

1970

1999

'Austerity Look'
A shortage of fabrics after the Second World War meant that fashions were simple.

1970 Bright colours and short skirts were the height of fashion.

Farms and farming

Food and nutrition p.138 · The rise of civilisation p.208 ·
Cooking, food and drink p.230 · Fact File p.354

About half of the Earth's people work on the land, growing crops and raising livestock to provide food and drink, as well as raw materials such as wool and cotton. Modern farming methods, which rely on chemicals, are very efficient, but many people now prefer food that has not been treated with chemicals.

CROP PRODUCTION

There are big differences in the way that farmers operate across the world. In rich countries, most food is produced using heavy machinery and mass-production methods, in contrast to the developing world, where most farming is still done by hand. Organic farmers are those who use traditional methods to control pests and fertilise the soil.

Who were the first farmers?

Farming began around 10 000 BC, as people began sowing seeds in prepared ground, instead of gathering wild plants. The first farmers lived in the Middle East, where wild grasses – including early forms of wheat and barley – grew on the hills. These farmers also tamed the wild ancestors of today's cattle, sheep, geese and chickens.

Procession A man leads a cow and goats in a picture which is about 4600 years old.

Why plant different crops year by year?

All crops absorb minerals – such as potassium – from the soil in order to grow. However, different plants absorb different minerals, and some also return minerals to the soil. By planting various crops in rotation, farmers can help the soil to maintain a healthy balance of minerals.

Crop rotation The four crops shown below are often planted in rotation, provided the soil and weather are suitable in the area.

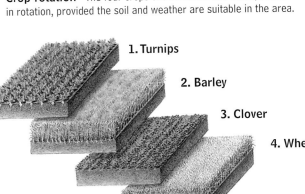

1. Turnips
2. Barley
3. Clover
4. Wheat

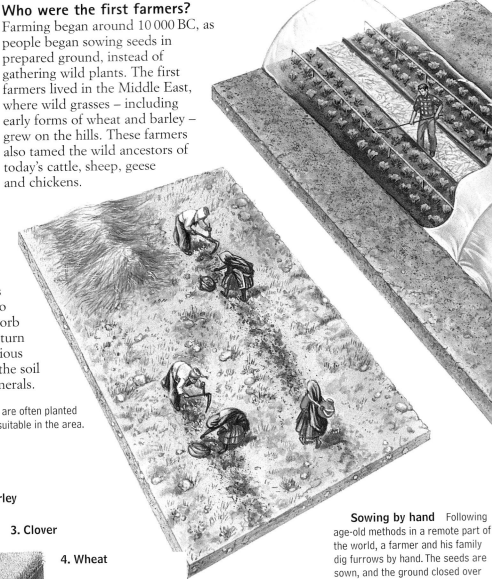

Sowing by hand Following age-old methods in a remote part of the world, a farmer and his family dig furrows by hand. The seeds are sown, and the ground closed over them. The furrows are dug in straight lines in order to make weeding easier.

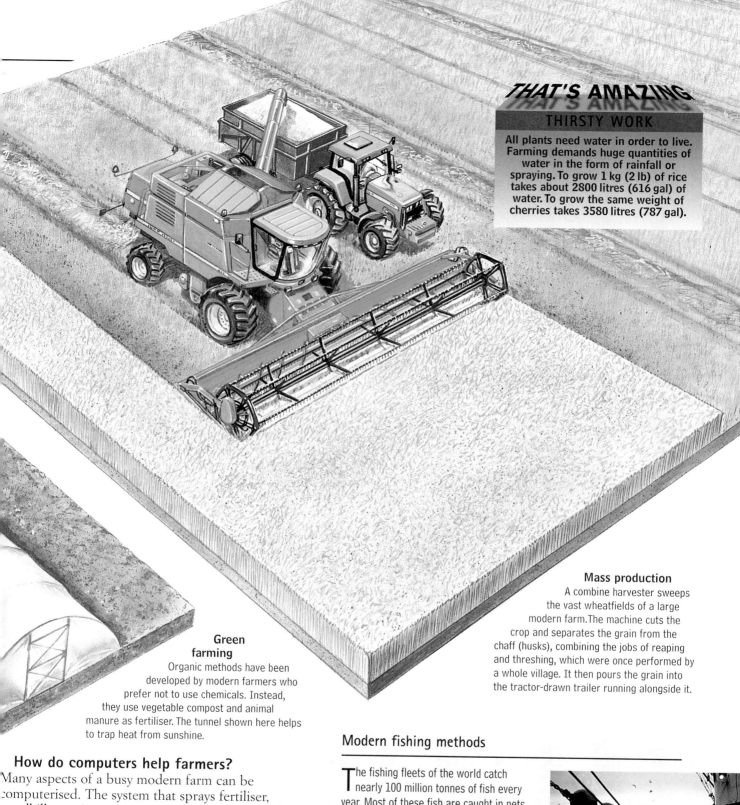

Mass production
A combine harvester sweeps the vast wheatfields of a large modern farm. The machine cuts the crop and separates the grain from the chaff (husks), combining the jobs of reaping and threshing, which were once performed by a whole village. It then pours the grain into the tractor-drawn trailer running alongside it.

Green farming
Organic methods have been developed by modern farmers who prefer not to use chemicals. Instead, they use vegetable compost and animal manure as fertiliser. The tunnel shown here helps to trap heat from sunshine.

How do computers help farmers?
Many aspects of a busy modern farm can be computerised. The system that sprays fertiliser, weedkiller, or just water onto crops knows exactly when and how much to spray. Another system can calculate precisely how much food to give livestock at feeding time.

Electronic farmer At this lettuce farm in Germany, a computer checks the daily needs of the plants.

Modern fishing methods

The fishing fleets of the world catch nearly 100 million tonnes of fish every year. Most of these fish are caught in nets, of which there are three main types. A trawling net is bag-shaped and is drawn behind the boat. A seining net lies on the seabed and is drawn up around a shoal of fish. Drift nets are suspended from floats on the surface; they hang like curtains to trap any fish which try to swim through them.

A modern fishing boat like this will have freezers to preserve its catch.

What is art?

⊜ The rise of civilisation p.208 · Architectural styles p.238 · Eye-catching design p.240 · Craft skills p.242 · Fact File p.364-6

Throughout history, artists have made paintings and sculptures to record the world around them, to tell stories, explain religious beliefs, and to provide objects of great beauty. Art is also an expression of the artist's own personality, and the spirit of his or her age. Even an abstract arrangement of colours or shapes can communicate a message that may be passionate, mysterious, calm or playful.

THAT'S AMAZING

CURIOUS COLOURS

Artists have sometimes obtained their colours from strange sources. In the past, a colour called Indian yellow was made from the urine of cows fed on mango leaves, while carmine red came from juice taken from a South American insect.

What's the story?

Painters include many clues to what is going on in a painting. Settings and costumes can be real, historical, mythological or dream-like, telling us what type of story it is. Weather and lighting suggest a mood. People's gestures and the expressions on their faces also provide hints. In portraits, objects are often included that tell us about the sitter – his or her background or profession, interests and character.

Joseph Wright, *An Experiment on a Bird in the Air Pump.*

WHY DOES IT LOOK LIKE THAT?

The way artists paint depends on the techniques and materials they use, on the way they see the world, and on the ideas of their time. Some artists use perspective, a system for showing how far away people and objects are, and use light and shadow to make everything look solid and real. Others are more interested in creating a particular mood.

Egyptian wall painting, *Musicians at an Entertainment* The figures are idealised – they are made to look as perfect and beautiful as possible. They are painted as flat shapes on a flat background, so do not look real.

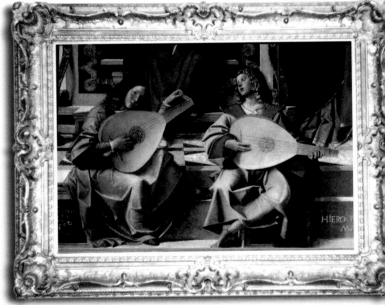

Caravaggio, *A Young Man Playing a Lute* In the late 16th century, artists were admired for their skill in painting solid-looking objects in realistic settings. Caravaggio used light and shade to model lifelike figures and objects.

How are statues made?

Some sculptures are made by carving into stone or wood, others by modelling in clay. A third method is more complex, and involves casting bronze statues by the *cire perdue* ('lost wax') technique. A wax model is made (1), and channels are added so the bronze will reach all of the figure (2). Clay is packed around the figure and allowed to harden. Then the wax is melted and run out to leave a hollow mould (3), into which molten bronze is poured (4). When the bronze has hardened, the mould is removed (5) and the figure is finished off (6).

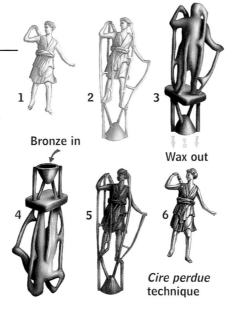

Bronze in

Wax out

Cire perdue technique

Artists' materials

Oil paints came into use in the Middle Ages. They are made from pigments ground up with linseed oil, and are usually applied to canvas, a tough linen or cotton fabric. Many modern artists use artificial paints called acrylics. Sometimes they mix sand or other materials into the paint to make it thicker.

Solid colour Lumps of substances called pigments are ground up to make artists' paints.

Pierre August Renoir, *The Daughters of Catulle Mendes at the Piano* Renoir belonged to a group of artists in the late 19th century called the Impressionists, whose main interest was to show the changing effects of light. Renoir has used bright colours and bold brushmarks to do this.

New forms of art

Artists in the 20th century have often astonished the public. In about 1911, a group of artists called the Cubists made collages, using materials such as newspaper clippings and menus in their paintings. In the 1950s, an American painter called Jackson Pollock poured and dripped paint onto canvas to achieve dramatic effects. Sculptors have experimented with the 'found art' of driftwood, rusted metal or wire. A Bulgarian artist named Christo believes that packaging is an art form. In the 1980s he wrapped whole buildings in canvas.

A building wrapped by Christo.

Georges Braque, *Man with a Guitar* Braque belonged to a group called the Cubists, who analysed the structure of the subjects they painted. In the painting on the right Braque has done this by combining different views of the same subject.

➲ Houses and buildings p.198 · Bridges, dams and tunnels p.200 · Home life p.228 · Fact File p.316, 364-6

Humans are not the only creatures that build. Birds weave nests, while rabbits make burrows and ants create anthills. All these homes provide shelter for the young. But humans build for a wider range of purposes: temples for worship, bridges for transport, theatres for entertainment and fortifications for defence. The art of designing buildings and other structures is called architecture. It improves the world we live in.

Why do we need architects?

Left to fend for ourselves, most of us could build a rough shelter. But could we design a 1000 m (3000 ft) wide bridge or a four-storey hotel that was guaranteed not to fall down? Architects decide what a building should look like and produce plans showing how it is to be constructed. They decide which are the best materials to use and how to keep costs down. They also have to solve questions like where to put windows for good lighting and how to roof an area safely without using massive, ugly supports.

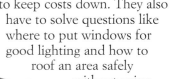

Preview
Architects make small models of the buildings they are designing.

CHANGING STYLES

The size, shape and style of new buildings have changed through the ages, depending on the intended use for a building, the materials and amount of space available, and the technology of the time. People's ideas about what looks beautiful have also changed over time.

Gothic church   The Gothic style of architecture was used by European architects in medieval times. Pointed windows, pinnacles and spires all direct the eye upwards. The use of stone meant that buildings could be taller than before.

PLASTIC BRIDGE

The Swiss engineer Urs Meier has produced plans for a bridge to link Europe and Africa across the Straits of Gibraltar. The structure would have a central span of 8400 m (27 600 ft) and be made of reinforced plastic.

Anglo-Saxon longhouse   This is a family dwelling where the extended family group would have lived. Buildings at this time consisted of simple structures. They were usually made from wood with a thatched roof. The floor is raised off the ground, with ladders up to the entrances.

How are domes built?

The Romans discovered how to bridge a gap between walls by building an arch made of specially shaped stones, which are wedged together so that they hold each other in place. Domes are, in effect, a collection of criss-crossing arches supporting the roof.

Hagia Sophia, Istanbul

Duomo, Florence

Dome shapes The basic structure can be adapted to produce domes that are shallow or high.

20th-century workplace The Lloyd's Building in London is constructed from glass and steel. Lifts and staircases are housed in towers attached to the outside of the building to give as much open space as possible inside.

Strange shapes

Modern architecture often surprises us with its unusual shapes. New building materials have permitted this. Concrete strengthened with steel rods is very strong. It is one of the most popular modern materials as it allows a variety of curved and sculpted shapes to be created. Tiles made from metal or glass can be used to build curved walls, and can be manufactured to fit any shape. The Guggenheim Museum in Bilbao is an arrangement of strange shapes covered with 30 000 shining titanium tiles.

The Guggenheim Museum in Bilbao.

Are glass buildings safe?

Glass is specially toughened to make it strong enough to use for office buildings. Extra-strong glass is produced either by using heat to toughen it or by a process called lamination (interleaving layers of glass with layers of plastic). Lamination can produce glass so tough that it is bulletproof.

Blending in Curving walls of mirrored glass reflect the building's surroundings.

Eye-catching design

⤵ Printing and publishing p.178 ·
The Industrial Revolution p.216 · Craft skills p.242

Just about everything that we use, read or wear has been carefully designed by someone. A well-designed object not only looks good, but works well, too. In an age of mass production, when items are manufactured in thousands, a badly designed product can cause major problems for a company. Designs are thoroughly examined and tested before production begins.

Who designed the chair?

Some everyday items work so well and are so widespread that we hardly think of them as being designed. No one can say who made the first chair, but exquisite four-legged examples were fashioned in ancient Egypt. Over the centuries, designs have changed according to taste and needs. Recliners, rocking chairs and swivel chairs are three adaptations of the traditional type. Some modern chairs dispense with legs altogether.

Sitting pretty   These four types of chair show how an idea can develop. They are all stylish, but only one looks as if it might be comfortable.

What makes a design successful?

Designs do not need to be complicated to be successful. Some are very simple, but are so reliable that they hardly ever change. Pop-up electric toasters, for example, were first made in the 1920s and have altered little over the years. The ball-point pen has also been very successful, probably because it is so simple and works so well.

Classics   The electric kettle and the anglepoise lamp are elegant and useful at the same time.

BIRTH OF A NEW TRAINER

A great deal of work goes into the design of a new product, such as a trainer. It must be comfortable and hard-wearing, and fashionable, too. It must also be straightforward to manufacture. A popular brand name will help to sell the trainer, and so will attractive packaging.

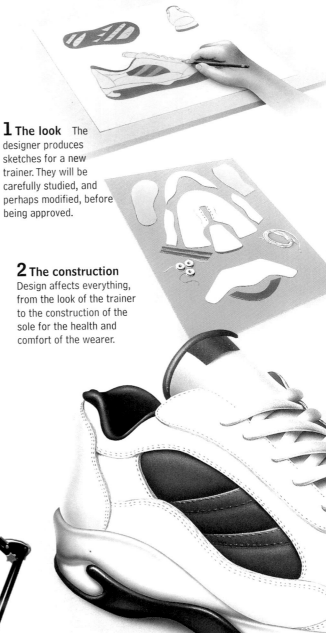

1 The look   The designer produces sketches for a new trainer. They will be carefully studied, and perhaps modified, before being approved.

2 The construction   Design affects everything, from the look of the trainer to the construction of the sole for the health and comfort of the wearer.

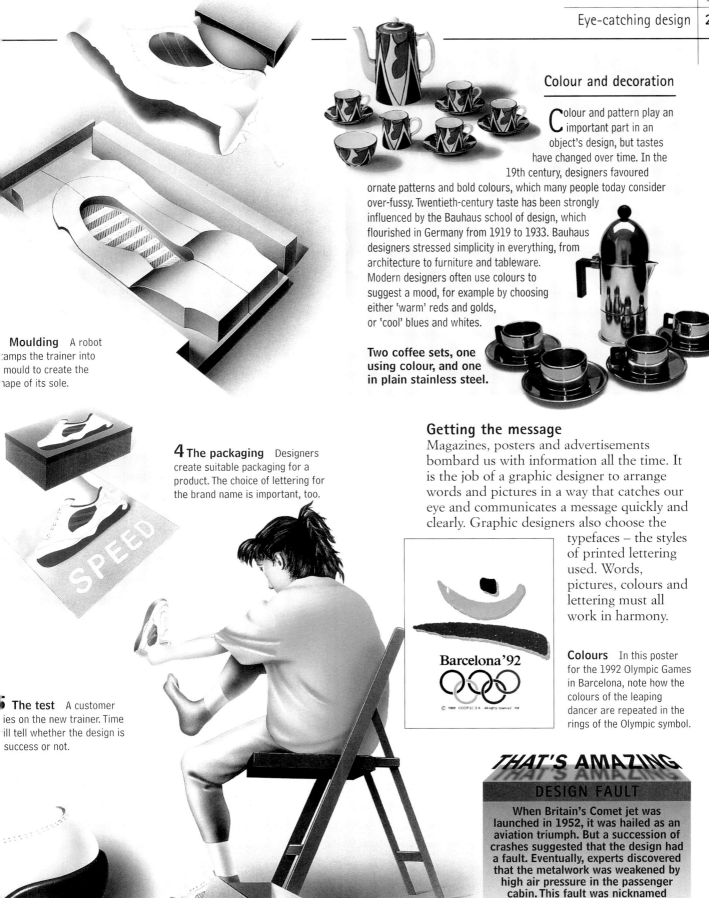

Moulding A robot
clamps the trainer into
a mould to create the
shape of its sole.

4 The packaging Designers
create suitable packaging for a
product. The choice of lettering for
the brand name is important, too.

5 The test A customer
tries on the new trainer. Time
will tell whether the design is
a success or not.

Colour and decoration

Colour and pattern play an
important part in an
object's design, but tastes
have changed over time. In the
19th century, designers favoured
ornate patterns and bold colours, which many people today consider
over-fussy. Twentieth-century taste has been strongly
influenced by the Bauhaus school of design, which
flourished in Germany from 1919 to 1933. Bauhaus
designers stressed simplicity in everything, from
architecture to furniture and tableware.
Modern designers often use colours to
suggest a mood, for example by choosing
either 'warm' reds and golds,
or 'cool' blues and whites.

**Two coffee sets, one
using colour, and one
in plain stainless steel.**

Getting the message

Magazines, posters and advertisements
bombard us with information all the time. It
is the job of a graphic designer to arrange
words and pictures in a way that catches our
eye and communicates a message quickly and
clearly. Graphic designers also choose the
typefaces – the styles
of printed lettering
used. Words,
pictures, colours and
lettering must all
work in harmony.

Barcelona '92

Colours In this poster
for the 1992 Olympic Games
in Barcelona, note how the
colours of the leaping
dancer are repeated in the
rings of the Olympic symbol.

THAT'S AMAZING

DESIGN FAULT

**When Britain's Comet jet was
launched in 1952, it was hailed as an
aviation triumph. But a succession of
crashes suggested that the design had
a fault. Eventually, experts discovered
that the metalwork was weakened by
high air pressure in the passenger
cabin. This fault was nicknamed
'metal fatigue', and designers took it
into account in planning all later jets.**

The rise of civilisation p.208 · The Industrial Revolution p.216 · Eye-catching design p.240 · Fact File p.344

Factories turn out identical, machine-made products in their thousands, but some people still produce handmade goods that are valued for their exclusiveness and for the skill with which they were made. In many cases, the techniques have changed little since ancient times. The ancient Egyptians, Greeks and Romans were all familiar with the crafts of the potter, glass-maker, weaver, jeweller, woodworker and leatherworker.

How is cloth woven?
At least 5000 years ago, the skill of weaving provided an alternative to animal skins for clothing and blankets. Wool was probably the first fibre used. Then, as now, cloth was woven on a loom, which was basically no more than a square-sided wooden frame. Weaving uses two sets of yarn, called the warp and the weft. Warp threads run along the length of the cloth. Weft threads are woven across the warp threads, over one and under the next.

Traditional carpets Turkish carpets are famous for their rich colours. The designs are often specific to the area or village in which they are made.

Carrier bags These colourful woven bags, known as *bilums*, are made in Papua New Guinea.

Tribal elegance
Twentieth-century artists have often found inspiration in the tribal art of Africa, Asia, Australia and the Americas. Pottery containers, ritual masks, patterned rugs – these and other objects made in tribal communities are often beautifully designed and full of character. The necessary skills are passed on within the community, and the shapes and patterns become perfected, while the techniques can become increasingly complex.

Making a basket, Mexico The Seris Indians of Mexico make woven baskets that are so large and delicate that they take years to complete.

How are glass objects made?
Individual objects can be made by 'blowing' glass. The glass-blower puts a dab of red-hot molten glass on the end of an iron tube. Then he blows through the tube to expand the glass into a hollow object, rather like blowing up a balloon. The glass hardens as it cools.

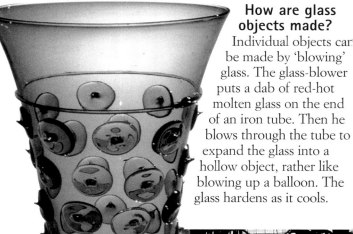

Hot work Glass-blowers shape an object by turning the molten glass as they blow. The vase above was made in this way.

MAKING POTS

Around 9000 years ago, people discovered that a container could be made by scooping out a hole in a lump of wet clay and waiting for it to dry. Then people began shaping pots, or building up coils of clay. Later, pots were made by hollowing out a ball of clay on the middle of a spinning wheel. Potters' wheels are still in use today.

A kiln Firing is done in a kiln – a kind of oven that heats the pots to very high temperatures.

On the wheel As the clay spins, the potter hollows out the centre and shapes the object. The potter must keep the clay absolutely central on the wheel or the pot will become crooked.

Firing and decorating
The pot is fired in a kiln to dry out the clay and harden it. Then it is decorated and covered with a glaze, a transparent liquid that makes the pot waterproof. The pot is then fired again.

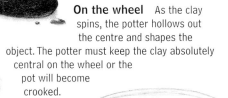

Make a silver badge

This project uses the metalwork technique of engraving. You will need a piece of tracing paper, a sheet of thin metal or tinfoil, card for backing, and sticky tape and a safety pin for pinning on the badge. You can use the design below for the badge, or design your own. People get ideas for their designs from objects in museums, from patterns in things they find, such as shells and stones, or from stories. This design came from a bottle label in a museum.

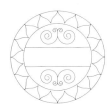

1 Draw out your design. Write your name in the space.

2 Transfer the design onto tracing paper.

3 Trace the design onto the metal sheet using a sharp pencil.

4 Stick the badge to card, and cut it out. Attach the safety pin.

Finishing off
Glazes are made from ingredients that change colour when heated, so the second firing brings out the colours in the glaze and sets, or hardens, it.

The world of literature

Printing and publishing p.178 · The written word p.210 · Myths, legends and folk beliefs p.226 · Fact File p.346, 378, 381

Shaped with power and skill, words have a tremendous power to excite a reader's imagination, whether in poetry, prose or drama. Yet stories and poems offer more than entertainment. Whether true to life or exploring realms of fantasy, good writing helps people to understand themselves and the world around them.

Real or not?

James Bond, Alice in Wonderland, Robinson Crusoe, these and other great characters of fiction can seem as real as living people. When Sir Arthur Conan Doyle invented Sherlock Holmes in 1887, he had no idea that his detective would become so popular. Conan Doyle became bored with his creation and killed off Holmes in a story in 1893. The public was so angry that he had to bring Holmes back again. Though fictional characters are products of the imagination, many had real-life counterparts. James Bond was based on men that author Ian Fleming had known in British Naval Intelligence during the Second World War.

James Bond, secret agent.

Story time
Rudyard Kipling tells his *Just So Stories* to a group of children.

Why do people tell stories?

Stories give shape and meaning to human fears and desires. Some stories grew from simple tribal tales to become epics – long narratives dealing with heroes and heroic deeds. Examples include the *Odyssey* of ancient Greece and the Indian *Ramayana*. The novels of some 19th-century writers, such as *Oliver Twist* and *Great Expectations* by Charles Dickens, and *War and Peace* by the Russian writer Leo Tolstoy, also have an epic quality, as they mirror the life and dreams of entire societies.

Pattern poem The words have been arranged to express a shape – *apfel* is German for apple.

Why write in verse?

Before books were invented, tales were passed on by word of mouth. Storytellers used a foot-tapping beat to remember the words. Rhyme and rhythm in songs have also influenced poetry. Poems achieve their effects through combinations of features such as rhythm and rhyme with striking, expressive language and sound patterns. Some poems tell a story, but many explore the meaning of a single event, object, experience, idea or feeling.

IMAGINARY WORLDS

In novels, authors use their skill with words to create imaginary worlds that we can believe in, even if the characters and events are far-fetched. In *Gulliver's Travels* by Jonathan Swift, published in 1726, the hero visits a series of strange lands. Swift uses his story to ridicule human foolishness.

What makes a popular classic?

Some books remain popular long after the time they were written. The quality of the writing is part of their success. Suspense – keeping the reader guessing about what is going to happen next – is also important, and not only in adventures and mysteries. In romances, the reader may be teased by doubts as to whether two lovers will be happily united. Not all favourite books are action-packed adventures. The appeal of Jane Austen's novels lies in her insight into human affairs as they unfold in outwardly uneventful situations. Character is also vital. Colourful heroes and heroines are valuable, but a good villain – such as the thief-master Fagin in Dickens's *Oliver Twist* or peg-legged Long John Silver in R.L. Stevenson's *Treasure Island* – is even more important.

Everlasting favourites
Great authors invent characters that we identify with. We share Charlie's wonder in *Charlie and the Chocolate Factory* and Alice's confusion in *Alice Through the Looking Glass*.

Gulliver in Lilliput
Gulliver is shipwrecked on an island called Lilliput. The inhabitants are only 15 cm (6 in) tall, but take themselves and their petty squabbles very seriously.

The magic of music

Sound: making waves p.156 · Sound recording p.162 ·
The art of dance p.248 · Fact File p.366, 380

Bone flutes and whistles have been found in prehistoric caves, along with rattles and castanets made from mammoths' jawbones. From such basic elements as clapping hands and tapping sticks on a log, the entire musical heritage of the world has grown. Music consists of sounds arranged, or composed, into pleasing patterns to express moods and to delight the ear.

THAT'S AMAZING

VOICE POWER

Because music is so popular, it is easy to think that all cultures around the world have musical instruments. This is not true. The Vedda people of Ceylon and certain tribes in Patagonia have no instruments. They sing, unaccompanied even by clapping.

The human voice

Singing is produced by air making the vocal cords vibrate as the singer breathes out. The higher, louder and longer the note being sung, the more breath is needed. The pitch of the voice is varied by tensing and relaxing muscles in the throat.

In harmony This is created when people sing at the same time on different notes.

LISTEN TO THE BAND

All musical sound, whether from string, reed or cymbal, is created by vibrations. These travel as pressure waves in the air. Fast vibrations produce high-pitched notes; slower vibrations produce low-pitched notes. When the rate of vibrations changes, so does the note. Different instruments create vibrations in different ways to produce a different range of notes.

French horn Air blown into the brass tube vibrates to create sound. High and low notes are produced by opening and closing valves to make the tube longer or shorter.

Cello The cello's low notes are made by bowing on long strings that vibrate slowly.

Why is fast music exciting?

Rhythm is related to the human heartbeat and to activities such as walking. A fast rhythm suggests excitement because it reminds us of a racing heart or a running pace. Dance music played in clubs is generally produced at 120 beats per minute, roughly double the rate of the normal heartbeat.

Dance music A fast rhythm makes people want to dance.

The story of the guitar

The first sounds from stringed instruments were probably made by prehistoric hunters twanging their bows. Small harp-like instruments called lyres, with strings stretched across a soundbox to increase the volume, were used in Mesopotamia in about 2500 BC. The medieval lute, cittern and cithara are descended from these. The guitar itself was Moorish in origin and spread to Spain during Moorish rule there. It was seen as an instrument of the common people. By the 19th century, the modern six-string guitar was in widespread use. The electric guitar, which is connected to an amplifier and speakers, first became popular among blues and jazz musicians in 1935.

A 15th-century 'gitterne' or cittern.

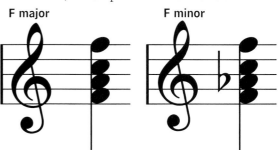
An electric guitar.

Why does some music sound sad?

Music may sound sad because it is slow, and recalls the slow heartbeat and movements of someone who is depressed. The pattern of notes can also suggest sorrow. A chord is a group of three or more notes played together, and a major chord yields a simple, pleasant sound. In a minor chord, the pitch of one note is lowered, which produces a sad effect.

Percussion Drumskins and metal cymbals vibrate to create different textures (patterns) of sound.

Clarinet Woodwind instruments such as the clarinet and oboe have a reed in the mouthpiece. When blown, the reed vibrates to make musical sound.

Guitar The player plucks the strings with one hand, causing them to vibrate and create notes. The player 'stops' the strings with the other hand, which shortens the string and creates higher notes.

The art of dance

The magic of music p.246 ·
On stage p.250 · Fact File p.381

All through human history, dance has been important as a social activity, as entertainment and as a means of self-expression. In ancient times, people danced to make magic, or to tell sacred stories, or to bind themselves together as a tribe. Different forms of dance, such as folk, ballet and contemporary, have developed their own languages and conventions.

How did dancing begin?

The dances of our ancestors were group activities and provided a way of rejoicing and sharing an experience of togetherness. Many celebrated times of importance to the group: the harvest, the battle or the hunt, for example. People also danced to please their gods. Indian dance still expresses themes from the Hindu religion.

Tribal dance Zulu warriors celebrate the traditional ceremony of the Reed Dance.

TELLING STORIES IN DANCE

Indian dance and traditional Western ballet both use a highly developed language of steps, movements and gestures. Series of movements are linked together in different combinations to tell a story or create a mood. Many years of intensive training are needed to master the intricate steps and movements and develop the necessary suppleness and strength.

Expression Movement, hand gestures and facial expressions are used to tell stories of the gods. Here, Krishna and a cowherd play with a ball.

Abstract patterns
Three stages in a spiral movement. Set movements can be combined to create decorative patterns.

1

2

3

THAT'S AMAZING

THE TARANTULA DANCE

A whirling dance called the tarantella has been popular since the 15th century. It was first performed in Italy, and people believed that it was the only way a victim could overcome the effects of the tarantula spider's poisonous bite. There is a condition called tarantism, or dancing mania, in which victims are seized by a wild urge to dance.

Take your partner

Dance has always offered young men and women the chance to meet. Ancient tribal courtship dances were performed by groups of men and women. In the villages of medieval Europe, group dancing was common. In the English country dance called the Sir Roger de Coverley, each man danced with each woman in turn. There were dances for couples, too. The minuets and gavottes danced by peasants in 17th-century France involved much flirting. The Spanish flamenco and Argentinian tango are dances for couples that express great passion.

Dancing couple
The lambada was invented in Brazil.

Folk dance

Ancient folk dances may be performed to ask for good luck or a bumper harvest, to celebrate a wedding or to frighten away evil spirits. Some take the form of a circle dance, in which men and women link arms. Others involve movements that mime the sowing of seed or harvesting. The maypole dance, in which people circle around a tall pole hung with garlands and ribbons, is a survival from times when people danced round a tree to ask for their crops to grow.

Couples dance at a village wedding in medieval times.

Attitude
One leg is raised and bent.

Ballet practice Dancers work to develop skill, balance and grace, and to produce a good 'line' – the flowing lines and curves that can be traced through a dancer's body.

Ronde de jambe
'Circles of the leg', being done here on *pointe*.

Basic positions
Most ballet steps begin and end in one of the five basic positions. This is the fifth position.

Arabesque The dancer creates a long line from the ends of the fingers to the tips of the toes.

When did ballet begin?

The first ballet was staged in 1489, when the Duke of Milan was entertained by the story of Jason and the Golden Fleece enacted in dancing and mime. Ballet performances were later staged in public theatres. In the 19th century, dancing on the tips of the toes, called on *pointe,* was introduced, and ballets with romantic stories, such as *Swan Lake,* were composed. In the 20th century, some dancers reacted against the formality and romanticism of traditional ballet. Modern ballet uses a freer style. In some modern ballets, stark costumes and jerky movements are used to express emotion.

Planted Seeds This contemporary dance is based on people's stories of the war in Bosnia.

Pirouette Turns, or spins, can be done on the spot or travelling across the stage.

🌐 The art of dance p.248 · Moving pictures p.252 · Fact File p.369, 378-9, 382

The plays staged in ancient Greece's vast open-air arenas developed from early religious ceremony. The bare sets and masked actors of Japan's Noh plays also recall ancient ritual. From early times, plays were performed by professional actors, but in Europe until the 17th century there were no actresses – women's parts were played by boys.

AT THE THEATRE

Drama, dance and opera are all produced on stage. The world that we see and hear in the theatre is created through scenery, props (articles used on stage), lighting, sound, music and costumes. Beyond the stage, there are large backstage areas, workshops and rehearsal rooms, where the work of preparing a production goes on.

Why do actors need make-up?

Stage actors and actresses have to project the character they are playing to a large audience. They do this through the way they move and speak, and through their costume and facial expressions. Stage make-up helps to reinforce the actors' features, making it easier for the audience to see their expressions. It also combats the effect of stage lighting, which is very strong and can make it hard to see the actors' features. In ancient Greece, actors solved this problem by using bold, colourful masks to project their characters.

Making up Make-up is exaggerated close up, but natural from a distance.

Rowing along A revolving stage creates the impression of movement in *Wind in the Willows*.

All done with mirrors

Victorian audiences delighted in spectacular effects on stage. Ghosts were made to appear by bouncing images off mirrors. So-called 'hippodramas' involved horse-races onstage – using real horses on moving platforms. A production in 1900 of Shakespeare's *A Midsummer Night's Dream* used a carpet of real grass with rabbits running around the stage.

Make 'em laugh, make 'em cry

It is easy enough to understand why people go to a comedy. But why do people go to see a play that frightens them, or makes them cry? All of us have secret fears, desires and worries. Comedy and tragedy release these emotions in the form of a good laugh or a good cry without a real misfortune or tragedy occurring – after all, a stage production has an advantage over real life in that 'it's just a play'. The Greek philosopher Aristotle called this releasing of emotions 'catharsis'.

Clowns make us laugh by exaggerating aspects of human behaviour.

Auditorium
The area occupied by the audience.

Lighting
Spotlights beam light down from above.

Does all drama need a theatre?

A drama is the acting out of a story – it does not require a building. Roofed theatres became widespread in the 17th century, to protect lavish scenery from bad weather. Until then, dramas were usually performed in the open air with little scenery. In the Middle Ages, morality plays, based on religious themes, were staged on wagons in inn courtyards.

Street theatre
Street entertainers are still popular today.

The 'set' The stage with its grouping of scenery. Movable pieces of scenery mounted on frames are called 'flats'.

The wings The unseen area at the sides of the stage. The scenery is arranged so that the cast can enter and exit.

Orchestra pit The area where the orchestra plays. Performers and orchestra can see the conductor.

THAT'S AMAZING

UNLUCKY PLAY

It has long been rumoured that Shakespeare's *Macbeth* contains a real black-magic spell. Actors consider the play to be unlucky, and they never quote from it in the dressing room. They even avoid referring to it by name, calling it 'the Scottish play' instead.

➡ Television and video p.170 ·
The mass media p.254 · Fact File p.368–9, 382

From the early 20th century, families throughout the Western world used to visit the cinema every week. Picture palaces opened in every major town, and films were watched by millions in the village halls of Russia and India, too. The invention of television seemed to threaten the cinema's existence, but blockbusters such as *Star Wars* with their spectacular special effects have restored its popularity.

The first talkie
The Jazz Singer was the first film to have synchronised speech as well as music and sound effects.

How do movies work?
A film camera produces a series of pictures, called frames, at a rate of about 24 per second. Light shining through the film throws the pictures onto a screen, and the changes from frame to frame occur so fast that motion seems continuous to the human eye. Sound is carried on a strip at the side of the film, and is matched to the pictures.

Wide-screen films
The image is 'squeezed' during filming (top). The projector 'stretches' the image again.

Film strip This series of frames shows a close-up shot. The soundtrack is on the strip down the left-hand side.

When were talking pictures invented?
The first commercial showing of a film was in Paris in 1895. Like all the movies that followed for years to come it was silent. Sound arrived with *Der Brandstifter* (*The Arsonist*), a German film made in 1922. But at first it seemed no more than a gimmick. 'Talkies' replaced 'silents' after the release in 1927 of *The Jazz Singer*, starring Al Jolson. It was such a success that other movie-makers quickly followed suit.

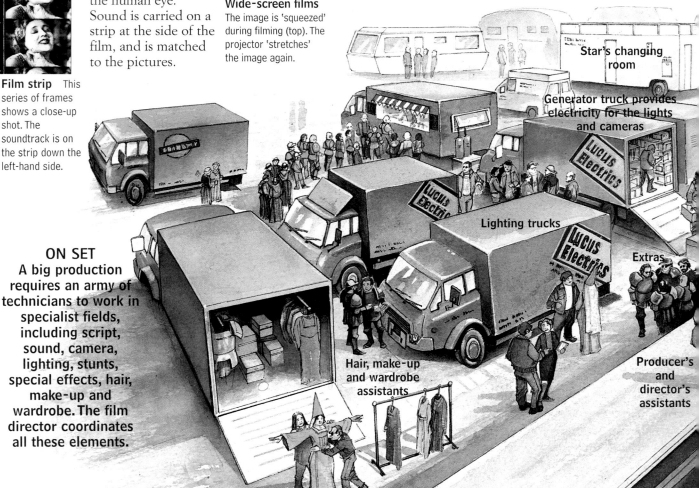

ON SET
A big production requires an army of technicians to work in specialist fields, including script, sound, camera, lighting, stunts, special effects, hair, make-up and wardrobe. The film director coordinates all these elements.

Star's changing room

Generator truck provides electricity for the lights and cameras

Lighting trucks

Extras

Hair, make-up and wardrobe assistants

Producer's and director's assistants

How are cartoons made?

Series of drawings, each slightly different from the previous one, are made and photographed. Seen as a rapid sequence, the drawings produce the illusion of movement. In the past, all the drawings were done by hand, and a film could take years to complete. Today, computers are usually used to generate sequences of drawings, although people still create the key frames at the beginning and end of the sequences.

Special effects

Film technicians create wonders through special effects. Miniatures and life-size models of monsters, for example, can be brought to life by moving their position frame by frame. Back projection is another common trick. The makers of *King Kong* (1933) created the illusion of a colossal ape looming over the heroine by projecting film of the monster onto a screen behind the actress and then filming the two together. The effect terrified audiences at the time. The makers of *Jurassic Park* used computers to generate sequences involving lifelike dinosaurs.

The mechanical gorilla's head made for *Buddy*.

The set is constructed from lightweight materials such as plywood and painted to look solid. Scenery is constantly being moved during filming.

Lighting rig

Standby crew – carpenter, painter, stage hand, rigger and plasterer

Second camera unit records action from a different angle

People who play in crowd scenes are called extras

Extras

Focus puller

Camera on rails follows the action

Fight arranger

Sound recording

Light reflector fills in shadows

Director of photography

Director follows video playback

Sound mixer

➜ Radio communications p.164 · Television and video p.170 · Printing an publishing p.178 · Government and politics p.260 · Fact File p.381-3

Television, radio, newspapers and magazines are powerful sources of information and entertainment. Through advertising, they can also persuade millions of people to buy certain products or vote for particular political parties. The media have this power because they reach into people's homes. In Britain, the average person watches almost 26 hours of television every week.

TV studio The action is filmed in a studio, which is specially lit and soundproofed.

Studio camera A small TV screen on top of the camera shows the operator what is being filmed.

How is the news brought to us?

When a newsworthy event occurs, the media send reporters and photographers to the scene. These people investigate and record the incident, and prepare the reports that will be printed in the newspapers or appear on television. Satellites are often used to transmit live television reports from the other side of the Earth.

On the scene A TV journalist files his report.

How did soap operas get their name?

Soap operas are TV or radio dramas that are spread over many episodes. These programmes got their nickname because they were originally sponsored in the United States by manufacturers of soap powder. While a novel or play is generally written by a single author, whole teams of scriptwriters are responsible for the plots of soap operas.

High drama The TV series *Eastenders* is a classic soap opera.

TV DIRECTORS

A director controls all the different elements in a TV production. Several cameras are used at the same time in a TV studio. Some give the general picture, while others are focused more closely on details, such as facial expressions. The director selects shots from the various cameras, cutting from one to another. Next time you watch a TV drama, notice how often the camera angle changes.

Holding the reins The director gives instructions to sound and camera operators working in the studio.

Sound check A technician monitors sound levels. If actors speak too softly, they will not be heard; too loudly, and the sound will be distorted.

TV screen Electrical signals create a picture made up of hundreds of horizontal lines.

The control room All the sounds and images being recorded are monitored here.

How do advertisements work?

Advertisements work by trying to make people remember a product, so they often use images or scenes that will stay in people's minds. One trick is to use children or animals, which make a strong impression.

Tea time The tea-drinking chimpanzee is a memorable image.

The sporting world

Muscles and movement p.108 · Lungs and breathing p.112 · Fact File p.384

Events such as the World Cup and Olympic Games are watched by millions worldwide, and attract huge sums of money in advertising sponsorship. Yet the original sports, such as marathon running or throwing the javelin, were based on training for war. Team games and individual contests provide outlets for the competitive spirit, and give everyone the opportunity to keep fit.

HIGHER AND HIGHER
In 1924, the American high-jumper Harold Osborn made a record jump of 2.03 m. The present record of 2.45 m was set in 1993 by Cuba's Javier Sotomayor.

World Cup 1998 Zinedine Zidane scores the first goal for France in the final. The total TV audience for all the matches is thought to have been around 38 billion viewers.

What is the most popular sport?

Soccer draws the biggest crowds around the world and arouses strong emotions in its followers. In 1969, a dispute in a World Cup qualifying match between El Salvador and Honduras led to a five-day war between the two countries; 2000 people died and much of the Honduran air force was destroyed. Football is a game with ancient roots. Around 400 BC, the Chinese played a game called *Tsu-Chu* ('to kick the ball with the feet'). The Romans brought football to Britain. Matches were played between villages in the Middle Ages. The rules of Association Football were drawn up in England in 1863.

The martial arts

The ancient tradition of the martial arts grew out of the self-defence skills of Zen Buddhist monks in medieval China, and involves spiritual philosophy as well as physical training. The term kung fu comes from the Chinese *gong fu*, which simply means 'skill'. Kung fu is a system of unarmed fighting that uses sharp blows struck with the hands and feet. The combat sport of *karate* (which means 'open hand') derived from the kung fu tradition. Another martial art is the Japanese combat sport of *kendo* (meaning 'sword way'). Kendo was associated with the swordfighting skills of the samurai, the warriors of feudal Japan. Contestants wear protective armour and use bamboo staffs or wooden swords to try to hit specific targets on their opponent's body. Two hits result in a win.

Japanese schoolchildren in a kendo class.

THAT'S AMAZING

TENPIN BOWLING

Ninepin bowling was once all the rage (hence the expression 'to go down like ninepins'). In the United States during the 1840s, it attracted so many gamblers and crooks that several states banned the game. Promoters dodged the law by adding an extra pin – and the new sport of tenpin bowling was born.

Winter Games Martina Accola of Switzerland competes in the women's slalom in the 1998 Winter Olympic Games in Japan.

When did the Olympics start?

The original Olympic Games were staged every four years between 776 BC and AD 394, at Olympia in ancient Greece. They began as a religious festival, and the main events included contests still held today: running, wrestling, boxing, the long jump, throwing the discus and throwing the javelin. In 1896, France's Baron Pierre de Coubertin revived the Olympics at Athens. They have been held every four years, except in 1916, 1940 and 1944, when world war intervened. The first Winter Olympics were held in 1924.

Fosbury flop

British high-jumper Steve Smith uses the Fosbury flop. This technique is named after the 1968 US Olympic champion Richard Fosbury. He invented the technique of going over the bar head first and feet last. Previously, high-jumpers had used a scissors action or a sideways roll.

Can athletes go on breaking records?

At one time, it was thought impossible for a person to run a mile in 4 minutes, but on May 6, 1954, a 25-year-old British student named Roger Bannister achieved it in 3 minutes 59.4 seconds. Today, top runners regularly run inside 4 minutes, and the world record stands at 3 minutes 44.39 seconds. A time will come when no more records are broken because factors like the length of the human leg and the pump rate of the heart will prevent further improvements.

1900 Bennett 4:6.2

1915 Taber 3:55

1930 Ladoumègue 3:49.2

1945 Hägg 3:43

1960 Elliott 3:35.6

1975 Bayi 3:32.16

1990 Aouita 3:29.46

1998 Guerrouj 3:26

1500 metres
Between 1900 and 1998, the world record has fallen from 4 minutes 6.2 seconds to 3 minutes 26 seconds.

🌐 The rise of civilisation p.208 · Government and politics p.260 · Fact File p.346, 351

Coins and banknotes are what we use to measure wealth and pay for things, and their value can go up and down. Today, people use credit cards and cheques as substitutes for cash, and computer technology allows sums of money to be added to or subtracted from bank accounts without coins or banknotes changing hands.

Why do we need money?

The earliest form of trade was barter, where people exchanged goods of similar usefulness – an animal skin for an earthenware pot, for example. Later, the idea dawned of using one type of object as the measure for valuing goods and services. Spearheads, cattle, sacks of corn or metal bars would be chosen, and everything was valued against it. Within an area or community, everyone used the same type of money. All sorts of things have been used, but the most successful have been small and portable. Cowrie shells were used in Africa and Asia. Bronze tokens, in the form of coins and small blades, were in use in China by the 7th century BC. Paper money was introduced later, also in China.

Decorative money Native Americans used wampum beads, which were made from shells, as money and for jewellery.

Money token This 10th-century BC bronze blade was used as money in ancient China.

THE MONEY GAME
People can save money in a bank, invest it in a company, or spend it. Bank loans and investment help businesses to finance the factories and shops in which products are made and sold. Money is safe in a piggy bank, but it will not provide any benefit.

COMPGAME INTERNATIONAL HQ

Tom receives dividend

Tom buys shares in Compgame

Investing Tom can put his money directly into a company by buying 'shares' in it. If the company makes a profit, it will pay him a share of the profits, called a dividend.

Compgame receives profit on sales of its products

Compgame uses the bank loan to build a new factory

Tom receives pocket money from Dad

COMPGAME FACTORY

THAT'S AMAZING

TULIP MANIA

In 1634, there was a craze for rare tulip bulbs in Holland. Prices rocketed, and a particularly unusual bulb could cost the buyer a house, a coach and horses, or a whole farm. Tulips became a form of currency, and Tulip Notes were even issued, bearing a promise to pay a stated number of bulbs. In April 1637 the craze ended, producing a sudden fall in prices, or crash, and many people lost money.

Roman money These are examples of the denarius, the main silver coin used by the Romans.

What do banks do?

Merchants long ago took to storing their money in banks to avoid carrying cash about. These banks also lent money so that traders could, for example, set up businesses. When someone paid back a loan, the banks charged an additional sum, known as 'interest'. This was how they made their profit. By the end of the Middle Ages, the main features of the modern banking system – such as deposits and loans, accounts against which cheques could be drawn, and exchanging foreign money – had been established. An important development in recent times has been the number of ordinary people who use banks to look after their money.

This 14th-century Chinese banknote was worth 1000 coins.

Paper money

Paper money was in use in China by the 9th century AD. It was introduced there at a time when coins were in short supply. In medieval Europe, merchants started exchanging 'letters of credit' to avoid dealing in sacks of coins. In the 17th century, banks started to issue such letters. Banknotes originally represented a bank's promise to pay cash to the bearer of the letter, but they quickly became a form of money in themselves. Banknotes are printed with complex patterns to make them difficult to forge.

In Germany in the 1920s the value of money fell so fast that notes became worthless and were used as toys.

Bank provides a loan

Compgame pays interest

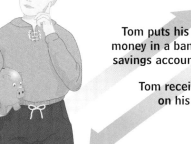

BANK

Tom puts his money in a bank savings account

Tom receives interest on his savings

Shopping centre pays interest on the loan

Saving Tom can put his money in a bank savings account, and the bank will pay him additional money, called interest, in return for the use of his money.

Bank provides finance for a shopping centre

Tom spends his savings

Compgame

WHAT SHOULD TOM DO WITH HIS POCKET MONEY?

SHOPPING CENTRE

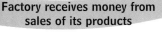

Factory receives money from sales of its products

Factory supplies products to shopping centre

Why do we have to pay taxes?

In ancient times, rulers forced conquered peoples and peasants to pay financial contributions called taxes. This was how the rulers funded wars and their own wealthy lifestyles. Even in free societies today, citizens and businesses have to pay taxes. National and local governments need the money in order to provide schools, hospitals, police, firefighting services, armed forces and refuse collection for everyone. Taxes are usually raised according to a person's income; the rich pay more and the poor pay less. Governments can sometimes cut taxation by running services more efficiently. They may also ask individuals to pay more towards their healthcare or their children's schooling.

The rise of civilisation p.208 · The mass media p.254 · Money matters p.258 · Fact File p.324-43, 362, 388

E ven in the most peaceful countries, people often disagree about important issues such as taxation, law and order, defence and so on. Most societies deal with these issues through some form of national government – a body of people who set the rules, pass the laws, and make sure that they are carried out.

Anarchist
Many anarchists are peaceful, but some believe that violence is the only way to change society.

Could we cope without government?

There is a belief, called anarchism, which holds that people should abolish organised government and live through cooperation. No truly anarchist society has existed in the modern industrial world, though certain tribal communities survive without a chief or governing group. Tribe members discuss policy among themselves, and each person acts on what has been decided. These communities are rare, and tend to be found where possessions are few and life is relatively simple. In a society where millions of individuals do a range of different jobs, it is difficult for everyone to take part in all decision-making. Most people prefer to elect representatives to make decisions for them.

What is democracy?

Democracy means 'government by the people'. It is a system which originated in ancient Athens, where all free men were entitled to meet and vote on important issues in a general assembly. However, neither women nor slaves were allowed to vote. In the modern world, democracy usually means that all adult citizens have the right to elect representatives to a government, which should make decisions on behalf of everyone. Democracy today is often defined as 'one person, one vote'.

Secret ballot The voter on the right places his vote in a sealed box, so no one can know his choice.

1 Campaigning
Candidates travel around the country, making speeches and meeting as many people as possible.

2 Mass rallies
Large meetings give the candidates a chance to explain their policies to supporters.

How does government work?

Democratic government takes different forms around the world, but it generally has two main branches: the legislature and the executive. The legislature – usually called a parliament, congress or assembly – is made up of elected representatives from different political parties, who debate what laws should be passed, or measures taken, for the well-being of the country.

The executive is the branch of government which puts these laws or measures into effect. It is usually headed by a president or prime minister.

ELECTING THE PRESIDENT OF THE UNITED STATES OF AMERICA

The American people have to choose a president every four years, or sooner if the president dies or is thrown out of office. The country has two main parties – Democrats and Republicans – but anyone can stand as an independent candidate if he or she has enough money. The cost of funding an election campaign can run into many millions of dollars.

4 Celebration!
Victory for the new president is announced after the votes have been counted. He or she is now known as the 'president-elect'.

Could a world parliament work?

The closest thing we have to a world parliament is the United Nations (UN), which was created in 1945, at the end of the Second World War. The UN provides a meeting place, where the nations of the world can discuss their problems, and try to find solutions. At certain times, the UN has been called upon to send troops when one country has attacked another, such as when Iraq invaded Kuwait in 1990. In other cases, the UN has stated its disapproval of a country by imposing economic sanctions (punishment), such as when Serbia sent troops into Bosnia. But often the UN has been unable to impose its decisions, especially when a powerful country such as the United States has opposed them. Many people would like to see a stronger UN.

UN peacekeeping soldier in the Bosnian city of Sarajevo.

3 Media event
TV interviews provide opportunities for the candidates to be questioned about their ideas. Such interviews play an important role in shaping, or changing, public opinion during an election campaign.

5 Inauguration
The president-elect takes the oath of office during an inauguration ceremony. At this point, he or she becomes the country's president.

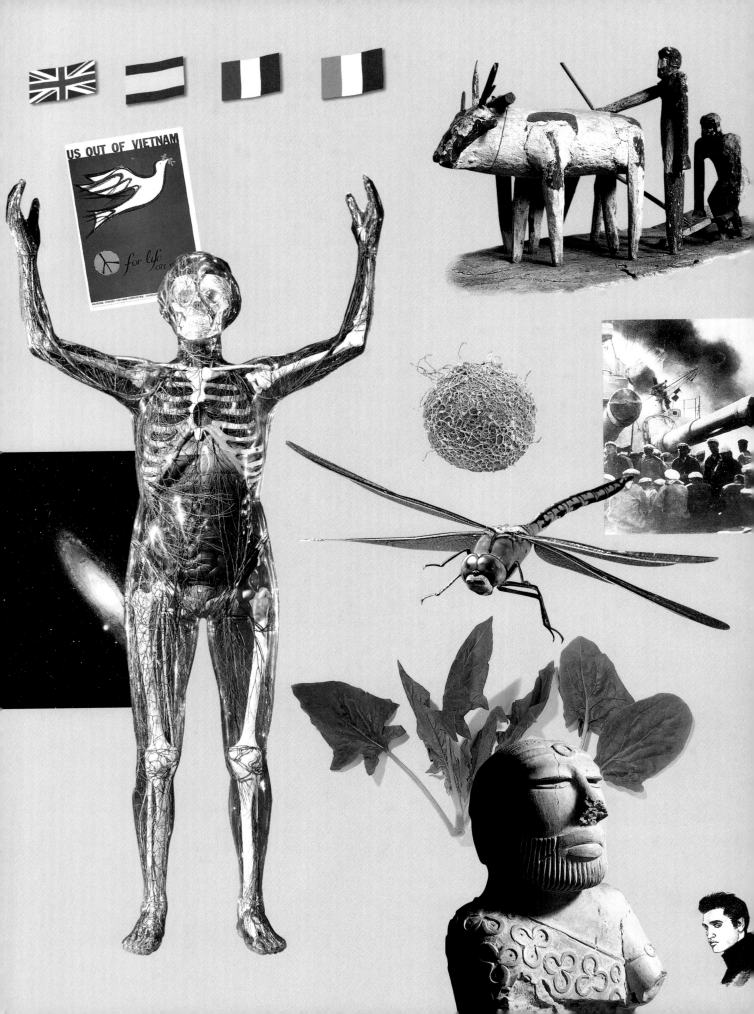

US OUT OF VIETNAM

for life
on e

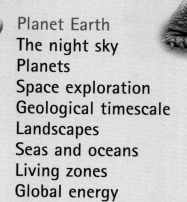

Fact File

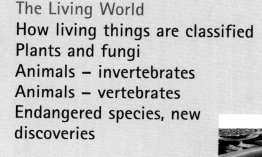

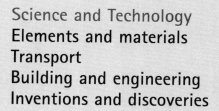

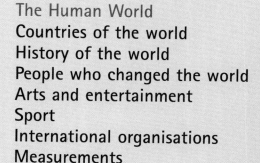

The night sky

In all, about 5800 stars are bright enough to be seen with the naked eye in perfect conditions – on a clear, moonless night. With binoculars or a small telescope, you can see many more. The stars seem to move in a circle around the North and South Poles. In fact it is the Earth that moves, not the stars.

Nebulae

Even without binoculars, some stars look fuzzy. One example appears in the middle of Orion's 'sword'. Through binoculars, you can see that it is not a true star at all, but a glowing cloud of dust and gas called a nebula. It is known as the Great Nebula.

Galaxies

Other fuzzy objects turn out to contain stars as well as gas and dust. These are galaxies – huge swirling masses of billions of

▼ **Visible galaxy** The Andromeda Galaxy contains some 200 billion stars. It is so far away that its light takes about 2 300 000 years to reach us. It is the most distant object you can see with the naked eye.

stars. The only whole galaxies you can see with the naked eye are the Andromeda Galaxy in the Northern Hemisphere, and the Large and Small Magellanic Clouds in the Southern Hemisphere.

Astronomers have observed millions of galaxies, and believe that about 100 billion of them exist in the Universe. The Milky Way – the galaxy of which our Sun is a member – is shaped like a spiral, with curving arms of stars.

The Milky Way

The Milky Way is a band of light and stars stretching right across the sky. All the stars you can see in the sky are part of this same galaxy.

The Milky Way would look very much like the Andromeda Galaxy if you could see it from far enough away. It is about 100 000 light-years in diameter and contains about 200 billion stars. It is about 10 billion years old, and rotates around its central bulge. The Sun is about 30 000 light-years from the centre and takes 225 million years to make a complete circuit of the galaxy.

Biggest and smallest galaxies

The biggest galaxies contain more than a trillion stars, and are more than 5 million light-years across. The smallest, dwarf galaxies, have fewer than a billion stars and are less than 2000 light-years across.

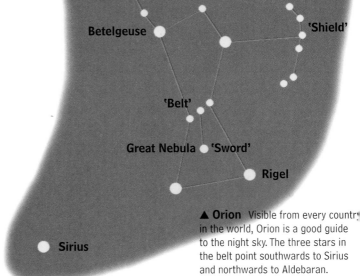

▲ **Orion** Visible from every country in the world, Orion is a good guide to the night sky. The three stars in the belt point southwards to Sirius and northwards to Aldebaran.

Nearest and farthest galaxies

The closest known galaxy outside the Milky Way is a dwarf galaxy in the constellation Sagittarius; it is about 82 000 light-years away. The most distant known galaxies are estimated to be more than 13 billion light-years away.

Constellations

Groups of stars seem to form shapes, called constellations, in the sky. Thousands of years ago, people gave names to the constellations and made up stories, or myths, about them. Astronomers still use these constellation names to identify stars. There are 88 constellations covering the whole sky.

Northern Hemisphere

Some constellations are easy to recognise. They include the Plough (or Big Dipper), which is actually part of a bigger constellation called Ursa Major (or the Great

Bear), and Cassiopeia, which forms a 'W' shape in the sky. Both these constellations are visible only in the Northern Hemisphere and Tropics, and can be used like a compass to find north (*see opposite page*).

The constellation Orion can be seen for part of the year in both the Northern and Southern Hemispheres. Orion (a great hunter in Greek mythology) has a distinctive 'belt', 'sword' and 'shield'.

Southern Hemisphere

The best known Southern Hemisphere constellation is Crux, or the Southern Cross, which looks like a cross or a diamond-shaped kite. It can be used to find south.

How long is a light-year?

A light-year is the distance light travels in a year. Light moves at 299 792 km (186 287 miles) per second. So a light-year equals about 9.46 trillion km (5.88 trillion miles).

▲ **Sirius** Also called 'the Dog Star', Sirius (burning brightly in the bottom left of this telescope image) is the brightest star in the night sky.

Stars and stargazing

There are so many stars that no one has ever been able to count them all. Astronomers estimate that there are about 100 billion galaxies in the Universe, each with an average of 100 billion stars. So, in all, there are about 10 billion trillion stars – 10 followed by 21 zeros.

Once you can recognise some of the constellations, you can find many interesting stars – especially if you have a small telescope or pair of binoculars.

The brightest star in the sky is called Sirius. You can find it by following an imaginary line from Orion's 'belt'.

If you look carefully, you can see that stars are various colours. Betelgeuse, at Orion's right 'shoulder', looks quite reddish, even without binoculars. This means that its surface is much less hot (2800°C) than Rigel (28 000°C), on the opposite side at Orion's left 'foot', which is bluish-white.

Many stars are 'doubles' – two stars very close together. One example is Mizar, in the 'handle' of the Plough or Big Dipper. On a clear, dark night, you may be able to see the nearby second star, Alcor, with the naked eye – and you certainly should be able to see it with binoculars.

Some stars vary in brightness at different times. Betelgeuse varies in brightness by about 2½ times over a period of almost seven years.

Some stars suddenly become much brighter than normal, sometimes in a matter of hours, and then gradually fade over the following months or years. The cause is a gigantic nuclear explosion. Such stars are called novae ('new' stars) and supernovae.

Supernovae

A supernova occurs when a large star – at least 1½ times as heavy as the Sun – is near the end of its life. It has used up most of its nuclear fuel and either explodes or collapses in on itself within a few seconds. In both cases, the supernova may give off billions of times more energy than the Sun for a period of months, or even a year or two.

The last supernova in the Milky Way was seen in 1604. In 1987 the closest supernova of recent times was observed in the Large Magellanic Cloud, a galaxy about 169 000 light-years away. At its peak it gave out 250 million times more light than the Sun.

The Crab Nebula, 6000 light-years away, is the remains of a supernova explosion in AD 1054 recorded by Chinese and Japanese astronomers. It was visible even in daylight. A pulsar is now where the original star used to be.

Pulsars are small, dense stars that spin very rapidly. They send out radio waves in a narrow beam like a lighthouse. As the beam crosses the Earth, a radio observatory can detect a pulse or 'blip'. The pulses may be a few seconds apart or up to hundreds of times each second. The fastest known pulsar pulses about 642 times each second.

Closest star

Proxima Centauri, our nearest star apart from the Sun, is close to Alpha Centauri, the brightest star in the constellation Centaurus. Proxima Centauri is 4.25 light-years away, while Alpha Centauri is only a little farther away, at 4.4 light-years.

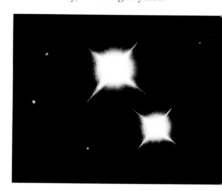

▲ **Double star** Alpha Centauri is a double, or binary, star – two stars very close to each other, which orbit each other every 80 years. It is visible to the naked eye. After our Sun and Sirius, it is the third brightest star.

The most distant space probe, Pioneer 1, will take nearly 80 000 years to travel a similar distance.

Farthest star

The farthest star yet detected was a supernova in a galaxy about 5 billion light-years away. It was first seen in August 1988.

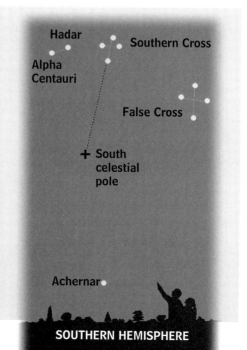

Cassiopeia

Polaris (Pole Star)

North celestial pole

Dubhe

Merak

Mizar

Plough or Big Dipper

NORTHERN HEMISPHERE

Finding your way

Northern Hemisphere
The Pole Star, or Polaris, is directly above the North Pole, and always points north. You can find it by following the line of the two 'pointer' stars of the Plough or Big Dipper, Merak and Dubhe. The 'W' of Cassiopeia also faces towards Polaris.

Southern Hemisphere
There is no bright star above the South Pole, so you have to imagine a line drawn from the longest 'arm' of the Southern Cross. If you extend it about 3½ times the distance between the two stars at each end of the arm, that spot marks the position of the South Pole.

Hadar

Southern Cross

Alpha Centauri

False Cross

South celestial pole

Achernar

SOUTHERN HEMISPHERE

Hottest and coldest stars

A nebula called NGC 2240 contains the hottest known star. Its surface temperature is about 220 000°C. The coolest stars are 'dead' stars called brown dwarfs, whose temperature is only a few hundred degrees.

Biggest stars

Betelgeuse is a red supergiant. It is the biggest star whose

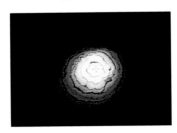

▲ **Betelgeuse** A halo of gas surrounds the red supergiant Betelgeuse, in the constellation of Orion. It is 17 000 times brighter than the Sun.

exact size is known. It varies in size, swelling and shrinking regularly. At its biggest, it is 980 million km (609 million miles across) – 700 times bigger

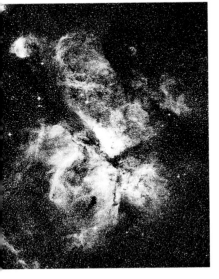

▲ **Bright star** The bright area in the centre of this nebula (cloud of dust and gas) is the star Eta Carinae.

than the Sun, or 6½ times bigger than the orbit of the Earth around the Sun. It would even dwarf the orbit of the planet Jupiter. Other stars may be even bigger but are surrounded by huge shells of gas and cannot be seen properly.

Smallest stars

Neutron stars are only about 10-20 km (6-12 miles) in diameter. They cannot be seen, but give off powerful radio signals. They are so dense that a piece the size of a pinhead would weigh tens of thousands of tonnes.

Brightest stars

How bright a star looks depends on how far away it is and how luminous it is – that is, how much energy it gives off. The most luminous known stars are so far away that they can be seen only with a telescope. Eta Carinae, in the constellation Carina, is estimated to generate 6.5 million times more energy than the Sun, and S Doradus (in the Large Magellanic Cloud) is at least a million times stronger than the Sun. Supernovae may be even more luminous, but only for short periods.

Heaviest stars

Eta Carinae is also probably the heaviest star – 150-200 times more massive than the Sun. Plaskett's Star, a binary star (pair of stars), is the heaviest whose weight has actually been calculated. Each star in the pair is at least 55 times heavier than the Sun.

Oldest and youngest stars

The oldest known stars are about 14 billion years old – about a billion years younger than the Big Bang that formed the Universe. The youngest known stars, known as IRAS 4, are in the nebula NGC 1333; they are still forming and will not be real stars for another 100 000 years. The Orion Nebula, M42, is another place where stars are being born.

Planets

The stars move, but they do so too slowly to see. The planets, on the other hand, can be seen to move from day to day or from week to week as they circle the Sun. Astrologers believe that, as the various planets move through the different constellations, they affect events in people's lives.

▲ **Planets at night** The bright tracks of Jupiter (top) and Venus appear in the night sky over Mount Fuji in Japan.

Planets shine because the Sun's light reflects off them. Their distance from the Earth varies over the months, so their brightness in the night sky varies too. At their brightest, some planets are the brightest objects in the sky apart from the Sun and Moon.

Mercury and Venus are the closest planets to the Sun – even closer than the Earth – and can sometimes be seen together shining very brightly in the westerly evening sky soon after sunset. They may also be seen in the eastern morning sky just before sunrise.

The Moon

The Moon looks by far the biggest and brightest object in the night sky, but that is only because it is much closer to Earth than any other. It is quite small compared to stars and even planets, and is only lit up

▼ **Lunar eclipse** The Moon gradually enters and then leaves the shadow cast by the Earth.

▲ **Return of the comet** Hale-Bopp, one of the brightest comets of the 20th century, passes above the Keck I and II telescope domes in Hawaii in 1997.

by reflected sunlight. Even through ordinary binoculars, you can see quite clearly the craters on the Moon's surface.

The Moon moves in a circular orbit around the Earth about every four weeks. But it also turns as it moves, so that the same side always faces us. As the angle between Sun, Moon and Earth changes, the amount of the Moon's visible side lit by the Sun varies. As a result, we see the various 'phases' of the Moon, from an almost invisible 'new' Moon, through the 'first quarter' to a round 'full' Moon, then through the 'last quarter' back to new Moon. Sometimes the

Moon passes through all or part of the shadow cast by the Earth itself. Then there is an eclipse of the Moon. When the Earth passes through the shadow cast by the Moon, there is an eclipse of the Sun.

Other objects

A comet can look spectacular – a small bright 'head' with a long 'tail' streaming from it. It consists of a ball of rock, dust and ice that travels around the Sun and then far out into space again. The tail is formed by the heat of the Sun boiling the ice and dust.

Some comets are seen regularly. Halley's Comet is near the Earth and Sun every 76 years (next appearance: 2061). Some large comets take longer. Comet Hyakutake was seen in 1996 for the first time in 9000 years and Comet Hale-Bopp in 1997 for the first time in 4000 years.

Shooting stars – bright, fast-moving streaks of light across the sky – consist of particles of dust or rock that get white-hot and burn up as they hit the Earth's atmosphere. They are properly called meteors. At certain dates in the year they are particularly common. These 'meteor showers' seem to come from a particular point in the sky, and are named after the constellation covering that area. They occur when the Earth's orbit around the Sun passes

through debris left by a comet. If you see a steadily moving 'star' crossing the night sky, it is probably an artificial satellite or part of an old rocket circling the Earth.

The Aurora Borealis, or Northern Lights, may be seen

▲ **Solar eclipse** A total eclipse of the Sun occurs when the Moon (black circle) blocks the Sun's disc.

on clear nights in the far north. It is caused by electrically charged particles thrown out from the Sun reacting with the upper atmosphere. Similar lights – the Aurora Australis – occur in the Southern Hemisphere, but are rarely seen in inhabited areas.

Major meteor showers

NAME	DATE OF PEAK
Quadrantids	Jan 4
Lyrids	Apr 21
Eta Aquarids	May 5
Delta Aquarids	July 28
Perseids	Aug 12
Orionids	Oct 22
Taurids	Nov 3
Leonids	Nov 17
Geminids	Dec 14
Ursids	Dec 23

Watch out for meteor showers on these dates.

▲ **Northern lights** Bands of light are caused by solar particles entering the upper atmosphere.

Planets

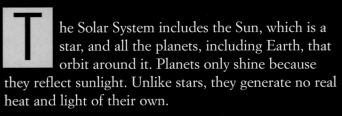

T he Solar System includes the Sun, which is a star, and all the planets, including Earth, that orbit around it. Planets only shine because they reflect sunlight. Unlike stars, they generate no real heat and light of their own.

▼ Solar System scale
The distances of the planets from each other and from the Sun are shown to scale.

Earth
Mars
Venus
Mercury
Jupiter
Saturn
Uranus
Neptune
Pluto

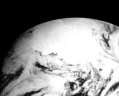
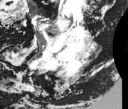

Other moons
The Solar System also includes the Moon (which orbits Earth) and the moons that circle other planets. All the planets except Mercury and Venus have moons. Altogether, over 60 moons are known about, but many of them are very small. Most were discovered only when unmanned space probes passed the outer planets and took photographs. The smallest known moon, Leda, a moon of Jupiter, is only about 10 km (6 1/4 miles) across.

Mercury
The four inner planets (those nearest the Sun) – Mercury, Venus, Earth and Mars – are all rocky on the surface. They are much smaller than the next four – the so-called giant planets. Mercury, the fastest-moving planet, is scorched by the Sun during the day and frozen by night.

Venus
Of all the planets, Venus is the most similar to Earth in size, and the brightest. Yet its features are obscured by clouds. Its surface is a wasteland of rocks roasted by the highest temperatures of all the planets.

Earth
Only the Earth has life-giving water in its three forms: solid (as ice), liquid (in seas, lakes and rivers) and vapour (in air). It is close enough to the Sun to receive warmth and light, and far enough not to burn up.

Mars
Because it seemed similar to Earth, scientists assumed that there might be life on Mars. The planet has the same length of day, and there are ice caps at its poles. But spacecraft landing on Mars have found no evidence of life.

	Mercury	Venus	Earth	Mars
Distance from the Sun (minimum)	45 900 000 km (28 520 000 miles)	107 400 000 km (66 740 000 miles)	147 000 000 km (91 340 000 miles)	206 700 000 km (128 440 000 miles)
Distance from the Sun (maximum)	69 700 000 km (43 300 000 miles)	109 000 000 km (67 730 000 miles)	152 000 000 km (94 450 000 miles)	249 000 000 km (154 730 000 miles)
Period of orbit around the Sun	87.97 days	224.7 days	365.3 days	687 days
Diameter (at Equator)	4878 km (3031 miles)	12 104 km (7521 miles)	12 756 km (7926 miles)	6794 km (4222 miles)
Diameter × Earth	0.38	0.95	1	0.53
Mass × Earth	0.055	0.815	1	0.11
Spin period (at Equator)	58 days 15 hours 28 mins	243 days 3 hours 50 mins	23 hours 56 mins	24 hours 37 mins
Surface temperature	350°C (day); −170°C (night)	480°C (average)	22°C (average)	−23°C (average)
Atmosphere	Very thin; some helium	Dense; mainly carbon dioxide	Mainly nitrogen and oxygen	Thin; mainly carbon dioxide
Number of moons	0	0	1	2
Names of main moons			Moon	Phobos; Deimos

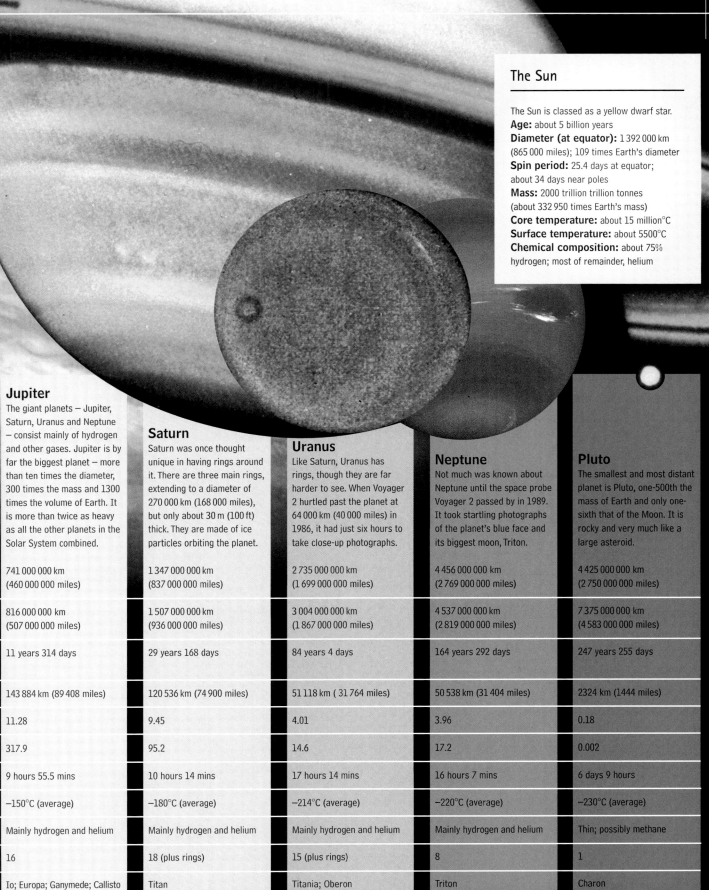

The Sun

The Sun is classed as a yellow dwarf star.
Age: about 5 billion years
Diameter (at equator): 1 392 000 km
(865 000 miles); 109 times Earth's diameter
Spin period: 25.4 days at equator;
about 34 days near poles
Mass: 2000 trillion trillion tonnes
(about 332 950 times Earth's mass)
Core temperature: about 15 million°C
Surface temperature: about 5500°C
Chemical composition: about 75%
hydrogen; most of remainder, helium

Jupiter

The giant planets – Jupiter, Saturn, Uranus and Neptune – consist mainly of hydrogen and other gases. Jupiter is by far the biggest planet – more than ten times the diameter, 300 times the mass and 1300 times the volume of Earth. It is more than twice as heavy as all the other planets in the Solar System combined.

Saturn

Saturn was once thought unique in having rings around it. There are three main rings, extending to a diameter of 270 000 km (168 000 miles), but only about 30 m (100 ft) thick. They are made of ice particles orbiting the planet.

Uranus

Like Saturn, Uranus has rings, though they are far harder to see. When Voyager 2 hurtled past the planet at 64 000 km (40 000 miles) in 1986, it had just six hours to take close-up photographs.

Neptune

Not much was known about Neptune until the space probe Voyager 2 passed by in 1989. It took startling photographs of the planet's blue face and its biggest moon, Triton.

Pluto

The smallest and most distant planet is Pluto, one-500th the mass of Earth and only one-sixth that of the Moon. It is rocky and very much like a large asteroid.

Jupiter	Saturn	Uranus	Neptune	Pluto
741 000 000 km (460 000 000 miles)	1 347 000 000 km (837 000 000 miles)	2 735 000 000 km (1 699 000 000 miles)	4 456 000 000 km (2 769 000 000 miles)	4 425 000 000 km (2 750 000 000 miles)
816 000 000 km (507 000 000 miles)	1 507 000 000 km (936 000 000 miles)	3 004 000 000 km (1 867 000 000 miles)	4 537 000 000 km (2 819 000 000 miles)	7 375 000 000 km (4 583 000 000 miles)
11 years 314 days	29 years 168 days	84 years 4 days	164 years 292 days	247 years 255 days
143 884 km (89 408 miles)	120 536 km (74 900 miles)	51 118 km (31 764 miles)	50 538 km (31 404 miles)	2324 km (1444 miles)
11.28	9.45	4.01	3.96	0.18
317.9	95.2	14.6	17.2	0.002
9 hours 55.5 mins	10 hours 14 mins	17 hours 14 mins	16 hours 7 mins	6 days 9 hours
−150°C (average)	−180°C (average)	−214°C (average)	−220°C (average)	−230°C (average)
Mainly hydrogen and helium	Mainly hydrogen and helium	Mainly hydrogen and helium	Mainly hydrogen and helium	Thin; possibly methane
16	18 (plus rings)	15 (plus rings)	8	1
Io; Europa; Ganymede; Callisto	Titan	Titania; Oberon	Triton	Charon

Space exploration

For centuries, people dreamed of leaving Earth for outer space. Only in the second half of the 20th century did the dream become reality, with the help of lightweight, heatproof materials, rockets, electronics, radar and computers. Since 1957, hundreds of probes and satellites have been sent into space.

1232
The Chinese made the **first rockets** at least 800 years ago, using gunpowder to propel them. These rockets were small, and were mainly used in firework displays. In 1232, the Chinese used them in battle against Mongol invaders.

1812
The British Army used the **first modern military rockets**, developed by William Congreve, in the war of 1812 against the United States and at the Battle of Waterloo in 1815. William Hale, a British inventor, was the first to add fins to guide rockets, in the 1840s.

1926
Robert Goddard, an American, launched the **first liquid-fuelled rocket** in 1926. It was 1.2 m (4 ft) high and rose only 56 m (184 ft), reaching a speed of about 100 km/h (60 mph). By 1937, Goddard's rockets rose 3 km (almost 2 miles).

▲ **Rocket scientist** American rocket pioneer Robert Goddard poses beside his first successful liquid-fuel rocket in 1926.

1942
In Germany during the Second World War, Wernher von Braun developed the A4 (also known as **V2**) liquid-fuelled rocket as a weapon to attack Britain. It first flew in 1942. It

▲◄ **Rocket weapons** German scientists, including von Braun (above, second from right), examine a rocket in the 1930s. Their experiments resulted in the V2 (left).

reached a height of 85 km (53 miles) and a speed of 5500 km/h (3400 mph).

1949
After the war, von Braun moved to the United States. In 1949 he built the **first two-stage rocket** – a vital step towards space travel. It reached a height of 400 km (250 miles).

August 1957
The Soviet Union fired its first long-range two-stage **R7 rocket** 8000 km (5000 miles). It was used to launch the first artificial satellite.

October 4, 1957
The Soviet Union launched the **first artificial satellite**, the 85 kg (38 1/2 lb) Sputnik 1, into orbit around the Earth. It was carried by an R7 rocket.

November 3, 1957
The **first animal in space**, a dog called Laika, orbited the Earth in the Soviet Sputnik 2.

January 31, 1958
The **first American satellite**, Explorer 1, was launched.

September 13, 1959
The **first man-made object to reach the Moon**, the Soviet probe Luna 2, crashed on the Moon's surface.

October 7, 1959
Luna 3 (USSR) sent back to Earth the **first photographs of the hidden far side of the Moon**. (The Moon spins on its axis in exactly the same time as it travels around the Earth, so we always see the same side.)

April 12, 1961
Yuri Gagarin (USSR) was the **first person to orbit the Earth**,

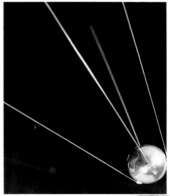

▲ **Explorer 1** The first American satellite, launched in 1958, was smaller than the Soviet Sputniks.

in the spacecraft Vostok 1. His flight lasted 1 hour 38 minutes before the craft returned to Earth by parachute.

May 5, 1961
Alan Shepard became **the first American in space**. His flight in Freedom 7 lasted 15 minutes.

February 20, 1962
John Glenn was the **first American in orbit**, doing three orbits of Earth in his Mercury capsule in just under five hours.

◄▼ **Sputnik story** Sputnik 1, the world's first satellite (left), was launched in October 1957. The following month, Laika the dog (below) orbited Earth in Sputnik 2.

▲ **Space hero** A postage stamp celebrates the Russian Yuri Gagarin, the first person to orbit the Earth, in 1961.

December 14, 1962

Mariner 2 (USA) successfully flew by Venus and sent back data about the planet. Later American and Soviet probes mapped Venus's surface. Venera 7 (USSR) was the first probe to reach the surface of Venus, in 1970.

June 16, 1963

Valentina Tereshkova (USSR) became the **first woman in space**, in Vostok 6.

▲ **First American in space** The astronaut Alan Shepard was rescued by a US Marine helicopter after his space flight in 1961.

March 18, 1965

Alexei Leonov (USSR) was the **first person to 'walk' in space**. He left the two-man Voskhod 2 spacecraft for 10 minutes while wearing a space suit. It was orbiting 500 km (300 miles) above the Earth.

July 14, 1965

Mariner 4 (USA) flew by Mars and sent back photographs showing the planet to have many craters.

February 3, 1966

Luna 9 (USSR) made the **first soft landing on the Moon**. Later Luna probes took small remote-controlled vehicles and returned lunar soil samples to Earth. An American Surveyor probe followed four months later. The first of several American Lunar Orbiters went into orbit around the Moon in August 1966. They surveyed it ready for manned landings.

March 16, 1966

The two-man Gemini 8 capsule (USA) made the **first docking with another space vehicle**, an Agena rocket. Astronauts had to be able to dock spacecraft for long-distance space travel or long-term space stations to be successful.

January 27, 1967

A fire in the cabin of the **first manned Apollo spacecraft** killed three American astronauts. They were on the launch pad, testing systems ready for the first test flight. The disaster delayed the American manned space flight programme by more than a year. The fire was blamed on an electric spark in the capsule's atmosphere, which was pure oxygen.

April 24, 1967

Soviet cosmonaut Vladimir Komarov was killed trying to land after the **first manned flight of the Soyuz 1** spacecraft.

November 11, 1967

The **most powerful, successful rocket** ever built was the three-stage Saturn 5, which was later used to take the first men to the Moon. Its thrust at liftoff was about 3435 tonnes. It could launch a load of 48 tonnes to the Moon. The

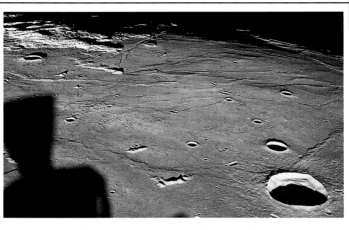

whole spacecraft was 110.6 m (363 ft) high and burnt more than 2 120 000 litres (over 466 000 imperial gallons) of fuel in less than 3 minutes.

December 21, 1968

Apollo 8 (USA) took off on the **first manned flight to the Moon**. During a six-day flight, the three astronauts orbited the Moon ten times before returning to Earth. They splashed down in the Pacific Ocean only 5 km (3 miles) from the rescue ship, after travelling more than 750 000 km (470 000 miles).

July 20, 1969

Neil Armstrong and 'Buzz' Aldrin (USA) became the **first men to step onto the Moon's surface** during the Apollo 11 mission. Their lunar module, *Eagle*, stayed on the Moon just under a day. They brought back

▶ **First woman in space** The Russian cosmonaut Valentina Tereshkova poses in a space suit in 1963, the year of her historic flight.

▲ **Moon landing** You can see the shadow of the Apollo 11 lunar module as it approaches the Moon's cratered surface in July 1969.

rock and soil samples, photographs and scientific measurements.

November 1969 – December 1972

Six more Apollo missions were sent to the Moon. One of them – Apollo 13 – did not land. It almost ended in disaster when there was an explosion on board. But the astronauts managed to return safely to Earth after circling the Moon.

Space exploration

▲ **Station in space** Skylab photographed by a new crew just before their command module docked with the space station.

Apollo 15, in July 1971, was the first to use a wheeled vehicle – the battery-powered Lunar Roving Vehicle, or 'Moon Buggy' – on the Moon's surface.

1966 – 1972
The Soviet Moon-landing programme – kept secret until the late 1980s – failed. There were serious faults in the giant N1 rocket built for the journey. Most test firings blew up. There were also serious

▼ **International partners** An American astronaut and a Russian cosmonaut shake hands, as an Apollo capsule (USA) links up with a Soyuz capsule (USSR) in 1975.

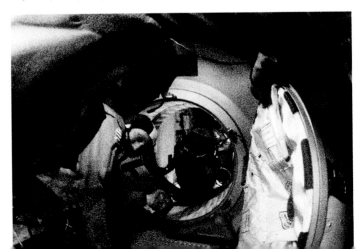

problems with the L1 lunar vehicle, planned to carry two cosmonauts.

1971 – 1982
The USSR launched a series of **Salyut space stations**. Salyut 6 was the first to be sent supplies and fuel while in orbit. It was operated for nearly five years. Crews spent up to eight months on board Salyut 7 in 1982-6.

November 13, 1971
Mariner 9 (USA) went into orbit around Mars. For 11 months it sent back photographs and data, showing that Mars's atmosphere was thinner than expected.

May 14, 1973
The **Skylab space station** (USA) was launched. It was manned by three crews sent up over the following nine months. The third crew stayed for 84 days – a record at the time. Skylab eventually broke up in the atmosphere, and fell to Earth in July 1979.

December 3, 1973
Pioneer 10 (USA) passed by Jupiter, followed by Pioneer 11 in December 1974.

July 15, 1975
An **Apollo capsule** (USA) **linked up in space with a Soyuz capsule** (USSR). This was a first

step to building and operating international space stations.

October 21, 1975
Venera 9 and 10 (USSR) sent back the **first photographs of the surface of Venus.**

July 20, 1976
Viking 1 (USA) landed on Mars and sent back photographs. Tests on the Martian soil showed no signs of life. **Viking 2**, which landed six weeks later, showed similar results.

March 5, 1979
Voyager 1 (USA) flew by Jupiter and sent detailed photographs. It then flew on to Saturn (November 12, 1980), and surveyed the planet and its moon Titan before heading out of the Solar System.

July 9, 1979
Voyager 2 (USA) flew by Jupiter. It then flew on to Saturn (August 25, 1981), Uranus (January 24, 1986) and Neptune (August 25, 1989). As it passed each planet in turn, the planet's gravity changed the space probe's direction towards the next planet.

April 12, 1981
The **first re-usable rocket**, the American space shuttle *Columbia*, made its first flight into space. It was re-used for the first time in November 1981. The very first shuttle, *Enterprise*, had made test gliding flights and landings from 1977. It had been launched in midair from a jumbo jet. Many successful shuttle missions followed *Columbia*'s first 54 hour space flight. Some launched commercial or military satellites, or carried out repairs to satellites (including the Hubble Space Telescope). Many flights involved experiments in a laboratory called the Spacelab, which was built in Europe.

January 28, 1986
The tenth launch of the **space shuttle Challenger** ended in disaster 73 seconds after liftoff.

▲▼ **Space shuttles** The first space shuttle, *Columbia*, was launched successfully in 1981 (above); a later shuttle, *Challenger*, exploded tragically in 1986 (below).

The spacecraft broke apart and exploded because of a fault in one of the booster rockets. All seven crew members died.

February 20, 1986
The space station Mir (USSR) was launched. It was followed by several extra modules (parts), which linked up with Mir to form **the biggest space station yet built**. It has since been visited several times by American space shuttles, and has carried many non-Russian astronauts among its crew.

March 13, 1986
Several probes visited Halley's Comet in 1986 on its closest approach to Earth for 76 years. The British-built **Giotto** took photographs of the comet's nucleus (head) from 1675 km (1040 miles) on March 13. It passed closer, but the camera was damaged by a flying particle.

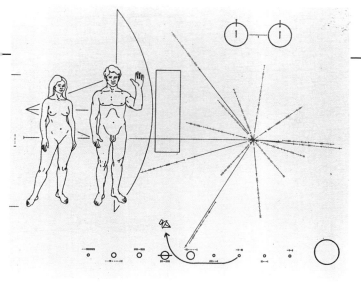

It carried a small roving vehicle called Sojourner, which crawled about the surface and analysed what the rocks were made of.

February 15, 1998
Voyager 1 overtook Pioneer 10 to become the **most distant space probe**. By December 31, 1999, it was expected to be about 11.5 billion km (over 7 billion miles) away from Earth.

November 20, 1998
A Russian rocket launched the first part of the **International** Space Station. The second part was launched and connected two weeks later by American astronauts. Altogether, the project involves 15 countries. It is planned to be complete in 2004. Then it will have more than 100 units, including laboratories and living quarters for six or seven astronauts.

November 4, 1998
John Glenn returned to space on the space shuttle *Discovery*, 36 years after becoming the first American in orbit.

October 17, 1986
Pioneer 10 crossed the orbit of the most distant planet, Pluto – becoming the **first man-made object to leave the Solar System**. It carried a plaque with messages and pictures for any other civilisation that may find it.

April 24, 1990
The **Hubble Space Telescope** (USA and European Space Agency) was launched into Earth orbit. It was able to take clearer and more detailed pictures of planets, stars and galaxies than any previous telescope. However, a small fault was found in its mirror that blurred the images slightly.

August 10, 1990
Magellan (USA) went into orbit around Venus and began detailed radar mapping of the planet's surface.

▼ **Space station** With its solar panels spread like wings, Mir has compartments for docking, working, living, and for its engines.

▲ **Space salute** Pioneers 10 and 11 carried a plaque. The symbols were devised so that an intelligent extraterrestrial being could interpret it. A naked man raises his hand in greeting.

December 1993
The crew of space shuttle **Endeavour** repaired the Hubble Space Telescope. They installed extra mirrors to correct the fault in the instrument.

March 22, 1995
Valeri Polyakov (Russia) returned to Earth from Mir after setting a **new record for manned space flight**. He had spent more than 14 months in space.

December 7, 1995
Galileo (USA; launched 1989) reached Jupiter. One section plunged into Jupiter's atmosphere. The other went into orbit around the planet. Over the following months, Galileo sent back many images of Jupiter and its moons.

June 25, 1997
An unmanned supply craft **collided with Mir**, damaging the space station's power supply and threatening the lives of the crew. Mir was later repaired and continued to work.

July 4, 1997
Pathfinder (USA) landed in an ancient river valley on Mars.

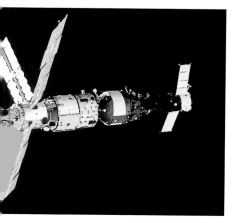

▲ **Life in space** The International Space Station (above) is due to be finished early in the 21st century. It could help humankind to set up home in space.

▶ **Return to space** At the age of 77, John Glenn (below) became the oldest man in space. He performed tests to study the effects of zero-gravity on a man of his age.

Geological timescale

The history of the Earth is divided into aeons, eras and periods, reflecting changes in rock formation dating back as far as 4 billion years. Plant and animal fossils found in each type of rock indicate major geological and climatic changes.

Dividing time – aeons

The 4.6 billion year history of the Earth is divided into four aeons. The earliest, called the Hadean, includes the formation of the Earth before any life began. The next is the Archean, which began 3.8 billion years ago (bya). It is marked by the origin of primitive life and lasted 1.3 billion years. The Proterozoic ('earlier life') began 2.5 billion years ago, and saw the evolution of more complex

4.6 billion years ago

1. Oldest rocks on Earth
The oldest known minerals are Hadean in age and come from north-western Canada. They have been dated as 3.962 billion years old. At that time, much of the Earth's surface was covered with active volcanoes.

3.8 bya

2. First evidence of life
The oldest fossil organisms, of single-celled bacteria smaller than specks of dust, have been buried in Archean seabed sediments 3.5 billion years old. The fossils were found in South Africa and Western Australia.

2.5 bya

3. First animal fossils
Burrow traces, made by worm-like organisms 1 billion years ago, have been found in Proterozoic rock in northern India. These are the oldest remains of multicelled animals.

580 million years ago

4. The Ediacarans
Fossils of jellyfish and flatworm-like organisms have been found in late Proterozoic seabed sediments. They are known as Ediacarans, after Ediacara in South Australia, where the first fossils were found.

150 mya

16. Feathered dinosaurs
Until recently, only birds were thought to have feathers, but feathered dinosaurs, such as *Protarchaeopteryx*, have been found in China. The fossils have been preserved in 145 million-year-old Jurassic Period rocks.

150 mya

15. First birds
The oldest fossil bird, *Archaeopteryx*, was found drowned and fossilised in 150 million-year-old Jurassic Period seabed deposits in Germany.

215 mya

14. First mammals
The first true mammal, which gave birth to live young, was probably a tiny, furry, shrew-like animal called *Adeliobasileus*. It lived in the Triassic Period deserts of Texas around 215 million years ago.

248 mya

13. Biggest extinction
Around 248 million years ago, 96 per cent of all species of animals and plants were wiped out, although scientists don't yet know what the causes were. It marks the end of the Palaeozoic Era and beginning of the Mesozoic.

150 mya

17. First flowering plants
Most kinds of living plants, from grasses to trees, are flowering plants. The first flowering plants, called *Archaefructus*, evolved in the Jurassic Period around 150 million years ago. Their fossils were found in China in 1998.

65 mya

18. End of the dinosaurs
An asteroid hit the Earth 65 million years ago at the end of the Cretaceous Period. Experts think the impact may have contributed to the extinction of the dinosaurs and 76 per cent of all species. The event marks the end of the Mesozoic Era.

53 mya

19. First whales
The first fossil whale remains, called *Himalayacetus*, were found in 1998 embedded within 53.5 million-year-old, Eocene Period seabed sediments. The sediments were once part of an ancient ocean called Tethys and now form strata within the foothills of the Himalayas.

30 mya

20. Building the Himalayas
The continent of India began colliding with Asia around 55 million years ago. The slow impact had so much force that by the Oligocene Period, around 30 million years ago, it had crumpled the edge of Asia into the Himalayan mountains.

life. It is followed by the Phanerozoic ('abundant life'), which began 545 million years ago (mya), during which life as we know it today evolved.

The eras of life
The Phanerozoic Aeon is divided into three eras. The first is called the Palaeozoic ('ancient life'), which began 545 million years ago. At first, life was largely confined to the seas. The later Palaeozoic, which began 354 million years ago, saw the growth of the first forests and the reptiles and amphibians that lived in them.

The second era, called the Mesozoic ('middle life'), began 248 million years ago and was the era of the dinosaurs. The most recent era is called the Cenozoic ('recent life'). It began 65 million years ago and is dominated by mammals and flowering plants.

Periods of time
The eras are subdivided into periods. The boundaries between periods are marked by environmental changes recorded in the rocks, along with the fossil remains of animals and plants. The first period is called the Cambrian.

545 mya | **530 mya** | **470 mya** | **450 mya**

5. First fossil shells
The first fossil shells appear in Cambrian sediments deposited on the seabed 545 million years ago. They are tiny mineral cones, just 1 mm or so in size, that belonged to snail-like creatures.

6. Our oldest ancestor?
A tiny eel-like animal (4 cm/ 1 1/2 in long), called *Pikaia*, may be our oldest known ancestor. It had a spine-like structure, a feature that eventually evolved into the backbone of the vertebrates to which we belong.

7. First fish
The oldest known fish fossils, called *Sacabambaspis*, have been found in seabed deposits of the Ordovician Period in Bolivia. These primitive fish, called agnathans, were the first backboned animals.

8. First land plants and animals
Fossils of the first land plants have been found in 450 million-year-old rock in North Africa. Footprints of the first centipede-like animals have been found in sediments of similar age in the Lake District of Britain.

310 mya | **325 mya** | **360 mya** | **420 mya**

12. Eggs and independence
The first vertebrates to be fully independent of water were egg-laying reptiles. *Hylonomus*, the oldest known reptile, lived in the Carboniferous Period coal-swamps of Nova Scotia, Canada.

11. First forests
The land was first forested with tree-size plants during the Carboniferous Period. There were so many plants that their remains formed huge coal deposits and changed the gases in the atmosphere.

10. Four-legged animals with backbones
Our first vertebrate ancestors with arms and legs appear in 360 million-year-old Devonian Period river deposits. The fossils were found in Greenland.

9. Advanced plants begin
Plants capable of growing upright require advanced cell structures and did not evolve until Silurian times. The oldest known, called *Cooksonia*, were found in Wales and are some 420 million years old.

20 mya | **5 mya** | **500 000 ya** | **6 000 ya**

21. Grasses and horses
The first grasslands appeared in the shadow of the North American Rockies over 20 million years ago in the Miocene Period. The primitive horse *Parahippus* was able to eat these grasses.

22. The last Ice Age
The world's climate began cooling around 5 million years ago, and around 2 million years ago the first glaciers and ice-sheets began forming at the start of the last Ice Age. The ice had retreated by 10 000 years ago, but scientists are not sure whether it has gone for ever.

23. Modern humans
The first type of humans who looked similar to modern humans are known as *Homo heidelbergensis*. They appeared 500 000 years ago in Africa. By 40 000 years ago, humans had spread throughout the world.

24. Last mammoths
Woolly mammoths are among the most famous Ice Age animals. Some dwarf mammoths survived on Wrangel Island in the Arctic Ocean until 6000 years ago, when pyramids were being built in Egypt.

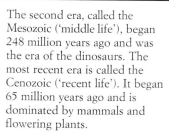

Proterozoic

545 mya | **Phanerozoic** | **Today**
Palaeozoic | Mesozoic Cenozoic

Landscapes

The surface area of the Earth is over 500 million km2 (nearly 200 million sq miles), but just 29 per cent of this is land. The rest is covered by seas and oceans. During the last Ice Age, over 20 000 years ago, sea levels were a lot lower (around 150 m/ 500 ft), so there was more land above sea level.

Biggest continent

Eurasia is about 53.7 million km2 (nearly 20.7 million sq miles) in area and makes up 30 per cent of the Earth's land surface. Africa is next biggest at 20 per cent.

Deepest valley on land

The Bentley trench in Antarctica reaches 2538 m (8327 ft) below sea level, far deeper than any other part of a continent. It is not possible to go there because the valley is buried below the Antarctic ice cap, the weight of which is responsible for its great depth.

Deepest cave

The Jean Bernard cave in France is the deepest known cave. It plunges 1602 m (5256 ft) below the surface. Caves like this have been hollowed out by slightly acid rainwater, which dissolves the limestone rock as it soaks through the ground.

Largest cave

The largest single cave chamber is Lubang Nasib Bagus on the Indonesian island of Sarawak. It was not discovered until 1980 and is 700 m (2300 ft) long, 300 m (980 ft) wide on average and at least 70 m (230 ft) high. The West End district of London would fit inside it.

Biggest island

Greenland is by far the biggest island. With an area of 2 175 000 km2 (840 000 sq miles), it is nearly ten times the size of the British Isles.

Roof of the world

The Himalayan mountain belt and the Tibetan plateau to its north are often referred to as the 'Roof of the World'. The Tibetan plateau is the most extensive uplifted area on Earth, being over 5 million km2 (2 million sq miles). It is bigger

▲ **Underground world** Deer Cave on Sarawak, Indonesia, is the world's largest cave passage.

▶ **Smouldering giant** Popocatépetl, near Mexico City, is the highest active volcano in the world.

than India, and has an average height of 5 km (3 miles).

Highest peak

The Himalayan peak of Mount Everest on the Nepal-China border is the highest mountain, being 8848 m (29 029 ft) at present. The top 30 highest mountains are all in Asia. Mountain heights can never be exact because such high peaks are always being worn down by ice shattering and rock falls, although the Himalayan mountain range is also being pushed upwards by forces within the Earth.

Highest volcano

Aconcagua in Argentina is the highest volcano, reaching some 6959 m (22 864 ft) above sea level but it is now extinct. The highest active volcano is Popocatépetl (5465 m, 17 929 ft), which looms over Mexico City and last erupted in 1943.

Best-preserved meteor crater

Meteor or Barringer Crater, near Wimslow, Arizona, discovered in 1891, is 1300 m (4200 ft) wide and now about 180 m (600 ft) deep. Its circular rim is raised 40 m (130 ft) above the surrounding landscape. It was formed by a meteor that hit this region 27 000 years ago.

Longest river

Two river systems compete to be the longest: the Nile in North Africa and the Amazon in South America. Rivers are difficult to measure exactly and are constantly changing their courses. The Nile seems to have the edge at the moment and is measured at 6670 km (4145 miles), while the Amazon is 6450 km (4010 miles). But the

▼ **On top of the world**
The highest mountains on each continent are shown here.

K2, Pakistan-China 8611 m (28 251 ft)

Mount McKinley, USA 6194 m (20 321 ft)

Mount Kilimanjaro Tanzania 5895 m (19 340 ft)

Mont Blanc France 4807 m (15 770 ft)

Ben Nevis, Scotland 1343 m (4409 ft)

Mount Fuji, Japan 3776 m (12 388 ft)

▲ **Heat and shade** There is no escaping the heat in the Sahara desert, the hottest place on Earth.

flow (the quantity of water on the move per second) of the Amazon is 60 times greater than that of the Nile.

Highest waterfall
The Angel Falls on the Carrao River in Venezuela have a spectacular total drop of nearly 1000 m (over 3200 ft), with the longest single drop being 807 m (2648 ft).

Average height of the land
Despite all the high mountains in the world, the average height of the continental landmasses is only about 300 m (1000 ft) above present sea level. In comparison, the average depth of all the oceans is some 4000 m (13 125 ft) below present sea level.

Biggest desert
The Sahara in North Africa is eight times bigger than any other desert. A world record for the highest temperature of 58° C (136° F) in the shade was recorded in the Libyan part of the Sahara in 1922. The Sahara covers over 9 million km2 (3.5 million sq miles) and is getting

bigger as the global climate warms. Yet only a few tens of thousands of years ago, much of the area was covered with plants, rivers and lakes.

Biggest and deepest lakes
The Caspian Sea in Russian Asia is by far the biggest lake, being 371 800 km2 (143 550 sq miles) in area and up to 1025 m (3360 ft) deep. In fact it is an inland sea with salty water. Lake Baikal in Russia is the deepest lake, reaching a maximum of 1637 m (5371 ft) deep and contains 20 per cent of the world's readily available, surface supply of fresh water. It

▶ **Winding course**
This satellite photograph shows the Amazon river running through the Amazon basin (the green area).

contains many unique animals including the freshwater seal.

Freshwater supply
Only a small proportion of the water on Earth is fresh, and over 77 per cent of that is locked up in ice caps and glaciers. Most of the remaining 23 per cent of fresh water is underground, and only 3 per cent is in the atmosphere, rivers and lakes.

Biggest, highest and most active volcanoes
Mauna Loa is an active Hawaiian volcano rising 4170 m (13 681 ft) above sea level. It is one of the highest mountains on Earth because it extends down about 6000 m

(19 685 ft) to the ocean floor, giving it a total height of over 10 200 m (33 480 ft). Kilauea in the Hawaiian islands is the most continuously active volcano. Lava has being pouring out of it at the rate of 5 m3 (176 cu ft) per second since 1983.

▼ **Long drop** Angel Falls have the tallest single drop of any waterfall in the world.

Mount Everest,
Nepal-China
8848 m (29 028 ft)

Aconcagua,
Argentina
6959 m (22 864 ft)

Popocatépetl,
Mexico
5465 m (17 929 ft)

Vinson Massif,
Antarctica
4897 m (16 066 ft)

Seas and oceans

A bout 70 per cent of the Earth's surface is covered in seawater, most of it in the Southern Hemisphere. The Pacific is the biggest ocean. It has an average depth of 4000 m (13 000 ft) and covers an area of over 181 million km2 (70 million sq miles) – three times more than Asia, the largest continent.

▲ **Pacific Ocean** From this angle the planet's surface appears to be almost completely covered by water.

Sea-ice
Seawater freezes slowly and the salt dissolved in it gradually drains out, leaving ice that contains little salt. The Inuits of the Arctic melt sea-ice and use it for drinking water.

Saltwater
Seawater is a solution of 96 per cent freshwater and 3 per cent salt, so every 100 tonnes of seawater contains 3 tonnes of salt. If all the salt were taken from the seas and spread over the land, it would form a layer 152 m (500 ft) thick. The remaining 1 per cent of seawater is made up of tiny amounts of some 80 other elements, including gold. By far the biggest gold reserves on Earth are in the oceans, but nobody has yet found an economic way of extracting it.

Jigsaw puzzle Earth
The Earth's surface is made up of nine huge continental plates and many smaller ones, which are on average 64 km (50 miles) thick. They have been shuffled

▶ **Frozen water supply** An Inuit hunter in Alaska collects ice for drinking water.

around the Earth's surface for over 3 billion years. As they split up and bumped into one another, new continents formed, together with volcanoes and mountain chains. Over 400 million years ago, North America, Europe and many other parts of today's Northern Hemisphere lay south of the Equator.

Moving oceans
The Earth's crust beneath the oceans is broken into enormous rocky plates, like those of the continents. The ocean plates can move at speeds of up to 20 cm (8 in) a year by a process known as mid-ocean spreading. Mid-ocean ridges, which are mountain ranges on the ocean floor, split apart, allowing volcanic lava to pour out and harden, forming new ocean-floor rocks.

Hot-water life
Many new kinds of animals have been discovered over the last 20 years, living in the active volcanic areas of mid-ocean ridges. In the crest of a ridge, at depths of around 2-4 km (1-2¹/2 miles), there are

▶ **Feeding time**
A large mass of bacteria feed around a deep-sea vent, where the water is rich in minerals that pour out from under the sea floor.

numerous chimney-like structures called vents that belch out water and mineral particles at temperatures of up to 350°C (662°F). The minerals are 'food' for bacteria, which are consumed by clams and worms. Crab-like crustaceans and shrimps feed on fragments of organic matter. Altogether they form a unique chain of life that survives without light.

Moving magnetism
Volcanic rock in the mid-ocean ridges records changes in the direction of the Earth's magnetic field. It seems that the magnetic north and south poles swop places every half million years or so, although the process takes about 1000 years to complete. Scientists do not know exactly how the switch happens because it has not occurred within human history.

Young oceans
None of the rocks in the ocean floor are more than 200 million years old. Lava is still spilling out along the mid-ocean ridges and hardening into new rock. Because the Earth cannot expand, ocean floor in some areas is destroyed as new rock is created.

Ocean mountains
The longest mountain chain on Earth is under the sea. It stretches south from the Arctic Ocean, following a wiggly path midway between the continents of North America and Europe and South

Baltic Sea

EUROPE

Black Sea

Caspian Sea

Mediterranean Sea

Red Sea

AFRICA

INDIAN OCEAN

Atlantic-Indian Ridge

America and Africa. In the southern South Atlantic it splits in two, with one branch going into the Pacific Ocean and the other extending up into the Indian Ocean. It extends altogether for over 50 000 km (30 000 miles) – four times the diameter of the Earth – and contains thousands of individual peaks, many of them extinct volcanoes. Most have their summits well below sea level, but some appear above the surface, forming active volcanoes like those of the Hawaiian Islands in the Pacific.

Ocean valleys
The ocean floor forms deep valleys in some parts of the world. At the bottom of these valleys the water is icy cold, pitch black and under pressure from the weight of water above. Yet a whole range of creatures, including fish, worms and shellfish, have adapted to living in these extreme conditions. The valleys, called deep-ocean trenches, form the most exaggerated features on the Earth's surface. The Mariana

▲ Deepest and highest
The Mariana Trench (left) is slightly deeper than Mount Everest (right) is high.

(30 000 ft), the pressure amounts to the equivalent of a 1 tonne weight resting on an adult human thumb.

Deep dives
The record for the deepest breath-held dive is 125 m (410 ft); it took the diver 2 minutes

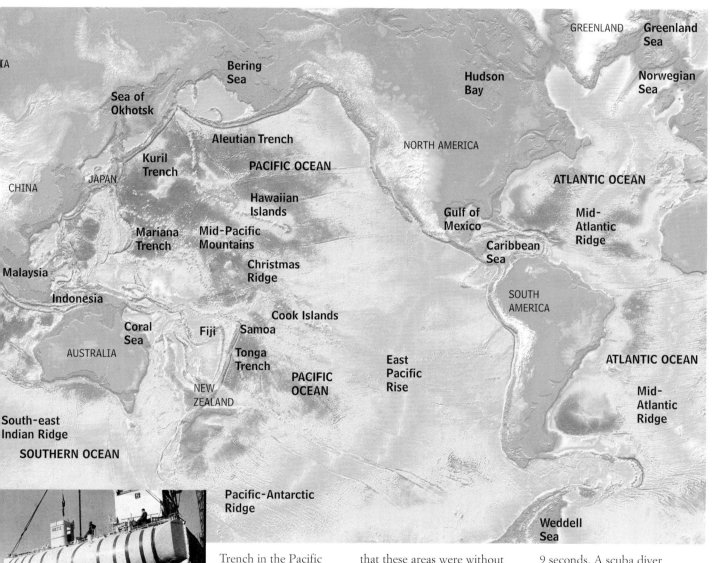

GREENLAND **Greenland Sea**

Hudson Bay

Norwegian Sea

IA

Bering Sea

Sea of Okhotsk

Aleutian Trench

NORTH AMERICA

Kuril Trench

CHINA   JAPAN   **PACIFIC OCEAN**

Hawaiian Islands

ATLANTIC OCEAN

Gulf of Mexico

Mid-Atlantic Ridge

Mariana Trench   **Mid-Pacific Mountains**

Caribbean Sea

Christmas Ridge

Malaysia

Indonesia

SOUTH AMERICA

Cook Islands

Coral Sea   Fiji   **Samoa**

AUSTRALIA

Tonga Trench

East Pacific Rise

ATLANTIC OCEAN

PACIFIC OCEAN

NEW ZEALAND

Mid-Atlantic Ridge

South-east Indian Ridge

SOUTHERN OCEAN

Pacific-Antarctic Ridge

Weddell Sea

▲ Deep diver In 1960, the US Navy bathyscaph (a manned submersible) called the *Trieste* reached a depth of 10.9 km (6³/₄ miles) in the Mariana Trench in the northern Pacific.

Trench in the Pacific descends to 11 034 m (36 200 ft). Trenches mark the places where areas of ocean floor are crumpled and pushed down into the Earth to be melted and recycled.

Ocean plains
Much of the ocean floor consists of flat plains of mud at depths of around 4 km (2¹/₂ miles). Experts used to think

that these areas were without life. But deep-sea photography has revealed that they are alive with fish, sponges, sea urchins, sea lilies and burrowing worms.

Heavy water
The deeper a diver or submersible goes below the surface, the greater the pressure becomes. The pressure increases with the increasing height and weight of the column of water above. At a depth of about 9000 m

9 seconds. A scuba diver managed a depth of 133 m (437 ft) in 1968, and a helmeted diver 176 m (577 ft).

Tides
The rise and fall of the ocean surface is seen along seashores by rising and falling tides. Normally the difference between high and low tide is less than 1 m (2¹/₂ ft), but in Canada's Bay of Fundy there is a rise and fall of 14 m (45 ft), the greatest in the world.

Living zones

Differences in climate and vegetation create a range of living zones. Each of these zones is a home where different kinds of plant and animal life can flourish. Some plants and animals can survive only in zones like tropical forests, where it is warm and damp. Others can cope with zones where drought is common. Others again prefer zones with bitter cold for many months each year.

► **Land of extremes**
In the northern coniferous forests, winters are long and very cold and many of the animals hibernate.

Deserts
Deserts cover more than a quarter of the Earth's land surface. The Sahara is one of the hottest places on Earth. It can reach 50°C (122°F) in the day. The Gobi is hot in summer but can be as cold as –20°C (–4°F) in winter. The plants and animals that live in deserts have developed adaptations to protect themselves from heat and drought.

Mountains
Mountains have several temperature and vegetation zones between the base and the top. The tops of some mountains are covered with snow all the year round. The Himalayas have 96 of the world's highest mountains, including Everest – at 8848 m (29 029 ft) the tallest of the lot.

Tropical forests
Tropical rain forests run in a belt around the Equator, where the weather is warm and wet. Once, they occupied about one-fifth of the Earth's land surface, but large parts have since been cut down. The rain forests contain around 1.5 million species of plants and animals, over half the known total for the world. The largest area of tropical forest is the Amazon basin in Brazil, covering 5.3 million km² (2 million sq miles).

Monsoon forests also grow in the tropics, but farther away from the Equator, in north-east Australia, West Africa and parts of India. Unlike rain forests, they get very little rain for several months each year.

Temperate forests
Temperate regions have mild summers but cold winters. In the wettest areas, such as New Zealand's South Island or the north-west coast of North America, giant trees form temperate rain forest. Most of these trees are evergreen, but in other temperate forests, trees drop their leaves in winter.

Boreal (northern) forests
In the cold northern reaches of the Northern Hemisphere, the only trees that can survive are conifers, such as spruces, pines and firs. Most of these trees are evergreen and they make up the biggest forest in the world, stretching in a broken band across Scandinavia, northern Russia and the north of North America.

Grasslands
Grasslands are found on every continent except Antarctica. They are given different names in different parts of the world: prairies in North America, pampas in Argentina, veld in South Africa and steppes in Russia. In tropical parts of the world grasslands are called savannah. The largest areas of savannah are in Central and East Africa, Venezuela and north Australia.

Coral reefs
Australia's Great Barrier Reef, the biggest coral reef of all, is over 3200 km (2000 miles) long. Coral reefs also occur in the Indian Ocean and in the Caribbean.

Poles and tundra
The North and South Poles are the coldest places on Earth. The South Pole is in the middle of Antarctica, where the ice is up to 4000 m (13 000 ft) thick. At the North Pole, the ice covering the Arctic Ocean can be as much as 5 m (16 ft) thick.

Land in the far north of the Northern Hemisphere, around the edge of the Arctic Ocean, is called tundra. The ground below the surface is permanently frozen.

Alaska

GREEN[LAND]

NORTH AMERICA

Prairies

NORTH ATLANTIC OCEAN

CARIBBEAN SEA

Amazon basin

SOUTH AMERICA

Andes

Pampas

- Boreal forest
- Temperate forest
- Tropical forest
- Grasslands
- Desert
- Mountains
- Tundra
- Coral reef

◄ **Autumn glow** The trees in temperate forests lose their leaves in winter. These forests are home to small birds and mammals.

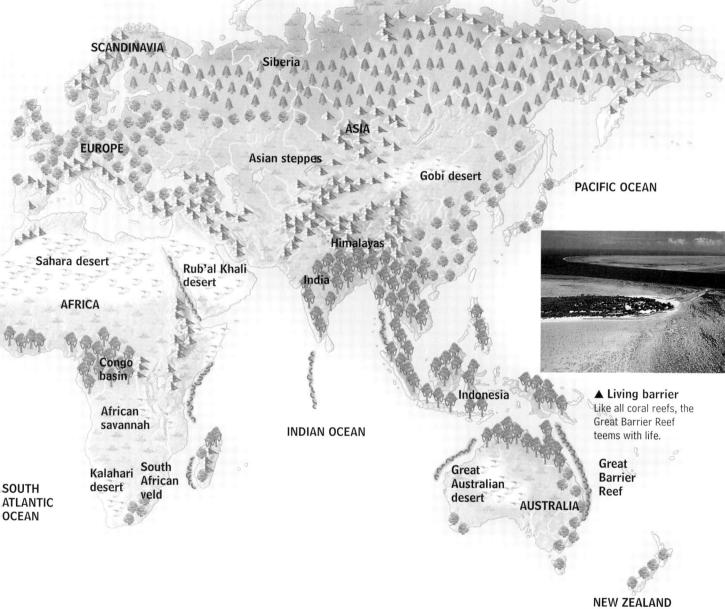

ARCTIC OCEAN

SCANDINAVIA

Siberia

EUROPE

ASIA

Asian steppes

Gobi desert

PACIFIC OCEAN

Sahara desert

Rub'al Khali desert

Himalayas

India

AFRICA

Congo basin

African savannah

INDIAN OCEAN

Indonesia

▲ **Living barrier** Like all coral reefs, the Great Barrier Reef teems with life.

Kalahari desert

South African veld

Great Australian desert

AUSTRALIA

Great Barrier Reef

SOUTH ATLANTIC OCEAN

NEW ZEALAND

ANTARCTICA

◄ **Midnight sun** In Antarctica, the Sun never sets in mid summer.

By far the biggest energy sources today are fossil fuels, but they are constantly being used up. Renewable energy sources such as wind and solar power have yet to make a major contribution on a global scale, but they can be very important locally.

Fuelling the planet

Fossil fuels – oil, gas and coal – provide over 90 per cent of the world's energy. They formed underground over hundreds of millions of years, and cannot be renewed. The remaining energy supplies are renewable and come primarily from nuclear power and hydroelectric (water) power. Other renewable sources are fuelwood, underground heat (geothermal power), wind and solar power.

▲ **Wind power** Rows of windmills in California drive turbines that generate electricity.

Oil and gas

These two fossil fuels provide 63 per cent of the world's energy. They took many millions of years to form under the ground from the remains of dead microscopic organisms. We have burned a large proportion of these reserves during the last 150 years, and it is estimated that by the end of the 21st century most will be used up. Much of the world's oil reserves are in Middle Eastern countries, especially Saudi Arabia. Russia, the southern countries of the former USSR and the Middle East have the biggest gas reserves.

Coal

Coal was the first fossil fuel to be discovered and used extensively. Today it provides

Energy production

The map shows the main sources of energy and annual production for each country.

mt = million tonnes
Gw = gigawatts
bm3 = billion cubic metres

●	Major oilfield	**G**	Geothermal
▪	Major gasfield	**W**	Wind
▲	Major coalfield	**S**	Solar
H	Hydroelectric	**FW**	Fuelwood

27 per cent of the world's energy needs. The use of coal in factories brought about the Industrial Revolution, but caused pollution of the environment and atmosphere. Burning coal releases 'greenhouse' gases, which contribute to global warming. Although coal has been largely replaced by oil and gas in the developed world, developing industrial nations such as China and India still rely on coal.

Water power

Waterfalls remind us how much energy is produced by rapidly flowing water. Since the 19th century, increasingly big dams have been built to hold back enormous reservoirs of water. By controlling the flow of this water through a dam and its turbines, electricity can be produced. This is known as hydroelectric power, and it provides 2 per cent of the world's energy. Around 20 countries, including Norway, Paraguay, Zambia, Brazil and Sri Lanka, supply over 90 per

cent of their energy from hydroelectric power, but several have relatively small energy needs. The USA supplies 9 per cent of its energy needs from hydroelectric power, but that 9 per cent amounts to three times the hydroelectric power generated in the whole of Africa.

Hot rocks

Iceland has active volcanoes and the rocks below ground are far hotter than in most places. When water is pumped through them, its temperature is raised enough for it to be used to heat whole towns, including houses, factories and swimming pools. Reykjavik, the capital, is supplied by this kind of geothermal energy, which produces 250 litres (55 gallons) of boiling water every second.

Energy from the Sun

Plants have always made use of light energy from the Sun, but humans have only begun to do this in a sophisticated way during the 20th century. Solar panels can trap light energy and use it to heat water. Panels with

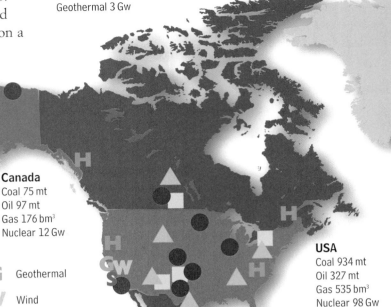

NORTH AMERICA
Hydroelectric 16 Gw
Geothermal 3 Gw

Canada
Coal 75 mt
Oil 97 mt
Gas 176 bm^3
Nuclear 12 Gw

USA
Coal 934 mt
Oil 327 mt
Gas 535 bm^3
Nuclear 98 Gw
Geothermal 3 Gw

Mexico
Coal 12 mt
Oil 140 mt
Gas 27 bm^3
Geothermal 0.7 Gw

Venezuela
Oil 145 mt
Gas 30 bm^3

Brazil
Coal 5 mt
Oil 36 mt
Gas 4 bm^3

Colombia
Coal 26 mt
Oil 30 mt
Gas 5 bm^3

SOUTH AMERICA
Hydroelectric 7.5 Gw
Fuelwood 80 mt

Ecuador
Oil 20 mt

Argentina
Oil 38 mt
Gas 26 bm^3

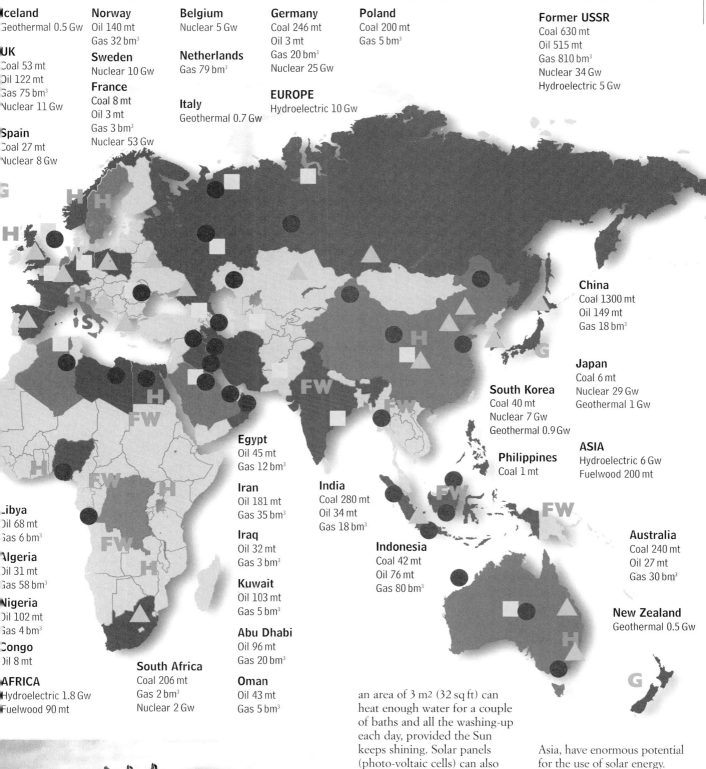

Iceland
Geothermal 0.5 Gw

UK
Coal 53 mt
Oil 122 mt
Gas 75 bm³
Nuclear 11 Gw

Spain
Coal 27 mt
Nuclear 8 Gw

Norway
Oil 140 mt
Gas 32 bm³

Sweden
Nuclear 10 Gw

France
Coal 8 mt
Oil 3 mt
Gas 3 bm³
Nuclear 53 Gw

Belgium
Nuclear 5 Gw

Netherlands
Gas 79 bm³

Italy
Geothermal 0.7 Gw

Germany
Coal 246 mt
Oil 3 mt
Gas 20 bm³
Nuclear 25 Gw

EUROPE
Hydroelectric 10 Gw

Poland
Coal 200 mt
Gas 5 bm³

Former USSR
Coal 630 mt
Oil 515 mt
Gas 810 bm³
Nuclear 34 Gw
Hydroelectric 5 Gw

China
Coal 1300 mt
Oil 149 mt
Gas 18 bm³

Japan
Coal 6 mt
Nuclear 29 Gw
Geothermal 1 Gw

South Korea
Coal 40 mt
Nuclear 7 Gw
Geothermal 0.9 Gw

Philippines
Coal 1 mt

ASIA
Hydroelectric 6 Gw
Fuelwood 200 mt

Egypt
Oil 45 mt
Gas 12 bm³

Iran
Oil 181 mt
Gas 35 bm³

Iraq
Oil 32 mt
Gas 3 bm³

Kuwait
Oil 103 mt
Gas 5 bm³

Abu Dhabi
Oil 96 mt
Gas 20 bm³

Oman
Oil 43 mt
Gas 5 bm³

India
Coal 280 mt
Oil 34 mt
Gas 18 bm³

Indonesia
Coal 42 mt
Oil 76 mt
Gas 80 bm³

Australia
Coal 240 mt
Oil 27 mt
Gas 30 bm³

New Zealand
Geothermal 0.5 Gw

Libya
Oil 68 mt
Gas 6 bm³

Algeria
Oil 31 mt
Gas 58 bm³

Nigeria
Oil 102 mt
Gas 4 bm³

Congo
Oil 8 mt

AFRICA
Hydroelectric 1.8 Gw
Fuelwood 90 mt

South Africa
Coal 206 mt
Gas 2 bm³
Nuclear 2 Gw

an area of 3 m² (32 sq ft) can heat enough water for a couple of baths and all the washing-up each day, provided the Sun keeps shining. Solar panels (photo-voltaic cells) can also produce electricity that can be stored in batteries and used to power vehicles on Earth or in space. Countries such as India and Australia, and parts of Asia, have enormous potential for the use of solar energy.

Consuming energy
America uses over 20 per cent of the world's energy resources, but has only 5 per cent of the world's population. The average American uses twice as much energy as a European and 1000 times as much as a Nepali.

◄ **Blue lagoon** People swim in the outflow from a geothermal power station in Iceland.

Natural disasters

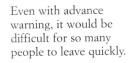

Earth's systems – the heat at the Earth's core, the shifting continents at the surface, the ocean currents and the weather – can unleash powerful forces in the form of volcanoes, earthquakes, floods and storms with devastating results.

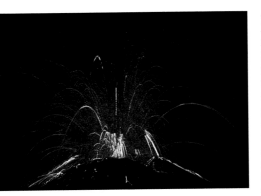

▲ **Big Bang** Krakatoa, which in 1883 was responsible for the loudest volcanic explosion in recorded history, is still active.

The most violent volcanoes

The eruption of Tambora, a volcano in Indonesia, in 1815 caused the deaths of 92 000 people, although many of these were the result of famine as the volcanic ash destroyed crops. The gigantic explosion threw so much dust into the atmosphere that it changed the global climate, and the following year, 1816, was known as 'the year without a summer'.

In November, 1985, over 23 000 people and 15 000 domestic animals were killed by the eruption of Nevado

▶ **Caked in mud** A rescue worker carries a child saved from the mud flows following the Nevado del Ruiz volcano eruption in Colombia.

del Ruiz in Colombia. Most were killed by mud flows over 60 km (37 miles) away from the volcano. The flows were mixtures of rain, water from melting glaciers, volcanic ash and debris that ran in torrents down valleys, overwhelming the town of Armero and burying its inhabitants under 5 m (16 ft) of mud.

Naples, a city with over 1 million inhabitants, lies in the shadow of Vesuvius, an active volcano that destroyed the ancient Roman towns of Herculaneum and Pompei in AD 79. Popocatépetl is possibly even more dangerous because it overlooks Mexico City, which has a population of over 15 million.

Even with advance warning, it would be difficult for so many people to leave quickly.

Loudest explosion

On August 27, 1883, the volcanic island of Krakatoa in Indonesia blew up. It made the loudest bang in recorded history, heard 4 hours later 4776 km (2968 miles) away on the island of Rodrigues in the Indian Ocean. Although no one was killed directly, the shock generated giant waves that drowned more than 36 000 people along the coasts of surrounding islands.

The volcano's killer clouds

In recent years, scientists have discovered that erupting volcanoes produce burning hot clouds of gas and ash, called nuées ardentes. These can travel at speeds of over 100 km/h (60 mph) and, at temperatures of around 700°C (1292°F), burn everything they engulf within seconds.

The most destructive earthquakes

The worst known earthquake in human history occurred on February 2, 1556. It struck the heavily populated provinces of Shaanxi and Henan in China. More than 830 000 people are thought to have been killed.

On July 27, 1976, the city of Tangshan in China was hit by an earthquake that measured 8.2 on the Richter scale. The city was totally destroyed and more than 242 000 people were killed.

▲ **Washed up** The tidal wave following Krakatoa's eruption in 1883 carried a ship inland and dumped it in the jungle.

Many of the worst earthquakes of the last few hundred years have happened in heavily populated regions of China, and it is most likely that future deaths will be in China. But many other regions are at risk, such as the Japanese Islands, southern Greece and Italy and the San Francisco area of California, situated over the San Andreas fault system.

Tsunamis – killer waves

Earthquakes that occur beneath the Earth's surface can create waves, called tsunamis, which can travel at up to 650 km/h (400 mph) across open ocean, and reach heights of 30 m (100 ft) in coastal waters. Tsunamis can cause immense destruction when they hit coastal communities. Tsunamis are fairly common in parts of the Pacific Ocean, especially around Hawaii and the Japanese Islands. The highest recorded number of deaths from a tsunami happened in

Major volcanic eruptions

	Date	Place	Deaths
1	1902	Mont Pelée, Martinique	29 000
2	1985	Nevado del Ruiz, Colombia	23 000
3	1919	Kelud, Java	5500
4	1951	Mount Lamington, Papua New Guinea	5000
5	1986	Nyos, Cameroon	1700

the Atlantic on November 1, 1775. One of the most violent earthquakes in modern history occurred off the coast of Portugal. It created a 16 m (52 ft) wave that hit Lisbon to the east and travelled across the Atlantic, reaching the West Indies on the other side. Some 60 000 people were killed.

The biggest wave ever
The impact of the Chicxulub asteroid, which crashed 65 million years ago in Mexico, is believed to have generated a tsunami 1 km ($^{1}/_{2}$ mile) high.

Major earthquakes

	Date	Place	Magnitude	Deaths
1	1976	Tangshan, China	8.2	242 000
2	1927	Nan-Shan, China	8.3(est)	200 000
3	1948	Turkmenistan	7.3	110 000
4	1920	Gansu, China	8.6(est)	100 000
5	1923	Tokyo, Japan	8.3(est)	99 330

When it hit the shores of the Caribbean and Gulf of Mexico, it swept inland for 100 km (60 miles) or more, killing dinosaurs and everything else in its path.

On July 9, 1958, some 90 million tonnes of rock, part of a mountainside, fell 1000 m (3000 ft) into Lituya Bay in Alaska. The splash created a tsunami-like wave, the highest in recorded history, that raced across the bay and surged up a mountainside on the other side of the bay to a height of 530 m (1740 ft), twice the height of the Eiffel Tower. No one was killed, but evidence of the power of the wave was there for all to see: 10 km² (4 sq miles) of forest had been washed off the mountainside.

River floods
Many rivers flood when they become overfilled with rainwater in the rainy season. The bigger the river, the bigger the flood. The worst recorded flood occurred in 1887. The Hwang-Ho (Yellow River) in China burst through its 20 m (70 ft) embankments, and some 900 000 people were drowned in the flood.

◀ ▼ Natural devastation
The Tangshan earthquake in 1976 destroyed this factory. Inset: Cyclone damage in Bangladesh.

Invasions by the sea
Even Europe, with its less extreme climate, can suffer on a large scale. In November, 1421, a major storm battered and broke the sea defences of south-west Holland, much of which is below sea level. At least 100 000 people lost their lives in the resulting floods.

Cyclones
Bangladesh borders the Bay of Bengal and is one of the most populated nations in the world. Much of the country is close to sea level; it is crisscrossed by two of the world's great rivers, the Ganges and the Brahmaputra; and it lies in the path of regular tropical storms (cyclones). At times, these elements have combined to cause disastrous flooding. In June, 1974, monsoon storms dropped over 5080 mm (200 in) of rain in a few weeks. The rivers flooded 38 850 km² (15 000 sq miles) of land – over half the country – destroying 800 000 homes. On November 12, 1970, a cyclone occurred at high tide and drove a 6 m (20 ft) high wall of seawater inland, drowning thousands. A million people died from drowning, disease, starvation and lack of fresh water.

There are at least 2 million kinds of living things on Earth, and probably many more. Scientists classify them in five major groups, known as kingdoms. On the next four pages, you can find out about the five kingdoms – bacteria, protists, fungi, plants and animals – and the species they contain.

Bacteria

What they are
Bacteria are the simplest living things on Earth. They are too small to be seen with the naked eye, yet they outnumber all other living things put together.

Where they live
Bacteria live in all kinds of places. They are found in soil, in milk, and even inside other living creatures. Some bacteria help us to digest the food we eat, but others can cause illnesses such as cholera, tetanus and food poisoning.

Number of species
At least 10 000.

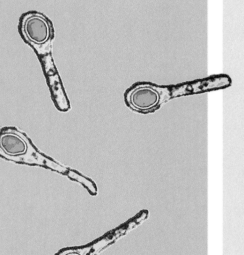

▲ Tiny germs
The bacteria seen here are dangerous. They are responsible for causing the disease tetanus.

Fungi

What they are
Some fungi look like plants, but they live in a very different way. They grow slender threads that break down and absorb any food they touch. Many fungi are microscopic, but some grow large mushrooms or toadstools in order to reproduce. These are called the 'fruiting bodies' of a fungus.

Where they live
Almost all fungi live on land. Some live in the soil, but many grow inside the remains of dead plants and animals, helping to break them down.

Number of species
About 100 000.

Protists

What they are
These tiny creatures are bigger and more complicated than bacteria, but they are still too small to be visible to the naked eye. Some protists eat food, as if they were animals; others live like plants, getting their energy from sunshine.

Where they live
Most protists live in water or damp places on land. Some live inside larger animals, and can cause diseases such as malaria.

Number of species
About 42 000 different species have been identified, but there are probably many more.

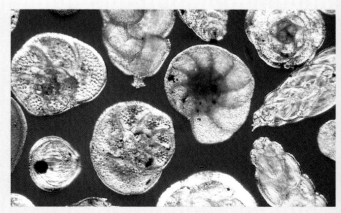

▲ Safe home Single-cell protists live inside these microscopic shells.

Plants

What they are
The plant kingdom contains living things that need sunlight to survive. They absorb sunlight with their leaves, and use its energy to manufacture food for themselves. Four of the most important groups of plants are shown here.

Where they live
Plants live almost everywhere on land, except places where it is very cold or dry. They also live in fresh water, but only a few grow in the sea.

Number of species
Over 400 000 plant species have been identified.

SIMPLE PLANTS
Mosses and liverworts are typical of simple plants. They live in damp places, and do not have true roots or leaves. They reproduce by scattering spores. Spores work like seeds, but are much smaller and simpler.
Number of species About 16 000.

▲ **Mossy wall** A dark, damp wall in Scotland is ideal for moss.

FERNS
Unlike simple plants, ferns have roots and leaves, yet they also reproduce by scattering spores. In the tropics, some ferns are over 15 m (50 ft) high.
Number of species About 11 000.

▲ **Fern fronds** Many ferns grow in dense, dark rain forests.

CONIFERS
These plants have long, needle-shaped leaves, and they reproduce by growing seeds inside cones. Most conifers keep their leaves all year round, making them 'evergreen'.
Number of species 550.

▲ **Pin-sharp** The leaves of conifers are often called 'needles'.

FLOWERING PLANTS
As their name suggests, flowering plants reproduce by growing flowers. Some have tiny flowers that are difficult to see, but others have huge blooms, which are impossible to miss. This giant group of plants includes grasses, cacti and orchids, as well as all the world's broadleaved trees.
Number of species About 250 000.

▶ **Show off** The colourful and unmistakable sunflower has one of the largest flowers of any plant.

Animals

What they are
The animal kingdom contains the most varied living things on Earth. Animals have sense organs that tell them about their surroundings, and they live by eating food. There are two main groups of animals: those that have backbones and those that do not.

Where they are found
Animals live in an incredible variety of places. Different species can survive in deserts, on ice near the Poles, and even in caves far beneath the ground.

Number of species
At least 1.3 million, and probably many more.

Invertebrates
Animals that do not have a backbone are called invertebrates. They include everything from simple sponges to complex creatures such as crustaceans and insects.
Number of species At least 1 million.

SPONGES
These are among the world's simplest animals. They live by sucking in water, and filtering it for small particles of food.
Number of species About 5000.

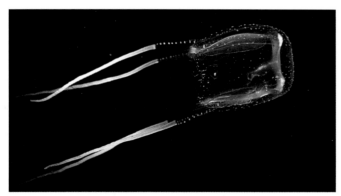

▲ **Stinger** The sea wasp jellyfish can kill an adult human.

CORALS, JELLYFISH AND SEA ANEMONES
Jellyfish can move through the water, but sea anemones and corals spend most of their lives fastened in one place. They all have stinging cells, which they use for catching their food.
Number of species About 9000.

ROUNDWORMS
The worms of this group have thin, rounded bodies that are pointed at both ends. They live in an amazing variety of habitats, including inside plants and other animals.
Number of species At least 15 000 – perhaps many more.

FLATWORMS
Many flatworms live in water or damp places, but some are parasites that live inside other animals. These parasites include tapeworms, which sometimes live in people.
Number of species About 18 500.

MOLLUSCS
There are several distinct types of molluscs, including snails, mussels and clams, octopuses and squid. Most are soft-bodied animals that are often protected by a hard shell.
Number of species About 50 000.

▲ **Land mollusc** Snails are related to mussels as well as squid.

SEGMENTED WORMS
As their name indicates, segmented worms have bodies that are made up of long rows of segments, or rings. They include earthworms, leeches and many worms that live in the sea.
Number of species About 12 000.

STARFISH, SEA URCHINS, SEA CUCUMBERS
This group contains the only animals that have bodies divided into five equal parts. They all live in the sea – some along the shore, others on the deep seabed.
Number of species About 6 500.

▼ **Predator** Sea urchins often eat mussels, as this one is doing.

CRUSTACEANS
Crabs, lobsters, shrimps and woodlice are crustaceans. They have antennae, or 'feelers', like insects. Most of them live in salt water, but there are also many freshwater species, and a few – such as woodlice – live on land. Most crustaceans have eight or ten legs, unlike insects, which have only six.
Number of species About 44 000.

SPIDERS, MITES AND SCORPIONS (ARACHNIDS)
The animals of this group walk on eight legs. They are similar to insects, but do not have antennae. Instead, they have bristles on their bodies for sensing what is happening around them. Most arachnids are hunters, catching their prey by biting, crushing or stinging it.
Number of species About 70 000.

▲ **In step** Millipedes have many legs to coordinate.

CENTIPEDES AND MILLIPEDES
These long-bodied animals are famous for having lots of legs. They are easy to tell apart: centipedes have two legs on each body segment, while millipedes have four. Another important difference is that centipedes are hunters, with a poisonous bite, while millipedes feed only on decaying plants or animals.
Number of species About 13 000.

◀ **Taking off** Dragonflies use their wings to hover or dart through the air at high speed.

INSECTS
Insects live almost everywhere on land and in fresh water, but very few are found in the sea. Most insects have wings when they are adults, making them the only invertebrates capable of flight. With few exceptions, their bodies are divided into three main sections: a head, thorax and abdomen. There are more species of insects than all other types of animals put together.
Number of species About 800 000 species have been identified; millions more may await discovery.

Vertebrates
Animals that have a backbone are called vertebrates. They make up less than 3 per cent of the world's animal species, but they include the fastest and most intelligent animals on Earth.
Number of species About 48 000.

BIRDS
Of all the world's animals, only birds have feathers. All birds lay eggs, and most can fly, although some have lost this ability: penguins, for example, and ostriches.
Number of species About 9000.

▲ **Fisher** The powerful beak of a kingfisher is used for spearing fish.

AMPHIBIANS
Frogs, toads, salamanders and newts are amphibians, a name which means that they can live both in the water and on land. They develop the ability to live on land as they grow up.
Number of species About 4350.

MAMMALS
Like lions and whales, human beings are mammals – animals that feed their young on milk. Most mammals live on land, but whales and dolphins spend all their lives at sea. Three types of mammals lay eggs, but all others give birth to live young.
Number of species About 4000.

REPTILES
The best known reptiles are snakes, lizards, crocodiles, turtles and tortoises. Most reptiles lay eggs, but a few give birth to live young. They have a tough skin covered with hard scales.
Number of species About 6000.

FISH
All fish have streamlined bodies that make it easy to move about in water. Most of them breed by laying eggs, but some – notably sharks – give birth to living young.
Number of species About 25 000.

Plants and fungi

Plants

Biggest
The biggest plants are trees. 'General Sherman', a giant sequoia growing in California, weighs about 2500 tonnes. This makes it the heaviest tree, and also the heaviest living thing in the world. Its weight is equivalent to about 19 fully grown blue whales, or more than 400 African elephants.

▲ **Forest giant** The huge sequoia called 'General Sherman' is thought to be about 3500 years old.

Tallest
The tallest living plant is a redwood tree growing in California. It is about 112 m (367 ft) high – nearly twice the wingspan of a jumbo jet. In the past, some trees have been even bigger than this. An Australian eucalyptus, which was measured in 1872, was 132 m (433 ft) high. Its top had broken off, so it probably reached over 152 m (500 ft) before it was damaged.

Smallest
The smallest flowering plants are duckweeds, which float on the surface of ponds. One species from Australia measures about 0.35 mm (0.014 in) across, which is about one-third as wide as a pinhead. Despite being so tiny, duckweeds can cover ponds completely, turning them bright green.

Biggest flower
The biggest single flowers are grown by a plant called *Rafflesia arnoldii*, which lives in the rain forests of South-east Asia. The flowers grow on the ground, and measure up to 90 cm (3 ft) across. They have rubbery petals and a horrible smell.

Biggest flowerhead
Many plants grow their flowers in clusters, called flowerheads. The biggest of these are grown by a plant from Bolivia called *Puya raimondii*. They can be over 10 m (33 ft) high, and contain up to 8000 separate flowers. The plant waits up to 150 years before growing its flowerhead, and then dies.

Fastest-growing
In good conditions, giant bamboo can grow 90 cm (3 ft) a day. If you sat

▼ **Rotten meat** The flower of the *Rafflesia* plant can weigh 11 kg (24 lb). It gives off a smell like rotting meat to attract flies, which pollinate it.

Plants

What they eat
Most plants make their own food and collect minerals from the ground. A few species – such as the Venus flytrap – obtain extra minerals by catching insects.

How they reproduce
By releasing spores or seeds, or by growing parts that separate and become new plants.

How they develop
Some plants reproduce once and then die, but many reproduce every year for years on end.

How long they live
From a few weeks to 5000 years, or even longer.

Interesting facts
Green plants are essential for life on Earth. They give off oxygen, which is needed by many other creatures, including humans.

beside a giant bamboo shoot and watched it carefully, you would be able to see it grow.

Oldest
The oldest individual plants are thought to be bristlecone pines, which grow in the Rocky Mountains of North America. Some of them are at least 4600 years old. This means that they started growing when the first of the Pyramids was being built in ancient Egypt.

Oldest clump
In California, some clumps of creosote bushes are over 11 500 years old. The plants that started each clump died long ago, but their 'babies' are still going strong.

Shortest-lived
Some desert plants germinate, flower and die in less than a month. They spring up after rare rainstorms and grow very quickly because the desert soon dries out again.

▲ **Oldest living thing** This bristlecone pine may look dead, but it continues to grow as it has for thousands of years.

Worst weed
A floating plant called the water hyacinth is probably the most troublesome weed in the world. It grows so quickly that it can clog up lakes and rivers, trapping boats and jamming the turbines in dams.

Toughest leaves

A desert plant called *Welwitschia mirabilis*, which lives in Namibia, has the toughest leaves in the world. Each plant has just two leaves, but they can last for over a thousand years.

Biggest seeds

A rare palm tree called the coco-de-mer has by far the biggest seeds in the world. Each one weighs up to 20 kg (44 lb) and takes about ten years to ripen. In ancient times, sailors thought that these trees grew at the bottom of the sea. In fact, they grow in the Seychelles, in the Indian Ocean.

Most seeds

Some orchid flowers can produce over a million seeds – more than any other kind of plant. Their seeds are like dust, so they can blow far and wide on the wind.

Longest-living seeds

If seeds get buried in very dry or cold ground, they sometimes stay alive for a very long time. The record is held by some Arctic lupin seeds, which were found in frozen ground in 1954. The seeds germinated when they were thawed out, even though they were at least 8000 years old.

Biggest cactus

Saguaro cacti in the deserts of Arizona and Mexico can grow over 15 m (50 ft) high, making them the tallest and heaviest cacti in the world.

Biggest seaweed

Giant kelp from California is the world's biggest seaweed, and also the fastest growing. It can grow over 60 m (196 ft) long in just one year.

Deepest seaweed

Off the Bahamas, red seaweeds have been found growing at a depth of 268 m (879 ft). Like other seaweed, they need light to survive, but at such depths sunlight is a thousand times dimmer than at the surface.

Longest roots

In 1960, miners in Arizona found roots 53 m (174 ft) below the surface. The roots belonged to mesquite bushes, which live in deserts by getting water from deep underground. Some fig trees reach even farther than this. One in South Africa has roots 120 m (390 ft) deep.

Fungi

Biggest

Some fungi grow slender feeding threads that can cover huge areas of ground. In an American forest, scientists have

▲ **Yeast colony** Each of these 'sausages' is a microscopic yeast cell.

found one network of threads that covers 15 ha (37 acres). This fungus probably started to grow at least 1500 years ago.

Smallest

Yeasts are among the tiniest fungi in the world. Each one consists of just a single cell, which can only be seen through a powerful microscope.

Most poisonous

Some of the world's most poisonous fungi grow in Europe's woodlands. Two of the most deadly are the destroying angel and the death cap, which should not even be touched. If they are eaten, their poisons slowly destroy a person's inner organs, causing death about two to three days later.

Most valuable

Many fungi are valued for their flavour, but truffles are the most prized of all. They grow underground, and the only way to find them is to use a dog or a pig to sniff them out. The Perigord truffle from France is the world's most costly – a whole one can be worth up to £500.

▶ **Puff of smoke** A puffball fungus releases its spores into the air.

Most spores

Fungi make microscopic spores for the same reason that plants make seeds – so that they can spread. All fungi make lots of spores, but giant puffballs can make over a billion, more than any other species. Puffballs, large and small, release their spores in a burst.

▲ **Reaching up** A saguaro cactus of North America can weigh up to 8 tonnes when mature.

Simple animals

Simplest
The simplest animal in the world doesn't have a common name. Scientists call it *Trichoplax*. It is only about 2 mm (0.1 in) across, and is transparent and flat, without a head, eyes, mouth or legs. *Trichoplax* was first discovered in a seawater aquarium, but has never been seen in the wild.

Sponges

Biggest
Giant vase sponges can be over 2 m (6 ft) high and over 1 m (3 ft) across. These huge sponges live in the sea round Antarctica, and they grow extremely slowly.

Smallest
Some sponges are only 4 mm (0.15 in) high.

Best borers
Some sponges make acids that help them to bore through rocks and shells. The most successful of these borer sponges can dig its way through shells 1 cm (³/₈ in) thick.

Corals, jellyfish and sea anemones

Biggest coral reef
The Great Barrier Reef, off the northeast coast of Australia, is about 2000 km (1250 miles) long, 120 m (390 ft) high and as much as 145 km (90 miles) across in places.

Biggest jellyfish
A species of jellyfish in the Arctic Sea can be over 2 m (6 ft) across. When its tentacles are stretched out, they are at least 30 m (100 ft) long.

Deadliest jellyfish
The Australian box jellyfish, or sea wasp, kills more humans than any other type of jellyfish. Although it can be 25 cm (10 in) across, it is almost transparent. This makes it difficult for swimmers to spot and avoid.

Biggest sea anemone
In the waters around Australia's Great Barrier Reef, one species of sea anemone grows to be 50 cm (20 in) across.

Flatworms

Biggest
The world's biggest flatworms are those that live and feed inside other animals. Called tapeworms, they can be over 30 m (100 ft) long, but their flat bodies are not much thicker than a sheet of paper.

▼ **Almost invisible** The deadly box jellyfish lives in the warm waters of the Great Barrier Reef.

Most eggs
Some tapeworms release three-quarters of a million eggs a day. They can keep doing this every day for several years.

Roundworms

Biggest
A type of roundworm that lives inside sperm whales can be up to 9 m (29 ft) long, making it the biggest yet found.

Smallest
Many roundworms that live in soil are only 0.5 mm (0.02 in) long – just big enough to be seen with the naked eye.

Strangest habitat
Roundworms live on or in almost anything. One species lives in vinegar, where it feeds on bacteria and moulds.

Molluscs

Biggest
The giant squid is the biggest mollusc, and also the biggest animal without a backbone. Giant squids live in the deep sea, and no one has ever seen

▲ **Parasite** Tapeworms are often found in the intestines of dogs and cats. They can also affect humans.

one alive. Dead ones washed up on beaches have measured up to 18 m (60 ft) long, with suckers 5 cm (2 in) across.

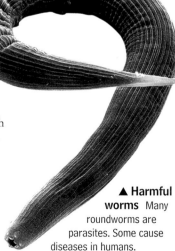

▲ **Harmful worms** Many roundworms are parasites. Some cause diseases in humans.

Heaviest shell
The giant clam, which lives in the warm waters around coral reefs, can weigh over 300 kg (660 lb). Most of this weight is made up by its shell, which can be 120 cm (48 in) wide.

Arthropods

What they are
About three-quarters of all the animal species in the world belong to a huge group known as the arthropods - a name which means 'jointed feet'. They include crustaceans; centipedes and millipedes; spiders, mites and scorpions; and insects. All arthropods have a hard outer body case and six or more jointed legs. Some of them have wings.

What they eat
All kinds of food, from plant remains to pollen, nectar, other animals and even blood.

How they reproduce
Usually by laying eggs, though some give birth to living young.

How they develop
Because they have a tough body case, arthropods have to shed this in order to grow bigger. They then develop a new body case. This process is known as moulting, and may occur several times during the animal's life.

Smallest shell
The smallest shelled mollusc is a snail from the South China Sea. It is just 0.4 mm (0.015 in) long.

Most dangerous
Two molluscs – the blue-ringed octopus and the geographer cone shell – can kill people with poison. The octopus has a deadly bite, and the cone shell shoots a dart into its victim.

Segmented worms

Biggest
The biggest earthworms live in South Africa. When fully stretched out, some of them can

be over 6.5 m (21 ft) – as long as some of the world's biggest snakes.

Starfish, sea urchins and sea cucumbers

Biggest starfish
A starfish found in the Gulf of Mexico has an 'armspan' of 1.38 m (4 ft) – making it the largest in the world.

Most arms
Most starfish have five arms, but some have many more. The record – about 50 – is held by some starfish that live in the northern Pacific Ocean.

Spiniest sea urchin
In the Indian Ocean, some sea urchins have spines that are over 15 cm (6 in) long. These

break off easily, and often get stuck in people's feet if they tread on the urchins.

Fattest sea cucumber
A sea cucumber that lives in the western Pacific Ocean is over 20 cm (8 in) across. When stretched out, it can be 1 m (3 ft) long.

Crustaceans

Biggest
The world's biggest crustacean is the Japanese spider crab, which lives on the seabed. It has a small body, but its legs can be over 3.5 m (11 ft) from one side to the other. Its legs are too weak for it to walk on land.

Heaviest
The heavyweights of the crustacean world are lobsters, which can weigh 20 kg (44 lb). Lobsters belong to a larger group called arthropods, which

▲ **Claws** Lobsters live among the rocks on the seabed.

includes insects and spiders. Arthropods living on land can never get this big, because they would not have the strength to move their heavy shells. Lobsters have the advantage of living under water, where things are lighter than on land.

Centipedes and millipedes

Most legs
Centipedes and millipedes have more legs than any other animal. The record for a centipede is about 340 legs, while the biggest millipedes have over 700.

▼ **Balancing act** The word 'millipede' means 'thousand legs', but many smaller millipedes have fewer than 200 legs.

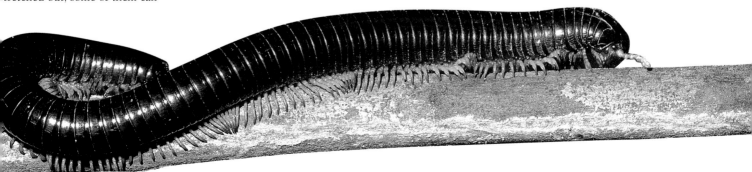

Animals – invertebrates

Insects

Biggest insects

Tropical stick insects are the longest insects living in the world today. With their legs fully stretched out, some of them measure over 50 cm (20 in). However, because stick insects are so thin, they do not weigh much. The heaviest insect is the African goliath beetle, which can weigh up to 100 g (3 oz) – about six times as much as a fully grown mouse.

Biggest insect ever

Some prehistoric insects were much bigger than the biggest ones alive today. Millions of years ago, dragonflies had wingspans of up to 75 cm (30 in). Their wings would have made a loud rustling sound as they flew past.

▼ **Big as a bird** The biggest butterflies live in the tropics. Queen Alexandra's birdwing butterfly has a wingspan of 28 cm (11 in) – far bigger than many birds.

▲ **Walking stick** It is not difficult to see how the stick insect got its name.

Smallest

Feather-winged beetles are probably the smallest insects alive today. They live on the remains of rotting plants, and some of them are only 0.2 mm (0.008 in) long. If they were any smaller than this, they would be impossible to see with the naked eye.

Most numerous

Springtails are the most common insects in the world. These tiny wingless animals live on blades of grass, on fallen leaves, and even on the surface of snow. They are so small that people rarely notice them, but if you lie down on grass, the chances are that thousands will be hopping about beneath you.

Biggest swarm

In 1875, a giant swarm of Rocky Mountain locusts in Nebraska was estimated to contain about 12.5 trillion insects, making it the biggest ever seen. Together, the locusts weighed at least 25 million tonnes. Today, locusts still swarm in other parts of the world, but the Rocky Mountain locust has died out.

Fastest flier

Dragonflies hold the speed record for insects in the air. Some of them can fly at over 55 km/h (34 mph), although they cannot keep this speed up for long.

Biggest wings

Queen Alexandra's birdwing, a rare butterfly from New Guinea, has wings that can measure over 28 cm (11 in) across. The owlet moth from Brazil is even bigger, with a wingspan of 30 cm (12 in). With its wings outstretched, it would easily cover a dinner plate.

Fastest runner

Cockroaches have a top speed of about 5 km/h (3 mph), which is the highest land speed in the insect world. This is amazingly fast. Scaled up to human size, it would be the same as running at 320 km/h (200 mph).

Noisiest

Many insects have loud calls, but the noisiest of all are tropical cicadas and burrowing insects called mole crickets. Some of them are so loud that they can be heard almost 2 km (1.2 miles) away.

Most frozen

In cold places, some insects freeze solid in winter, and then come back to life when they

Insects

What they eat
Plant or animal food, including seeds, leaves and blood, as well as other insects.

How they reproduce
Usually by laying eggs, although some insects can give birth to living young.

How they develop
Most insects change shape as they grow up. Moths and butterflies, for example, are born as caterpillars. They then make a cocoon, and emerge from this as adults with wings. This process is known as metamorphosis. Other insects go through the same process in a different way.

How long they live
Usually only a few months, but some survive for several years, or even decades.

Spiders

What they eat
Small animals, particularly insects.

How they reproduce
By laying eggs.

How they develop
Young spiders get bigger as they get older, but they do not change shape. They look like miniature copies of their parents, even when they first hatch.

How long they live
From a few months to 25 years.

Interesting facts
Spiders have three pairs of glands, called spinnerets, for making their silk. Spiders can produce many types of silk for different purposes, such as spinning a web, binding up prey, or floating on air currents.

▲ **Hairy monster**   The Goliath bird-eating spider feels for food using its long, hairy legs.

haw in spring. A tiger moth that lives in the high Arctic is expert at coping with low temperatures. Its deep-frozen caterpillars can survive at –50°C –58°F) for months on end.

Longest tongue
A hawkmoth from Madagascar has a tongue that is 28 cm 11 in) long. Like other moths and butterflies, it rolls up its tongue when it is not in use.

Most dangerous
Some insects have painful stings, which can kill people who are allergic to them. But the most dangerous of all are those that transmit

diseases. Mosquitoes are at the top of the list because they spread malaria. This disease kills several thousand people every day of the year.

Longest life span
Queen termites often live longer than 20 years, but beetles that feed on wood can survive twice this long. The record holder is a beetle that was estimated to be nearly 50 years old when it was caught clambering out of an old piece of timber in a house in England.

Shortest life span
If they have enough food, some insects grow up, breed and die very quickly. Houseflies are among the fastest of all; in warm weather, they often have a life span of less than six weeks. If the weather is colder, they take longer to grow up, and can live for several months.

Best jumper
For their size, fleas are by far the best jumpers in the insect world. Many of them can jump over 30 cm (12 in) – equivalent to a human jumping over 200 m (660 ft). Instead of jumping forwards, fleas leap backwards, spinning head-over-heels in the air.

◀ **Leg power**   A flea uses its hind legs to leap onto a passing animal, or to escape being caught.

Biggest nest
Termites build by far the biggest nests in the entire animal world. Some of them are over 12 m (40 ft) high, and the widest are about 10 m (33 ft) across at the base. Most termite nests are made of mud, which is stuck together and then left to dry in the sun. Once it has dried out, the mud turns rock-hard.

Spiders

Biggest
The Goliath bird-eating spider from South America has a legspan of 28 cm (11 in), which is bigger than any other spider in the world. Females can weigh over 120 g (4.2 oz) – about the same as a starling.

Smallest
The smallest spider that scientists have yet discovered measures just 0.37 mm (0.014 in) across – about a third as wide as a pinhead. It lives in the forests of South America. This tiny spider hunts animals that are even smaller than itself.

Biggest size difference
Female spiders are often much bigger than males. This size difference is most extreme in golden orb-weaver spiders, which are common in the tropics. In some cases, the females are a thousand times heavier than the males.

Fastest
Spiders are good at sitting and waiting, but not so good at getting about at speed. House

spiders are among the fastest; over short distances, they can reach a top speed of nearly 2 km/h (1.25 mph).

Most dangerous
Almost all spiders have poisonous fangs, but fortunately for us, very few can pierce human skin. The most deadly spider of all is probably the wandering spider, which lives in

▲ **Wife and husband**   The larger of these two golden orb-weaver spiders is the female; the smaller one is her mate.

South America. This spider often enters houses, and is thought to kill more than a hundred people every year.

Longest web
The longest webs are made by social spiders, which join forces to catch their prey. Up to 10 000 spiders work together to build huge webs that stretch for hundreds of metres.

Fish

Biggest sea fish
Whale sharks are the biggest fish of all. They can be over 12 m (40 ft) long, and weigh up to 20 tonnes. Despite being so enormous, whale sharks are not dangerous. They feed by swallowing huge mouthfuls of tiny animals, which they sieve out of the water with their gills.

Biggest freshwater fish
Several freshwater fish can grow to be over 3 m (10 ft) long. They include sturgeons, catfish and some freshwater eels. The biggest on record was a catfish caught in Russia, which measured 4.5 m (14 ft 8 in) from head to tail. One giant catfish was found to have a human head and arm in its stomach.

Smallest
Adult marine dwarf gobies measure just under 1 cm (3/8 in) long, making them the smallest fish in the world. They are also the smallest vertebrates (animals with backbones). These tiny fish live in shallow water in the Indian Ocean.

Most numerous
Small fish are much more numerous than big ones. The most abundant of them all are probably bristlemouths, which live in the deep sea all over the world. They are only about 7.5 cm (3 in) long, and often fall apart when they are brought to the surface.

Fastest
Over short stretches, the sailfish can swim at over 100 km/h (60 mph), which makes it faster than anything else in the sea. It has a sword-like beak, and a big sail-shaped fin on its back. When the fish is moving at full speed, this fin folds flat.

Slowest
Even at full speed, small seahorses would have trouble overtaking a snail. These fish swim with their bodies upright, and they push themselves along with a tiny fin on their backs.

▲ Feelers The catfish gets its name from its 'whiskers', or barbels, which it uses for finding prey.

Best traveller
Many fish travel thousands of kilometres every year. The record distance known to have been travelled by a a single fish is 9335 km (5800 miles). The fish was a bluefin tuna that swam all the way from Mexico to the Sea of Japan.

Longest fins
The upper part of a thresher shark's tail fin is as long as the rest of its body. Thresher sharks probably use their long tails to herd smaller fish into groups, where they are easier to attack. However, no one has yet seen them do this, so their long tails may have another purpose.

▲ Waiting for food Gobies are found throughout the world. This triplefin goby is hiding among corals in the Pacific Ocean.

Most dangerous sea hunter
Many fish feed by hunting, but sharks are the only sea fish that regularly attack humans. The great white shark is the world's biggest hunting fish, sometimes growing to over 7.5 m (25 ft) in length. It is quite capable of eating people, but it usually attacks seals, dolphins and other sharks.

Most dangerous freshwater hunter
Compared to the great white shark, piranhas are tiny, but these freshwater fish attack in packs hundreds strong. Working together, they can kill a person in less than a minute.

Most poisonous
Many fish have poisonous spines on their backs, but the most deadly of all is the stonefish from the Indian and Pacific Oceans. These fish lie on the seabed in shallow water, and sometimes kill people who tread on them.

▶ Weak swimmer Sea horses often live among seaweed, which protects them from strong ocean currents.

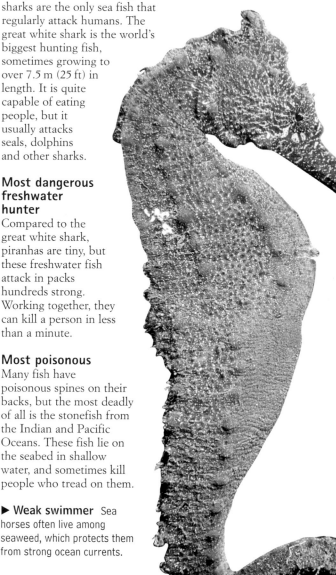

▲ **Jaws** Great white sharks have been known to attack small boats in their quest for a meal.

▼ **See-through** The transparent body of the glassfish gives it the appearance of an X-ray photograph.

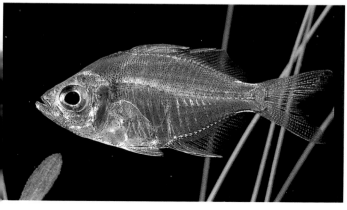

Longest life span
Scientists can estimate the age of a fish by looking at the growth rings or structure of its scales. They believe that sturgeons and the larger species of sharks – like great whites – probably live longer than any other fish. Both may live to the age of 80 or more.

Deepest swimmers
Fish called brotulids have been seen in water 8 km (5 miles) deep, and it is possible that other fish live even deeper. At such depths, the water is totally without light, and the pressure is hundreds of times higher than at the surface.

Most eggs
Many fish produce a vast number of eggs when they breed, but the record probably goes to the sunfish – a huge animal shaped like an upright dinner plate with fins. Female sunfish can be over 3 m (10 ft) across, and they can produce 300 million eggs a year.

Best air-breather
Some fish can survive in air for a few hours, but lungfish can survive out of water for months at a time. These fish live in lakes in Africa, South America and Australia. They spend the dry season curled up in lake-bed burrows, and they come to life when the next rainy season begins.

Best flier
Flying fish can't really fly, but they are good at gliding above the waves. They use one or two pairs of fins as wings, and can glide over 150 m (500 ft) before dropping back into the sea. Flying fish usually take to the air to escape from their enemies.

Most invisible
Many fish are camouflaged, which makes them hard to see, but some have transparent bodies, making them almost invisible. The only parts of the fish that have colour are their eyes, bones and internal organs. Called glassfish, they live in Australia, Africa and Asia.

Fish

What they eat
Small fish eat plankton – tiny living things that drift near the surface of the water. Most other fish are predators. They hunt and catch fish smaller than themselves.

How they reproduce
Most sea fish lay vast quantities of eggs, which float away in the water. Freshwater fish often lay their eggs among waterplants. Only a few types of fish – notably sharks – give birth to living young.

How they develop
Most fish start life as 'fry' – tiny fish that often swim in shoals. Some change shape as they grow up.

How long they live
From a few months to over 80 years.

Interesting facts
Most fish live in fresh water or salt water, but some can live in both. Salmon are born in fresh water, spend most of their lives at sea, and then return to fresh water to breed.

Most shocking
The electric eel is like a living battery that can deliver a deadly shock. This South American freshwater fish can deliver a shock of 650 volts – powerful enough to kill other fish, to stun a person, and to knock a horse off its legs.

▼ **Stunner** Electric eels move slowly through the water, catching their prey by shocking it.

Animals - vertebrates

Amphibians

Biggest salamander

Chinese giant salamanders can be over 1.8 m (6 ft) long, and can weigh over 60 kg (132 lb). Unlike most amphibians, these wrinkly skinned giants spend all their lives in fast-flowing water, and are now very rare.

Biggest frog

The Goliath frog from West Africa often weighs more than 3 kg (6.6 lb) – as much as a fully grown rabbit. With its hind legs

▲ **Pot luck** A fisherman in West Africa holds up a Goliath frog, which will soon be his dinner.

Amphibians

What they eat
When they are adult, all amphibians feed on other animals. They only eat things that move.

How they reproduce
Most amphibians lay eggs, which do not have shells, but are protected by a thick layer of jelly.

How they develop
Amphibians start life as tadpoles living in water. Most of them slowly change shape, growing legs for moving about on land. As adults, they can live on land or in water.

How long they live
Up to 40 years.

Interesting facts
Frogs living in areas that get little rain can spend months buried in mud, emerging only when the rains return.

---

stretched out, this giant frog can be nearly 90 cm (3 ft) long from its nose to its toes.

Smallest

In Central and South America, several frogs are under 1 cm (3/8 in) long, which makes them the smallest amphibians in the world. Many of these frogs live among leaves on the forest floor, where they are very difficult to find.

Best jumper

The prize for the record leap goes to the South African sharp-nosed frog, which can jump 5.35 m (17 ft). This frog is only about 7 cm (2 3/4 in) long when its legs are tucked up. This means that it can jump 76 times its own length.

Most poisonous

Many amphibians make poisons to stop other animals from eating them. The most poisonous of all are arrow-poison frogs from Central and South America. Although many are less than 2.5 cm (1 in) long, a single frog can have enough poison to kill a thousand people.

Noisiest

Many frogs and toads make loud noises in the breeding season, but tree frogs are the noisiest amphibians of all. Some have high-pitched calls that can be heard 1 km (650 yards) away. The painted frog, from South-east Asia, makes one of the strangest calls: it sounds like a cow groaning.

Longest life span

Common toads can live to at least 40, but some large salamanders may reach an even greater age.

Reptiles

Biggest crocodile

The saltwater crocodile is the biggest crocodile in the world, as well as the biggest living reptile. The largest ones ever found have been over 5.5 m (18 ft) long, and in the past they may have reached over 8 m (26 ft). Saltwater crocodiles are dangerous animals. They probably kill at least a thousand people every year.

Smallest crocodile

Cuvier's dwarf cayman, which lives in South America, never grows longer than 1.5 m (5 ft). It feeds mainly on fish and frogs, and has backward-pointing teeth to help it to grip its food.

Biggest sea turtle

The leatherback turtle can be over 2 m (6 ft) long, and can weigh nearly half a tonne (1100 lb). These huge turtles get

▲ **Tough hide** Swimming lazily through the Atlantic Ocean, this leatherback turtle is accompanied by pilot fish, which eat its food scraps.

▲ **Cruel smile** Saltwater crocodiles, known in Australia as 'salties', frequently kill unwary swimmers.

▲ On the prowl The Komodo dragon can live up to 100 years.

their name because they have a tough leathery back instead of a hard shell.

Biggest freshwater turtle

The alligator snapping turtle, from the south-east USA, can grow to a length of 80 cm (32 in), and weigh over 140 kg (308 lb). These turtles lie at the bottom of lakes and rivers. They

---

Reptiles

What they eat
Most reptiles eat animals, but some eat leaves and fruit.

How they reproduce
Most reptiles lay eggs with soft shells, but some give birth to living young.

How they develop
Young reptiles look like miniature versions of their parents when they hatch. Usually, they grow up on their own, without protection from their parents.

How long they live
Some reptiles can live to be over 100 years old.

Interesting facts
Reptiles are cold-blooded, which means that they cannot control their body temperature. This is why they are often seen lying in the sun – to warm themselves up.

---

lure fish into their mouths by waving their little pink tongues, which look like worms to passing fish.

Smallest turtle

The common musk turtle, from eastern North America, is the smallest reptile with a shell. The biggest one yet found measured just over 13 cm (5 in) from nose to tail. Despite its small size, this turtle is a good climber, and can often be seen sunbathing on trees overhanging the water.

Biggest lizard

The rare Komodo dragon from Indonesia is the biggest and most dangerous lizard in the world. Adult males can be over 2.2 m (7 ft) long. Young Komodo dragons feed on insects and other small animals, but the adults have been known to tackle wild pigs, deer and even people.

Smallest lizard

Insect-eating lizards called geckos are often very small. One species from the Caribbean measures just 4 cm (1.5 in) from nose to tail,

---

making it the smallest lizard, and also the smallest reptile, in the world. Each time it breeds, it lays just a single egg.

Biggest snake

People often think that snakes are longer than they really are, but some do grow to an astounding size. The longest is the reticulated python, which has been known to reach 10 m (33 ft). This snake does not kill its prey with poison; instead, it squeezes its victims to death, and then swallows them whole.

Smallest snake

A thread snake from the West Indies rarely grows more than 10 cm (4 in) long. Its body is thinner than a shoelace.

Most poisonous snake

The king cobra from southern Asia is the biggest of the world's poisonous snakes, and also the most venomous. Fortunately, it feeds entirely on other snakes, and rarely attacks people. The Indian cobra, a smaller snake, is much more aggressive. It kills more than 5000 people every year.

Longest fangs

The gaboon viper's fangs are 5 cm (2 in) long – longer than any other snake's. They fold back when its mouth is closed, but swing forwards when it is about to bite.

Fastest reptile

Lizards called spiny-tailed iguanas can run at a speed of 35 km/h (22 mph) for short bursts, which is faster than any other reptile.

Longest life span

Big reptiles often live to a great age because they spend a lot of their time resting or basking in the sun. Crocodiles can live to be 80 years old, but giant tortoises often survive well past their 100th birthday. The record known age for a giant tortoise is 152, but in the past some may have lived to be 200.

▼ Cannibal Snakes often eat other snakes. This Indian king cobra is swallowing a smaller rat snake.

Birds

Biggest bird
The biggest bird alive today is the ostrich, which is flightless and lives in Africa. Males can be up to 2.7 m (9 ft) tall, and can weigh over 150 kg (330 lb).

▲ **Lost eggs** An ostrich collects its eggs, which have been scattered.

Biggest bird ever
The tallest bird that has ever lived was the giant moa in New Zealand, which stood over 3.5 m (11 ft) high. For its size, this flightless giant was quite light, weighing about a quarter of a tonne (550 lb). The heaviest bird ever was another flightless species, called *Dromornis stirtoni*, which lived in Australia. It could weigh up to half a tonne (1100 lb).

Smallest
The bee hummingbird, which lives in Cuba, is just under 6 cm (2¹/₂ in) long. It weighs about 1.6 g (0.056 oz) – less than a sugar cube. Lots of moths and butterflies are much bigger than this tiny bird.

Most numerous
The most numerous bird in the world is a seed-eating finch called the red-billed quelea, which lives in Africa. A single flock can contain 10 000 birds, but up to a million queleas may come together to roost.

Most widespread
The barn owl and the peregrine falcon are both found on every continent except Antarctica; no other land bird is so widespread.

Most dangerous
Some birds will attack people who come near their nests, but they rarely do any harm. The only really dangerous birds are ostriches and the smaller cassowaries, which live in northern Australia and New Guinea. Although neither of these birds can fly, they have powerful legs and huge claws that can cause serious and sometimes deadly wounds.

Greatest wingspan
The wandering albatross, a sea bird, has a wingspan of over 3.5 m (11 ft), giving it the longest wings of any bird alive today. Among land birds, those with the biggest wings are the African marabou stork and the Andean condor. Their wings can measure 3 m (nearly 10 ft) from tip to tip.

Heaviest flying bird
Flying is difficult for heavy birds. The great bustard, which can weigh up to 21 kg (46 lb), is the heaviest flying bird, yet it is still only one-seventh as heavy as the flightless ostrich.

Fastest flier
During a dive, a peregrine falcon probably reaches a speed of over 200 km/h (125 mph). However, because measuring its speed is difficult, no one is quite sure how fast it can go. Flying on the level, it probably reaches about 100 km/h (60 mph) in short bursts.

Highest flier
In 1973, a Rüppell's griffon (a kind of vulture) was sucked into the engine of a plane flying over western Africa. The plane was travelling at about 11 300 m (37 000 ft), making this the greatest height ever recorded for a bird.

Fastest wingbeats
The fastest flappers by far are tiny hummingbirds. Some of the smallest species beat their wings up to 90 times a second – so fast that they become completely blurred. Hummingbirds are the only birds that can fly backwards and sideways just as easily as they can forwards.

Slowest flier
Barn owls move very slowly when they are out hunting, but the slowest bird of all is probably the American woodcock. It flies along at just 8 km/h (5 mph). Woodcocks have broad wings, which allow them to fly slowly without falling out of the air.

Deepest diver
Scientists working in Antarctica have found that emperor penguins can dive to at least

▲ **High diver** Peregrine falcons fly high in the air, then dive, or 'stoop', onto their prey at great speed.

250 m (820 ft). They hold their breath for over 15 minutes under water. Flying seabirds cannot dive this deep, but some – such as guillemots and razorbills – have been accidentally caught by fishing nets over 70 m (230 ft) below the surface.

Longest beak
The Australian pelican's beak can be over 45 cm (18 in) long, which makes it the biggest in the bird world. However, in

▲ **Great flier** A wandering albatross looking for food for its chick has been tracked by satellite for up to 15 000 km (9320 miles) on a single flight.

Birds

What they eat
Plants (particularly seeds, nectar and fruit) and small animals.

How they reproduce
All birds lay hard-shelled eggs.

How they develop
Some birds, such as ducklings, can feed themselves as soon as they hatch. But others are born helpless, and have to be fed by their parents until they can look after themselves.

How long they live
From one year to over 80 years.

Interesting facts
Many birds migrate thousands of kilometres to avoid the cold of winter. Experts believe that they use the Sun and stars to guide them.

proportion to its body, the sword-billed hummingbird's beak is even longer. Its beak measures about 10 cm (4 in) from base to tip, making it the only bird whose beak is longer than its body.

Longest legs
Ostriches have the longest legs of all, but a bird called the black-winged stilt has more of its share of leg than any other. Its pencil-thin legs are up to 24 cm (9½ inches) long, about three-fifths the length of its body. Stilts need long legs because they get their food by wading in water.

Shortest legs
Swifts have such short legs that they find it difficult to move about on the ground. They cannot walk, but this is not a problem for them

because they only land when they nest. They feed, and even sleep, in the air.

Longest feathers
Some pheasants have tail feathers that are over 2 m (6 ft) long. These are the longest feathers in the wild, but they are not the longest feathers of all. In Japan, jungle fowl are specially bred for their long tails, and some of these have tail feathers that measure over 10 m (33 ft).

Loudest song
Bitterns make a loud booming call that can be heard up to 5 km (3 miles) away, but the loudest call of all is made by the kakapo, a rare flightless parrot in New Zealand. On a still night, the male's deep boom echoes off the mountainsides, and carries up to 7 km (4 miles).

Best at talking
Parrots are unrivalled experts at imitating human speech, and pet budgerigars (which are small parrots) are best of all. One tame budgie in California managed to learn more than 1700 words. Talking birds may sound intelligent,

but they are merely imitating sounds, and don't understand what they are 'saying'.

Biggest eggs
Ostriches lay bigger eggs than any other bird. They can be up to 20 cm (8 inches) long, and they have such thick shells that a man can stand on one without it breaking. A single ostrich egg is equivalent to 24 hens' eggs.

Smallest eggs
Some hummingbird eggs are less than 1 cm (3/8 in) long, making them not much bigger than a pea.

Most eggs
Game birds, which include pheasants, partridges and quails, are famous for

▲ **Fish scoop**
Pelicans feed on fish, which they scoop up in the flexible pouch that lies under their long beaks.

▲ **House proud** A pair of wild budgies build their nest in Australia.

laying lots of eggs. The grey partridge can lay up to 20 eggs at a time. Unlike many smaller birds, however, it lays its eggs only once a year.

Longest incubation
The time that it takes for a bird's eggs to hatch after they have been laid is called the incubation period. Some small birds lay eggs that hatch after just ten days. Ostriches incubate their eggs for about five weeks. Yet some albatrosses sit on their eggs for nearly 11 weeks. Albatrosses usually lay a single egg, and both parents share the job of incubating it. While one keeps the egg warm, the other parent collects food, sometimes from thousands of kilometres away.

Shortest life span
Many small songbirds, such as wrens and robins, die before they are even one year old. However. if they manage to survive the dangerous first year, they have a good chance of reaching 'old age' – between five and ten years.

Longest lived
Albatrosses probably live longer than any other birds in the wild, surviving well into their 50s. In captivity, birds live even longer. A cockatoo at London Zoo was at least 80 when it died in 1982.

Animals – vertebrates

Sea mammals

Biggest

The blue whale is easily the biggest sea mammal, and also by far the largest animal on Earth. The largest blue whale ever measured was 33.5 m (110 ft) from head to tail, and probably weighed at least 180 tonnes – more than 20 fully grown elephants. Whales can grow this

▲ **Biggest ever** Blue whales are the biggest creatures ever to have lived on Earth.

large only because they live in water, which helps to support their huge bodies. No land animal could grow to this size, as its muscles would not be strong enough to move it.

Smallest

The vaquita – a porpoise that lives in the Gulf of California – is only 1.5 m (5 ft) long, making it the smallest of all sea-going mammals. Vaquitas are very rare, so scientists still know little about how they spend their lives.

Most numerous

There are probably more crabeater seals than any other mammal in the sea. They live around Antarctica, which makes it difficult to count them, but experts think there may be as many as 40 million. Despite their name, they feed on shrimp-like animals called krill, not crabs. As well as being the most numerous mammals in the sea, crabeater seals are probably the most common large mammals on the entire planet.

Biggest brain

A sperm whale's brain weighs about 9 kg (20 lb) – seven times as much as an adult human's. However, despite having the largest brains in the world, these whales are not the cleverest creatures; they are probably less intelligent than most dolphins.

Fastest

Dolphins, porpoises and killer whales (orcas) are all hunters and flesh-eaters, and so can swim at high speeds to catch their prey. The fastest of all is thought to be Dall's porpoise, a barrel-shaped animal that lives in the northern Pacific Ocean. It can power through the water at 55 km/h (35 mph). At

this speed, it is easily able to overtake most boats and ships.

Deepest diver

Sperm whales are by far the best divers in the mammal world. They can dive down to a depth of at least 2 km (1 1/4 miles), where they hunt for giant squid. During a dive, sperm whales can stay underwater for over an hour.

Best traveller

Grey whales migrate farther than any other mammal. Every year, they swim from Mexico to the Arctic Ocean and back again – a total distance of up to 20 000 km (12 400 miles). Many other large whales travel almost as far.

Longest lived

No one knows exactly how long whales can live. Some have survived into their 80s, but most probably die before they get this old.

Land mammals

Biggest

The African elephant is the world's largest land mammal. Males can weigh over 6 tonnes (13 200 lb). To keep themselves alive, these big males have to eat nearly a quarter of a tonne

◀ **Lookout** Although crabeater seals can weigh up to 225 kg (500 lb), they are often eaten by killer whales.

(550 lb) of food a day. They strip bark from trees with their tusks, and pluck down leaves with their trunks. They chew up their food with giant back teeth, or molars, each the size of three bricks put together.

▶ **Family group** Elephants stay together and look after each other. This little group is heading for a waterhole in Namibia.

▼ **Leaf-eater** Giraffes can reach up to the top of a tree, where the youngest, tastiest leaves are found.

Biggest hunter

Brown bears from Kodiak Island in Alaska are the biggest predators that live on land. The biggest males can weigh over half a tonne (1100 lb).

Tallest

For height, no other animal comes close to the giraffe. The tallest on record stood just over 6 m (20 ft) high. When they are

Mammals

What they eat
Other animals and plant food, particularly grass and leaves.

How they reproduce
Two types of mammals, known as monotremes, lay eggs. They are the platypus and a type of anteater called an echidna. All other mammals give birth to living young.

How they develop
Young mammals are fed on milk. Marsupials, such as kangaroos, give birth to babies so tiny that they are barely recognisable for what they are. The young marsupial spends the first months of its life clinging to its mother's nipple, which is usually hidden in a pouch.

How long they live
From a few weeks for small rodents to more than 70 years for large whales, elephants and humans.

Interesting facts
Sea mammals such as dolphins and whales breathe air, rather than water, as fish do.

feeding, giraffes can reach even farther than this, because their tongues are 45 cm (18 in) long – handy for reaching the highest leaves on a tree.

Smallest
Including their tails, Etruscan pygmy shrews measure just 8 cm (3 in) in length, making them smaller than any other land mammal. However, they are not the smallest mammals of all. Bumblebee bats, from Thailand, are only 3.3 cm ($1^1/4$ in) long. They weigh 2 g (0.07 oz) – less than a sugar cube.

Fastest
Over short distances, cheetahs can run at just over 100 km/h (60 mph) – faster than any other animal on land. After the cheetah, the next fastest is the pronghorn antelope from North America. It can reach speeds of 88 km/h (55 mph).

Slowest
Sloths can remain in the same tree for a whole week, and they often stay perfectly still for hours at a time. When they are

▶ **No contest** Try as it might, a young gazelle has little chance of escaping from an adult cheetah.

on the ground, moving from one tree to another, their speed is about 0.2 km/h (0.1 mph).

Biggest wingspan
Australian bats called flying foxes have a wingspan of more than 1 m (39 in) – bigger than that of many birds.

Most intelligent
Intelligence is difficult to measure, but scientists think that chimpanzees are the most intelligent mammals after humans. Chimps know how to make tools, and communicate with each other using more than 30 'words'.

Longest hibernation
Animals that spend the winter asleep are said to hibernate. Some of the mammals that hibernate are bears and bats. Mountain rodents called marmots can hibernate for nine months each year. This means that a marmot spends three-quarters of its life in a deep sleep.

Lowest body temperature
When a mammal is hibernating, its heartbeat slows down and its temperature can drop to just a few degrees above freezing. The lowest temperature in mammals that are not hibernating is

found in sloths. Their normal body temperature can be as low as 24°C (75°F), compared with 37°C (98.6°F) for humans.

Highest
During summer in Tibet, mountain cattle called yaks sometimes climb above 6000 m (nearly 20 000 ft). At this altitude, the air is so thin that most people would be left gasping for breath.

Longest gestation period
A mammal's gestation period is the time it takes for its young to develop before they are ready to be born. In elephants, this is about 20 months, compared with nine months for humans.

Longest life span
Humans live longer than any other mammal, sometimes reaching the age of 100 or more. After us, those that live longest are large whales and elephants, which can live to be more than 70 years old.

Endangered species

Plants

Number of threatened species: more than 25 000.

Many plants have become rare over recent years, but some trees are now so rare that only one living specimen is left. They include the caffe marron, from the island of Rodrigues in the Indian Ocean, and the St Helena olive, from the island of St Helena in the Atlantic Ocean.

Insects

Number of threatened species: unknown.

Because there are so many kinds of insects, it is difficult to know which ones are most in danger. However, scientists believe that at least 400 species of beetles, and more than 300 species of butterflies and moths, could soon be lost forever. Queen Alexandra's birdwing – the biggest butterfly in the world – is one of the most threatened insects of all.

▲ **Fierce looks** In spite of its appearance, the Mexican red-kneed tarantula is harmless to humans.

Spiders

Number of threatened species: unknown.

Some of the world's biggest spiders have become extremely rare in the wild because so many have been collected and sold as pets. One that has been

threatened by over-collection is the Mexican red-kneed tarantula, a species that lives in the deserts of Mexico.

Molluscs

Number of threatened species: 1200.

People have always been fascinated by shells, and this is one of the reasons why some molluscs are now very rare. Collecting empty shells at the seaside does no harm, but buying shells encourages people to collect molluscs while they are still alive. Many species of cowrie are endangered because too many have been collected for their shells.

Fish

Number of threatened species: unknown.

About 1000 species of fish are thought to be endangered. Most of them are freshwater species that have been harmed by pollution or over-fishing. There may, however, be many more at risk.

Amphibians

Number of threatened species: about 170.

Frogs are among the most endangered animals on Earth. Throughout the world, many species have mysteriously declined in recent years, and scientists have yet to work out why. One of the world's most colourful species – the golden toad of Costa Rica – suddenly vanished in the late 1980s. Over 100 other species are at risk of sharing the same fate.

Reptiles

Number of threatened species: more than 300.

For many centuries, reptiles have suffered by being hunted for their skins or shells. Today, turtles and tortoises are among the most threatened

▲ **Sought after** Right whales got their name because whalers considered them the 'right' whales to hunt and kill.

reptiles in the world. Giant tortoises, which live on the Galapagos Islands, are now carefully protected, but many sea turtles are threatened because people continue to collect their eggs. The same people also often kill the turtles when they have laid their eggs.

▶ **Last of many** Huge numbers of giant tortoises were taken from the Galapagos Islands as food for the crews of whaling ships.

Birds

Number of threatened species: about 1000.

Many birds are now so rare that only a handful of them are left. Among the most endangered of all is Spix's macaw, which lives in the rain forests of South America. About 30 are living in captivity, but over the last ten years only one bird has been seen in the wild.

Sea mammals

Number of threatened species: about 90.

After centuries of being hunted by many nations, whales are now protected. However, scientists think that some of them might still be in danger of extinction. One of the most threatened is the northern

◄ **New hope** A mother mountain gorilla suckles her baby in the highlands of Rwanda.

Molluscs
In 1952, a research ship working off the coast of Mexico hauled up a species of mollusc that was thought to have died out more than 300 million years ago. These survivors from the Earth's distant past are called monoplacophorans. They look like limpets, and live on the deep seabed.

Fish
A fish called the coelacanth was the most important animal discovery of the 20th century. It was thought to have died out about 60 million years ago, but in 1938 one was caught by a fishing boat off the coast of southern Africa. Coelacanths have fins that look like stumpy legs. They probably resemble the first animals that crawled out of the sea to take up life on land.

Amphibians
One of the world's largest toads, a species called *Bufo blombergi*, was not discovered until 1951. It lives in Colombia, in South America, and can grow up to 25 cm (10 in) long.

Reptiles
Scientists did not find out about the world's biggest lizard – the Komodo dragon – until 1912. The first one to live outside the island of Komodo arrived at a zoo in New York in 1926.

Birds
One of Australia's rarest birds – the night parrot – was thought to have died out early in the 20th century, but in 1990 a motorist found one dead by the side of a road. This chance discovery means it likely that others are still alive.

Mammals
One of the most recent discoveries among mammals is the bondegezou, a small tree kangaroo that lives in some high mountain forests of New Guinea. It was first recorded by a photographer in 1990.

▼ **Shy and retiring** The rare bondegezou lives in remote forests of Irian Jaya, in western New Guinea. Very little is known about it.

right whale. These whales have been protected since 1937, but there may be fewer than 700 of them left. Since some countries want to start hunting whales again, other species may also soon be at risk.

Land mammals
Number of threatened species: about 650.

The list of endangered land mammals is a long one, but big cats, monkeys and apes are probably the most threatened of all. Tigers are rapidly disappearing all over southern Asia, and soon there will be very few left in the wild. In central Africa, mountain gorillas are in danger of extinction, with only about 600 animals left. There are only about 50 Javan rhinos left in the forests of Indonesia.

New discoveries

Plants
New species of plants are being discovered all the time. One of the most exciting finds of recent years was made in 1994, when a ranger found some unknown trees in a remote gorge in eastern Australia. Called Wollemi pines, they have survived since the age of the dinosaurs, but had never been seen before.

Insects
The 'Cooloola monster' is one of the strangest insects to be discovered in recent years. Found in 1976 in Australia's Cooloola National Park, it looks like a stubby, wingless grasshopper, and spends almost all of its life underground.

How we work

Every part of your body, from skin to muscles, bones and internal organs, is made up of different types of cells. A healthy diet containing vitamins and minerals is essential to keep the different parts working properly, but sometimes the body may be affected by disease.

Cells
A human body is made up of about 50 000 billion building blocks, known as cells. Most of these are too small to be visible without a microscope, but if all of them were laid out in a line, they would go round the Earth 25 times.

Cell types
The human body has over 200 different kinds of cells. They are arranged in groups, called tissues, according to the different functions they perform. The different kinds of tissues are organised into organs, such as the liver, the heart and the kidneys. Organs make up the body's systems. There are more than ten of these, including the skeletal system, the respiratory system, the digestive system, the circulatory system, and the reproductive system.

Biggest human cells
Some nerve cells can be 1.2 m (4 ft) long, but they are so slender that they are invisible to the naked eye. The bulkiest cells are egg cells, which develop into babies if they are fertilised.

These are over 0.1 mm (0.004 in) across, just big enough to be visible.

Smallest human cells
Some cells in the brain are only 0.005 mm (0.0002 in) across, which is much smaller than some bacteria. The brain contains billions of these cells, and they help control the rest of the body.

Shortest-lived cells
Cells that get a lot of wear and tear only live for a short time. The shortest-lived cells are ones that make up the lining of the

▲ **Short life** These cells are from the lining of the mouth.

mouth, stomach and intestines. On average, these last for just three days before they wear out and die. They are constantly replaced by new cells, which form beneath the surface layer.

Longest-lived cells
Nerves form before we are born. Unlike most other cells, they cannot be replaced, so they have to last for life.

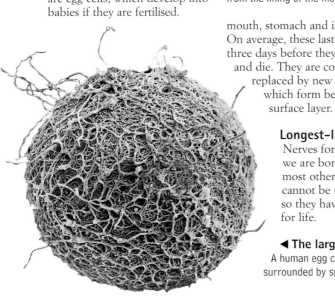

◀ **The largest cell** A human egg cell, or ovum, surrounded by sperm cells.

▲ **Hard head** This X-ray of the head shows how the upper and back part of the skull protects the brain (the pink area).

Skeleton
The average person has 206 bones. Two-fifths of them make up the central part of the skeleton, which includes the skull, backbone and ribcage. The remaining three-fifths make up the arms, legs, shoulders and hips.

Loose bones
Most of your bones are attached to another bone, but some bones are fixed to tendons instead, and these bones are known as sesamoid bones. The biggest sesamoid bones are the kneecaps, which protect the knee joints from damage. We also have a loose horseshoe-shaped bone at the top of the throat that helps the tongue to work.

Strongest and weakest bones
The strongest bones in the human body are those that protect the brain. The weakest ones are inside the head, around the air

spaces behind the nose. These bones are paper-thin, but they are protected by the rest of the skull.

Muscles
The body has over 600 skeletal muscles, which we use to move about. It also has lots of 'involuntary' muscles that work automatically. These include the muscles that move food through the intestines, and those that make your hair stand on end when you are cold.

▼ **Eye muscles** Involuntary muscles inside the eye keep the objects that you are looking at in focus.

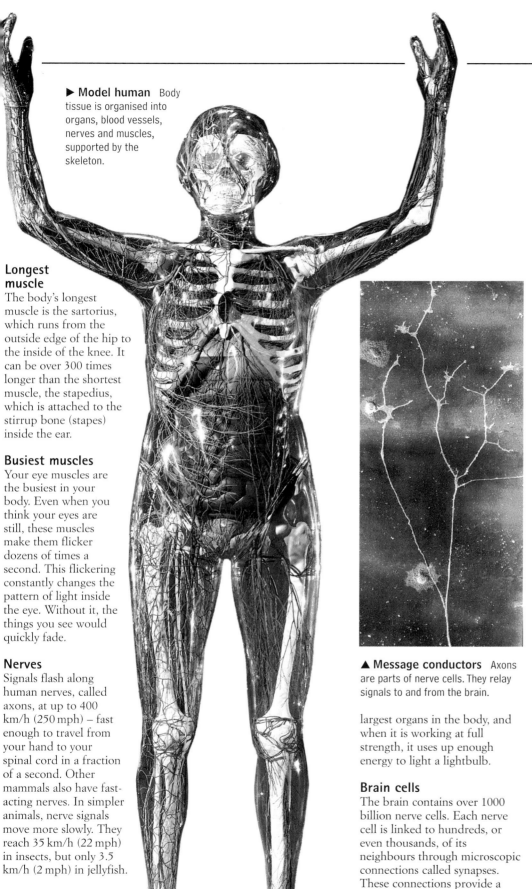

▶ **Model human** Body tissue is organised into organs, blood vessels, nerves and muscles, supported by the skeleton.

Longest muscle

The body's longest muscle is the sartorius, which runs from the outside edge of the hip to the inside of the knee. It can be over 300 times longer than the shortest muscle, the stapedius, which is attached to the stirrup bone (stapes) inside the ear.

Busiest muscles

Your eye muscles are the busiest in your body. Even when you think your eyes are still, these muscles make them flicker dozens of times a second. This flickering constantly changes the pattern of light inside the eye. Without it, the things you see would quickly fade.

Nerves

Signals flash along human nerves, called axons, at up to 400 km/h (250 mph) – fast enough to travel from your hand to your spinal cord in a fraction of a second. Other mammals also have fast-acting nerves. In simpler animals, nerve signals move more slowly. They reach 35 km/h (22 mph) in insects, but only 3.5 km/h (2 mph) in jellyfish.

Brain

A typical fully grown human brain weighs about 1.3 kg (3 lb). It is one of the

▲ **Message conductors** Axons are parts of nerve cells. They relay signals to and from the brain.

largest organs in the body, and when it is working at full strength, it uses up enough energy to light a lightbulb.

Brain cells

The brain contains over 1000 billion nerve cells. Each nerve cell is linked to hundreds, or even thousands, of its neighbours through microscopic connections called synapses. These connections provide a huge number of pathways for nerve signals. They work like the electronic circuits in a computer chip, but are much more complicated.

Blood

An average adult has about 5 litres (8 pints) of blood, making up about 8 per cent of the body's total weight. Blood is heavier than water, and it is also about five times thicker.

Blood cells

On average, a typical red blood cell lasts for about four months, and travels around the body nearly 200 000 times. White blood cells can last for much longer – sometimes as long as several years.

Blood groups

Everybody's blood belongs to one of four blood groups: A, B, AB or O. When people have a blood transfusion, they are normally given blood that matches their own group. In emergencies, they can be given type O blood, because this can be given to anyone without causing ill-effects. Mixing blood from the other blood groups can be dangerous.

Biggest blood vessels

The largest artery in the body is called the aorta. In adults, its widest part is about 2.5 cm (1 in) across. The largest vein, called the vena cava, has less thick walls than the aorta, but is the same width inside.

Smallest blood vessels

Tiny blood vessels called capillaries can be just 0.001 mm (0.00004 in) across. Their walls are only one cell thick, which means that oxygen can easily travel through them and into nearby cells.

▼ **Tiny supplier** This capillary is transporting blood through muscle.

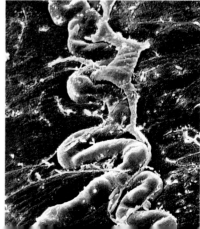

Vitamins

Vitamins are complicated chemicals that your body needs, but which it cannot make for itself. Instead, it gets them from food. Altogether, there are 13 different vitamins. This page shows which foods contain lots of vitamins, and what each vitamin does.

Vitamin A (retinol)
Where it comes from
Milk and dairy products, leafy vegetables, eggs.
What it does
Important for bone growth and healthy skin; also keeps your corneas (the outer layer of your eyes) in good health.

▼ **Strong bones** Cheese is good for growth and for healthy bones and teeth.

Vitamin B1 (thiamine)
Where it comes from
Bread, meat, peas, beans, nuts.
What it does
Makes nerves and muscles work.

Vitamin B2 (riboflavin)
Where it comes from
Dairy products, leafy vegetables.
What it does
Helps release energy from food; keeps skin healthy.

▼ **Healthy cells**
Spinach provides Vitamin C and folic acid.

▲ **Quick responses** Vegetables help nerve cells work well.

Vitamin B3 (niacin)
Where it comes from
Wide range of foods, including fish, whole-grain cereals, peas and beans.
What it does
Helps release energy from food; makes hormones, the chemicals that regulate the way your body works; keeps skin healthy.

Vitamin B6 (pyroxidine)
Where it comes from
Meat, fish, liver, dairy products, fruit and vegetables.
What it does
Helps your body to make haemoglobin – the red pigment in blood – and substances used for fighting disease; important for nervous system.

Vitamin B12 (cyanocobalamin)
Where it comes from
Meat, fish, dairy products, eggs.
What it does
Essential for the growth of new cells; also helps your nervous system to work well.

Folic acid
Where it comes from
Leafy vegetables, whole-grain foods, peas and beans, nuts.
What it does
Needed for making new cells; also helps your nervous system to work.

Vitamin C (ascorbic acid)
Where it comes from
Fresh fruit and vegetables, particularly citrus fruit such as lemons and oranges, salad vegetables, potatoes.
What it does
Essential for the growth and repair of cells, and for healthy bones and teeth; also helps your body to fight off infections.

Vitamin D
Where it comes from
Milk and dairy products, cereals, fish, cod liver oil. Also made by skin when the Sun shines on it.
What it does
Helps your body to absorb calcium, which is needed for strong teeth and bones, and to make muscles and nerves work normally.

Vitamin E (tocopherol)
Where it comes from
Vegetable oils, leafy vegetables, whole-grain foods, eggs, fish.
What it does
Helps your body to produce red blood cells, and protects all cells from damaging chemicals.

Vitamin K
Where it comes from
Leafy vegetables, eggs, cheese and liver. Also made by bacteria that live in your intestines.
What it does
Essential for healthy bones, and for helping to make blood clot after an injury in order for wounds to heal.

Biotin
Where it comes from
Eggs, liver, kidneys. This vitamin is also made by bacteria that live in your intestines.
What it does
Helps make substances needed by cells.

▲ **Light and refreshing**
Salad vegetables, including cucumber, provide Vitamin C.

Pantothenic acid
Where it comes from
Liver, kidneys, green vegetables, cereals.

▲ **Fighting infections**
Grapefruit are full of Vitamin C.

What it does
Pantothenic acid helps your body release energy from food; and is used in making hormones.

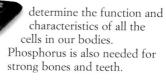
Minerals

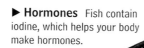

Minerals are simple substances that are formed in the ground. Your body needs 16 minerals, which it gets from food, salt, and the water that you drink. You need large amounts of some minerals, but only tiny traces of others.

Calcium
Where it comes from
Milk and dairy products, green vegetables, nuts.
What it does
Essential for strong bones and teeth; and plays a part in clotting – the process that brings bleeding to a halt.

▲ **Healthy teeth** In some areas, tapwater contains calcium and fluorine.

Chlorine
Where it comes from
Mainly from salt.
What it does
Enables your body to keep an equal balance between the amount of water you drink each day and the amount your body gets rid of. Also essential for making the acid your stomach uses to break down food.

Chromium
Where it comes from
Meat, dairy products, whole-grain foods, yeast.
What it does
Helps your body to adjust the level of sugar in your blood.

▶ **Energy** Eggs are rich in the nutrients for growth and for releasing energy.

▶ **Hormones** Fish contain iodine, which helps your body make hormones.

Cobalt
Where it comes from
Meat and dairy products.
What it does
Essential for producing red blood cells.

Copper
Where it comes from
Liver, meat, fish, seafood, green vegetables, whole-grain cereals.
What it does
Copper is needed in many of the chemical reactions that your body carries out. Without it, your body cannot make haemoglobin or many other important substances.

Fluorine
Where it comes from
Fish and seafood, tea, fluoridated tapwater (tapwater with fluorine added to it).
What it does
Needed to make strong bones and teeth.

Iodine
Where it comes from
Sea fish, seafood, dairy products, sea salt.
What it does
Used by your thyroid gland to make hormones. These hormones control how fast your body uses energy.

Iron
Where it comes from
Red meat, liver, green vegetables, nuts.
What it does
Helps the body to make haemoglobin, the red chemical that carries oxygen in your blood. Iron is also needed to make muscle cells.

Magnesium
Where it comes from
Milk, fish, whole-grain cereals, green vegetables, peas, beans, fruit, tapwater (in some areas).
What it does
Essential for healthy teeth and bones, and for making nerves and muscles work normally.

Manganese
Where it comes from
Meat, whole-grain food, nuts, tea, coffee.

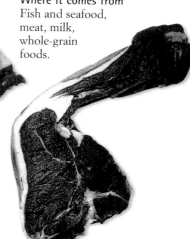

▲ **Growth** Meat is important for the development of new cells.

What it does
Manganese is used to make enzymes – substances that speed up chemical reactions.

Phosphorus
Where it comes from
Meat, milk and dairy products, whole-grain foods, green vegetables, fruit, nuts.
What it does
Needed to build many of the substances used inside your body, including genes – the chemical instructions we inherit from our parents, carried in the nucleus of each cell, that determine the function and characteristics of all the cells in our bodies. Phosphorus is also needed for strong bones and teeth.

Potassium
Where it comes from
Bread and whole-grain cereals, green vegetables, beans, fruit.
What it does
Potassium is an essential ingredient in all of your body's fluids. It enables nerves to carry signals around the body.

Selenium
Where it comes from
Fish and seafood, meat, milk, whole-grain foods.

What it does
Helps to protect cells from any damaging chemicals that build up inside them.

Sodium
Where it comes from
Table salt, and salty food including fish and cheese.
What it does
Sodium helps to keep your body's water balance correct, and enables nerves to work.

Sulphur
Where it comes from
Meat, eggs, dairy products.
What it does
Helps to make proteins.

Zinc
Where it comes from
Meat, eggs, fish, cereals, beans, nuts.
What it does
Used by cells to grow and to release energy.

Major diseases

Infectious diseases

An infectious disease is a disease that is caused by bacteria, by viruses, or by other forms of microscopic life. These tiny organisms live in or on the body, and they can be passed on from one person to another. Some infectious diseases are quite mild and our bodies soon fight them off. Others can be much more dangerous. Here you can find out about some of the most important of these infectious diseases.

Chickenpox
What causes it
A virus.
Effects
Produces itchy blisters all over the body.
How it spreads
Through the air. Most people catch this disease during their childhood.

▲ ▶ **Feeling ill** The chickenpox virus causes a rash and fever.

Cholera
What causes it
A bacterium.
Effects
Causes severe diarrhoea and water loss.
How it spreads
Through infected water. Cholera sometimes breaks out after disasters such as earthquakes, when water supplies become polluted.

Common cold
What causes it
Over 200 kinds of virus.
Effects
Inflames the lining of the mouth, nose and throat, making them sore and the nose 'run'.
How it spreads
Mainly through the air. Colds are very difficult to prevent, because cold viruses spread very easily when people sneeze.

Influenza (flu)
What causes it
Viruses.
Effects
Headaches, aching joints, high temperature.
How it spreads
Through the air. The viruses that cause flu are difficult for the body to fend off, because they change quite frequently.

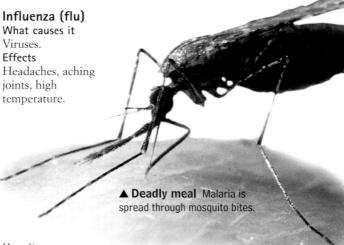

▲ **Deadly meal** Malaria is spread through mosquito bites.

Malaria
What causes it
A tiny single-celled parasite that is carried by mosquitoes.
Effects
Causes severe fever, and chills, and it can damage the liver and kidneys.
How it spreads
Through mosquito bites. Malaria is widespread in warm countries, and is one of the world's most dangerous diseases.

Measles
What causes it
A virus.
Effects
High temperature and a rash across the skin.
How it spreads
Through the air. This was once a very common childhood disease, but today many children are vaccinated against it.

Meningitis
What causes it
Either a virus or a bacterium.
Effects
Headache and fever caused by microbes infecting the lining around the brain.
How it spreads
Usually through the air. The kind of meningitis caused by viruses is usually mild; bacterial meningitis can be dangerous.

Mumps
What causes it
A virus.
Effects
Swollen salivary glands in the mouth, producing a 'puffy-faced' look.
How it spreads
Through the air. Mumps is a common childhood illness. It can be prevented by vaccination.

Pneumonia
What causes it
Bacteria, viruses and some other microorganisms.
Effects
Coughing and difficulty in breathing caused by microorganisms infecting the lungs.
How it spreads
Usually through the air. Pneumonia is a serious disease. People often catch it when they are already suffering from some other illness, which makes it harder for their immune systems to fight off an attack.

Rubella (German measles)
What causes it
A virus.
Effects
Produces a spotty red rash on the skin.
How it spreads
Through the air. Rubella is usually harmless, but it can damage unborn babies when it infects women who are pregnant. Nowadays, most children are vaccinated against the disease.

Tetanus
What causes it
A bacterium.
Effects
Interferes with the nervous system, paralysing muscles.
How it spreads
From soil contaminated with bacteria. Unlike most other infectious diseases, tetanus does not spread from person to person. Although it is very dangerous, it is easy to prevent by vaccination.

Tuberculosis
What causes it
A bacterium.
Effects
Difficulty in breathing, caused by bacteria infecting the lungs.
How it spreads
Through the air. At one time, tuberculosis used to be a major killer throughout the world. It can now be treated, but it still affects poor people who live in unhealthy conditions.

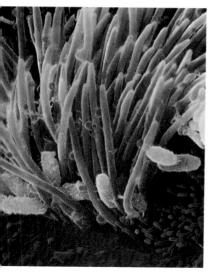

Whooping cough (pertussis)
What causes it
A bacterium.
Effects
Severe coughing, caused by an infection of the windpipe (trachea).
How it spreads
Through the air. This disease is prevented by vaccination.

Noninfectious diseases

Unlike infectious diseases, non-infectious diseases are not caused by bacteria or by viruses, so they cannot be passed on from one person to another. Some non-infectious diseases are caused by natural wear and tear as people get older. Others are caused by defects in genes – the chemical instructions that control the body.

Arthritis
What causes it
Usually natural wear and tear on the joints. One form of this disease, called rheumatoid arthritis, is caused by the immune system – the body's defence system against invading bacteria – attacking the body by mistake.
Effects
Arthritis can make a person's joints stiff and painful, making it difficult for them to hold objects or move about.

◀ **Causing a cough**
The yellow discs are whooping cough bacteria lodged in the lining of the windpipe.

Asthma
What causes it
Often caused by allergies. Substances in the air, changes in temperature, or sudden anxiety can bring on attacks.
Effects
During an asthma attack, the airways leading to the lungs become narrow, making it hard to breathe. Asthma often affects children, particularly those who live in cities where the air is polluted.

Cancer
What causes it
Defects in genes, over-exposure to strong sunlight resulting in sunburn, X-rays, and some chemicals, including those in tobacco smoke.
Effects
When someone has cancer, the cells in a part of their body start to divide, producing a lump called a tumour. Tumours can get so big that they stop nearby organs working properly, and they can spread to other parts of the body. Cancer is a serious disease, and scientists do not yet know how to prevent it. Once it has begun, it can be treated with drugs and with radiotherapy – using X-rays to kill the cancerous cells – and by surgery.

Diabetes
What causes it
A shortage or lack of insulin, the hormone that controls the level of sugar in the blood.
Effects
Without insulin, the blood's sugar level becomes dangerously high, and this can damage the eyes, kidneys and other organs. People with diabetes often have to inject themselves with insulin every day to keep their blood sugar at a safe level.

Eczema
What causes it
Sometimes caused by chemicals, including soaps and detergents, but in many people the cause is unknown.
Effects
Makes the skin dry and itchy. It can be treated with creams and ointments, but it sometimes disappears on its own.

Leukaemia
What causes it
Unknown.
Effects
Leukaemia is a kind of cancer that causes the body to produce an abnormally high number of white blood cells. Unlike other kinds of cancer, it affects children as much as adults. It is treated by

◀ **Breathing trouble**
An asthma sufferer wears a mask to protect him from air pollution.

drugs, and sometimes by replacing a person's bone marrow, the substance that produces white blood cells.

Multiple sclerosis (MS)
What causes it
Unknown.
Effects
The protective material that is normally wrapped around nerves starts to break down. This can make parts of the body feel numb, and it can also make it hard to balance and to move about. At present, there is no known cure.

Muscular dystrophy
What causes it
Inherited genes.
Effects
The body's muscles gradually weaken, making it difficult to move about. There are several kinds of this childhood disease, but all of them are rare.

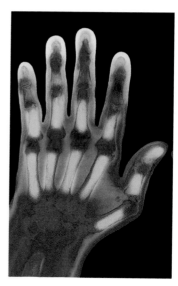

▲ **Arthritic hands** The pink areas in this X-ray of a hand indicate swelling in the joints of a person suffering from rheumatoid arthritis.

Rheumatism
What causes it
Several different disorders; arthritis is one of the most common.
Effects
Pain and stiffness in the joints. Many people suffer from rheumatism as they get older, but it only becomes a serious problem when someone's joints are damaged.

Elements and materials

Different materials have different qualities, making them good for different jobs. Diamonds, for example, are so hard that almost nothing can scratch them, so they are used for specially accurate drills and cutting tools. Nowadays, we use many synthetic (man-made) materials as well as those found in nature.

Metals and alloys

Metals are chemical elements or alloys (mixtures of elements) that are good conductors of heat and electricity. Most metals are hard and shiny.

Densest and least dense
The densest metallic element is osmium. Just 1 cm³ of it weighs 22.6 g (1 cu in weighs 13 oz) – very nearly twice as much as a piece of lead of the same size. At the other end of the scale, the least dense metallic element is lithium, weighing 0.53 g per cm³ (0.31 oz per cu in).

Highest melting point
Tungsten is the metallic element with the highest melting point – 3410°C (6170°F). That is why tungsten is used to make the filaments (thin wires) inside light bulbs, which must withstand very high temperatures.

Lowest melting point
The metal with the lowest melting point is mercury. It is liquid at room temperature and freezes at –38.8°C (–37.8°F). It is used in thermometers, though not for measuring very cold temperatures.

Best conductor
The best conductor of heat and electricity is silver, but copper is almost as good and is much cheaper than silver. So copper is generally used for electric wires.

Rust-resistant
Iridium is the metal that resists rusting and other kinds of corrosion best. It is also extremely hard and resists scratching. That is why rods and bars used for standard weights and measures are generally made of iridium. These standards are used to check other weights, rulers and measures. Gold and platinum also resist attack by almost all chemicals, and stay bright and shiny. That is why they are used for jewellery.

Malleable and ductile
Most metals are malleable – they can be shaped by beating or pressing. And most are ductile – they can be drawn into a wire. The most malleable and ductile metal of all is gold. It can be beaten to gold leaf less than one-10 000th of a millimetre thick, and 1 g (0.04 oz) can be drawn into a wire thread as long as 2.4 km (1¹/₂ miles).

Hardest
The hardest metals in wide use are alloys. Alloys usually remain harder at high temperatures than pure metallic elements. For example, tungsten steel and Stellite (an alloy of cobalt, chromium and tungsten) are both used in cutting tools and drills. Carboloy (an alloy of tungsten, carbon and cobalt), is almost as hard as diamond.

▲ **Drill head** Tiny chips of diamond on the tip of a dentist's drill, magnified nearly 10 000 times.

Steel alloys
The most widely used alloys are forms of steel. There are many types, all based on iron with small amounts of carbon, manganese and other elements. Examples include mild or carbon steel, which contains a small amount of carbon and is used for car bodies and girders. Stainless steel, which resists rust, contains chromium and often nickel. The various types of tool steel, which are very hard, contain elements such as tungsten, cobalt or molybdenum.

Lightweight alloys
The most widely used lightweight alloys are those based on aluminium, mixed with copper, magnesium, manganese or other elements. Some of these alloys are almost as strong as steel but are only one-third as heavy. For this reason, they are widely used in building aircraft. Aluminium is the most common metallic element in the Earth's crust, but it is expensive to refine.
Aluminium alloys are much more expensive than steel.

Nonmetallic elements

Nonmetallic elements are gases, liquids or solids that do not conduct heat well. Some of the solids are hard and shiny, but more like rocks than metals.

Hard as diamond
Diamond, a form of carbon, is the hardest nonmetal and the hardest known element. (Another form of carbon, graphite, is soft and slippery.) However, a man-made substance called borazon – a compound of boron and nitrogen – is as hard as diamond. It is the only known substance that can scratch diamond. Diamond will also scratch borazon.

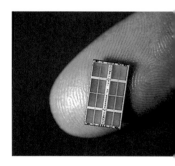
▲ **Fingertip chip** Silicon, used to make microchips, has become a vital element in the computer age.

Lowest melting point
The nonmetal with the lowest melting point is the gas helium. It becomes a liquid at –268.93°C (–452.07°F), only a few degrees above absolute zero, –273.16°C (–459.69°F), the lowest possible temperature. Helium never freezes to a solid unless it is compressed at about 25 times the pressure of the atmosphere and cooled to –272.2°C (–458°F). Liquid helium is a very peculiar substance. It is *superfluid* – that is, it has no friction – and can flow *up* the surface of its container and down the outside without any help.

◄ **Space frame** The German carmakers Audi use an aluminium alloy 'space frame' to give their cars extra strength in case of a crash.

Like a metal, but not a metal

Silicon is a metalloid – a substance that acts in some ways like a metal and in some ways like a nonmetal. It is also a semiconductor: it conducts electricity better than most nonmetals but not as well as metals. It is used to make computer chips. Silicon is by far the most common solid element in the Earth's crust, making up 28 per cent of its weight. Sand is mainly silica – a compound of silicon and oxygen.

Ceramics

Ceramics are the most ancient man-made materials. Pottery dates from prehistoric times, about 13 000 years ago. Nowadays, ceramics are important in industry and engineering.

Heat-resistant
Ceramics are among the most heat-resistant of all materials. They are used where metals would melt or become weak. For example, the space shuttle has ceramic tiles or pads made of woven fibres of silica (purified sand) to resist the heat generated when it re-enters the Earth's atmosphere.

Superconducting
Some ceramics are *superconductors*: they conduct electricity without any loss of power. Mostly they do this at very low temperatures. One ceramic, made from oxides of barium, calcium, copper and mercury, becomes superconducting at a relatively 'warm' –141°C (–222°F).

▲ ▼ **Synthetic fibres** Nylon is used in chemical warfare suits. Nylon fibres, magnified 16 500 times.

Plastics and fibres

Both plastics and synthetic fibres are polymers – substances made of very long chains of atoms. Many are made from by-products of oil refining.

First plastics
These were made by treating cellulose, a natural polymer found in cotton and other plant materials. The first, in 1869, was called Celluloid, and was used for making billiard and table-tennis balls. Starting in 1884, scientists discovered ways of making synthetic cellulose fibres known as rayon, or 'artificial silk'.

Thermoplastics
Plastics that get soft and can be reshaped when they are hot are called *thermoplastics*. They include nylon, polyethylene, polystyrene and synthetic rubbers. *Thermosetting* plastics harden and cannot be reshaped when hot. One of the first was Bakelite, invented in 1909 and long used to make telephones. Melamine and polyurethane are newer thermosetting plastics.

Strongest plastics
Some synthetic fibres, such as Kevlar, are five times stronger than steel. They are used to make bullet-proof vests, the sails of racing yachts and the strings of archery bows.

Composite materials

Composite materials are two or more different materials that are combined to make something that is better than either on its own. The earliest composite dates from over 2000 years ago, when the ancient Greeks used metal bars to strengthen marble.

Most widely used
Reinforced concrete – concrete containing steel (or sometimes plastic) rods – is more widely used than any other composite.

Concrete is very strong in *compression* (it cannot be crushed easily) while steel is strong in *tension* – it bends if crushed but is very strong when pulled. The combination is used for buildings, bridges and roads.

Plastic composites
These include plastic resins containing hair-like fibres of glass or graphite (carbon). They have been used for car bodies, baths and parts of aircraft.

Honeycomb composites
Some of the lightest and stiffest materials used in engineering are honeycombs. These consist of lightweight hollow cross-pieces (like a bee's honeycomb) sandwiched between surface layers. Honeycombs of metals and plastic composites are used in the bodies of some aircraft and spacecraft.

▲ ▼ **Reinforced bridge** The steel 'cage' goes up first, then the concrete. Below: A tennis racket made from a composite of graphite (carbon) fibres and synthetic resin.

A ir transport is the newcomer on the scene. Our ancestors started using wheeled vehicles on land and sailing boats at sea thousands of years ago. Nowadays, we take air travel for granted, but the first 'vehicle' to carry a human through the air was a hot-air balloon a little over 200 years ago.

On land

5000 BC

The **first vehicles** were sledges. People in prehistoric times used them to drag loads.

3500 BC

The **wheel was invented** in Mesopotamia (modern Iraq). It was first used on funeral carts.

2000–1500 BC

Wheels with spokes were invented. They were light enough for horse-drawn chariots, the fastest vehicles of the ancient world.

AD 800–1000

Three inventions in Europe made horse transport faster and more reliable: the iron **horseshoe** (which protected horses' hooves), the **rigid horse-collar** (which meant horses could haul heavy loads without being choked) and the **wiffletree** (a crossbar on a wagon so that a team of horses could pull it efficiently).

1825

The **first public steam railway** was the Stockton-Darlington Railway in north-eastern England.

1839

The **first pedal-cycle** was made in Dumfries, Scotland.

1863

The **first underground railway** was opened, in London, using steam trains.

1885

The **first petrol-engined vehicles** were built in Germany. Gottlieb Daimler built a motorcycle with two wheels. Karl Benz made a three-wheeled carriage.

1890

In France, René Panhard and Emile Levassor built the **first petrol-engined motor car** with four wheels.

1913

The age of **mass-produced cars began** when Henry Ford opened a factory where workers assembled Model T Fords on conveyor belts known as production lines.

1916

The world's **longest continuous railway track** was completed: Russia's Trans-Siberian Railway, stretching about 9300 km (5780 miles) from Moscow to Vladivostok.

▲ **First bike** This pedal-less bicycle, made in about 1818, was called a hobbyhorse or dandy horse.

1936

The **most successful car** ever made was the Volkswagen 'Beetle', first built in Germany.

▼ **Trans-Siberian Railway** At a station along the way, women use old prams to sell snacks to passengers on board the train.

Some 21 million were made in five countries over 60 years.

1990

A French electric TGV (*Train à Grande Vitesse*) reached 515.3 km/h (320.2 mph) between Courtelain and Tours in western France. This set the **speed record for a train on a public rail network**.

1997

The **world land-speed record** was set in Nevada, USA, by Andy Green of Britain. His jet-powered *ThrustSSC* was the first car to travel faster than the speed of sound, setting a record of 1227.985 km/h (763.035 mph)

At sea

3200 BC

The **first sailing boats** we know of were built in Egypt.

650 BC

The Greeks built triremes – ships propelled by three banks of oars, one above the other, on each side. They were the **biggest ships ever powered by human muscles**.

AD 950

The Vikings were the **first Europeans to cross oceans**. They reached Greenland and Newfoundland.

Moscow

Vladivostok

Blue riband The famous trophy awarded to the liner that made the fastest transatlantic crossing.

769
The Spanish navy's *Santísima Trinidad* was the **most powerful wooden warship** built in the age of sail. It had up to 144 guns, in four banks, on either side.

787
The **first successful steam-powered vessel** was a paddle boat built in the USA.

837
Brunel's *Great Western* was the first ocean-going iron ship.

952
Setting out from New York, the *United States* made the **fastest-ever transatlantic crossing by a liner**. It reached Cornwall in three days and ten hours, winning the Blue Riband trophy for the fastest crossing.

960
The globe-shaped bathyscaph *Trieste* made the **deepest dive** by submersible. Jacques Piccard and Donald Walsh took it down some 11 000 m (36 000 ft) in the Marianas Trench in the Pacific.

1976
The 564 763 tonne oil tanker *Seawise Giant* (later *Jahre Viking*) was launched. It is the **biggest ship ever built**, almost 460 m (1510 ft) long.

In the air

350 BC
The Chinese flew **kites** – really a type of glider – as early as the 4th century BC.

1483
The artist Leonardo da Vinci drew a **helicopter design**.

1783
In France, the Montgolfier brothers flew the first hot-air balloons. One, on October 15, **carried a man into the air for the first time**.

1853
The **first manned flight by a glider**, built in England by Sir George Cayley.

1903
On December 17, in the USA, Orville Wright made the **first controlled flight** in a powered, manned, heavier-than-air craft.

1909
The **first commercial passenger airship**, the Zeppelin *Deutschland* of Germany, went into service.

The Frenchman Louis Blériot made the **first international aeroplane flight**, when he flew from France to England.

1919
Britain's James Alcock and Arthur Brown made the **first nonstop transatlantic air crossing**.

The Australian brothers Ross and Keith Smith made **the first flight from Britain to Australia**.

1937
The **German airship Hindenberg exploded** on arrival in the USA, killing 35 of its 97 passengers.

1939
The first flight of the German Heinkel 178, the **first jet aircraft**.

◄ ▼ **Balloon crossing** In 1785 a Frenchman, Jean-Pierre Blanchard, and an American, John Jeffries, became the first people to cross the English Channel by air – in a balloon. Below: Chicago's O'Hare airport.

▲ **Helicopter experiment** In March 1908, Frenchman Paul Cornu stayed in the air for 20 seconds in this early version of a helicopter.

Igor Sikorsky in the USA flew the **first successful single-rotor helicopter** of the modern type.

1952
The **first jet airliner**, Britain's De Havilland Comet, entered service.

1970
The **first Boeing 747 'jumbo jet'** went into service.

1976
The **British-French supersonic airliner Concorde** entered service.

1990s
The world's **busiest airport** was Chicago's O'Hare airport, handling nearly 70 million passengers each year.

1999
Bertrand Piccard from Switzerland and Brian Jones from Britain made the **first non-stop round-the-world balloon flight** in just under 20 days.

Building and engineering

C anals, dams, bridges, tunnels – the human race has been building them for thousands of years. And the more advanced our technology becomes, the more ambitious the projects we undertake: office buildings that soar hundreds of metres in the air, giant telescopes to study the Universe.

Dams and reservoirs

Oldest dams
These were built in ancient Egypt and Mesopotamia about 3000 BC. They controlled the flooding of the Nile and Tigris rivers and provided water for their crops. The Romans built dams in Italy, Spain and North Africa about 2000 years ago. Some are still in use today.

Biggest dam
The New Cornelia Tailings dam in Arizona, USA, contains 210 million m³ (270 million cu yd) of earth. Two even bigger dams are being built in Argentina; the Chapetón dam will be 296 million m³ (387 million cu yd).

Highest and longest dams
The Rogun dam in Tajikistan is 335 m (1099 ft) high, made of earth and rock. The highest concrete dam is the Grande Dixence in Switzerland, 285 m (935 ft) high.

▼ **Panama Canal** SS *Ancan*, the first ship to pass through the canal on its opening day, August 15, 1914.

The longest dam is the Yaciretá-Apipé dam, on the Paraná river between Argentina and Paraguay. Its crest is some 70 km (40 miles) long.

Largest reservoir
Central Siberia in Russia has the world's largest wholly man-made reservoir: the Bratsk reservoir on the Ankara river. It holds about 170 km³ (40 cu miles) of water.

Canals and aqueducts

Longest canal
The Chinese built the longest canal, the Grand Canal, which stretches from near Beijing about 1780 km (1110 miles) to Hangzhou. It was begun about 540 BC and completed nearly 2000 years later.

Busiest canals
The Kiel Canal in Germany, linking the North and Baltic seas, carries more than 40 000 ships a year. But the Suez Canal in Egypt (joining the Mediterranean and Red Sea) carries the greatest tonnage of shipping – over 400 million

tonnes a year, most of them large oil tankers.

Greatest short cut
The Panama Canal links the Atlantic and Pacific oceans. It reduces the distance ships have to travel between the American east and west coasts by as much as 11 250 km (7000 miles).

Early aqueducts
The earliest aqueducts may have been those supplying water to Jerusalem and Athens, but ancient Rome had the most extensive ancient water-supply system. Its aqueducts eventually totalled about 610 km (380 miles).

Longest aqueduct
A 1670 km (1040 miles) long aqueduct supplies water to Tripoli in Libya.

Roads, bridges and tunnels

Early roads
The wheel was invented in the Middle East about 3500 BC; the first roads were built soon after that. The Romans were the first to build a network of paved (smooth-surfaced) roads around 2000 years ago. By the 3rd century AD the Roman Empire had more than 80 000 km (50 000 miles) of good roads.

▲ **Sydney Harbour Bridge** Opened in 1932, Sydney's bridge was soon famous across the world.

Longest highways
The old Silk Road, which ran between China and Europe via India and Persia, extended nearly 6400 km (4000 miles).

Nowadays, the longest highway that has a name and can be used by motor traffic is the Pan-American Highway. It extends from Alaska to southern Chile, then across to Buenos Aires, Argentina, and north again to Brasília, the capital of Brazil. Apart from a section called the Darién Gap, in the jungles of Panama and Colombia, it stretches continuously for over 24 000 km (15 000 miles).

Widest bridge
Australia's Sydney Harbour Bridge has the widest deck of any bridge. It is 49 m (160 ft) across and carries eight lanes of road traffic, two railway tracks, a cycle path and a footpath.

Longest bridges
The Second Lake Pontchartrain Causeway in Louisiana, USA, is 38 km (24 miles) long, but consists of many arches. The longest single span is that of the Akashi-Kaikyo suspension bridge in Japan. Its main span is 1991 m (6532 ft) long.

Longest tunnel
The Seikan rail tunnel between the islands of Honshu and Hokkaido in Japan is 54 km (34 miles) long. The Channel Tunnel between England and France is shorter at 50 km (31 miles), but has a longer undersea section of 38 km (24 miles). The longest road tunnel is the 16 km (10 mile) St Gotthard Tunnel under the Alps in Switzerland.

Deepest mineshaft
The Western Deep Levels gold mine in South Africa has the deepest mineshaft in the world. It is 3581 m (11 748 ft) deep.

49 m (161 ft) steel pinnacles. The Sears Tower in Chicago, USA, is 443 m (1454 ft) tall to the roof, or 520 m (1706 ft) including its TV aerials. Both will be beaten in 2001 by the World Financial Centre in Shanghai, China, whose roof will be 460 m (1509 ft) high.

The tallest building of any kind is Toronto's CN Tower. It is a broadcasting tower with a revolving restaurant near the top, and is 553 m (1815 ft) tall.

▲ **Arecibo telescope** The huge dish of the Arecibo radio telescope picks up signals from space.

▲ **Greenwich dome** The roof is made of a special fabric, supported by 90 m (295 ft) masts.

Buildings and machines

Tallest buildings
Malaysia's Petronas Towers are claimed as the world's tallest office building. They are 452 m (1483 ft) tall, but this includes

▼ **CN Tower** The tower soars from Toronto's Lake Ontario shorefront 553 m (1815 ft) into the air.

Biggest dome
The Millennium Dome at Greenwich, London, is 320 m (1050 ft) in diameter, 50 m (164 ft) tall inside, and covers 8 ha (nearly 20 acres).

Biggest buildings
The office building with the biggest floor area is the Pentagon – headquarters of the US Defense Department. Its floor area is

more than 60 ha (148 acres); 23 000 people work there.

The building with the biggest volume is the Boeing aircraft company's main assembly plant near Seattle, USA. It measures about 13 million m³ (more than 473 million cu ft).

Longest structure
The Great Wall of China is 3460 km (2150 miles) long, or 6325 km (3930 miles) including branches. In spite of its great length, it is not – as many people believe – visible from space.

Biggest telescopes
The two Keck telescopes on the

peak of Mauna Kea in Hawaii are the world's largest astronomical telescopes. Each has 36 mirrors fitted together to act like a single mirror 10 m (394 in) in diameter.

The biggest orbiting telescope is the Hubble Space Telescope; it has a 2.4 m (94 in) mirror. The biggest radio telescope dish is at Arecibo, Puerto Rico; it is 305 m (1000 ft) in diameter.

Most powerful laser
California's Lawrence Livermore Laboratory has the world's most powerful laser. It generates 100 trillion watts for one-billionth of a second and is 91 m (300 ft) long. It was built for research into ways of destroying enemy missiles.

Inventions and discoveries

Our far-distant ancestors learned how to grow crops rather than just gather them, and how to use metal rather than stone for their tools and weapons; in recent times, we have put men on the Moon. The human race's journey of discovery continues, and it is still transforming our lives.

Before 500 000 BC
Humans discovered how to set things alight, using the flames from natural bushfires. They could now **use fire**, but they did not yet know how to start fires.

About 30 000 BC
People started to use **bows and arrows** to hunt large animals. The new weapons allowed hunters to attack from a distance.

About 20 000 BC
Australian Aborigines produced **rock paintings** – some of the world's earliest art.

12 000 BC
Wolves were the first animals to be domesticated, or tamed. They helped people to hunt for food. These **tamed wolves** were the ancestors of today's dogs.

10 000 BC
People in the Middle East learned **how to grow crops**, and slowly gave up gathering their food in the wild. This new way of life allowed them to settle down in one place.

6000 BC
In the Middle East, people started to make things out of metal – **copper**. Before this, tools had to be made out of wood, bone or stone. The first implements used for

▼ **Ancient weapons** A copper dagger (below) and a flint one (bottom) from about 6000 years ago.

▲ **Farmers ploughing** This model came from an Egyptian tomb.

making fire also date from about this time.

3600 BC
People in the Middle East **made bronze** by mixing copper with tin. Unlike copper, bronze is hard enough to make sharp blades.

3500 BC
The Sumerians, living in present-day Iraq, began to use **one of the earliest known kinds of writing**. Using a piece of reed, they pressed wedge-shaped letters into pieces of soft clay.

The Sumerians also used the world's first **animal-driven ploughs**.

3200 BC
In the Middle East, **wheeled vehicles** appeared for the first time. They were made out of wooden planks fastened together, and the wheels were solid.

3000 BC
People in Egypt and the Middle East discovered how to make **arches out of stone**. The stones in an arch prop each other up, so they could be used to bridge rivers and make wide roofs.

2800 BC
At about this time, the ancient Egyptians devised one of the world's **first calendars**. They used it to predict the annual flood of the River Nile. The flood was an important event for Egyptian farmers, because it covered their fields with fertile mud.

1900 BC
People in the Middle East learned how to **make iron**.

1000 BC
In Egypt, **early sundials** were used to tell the time.

440 BC
A Greek philosopher called Democritus suggested that everything is made up of tiny particles called **atoms**. At the time, no one had any way of telling if atoms really existed, but over 2000 years later, scientists discovered that Democritus was right.

350 BC
A Greek philosopher called Aristotle decided that the **Earth must be round**, not flat as most people thought. One piece of evidence that convinced him was that ships seem to sink below the horizon when they sail out to sea.

270 BC
Ctesibius, a Greek inventor living in Egypt, designed a **water-operated clock**.

240 BC
A Greek mathematician called Eratosthenes correctly worked out that the **Earth is about 40 000 km (25 000 miles) round**.

85 BC
By this time, **water wheels were being used to grind up corn**. These early water wheels were developed in Greece. They turned horizontally, powering a pair of millstones on a platform above the water.

▲ **Hero's whizzer** Hero of Alexandria's steam engine.

AD 50
Hero of Alexandria invented the **first steam engine** – a hollow metal ball that spun around when water inside it boiled. The invention was ingenious, but had no practical use.

650
Windmills were used in Persia.

740
In Japan, carved wooden blocks were used to **print pictures and words**.

810
Muhammad Al-Khwarizmi, an Arab mathematician, used the **number zero** in calculations. Before this, there was no mathematical symbol for 'nothing'. This new idea was one of the most important developments ever made in mathematics.

About 950
Gunpowder was invented in China. Two centuries later, it was being used in Europe.

1090
Magnetic compasses were invented in China.

▲ **Specs on his nose** A priest with spectacles, painted in 1352.

1250
Italian glassmakers produced **spectacles**, perhaps copying discoveries made by the Chinese.

◄ **Star-gazers** Galileo's telescope, now in a museum in Florence.

1455
In Germany, Johannes Gutenberg produced Europe's **first printed book** – a copy of the Bible. He used movable type, a system that had already been used in China for more than 400 years. Gutenberg invented a new machine for pressing the type onto the paper – the printing press.

1504
The **first pocket watch** was made in Germany. Unlike other clocks of the time, it was powered by a wind-up spring.

1519
A Portuguese-born explorer, Ferdinand Magellan, set off from Spain on the **first sea journey around the world**. Magellan was killed in the Philippine Islands in 1521. Many other members of the expedition died in accidents and storms, but after a journey lasting three years, 18 men led by Juan Sebastian del Cano managed to complete the journey back to Spain.

1543
Only a few months before he died, the Polish astronomer Nicolaus Copernicus published a book **claiming that the Earth orbits around the Sun**. At the time, most people believed that the Sun orbited around the Earth, and Copernicus's ideas caused a storm of protest.

1590
In the Netherlands, Zacharias Janssen invented the **first microscope**. Janssen's instrument was a compound microscope, meaning that it contained several lenses.

1592
Galileo Galilei, a professor at the University of Padua and one of Italy's most famous scientists, invented the **first thermometer**. It contained air sealed in a tube by water. The air expanded when it got warm, moving the water level.

1608
A Dutch spectacle-maker called Hans Lippershey was probably the first person to build a **telescope**.

1610
While he was looking at Jupiter through a telescope, the Italian scientist Galileo noticed four moons orbiting around it. This was the **first time moons had been seen** circling another planet. Galileo was also the first person to see sunspots.

1624
The **first submarine** set off on its maiden voyage beneath the River Thames near London. Made of wood and waterproofed with animal fat, it was powered by men pulling oars.

1628
William Harvey, an English doctor, published a book in which **he explained how blood circulates**. He correctly worked out that blood flows in two loops – first around the lungs, and then around the rest of the body.

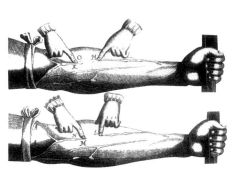

▲ **Veins and arteries** An illustration from Harvey's book.

1633
Church authorities forced Galileo to deny that the Earth orbits around the Sun. Threatened with torture, **Galileo gave in**.

1642
Blaise Pascal, a French mathematician, invented a **mechanical adding machine**. It did not become popular.

▼ **Calculator** A pascaline, Pascal's original calculating machine.

Inventions and discoveries

◄ **Measuring pressure**
Torricelli's barometer.

1643
Evangelista Torricelli, Galileo's assistant, invented the world's **first barometer** – a device for measuring the pressure of the atmosphere.

1648
Experiments carried out in France showed that **air pressure on high mountains is less than air pressure lower down**. From this, scientists worked out that there cannot be any air in space.

1658
Using a microscope, Jan Swammerdam, a Dutch scientist, became the **first person to see red blood cells**.

1666
Isaac Newton, an English mathematician and physicist, **split a beam of sunlight with a glass prism**, and showed that the beam of light was actually a mixture of many different colours. The colours

▼ **Prism light** The prism Newton used, and some of his writings.

he found were the same ones that make up rainbows.

1675
Olaus Roemer, a Danish astronomer, became the **first person to calculate the speed of light**. He estimated that it travels at about 227 000 km (141 000 miles) per second – only about 20 per cent less than the true figure.

1676
Antoni van Leeuwenhoek, a Dutch microscope-maker, became the **first person to see microorganisms in pond water**. Until then, nobody realised that such tiny living things existed.

1698
The world's **first steam-powered pump** was put to work in England. It was called the Miner's Friend, because it helped to stop flooding in mines.

1751
The American Benjamin Franklin flew a kite during a thunderstorm, and showed that lightning is a kind of electricity. His experiment led him to invent **lightning conductors**. These protect buildings by conducting the electricity straight down to the earth without passing through the building and damaging it.

▼ **Safe from lightning**
Some of Benjamin Franklin's lightning conductors.

1759
The engineer John Smeaton built **a new lighthouse on the Eddystone Rocks** off Plymouth, England. It was built in a way that would be copied in many other lighthouses around the world. The blocks of stone interlocked for extra strength, and the lighthouse tapered towards the top so that waves would lose some of their energy as they smashed against it.

1769
English inventor Richard Arkwright built the **Spinning Frame** – a machine for making cotton thread.

In France, the **first steam-powered carriage** went for a test drive. Designed by Nicolas Cugnot, its first outing ended in disaster when it crashed into a wall.

1783
Joseph and Etienne Montgolfier made the world's **first hot air balloon** flight near Paris.

1790
In France, scientists devised a new system of measurements. It was based on multiples of

▶ **Ballooning** The Montgolfiers' balloon was brightly coloured, like a huge Japanese lantern.

ten, which made it very easy to use in calculations. Known as **the metric system**, it is now used by scientists all over the world.

1796
An English doctor, Edward Jenner, successfully **vaccinated a young girl against smallpox**, a disease that killed many people at the time. Although Jenner did not invent vaccination, his work made its use much more

Dr Jenner's jab Jenner performs his first vaccination.

...idespread, helping to combat ...any infectious diseases.

800

...n Italian physicist, Alessandro ...olta, made the **first battery**, ...sing plates of copper and zinc.

... newly discovered gas, nitrous ...xide, became the world's **first ...hemical anaesthetic**. Before ...is time, operations were

carried out without any kind of pain relief, apart from brandy and other alcoholic drinks.

William Herschel, a British astronomer, discovered that **light contains invisible heat rays** – infra-red rays.

1803

The English engineer Richard Trevithick demonstrated the **first ever steam engine to run on rails** at an ironworks in South Wales. It was used to haul men and iron to and from the ironworks.

▶ **Steam-driven** A model based on drawings of a Trevithick locomotive.

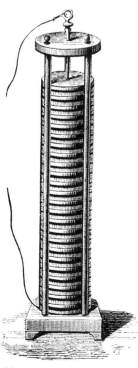

First battery Volta's electric ...ttery with discs of zinc, copper ...d cloth soaked in acid.

1816

René Laennec, a French doctor, invented the **stethoscope** – a device for listening to the sound of a person's heart or breathing. It quickly became an important medical instrument.

1820

In Europe, several physicists discovered that when electricity flows through a wire it produces a **magnetic field**.

1821

Michael Faraday, a British scientist, invented the **electric motor**.

1822

Gideon Mantell, a British geologist, discovered the fossilised remains of a giant reptile. Called Iguanodon, it was the **first dinosaur to be studied** by scientists.

1827

Joseph-Nicéphore Niépce took the world's **first photograph** – a view from the window of his workshop in France. He made the photo by focusing daylight

onto a metal plate covered with bitumen (tar).

1837

Louis Agassiz, a Swiss geologist, realised that long ago, much of the Northern Hemisphere must have been covered by ice. His work showed that **the Earth's climate changes** as time goes by.

1839

Charles Wilkes, an American explorer, led the **first expedition known to have set eyes on Antarctica**. His discovery meant that humans had now reached all the continents on Earth.

1854

Engineers laying a cable across the Atlantic discovered a **huge range of submerged mountains**.

1855

Alexander Parkes, a British chemist, made a flexible material called **Parkesine** from chloroform and castor oil. This discovery led to the first plastics.

1859

Charles Darwin, a British naturalist, published a book called **On the Origin of Species**. The book explained evolution – the process that makes living things gradually change as time

goes by. Darwin's book caused fierce arguments, but eventually most scientists accepted his idea.

The Belgian inventor Etienne Lenoir built the **first internal-combustion engine**, powered by gas. It was called an internal-combustion engine because it burned fuel inside the engine, and not outside it as a steam engine does.

Inventions and discoveries

1861
Quarry workers in Bavaria, in the southern part of Germany, discovered the fossilised remains of **Archaeopteryx**, a prehistoric 'missing link' between reptiles and birds.

1862
Louis Pasteur, a leading French biologist, decided that **infectious diseases are caused by germs and other microorganisms**. Once he had made this breakthrough, work started on ways to stop germs from spreading diseases.

1865
An Austrian monk called Gregor Mendel published the results of his experiments on pea plants. Mendel had worked out the **basic rules of genetics**, but his work went unnoticed for the next 35 years.

1866
The Swedish chemist Alfred Nobel invented a new explosive, which he called **dynamite**. Unlike the explosives used at the time, it did not go off if it was accidentally knocked or dropped.

1876
After spilling battery acid on his clothes, the Scottish-born American scientist Alexander Graham Bell made the world's **first phone call**. He used his newly invented device, the telephone, to call a colleague: 'Watson, please come here. I want you!'

Robert Koch, a German biologist, **discovered a way of growing bacteria in the laboratory**, enabling him to test methods of fighting disease. Before this, disease-causing bacteria could only be grown in animals.

▶ **Fit for a queen** Bell gave a demonstration of this phone to Queen Victoria.

1879
Thomas Edison invented the world's **first reliable electric light bulb**.

1884
Gottlieb Daimler made the **first lightweight petrol engine**. A year later, he tested it out on a prototype motorbike.

1885
Karl Benz produced one of the world's **earliest motor cars**.

▲ **Lighting up** An example of an Edison light bulb.

English scientists discovered that no two people – apart from identical twins – have the same **fingerprints**. This became a valuable way of identifying

people at the scene of a crime, and was used by Scotland Yard from 1901 onwards.

1895
Guglielmo Marconi built the world's **first radio transmitter**. Six years later, he managed to send a radio signal across the Atlantic Ocean, from Europe to North America.

Wilhelm Röntgen, a German physicist, accidentally discovered **X-rays** while experimenting with a cathode-ray tube. To his amazement, he found that the rays could pass straight through many solid objects, almost as if they were not there.

1896
Henri Becquerel, a French physicist, discovered that crystals of uranium give off invisible radiation. His breakthrough marked the start of **intensive research into radioactivity**. Soon, other elements, including radium, were also found to be radioactive.

1898
Scientists realised that some diseases are caused by things that are much smaller than bacteria. They called these unknown objects **viruses**, from a word meaning poison.

1900
Karl Landsteiner, an Austrian doctor, discovered that people all belong to one of **four blood groups**. His find made blood transfusions safe for the first time.

1903
Orville Wright made the world's **first powered plane flight**, aboard an aircraft he had built with his brother, Wilbur. The flight lasted 12 seconds.

1908
Wilhelm Geiger, a German physicist, invented a device that could detect radioactivity. It is called a **Geiger counter**, because it counts the number of radioactive particles that it picks up.

1912
A German geologist called Alfred Wegener suggested that the **continents slowly drift**

▲ **Wright flight** Orville hovers above the ground in his plane.

across the surface of the Earth. At the time, hardly anyone believed him.

1916
Albert Einstein completed his **general theory of relativity** – a new explanation of the way space and time are related. Among other things, Einstein's theory correctly predicted that light is bent by gravity.

1926
John Logie Baird demonstrated his **newly invented television set** – the world's earliest. Unlike modern televisions, it was mechanical and had lots of moving parts.

1928
While working in a hospital in London, Alexander Fleming discovered **penicillin**. It turned out to be the

▲ **TV pioneer** Baird with an early television transmitter.

world's first antibiotic drug – a substance that kills bacteria without harming the body's cells.

1929
By examining light coming from distant galaxies, the American astronomer Edwin Hubble showed that the **Universe is expanding**. This helped to convince many scientists that the Universe started in a 'Big Bang'.

1933
British chemists Reginald Gibson and Eric Fawcett discovered **polythene**, a new kind of plastic. Unlike existing plastics, it was both tough and flexible.

1938
Biologists all over the world were amazed to hear about the discovery of a **living coelacanth** off the coast of Madagascar. Until 1938, this primitive fish was thought to have been extinct for millions of years.

1939
Swiss chemist Paul Müller discovered that a chemical called **DDT** is deadly poisonous to insects. DDT was soon being used worldwide, but in later years it became clear that it harms other animals as well as insects.

1942
Italian physicist Enrico Fermi built and tested the world's **first nuclear reactor** in a squash court at the University of Chicago. The reactor showed

that huge amounts of energy are released when atoms of uranium break down.

1943
French diver and naturalist Jacques Cousteau invented the **aqualung** – a portable breathing device that revolutionised underwater exploration.

1945
Two **atomic bombs** were dropped on cities in Japan – the first and as yet the only time that these devastating weapons have been used in warfare.

1946
One of the world's **first computers** was built in America. Called ENIAC (short for Electronic Numerical Integrator And Calculator), it filled an entire room, and used enough electricity to power a hundred homes.

▲ **Atomic blast** The mushroom cloud after the second atomic bomb was dropped on Nagasaki.

1948
In America, John Bardeen and Walter Brattain invented the **transistor**, a tiny electronic device that makes electric signals stronger, or 'amplifies' them. Before that, electrical amplifiers used tubes called valves. These were big and fragile, and they often broke down.

1953
Cambridge scientists James Watson and Francis Crick successfully uncovered the structure of **DNA** – the chemical that makes up genes.

1957
The Soviet Union launched the world's **first artificial satellite**, called Sputnik. This marked the beginning of the Space Age.

1960
Geologists discovered that the floor of the **Atlantic Ocean is spreading**, pushing North and South America farther away from Africa and Europe. This proved that Alfred Wegener's theory of continental drift (see 1912) was right.

1961
The Soviet Union took a lead in the space race when cosmonaut Yuri Gagarin became the **first person to orbit the Earth**. Gagarin completed just one orbit, but a few months later another Russian cosmonaut – Gherman Titov – circled the Earth 17 times.

1962
Astronaut John Glenn became the **first American in space**.

1967
At Cape Town in South Africa, Dr Christiaan Barnard carried out the world's **first heart transplant operation**.

1969
Two American astronauts, Neil Armstrong and 'Buzz' Aldrin, became the **first human beings to land on the Moon**. After spending 21 hours on the Moon's surface, they successfully returned to Earth in the spacecraft *Apollo 11*.

1971
The Soviet Union launched the **first space station**, Salyut 1.

1973
American scientists managed to insert pieces of DNA into the cells of bacteria. This marked the start of **genetic engineering**, in which scientists alter the genetic material in living things. In this

way they can 'breed' useful qualities into them. For example, bacteria can be genetically modified to produce useful drugs. Genetic engineering has been one of the most important developments in the whole of 20th-century science.

1975
The **first microchips** went into mass production. Within a few years, they made computers small and cheap enough for millions of people to use.

1979
American geologists uncovered evidence that a **huge meteorite may have struck the Earth 65 million years ago**, killing off the dinosaurs.

▲ **New heart** One of Jarvik's aluminium and plastic hearts.

1982
American surgeon Robert Jarvik carried out an operation to give a patient an **artificial heart**. The patient survived for nearly four months.

1986
Scientists began work on the **Human Genome Project**, an international project to identify all the genes in human beings.

1997
Genetic engineers produced a **sheep by cloning**: they used one of its mother's cells to create a baby sheep whose genes were an exact copy of its mother's. This raised fears that human cloning may become possible.

Countries of the world

Northern Europe

Short stretches of sea separate Ireland from Britain, and Britain from Continental Europe. Parts of the Netherlands are below sea level, but Austria rises into the Alps.

▲ **German castle** The eccentric King Ludwig II of Bavaria built this dreamy masterpiece, called Neuschwanstein, in southern Germany in the late 19th century.

Sweden

- Stockholm
- 8 850 000
- Swedish krona
- Swedish
- 449 964 km²/173 732 sq miles

Sweden has many lakes, and about half the country is covered by forests. In the south, there are some 20 000 islands around the coast. The northern part of Sweden, which extends into the Arctic Circle, is dark for most of the winter and bitterly cold. Most people live in the south, which is where the capital, Stockholm, is located. Swedes pay more taxes than any other nation.

Finland

- Helsinki
- 5 140 000
- markka
- Finnish, Swedish
- 338 144 km²/130 558 sq miles

Finland is covered in lakes and forests. In northern Finland, which is called Samiland, the midsummer sun shines throughout the night.

Norway

- Oslo
- 4 410 000
- Norwegian krone
- Norwegian
- 323 877 km²/125 050 sq miles

One-third of Norway lies north of the Arctic Circle. This is a land of mountains, glaciers, deep lakes, great pine forests and spectacular fiords – narrow inlets that pierce the coast. Reindeer herders called Lapps live in the far north.

United Kingdom

- London
- 58 800 000
- pound sterling
- English
- 241 752 km²/93 341 sq miles

Germany

- Berlin
- 82 070 000
- Deutschmark
- German
- 356 974 km²/137 828 sq miles

Germany has the largest population of any country in Europe. It stretches from the Baltic Sea in the north to the Alps in the south.

For many years after the Second World War, Germany was divided into a communist east and a capitalist west, with Berlin split by a concrete wall. After the fall of communism in eastern Europe, Germany was reunited in 1990.

Since then, Germany has become the most successful country in Europe, with good farmland and busy industries.

The United Kingdom is made up of Great Britain (England, Wales and Scotland) together with Northern Ireland. The head of government is a monarch, but the country is run by Parliament. The British Parliament has been the model for democracies around the world, which is why it is called 'the mother of parliaments'.

Until the 20th century the United Kingdom was one of the most powerful states in the world, with a great empire stretching to the Far East. Although that empire has crumbled, the capital, London, remains one of the world's major financial centres.

Iceland

Norway

Sweden

Finland

Denmark

Ireland

United Kingdom

Netherlands

Belgium

Luxembourg

Germany

Austria

Iceland

- Reykjavik
- 270 000
- Icelandic krona
- Icelandic
- 103 000 km²/39 769 sq miles

Iceland is known as 'The Land of Fire and Ice' because of its many glaciers and volcanoes. Bubbling hot springs provide the capital, Reykjavik, with natural heating. However, large areas are unpopulated because nothing can be grown there.

Austria

- Vienna
- 8 070 000
- schilling
- German
- 83 858 km²/32 378 sq miles

Much of Austria is covered by mountains, which makes it popular for skiing and other winter sports. The winter Olympics have twice been held at Innsbruck, in the south-west.

Austria is also famous for its music. Its capital, Vienna, gave its name to a dance, the 'Viennese Waltz', and Salzburg, Austria's second biggest city, has a music festival which draws people from all over the world.

For many centuries Austria's ruling family, the Habsburgs, was one of the most powerful in Europe. Austria built a rich empire for itself, but this collapsed at the end of the First World War, in 1918.

Ireland

- Dublin
- 3 520 000
- Irish pound (punt)
- Irish, English
- 70 285 km²/27 137 sq miles

Ireland is a state covering most of the island of Ireland. It is also known by its Irish name, Eire. The rest of the island is the province of Ulster, or Northern Ireland, which is part of the United Kingdom.

Lying to the west of Britain, Ireland is swept by rain from the Atlantic Ocean. This gives it a beautiful green landscape, which has earned it the name 'The Emerald Isle'. The capital, Dublin, is on the River Liffey in the east.

Ireland was ruled by Britain until 1922. Many Irish people would prefer their country to include the northern province of Ulster as well.

Denmark

- Copenhagen
- 5 280 000
- Danish krone
- Danish
- 43 094 km²/16 639 sq miles

Denmark's first Christian king was the Viking, Harold Bluetooth, whose son, Sweyn, conquered England in 1013.

The country consists of over 450 islands, together with the Jutland peninsula, which is part of mainland Europe. Denmark grew rich because it controlled the narrow entrance to the Baltic Sea. It could therefore tax ships trading with much bigger countries, such as Finland, Norway and Russia.

The capital, Copenhagen, was the birthplace of Hans Christian Andersen, author of many well-known children's stories. The Tivoli gardens are a favourite attraction.

Netherlands

- Amsterdam
- 15 600 000
- guilder
- Dutch
- 33 939 km²/13 104 sq miles

About 40 per cent of the Netherlands lies below sea level, so there is a constant struggle to keep the sea from flooding in. The country is often called Holland, though this name really refers to a historical region around the capital, Amsterdam. There are now two provinces called North and South Holland.

Belgium

- Brussels
- 10 160 000
- Belgian franc
- Flemish, French
- 30 528 km²/11 787 sq miles

Belgium is divided into two separate regions: Flanders in the north-west, where people speak Flemish; and Wallonia in the south-east, where the language is French. Each group has its own distinct culture.

The capital, Brussels, is the seat of the European Union. This is a rich city; like Bruges and Antwerp, it has built its wealth on trade.

Luxembourg

- Luxembourg
- 420 000
- Luxembourg franc
- Letzeburgish, French, German
- 2587 km²/999 sq miles

Luxembourg is unique in being the last of Europe's small, independent duchies, dating back to the medieval Holy Roman Empire. Its ruler is a Grand Duke.

◄ **London's pride** St Paul's Cathedral was built after the Great Fire of London destroyed an earlier building of the same name in 1666. Designed by Sir Christopher Wren, it is widely admired as one of the finest buildings in London.

Countries of the world

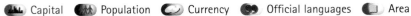

Key Capital Population Currency 👀 Official languages 🔲 Area

Southern Europe

Hills or high mountains dominate the countries of this area, though some parts are flat. The climate and cultures in the far south are quite different from those farther north.

France

- 🏛 Paris
- 👥 58 610 000
- 💰 French franc
- 👀 French, Breton, Basque
- 🔲 543 965 km²/210 026 sq miles

France is the biggest country in western Europe, and so has many different kinds of landscape. In the east are the Alps, which are popular with skiers and climbers. On the Mediterranean coast, in the south, lies the sunny Riviera. Inland, there is rolling, fertile countryside, which produces many fine foods and wines.

Paris, the capital, is one of the most important cities in the world, famous as a centre of fashion, culture and style. France became the world's first modern republic after the French Revolution of 1789, when the king was overthrown.

Spain

- 🏛 Madrid
- 👥 39 320 000
- 💰 peseta
- 👀 Spanish
- 🔲 504 782 km²/194 897 sq miles

The beaches of southern Spain attract millions of tourists each year, but few go inland, where the country is wilder, with remote mountain villages and ancient traditions.

The country is divided into several regions, with strong local cultures and even their own languages. In the east is Catalonia, where people speak Catalan, and in the north is the mountainous Basque country, where the language is unlike any other in Europe.

The Spanish are associated with bullfights and passionate flamenco dancing. They once had a great empire, which included most of Central and South America, and even part of what is now the USA.

◀ **Symbol of Paris** The Eiffel Tower was built out of wrought iron in 1887–9. It stands 300 m (984 ft) high.

▲ **Spain's daring designs**
The church of the Sagrada Familia ('Holy Family') in Barcelona is adorned by this imaginative cross.

Italy

- 🏛 Rome
- 👥 57 520 000
- 💰 lira
- 👀 Italian
- 🔲 301 323 km²/116 341 sq miles

Italy is often said to be shaped like a boot, with the heel and toe in the south, which is the poorest part of the country. In the north are the big industrial cities of Milan and Turin, where most of the country's business takes place. Rome, the capital, is in the centre, and is the site of the Vatican, where the Pope lives. The country includes the islands of Sicily and Sardinia.

Italy is full of ancient ruins from the days of the Roman Empire. There are also many magnificent works of art from the Renaissance, when artists like Michelangelo, Leonardo da Vinci and Raphael flourished. The city of Venice is unique; it is built on 118 small islands, and has canals, instead of roads, between its buildings.

France
Liechtenstein
Switzerland
San Marino
Monaco
Italy
Andorra
Spain
Vatican City
Portugal
Malta

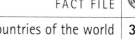
Portugal
- Lisbon
- 9 810 000
- escudo
- Portuguese
- 92 270 km²/35 626 sq miles

Portugal is one of the poorest countries in the European Union, and is a land of strong contrasts. Its big cities, though old, are modern and up to date; but life in the countryside is much more old-fashioned and traditional.

In the late 15th century Portuguese seafarers helped to build an empire, which brought the country great wealth. For a while, Portugal led the world, but it was soon overtaken by Spain and England.

The country has long been known for one of its wines, called port. This was exported from the northern city of Oporto. The south has become popular for its hot beaches, which attract tourists.

Switzerland
- Bern
- 7 090 000
- Swiss franc
- German and three others
- 41 284 km²/15 940 sq miles

Switzerland is the country most people associate with the Alps. A land of mountains and lakes, it is popular with tourists who can afford its high prices.

Switzerland is a wealthy country. For centuries it has made money by taxing traders crossing its mountain passes. It is famous for its banks, which have a reputation for being secret and trustworthy. The country is also known for its neutrality – its refusal to get involved in any war.

There are 23 different regions, called cantons, which are all self-governing.

▼ **Roman circus** The Colosseum was built in Rome in AD 69-82, and seated 50 000 spectators.

Andorra

- Andorra la Vella
- 70 000
- French franc, Spanish peseta
- Catalan
- 468 km²/181 sq miles

Andorra is a tiny country high in the mountains of the Pyrenees. It is self-governing, but has two heads of state: the Bishop of Urgel, in northern Spain, and the President of France.

Malta

- Valletta
- 370 000
- Maltese lira
- Maltese, English
- 316 km²/122 sq miles

The state of Malta consists of three islands in the middle of the Mediterranean Sea; they are Malta, Gozo and Comino. The island of Malta has been an important naval base for over 2500 years. The islands were ruled by many foreign powers, and came under British control in 1800. The British built much of the capital, Valletta. Malta has been independent since 1964.

Liechtenstein
- Vaduz
- 30 600
- Swiss franc
- German
- 160 km²/62 sq miles

Sandwiched between Austria and Switzerland, Liechtenstein is a tiny, mountainous country ruled by an old family of princes. It has very low taxes.

San Marino
- San Marino
- 30 000
- Italian lira
- Italian
- 61 km²/24 sq miles

Surrounded entirely by Italy, this tiny independent state gets most of its money from tourists, who come to admire its medieval buildings.

Monaco
- Monaco
- 30 000
- French franc
- French
- 1.95 km²/0.75 sq miles

Monaco has been ruled by princes of the Grimaldi family since the 13th century. It is a playground for rich people, many of whom arrive in their yachts to gamble in the casinos, stroll along the beaches and shop in the town's many exclusive stores.

Vatican City
- Vatican City
- 1000
- Italian lira
- Italian, Latin
- 0.44 km²/0.17 sq miles

The world's smallest state consists of the Vatican and St Peter's Basilica in the centre of Rome, together with 12 other buildings in and around Rome.

▼ **Vatican masterpiece** In this painting by Michelangelo, God has just created Adam.

Countries of the world

Key Capital ![icon] Population ![icon] Currency ![icon] Official languages ![icon] Area

Central Europe

From the wide, flat plains of Poland to the deeply indented coast of Greece, the countries of this area form the border between East and West, and are influenced by both.

Poland

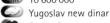

- Warsaw
- 38 650 000
- zloty
- Polish
- 312 685 km²/120 728 sq miles

Since it became a state in the 10th century, Poland has had to fight for its territory on many occasions. The capital, Warsaw, has been totally rebuilt after being destroyed in the Second World War. Poland led the communist countries of eastern Europe in the fight for democracy, and held its first free elections in 1989.

▲ **Athenian temple** The Parthenon in Athens was dedicated to Athena, the goddess of wisdom.

Greece

- Athens
- 10 480 000
- drachma
- Greek
- 131 957 km²/50 949 sq miles

Greece and its capital, Athens, were the birthplace of Western civilisation 2500 years ago.

Greece is a country of mountains and more than 2000 islands, only 200 of which are inhabited. The bigger ones include Crete and Rhodes. Because the country is so hilly the most successful crops are olives, figs and citrus fruits.

Yugoslavia

- Belgrade
- 10 600 000
- Yugoslav new dinar
- Serbo-Croat
- 102 173 km²/39 449 sq miles

Since 1992, the six countries which once formed the Federal Republic of Yugoslavia have split apart, leaving only Serbia and Montenegro to make up modern Yugoslavia. The country is very varied, from the beautiful resorts along the Adriatic coast to the arid Dinaric Alps in the south.

Hungary

- Budapest
- 10 150 000
- forint
- Hungarian
- 93 030 km²/35 919 sq miles

This landlocked country, cut in half by the River Danube, was part of the Austro-Hungarian Empire until 1918. Its capital, Budapest, is a union of two cities – Buda and Pest – on opposite sides of the Danube. The country turned away from communism in 1989.

Czech Republic

- Prague
- 10 300 000
- Czech koruna
- Czech
- 78 864 km²/30 450 sq miles

Until 1993, the Czech Republic was joined to Slovakia, with which it was jointly known as Czechoslovakia.

The country includes the ancient land of Bohemia. Its capital, Prague, is one of the world's most beautiful cities, dating back to the 14th century.

Croatia

- Zagreb
- 4 490 000
- kuna
- Serbo-Croat
- 56 610 km²/21 857 sq miles

Croatia used to be part of Yugoslavia, but separated in 1992 in a bitter civil war. The most frequently visited part of Croatia is its amazing coastline, with beautiful old cities. They include buildings by Romans, Venetians and Turks.

Bosnia and Herzegovina

- Sarajevo
- 4 510 000
- Bosnia & Herzegovina dinar
- Serbo-Croat
- 51 129 km²/19 741 sq miles

The combined country of Bosnia and Herzegovina was part of Yugoslavia until 1992. It then suffered from a vicious civil war, which has left it badly scarred. The country is rugged and mountainous.

Slovakia

- Bratislava
- 5 380 000
- Slovak koruna
- Slovak
- 49 036 km²/18 933 sq miles

Until 1993, Slovakia was part of Czechoslovakia.

Albania

- Tirana
- 3 670 000
- lek
- Albanian
- 28 748 km²/11 100 sq miles

Albania is one of the poorest countries in Europe.

Macedonia

- Skopje
- 2 160 000
- Macedonian denar
- Macedonian
- 25 713 km²/9928 sq miles

Until 1992, Macedonia was part of Yugoslavia.

Slovenia

- Ljubljana
- 1 990 000
- tolar
- Slovene
- 20 253 km²/7820 sq miles

Slovenia broke away from Yugoslavia in 1991.

Cyprus

- Nicosia
- 740 000
- Cyprus pound
- Greek
- 9251 km²/3572 sq miles

Since 1974, northern Cyprus has been occupied by Turkey.

Poland

Czech Republic

Slovakia

Slovenia

Hungary

Croatia

Bosnia & Herzegovina

Yugoslavia

Macedonia

Albania

Greece

Cyprus

Russia and its western neighbours

The Baltic countries are generally flat and featureless, but the ground rises to the Carpathian Mountains, which dominate Romania. Much of Russia is frozen tundra and huge forests.

Russia

- Moscow
- 147 740 000
- Russian rouble
- Russian
- 17 075 400 km²/6 592 850 sq mi.

Russia is the biggest country in the world, stretching from the Baltic sea in the west to the Sea of Japan in the east. Its most important cities are Moscow and St Petersburg.

Vast areas of Russia are featureless plains and dense forests. Winter temperatures often drop to –50°C (–58°F), and in the north the ground is permanently frozen.

Until 1991, Russia was the centre of the Soviet Union.

Romania

- Bucharest
- 22 570 000
- Romanian leu
- Romanian
- 238 391 km²/92 043 sq miles

Romania is made up of three parts: Wallachia in the south, Moldavia in the east and Transylvania (home of Count Dracula!) in the north-west. The Carpathian Mountains form a horseshoe in the middle, where people go skiing and hiking.

Bulgaria

- Sofia
- 8 310 000
- lev
- Bulgarian
- 110 994 km²/42 855 sq miles

Modern Bulgaria emerged as an independent nation only in 1908, when it threw off almost 500 years of Turkish rule.

Lithuania

- Vilnius
- 3 717 700
- litas
- Lithuanian
- 65 300 km²/25 212 sq miles

Lithuania was part of the Soviet Union until 1991, when it gained its independence.

Estonia

- Tallinn
- 1 470 000
- kroon
- Estonian
- 45 227 km²/17 462 sq miles

Like Latvia and Lithuania, this Baltic country broke away from the Soviet Union in 1991. Most of the country is dominated by marshes, lakes and forests.

Moldova

- Kishinev
- 4 310 000
- Moldovan leu
- Moldovan (Romanian)
- 33 700 km²/13 010 sq miles

Moldova was part of Romania until it was seized by the Soviet Union in 1940. It gained its independence in 1991.

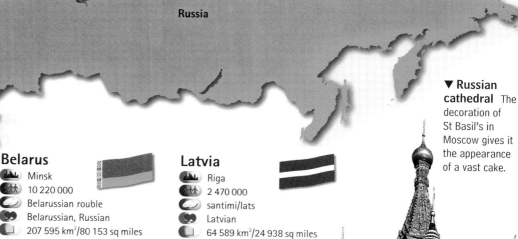

▼ **Russian cathedral** The decoration of St Basil's in Moscow gives it the appearance of a vast cake.

Ukraine

- Kiev
- 50 700 000
- hryvnya
- Ukrainian
- 603 700 km²/233 090 sq miles

The Ukraine was part of the Soviet Union until it became independent in 1991. It consists mostly of vast rolling plains with more than 3000 rivers and few hills.

The capital is Kiev, which was the capital of medieval Russia until replaced by Moscow. Only 90 km (55 miles) north of Kiev is Chernobyl, site of the world's worst nuclear accident in 1986.

Belarus

- Minsk
- 10 220 000
- Belarussian rouble
- Belarussian, Russian
- 207 595 km²/80 153 sq miles

Belarus was a part of the Soviet Union until 1991, when it became independent. It is also often known as 'White Russia'.

For centuries Belarus has been fought over by its more powerful neighbours, Poland, Lithuania and Russia, before being taken over by the Soviet Union in 1939. It was then devastated by German forces during the Second World War.

Much of the land is boggy, with many lakes and swamps fed by heavy summer rains.

Latvia

- Riga
- 2 470 000
- santimi/lats
- Latvian
- 64 589 km²/24 938 sq miles

Latvia is a country of rivers, lakes and forests – almost 40 per cent is covered in trees. Since the 13th century, Latvia has been independent only twice: between 1918 and 1940, and since breaking free from the Soviet Union in 1991. The capital, Riga, is the country's main port. Its old quarter retains a strong feel of the Middle Ages.

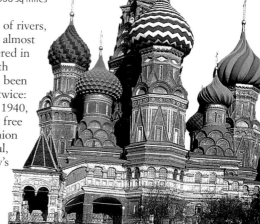

Countries of the world

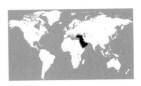

Key  Capital  Population  Currency  Official languages  Area

The Middle East and The Gulf

Turkey is very mountainous, and gets some rain. Farther south, the land becomes more arid, until it turns into desert. Saudi Arabia's harshest desert is called 'The Empty Quarter'.

Saudi Arabia

- Riyadh
- 18 840 000
- Saudi riyal
- Arabic
- 2 240 000 km²/864 869 sq miles

This is the only country that is named after its ruling family – the Al Sauds. It is mostly desert, but has the biggest oil reserves in the world.

Turkey

- Ankara
- 63 750 000
- Turkish lira
- Turkish
- 779 452 km²/300 948 sq miles

Turkey has been part of many great empires, most recently that of the Ottoman Turks. Modern Turkey was founded in 1923. Its capital, Istanbul, used to be known as Constantinople and Byzantium.

Yemen

- San'a
- 16 480 000
- Yemeni rial
- Arabic
- 536 869 km²/207 286 sq miles

Present-day Yemen was formed in 1990 when mountainous North Yemen united with South Yemen. Society is still strongly tribal and traditional.

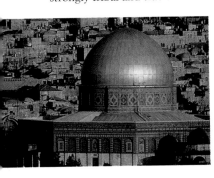

◀ **Sacred site**
The Dome of the Rock in Jerusalem, Israel, is one of the holiest places in the Muslim faith.

Iraq

- Baghdad
- 20 610 000
- Iraqi dinar
- Arabic
- 438 317 km²/169 235 sq miles

Iraq is the site of the world's earliest cities, such as Ur and Babylon. It is mostly desert, with rich lands between the rivers Tigris and Euphrates. Oil provides most of its income.

Oman

- Muscat
- 2 300 000
- Omani rial
- Arabic
- 309 500 km²/119 500 sq miles

Oman consists of two parts: a large area north of Yemen, and a tiny sector in the eastern United Arab Emirates.

Syria

- Damascus
- 14 620 000
- Syrian pound
- Arabic
- 185 180 km²/71 498 sq miles

Modern Syria was formed in 1946, but its history goes back for thousands of years.

Jordan

- Amman
- 5 580 000
- Jordanian dinar
- Arabic
- 97 740 km²/37 738 sq miles

Most of Jordan is desert, and it does not have any oil, yet it is a prosperous country through industry and exports.

United Arab Emirates

- Abu Dhabi
- 2 580 000
- UAE dirham
- Arabic
- 77 700 km²/30 000 sq miles

Formed in 1971, the Emirates depends entirely on oil for its wealth. Apart from a few oases on the coast, the land is desert.

Israel

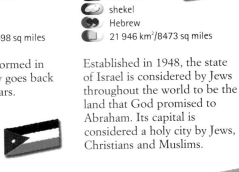

- Jerusalem
- 5 830 000
- shekel
- Hebrew
- 21 946 km²/8473 sq miles

Established in 1948, the state of Israel is considered by Jews throughout the world to be the land that God promised to Abraham. Its capital is considered a holy city by Jews, Christians and Muslims.

Kuwait

- Kuwait City
- 1 810 000
- Kuwaiti dinar
- Arabic
- 17 818 km²/6880 sq miles

Kuwait is a small desert state at the top of the Gulf. It became hugely rich in the 1960s from the discovery of oil.

Qatar

- Doha
- 560 000
- Qatar riyal
- Arabic
- 11 437 km²/4416 sq miles

Qatar gained independence in 1971. It relies on oil and gas for its huge wealth.

Lebanon

- Beirut
- 3 080 000
- Lebanese pound
- Arabic
- 10 452 km²/4036 sq miles

Once the most advanced state in the Middle East, Lebanon is recovering after a long civil war.

Bahrain

- Manama
- 620 000
- Bahrain dinar
- Arabic
- 695 km²/268 sq miles

Bahrain consists of a collection of 35 islands in the Gulf.

Indian subcontinent and neighbours

The Indian subcontinent is bordered by the world's highest mountains. To the west, smaller mountains continue into Afghanistan and Iran, which are largely arid countries.

India

- New Delhi
- 955 220 000
- rupee
- Hindi
- 3 287 263 km²/1 269 219 sq mi.

This vast country stretches from the freezing heights of the Himalayas in the north, to the steamy tropics of the south. It is the world's most heavily populated country after China.

Indian civilisation goes back for thousands of years, and gave birth to two of the world's great religions – Hinduism and Buddhism. The country was part of the British Empire until 1947. It then split into present-day India and Pakistan. Many people in India live in terrible poverty, especially in the cities.

Pakistan
- Islamabad
- 138 150 000
- Pakistani rupee
- Urdu
- 796 095 km²/307 374 sq miles

Until 1947 Pakistan was part of British India. When Britain left the region in that year, India's Muslims decided to form their own country, which they called Pakistan ('Land of the Pure').

Parts of the country are very mountainous, especially in the north. In the centre are wide plains, fed by the River Indus.

Afghanistan
- Kabul
- 20 880 000
- Afghani
- Pashto, Dari
- 652 225 km²/251 773 sq miles

This is a country of mountains, deserts and fierce, independent people. Many nations have tried to defeat them, but none has yet succeeded.

Iran

- Tehran
- 60 690 000
- Iranian rial
- Farsi
- 1 648 000 km²/636 296 sq miles

Iran, which used to be called Persia, was once the centre of a great empire. Today it is a strict Islamic country, strongly opposed to Western culture.

Much of Iran is desert, but the north-west is fertile. Most of its money comes from oil.

Bangladesh

- Dhaka
- 120 070 000
- taka
- Bengali
- 147 570 km²/56 977 sq miles

Bangladesh is a young country, winning independence in 1971.

Nepal

- Kathmandu
- 21 130 000
- Nepalese rupee
- Nepali
- 147 181 km²/56 827 sq miles

Nepal includes Mount Everest, the world's highest mountain, rising to 8848 m (29 028 ft).

Azerbaijan
- Baku
- 7 630 000
- Azerbaijani manat
- Azerbaijani (Azeri)
- 86 600 km²/33 400 sq miles

In 1991 Azerbaijan won its independence from the Soviet Union. It gets most of its money from oil.

Georgia

- Tbilisi
- 5 410 000
- lari
- Georgian
- 69 700 km²/26 911 sq miles

Georgia is another former Soviet republic which won its independence in 1991. The country has high mountains, as well as fertile plains and valleys.

▲ **Indian tomb** The Taj Mahal was built in the 1630s by Emperor Shah Jahan as a memorial to his wife.

Sri Lanka

- Colombo
- 18 550 000
- Sri Lanka rupee
- Sinhala
- 65 610 km²/25 332 sq miles

Formerly known as Ceylon, Sri Lanka was ruled by Britain until 1948.

Bhutan

- Thimphu
- 1 810 000
- ngultrum
- Dzongkha
- 46 500 km²/17 954 sq miles

This tiny kingdom lies high in the Himalaya mountains.

Armenia

- Yerevan
- 3 770 000
- dram
- Armenian
- 29 800 km²/11 500 sq miles

This former Soviet republic won independence in 1991.

Maldives

- Malé
- 260 000
- rufiyaa
- Divehi
- 298 km²/115 sq miles

A chain of nearly 2000 coral islands in the Indian Ocean.

Countries of the world

Key Capital Population Currency Official languages Area

Central and East Asia

High plateaus dominate Central Asia, reaching their greatest height in Tibet. Most are cold and dry, but the landscape becomes more varied and fertile towards the east.

China

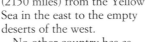

- Beijing
- 1 232 086 310
- yuan
- Mandarin, Cantonese
- 9 571 300 km²/3 695 500 sq mi.

China is a huge country, home to the world's oldest civilisation. Since 1951, China has included Tibet, which many people regard as a separate country.

To keep out invaders from the north, the ancient Chinese built the Great Wall, the world's biggest man-made structure. It runs for 3460 km (2150 miles) from the Yellow Sea in the east to the empty deserts of the west.

No other country has as many people as China, which is home to a quarter of all the world's population. There are great contrasts between its different regions. Most people live in the east, on the fertile plains beside the country's largest rivers, the Yangtze and the Yellow River.

The Chinese government claims that the island of Taiwan also belongs to it, but the people of Taiwan disagree.

Kazakhstan

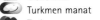

- Astana
- 15 920 000
- tenge
- Kazakh
- 2 717 300 km²/1 049 150 sq mi.

Part of the Soviet Union until 1991, Kazakhstan stretches for 3000 km (1875 miles) from the Caspian Sea in the west to China in the east. Much of it is flat, desert landscape or open plains, which experience bitter winters and very hot summers.

Mongolia

- Ulan Bator
- 2 350 000
- tugrik
- Khalkha Mongolian
- 1 566 500 km²/604 829 sq miles

In the 13th century Mongolia was the centre of the biggest empire the world has ever seen. Modern Mongolia emerged in 1924, when it broke free from China. It is mostly mountainous grasslands and deserts.

◄ **Army of the dead** An army of clay warriors stands guard at the tomb of the Chinese emperor Qin Shi Huangdi, who died in 206 BC.

▼ **Chinese hills** The area around Guilin, in southern China, is full of strange hills, which have inspired artists for hundreds of years.

Turkmenistan

- Ashgabat
- 4 570 000
- Turkmen manat
- Turkmen
- 488 100 km²/188 456 sq miles

Turkmenistan was part of the Soviet Union until 1991. It is a wild, empty country covered mostly by desert and stony plains, where nothing grows. Most people live in the south, where there are oases, rivers and the Kara-Kum canal, which carries water across 800 km (500 miles) of desert.

Uzbekistan

- Tashkent
- 23 440 000
- som
- Uzbek
- 447 400 km²/172 740 sq miles

Uzbekistan declared itself independent from the Soviet Union in 1991. Much of the country is desert, but there are also fertile lands in the east.

The oasis cities of Bukhara and Samarkand lay on the old Silk Road that linked Europe with China. Both grew rich from the trade, and are still the most impressive cities in Central Asia.

The country's main exports are gold, oil and textiles made from cotton, wool and silk.

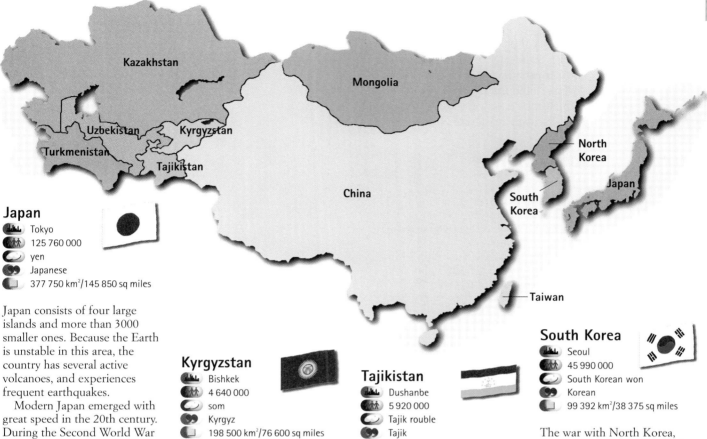

Japan

- Tokyo
- 125 760 000
- yen
- Japanese
- 377 750 km²/145 850 sq miles

Japan consists of four large islands and more than 3000 smaller ones. Because the Earth is unstable in this area, the country has several active volcanoes, and experiences frequent earthquakes.

Modern Japan emerged with great speed in the 20th century. During the Second World War Japan invaded many of its neighbours. It surrendered only after America dropped atomic bombs on two of its cities.

Since then Japan has built itself into a great economic power, second only to the USA. Its cars, electronic goods and cameras are known throughout the world. The Japanese are renowned for their hard work. Most of them live in the cities, which are very crowded.

Kyrgyzstan

- Bishkek
- 4 640 000
- som
- Kyrgyz
- 198 500 km²/76 600 sq miles

After parting from the Soviet Union in 1991, this small, mountainous country adopted the name Kyrgyzstan, which means 'Land of Nomads'. These days most people are not nomads, but remain proud of their nomadic past.

▼ Japanese mountain Mount Fuji is a dormant volcano. At 3776 m (12 388 ft) it is Japan's highest peak.

Tajikistan

- Dushanbe
- 5 920 000
- Tajik rouble
- Tajik
- 143 100 km²/55 251 sq miles

Tajikistan separated from the Soviet Union in 1991, and was at once torn by civil war. It is a landlocked country with a dry climate and high mountains. Most people live in its valleys.

North Korea

- Pyongyang
- 22 470 000
- North Korean won
- Korean
- 120 538 km²/46 540 sq miles

The peninsula of Korea was divided into two separate nations in 1945. North Korea has been communist ever since, and strongly opposed to the non-communist South. In 1950, North Korea invaded the South to unite the two countries, but was driven back by American and United Nations forces.

The country is mountainous and covered in forests. Only 19 per cent of the land is cultivated. Many people live in great poverty, made worse by a long famine in the late 1990s.

South Korea

- Seoul
- 45 990 000
- South Korean won
- Korean
- 99 392 km²/38 375 sq miles

The war with North Korea, from 1950 to 1953, shattered the South Korean economy. Since then, South Korea has made an incredible recovery. It has become one of the most important producers of ships, steel, cars and electronic goods. Seoul, the capital, was host of the 1988 Olympic Games.

The South is much warmer than the North, and grows more food. However, it is just as mountainous, so farming land is in short supply. Fishing is an important industry.

Taiwan

- Taipei
- 21 500 000
- dollar/yuan (NT$)
- Mandarin
- 36 000 km²/13 900 sq miles

This island state calls itself the Republic of China. It was founded in 1949, when supporters of the nationalist leader Chiang Kai-Shek were defeated by communists on the mainland. Since then, Taiwan has become a major economic success.

Countries of the world

Key  Capital · Population · Currency · Official languages · Area

South-east Asia

Lying on or close to the Equator, South-east Asia is generally hot and humid. The mainland is very hilly, which makes farming difficult. The area has several active volcanoes.

Myanmar
Laos
Thailand
Vietnam
Cambodia
Philippines
Brunei
Malaysia
Singapore
Indonesia
Indonesia

Indonesia

- Jakarta
- 201 390 000
- rupiah
- Bahasa Indonesia
- 1 919 317 km²/741 053 sq miles

Indonesia consists of almost 14 000 islands, including Java, Sumatra, Sulawesi and parts of Borneo and New Guinea. The country has the world's fourth largest population, speaking about 580 different languages.

Most people live on the island of Java, which is where the capital, Jakarta, is located. The country's chief exports are rubber, palm oil and timber. This is one of the world's wealthiest countries.

▼ **Indonesian dancer** Every gesture made by this dancer is full of significance.

Myanmar

- Yangon
- 46 400 000
- kyat
- Myanmar
- 676 553 km²/261 218 sq miles

Myanmar was called Burma until 1989, when it was renamed following a military rebellion. The name of the capital was also changed from Rangoon to Yangon.

Myanmar is a country of dense tropical forests and mountains. It has many fine Buddhist temples.

Thailand

- Bangkok
- 60 600 000
- baht
- Thai
- 513 115 km²/198 115 sq miles

Thailand, which was called Siam until 1939, is the only country in South-east Asia which was never a European colony – 'thai' means 'free'.

The country has developed rapidly since the late 1940s, mostly from exports of timber and rubber. It is also popular with tourists.

Vietnam

- Hanoi
- 75 180 000
- dông
- Vietnamese
- 331 114 km²/127 844 sq miles

Until 1976 Vietnam was split between the North, which was communist, and the South, which was not. After many years of war, the communists took over the whole country.

The land is hilly, with green rice fields where its great rivers flow down to the sea.

Malaysia

- Kuala Lumpur
- 21 670 000
- ringgit
- Bahasa Malaysia
- 329 758 km²/127 320 sq miles

Malaysia is split into two parts, which are 700 km (435 miles) apart. West Malaysia is on the Malay Peninsula, and East Malaysia is in the north of the island of Borneo.

Philippines

- Manila
- 73 530 000
- Philippine peso
- Filipino
- 300 000 km²/115 831 sq miles

The Philippines is a group of over 7000 mountainous islands, ruled by Spain until 1898, and then by America until 1946.

Laos

- Vientiane
- 5 040 000
- new kip
- Laotian
- 236 800 km²/91 400 sq miles

This communist country was closed to the outside world from 1975 until 1990. It is one of the least developed countries in the region, and the poorest.

Cambodia

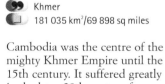

- Phnom Penh
- 10 270 000
- riel
- Khmer
- 181 035 km²/69 898 sq miles

Cambodia was the centre of the mighty Khmer Empire until the 15th century. It suffered greatly in the later 20th century from war and the bloody policies of the communist Pol Pot.

Brunei

- Bandar Seri Begawan
- 300 000
- Brunei dollar
- Malay
- 5765 km²/2226 sq miles

This tiny state, ruled by a Sultan, has large deposits of oil and natural gas, which have made it very wealthy.

Singapore

- Singapore
- 3 740 000
- Singapore dollar
- Malay
- 646 km²/249 sq miles

Singapore has built a strong industrial economy, and is also a major financial centre.

Oceania

The islands of Oceania are tropical gems surrounded by coral reefs. Australia has its own Great Barrier Reef, as well as arid deserts. New Zealand is more mountainous.

Australia

- Canberra
- 18 530 000
- Australian dollar
- English
- 7 682 300 km²/2 966 153 sq mi.

Australia may have been inhabited for the last 60 000 years by Aboriginal people; Europeans arrived to live here only in 1788. The country has one of the oldest landscapes on Earth, with most of its features worn down by millions of years of wind and rain.

It is also a young, exciting country, with people from all over the world working to build their future there.

Papua New Guinea

- Port Moresby
- 4 210 000
- kina
- Pidgin, English, Motu
- 462 840 km²/178 704 sq miles

Papua New Guinea, or PNG as it is often called, occupies the eastern half of the island of New Guinea. It was ruled by Australia until 1975.

New Zealand

- Wellington
- 3 760 000
- New Zealand dollar
- English
- 270 534 km²/104 454 sq miles

New Zealand is made up of two major islands – North Island and South Island – and some smaller ones. The original inhabitants came from Polynesia, with the Maori arriving about 1000 years ago. European settlers began arriving in the 1820s. The country is renowned for its fine scenery, which includes glaciers.

Solomon Islands

- Honiara
- 390 000
- Solomon Island dollar
- English
- 27 556 km²/10 639 sq miles

The Spanish named these islands after King Solomon in the Bible. They are spread over 1450 km (900 miles) of ocean.

Fiji

- Suva
- 800 000
- Fiji dollar
- Fijian, Hindi
- 18 376 km²/7095 sq miles

Fiji is made up of hundreds of small islands, but only 110 have people living on them.

Vanuatu

- Port Vila
- 170 000
- vatu
- Bislama, English, French
- 12 190 km²/4707 sq miles

This chain of 83 islands was called the New Hebrides until it became independent in 1980.

Samoa

- Apia
- 170 000
- tala
- Samoan, English
- 2831 km²/1093 sq miles

Samoa consists of two large islands and seven small ones.

Kiribati

- Bairiki
- 80 000
- Australian dollar
- I-Kiribati, English
- 810 km²/313 sq miles

A string of 33 tiny coral islands, formerly the Gilbert Islands.

Micronesia   Marshall Islands

Palau

Papua New Guinea   Nauru   Kiribati

Solomon Islands   Tuvalu

Vanuatu   Samoa

Australia   Tonga   Fiji

New Zealand

Tonga

- Nuku'alofa
- 100 000
- Tongan dollar (pa'anga)
- Tongan, English
- 748 km²/289 sq miles

The 170 islands of Tonga are ruled by a family that has been in power for 1000 years.

Micronesia

- Palikir
- 110 000
- US dollar
- English
- 700 km²/270 sq miles

Micronesia consists of more than 600 islands.

Palau

- Koror
- 20 000
- US dollar
- Palauan, English
- 508 km²/196 sq miles

Palau is a chain of about 200 islands which declared itself independent in 1994.

Marshall Islands

- Dalap-Uliga-Darrit
- 60 000
- US dollar
- English, Marshallese, Japanese
- 180 km²/70 sq miles

The Marshall Islands are made up of over 1000 coral islands.

Tuvalu

- Vaiaku
- 10 000
- Australian dollar
- Tuvaluan, English
- 26 km²/10 sq miles

Formerly known as the Ellice Islands, there are nine small islands in this group.

Nauru

- (none)
- 11 000
- Australian dollar
- Nauruan
- 21 km²/8 sq miles

Independent since 1968, Naura is the world's smallest republic.

▲ **Australia's red rock** Uluru, also known as Ayers Rock, lies in the middle of a desert. It is sacred to the Aboriginal people.

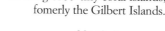

Countries of the world

Key Capital Population Currency Official languages Area

North and Central America

A line of mountains runs down the North American continent, from Alaska to Mexico. In the far north, the land is permanently frozen, but in the middle there are fertile prairies.

Canada

- Ottawa
- 30 280 000
- Canadian dollar
- English, French
- 9 958 319 km²/3 844 928 sq mi.

Canada is the second largest country in the world after Russia; crossing it by train takes four days and five nights. It has ten provinces with more lakes than any other country, as

United States of America

- Washington D.C.
- 267 900 000
- US dollar
- English
- 9 809 155 km²/3 787 319 sq mi.

This enormous country, 'land of the free and home of the brave', is made up of 50 states, including Alaska and Hawaii. The original inhabitants of the

▲ **Over the edge** The Niagara Falls lie on the border between Canada and the USA.

well as high mountain ranges and forests where bears and wolves roam. Winters are bitterly cold, so most farming is done in the south.

Nearly 7 million Canadians – around a quarter of the total population – live in the French-speaking province of Quebec, which was founded by the French explorer Samuel de Champlain in 1608. Many people in Quebec would like the province to break free from the rest of Canada.

mainland were the American Indians, who may have arrived 17 000 years ago.

Europeans began to settle on the continent from the 16th century, although Vikings explored its northerly points several centuries earlier. Since then, people have been coming to America from all over the globe, especially in the 19th and 20th centuries. As a result, American society is very varied.

America has the world's most powerful economy and armed forces, making it a global superpower. For much of the 20th century, the country led the world in many fields, such

▲ **Rain god** The ancient culture of Mexico can be seen in this temple, with its figure of a rain god.

as industrial development and space research.

Because of its vast size, the American landscape ranges from steamy swamps to arid deserts, to Arctic tundra.

Mexico

- Mexico City
- 96 400 000
- Mexican peso
- Spanish
- 1 958 201 km²/756 066 sq miles

Mexico City, the capital of Mexico, is inhabited by over 20 million people, and is the fastest growing city on Earth.

Mexico has a dramatic landscape of mountains and volcanoes. It is occasionally rocked by earthquakes: one in 1985 killed 7000 people in Mexico City.

The country was inhabited by the Maya Indians from about 2600 BC. The Aztecs arrived in the 13th century, and were conquered by the Spanish in the 16th century.

Mexico was once much bigger; between 1836 and 1848, it lost more than half its territory to the United States.

Nicaragua

- Managua
- 4 240 000
- gold cordoba
- Spanish
- 120 254 km²/46 430 sq miles

Nicaragua has coasts on two seas, the Pacific in the west and the Caribbean in the east. Most people live in the west, where the land is flat and good for farming. The east coast is known as the Mosquito Coast, and is dangerous because of the risk of catching malaria there.

The country has suffered from civil war for much of its history. Over 70 per cent of the population live in deep poverty.

Honduras

- Tegucigalpa
- 6 340 000
- lempira
- Spanish
- 112 088 km²/43 277 sq miles

Honduras was the original 'banana republic', which meant that it made all its money from bananas. Today, coffee, cattle and sugar are also farmed.

The capital, Tegucigalpa, was named by the Maya Indians. The name means 'silver hills', a reference to the fact that the Mayas mined silver here.

Belize

- Belmopan
- 230 000
- Belizean dollar
- English
- 22 965 km²/8867 sq miles

Belize is the only country in Central America where English is the official language, as it was colonised by British settlers in the 1600s. It has the biggest coral reef in the Western Hemisphere, as well as ancient temples of the Mayan kingdom buried deep in its jungles.

El Salvador

- San Salvador
- 5 800 000
- Salvadorean colón
- Spanish
- 21 041 km²/8124 sq miles

Since gaining independence in 1821, El Salvador has suffered much internal conflict. Its name means 'The Saviour', which is something the country badly needs. Since the 1970s more than 30 000 people have disappeared or been killed, and the economy is weak.

Guatemala

- Guatemala City
- 10 520 000
- quetzal
- Spanish
- 108 889 km²/42 042 sq miles

Guatemala is a country of mountains and dense jungle, which was part of the ancient kingdom of the Mayas. Now it has the biggest population in Central America, 2 million of whom live in the capital.

Panama

- Panama City
- 2 720 000
- balboa
- Spanish
- 75 517 km²/29 157 sq miles

Panama is a thin strip of a country, in some places only 58 km (36 miles) wide. Most of its money comes from its canal, which links the Caribbean and the Pacific Ocean.

Costa Rica

- San José
- 3 400 000
- Costa Rican colón
- Spanish
- 51 100 km²/19 730 sq miles

Costa Rica is the most peaceful country in Central America: it has not had an army since 1948. It is also the most careful with its environment, and is popular with tourists.

▶ **Torch of freedom** Since 1886, the Statue of Liberty has welcomed people arriving by ship at New York harbour. It is 93 m (305 ft) high.

Countries of the world

The Caribbean

Many Caribbean islands were formed by volcanoes, some of which are still active. It was here that Christopher Columbus first landed when he crossed the Atlantic in 1492.

Cuba

- Havana
- 11 060 000
- Cuban peso
- Spanish
- 110 860 km²/42 803 sq miles

Cuba, the largest island in the West Indies, is famous for its music, rum and cigars. Havana, the capital, is full of old colonial buildings and palm trees. Cuba has been ruled since 1959 by Fidel Castro.

The Bahamas

- Nassau
- 290 000
- Bahamian dollar
- English
- 13 939 km²/5382 sq miles

The Bahamas consist of over 700 tropical islands and about 1000 cays, or little coral islets.

The islands were occupied by Britain in the 17th century, and gained their independence in 1973. They derive most of their income from tourism, especially from the USA.

Trinidad and Tobago

- Port of Spain
- 1 260 000
- Trinidad and Tobago dollar
- English
- 5128 km²/1980 sq miles

Trinidad is the larger of these two islands.

Dominica

- Roseau
- 70 000
- East Caribbean dollar
- English
- 750 km²/290 sq miles

Dominica is a volcanic island with large forests; its name means 'Sunday' in Spanish.

Barbados

- Bridgetown
- 260 000
- Barbados dollar
- English
- 430 km²/166 sq miles

Barbados is the most easterly island in the Caribbean.

St Vincent and the Grenadines

- Kingstown
- 110 000
- East Caribbean dollar
- English
- 389 km²/150 sq miles

There is an active volcano called Soufrière on St Vincent.

Bahamas

St Kitts & Nevis

Antigua & Barbuda

Cuba

Dominican Republic

Dominica

St Lucia

Barbados

Haiti

St Vincent & the Grenadines

Jamaica

Grenada

Trinidad & Tobago

▲ **Tropical paradise** The island of Mustique is one of the Grenadines.

Dominican Republic

- Santo Domingo
- 8 050 000
- Dominican Republic peso
- Spanish
- 48 422 km²/18 696 sq miles

This country is located on the island of Hispaniola, which it shares with Haiti.

Haiti

- Port-au-Prince
- 7 490 000
- gourde
- French, Creole
- 27 750 km²/10 714 sq miles

Haiti became the world's first black republic after a slave rebellion in 1804. Mountains dominate the land.

Jamaica

- Kingston
- 2 550 000
- Jamaican dollar
- English
- 10 991 km²/4244 sq miles

One of the larger islands in the Caribbean, Jamaica is the home of rum and reggae music. It was seized by Britain from Spain in 1655, and was granted independence in 1962. Many foreign tourists visit Jamaica because of its beautiful beaches and friendly atmosphere. Unfortunately, these hide deep poverty among local people, many of whom have no work.

St Lucia

- Castries
- 140 000
- East Caribbean dollar
- English
- 616 km²/238 sq miles

St Lucia has one of the deepest harbours in the Americas.

Antigua and Barbuda

- St John's
- 70 000
- East Caribbean dollar
- English
- 442 km²/170 sq miles

These two small islands were settled by the British in 1674 to create sugar plantations.

Grenada

- St George's
- 100 000
- East Caribbean dollar
- English
- 344 km²/133 sq miles

Grenada includes the island of Grenada, and some of the islands called the Grenadines.

St Kitts and Nevis

- Basseterre
- 44 400
- East Caribbean dollar
- English
- 261 km²/101 sq miles

The island of St Kitts is also known as St Christopher.

South America

South America has three great features: the Amazon rain forest; the pampas, or plains, of Argentina and Uruguay; and the Andes mountains, which run the length of the continent.

Brazil

- Brasília
- 159 880 000
- real
- Portuguese
- 8 511 996 km²/3 286 500 sq mi.

Brazil is the only country in South America that has Portuguese as its official language. There are also about 120 Indian languages.

The northern part of Brazil is made up of dense Amazon rain forest and huge rivers. On the coast, the city of Rio de Janeiro is famous for its annual carnival. This used to be the capital until Brasília was built.

Argentina

- Buenos Aires
- 35 670 000
- peso
- Spanish
- 2 766 889 km²/1 068 302 sq mi.

Argentina consists of the massive Andes mountain chain in the west, forest in the north, and huge, flat grass plains, called pampas, in the centre. The country was conquered and settled by Spain, but in Patagonia, in the south, a few people speak Welsh. Their ancestors arrived from Wales in the mid-19th century.

Peru

- Lima
- 24 370 000
- nuevo sol
- Spanish, Quechua, Aymara
- 1 285 216 km²/496 225 sq miles

Peru was the centre of the Inca civilisation, which lasted for 300 years until conquered by Spain in 1532. The country includes part of the Andes mountains and Amazon forest.

Colombia

- Bogotá
- 36 160 000
- Colombian peso
- Spanish
- 1 141 748 km²/440 831 sq miles

Mountainous Colombia has ideal conditions for growing fine coffee, for which it is known throughout the world.

Bolivia

- La Paz, Sucre
- 7 770 000
- boliviano
- Spanish, Quechua, Aymara
- 1 098 581 km²/424 164 sq miles

Bolivia gets its name from Simón Bolívar, who brought about its independence from Spain in 1825.

Venezuela

- Caracas
- 22 210 000
- bolívar
- Spanish
- 912 050 km²/352 144 sq miles

Venezuela, which means 'Little Venice', has the world's largest waterfall – Angel Falls – which drops 979 m (3212 ft). It also has the snow-capped Andes mountains in the west, Amazonian jungles in the south, and the third-longest river in South America, the Orinoco. Oil has brought the country much wealth.

Chile

- Santiago
- 14 620 000
- Chilean peso
- Spanish
- 756 626 km²/292 135 sq miles

Chile is a narrow strip with the Andes mountains on one side and the Pacific Ocean on the other, with some of the most dramatic scenery in the world.

Paraguay

- Asunción
- 5 090 000
- guarani
- Spanish
- 406 752 km²/157 048 sq miles

This landlocked country won its independence from Spain in 1811. Wars with its neighbours have slowed its development.

Ecuador

- Quito
- 11 940 000
- sucre
- Spanish
- 272 045 km²/105 037 sq miles

The name Ecuador means 'Equator' in Spanish. There are two big active volcanoes here.

Guyana

- Georgetown
- 840 000
- Guyana dollar
- English
- 214 969 km²/83 000 sq miles

Guyana, meaning 'Land of Many Waters', was ruled by Britain until 1966.

Uruguay

- Montevideo
- 3 280 000
- Uruguayan peso
- Spanish
- 176 215 km²/68 037 sq miles

Uruguay has plenty of pasture, which makes it ideal for raising sheep and cattle.

Surinam

- Paramaribo
- 430 000
- Surinam guilder
- Dutch
- 163 265 km²/63 037 sq miles

This former Dutch colony became independent in 1975.

▼ **Protector** A giant statue of Jesus looks over Rio de Janeiro.

Countries of the world

Key Capital Population Currency Official languages  Area

North and East Africa

North Africa is dominated by the great Sahara desert, and East Africa has its own deserts. The landscape becomes milder in Kenya, while the Seychelles are a small paradise.

Sudan

- Khartoum
- 27 290 000
- Sudanese dinar
- Arabic
- 2 505 813 km²/967 500 sq miles

The largest country in Africa, Sudan includes the Sahara desert in the north, and tropical jungles in the south.

Algeria

- Algiers
- 28 570 000
- Algerian dinar
- Arabic
- 2 381 741 km²/919 595 sq miles

A country of mountains and deserts, Algeria has been torn by vicious civil war since 1990.

Libya

- Tripoli
- 5 590 000
- Libyan dinar
- Arabic
- 1 775 500 km²/685 524 sq miles

Most of Libya is covered by the Sahara desert. Oil made it rich.

Ethiopia

- Addis Ababa
- 58 510 000
- birr
- Amharic
- 1 133 380 km²/437 600 sq miles

Drought and civil war have created long famines, and have kept Ethiopia poor.

Egypt

- Cairo
- 62 010 000
- Egyptian pound
- Arabic
- 997 738 km²/385 229 sq miles

Egypt had a great civilisation 5000 years ago. Today its capital, Cairo, is the biggest city in Africa with a population of 16 million people, more than twice as many as London.

Tanzania

- Dodoma
- 30 800 000
- Tanzanian shilling
- Swahili
- 945 087 km²/364 900 sq miles

Tanzania is a country of huge open plains and the richest wildlife in East Africa. It also has Africa's highest mountain – Mount Kilimanjaro, which rises to 5895 m (19 340 ft).

▼ **Ancient tombs** The three pyramids of Giza, in Egypt, were built about 4500 years ago as tombs for three pharaohs, or kings. They are regarded as one of the wonders of the world.

Morocco

- Rabat
- 28 130 000
- Moroccan dirham
- Arabic
- 710 850 km²/274 461 sq miles

A land of contrasts, Morocco contains arid deserts, fertile lands and the Atlas Mountains, covered in winter snow.

Somalia

- Mogadishu
- 9 820 000
- Somali shilling
- Somali
- 637 657 km²/246 201 sq miles

A former colony of Britain and Italy, Somalia lies on what is called the Horn of Africa.

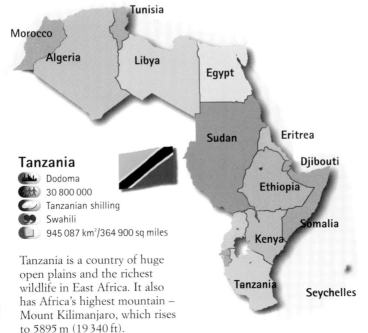

Kenya

- Nairobi
- 33 140 000
- Kenya shilling
- Kiswahili
- 580 367 km²/224 081 sq miles

Kenya is a big, hot country with high mountains, fertile farmlands and white beaches.

Tunisia

- Tunis
- 9 090 000
- Tunisian dinar
- Arabic
- 163 610 km²/63 170 sq miles

An Arab country, Tunisia has been independent since 1956.

Eritrea

- Asmara
- 3 280 000
- nafka
- Arabic
- 121 144 km²/46 774 sq miles

Until 1991, Eritrea was part of Ethiopia. It won its freedom after 30 years of war.

Djibouti

- Djibouti
- 620 000
- Djibouti franc
- Arabic
- 23 200 km²/8958 sq miles

This tiny country gets most of its income from its main port.

Seychelles

- Victoria
- 80 000
- Seychelles rupee
- Creole
- 454 km²/175 sq miles

The Seychelles is a group of 115 beautiful tropical islands lying off the east coast of Africa.

West Africa

West Africa ranges from mangrove swamps and dense tropical forests along the coast, to the barren sands of the Sahara desert in the north. In between, there are open grasslands.

▲ **Keeping cool** A group of African elephants takes shelter from the sun under an acacia tree.

Niger

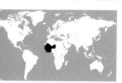

- Niamey
- 9 470 000
- CFA franc
- French
- 1 267 000 km²/489 191 sq miles

Niger gained its independence from France in 1960.

Guinea

- Conakry
- 7 520 000
- franc guinéen
- French
- 245 857 km²/94 926 sq miles

Ruled by France until 1958, Guinea gets most of its income from its mining industries.

Benin

- Porto-Novo
- 5 990 000
- CFA franc
- French
- 112 622 km²/43 484 sq miles

Benin has white beaches and quiet lagoons, surrounded by houses built on stilts.

Mali

- Bamako
- 11 130 000
- CFA franc
- French
- 1 240 192 km²/478 841 sq miles

Once part of a great empire, Mali is where the legendary city of Timbuktu can be found.

Togo

- Lomé
- 4 200 000
- CFA franc
- French, Kabiye, Ewe
- 56 785 km²/21 925 sq miles

Togo's landscape includes mountains, high wooded plateaus and grassy plains.

Mauritania

- Nouakchott
- 2 350 000
- ouguiya
- Arabic
- 1 030 700 km²/397 950 sq miles

Mostly desert, Mauritania is home to Africans and Arabs.

Guinea-Bissau

- Bissau
- 1 090 000
- CFA franc
- Portuguese
- 36 125 km²/13 948 sq miles

This is one of the poorest countries in West Africa.

Ivory Coast

- Yamoussoukro
- 14 780 000
- CFA franc
- French
- 322 462 km²/124 503 sq miles

The trade in elephant tusks gave this country its name.

Ghana

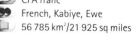

- Accra
- 17 830 000
- cedi
- English
- 238 537 km²/92 100 sq miles

Ghana used to be called the Gold Coast because it was a major source of gold.

Liberia

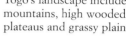

- Monrovia
- 2 880 000
- Liberian dollar
- English
- 97 754 km²/37 743 sq miles

Created by freed slaves returning from America in 1822, Liberia is the oldest African republic.

The Gambia

- Banjul
- 1 140 000
- dalasi
- English
- 11 295 km²/4361 sq miles

About half the size of Wales, The Gambia is the smallest country on mainland Africa.

Burkina

- Ouagadougou
- 10 780 000
- CFA franc
- French
- 274 200 km²/105 870 sq miles

Burkina is a poor country on the edge of the Sahara desert.

Senegal

- Dakar
- 8 800 000
- CFA franc
- French
- 196 722 km²/75 955 sq miles

This former French colony is famous for its distinctive music and folk traditions.

Sierra Leone

- Freetown
- 4 300 000
- leone
- English
- 71 740 km²/27 699 sq miles

Sierra Leone grew around a refuge for freed African slaves.

Cape Verde

- Praia
- 400 000
- Cape Verde escudo
- Portuguese
- 4033 km²/1557 sq miles

Discovered by the Portuguese in 1460, the 15 islands of the Cape Verde republic lie some 400 miles off the African coast.

Countries of the world

Key 🔲 Capital 🔲 Population 🔲 Currency 🔲 Official languages 🔲 Area

Central Africa

Northern Chad reaches into the arid Sahara desert. Farther south, there are dense equatorial forests, open plains and, in the east, mountain rain forests where rare gorillas live.

Democratic Republic of the Congo

- 🔲 Kinshasa
- 🔲 46 810 000
- 🔲 Congolese franc
- 🔲 French
- 🔲 2 344 885 km²/905 365 sq miles

Until 1997, this country was known as Zaire. It changed its name after a civil war.

Formerly ruled by Belgium, this huge country exports copper, silver and diamonds. Even so, it is one of the world's poorest nations.

Chad

- 🔲 N'Djamena
- 🔲 6 520 000
- 🔲 CFA franc
- 🔲 French, Arabic
- 🔲 1 284 000 km²/495 800 sq miles

Chad is famous for its carpets and cottons, which are handwoven and embroidered.

Most people live in the south, where the rains fall. The north is mostly desert.

Nigeria

- 🔲 Abuja
- 🔲 115 020 000
- 🔲 naira
- 🔲 English
- 🔲 923 768 km²/356 669 sq miles

With more than 115 million people, Nigeria is the most populated country in Africa. Since the discovery of oil and gas, it has become one of the richest in Africa. Yet most people still live in mud huts with no running water.

Central African Republic

- 🔲 Bangui
- 🔲 3 250 000
- 🔲 CFA franc
- 🔲 French
- 🔲 622 984 km²/240 535 sq miles

Partly desert and partly tropical forest, this landlocked country was ruled by France until 1960.

Cameroon

- 🔲 Yaoundé
- 🔲 13 560 000
- 🔲 CFA franc
- 🔲 English, French
- 🔲 475 442 km²/183 569 sq miles

Cameroon is home to 163 different ethnic groups, each with its own language.

Congo

- 🔲 Brazzaville
- 🔲 2 670 000
- 🔲 CFA franc
- 🔲 French
- 🔲 342 000 km²/132 047 sq miles

Although Congo exports oil, it remains one of the poorest countries in Africa because of political turmoil.

Gabon

- 🔲 Libreville
- 🔲 1 110 000
- 🔲 CFA franc
- 🔲 French
- 🔲 267 667 km²/103 347 sq miles

Gabon lies on the Equator, so it has a hot and rainy tropical climate. The capital, Libreville, was founded in 1849 by the French for freed slaves.

Uganda

- 🔲 Kampala
- 🔲 20 440 000
- 🔲 new shilling
- 🔲 English
- 🔲 241 139 km²/93 104 sq miles

Uganda is mostly a fertile, high plateau, with the huge Lake Victoria in the south and semi-desert in the north. The Ruwenzori mountains, in the south-west, are one of the last places where you can find the rare mountain gorilla in its natural habitat.

With its tropical climate, Uganda is very lush, and was once described as 'the pearl of Africa'. Political turmoil in the 1980s damaged the economy, which has still not recovered.

Equatorial Guinea

- 🔲 Malabo
- 🔲 410 000
- 🔲 CFA franc
- 🔲 Spanish
- 🔲 28 051 km²/10 830 sq miles

The capital of Equatorial Guinea is not on the mainland, but on the island of Bioko.

Rwanda

- 🔲 Kigali
- 🔲 5 400 000
- 🔲 Rwandan franc
- 🔲 French, English
- 🔲 26 338 km²/10 169 sq miles

Rwanda is a dramatic, rugged country of extinct volcanoes, and deep valleys.

Burundi

- 🔲 Bujumbura
- 🔲 6 190 000
- 🔲 Burundian franc
- 🔲 French
- 🔲 27 834 km²/10 747 sq miles

This is a small, mountainous country in the middle of Africa.

São Tomé e Príncipe

- 🔲 São Tomé
- 🔲 140 000
- 🔲 dobra
- 🔲 Portuguese
- 🔲 1001 km²/386 sq miles

The main crop of these two rugged islands is cocoa.

(Map showing Chad, Nigeria, Central African Republic, Cameroon, Equatorial Guinea, São Tomé e Príncipe, Gabon, Congo, Democratic Republic of the Congo, Uganda, Rwanda, Burundi)

▲ **Big and small** A hippopotamus calf stays close to its mother. These animals are excellent swimmers.

Southern Africa

Although the northern part of this area gets tropical rains, there are also two large deserts – the Namib and the Kalahari – which have wide areas of semidesert around them.

Angola

- Luanda
- 11 190 000
- kwanza
- Portuguese
- 1 246 700 km²/481 354 sq miles

Angola could be one of Africa's richest countries, but it has been ruined by civil war since gaining independence in 1975.

South Africa

- Pretoria
- 42 390 000
- rand
- English, Afrikaans, nine others
- 1 219 080 km²/470 689 sq miles

South Africa is often described as 'a world in one country'. In the north there is dry African bush, while in the south, where grapes and fruit are grown, the countryside looks more like Europe. This country is the most industrialised in Africa.

Namibia

- Windhoek
- 1 580 000
- Namibian dollar
- English
- 824 292 km²/318 261 sq miles

Namibia is mostly desert, but has huge deposits of diamonds, uranium and copper. It became independent in 1990.

Mozambique

- Maputo
- 17 800 000
- metical
- Portuguese
- 799 380 km²/308 641 sq miles

Mozambique was ruled by Portugal until 1975, when it became independent. A long civil war lasted until 1992.

Zambia

- Lusaka
- 8 280 000
- Zambian kwacha
- English
- 752 614 km²/290 586 sq miles

Zambia gets its name from the River Zambezi, which runs along its southern border with Zimbabwe. The country is the second biggest producer of copper in the world after the United States.

Madagascar

- Antananarivo
- 15 350 000
- franc malgache (MG)
- Malagasy, French
- 587 041 km²/226 658 sq miles

The fourth largest island in the world, Madagascar is famous for its unique animals – such as lemurs, which have long noses but are related to monkeys.

Botswana

- Gaborone
- 1 530 000
- pula
- English
- 581 730 km²/224 607 sq miles

Most of Botswana is desert, but one area, called the Okavango Delta, is a treasury of wildlife.

Zimbabwe

- Harare
- 12 290 000
- Zimbabwe dollar
- English
- 390 759 km²/150 873 sq miles

Zimbabwe was the British colony of Southern Rhodesia. It declared independence in 1965, and after 15 years of war, became Zimbabwe in 1980. It is the most developed state in the area after South Africa.

Malawi

- Lilongwe
- 10 440 000
- Malawian kwacha
- English
- 118 484 km²/45 747 sq miles

Malawi takes its name from its lake – the third largest lake in Africa – which runs almost the entire length of the country.

Lesotho

- Maseru
- 2 080 000
- loti
- English, Sesotho
- 30 355 km²/11 720 sq miles

Surrounded entirely by South Africa, most of this tiny kingdom is made up of high mountains and deep valleys.

Swaziland

- Mbabane
- 940 000
- lilangeni
- English, siSwati
- 17 363 km²/6704 sq miles

This is one of Africa's last few traditional monarchies.

▼ **On the border** The magnificent Victoria Falls lie on the border between Zimbabwe and Zambia.

Mauritius

- Port Louis
- 1 150 000
- Mauritian rupee
- English
- 2040 km²/788 sq miles

Mauritius is a volcanic island surrounded by coral reefs.

Comoros

- Moroni
- 630 000
- Comoros franc
- Comorian, French, Arabic
- 1862 km²/719 sq miles

Comoros consists of four islands in the Indian Ocean.

History of the world

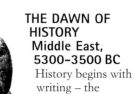

T he history of humankind is the story of nations rising and falling; of great empires that triumph for a while over all around them, before fading and being replaced by others. It is also the story of how humanity has come to dominate the Earth, and even threaten its continued existence.

THE FIRST POPULATION EXPLOSION
Around 10 000 BC
Before long, our farming ancestors found that they had an excess of food, which they could store for when times were hard. Famine became less of a threat, and the world's population started to soar. Adventurous groups of people split away from their tribes, looking for new lands to farm. Those who left and those who stayed stored their food in woven baskets, and in pots made from clay.

WORLD

▶ **Mother goddess** The people of Çatal Hüyük, in Turkey, made this figure of a woman in about 5500 BC.

THE FIRST CITIES
Middle East, 9000 BC
Settlements grew larger as those with a talent for making things began to exchange the products of their skills for food or other items they needed. Some became shoemakers, others builders, and so on. The first known city, protected by a massive stone wall, was built about 9000 BC at Jericho in Jordan.

Nearly 3000 years later, Çatal Hüyük in Turkey had a population running into several thousands.

ASIA

THE DAWN OF HISTORY
Middle East, 5300–3500 BC
History begins with writing – the keeping of records – and a recent discovery suggests that the Egyptians were using hieroglyphic (picture-symbol) writing as early as 5300 BC for their tax records.

The Sumerians, a very creative people who lived in Mesopotamia (modern Iraq) more than 5000 years ago, also invented writing, and many other things that are part of civilisation. They built great cities, such as Babylon and Ur, and were the first people known to use the wheel.

ASIA

| 50 000 BC | 10 000 BC | 9000 BC | 8000 BC | 7000 BC | 6000 BC | 5000 BC | 4000 BC | 30 |

STONE AGE HUNTERS
World, 50 000 BC
By 50 000 years ago, early types of modern humans had slowly spread across much of the face of the Earth. Our ancestors made tools and weapons of bone, antlers, wood and flint. They gathered fruit, berries and juicy grubs to eat, and hunted wild animals, using dogs bred from wolf cubs as their partners. They lived in caves or built huts, wore furs, and knew the secret of making fire by rubbing dry sticks together.

Another reason for their success was their skill in language, which meant that they could communicate – and so cooperate with each other – more effectively.

AFRICA

THE FIRST FARMERS
Middle East, 10 000 BC
Wild seeds, from plants gathered for food, must often have sprouted after being dropped near the camps of Stone Age hunters. It must have taken a gigantic leap of the imagination to begin planting the seeds on purpose, but this is precisely what happened.

▼ **Tally-ho!** The first hunters often painted the animals they pursued on cave walls.

ASIA

MASTERS OF METAL
Western Asia, 6000 BC
Gold and copper were probably the first metals used, because they could be found lying on the ground. In Iran and Turkey they were smelted (melted at high temperatures), then made into jewellery and ornaments. Metal-workers in Europe used copper to make axes, knives and other tools.

Mixing copper and tin produces bronze, which is harder than either of the original metals. Bronze was being made in China by 3000 BC, but the Bronze Age took another 1000 years to reach Europe, and by that time an even harder metal was in use in western Asia – iron. The Iron Age reached Europe about 700 BC.

ASIA

GODS, PEASANTS AND PYRAMIDS
Egypt, 3100–1780 BC
Egypt depended for its very life on the annual flooding of the river Nile, which brought down rich silt, on which crops could be grown. Seeds had to be sown at the right time, so power was in the hands of the priests who, by studying the stars, created a 365 day calendar that helped them to predict when to sow. Farmers grew wheat and barley, and peasants lived mainly on bread, onions, leeks and beer. Noblemen had a more luxurious diet with meat.

The Egyptians saw this life as a journey to the next one, so important people were preserved as mummies when they died. The kings, or pharaohs, were buried in pyramids.

AFRICA

◀ **Stone circle** Stonehenge is now ruined, but still has the power to impress visitors.

THE MONUMENT BUILDERS
Europe, 2510–1500 BC

The early peoples of western Europe built monuments of enduring mystery and astonishing size. Four thousand years ago, at Carnac in Brittany, nearly 3000 standing stones were set in lines more than a kilometre (1/2 mile) long. Some 500 years earlier, at Stonehenge in England, work had begun on a monument that must have been a marvel of its age. A circle of gigantic stones stood upright, with huge blocks of stone linking the top of each stone with its neighbour. The standing stones weigh about 25 tonnes each.

THE WORSHIP OF ONE GOD
Middle East, 2100–1200 BC

Most early societies worshipped many gods, but Abraham, who became the father of the Jewish race, believed in only one. He left his home in Mesopotamia to spread the message of one God, and the Bible tells how God promised the land of Canaan (Palestine) to Abraham and his descendants, the Israelites.

When famine struck in Canaan, the Israelites fled to Egypt, where they became slaves. Moses led them out of slavery to the edge of the promised land.

ASIA

THE FIRST GREAT LAW–GIVER
Babylon, 1792–1750 BC

After a period of fighting with one another, the Sumerian city-states fell prey to invaders. Babylon was taken over by new kings from Syria, and one of these, Hammurabi, left behind a code of laws. His principles of justice may seem harsh today, but in their time they were intended to be fair, setting a limit to how far the strong could punish the weak in the name of revenge.

In 1595 BC, Babylon fell again, to Hittites from Anatolia in Turkey, who were invincible with their war chariots and their superior iron weapons.

ASIA

THE BIRTH OF THE CASTE SYSTEM
Indus Valley, 1500 BC

The Aryans, fierce invaders on horseback, swarmed into the Indus Valley about 1500 BC, bringing with them a tradition of dividing society into priests, warriors and farmers. They overran the darker-skinned Dravidians and put them into a fourth group: servants. This was the origin of the rigid caste system, with those doing the most menial jobs – such as clearing human waste – classed as Untouchables.

The Aryans had no written language, but passed on stories of their gods and heroes in poems known as the Vedas, which became the basis of the Hindu religion.

ASIA

| 0 BC | 2500 BC | 2000 BC | 1500 BC | 1200 BC |

CITIES OF THE INDUS
Indus Valley, 2500–1500 BC

More than 4000 years ago, people of the Indus Valley, in what is now Pakistan, were living in cities that had streets laid out on a grid system, like modern American cities. They had baths and drains, too.

The citizens of Harappa and Mohenjo-Daro grew wheat, barley, rice and cotton, and traded as far away as Mesopotamia. They deserted the cities in about 1500 BC, but nobody knows why.

◀ **Haughty gaze** This figure of a man is thought to be that of a priest. It was found at the city of Mohenjo-Daro.

BULL-LEAPERS AT KNOSSOS
Crete, 2000–1400 BC

EUROPE

The Minoan civilisation in Crete, named after King Minos, grew rich on commerce. Its wine and olive oil were traded for such luxuries as gold and pearls from Egypt, and ivory from Syria. In the royal palace at Knossos, youths and girls played the sacred game of bull-leaping, seizing the horns of a charging bull and somersaulting over its back.

According to a legend, King Minos kept a monster, half-man and half-bull, hidden in an underground maze known as the labyrinth. The Cretan civilisation came to a rapid end after an immense volcanic eruption on a nearby island, and Knossos was invaded by a warrior race from mainland Greece – the Mycenaeans.

TRADERS WHO USED THE ALPHABET
Lebanon, 1700–1050 BC

ASIA

The alphabet – writing based on the sound of words, rather than on using thousands of pictures that have to be memorised – was born in Syria and Palestine about 1700 BC. By 1050 BC the Phoenicians, in Palestine and present-day Lebanon, had an alphabet of 22 letters, on which all today's Western alphabets are based. It had no vowels, however; these were added later by the Greeks.

The Phoenicians wrote on flexible papyrus – a sort of rough paper – made from papyrus reeds; their inks were made of gum mixed with soot or dye. They were outstanding traders, and their alphabet made it easy for them to keep records of their commercial transactions around the Mediterranean.

PHARAOH WHO DEFIED THE PRIESTS
Egypt, 1377 BC

AFRICA

The ancient Eyptians worshipped hundreds of gods. But in 1377 BC Pharaoh Amenhotep ruled that there was only one god – Aton, the sun-god. He even changed his name to Akhenaton, which means 'Pleasing to Aton'.

▼ **Worship** Akhenaton prays to Aton, the Egyptian sun god.

History of the world

EMPIRES IN COLLISION
Middle East, 1200–612 BC
For reasons not yet fully known, social order broke down along the eastern coasts of the Mediterranean around 1200 BC. A group of refugees, pirates and bandits known as the Sea Peoples caused havoc, and only Egypt stood firm. In Mesopotamia, the Assyrians built an empire based on fear. Slaves and plunder poured into their cities, and over the centuries they forged the most powerful empire that the world had yet seen. In 612 BC, however, an alliance of Medes and Babylonians captured the Assyrian capital, Nineveh, and their reign of terror was over.

ASIA

THE FIRST MONEY
Lydia, 8th century BC
Before the invention of money, people traded by the clumsy method of bartering. If, for example, you had a spare cloak but no fish, you had to find somebody who had spare fish and needed a cloak. Money made trading simpler. The first coins, made of a mixture of gold and silver, appeared in Lydia, in eastern Turkey, and in China, in the 8th century BC. Later, in the 6th century BC, Lydia's King Croesus ruled that his coins should have a set weight and be worth a fixed amount. The phrase 'as rich as Croesus' is still used today.

ASIA

EMPIRE OF A 'KING OF KINGS'
Asia 539–486 BC
The great city of Babylon fell in 539 BC to a surprise attack by Cyrus, King of Persia, who allowed the captive Jews to return to Jerusalem. Under a later king, Darius the Great, Persia's empire stretched from the Mediterranean to India. In letters carved on a cliff face he boasted: 'I am Darius, king of kings.' He died in 486 BC.

ASIA

◀ **Royal bowmen** The Persian king Darius the Great celebrated his military triumphs by depicting his army on the glazed brick walls of his winter palace at Susa.

THE WISDOM OF CHINA
China, 6th century BC
Isolated from other lands by mountains, deserts, seas and huge distance, the Chinese developed a civilisation based on respect for tradition and authority. The sage (wise man) Confucius taught that children should obey their parents, people should know their place in society, and those in authority should behave justly. Another system of thought, Taoism, taught that the way to inner peace was to follow nature. Just as water flows downhill, so human life should be lived without effort.

ASIA

1200 BC — 1000 BC — 800 BC — 700 BC — 600 BC — 500 BC

HEROIC BATTLES
Troy, 1200 BC
ASIA

The Mycenaeans, rulers of Greece and Crete after the collapse of the Minoan civilisation, were the most fearsome warriors of the Bronze Age. Around 1200 BC, they came into conflict with the city of Troy, which controlled trade from the Black Sea area.

This conflict inspired one of the world's most powerful stories – *The Iliad*, composed about 400 years later by the poet Homer. This tells how the Greeks fought the Trojans for ten years, and how they finally got into Troy by hiding some warriors inside a huge wooden horse.

▶ **In action** The Greek hero Achilles meets the Trojan hero Hector in face-to-face combat.

WONDER OF THE WORLD
Babylon, 630–562 BC
ASIA

King Nebuchadnezzar II, who ruled Babylon from about 630-562 BC, made it the world's most splendid city. It was entered by massive gates, 15 m (50 ft) high, set in a wall 17 km (10.5 miles) long. The hanging gardens of Babylon were one of the Seven Wonders of the World.

In 586 BC, Nebuchadnezzar captured Jerusalem, and took the Jews to Babylon as slaves. The Bible records this period, which has become known as the Babylonian captivity.

VISION OF THE BUDDHA
India, 528 BC
ASIA

Gautama Siddhartha was brought up in luxury, as a prince in northern India, but turned his back on comfort when he saw the results of human suffering. After years of searching he stopped to meditate under a fig tree. There he found the spiritual knowledge he was looking for, and became the Buddha ('Enlightened One').

His vision was that human suffering will end when people are freed from selfish desires. Believing in the Hindu doctrine of rebirth, Buddha taught that the way we live determines our next life, which we are born into after death. He also taught that all life is sacred.

Buddha's teachings spread throughout Asia, becoming one of the world's most important religions.

THE GLORY THAT WAS GREECE
Greece, 5th century BC
EUROPE

Greek-speaking Dorians from the north, who began moving into southern Greece about 1200 BC, gradually built up a dazzling civilisation, based on isolated city-states. Most famous was Athens, where democracy had its beginnings around 510 BC, when the right to vote was given to every free adult man – though not to women or slaves.

Greek thinkers explored the secrets of the Universe. One of them, Democritus, even concluded that matter is made up of invisible atoms. Philosophers such as Socrates and Plato sought to discover the meaning of life and the right way to live. The Greeks had a deep insight into human nature, revealed in their myths, poetry, drama, sculpture and vase paintings.

◀ Conqueror Alexander the Great rides to battle on his warhorse.

◀ Switchback The Great Wall of China crosses some of the country's most mountainous areas, yet continues unbroken, always running along the crest of a ridge.

GREEK AGAINST PERSIAN
Greece, 490–480 BC

King Darius of Persia sent an army to invade Greece in 490 BC, but was defeated at Marathon. Tradition says that the Greek Pheidippides ran the first marathon – nearly 42 km (26 miles) – to bring news of the victory to Athens, then fell dead. Ten years later, Darius's son, Xerxes, built two bridges of boats to allow his army to cross into Greece.

ASIA

ALEXANDER THE GREAT
Persia and India, 336–323 BC

An ancient legend said that whoever could untie the Gordian knot would rule the world. Many men had tried and failed, but Alexander the Great simply drew his sword and hacked through the knot. He went on to conquer the vast Persian Empire in 11 years, with just 35 000 men.

Alexander's campaigns took him deep into Central Asia and then India, where it is said that he wept because there were no worlds left to conquer. He was only 33 when he died.

ASIA

CHINA'S FIRST EMPEROR
China, 221–206 BC

A warlord and outstanding cavalry leader, Qin Shi Huangdi, made himself China's first emperor in 221 BC. He could not tolerate opposition; he burnt books that displeased him, and executed more than 400 scholars. Using the forced labour of 700 000 troops and peasants, he started building China's Great Wall, to keep out invaders from the north. When he died, an army of life-sized pottery soldiers was buried with him.

EUROPE

THE MURDER OF JULIUS CAESAR
Rome, 44 BC

From small beginnings as a settlement beside the river Tiber, Rome grew into a mighty empire. The city started as a republic, ruled by a senate and elected consuls. Its tough legions expanded Rome's borders and Julius Caesar was made dictator for life after adding Gaul to the conquests. But many saw him as a threat, and in 44 BC a group of plotters in the Senate, led by Brutus, stabbed Caesar to death.

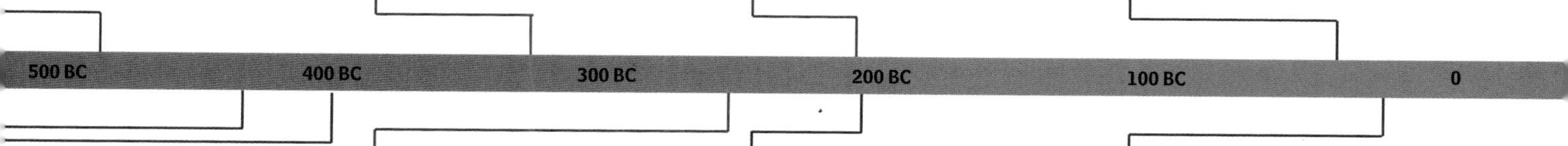
500 BC
400 BC
300 BC
200 BC
100 BC
0

GREEK AGAINST GREEK
Greece, 431–404 BC

Athens, renowned in all Greece for its learning and culture, had little chance when war broke out with the warrior city of Sparta. From birth, Spartans learned to endure hardship. Sickly babies were left out on hillsides, to live or die, and boys were trained as soldiers from the age of seven.

ASIA

AN EMPIRE BUILT ON PEACE
India, 269–238 BC

An uprising broke out in India soon after the departure of Alexander the Great. Its leader, Chandragupta Maurya, went on to establish India's first empire, which reached its height under his grandson, Asoka.

Thousands were killed as Asoka extended the empire. But the slaughter reached a point that sickened him. Asoka became Buddhist and renounced war, proclaiming: 'All men are my children.' Asoka's missionaries carried the Buddha's message of peace as far away as Greece.

EUROPE

HANNIBAL CROSSES THE ALPS
Italy, 218 BC

In one of the most astonishing feats of military history, the Carthaginian general Hannibal led 40 000 men and 38 elephants across the Alps in 15 perilous days, to attack the rising power of Rome. Only 12 of the elephants survived, but they caused great terror.

For 14 years Hannibal made war in Italy, but when he returned to Carthage in North Africa, he was defeated by the Roman general Scipio at Zama. Hannibal fled, and in 183 or 182 BC took poison to avoid capture. Rome gained a final victory over Carthage in 146 BC, and full control of the Mediterranean.

EUROPE

ROME'S FIRST EMPERORS
Rome, 27 BC–AD 63

Octavius emerged as victor in the power struggle that followed the murder of Julius Caesar. In 27 BC he was granted the title Augustus ('Revered One'), making him emperor in all but name.

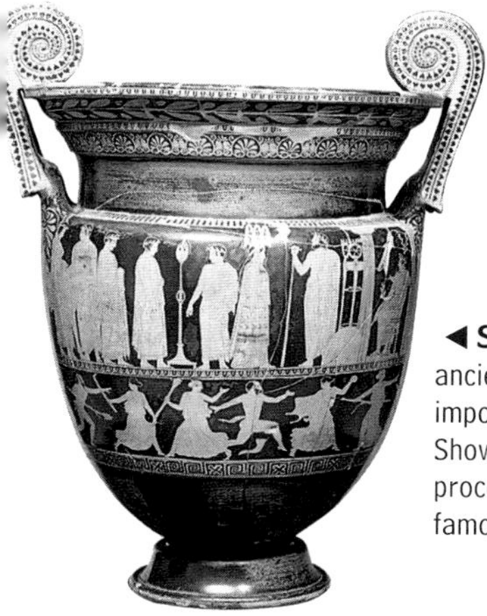

◀ Sacred procession The ancient Greeks depicted many important events on their pottery. Shown here is a sacrificial procession at Delphi, site of a famous shrine to the god Apollo.

▶ Waterway Roman triumphs include this fine aqueduct, for carrying water, in France.

▶ **Crucifixion** Jesus dies on the cross.

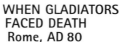

THE CRUCIFIXION
Jerusalem, AD 33
Nobody has done more to change the world than Jesus Christ. He performed miracles, and taught that we should love one another – even our enemies. His followers in Palestine, the disciples, believed he was the Messiah, come to lead the Jewish nation to freedom. But Jewish leaders regarded him as a trouble-maker, and asked the Romans to execute him.

ASIA

WHEN GLADIATORS FACED DEATH
Rome, AD 80
The Roman Empire was built on violence, and the Roman crowds loved to watch gladiators fighting to the death in an arena called the Colosseum. Slaves, criminals, prisoners of war and sometimes Christians would be set against each other or thrown to lions, bears and other wild animals. When the Colosseum was opened, in AD 80, the 'games' lasted 100 days.

EUROPE

A NEW ROME IN THE EAST
Turkey, 330
Fierce tribes attacked Rome's long borders, and enormous taxes were needed to pay its army of half a million men. To make the empire easier to rule it was divided into two, but fighting broke out between rivals for the western half. The victor, Constantine, turned the empire to Christianity after winning a decisive battle outside Rome. Some say that before the battle he saw a cross in the sky, others that he saw Christ's name in a dream.

In 330 Constantine founded the city of Constantinople as a new Rome in the East. It grew rich and powerful as the old Rome fell into decline.

ASIA

THE FALL OF ROME
Rome, 410
At the beginning of the 5th century, Rome was rich but weak. The upper classes lived in luxury, while the poor survived on handouts of free bread. The slaves, meanwhile, hated their masters, and so-called 'barbarian' tribes swarmed at the borders of the empire, eager for plunder.

In 410 the Visigoths, led by Alaric, burst into Rome. For three days they slaughtered, looted and burned what was once the world's most powerful city. Only the Christians were spared, for the barbarian Alaric had joined the new religion.

EUROPE

| 0 | AD 100 | 200 | 300 | 400 | 50 |

LAST STAND AT MASADA
Palestine, AD 73
A Jewish sect called the Zealots rebelled against Roman rule and captured the fortress of Masada. When they realised that they were about to be defeated, the Zealots decided to kill one another, rather than fall into Roman hands.

ASIA

THE ROMAN WALL
Britain, 122–383
Wherever the legions of Rome marched, Roman builders followed. They made roads that were long and straight, brought water to cities along aqueducts, laid drains, and built villas with underfloor heating. In Britain, the emperor Hadrian had a 117 km (73 mile) wall built to mark and protect Rome's north-west frontier. It had watchtowers, forts stood along its length, and troops were stationed in 'milecastles' every Roman mile (1480 m).

EUROPE

◀ **Mountain fort**
Masada was considered safe from attack, but the Romans built a huge ramp up to it to defeat the Zealots inside.

FROM TRIBES TO NATIONS
Europe, 4th and 5th centuries
The Huns, famed for their horsemanship and feared for their savagery, terrified Europe when they erupted from their Asian heartlands. Other tribes fled before them, in a wave of migrations that shaped the future of nations.

The Visigoths fled to Spain, Ostrogoths moved into Italy, and Franks into Gaul (modern France). With Roman power crumbling, Angles, Saxons and Jutes crossed the North Sea, taking over what became England. In 452, Attila the Hun threatened Rome itself.

EUROPE

▶ **Golden eagle** Visigoth craftsmen made this beautiful brooch, which was found in a cemetery in Spain.

THE MARCH OF ISLAM
Arabia, 622

Muhammad, the founder of Islam, had to flee his home city of Mecca in 622 because people who worshipped idols were angered by his message that there was only one God, Allah. Muhammad set up the first Muslim state in Medina and his flight from Mecca,

▲ **Islam in Europe** For several centuries, Spain was the centre of a rich Islamic culture, as this mosque at Cordoba shows.

called the Hegira, marks the start of the Muslim calendar.

Muhammad, as a prophet, or messenger, wrote down Allah's message in the Koran, the holy book of Islam.

PEOPLING THE VAST PACIFIC
New Zealand, 1500 BC–AD 1350

Polynesian voyagers reached New Zealand in open canoes around 800, with another group following in about 1350. They were completing an adventure of exploration that had begun as early as 1500 BC. With no charts and no knowledge of the compass, the Polynesians spread from India and Indonesia across the immensity of the Pacific.

They reached Tonga around 1140 BC and Tahiti about AD 300. By about AD 500 they were in Hawaii and Easter Island, where they left behind a mystery – over 600 faces carved in stone, some of them 20 m (65 ft) high.

OCEANIA

THE FURY OF THE VIKINGS
Scandinavia, 8th–10th centuries

Late in the 8th century, the Vikings burst out of their homelands in Scandinavia and began a series of raids that brought terror to Europe. Monasteries were their first prey – at Lindisfarne in Britain they stole sacred treasures and murdered monks or carried them off into slavery.

In their graceful longships, the Vikings sailed up rivers to raid cities as far inland as Paris. They were traders and farmers as well as pirates, settling in Iceland and Greenland, Normandy and England. They became overlords of the Russian Slavs, and even reached North America.

EUROPE

---

600 — **600** — **700** — **800** — **900** — **1000**

ASIA

AN AGE OF SAINTS
Europe, 435–529

The sparks of Christianity and learning were kept alive after the fall of Rome by monks. St Patrick began his mission in Ireland about 435. Irish monks, who made converts in Britain and on the Continent, created beautifully illuminated (decorated) books, like the Book of Kells. Their rules were strict – even in the cold of winter, prayers began at 2 am.

The rules of St Benedict, who founded a monastery at Monte Cassino in Italy in 529, were firm but less severe. The day was divided into work, rest and prayer, but monks had hot meals and were allowed to make their own wine, and drink it.

THE TALES OF THE 1001 NIGHTS
Baghdad, 786

Harun al-Rashid was the most splendid of the caliphs who ruled the Islamic world after Muhammad's death. His court at Baghdad received gold and ivory from Africa, perfumes from Arabia, carpets from Armenia and slaves from every part of the Arab empire.

Harun's reign (786-809) was the imaginary setting for the legend of the *Arabian Nights*. Every night for 1001 nights, it is said, Queen Scheherazade kept her easily bored husband entertained by telling cliff-hanging stories about Sinbad the Sailor, Aladdin, Ali Baba and other remarkable heroes.

EUROPE

THE EMPIRE OF CHARLEMAGNE
Europe, 800

On Christmas Day 800, Pope Leo III crowned Charlemagne, King of the Franks, as Holy Roman Emperor. It was a reward for what he had done for the Church, and a recognition of the power of a ruler whose empire stretched from the Baltic coast to Italy. Charlemagne led his armies against heathen Saxons and Avars, forcing them to become Christians.

He was ruthless: he once had 4500 Saxons beheaded after a battle. But he was also a friend of learning, encouraging scholars throughout his empire.

▼ **Holy Roman Emperor** A panel on Charlemagne's golden tomb shows him on his throne.

THE BATTLE OF HASTINGS
England, 1066

In 1066, England was being attacked from all sides. Harald Hardrada, King of Norway, invaded from the north, while Duke William of Normandy landed an army of 8000 men in the south. The English king, Harold, defeated the Norwegians at Stamford Bridge, then marched south for 19 days to face the Normans at Hastings.

Swinging their two-handed axes to terrible effect, the English beat off charge after charge, but they were footsoldiers, fighting cavalry. After their king was wounded – probably by an arrow – the English lost the battle and Harold was killed.

EUROPE

PENANCE IN THE SNOW
Italy, 1077

Popes and Holy Roman Emperors clashed in 11th-century Europe over who was in control of church lands and who had the authority to appoint bishops. The struggle reached a crisis point when the Emperor Henry IV declared that Pope Gregory VII was fired. In reply, the Pope excommunicated Henry – that is, he expelled him from the Catholic Church, which also meant denying him any hope of getting into Heaven. This punishment was so serious that Henry lost the support of other German rulers. He had to cross the Alps in winter, to beg forgiveness. The Pope left Henry standing barefoot in the snow at Canossa for three days before granting it.

EUROPE

KNIGHTS AND SQUIRES
Europe, 12th–14th centuries

A knight in the Middle Ages had a duty to serve his lord, protect the weak and defend the honour of women. Training began at the age of seven, when a boy became a page in the castle of a lord. At 14 he could become a squire, looking after a knight, and after another seven years, if he did well, he would be made a knight himself. A knight on his warhorse was hard to stop, but if he was unhorsed, his heavy armour made him clumsy and slow.

EUROPE

▶ **Mongol ruler** In 1276, Kublai Khan, the grandson of Genghis Khan, became emperor of China.

THE MONGOL TERROR
Asia and Europe, 1206

The Mongols of Central Asia were warriors from birth. Hardened by freezing winds and the baking sun, they learned to ride almost before they could walk. Genghis Khan, proclaimed their leader in 1206, made the Mongols feared throughout Asia and Europe. They would massacre all the citizens of a city that refused to surrender to them.

ASIA

| 1000 | 1050 | 1100 | 1150 | 120 |

THE NORMAN CONQUEST
England, 1066–87

EUROPE

Duke William, crowned William I in London, ruled his new realm with an iron fist. He put down rebellions brutally, and destroyed large areas of the north from York to Durham. Under the feudal system, William handed out land to his followers, and they in return promised him support in war. The Normans built 500 castles to impress their unruly subjects, and laid down savage penalties for anyone caught poaching in the royal forests.

William also commissioned the Domesday Book, which was completed in 1087. It was a survey of the wealth of all England, to discover what the land could provide by way of taxes and soldiers. This is a remarkable historical record of the period.

THE CRUSADES
Palestine, 1095–1272

ASIA

For nearly two centuries the Christian and Muslim worlds fought a vicious struggle over the land where Christ lived and died. The Crusades began in 1095, when Pope Urban II called on Christians to drive the Muslim Turks from the Holy Land. Jerusalem fell in 1099, and both Muslims and Jews were massacred. Eight other crusades followed.

CATHEDRALS
Europe, 12th–14th centuries

EUROPE

Cathedrals were built to glorify God. Early cathedrals had rounded arches and thick columns, in the Roman style. This gave way to a much lighter design when the pointed Gothic arch allowed the weight of the roof to be taken by slender columns. Now cathedral roofs seemed to soar towards Heaven, as at Notre Dame, in Paris.

ON THE ROAD TO FREEDOM
England, 1215

EUROPE

King John of England, brother of Richard the Lionheart, had to find a way of paying for his costly but unsuccessful wars in France. He did so by increasing taxes, but this angered his barons, who rose in rebellion. At Runnymede, on the Thames, they forced the king to accept the Magna Carta ('Great Charter'). It dealt mainly with the rights of landowners, but was also a major step on the road to freedom, for it meant that the king could no longer impose taxes without the consent of his council, and no free man could be kept in prison without a trial.

◀ **To the Holy Land** King Richard I, 'the Lionheart', sets off on the Third Crusade in 1190. He was renowned as a great warrior.

▶ **Scottish hero** Robert the Bruce, shown here with his wife, won his country's freedom from England.

FORGING A NATION
Britain, 1277-1314
Edward I of England had an ambition to rule all Britain. He invaded Wales in 1277 and built a string of castles to keep his new subjects in order. In 1296, the king who became known as 'The Hammer of the Scots' sent his army against Scotland. The Scottish patriot William Wallace defeated the English at Stirling Bridge, but was later caught and executed.

According to legend, the Scottish king Robert the Bruce found the will to fight on after watching a spider spin its web despite all setbacks. He went on to defeat the English at Bannockburn in 1314.

THE HUNDRED YEARS' WAR
France, 1337-1453
Rivalry between the rulers of France and England came to a head in 1337, when the English king, Edward III, claimed the French crown. Early victories in the so-called Hundred Years' War went to the English. At Sluys (1340) they defeated a much larger

EUROPE

▲ **Victory** At the Battle of Agincourt, a small English army used its archers to defeat a much bigger force of French knights.

French fleet. Edward's son, the Black Prince, won stunning victories at Crécy (1346) and Poitiers (1356). At Agincourt (1415), English bowmen killed many French knights bogged down in mud. But Joan of Arc beat back the English at Orléans (1429), and after the Battle of Castillon (1453) only Calais was left in English hands.

PEASANTS IN REVOLT
France and England, 1358-81
Famine, disease, war and taxes made life a misery for peasants in Europe after the ravages of the plague, known as the Black Death. In France, a revolt called the Jacquerie (after a nickname for peasants) was brutally crushed in 1358, with the loss of 20 000 lives. In England, 60 000 men from Kent and Essex, led by Wat Tyler, marched on London in 1381 to protest against taxes.

They seized the Tower and beheaded the Archbishop of Canterbury. King Richard II, only 14 years old, bravely rode out to face the rebels, and Wat Tyler was wounded in a scuffle. Troops arrived and the rebellion failed.

EUROPE

| 200 | 1250 | 1300 | 1350 | 1400 |

THE TRAVELS OF MARCO POLO
China, 1271-95
Marco Polo was a Venetian merchant who travelled to China and lived there for about 16 years as personal representative of the emperor Kublai Khan. After he returned to Europe in 1295 he published an account of his travels. People were eager to believe his stories of men with the heads of dogs, but found it harder to accept that the Chinese used paper money and warmed their homes by burning a kind of black stone, which would later become known as coal.

Marco reached China along the 6400 km (4000 mile) Silk Road, the route by which silk and other goods had reached the West for centuries.

ASIA

A 'DIVINE WIND' SAVES JAPAN
Japan, 1281
A Japanese Samurai warrior was a fearsome figure, allowed to slice the head off a commoner with his razor-sharp sword if he felt he had been insulted. The Samurai code demanded courage, and never was this more needed than in 1281, when the Mongol emperor of China, Kublai Khan, sent an army of 150 000 men to invade Japan.

The battle raged for seven days, but the Samurai won when a hurricane called the kamikaze ('divine wind') wrecked the Mongol fleet. Real power in Japan at this time lay with a military dictator called the Shogun. The emperor was important, because people believed that he was descended from the gods, but he had no great power in the land.

AMERICAS

EMPIRE OF BLOOD
Mexico, 1345
The Aztecs of Central America created an empire based on war, because they needed a constant flow of captives. They believed that unless the Sun was fed with human blood it would not be strong enough to rise every morning. At their capital of Tenochtitlán, Aztec priests sacrificed prisoners on the steps of a great temple formed like a pyramid.

▶ **Sacrifice**
A human skull forms the basis of this mask, which is believed to represent one of the Aztec gods.

EUROPE

THE BLACK DEATH
Europe, 1348-52
A terrifying disease wiped out nearly one-third of the population of Europe in the Middle Ages. The Black Death, carried by the fleas of rats, spread along trade routes from China. By 1348 it was in Italy, France, Spain and England. People did not know what caused the painful swellings that gave the Black Death its name. Some blamed human sinfulness and wandered through towns whipping themselves as a punishment. The plague left Europe with a huge shortage of labour, and caused many villages to be completely deserted.

History of the world

JOAN OF ARC
France, 1431

France's fortunes in the war against England were at a low point when 17-year-old Joan of Arc arrived at the court of King Charles VII with a stirring vision: the voices of saints were telling her to drive out France's foes and have the king crowned at Rheims, then in English hands. Leading Charles's troops and wearing armour like a man, Joan defeated the English, and Charles was crowned at Rheims as promised. But Joan fell into the hands of the English, who burned her at the stake in 1431. Joan, the girl who inspired a nation, was made a saint in 1920.

EUROPE

◄ **Disaster** Constantinople falls to the Turks in 1453, to the horror of Christian Europe.

THE FALL OF CONSTANTINOPLE
Europe, 1453

Constantinople, capital of the Byzantine Empire, guarded Christian Europe for more than 1000 years. In 1453, however, it fell to the Ottoman Turks, and its great cathedral of Hagia Sophia became a Muslim mosque.

EUROPE

THE FIRST INFORMATION EXPLOSION
Germany, 1455

In about 1455, a German craftsman called Johann Gutenberg introduced to Europe the invention that was to bring the Middle Ages to an end: printing using movable type. Using a wine press, he began printing 200 copies of the Bible. Until then books had been copied by hand or printed from wooden blocks that had to be carved page by page. With movable type, the letters of the alphabet could be used over and over again to form words. A great explosion of knowledge followed. William Caxton printed the first book in English in 1475.

EUROPE

AFRICAN RICHES
Nigeria and Zimbabwe, late 15th century

A warrior king known as Oba Ewuare built a powerful trading empire in the rain forests of West Africa late in the 15th century. In his walled capital of Benin, craftsmen produced amazingly lifelike heads in bronze and ivory. Benin was also a centre of human sacrifice, and prisoners taken in war were sold as slaves.

More than 3500 km (2200 miles) to the south, the Shona people had grown rich by trading in gold, copper, tin and salt. At their religious centre, Great Zimbabwe, they built massive walls 9.5 m (31 ft) high, and a granite tower whose purpose still baffles the experts.

AFRICA

| 1400 | 1410 | 1420 | 1430 | 1440 | 1450 | 1460 | 1470 |

IN THE FORBIDDEN CITY
China, 1421

ASIA

The Mongol Empire's control of China was overthrown in 1368 in a rebellion led by a Buddhist monk, who was living as a beggar. He became China's first Ming emperor, taking the name Hong Wu and ruling his subjects firmly. In 1421, the third Ming emperor, Yung-lo, moved into the new capital he had built at Beijing. At its heart, filled with priceless vases, silks and statues, lay the huge Forbidden City – closed to all but the emperor and his official household.

GOLDEN CITIES OF THE INCAS
South America, 1438–1530

AMERICAS

From the small city of Cuzco in the Peruvian Andes, the Incas began to expand around 1438, under the emperor Pachacuti, who claimed descent from the sun god. In less than 100 years they ruled a vast empire, their palaces and temples crammed with treasures of gold and silver. They had no wheeled transport and no writing, but were great builders.

◄ **Growl** The shape and decoration of this Inca pot are meant to represent a fierce jaguar.

THE PRINCES IN THE TOWER
London, 1483

EUROPE

Two high-born families fought for the crown of England in the Wars of the Roses. Both had roses as their badges – a white rose for the House of York, and a red one for the House of Lancaster.

When the 12-year-old Yorkist prince Edward became king in 1483, the boy's uncle sent him and his 9-year-old brother to the Tower of London, and had himself crowned Richard III. Within weeks, both princes were dead. Suspicion fell on King Richard, and Henry Tudor led a rebellion against him. Richard was killed at Bosworth in 1485, and Henry united the country behind his red-and-white Tudor rose.

▶ **Exodus** The last Muslim king leaves Granada in 1492.

THE CONQUEST OF GRANADA
Spain, 1492

EUROPE

The last Muslims in Spain were expelled from Granada in 1492. It was the end of an epic struggle that had lasted for nearly 800 years.

The Muslim Moors left a lasting mark on the country in their mosques and palaces. Finest of all was the Alhambra, above Granada, with its courtyards, fountains, and ornamental stonework.

COLUMBUS FINDS A NEW WORLD
America, 1492

A taste for adventure and the prospect of riches from the gold, silks and spices of the East lay behind Europe's age of exploration. Vasco da Gama, from Portugal, reached India by sailing around Africa, but the Italian Columbus had the daring idea of reaching the east by sailing west.

In 1492 he crossed the Atlantic with three ships, reaching what he thought was the Indies. It was a new world, later known as the Americas.

NEW ART FOR A NEW AGE
Italy, 15th and 16th centuries

The Renaissance was a wave of artistic creativity that surged through the Italian city-states. Artists of genius were supported by patrons – the Medici in Florence, the Borgias in Rome. When it began, the Renaissance found its inspiration in the glories of ancient Rome.

Later artists studied nature, as well as tradition. The period produced men of many talents, such as Michelangelo, a painter and sculptor as well as a poet.

▲ **Renaissance ideal** Michelangelo's *David* stands in Florence.

LUTHER DEFIES THE POPE
Germany, 1517

The German monk Martin Luther started the Protestant Reformation when he nailed 95 theses (statements) to a church door in 1517, challenging the authority of the Pope. He was especially angered by the way Indulgences (pardons for sin) were being sold to pay the Pope's debts. Luther believed that human souls were saved by faith alone, not by obedience to the Church.

Summoned before the Holy Roman Emperor, Charles V, Luther declared: 'Here I stand. I can do no other.' As Protestants argued with Catholics, the printing of books and pamphlets helped to spread the debate.

THE CHURCH FIGHTS BACK
Europe, 1545-63

The Reformation spread rapidly in Europe. England broke from the Catholic Church after the Pope refused to grant King Henry VIII a divorce so that he could marry Anne Boleyn. Henry declared himself head of the English Church and seized the wealth of England's monasteries. In Geneva, John Calvin set up a regime that was committed to strict Protestant principles.

The Popes fought back at the Council of Trent (1545-63), which set out a clear and complete statement of Catholic doctrine. They received much support from the Jesuits – members of the Society of Jesus, founded in 1534 by St Ignatius Loyola.

| 1480 | 1490 | 1500 | 1510 | 1520 | 1530 | 1540 | 1550 |

THE BATTLE FOR ITALY
Italy, 1494-1559

The wealth and the weakness of the Italian city-states made Italy a rich prize for its greedy northern neighbours.

France's King Charles VIII began the Italian wars when he invaded Naples in 1494. These wars became a struggle to prevent Charles V, the Holy Roman Emperor and ruler of Spain, Austria and the Netherlands, from becoming too powerful.

Charles V defeated his rival, Francis I of France, at Pavia in 1525, and his troops entered Rome in 1527. But Charles's empire proved to be unwieldy. Before he died, he divided it between its Austrian and Spanish branches. Although France had to give up its claims in Italy, the balance of power in Europe had been preserved for the time being.

GOLDEN EMPIRES PUT TO THE SWORD
Mexico and Peru, 1519-33

Spanish conquerors, called *conquistadores*, who were hungry for gold, overthrew two mighty empires in the Americas. When Hernan Cortes landed in the territory of the Aztecs in 1519, he burned his boats so that there could be no turning back. The Aztecs had never seen guns or horses before, and thought that the Spaniards were gods. They were beaten in two years.

Francisco Pizarro won the Inca Empire in Peru with only 180 men. He was helped by a civil war between Inca leaders.

▶ **Mogul style** Babur, seated in the centre, brought the style and culture of Central Asia to north India in 1526.

THE 'TIGER' WHO WON INDIA
India, 1526

Babur 'The Tiger' was a prince from Central Asia, who in 1526 invaded the plains of India. At Panipat he defeated the huge army of the Sultan of Delhi with his secret weapon – artillery – to become the first of India's Mogul emperors.

▲ **Russian terror** Ivan IV was the first tsar of all Russia.

IVAN IV – THE TERRIBLE
Russia, 1533-84

Enemies, real and imagined, surrounded Ivan the Terrible on all sides. As the first tsar of Russia, Ivan ordered his secret police to torture and kill anyone who opposed him. In one fit of rage, he even struck and killed his own son.

THE WITCH HUNTERS
Europe, 15th–18th centuries

Tens of thousands of innocent people died during the centuries when the Western world lived in fear of witches. Crop failures, sickness and natural disasters were all blamed on witchcraft, which was thought to indicate a pact with the Devil. Both men and women were often tortured to make them confess.

◀ **Superstition** King James I of England examines four women accused of witchcraft.

THE MASSACRE OF ST BARTHOLOMEW
Paris, 1572

A wedding that was meant to halt an era of religious wars in France ended in a Catholic mob butchering 2000 Huguenots (French Protestants) in the streets of Paris. The victims had come to attend the marriage of the Huguenot Henry of Navarre to a Catholic princess. But some Catholics saw this as a chance to end the Huguenot threat, and so gave the signal for a massacre. Henry escaped, and in 1589 brought the wars to an end when he became King Henry IV of France. To win the crown, he turned Catholic with the words, 'Paris is worth a mass'.

▶ **Pilgrims** English Puritans set off to join the *Mayflower* for its voyage to America.

EXPLORING CANADA
Quebec, 1608

Samuel de Champlain was an explorer and fur trader who wanted to build a French empire in the New World. The fort he founded on the St Lawrence River in 1608 grew to become the city of Quebec, the centre of French power in Canada. Its first years, however, were very uncertain because of the cold.

Earlier, in 1534, another Frenchman, called Jacques Cartier, had voyaged up the St Lawrence while searching for the Northwest Passage – a sea route to China around the top of Canada.

VOYAGE OF THE MAYFLOWER
America, 1620

Crowded aboard the *Mayflower*, a ship less than 28 m (92 ft) long, 102 passengers set sail from England in 1620 for a new life in America. Among them were 35, later called the Pilgrims, who were seeking the freedom to worship in their own way. The first winter was so harsh that nearly half of them died.

| EUROPE | EUROPE | AMERICAS | AMERICAS |

1550   1560   1570   1580   1590   1600   1610   1620   1630   1640   165

| EUROPE | EUROPE | EUROPE | ASIA |

REVOLT IN HOLLAND
The Netherlands, 1568–1648

King Philip II of Spain, a devout Catholic, could not tolerate the fact that the Protestant faith had been taken up by his subjects in the Netherlands. In 1567 he sent the Duke of Alba to bring them under control, but Alba's brutality and high taxes caused a full-scale revolt. It was led by Prince William of Orange, who was known as William the Silent because of his self control as a diplomat. Alba executed 18 000 Protestants and sacked the city of Antwerp. This merely made the Protestants fight even harder. By 1609, seven northern provinces had won their freedom, though it was not recognised by Spain until 1648.

THE SPANISH ARMADA
England, 1588

When King Philip II of Spain sent a mighty Armada of 130 ships and over 19 000 soldiers to invade England, he was sure he would win. But the Armada was scattered by English fireships – small ships, which had been set ablaze. It was then pounded with cannons, and finally blown away by sudden storms from the Atlantic Ocean.

THE THIRTY YEARS' WAR
Europe, 1618–48

Rivalry between France and the Holy Roman Empire, ruled by the Habsburg family, prolonged the horrors of the Thirty Years' War. It began when Protestant nobles in Prague, in revolt against their Habsburg rulers, hurled two of their governors out of a window. Both men lived, and the rebellion was crushed. But the struggle spread.

In 1635 it became more complicated when France joined the fight against the Habsburgs. The Peace of Westphalia, ending the war, left France the strongest power in Europe, the Holy Roman Empire broken up and Germany devastated.

◀ **English hero** Sir Francis Drake was a fearless sea captain, who preyed on Spanish shipping. He helped to defeat the Armada.

THE MANCHU TAKE OVER CHINA
China, 1644

The last Ming emperor of China faced a peasant rebellion, and one of his generals made a major mistake. He turned for help to the Manchu, a warrior race living to the north-east of China. They passed through the Great Wall and put the rebels to flight. However, when the Chinese pursued the rebels, the Manchu seized the capital, Beijing, and made their leader the first Manchu emperor of China.

The Manchu admired Chinese culture, with its love of beautiful objects and respect for tradition. But they kept well apart from the Chinese people. They forbade intermarriage and made Chinese men wear long pigtails to show that they were inferior to the Manchu.

◀ **Royal pride** Louis XIV, in ermine cloak and other royal finery, shows that he has what it takes to be a king. This portrait was painted in 1701.

TURKS AT THE GATES OF VIENNA
Austria, 1683

Ever since they captured Constantinople in 1453, the Ottoman Turks had been a threat to Christian Europe. In 1683, the Turkish army stood right outside the gates of Vienna, capital of the Austrian Empire. An army of 300 000, led by the Turkish sultan's vizier (chief adviser) laid siege to the city. Inside it were no more than 15 000 soldiers. A number of German states sent help, but what made the difference was the arrival of the Polish king, Jan Sobieski, with 25 000 cavalry. The Turkish army was put to flight, and the Ottoman threat was over.

THE SUN KING
France, 1643–1715

Nobody believed more fervently that kings were appointed to rule by God than Louis XIV of France. He was called the Sun King because the affairs of the nation revolved around him like planets. 'I am the State', he declared. He built his great palace at Versailles, with 1400 fountains, roofs covered in gold leaf, and rooms full of mirrors to fill them with light.

THE INDUSTRIAL REVOLUTION
Britain, 1700–1851

The Industrial Revolution that began in Britain around the start of the 18th century was to change the world more dramatically than anything since the discovery of settled farming. Steam power

▲ **Industry** *The Iron Forge*, painted in 1772 by Joseph Wright.

replaced manpower and horse power; canals and railways crisscrossed the countryside; and towns grew at an astonishing rate as people left the land to work in new factories everywhere.

EUROPE EUROPE

| 50 | 1660 | 1670 | 1680 | 1690 | 1700 | 1710 | 1720 | 1730 | 1740 | 1750 |

EUROPE EUROPE

ROUNDHEADS AND CAVALIERS
England, 1649

The English civil war broke out soon after King Charles I marched into Parliament and tried to arrest five MPs. Those fighting for the king were named Cavaliers, while his opponents were called Roundheads, because of their close-cropped hair. The king was defeated and executed for treason in 1649.

▼ ▲ **Royal death** A crowd watches the execution of Charles I, after his death warrant (above) had been signed by 59 court officials.

PETER THE GREAT
Russia, 1682–1725

When Peter I became Tsar of Russia at the age of ten, it was a backward country with a mass of hard-working serfs (peasants) at the bottom, and princes and boyars (nobles) living in idleness and luxury at the top. Peter earned the title 'The Great' by his tireless campaign to modernise his country. To mark a complete break with the past, Peter began in 1703 to build the elegant new capital that became St Petersburg. The site was marshy, but it gave access to the Baltic Sea, and so to the West.

Peter was so ready to learn that he pretended to be an ordinary citizen, and worked in a London dockyard.

THE AGE OF REASON
Europe, 18th century

An exciting mixture of new ideas swept across France in the 18th century. In *The Social Contract*, published in 1762, Jean-Jacques Rousseau hurled a challenge at all rulers: 'Man is born free, and is everywhere in chains.'

A 35-volume encyclopedia, edited by Denis Diderot, rejected superstition and any belief that could not be supported by science and reason. The playwright and wit Voltaire caused a scandal when he attacked the Church. These thinkers of the 'Age of Reason' paved the way for the French Revolution of 1789, by raising a question which had already been asked in England by Thomas Hobbes and John Locke: Why should our rulers be obeyed?

History of the world

CLIVE WINS AN EMPIRE
India, 1757
Britons working for the East India Company in Calcutta made fortunes from trading in spices and cotton. But there were risks. In 1756, the nawab (ruler) of Bengal attacked Calcutta and had his British prisoners thrown into the Black Hole – a tiny cell, which was stiflingly hot. A story reached Britain that only 23 out of 146 people came out alive, causing a public outcry.

Robert Clive avenged the deaths at the Battle of Plassey in 1757 when, with only 3250 men, he defeated the nawab's army of 50 000. The victory gave the East India Company control over all Bengal and laid the foundations of Britain's empire in India.

ASIA

▲ **Voyager** Captain Cook is welcomed by Pacific Islanders.

CAPTAIN COOK
The Pacific, 1768–79
Captain James Cook was the greatest navigator of his day, perhaps of all time. From 1768 to 1779 he made three voyages in the Pacific, on the first of which he claimed the east coast of Australia for Britain. He was killed in Hawaii on his way home.

OCEANIA

THE FALL OF THE BASTILLE
Paris, July 14, 1789
For years, the ordinary people of France had suffered under a crushing burden of taxes. In 1789 their anger erupted, and an enraged crowd stormed the Bastille, a hated royal prison in Paris. So began the French Revolution. King Louis XVI and his queen were executed by the guillotine in 1793.

EUROPE

THE LIBERATORS
Latin America, 1791–1823
The ideas unleashed by the French Revolution soon spread beyond France. In 1791, a slave revolt broke out in a French colony on the other side of the Atlantic. Its leader, Toussaint l'Ouverture, died in prison, but the struggle went on, and in 1804 Haiti became the first country in Latin America to win independence.

Over the next 20 years, a tide of revolution swept through the entire continent. Argentina threw off Spanish rule in 1816. Simon Bolivar, 'The Liberator', drove the Spanish out of Colombia, Venezuela, Ecuador, Peru and Bolivia. Chile was liberated by Bernardo O'Higgins and José de San Martin, who also helped to free Peru.

AMERICAS

| 1750 | 1760 | 1770 | 1780 | 1790 | 18 |

WOLFE TAKES QUEBEC AND CANADA
Canada, 1759
AMERICAS

Canada was a land of lakes, forests and a prosperous fur trade when Britain and France went to war over who should control it. The French general, Montcalm, felt safe in his fort at Quebec, because it was protected by high cliffs. However, the British general James Wolfe surprised him by sending troops to climb the cliffs. The battle that followed lasted only ten minutes but won both Quebec and Canada for Britain. It also cost the lives of both generals – Wolfe and Montcalm.

▶ **Surprise attack**
The Americans' leader George Washington crosses the Delaware River on Christmas Day 1776.

AMERICA'S WAR OF INDEPENDENCE
America, 1775–81
AMERICAS

By 1773, Britain's colonies in America were frustrated at having to pay taxes, while having no say in how their government was run. In 1775 the first shots for American independence were fired at Lexington. The British redcoats were finally defeated at Yorktown in 1781.

THE RIGHTS OF MAN
France, 1789–94
EUROPE

The revolutionaries in France set out to change the world with their message of the Rights of Man and their slogan 'Liberty, Equality, Fraternity!' They abolished the monarchy and swept away the privileges of the upper classes and the Church. Talent, not birth, became the way to the top, and the only title that mattered was 'Citizen'. To mark a complete break with the past, the revolutionaries began a new calendar, with names like Brumaire (Foggy) and Ventose (Windy) for the months. And they created a new set of weights and measures – the metric system, with its kilograms and metres.

UNITE INDIVISIBILI
DE LA RÉPUBLIQU
LIBERTE EGALIT
FRATERNITE OULA MOR

▶ **New ideals**
France's First Republic proudly declared its intention to succeed, or die in the attempt.

THE RISE AND FALL OF NAPOLEON
France and Europe, 1796–1815

Napoleon Bonaparte was only 26 when he was appointed general of the French army fighting the Austrians in Italy. He found his troops half-starved and in rags, but led them to a series of victories that made him a national hero.

With his fame ever-growing, Napoleon crowned himself Emperor of the French in 1804. He went on to win dazzling victories over the Russians, Austrians and Prussians. His biggest mistake came in 1812, when he invaded Russia, with its ferocious winter weather.

Napoleon was eventually defeated at Waterloo in 1815 by the Duke of Wellington and Marshal von Blücher.

◀ **Free** This medal was made to celebrate the end of slavery in the British Empire.

THE FIGHT AGAINST SLAVERY
British Empire, 1833

More than 15 million human beings were shipped across the Atlantic and sold as slaves during the 400 years of the African slave trade. Conditions on the journey were so wretched that many died on the way. Those who survived were put to work on the sugar plantations of the West Indies or in the tobacco and cotton fields of America.

William Wilberforce led a long campaign against slavery by Britain. Success came a month after his death in 1833, when slavery was abolished within the British Empire.

▶ **Fatal error** On February 23, 1848, French troops fired on a crowd in Paris. The following day the king, Louis Philippe, abdicated, and the Second Republic was formed.

DEATH AND GLORY AT THE ALAMO
Texas, 1836

A handful of Americans – fewer than 200 – wrote themselves into legend when they died defending the mission fort of the Alamo, Texas, against 3000 Mexicans. Among them were Davy Crockett and Sam Bowie. A Texan army avenged their deaths six weeks later, and in 1845 Texas joined the rapidly growing United States.

YEAR OF REVOLUTIONS
Europe, 1848

National feelings were stirring among subject races in Europe in 1848, and unemployment was causing misery. The first major sign of trouble came in France, where the monarchy was overthrown. There was also trouble in Italy and Hungary, and Europe was soon in turmoil. Most of the revolutions failed, but the ideas behind them lived on.

EUROPE **AMERICAS** **EUROPE**

| 1800 | 1810 | 1820 | 1830 | 1840 | 1850 |

AFRICA **ASIA** **AMERICAS**

PEACE THAT RESTORED THE PAST
Vienna, 1815

The allies who defeated Napoleon gave no thought to national feelings when, at the Congress of Vienna (1815), they redrew the map of Europe. The country that later became Belgium was given to Holland; Norway went to Sweden; Austria kept Lombardy and Venetia, in Italy; and most of Poland fell under Russian control. Prussia became a watchdog over France, with territory on the Rhine. Most of these decisions simply stored up trouble for later.

Austria's Prince Metternich took the lead in finding ways to suppress the spirit of revolution, and the exiled Louis XVIII was restored to the throne of France. The frustrations in many countries would boil over in 1848.

THE GREAT TREK
South Africa, 1835–40

From the day that Britain seized the Cape Colony in 1806, the local Boers (Dutch farmers) began to fear that their future was under threat. Between 1835 and 1840, 14 000 of them packed their belongings and their Bibles into ox-drawn wagons and moved north to find new farmland. The Great Trek demanded courage. At the Battle of Blood River, in 1838, 468 Boers faced and defeated more than 10 000 Zulus.

THE OPIUM WARS
China, 1839–60

To keep foreigners out of China, the Manchu emperors ruled that trade with the West should be limited to one port – Canton. But British traders used the port to smuggle in opium from India, and millions of Chinese became addicts. When Chinese officials seized 20 000 chests of the drug, Britain sent out gunboats. Two Opium Wars forced China to open more ports to Western trade, and to give Hong Kong to Britain.

GOLD RUSH OF THE FORTY-NINERS
California, 1849

One of the most frenzied gold rushes in history hit America in 1849. It began when gleaming yellow grains were spotted in a stream at Sutter's sawmill in the Sacramento Valley, California. Clerks and cowboys, salesmen and barkeepers deserted their jobs and made for California.

Other 'Forty-Niners' came from as far away as Australia and China. Fortunes were made by panning – swirling stream water in a pan to separate grains of gold from sand. They were just as easily lost through drinking and gambling in camps with names like Peasoup Bar, China City and Skunk Flat.

◀ **Drug war** A British gunboat fires on Chinese junks (ships) at Canton during the Opium Wars.

THE TAIPING REBELLION
China, 1850–64

From about 1850, China had to deal with a visionary called Hong Xiuquan, who believed that he was the brother of Jesus Christ. Hong wanted to create a new era, called Taiping ('Great Peace'), and started a peasant revolt that was to cost 20 million lives.

Hong's rebels captured the city of Nanjing in 1853, and set up their own ideal state, with land shared out fairly and women having equal rights with men. The West decided to help the Chinese emperor when it realised that he was in serious trouble.

Western commanders, such as the American Frederick West and the Briton Charles 'Chinese' Gordon, helped the emperor's 'Ever Victorious Army' to recapture Nanjing and to defeat the rebellion.

ASIA

THE INDIAN MUTINY
India, 1857–58

For 200 years, the British East India Company ruled India, but many Indians resented the way it treated them. In 1857, Indian soldiers in the Company's army mutinied (rebelled). After the mutiny was crushed, the Company was abolished and India came under direct British rule.

ASIA

◀ **Trouble in the ranks**
Indian soldiers (sepoys) fight against their European officers during the fateful Indian Mutiny.

GARIBALDI AND THE REDSHIRTS
Italy, 1860

For Italians, 1860 was the 'Year of Miracles'. It was the year that Giuseppe Garibaldi and his Redshirts – just over 1000 volunteers – beat armies of twice their size to free Sicily and Naples from their Spanish Bourbon ruler.

Garibaldi was one of three towering figures in Italy's struggle for unification. The others were Giuseppe Mazzini, who inspired the struggle, and Camillo Cavour of Piedmont, who helped to force Austria out of northern Italy. A united Italy was proclaimed in 1861, though Rome still had to be won.

EUROPE

THE AMERICAN CIVIL WAR
USA, 1861–65

In 1861, the year Abraham Lincoln became President of the United States, slavery was forbidden in the North, but there were 4 million black slaves in the South. Fearing that they might lose their 'right' to their slaves, a group of Southern states broke away from the Union and formed their own rebel nation – the Confederacy.

War soon broke out, for Lincoln was determined to preserve the United States as one nation. The North had more men, more industries and more money, but the South fought gallantly and had an inspiring general in Robert E. Lee. The war ended on April 9, 1865, when Lee finally surrendered to General Ulysses S. Grant.

AMERICAS

| 1850 | 1860 | 1870 | 1880 |

EUROPE

THE CHARGE OF THE LIGHT BRIGADE
The Crimea, 1854

Forty years of peace in Europe came to an end in 1853, when Russia attacked Turkey. Britain and France, anxious to prevent Russia from becoming too powerful, sent armies to the Crimea.

Britain's Light Brigade – a cavalry brigade – won fame for the bravery of its men, when a mistake over orders sent it charging directly towards the Russian cannons.

EUROPE

THEORY OF EVOLUTION
England, 1859

Charles Darwin, an English scientist, shook the world in 1859 with his book *On the Origin of Species*. Darwin put forward the theory that species evolve (develop) through natural selection over long periods of time. Human beings, said Darwin, did not simply appear, but developed from apes, which themselves evolved from more primitive forms of life. This upset many people because it conflicted with the Bible's story of how God created the world in seven days.

◀ **Carer** The English nurse Florence Nightingale won praise for her work during the Crimean War, when she saved many lives.

OCEANIA

ACROSS THE OUTBACK
Australia, 1860–61

Robert O'Hara Burke, from Ireland, and William Wills, not long out of England, burned with the same desire: to be the first Europeans to cross Australia from south to north. Their team set out from Melbourne in 1860, and reached the Gulf of Carpentaria on the north coast after many hazards.

On the way back, they missed a rendezvous with a relief team by a few hours. By this stage they had been without adequate supplies for weeks. Both Burke and Wills died from hunger and exhaustion. Another member of their team, John King, was helped by Aborigines (local black people), who had the skills needed for survival in the desert. King was rescued by a search party in September 1861.

EUROPE

UNITED BY 'BLOOD AND IRON'
Germany, 1864–71

For Count Otto von Bismarck of Prussia, great issues were settled, not by speeches, but by 'blood and iron'. True to this policy, he set out to unite the many different states of Germany into a single nation.

First, he made war against Denmark, with Austria as an ally. Then he turned against Austria. In 1870, he provoked the French emperor, Napoleon III, into declaring war. The French were defeated at Sadowa, and Paris was starved into submission. France was further humiliated when Wilhelm I of Prussia was crowned Emperor of Germany at Versailles. To complete his task, Bismarck made the French sign a peace treaty surrendering the territories of Alsace and Lorraine to Germany.

▲ **Surrounded** Custer and his men face impossible odds.

CUSTER'S LAST STAND
USA, 1876

The Black Hills of South Dakota had been set aside as a hunting ground for the Sioux and Cheyenne people, but they were ordered to leave after gold was found. Two great chiefs, Sitting Bull and Crazy Horse, called their people to gather on the Little Bighorn River, and Colonel Custer rode to attack them with the 7th Cavalry. He and his 210 men were all killed.

THE BOXER REBELLION
China, 1899–1900

Western missionaries, diplomats and trading companies began moving into China after the Opium Wars. But the humiliation of those wars had produced strong anti-Western feelings among many Chinese.

In 1899 a semi-religious secret society called the Boxers (their full name was 'Righteous and Harmonious Fists') started by killing Western missionaries and Chinese Christian converts. Believing that their martial art – a form of boxing – protected them against bullets, the Boxers attacked the foreign embassies in Beijing. Rescue arrived after an eight-week siege, but the international relief force then went on to loot Beijing's Forbidden City.

ASIA

BLOODY SUNDAY
Russia, 1905

St Petersburg was bitterly cold on Sunday, January 2, 1905, as 200 000 people marched on the tsar's Winter Palace, singing hymns. With wages low, factories on strike, and no political freedom, they were turning to the tsar for help. Suddenly, the cavalry moved in, sabres flashing. Then the infantry opened fire. At the end, 500 marchers lay dead in the snow.

Riots and unrest spread to other cities, and in Odessa the sailors on the battleship *Potemkin* killed their officers.

EUROPE

◀ **Mutiny** Sailors pose on the battleship *Potemkin* during the Russian revolution of 1905.

THE LAST EMPEROR
China, 1912

With the power of the Manchu emperors crumbling, and warlords causing chaos in many areas, a full-scale revolution broke out in China in 1911. Its leader was a doctor called Sun Yat-sen, and he became president of the new Chinese Republic.

The six-year-old emperor, Puyi, abdicated in February 1912, and was allowed to continue living in Beijing's Forbidden City on a generous pension until 1924. However, Sun Yat-sen resigned after only two months, to make way for the real power behind the revolution, General Yuan Shikai. China then entered a long period of civil unrest.

ASIA

1890   **1900**   **1910**   **1920**

THE SCRAMBLE FOR AFRICA
Europe and Africa, 1880–1900

Most of Africa was still ruled by Africans in 1880, but 20 years later, apart from Liberia and Ethiopia, Europeans were in control everywhere. The 'Scramble for Africa' was a feverish competition between Britain, France, Portugal, Germany and Italy, with Belgium's King Leopold making a personal fortune out of labour in the Congo.

Yet profit was not the only motive. The explorer David Livingstone had exposed the miseries of the slave trade, and many colonisers thought they were bringing civilisation to what they still regarded as the 'Dark Continent.'

▶ **Success** Francisco ('Pancho') Villa sits in the Mexican presidential palace in 1914.

AFRICA

THE ANGLO–BOER WAR
South Africa, 1899–1902

The discovery of gold, in 1866, in the Boer republic of the Transvaal made some Britons very envious. War broke out in 1899, with early victories going to the Boers, who were skilled marksmen and good guerrilla fighters. Lord Kitchener defeated the Boers by burning their crops, and herding their women and children into the world's first concentration camps.

AMERICAS

MEXICO'S 30–YEAR REVOLUTION
Mexico, 1910–40

Three centuries of Spanish rule left Mexico with a huge gap between rich and poor. From 1910, the country had a series of revolutions, some of them led by legendary figures, such as Emiliano Zapata – a fierce champion of the Indians – and Pancho Villa, a former bandit. The troubles ended when the country's large estates were broken up and given to small farmers.

EUROPE

VOTES FOR WOMEN
Derby Day Martyr, Epsom, 1913

Emily Davison became a martyr (victim) in the cause of votes for women when she flung herself under the hooves of King George V's racehorse at the Epsom Derby in June 1913. Women in Britain and in many other countries at that time did not have the right to vote for a government. Those who campaigned for votes for women were known as Suffragettes – from the word *suffrage*, meaning 'the right to vote'.

▲ **Pioneer** Emmeline Pankhurst, whose image adorns this medal, led Britain's Suffragettes.

History of the world

ASSASSINATION AT SARAJEVO
Bosnia, 1914

The major powers in Europe were on a collision course in 1914. Nationalism increased many rivalries over trade and colonies, and Germany's Kaiser Wilhelm II had thrown down a challenge to Britain's power at sea.

The Balkans were specially tense, and when a Serbian fanatic assassinated the heir to the Austro-Hungarian throne at Sarajevo, Austria declared war on Serbia. Russia responded by calling up its armies, and within weeks Germany and Austria were at war with France, Russia and Britain. 'The lamps are going out all over Europe', said the British Foreign Secretary, Lord Grey. 'We shall not see them lit again in our lifetime.'

▲ **Fatal shot** The shooting in Sarajevo of Archduke Francis Ferdinand on June 28, 1914, led directly to the First World War.

EUROPE

THE EASTER RISING
Ireland, 1916

On Easter Monday, 1916, Irish patriots led by James Connolly seized the Post Office in Dublin, and declared an end to centuries of British rule. They gave up after five days of heavy bombardment, and 15 rebels were shot by firing squads.

One result of these executions was the formation of the Irish Republican Army, which fought a vicious war with the 'Black and Tans', recruited from British ex-servicemen. In 1921 this war was ended by a treaty that divided Ireland into a Catholic South and a Protestant North. The treaty led to civil war in the South, and IRA chief Michael Collins was assassinated by other Irishmen for signing it.

EUROPE

THE WALL STREET CRASH
New York, 1929

Americans went on a share-buying spree in the 'Roaring Twenties'. With share values soaring on Wall Street, they borrowed money to invest, in the hope that prices would be even higher by the time they sold. But shares can go down, as well as up, and in October, 1929, they fell sharply.

Men who had lost fortunes shot themselves or jumped out of skyscrapers. The Crash also led to a worldwide Depression. Banks called in loans, factories shut down, and workers lost their jobs. Unemployment reached 3 million in Britain, and nearly 6 million in Germany.

AMERICAS

1910   1920   193

THE FIRST WORLD WAR
Worldwide, 1914–18

Germany's plan in the war that broke out in 1914 was to knock out France, then turn east to face Russia. But the expected quick victory did not come. Instead, the Western Front was bogged down in trench warfare. Soldiers lived in a hell of bursting shells, machine-gun fire, barbed wire and deep mud. Ypres, the Somme and Verdun became places linked with heroism and sacrifice. The tide finally turned against Germany when America entered the war in 1917. An armistice (truce) was signed in November 1918.

▼ **Hell on Earth** A soldier takes cover in a trench in 1917.

WORLD

THE BOLSHEVIK REVOLUTION
Russia, 1917–20

There were two revolutions in Russia in 1917. The first, led by liberals and the moderate socialist Alexander Kerensky, overthrew the tsar. The second, led by Vladimir Lenin, drove out Kerensky and brought the communist Bolsheviks to power.

The tsar fell during an epidemic of strikes, food riots and military mutinies caused by shattering defeats in the war against Germany. Deserters were flocking home from the front, and Lenin won power because he offered land, bread and peace at any price. He found many supporters, but was opposed by the anti-Bolshevik White Russians, who started a civil war. They were eventually defeated by Leon Trotsky and the Red Army in 1920.

EUROPE

DECADE OF THE DICTATORS
Europe, 1930s

Three ruthless dictators rose to power in Europe during the 1930s. In Germany, Nazi Party leader Adolf Hitler became Chancellor in 1933, and turned Germany into a dictatorship. When he took over Austria and part of Czechoslovakia, Britain and France protested, but did nothing that might cause war.

The communist dictator Joseph Stalin ruled the Soviet Union with an iron fist. He forced peasants to give their land and crops to the state, causing a famine in which 7 million died. Opponents were shot, or sent to icy prison camps in Siberia.

In Italy, the Fascist dictator Benito Mussolini dreamed of rebuilding the Roman Empire, but got no further than invading Ethiopia.

EUROPE

THE LONG MARCH
China, 1934–5
Mao Zedong started the Long March in October, 1934, with 100 000 men. He finished, 368 days later, with 10 000. The rest had perished in a 9600 km (6000 mile) trek across mountains, ravines, deserts and swamps. The march was a desperate bid by Mao and his communist army to escape from the Nationalists of Chiang Kai-shek. The war was called off temporarily in 1936 for both sides to fight the Japanese.

◀ **Sitting pretty** As leader of the communists, Mao has the luxury of a pony, while everyone else walks on the Long March.

THE COLD WAR BEGINS
Worldwide, 1945–61
In the words of Britain's wartime leader, Winston Churchill, an 'Iron Curtain' fell across Europe after the Second World War. The Soviet Union was in control of countries captured by the Red Army, and was doing all it could to separate them from the rest of Europe.

In 1948, America helped to save West Berlin from a Soviet blockade. It also led United Nations forces in driving back communist invaders in the Korean War of 1950-3. However, there was little that anyone could do when the Soviets decided to build a wall dividing Berlin in 1961. This became a visible symbol of the Cold War.

FREEDOM AT MIDNIGHT
India, 1947
Nearly two centuries of British rule in India ended at midnight on August 14, 1947. India's Muslims, led by Muhammad Ali Jinnah, feared that they might be swamped by millions of Hindus, and so founded a separate nation, Pakistan.

In a terrible twist of fate, the Hindu leader Mahatma Gandhi was killed in 1948 by a Hindu fanatic for being 'too tolerant' to Muslims.

◀ **Man of peace** Mahatma Gandhi led the calls for Indian independence, but insisted that all campaigns must be nonviolent.

AMERICA'S TURBULENT YEARS
America, 1949–68
Americans, emerging rich and confident from the Second World War, became uneasy when the Soviets exploded an atomic bomb in 1949. Senator Joseph McCarthy began a hunt for communists that ruined many lives and careers. However, he went too far, and ended in disgrace when he attacked the US army.

President Kennedy brought hope to America, and his assassination in 1963 shocked the entire world. Martin Luther King, who led the struggle for black civil rights, was also assassinated – but not before setting out his vision of racial harmony with the words, 'I have a dream'.

WORLD   **ASIA**   **AMERICAS**

---

30   **1940**   **1950**

THE SPANISH CIVIL WAR
Spain, 1936–9
Spain in the Depression years had many problems and many people who thought they had the answers: the Church, the army, communists and socialists, among others.

In 1936, General Francisco Franco led the army in a nationalist revolt against the elected Republican government. Help for the left-wing Republicans came from Stalin and from various International Brigades – volunteers, mainly from France, Britain and America. However, Franco won after three years of savage war, helped by troops, weapons and planes supplied by Mussolini and Hitler.

WORLD

THE WORLD AT WAR
Worldwide, 1939–45
In September 1939, Hitler invaded Poland and plunged the world back into war. Russia was drawn in when it was invaded by the Germans in June 1941. And America had no choice after Japan's surprise attack on Pearl Harbor in December 1941. Peace returned to Europe in May 1945, and to the Far East in September that year.

ASIA

THE ARAB–ISRAELI CONFLICT
1948–
Since the early 1900s, Jews from all over Europe had dreamed of a haven in Palestine, their 'Promised Land'. But Arabs were already living there. Britain, which administered the area, tried to limit Jewish arrivals, then handed the problem over to the United Nations.

The UN decided to divide Palestine, to create the Jewish state of Israel. The birth of this country, in May 1948, led to the first of five Arab-Israeli wars. It also created a massive refugee problem as thousands of Palestinian Arabs fled from their homes into neighbouring countries.

◀ **Humiliation** A US military policeman searches a wounded German soldier in Normandy, France, in July 1944.

ASIA

UNDER MAO'S HEEL
China, 1949–69
Mao Zedong was ruthless in pushing through reforms after the communist victory in China. Women were given the vote, education was provided for all, and the peasants were given land. But 2 million landowners were executed, and opponents were crushed, under a system of control that even encouraged children to spy on, and denounce, their own parents.

In 1958, when Mao planned a 'Great Leap Forward' to modernise China, nobody dared criticise targets that were set too high. As a result, the 'Leap' brought famine instead of progress. In the Cultural Revolution of 1966-9, Mao unleashed schoolchildren – the Red Guards – to storm the land and root out his enemies, with devastating effects.

▶ **Peace** By 1970, many Americans wanted no more to do with Vietnam.

VIETNAM'S 30-YEAR AGONY
Vietnam, 1945-75
In 1945, when the French tried to reclaim their empire in Indochina, they clashed with the nationalist leader Ho Chi Minh. Ho, who was also a communist, fought for an independent Vietnam, and in 1954 he won the northern half of the country. America sent aid to the South, to prevent a communist takeover, and was gradually dragged deeper into a savage war against the communists. America withdrew in 1975, leaving behind a devastated land.

ASIA

THE SUEZ CRISIS
Egypt, 1956
President Gamal Abdul Nasser made himself wildly popular in Egypt when he nationalised the Suez Canal and declared that its profits would no longer go to shareholders in Britain and France. Both countries believed that control of the canal was vital to protect their oil supplies, so they hatched a plot with Israel.

After Israel attacked Egypt, the British and French landed troops, 'to keep Israeli and Egyptian forces apart'. This last gamble of old-style imperialism caused a world outcry, and the invaders had to withdraw.

AFRICA

THE WIND OF CHANGE
Africa, 1960
British Prime Minister Harold Macmillan said in 1960 that the demand for freedom was sweeping through Africa like a 'wind of change'. This wind was often resisted by white settlers, north and south.

In Algeria, independence was won in 1962, but only after a savage war. In Kenya, a murderous rebellion by a secret society, the Mau Mau, was crushed before the country gained independence in 1963. Northern Rhodesia became Zambia in 1964, but the following year the white government of Southern Rhodesia tried to set up its own nation. It gave up in 1980, after a long war against African guerrillas, and the country became Zimbabwe.

AFRICA

THE SWINGING SIXTIES
Britain, 1960s
A burst of youthful talent and energy in Britain brought about the 'Swinging Sixties'. The music of The Beatles and the Rolling Stones took the world by storm. Young men dressed like peacocks in London's Carnaby Street, while girls paraded down the King's Road, Chelsea, in Mary Quant designs. Revolution was in the air.

In America, where Bill Haley and Elvis Presley had spread the message of rock 'n' roll in the Fifties, Bob Dylan sang his protest songs, while the hippies made a gentler protest under their banners proclaiming 'Flower Power'. In France, however, protests turned to riots when students marched in the streets of Paris in May 1968.

EUROPE

1950   **1960**   **1970**

EUROPE

TOWARDS UNITY IN EUROPE
Europe, 1951-
After tearing itself apart in two great wars, Europe emerged in 1945 into a world of two superpowers: the USA and the USSR. The search for European unity arose against this background.

In 1951, France, West Germany, Italy, Belgium, the Netherlands and Luxembourg combined their iron and steel resources. The same countries, known as 'the Six', set up the Common Market in 1957. They were later joined in the European Union by nine other countries. Britain joined in 1973, but held back from the new currency, the Euro, which 11 EU members adopted in January 1999.

EUROPE

THE HUNGARIAN REVOLUTION
Hungary, 1956
When the new Soviet leader, Nikita Khrushchev, denounced Stalin's tyranny three years after the dictator's death, he released a pent-up demand for freedom in Eastern Europe. Riots in Hungary brought Imre Nagy to power, and he promised free elections. He also said that Hungary would withdraw from the Warsaw Pact – the Soviet military pact set up to oppose NATO, the Western military alliance. Khrushchev would not allow this, and sent Red Army tanks into Budapest. The Hungarians fought bravely, but were soon crushed. Nagy was executed in secret, and about 190 000 Hungarians fled to the West to escape communism.

WORLD

THE COMPUTER REVOLUTION
1960s
ENIAC, a computer used at Pennsylvania University in 1946, filled a large room, and contained 18 000 electronic valves. Since then, computers have became faster, smaller and cheaper – thanks to the silicon chip, which came into widespread use in the 1960s. Chips, with tiny electronic circuits printed on them, are now used in every aspect of life, from aircraft to domestic toasters. The company IBM introduced the personal computer (PC) in 1981.

▶ **Pride of place** The first two men on the Moon raise the American flag.

AMERICAS

THE FIRST MEN ON THE MOON
Space, 1969
The American astronaut Neil Armstrong set foot on the Moon on July 20, 1969, with the words: 'That's one small step for a man, one giant leap for mankind.' America had won a race that began in 1957, when the Soviet Union launched Sputnik 1, the first man-made satellite to orbit the Earth. Armstrong was joined on the Moon by Edwin (Buzz) Aldrin, while Michael Collins orbited above them.

▲ **Joint effort** West Germans climb onto the Berlin Wall on the night of November 9, 1989.

RETURN OF THE AYATOLLAH
Iran, 1979

There was wild celebration in Iran in 1979, over the return of the Ayatollah Khomeini, following the overthrow of the country's pro-Western ruler, the Shah. Khomeini had been exiled for opposing the Shah's attempts to modernise Iran, and he quickly enforced Islamic law in its full rigour. Thieves, for instance, could have their hands chopped off, and women were not allowed outdoors unless they were covered from head to toe.

THE WALL COMES TUMBLING DOWN
Berlin, 1989

On November 9, 1989, the people of Berlin began to tear down the Berlin Wall, for 28 years a symbol of division, oppression and the Cold War. The Wall fell in a year packed with drama: East Germany, Poland, Hungary, Bulgaria, Czechoslovakia and Romania all broke free from Soviet domination in 1989. The communist empire collapsed because it was incapable of delivering either prosperity or freedom to its many people.

The Soviet Union itself was to fall apart in 1991, when many of its republics declared themselves independent.

◄ **Air raid** Tracer bullets light the sky over Baghdad during the Gulf War.

THE GULF WAR
Iraq, 1990–1

Saddam Hussein, President of Iraq, threatened Western oil supplies when he invaded the tiny state of Kuwait in 1990. An America-led coalition of 29 nations defeated Saddam's forces in Operation 'Desert Storm', but did not succeed in toppling him. Instead, Iraq was placed under economic sanctions (restrictions) until Saddam could convince the United Nations that he was not building up weapons of mass destruction.

GOOD FRIDAY PEACE HOPES
Northern Ireland, 1998

An agreement made on Good Friday, 1998, set out to end a conflict that brought nearly 30 years of terror to Northern Ireland, and caused some 3500 deaths.

The violence began in 1968, when a demand by Catholics for civil rights led to riots. The British army was sent to keep the peace, but became a target of the rebel IRA. The Good Friday agreement won massive support in both Northern and Southern Ireland, but was tested to the limit by the IRA's refusal to give up its weapons for the sake of peace.

EUROPE **ASIA** **EUROPE**

1980   **1990**   **2000**

SOLIDARITY MAKES A STAND
Poland, 1981

People behind the Iron Curtain who objected to Soviet rule were normally dealt with ruthlessly. Lech Walesa was different, for he lived to fight on. Walesa was an electrician in the shipyard of Gdansk, Poland, when he helped to found Solidarity, the first free trade union in Eastern Europe. He was soon dismissed, but this, along with food shortages, led to riots and strikes. In 1981, the communist regime banned Solidarity and jailed Walesa, but he was freed in less than a year.

His treatment was less harsh than that of the Czechs, who tried to gain their own freedom in 1968. The 'Prague Spring' of Alexander Dubček was mercilessly crushed by Soviet tanks.

AFRICA

THE ROAD TO FREEDOM
South Africa, 1990

Apartheid, the racist system that kept a white government in power in South Africa, vanished with remarkable speed after Nelson Mandela was freed from jail. Mandela, who in 1964 had been given a life sentence for treason, went on to win the first elections in which black South Africans were allowed to vote. The struggle had cost many lives, with one of the worst incidents being a massacre of 69 African demonstrators at Sharpeville in 1960.

Under Apartheid, the best jobs, schools, houses and farmlands were reserved for whites, and Africans in white-only areas had to carry passes.

▶ **Fear in the Balkans** Ethnic Albanians flee from Serb police in the Yugoslav province of Kosovo, in March 1998.

EUROPE

THE BREAKUP OF YUGOSLAVIA
The Balkans, 1991

After the death in 1980 of Marshal Tito, the communist leader of Yugoslavia, the country began to fragment. Centuries of hostility between populations of Serbs, Croats, Slovenes, Christians and Muslims came to the surface. Croatia and Slovenia declared their independence. Civilians were murdered as war spread to Bosnia and Kosovo. In 1999 NATO launched attacks on Yugoslavia in defence of Kosovo's Albanian population.

WORLD

A STRICKEN PLANET
Worldwide

With 6 billion people on Earth, mankind has become, by sheer weight of numbers, a threat to the planet. Carbon dioxide in the atmosphere has risen by 25 per cent since 1800, increasing the risk of global warming. Rain forests are being destroyed in Amazonia. A hole in the ozone layer allows harmful rays to get through. Industrial pollution falls as acid rain.

In 1992 the United Nations held an 'Earth Summit' to begin tackling such threats.

People who changed the world

The great achievements of the human race belong to no one group, nation or time. They are spread among dedicated individuals who, through inspiration or sheer energy, broke new ground in art, music, entertainment or science – or led their nation to triumph or disaster.

Artists and architects

Botticelli, Sandro (1445–1510)

Artist of the Italian Renaissance in Florence. He painted mythical subjects like *The Birth of Venus* and *Primavera* ('Spring') in a graceful style of great beauty.

Botticelli was not his real name. He was born Alessandro di Vanni Filipepi, but he was sent to live with a goldsmith called Botticello, whose name he gratefully adopted.

Bruegel, Pieter, the Elder (c.1525–69)

Flemish painter famous for his landscapes, which show what everyday life was like in Holland in the 16th century.

His nickname was 'Peasant Bruegel' because of his lively and detailed pictures of village life. He shows the way that people farmed, what they ate and drank, and the customs and entertainments of the time.

Cézanne, Paul (1839–1906)

French painter, thought to be the greatest of the 19th century.

Cézanne started as one of the Impressionists, a group of artists who used paint to make an 'impression' of a subject. Cézanne moved on to create his own style, saying that he wanted 'to make of Impressionism something solid and durable, like the art of the Museums'.

One of his best friends was the French writer Émile Zola, but the two fell out after Zola published a book in which Cézanne thought he saw an unflattering account of himself.

Constable, John (1776–1837)

English landscape artist admired for his pictures of the English countryside.

Constable was skilled in painting a scene in a natural way, as if it was exactly as he had seen it. In fact, his paintings were all carefully planned. *The Hay Wain* and *View on the Stour* both won gold medals when they were exhibited in Paris in 1824, but many of his works remained unsold during his lifetime, causing him long bouts of depression.

Le Corbusier (1887–1965)

French architect who had a major impact on building styles in the 20th century.

Le Corbusier was the first architect to design multi-storey blocks of flats, and in the 1920s he created houses on stilts to make better use of space – he called them 'machines for living in'. He was also important for his ideas on town planning, which are still used today.

Giotto (c.1267–1337)

Italian painter and architect who is considered to be the founder of modern painting.

Giotto was the first artist to paint people in a natural way. The saints in his paintings are solid and lifelike, and his illustrations of Bible stories have more dramatic power than those by many earlier artists.

Not much is known about Giotto's life, but it is said that he was discovered at the age of ten by the painter Cimabue, who found him drawing a lamb on a flat stone. Cimabue took Giotto as his pupil, only to find that the boy was a better painter than he was.

Goya, Franciso de (1746–1828)

Spanish artist best known for his portraits of the Spanish royal family, and for his powerful images of war. Goya also painted simple scenes of everyday life.

Goya did not paint flattering portraits of the Spanish royal family; in fact, his paintings have been described as making them look like 'prosperous grocers'. Goya eventually got into trouble with the authorities over paintings which were considered indecent, and he had to appear before a Spanish religious court to defend himself and his work.

Kandinsky, Wassily (1866–1944)

Russian artist who led the way in creating abstract art, which avoids showing objects as they appear in the real world. Instead, it uses abstract colours and shapes.

Kandinsky was born in Moscow and spent much of his life in Russia. He also worked in Germany, where he founded an influential art group called 'The Blue Rider'. He left Germany when the Nazis came to power and settled in France.

Leonardo da Vinci (1452–1519)

Outstanding genius of the Renaissance in Florence. Leonardo da Vinci was a true

▼ **English idyll** Constable specialised in painting the English countryside.

▲ **Impressions** Monet created this misty view of Parliament in 1904.

Renaissance man, skilled in painting, architecture, sculpture and science.

His most famous work is the *Mona Lisa*, which he painted between 1500 and 1504. He also left behind him notebooks full of sketches of amazing inventions: aeroplanes, helicopters, even a submarine and a diving suit. He seems to have been interested in everything. It is thought that he nearly worked out how blood circulates – 150 years before this was officially discovered.

Michelangelo (1475–1564)
Italian sculptor, architect, painter and poet, and one of the greatest artists of the 16th century.

Michelangelo was outstanding both at sculpture and painting. His *David*, which is in Florence, is a masterpiece carved out of one huge slab of marble. He used to go to the marble quarries himself to choose his own materials. Between 1508 and 1512 Michelangelo completed one of his greatest works, the ceiling of the Sistine Chapel in the Vatican in Rome.

Monet, Claude (1840–1926)
French painter, thought to be the finest of the Impressionists.

It was a painting by Monet, called *An Impression, Sunrise*, that gave the Impressionist movement its name. Other works for which Monet is famous include his pictures of water lilies growing in his garden at Giverny, France. He often made a series of paintings of the same subject in different light.

Moore, Henry Spencer (1898–1986)
British sculptor who made huge abstract shapes and figures in wood, stone and metal.

Moore believed that sculpture should look natural. His style is easy to recognise because of its curving lines, and because many of his sculptures have a hole through them.

During the Second World War, when he was an official war artist, Moore made many powerful drawings of people taking refuge in air-raid shelters.

Palladio, Andrea (1508–80)
Italian architect who developed a mathematical method of planning buildings.

He was deeply influenced by Roman style and is best known for the churches he built in Venice, as well as his villas for rich families in the northern Italian countryside.

His real name was Andrea della Gondola. An admiring amateur architect called Trissino named him 'Palladio', after Pallas Athene – the ancient Greek goddess of wisdom – and the name stuck.

Picasso, Pablo (1881–1973)

'I paint objects as I think them, not as I see them.'

Spanish painter and sculptor – one of the most important artists of the 20th century.

Picasso was a pioneer of the movement called Cubism, an early form of abstract art.

One of his most famous paintings is *Guernica*, painted in 1937 during the Spanish Civil War. It offers a passionate comment on the savagery and destruction of war.

Rembrandt van Rijn (1606–69)
Dutch master painter, thought to be the greatest artist of the 17th century.

Rembrandt is famous for his portraits, particularly of old people. He also painted about 60 self-portraits, which show his growing sadness with life over the years. After the death of his wealthy wife in 1642, Rembrandt became steadily poorer, and by 1656 he was declared bankrupt. In later life he turned to painting more Biblical subjects.

Rodin, Auguste (1840–1917)
French sculptor whose realistic treatment of the human figure marked the beginning of a new direction in sculpture.

Some of his most famous works are *The Thinker* (1904) and *The Kiss* (1886). When Rodin first exhibited *The Age of Bronze* in 1877, people thought that he had taken the cast of the sculpture from a live model, as it was so lifelike.

Turner, Joseph Mallord William (1775–1851)
This great British artist painted highly unusual landscapes. He is famous for his use of colour to show how light changes at different times of day, and in different types of weather conditions.

He never married and lived a very private life. When he died he left 300 paintings and 20 000 watercolours and drawings to the nation. One of his best-known works is called *Rain, Steam and Speed*.

Van Gogh, Vincent (1853–90)
Dutch painter known for his self-portraits, landscapes of France, and his still-lifes such as *Sunflowers* (1888).

He influenced many modern painters. Van Gogh suffered from bouts of mental illness. After an argument with Gauguin, a fellow artist, he cut off part of his own ear.

In May 1890, he moved to the French village of Auvers-sur-Oise, where he shot himself two months later.

People who changed the world

Velázquez, Diego (1599–1660)

Spanish painter admired for his fine portraits.

Velázquez always paid great attention to detail, and painted in a very realistic way, whether his subject was the Spanish royal family, or his own household servants.

Other artists at the Spanish court were jealous of Velázquez and claimed that he could not paint anything other than heads, so the king organised a competition on a historical theme. Velázquez easily won with his painting of the expulsion of the Moors from Spain by Philip III.

Vermeer, Jan (1632–75)

Dutch artist who painted small masterpieces of domestic life.

Vermeer was little known during his lifetime and came to be recognised for the genius that he was more than 200 years after his death. Today, only about 35 paintings are accepted as his work.

Wren, Sir Christopher (1632–1723)

'If you seek his monument, look around you.'

One of Britain's greatest architects. Wren rebuilt more than 50 London churches after the Great Fire of 1666, among them St Paul's Cathedral, regarded as his masterpiece.

If he had died at the age of 30, Wren would have been remembered as a scientist. In 1657 he was Professor of Astronomy at Gresham College, London. After the Great Fire, he drew up plans for rebuilding the whole of London, with broad, straight streets. Most of these ideas were rejected.

Wright, Frank Lloyd (1869–1959)

Acclaimed American architect who was a brilliant engineer.

Frank Lloyd Wright designed many buildings to fit into their natural environment, like 'Fallingwater', a house of terraces over a waterfall (1936). Another radical design is the Guggenheim Museum in New York (1959), shaped like a continuous spiral.

Lloyd Wright also created interior designs and furniture that would harmonise with his ingenious buildings.

Composers

Bach, Johann Sebastian (1685–1750)

German composer who set new standards in music and was a major influence on Mozart.

Orphaned before he was ten, Bach went to live with his older brother, an organist. The young Bach would copy out music until late at night. He rose to be musical director for the German city of Leipzig. Among his best-loved works are the *St Matthew Passion* (1729) and the *Mass in B Minor* (1738).

Beethoven, Ludwig van (1770–1827)

The most influential composer of the 19th century. Beethoven was born in Germany, but went to live in Vienna. He wrote a wide range of music and was a brilliant pianist, but was forced to give up performing after he started going deaf in 1801.

He continued composing, and completed some of his finest work in the 1820s, when he could hear nothing.

▲ **In harmony** 'Fallingwater' is a memorial to Frank Lloyd Wright's genius.

Brahms, Johannes (1833–97)

German composer and pianist who wrote many songs and works for orchestra. He also composed the influential *A German Requiem* (1866), an important piece of Protestant church music based on Biblical texts rather than the Catholic Requiem Mass.

Brahms breathed new life into the great traditions of the past, when other composers were trying their hardest to be revolutionary.

Chopin, Frédéric (1810–49)

Polish composer and pianist who settled in Paris.

Chopin helped to establish the piano as a solo instrument. He played in public for the first time at the age of eight, and wrote his first composition when only 15. His melancholy piano nocturnes explored new depths of musical expression.

Gershwin, George (1898–1937)

American composer, perhaps best known for *Rhapsody in Blue* (1924), a concert piece for piano, which combines classical music with jazz.

Gershwin also composed the folk opera *Porgy and Bess* (1935) as well as many popular musicals and songs, with words written by his brother, Ira. He taught himself to play the piano, and went on to publish his first song at the age of 14.

Handel, George Frideric (1685–1759)

German-born composer who settled in London, becoming a British subject in 1726.

Handel's father intended his son to be a lawyer, but changed his mind when he realised how hard his son had practised music in secret. Handel wrote operas and oratorios, such as *Messiah* (1742). One of his most popular orchestral pieces is the *Water Music* (1717), written for George I. Handel is buried in Westminster Abbey, London.

Haydn, Joseph (1732–1809)

Austrian composer – the most celebrated of his day.

Haydn is considered to be the father of both the symphony and the string quartet. He wrote more than 100 symphonies, but was eventually overshadowed by two of his pupils – the young Mozart and, later, Beethoven.

Hildegarde of Bingen (1098–1179)

Mystical German nun who wrote religious music.

Hildegarde was a healer and philosopher, as well as a musician. As a child she was weak and ill. She was never taught how to read and write, though she did learn to sing psalms. She later composed music, which was largely forgotten until the 1980s.

Mozart, Wolfgang Amadeus (1756–91)

Austrian composer of genius – a child prodigy and one of the greatest

▲ **Music cover** Mozart composed his opera *Don Giovanni* in 1787.

composers ever. When he was six, Mozart and his older sister were taken on a tour of Europe by their father, performing to the wealthy families of Austria, France and England.

Mozart composed his first pieces for piano at the age of five. Later works included hugely popular operas such as *The Marriage of Figaro* (1786) and *The Magic Flute* (1791), choral music, concertos, sonatas and symphonies.

In spite of his genius, Mozart never found steady work. He died in poverty aged 35.

Schönberg, Arnold (1874–1951)

Austrian-born composer who invented the radical 'twelve-note method' of composing.

In 1925 Schönberg became a teacher at the Berlin Academy of the Arts but he left Berlin for Paris when the Nazis came to power. In 1933 he went to the USA and settled there. His music is also called 'atonal', a term which he disliked.

Schubert, Franz (1797–1828)

Austrian composer who is known for his many beautiful songs, called 'lieder'.

Schubert was a schoolteacher, but gave up his job to become a full-time composer. He was a admirer of Beethoven, but never had the courage to speak to him. Schubert wrote nine symphonies, together with piano works and some deeply expressive chamber music.

Stravinsky, Igor (1882–1971)

Russian-born composer whose ballet *The Rite of Spring* caused a riot at its first night in Paris in 1913. Stravinsky's other

well-known works include the ballets *The Firebird* (1910) and *Petrushka* (1912). He spent much of his professional life in Paris, before leaving for the USA in 1939.

Stravinsky's music had a profound effect on other composers in the 20th century, though he once said: 'My music is best understood by children and animals.'

Tchaikovsky, Piotr Ilyich (1840–93)

Russian composer, perhaps best known for his ballets *Swan Lake*, *The Sleeping Beauty* and *The Nutcracker*.

Tchaikovsky gave up his job as a civil servant to compose full time. He married one of his students, but suffered a nervous breakdown and separated from her after only a few weeks. A wealthy widow, whom he never met, gave him an annual grant, which enabled him to complete his 11 operas, six symphonies and many instrumental pieces.

He died after unwisely drinking unboiled water during a cholera epidemic.

Verdi, Giuseppe (1813–1901)

Italian composer who took 19th-century Italian opera to new heights.

During his long life – he was 87 when he died – Verdi composed 27 operas, including *Rigoletto*, *La Traviata*, *Aïda*, *Otello* and *Falstaff*.

For much of Verdi's life, the part of northern Italy where he lived was ruled by Austria. He often got into trouble with Austrian officials because they thought that his operas might encourage Italians to rebel. The Austrians may have had a point: the chorus of exiled Hebrew slaves in Verdi's opera *Nabucco* (1842) became a national song during Italy's struggle for unification in the 1860s.

Wagner, Richard (1813–83)

German composer whose operas had a major impact on 19th-century music, especially opera.

Wagner drew on German myths and legends for many of his operas, among them *Tristan and Isolde*, *Parsifal* and his giant four-part *The Ring of the Nibelung*. His music was bold and dramatic, inspiring strong feelings in admirers and opponents alike. As a composer, Wagner was unusual in that he wrote both the words and the music for his operas. He built his own opera house in the German city of Bayreuth.

⬤ Entertainers (stage, screen and sport)

Ali, Muhammad (1942–)

'Float like a butterfly, sting like a bee.'

US boxer who was world heavyweight champion three times between 1964 and 1980.

He was born Cassius Clay, but changed his name to Muhammad Ali after joining a movement called the Black Muslims. Never shy of publicity, he frequently referred to himself as 'The Greatest'.

Armstrong, Louis (1901–71)

US jazz musician, often known by the nickname 'Satchmo', short for 'Satchelmouth'. He was one of the most influential figures in the world of jazz.

Born in New Orleans, Louis Armstrong was brought up in extreme poverty. He learned to play the cornet, and went on to become a popular trumpeter and singer.

Astaire, Fred (1899–1987)

US singer and dancer who, with Ginger Rogers, formed one of the best-known partnerships in the history of film.

Born Frederick Austerlitz in Omaha, Nebraska, he toured and danced with his sister from the age of seven. Astaire revolutionised the film musical with new forms and styles of dance, which he both devised and performed.

Beatles, The

British pop group who became the most successful of the 20th century, selling more than 1 billion records worldwide.

Formed in Liverpool in 1960, The Beatles were John Lennon, Paul McCartney, George Harrison and Ringo Starr (Richard Starkey). Their first record, 'Love Me Do' (1962), became an instant hit. The group split up in 1970.

Bogart, Humphrey (1899–1957)

US film actor, who often played the part of a tough-guy.

Some of his best-known roles were as the club-owner Rick in *Casablanca* (1942), and the detective Philip Marlowe in *The Big Sleep* (1946). He won an Oscar for *The African Queen* (1951), in which he played a drunken boat captain.

▲ **Heart throb** James Dean starred with Elizabeth Taylor in the film *Giant*.

Brando, Marlon (1924–)

US stage and screen actor famous for his 'method' acting style, which meant being as natural as possible.

Brando shot to fame in *A Streetcar Named Desire* (1951), and won an Oscar for *On the Waterfront* (1954). After turning down an Oscar for his part in *The Godfather* (1972), he bought an island in the Pacific Ocean, where he became a recluse. He emerged to appear in *A Dry White Season* (1989), but has been rarely seen since.

Cagney, James (1899–1986)

US actor who often played the role of a gangster in films during the 1930s and 1940s.

Cagney also starred in comedies, and won an Oscar for his role in the film, *Yankee Doodle Dandy* (1942). He retired in 1961, but returned to make two more films. In 1974

he received a Life Achievement Award from the American Film Institute.

Dean, James (1931–55)

US film actor whose good looks and tragic early death in a car crash made him a legend.

Dean's parts in the films *East of Eden* (1955), *Rebel Without a Cause* (1955) and *Giant* (1956) made him a symbol of rebellious youth. The fact that he used the realistic 'method' style of acting meant that young people everywhere identified with him. He was just 24 when he died in his crashed Porsche.

Dietrich, Marlene (1901–92)

German-born actress and singer who became a Hollywood star and a US citizen in 1939.

Born in Berlin, she appeared in *The Blue Angel* (1930), the first German film with sound. Her acting and seductive, husky

voice caused a sensation, prompting her to move to the United States where she made numerous movies. One of her later films was *Witness for the Prosecution* (1957).

She was also a successful singer, making more than 500 appearances to Allied troops during the Second World War.

Hendrix, Jimi (1942–70)

US rock singer, songwriter, and influential guitarist.

Hendrix had a major impact on rock music with his guitar playing, which included playing the American national anthem by plucking his guitar strings with his teeth.

Born in a poor, black quarter of Seattle, Washington, Hendrix taught himself to play the guitar. With his band, The Jimi Hendrix Experience, he made three successful albums before dying of a drug overdose.

Jackson, Michael (1958–)

US pop star and songwriter who started his career singing with his brothers in their group, The Jackson Five.

Michael Jackson, who first appeared on stage at the age of five, is one of the most successful singers in the world. He has sold more than 45 million copies of his 1982 album, *Thriller*, and in 1991 he signed a recording deal with Sony for $890 million – the biggest such deal ever.

Jordan, Michael (1963–)

US basketball player considered to be the best all-rounder in the history of the game.

Jordan has led his team, the Chicago Bulls, to four victories in the National Basketball Association (NBA) championship. He has also won the NBA award for most valuable player four times.

Jordan caused much surprise when he retired in 1993 to play baseball, but he returned to basketball in 1994.

Monroe, Marilyn (1926–62)

US film star famous for her blonde beauty and image as a sex symbol.

Her real name was Norma Jean Mortenson and she had a hard childhood, spending time in foster homes on account of her mother's mental illness. Monroe starred in several films, including *Gentlemen Prefer Blondes* (1953) and *Some Like it Hot* (1959). She became depressed after the failure of her third marriage and died from an overdose of drugs.

Navratilova, Martina (1956–)

Czech-American tennis player who won the women's singles tournament at Wimbledon a record-breaking nine times.

Born in Prague in the former Czechoslovakia, she played for

her country until 1975, when she fled to the USA. She went on to win 167 singles titles, including the US Open four times, and the Grand Slam (the Australian, French and US Open Championships and Wimbledon) twice.

Olivier, Laurence (1907–89)

British actor, producer and director of stage and screen.

Olivier was a giant of the theatre. When he turned to film, he often produced, directed and starred in his own work, such as *Henry V* (1944), *Hamlet* (1948) and *Richard III* (1956). His Hollywood films included *Marathon Man* (1976). As well as performing, Olivier was also the director of the National Theatre from 1962 to 1973. He was knighted in 1947 and was made Lord Olivier in 1970 – the first actor to receive this honour.

Owens, Jesse (1913–80)

Black American athlete, and one of the greatest sprinters of his generation.

Owens won four gold medals at the Berlin Olympic Games in 1936, and records for sprinting, the relay and the long jump.

Seeing him win, the German leader Adolf Hitler left the stadium, apparently because he refused to award medals to a black man. In 1976 Owens was awarded the Presidential Medal of Freedom.

Presley, Elvis (1935–77)

US singer and actor, nicknamed 'the King', who was one of the world's first rock-and-roll stars.

Elvis began his singing career in a church choir, but was 'discovered' when he made a record privately during his lunch break for his mother at the Memphis Recording Service. He was working as a truck driver at the time.

He created a blend of country-and-western music with traditionally black rhythm-and-blues, selling more than 150 million copies of his records.

Sampras, Pete (1971–)

US tennis player, and one of the best in the history of the game.

Sampras was the youngest player to win the US Open at the age of 19. In December 1998 he became the world's number 1 player for the sixth consecutive year.

Explorers and pioneers

Amundsen, Roald (1872–1928)

Norwegian sailor and explorer, and the first person to reach the South Pole.

Between 1903 and 1906, Amundsen became the first explorer to sail through the Northwest Passage in northern Canada. In 1909 he was beaten

to the North Pole by the American Robert Peary. But Amundsen in turn beat Britain's Captain Scott to the South Pole in December 1911.

Armstrong, Neil (1930–)

'That's one small step for a man, one giant leap for mankind.'

US astronaut who on July 20, 1969 became the first man to set foot on the Moon .

Armstrong was an ace fighter pilot before becoming an astronaut. He flew in the Korean War and tested rocket planes for the US Air Force.

Cabot, John (1425– c.1500)

Italian explorer, the first European to discover the continent of North America.

Cabot was born Giovanni Caboto in Genoa. He was trying to find a route from England to Asia when he landed in Newfoundland, Canada, in 1497. He claimed the land, which he thought was part of Asia, for Henry VII of England, but the king was disappointed that Cabot returned without any gold. Cabot died during a second voyage shortly afterwards.

Columbus, Christopher (1451–1506)

Italian navigator financed by Spain, the first known European to land in the New World (the Americas).

In 1492 Columbus set sail westwards across the Atlantic

▼ Hard hitter Martina Navratilova heads for another Wimbledon victory.

Ocean with an expedition of three ships, in search of Asia. Instead, he discovered the Bahamas, Cuba and Hispaniola.

Columbus made three further voyages of discovery, and became governor of Spain's new colonies in the Caribbean.

▲ **Distant travels** Captain Cook's ships arrive in Tahiti.

Cook, James (1728–79)

British explorer and navigator who made three great voyages in the South Pacific.

On his first voyage (1768-71), Cook became the first European to land on the east coast of Australia, which he called New South Wales. On his second journey (1772-5), he crossed the Antarctic Circle, and on his third (1776-9) he discovered Hawaii, where he was killed by local inhabitants.

Drake, Sir Francis (c.1540–96)

English explorer and navigator, vice-admiral of the English fleet that defeated the Spanish Armada in 1588.

In his ship, *The Golden Hind*, Drake became the first Englishman to sail around the world, a feat for which he was knighted by Elizabeth I. Drake is thought to have introduced

tobacco to England from the West Indies in 1585.

Gagarin, Yuri (1934–68)

Soviet cosmonaut who, on April 12, 1961, became the first human to fly around the Earth in space.

Gagarin's orbit in his capsule Vostok reached a height of 327 km (203 miles) and lasted only 1 hour 48 minutes. He became a hero worldwide, but died in a plane crash while training for a later flight.

Gama, Vasco da (c.1469–1524)

Portuguese explorer and navigator who, in 1498-9, was the first to sail to India via the Cape of Good Hope.

He attempted to set up a colony in Kozhikode in India, but was driven out by Muslim merchants. Later he was appointed Viceroy of India, but lived there for only three months before he died.

Hillary, Sir Edmund (1919-)

New Zealand mountaineer who, in 1953, became the first to reach the summit of Mount Everest, the world's highest peak.

In 1958 Hillary led a British expedition to the South Pole, the first since the fatal journey of Captain Scott in 1911–12.

Livingstone, David (1813–73)

Scottish doctor and missionary who travelled deeper into Africa than any European before him.

Livingstone arrived in Africa in 1841, and discovered the Victoria Falls in 1855. Setting off on a second expedition to locate the source of the Nile, he disappeared in 1866. He was eventually tracked down in 1871 by the Anglo-American journalist Henry Morton Stanley, who greeted him with the words 'Doctor Livingstone, I presume?' Livingstone died of fever two years later.

Magellan, Ferdinand (c.1480–1521)

Portuguese navigator, and the first European to cross the Pacific Ocean.

Because the king of Portugal would not finance his voyage, Magellan offered his services to the king of Spain. He sailed around Cape Horn and reached the Philippines, where he was killed. One of his ships managed to return to Spain, completing the first voyage around the globe.

Polo, Marco (1254–1324)

Venetian merchant, explorer and author. In 1271 he travelled with his father and uncle to the court of Kublai Khan in China. He stayed on for about 16 years, serving as the Khan's ambassador. Returning to Europe, Marco published an account of his travels, which amazed his contemporaries.

 Leaders

Alexander the Great (356–323 BC)

King of Macedonia who conquered the Persian Empire and became ruler of most of the civilised world.

At the age of 20 Alexander inherited the tiny kingdom of Macedonia from his father Philip. By the time he died at the age of 33 he had conquered a vast empire, which stretched from Greece to Egypt, and east as far as Central Asia and India. He founded the Egyptian city of Alexandria, which would later become a centre of learning.

Caesar, Julius (c.100–44 BC)

'I came, I saw, I conquered.'

Roman general who conquered Gaul (France) and was the first to invade Britain.

Caesar was a brilliant soldier who was popular with his troops. He was also a politician, who introduced many reforms to help the poor people of Rome. Other politicians feared his popularity, but he defeated them in a civil war in 49-48 BC.

He was finally assassinated on his way to the Senate by a group opposed to his leadership.

▼ **Going home** In 1292 Marco Polo left China to return to Europe.

Charlemagne (c.742–814)

King of the Franks (later, the people of France and Germany), whose empire stretched over most of Western Europe.

Charlemagne promoted the arts, culture and learning from his court at Aix-la-Chapelle. He also spread Christianity among neighbouring pagan tribes, but was often ruthless in the way he did so. He was crowned Holy Roman Emperor by the Pope on Christmas day of the year 800.

Charles V (1500–58)

Charles, crowned Holy Roman Emperor at the age of 19, inherited a vast empire. He ruled over the Netherlands, Spain and Austria, as well as Spanish South America and parts of Italy.

During his long and difficult reign he had constant battles with Martin Luther and the Protestants. He eventually resigned to live in a monastery.

Churchill, Sir Winston (1874–1965)

British soldier and statesman who inspired his countrymen during the Second World War.

Churchill was a gifted orator. He had a long political career, and was 65 when he became Prime Minister in 1940. He guided Britain to victory in the war, but was defeated in the 1945 elections. He returned to power in 1951 at the age of 77.

Cleopatra (69–30 BC)

Queen of Egypt and last of the Macedonian Ptolemy dynasty,

loved by two Roman generals, Julius Caesar and Mark Antony.

In 48 BC Julius Caesar helped her to gain power from her brother. After Caesar was killed in Rome, she was visited by his friend Mark Antony, who fell in love with her. When Antony was killed in battle, Cleopatra committed suicide by getting a poisonous snake to bite her.

Cromwell, Oliver (1599–1658)

Leader of the Parliamentary party, or 'Roundheads', during the English Civil War.

In 1649, Cromwell helped to bring about the defeat and execution of Charles I. He became Lord Protector and ruler of England, Scotland and Ireland in 1653. Because he was a Puritan, he banned dancing and colourful clothes, and destroyed anything that had links with the Catholic Church.

Elizabeth I (1533–1603)

Queen of England during the time when England became a world power.

Elizabeth encouraged the Protestant faith. This made her the enemy of the country's Catholics, who gained the support of Spain, but the

▼ **Royal Profile** The portrait on this locket is that of Elizabeth I.

'Armada' Spain sent to invade England was destroyed before it could land.

Elizabeth never married, and was succeeded by her cousin James VI of Scotland, who became James I of England.

Frederick the Great (1712–86)

King of Prussia who turned his country into the strongest military power in Europe.

As well as being a successful soldier, Frederick was also a thinker. He wrote many volumes on politics, history and military subjects, and was a friend of the French philosopher Voltaire.

Gandhi, Mahatma (1869–1948)

Indian spiritual and political leader known as the Mahatma, which means 'Great soul'; his real name was Mohandas Karamchand Gandhi.

Gandhi was a lawyer with a passionate desire to see the end of British rule in India. He also believed that all violence was wrong, and so led hundreds of millions of Indians in peaceful protests. India won its independence in 1947, but Gandhi was killed by a religious fanatic the following year.

de Gaulle, Charles (1890–1970)

French general who led a government in exile during the Second World War.

When France was occupied by the Germans in 1940, de Gaulle fled to London, where he founded the Free French forces. After the war he was hailed as a national hero, and in 1958 he was made president. During his years in office, de Gaulle turned France into a

nuclear power and rebuilt relations with West Germany. He resigned in 1969.

Genghis Khan (c.1162–1227)

Mongol warrior who conquered an empire extending from the Yellow Sea in the east to the Black Sea in the west.

He was originally called Temujin, but changed his name to Genghis Khan – which means 'Universal Ruler' – after defeating all other Mongol tribes in 1206. Genghis then swept west across Asia, and south into China. His successors went on to build the biggest empire the world has ever seen.

Hannibal (247–182 BC)

Carthaginian general, who invaded Italy in 218 BC by crossing the Alps with his army, including elephants.

Hannibal was a brilliant commander. His crossing of the Alps is one of the great military achievements of history. Once in Italy, he defeated the Romans in several major battles, but was forced to withdraw because of a lack of reinforcements.

Henry VIII (1491–1547)

King of England who had six wives, Catherine of Aragon, Anne Boleyn, Jane Seymour, Anne of Cleves, Catherine Howard and Catherine Parr.

Henry was a cultivated and intelligent man. However, he wanted to divorce his first wife, Catherine of Aragon, because she had failed to give birth to a son and heir. The Pope refused to grant a divorce, and so Henry turned against the Pope and declared himself head of the Church of England.

People who changed the world

Hitler, Adolf (1889-1945)

German dictator who brought about the Second World War by invading Poland.

Hitler was born in Austria, but believed in the greatness of all the German people. He was also outraged by Germany's defeat in the First World War, and set about reversing it.

He was a powerful public speaker, who was able to convince many people to follow him. But he also sent millions of Jews, gypsies and others to their deaths in concentration camps.

Hitler committed suicide in his Berlin bunker as the Russian army took over the city in 1945.

Lenin, Vladimir Ilyich (1870-1924)

Russian revolutionary and first leader of the Soviet Union.

Lenin was active in the first Russian revolution of 1905, but had to escape when it failed. In April 1917 he returned to Russia, where he rallied the Bolsheviks and led them to power in October that year. After Lenin's death, his body was placed on public view in a crystal case.

▲ **Fiery speaker** A poster from about 1920 shows Lenin making a speech.

Kennedy, John Fitzgerald (1917-63)

JFK, as he was known, was the 35th and youngest president of the USA, yet he was in office for only three years before being murdered in Dallas on November 22, 1963.

Kennedy was glamorous and popular. He was also a tough leader, prepared to risk war with Russia over its plans to threaten America with nuclear missiles based on the island of Cuba. One of his lasting successes was his support for America's space programme, which placed a man on the Moon in 1969.

Lincoln, Abraham (1809-65)

Lincoln was known as 'Honest Abe' because of his high moral standards. He was president during America's civil war, and wanted to keep the southern, slave-owning states united with the north. He promoted the rights of slaves and granted them freedom in 1862. In his famous speech, the Gettysburg Address, he said that he believed in 'government of the people, by the people, and for the people'. He was murdered at a Washington theatre five days after the war ended.

Mandela, Nelson (1918-)

First black president of South Africa. Mandela was imprisoned in 1964 for his opposition to the country's white government, and released in February 1990. Four years later his party, the African National Congress, won the country's first multiracial elections. Since then, Mandela has been a leading figure in reforming South Africa. He retired from politics in 1999.

Mao Zedong (1893-1976)

Chinese communist dictator, the first leader of the People's Republic of China.

Mao took control of China in 1949. He was expert at getting people to follow him, and required everyone to learn his sayings from a 'Little Red Book'. However, many of his policies were disastrous, leading to the starvation of millions.

Napoleon Bonaparte (1769-1821)

French leader who conquered most of mainland Europe during the Napoleonic Wars.

Napoleon was a brilliant soldier and administrator. He built up France as a great power, and crowned himself emperor in 1804. In 1812 he invaded Russia, but was driven back by the savage winter. He was defeated in 1814, and again in 1815, by combined European forces. Napoleon died in exile on St Helena, a remote island in the Atlantic Ocean.

Stalin, Joseph (1879-1953)

Soviet communist leader who was one of the cruellest dictators of the 20th century.

Stalin ruled the Soviet Union for 27 years, and during that time he sent about 30 million people to their deaths. When he came to power the Soviet Union was chiefly a farming country. Stalin turned it into a powerful industrial nation with factories that produced everything from tanks to planes and tractors.

Tutankhamun (died c.1340 BC)

Egyptian pharaoh, or king, who came to power at the age of 12 and died when only 18.

Tutankhamun is most famous because of his tomb, which was discovered intact by Howard Carter in 1922. It contained amazing treasures, including gold statues, a solid gold coffin and a death mask decorated with precious stones.

Queen Victoria (1819-1901)

'We are not amused!'

British monarch who ruled over Great Britain for 63 years, at a time when it was the most powerful country in the world.

During her reign, which is called the Victorian age, Britain controlled an empire that included about a quarter of the Earth's population. Victoria married her German cousin, Albert, when she was 21. She was heartbroken when he died in 1861, and wore black for the rest of her life.

Washington, George (1732–99)

First president of the USA, from 1789 to 1797.

Washington commanded the American forces during the American Revolution, which ended British rule. He is sometimes referred to as the 'father of America'. The country's capital, Washington DC, is named after him.

William the Conqueror (1027–87)

Duke of Normandy who invaded England and defeated King Harold at the Battle of Hastings on October 14, 1066.

William became the first of a long line of Norman kings of England. The Normans brought the French language with them, and many aspects of French culture. English was not spoken again at court until the late 14th century.

Reformers

St Benedict (c.480–c.520)

Priest who founded the first Christian monasteries, where men could live as monks.

St Benedict was born in Nurcia, in central Italy. From there he went on to establish the monastery at Subiaco, and then Monte Cassino, which was to become one of the richest and most important in Europe.

Buddha (c.563–c.483 BC)

The name Buddha means 'Enlightened One'. It was the title given to Prince Gautama

Siddhartha, the founder of Buddhism. At the age of 29 he left his life of luxury to go and live in the wilderness. He is said to have found enlightenment (spiritual knowledge) while sitting under a fig tree in north India. He taught for 40 years and gathered many followers before he died at the age of 80.

Che Guevara (1928–67)

Latin American revolutionary who helped to bring about the communist revolution in Cuba in 1956-9.

Che was born in Argentina where he trained as a doctor. He joined the guerrilla army of Fidel Castro, and became the Cuban leader's trusted aide. He was later killed while organising a revolution in Bolivia.

St Francis of Assisi (c.1181–1226)

Spiritual leader and founder of the Franciscan order, which preached a rule of poverty, chastity and obedience.

St Francis was renowned for his gentleness, and for his love of animals. He was born into a wealthy family, but gave up everything he owned to look after the poor and the sick.

Garibaldi, Giuseppe (1807–82)

Italian revolutionary soldier and politician who played a leading role in the unification of Italy.

Garibaldi set out from Genoa in 1860 with 1000 volunteers. They went on to capture Sicily and Naples, which paved the way for Italy to become united as one country in 1870.

Earlier, he had been arrested for his part in an attempted revolution, and had spent 14 years in exile.

Jesus Christ (c.4 BC–c. AD 30)

Hebrew preacher whose teachings form the inspiration for the Christian religion.

Most of what we know about Jesus comes from the four Gospels in the New Testament. His teachings caused alarm among Jewish priests, who put him on trial for saying, according to them, that he was the Son of God. They then convinced the Romans to execute Jesus as a threat to peace in Jerusalem.

Joan of Arc (c.1412–31)

French patriot who became a great military leader.

Joan fought against the English during the Hundred Years War. She is sometimes known as the Maid of Orléans for her part in driving the English forces away from the city of Orléans in 1429. She

was later captured and burned at the stake by the English, who accused her of being a witch.

King, Martin Luther (1929–68)

American Baptist minister and civil rights leader.

Martin Luther King was an inspiring speaker who fought for equal rights for Americans of all races. He won the Nobel peace prize in 1964. Although he believed in non-violence, King had many enemies. He was murdered in Memphis, Tennessee, in 1968.

Luther, Martin (1483–1546)

German priest and reformer who brought about the Protestant Reformation.

Luther objected to a range of practices of the Catholic

▼ **Girl power** Joan of Arc believed she had a divine mission to save France.

People who changed the world

Church, and made his beliefs public in 1517 by nailing a list of 95 statements onto a church door in Wittenberg, Germany. This action grew into the Reformation – meaning the reform of the Church – as more and more people accepted his views. In 1534 Luther translated the Bible into German, so that ordinary people could read it.

Moses (c.15th–13th century BC)
Legendary Hebrew prophet and lawgiver who led the Israelites out of slavery in Egypt.

Moses is said to have written the first five books of the Old Testament in the Bible. He was brought up by the Egyptian pharaoh's daughter, but later discovered that he was a Jew.

He was told by God to lead the Israelites to the Promised Land of Israel, and he received the Ten Commandments from God on Mount Sinai.

Nobel, Alfred (1833–96)
Swedish chemist and engineer who invented dynamite and other explosives.

Nobel was also interested in the arts, and left most of his fortune to fund five annual Nobel prizes. The first prizes were awarded in 1901. They were for peace, literature, physics, chemistry and medicine. A prize for economics was established in 1968.

St Paul (died c.65)
Early Christian missionary who probably died for his faith.

St Paul was originally a Jewish lawyer opposed to the Christian Church. While he was travelling to Damascus he had a vision of Jesus, which changed his life. He dedicated himself to the new church, and made many converts. He was later arrested and sent to Rome, where he may have been killed by the emperor Nero.

St Peter (died c.64)
St Peter was among the first followers of Jesus, and leader of the Christians after Jesus's death.

Peter was originally called Simon. He was a fisherman on the Sea of Galilee when Jesus summoned him and gave him the name Peter, which means 'rock' in Greek. This shows that Jesus felt he was utterly reliable.

It is almost certain that St Peter was killed in Rome by the emperor Nero.

Robespierre, Maximilien (1758–94)
French politician in the French Revolution who helped to overthrow Louis XVI.

Robespierre was a strong defender of democratic principles. He was called 'The Incorruptible' because he could not be bribed. After sending many people to their deaths, he was himself overthrown and executed in 1794.

Teresa of Calcutta, Mother (1910–97)
Roman Catholic nun who dedicated her life to helping the abandoned children and the dying of Calcutta.

Mother Teresa was born in Macedonia. In 1928 she went to India, where she entered a convent. She opened the House for the Dying in 1952, and won the Nobel peace prize in 1979.

Science and medicine

Archimedes (287–212 BC)
Greek mathematician and inventor famous for applying science to everyday life.

He invented the Archimedes screw – a device for raising water from a lower level to a higher one. It is said that he once solved a difficult problem while sitting in his bath. He was so excited that he ran through the streets naked, shouting 'Eureka!', which means 'I have found it!'.

Copernicus, Nicolaus (1473–1543)
Polish astronomer who rejected the belief that the Sun and planets revolve around the Earth.

Copernicus placed the Sun at the centre of the Universe, rather than the Earth. One of his most important followers was Galileo. In 1616, however, the Catholic Church banned Copernicus's writings and made it an offence punishable by death to support his theories.

Crick, Francis (1916–)
British biophysicist who, together with the American, James Watson, determined the structure of DNA, the molecule that stores the unique genetic information of every living thing.

Their discovery led to a huge increase in our knowledge about all life on Earth.

▶ **Coded** DNA consists of two long spirals of codes.

Curie, Marie (1867–1934)
Polish physicist who, with her French husband Pierre, discovered two new chemical elements: radium and polonium.

In 1903 she was the first woman to win a Nobel prize, and in 1911 she became the first person to win it for a second time. Her discoveries advanced the medical use of X-rays.

Darwin, Charles (1809–82)
British scientist who developed the theory that evolution takes place through natural selection – the survival of the fittest.

Many people disagreed with Darwin on scientific grounds, but his most angry opponents were those who insisted that the only true story of creation was that told in the Bible.

Einstein, Albert (1879–1955)
Einstein is probably the most famous scientist of the 20th century.

He was born in Germany, but became an American citizen in 1940. He is best known for developing the Special and General theories of relativity, which have changed our perceptions of the Universe, space and time.

Einstein was opposed to war, but he was so worried by events in Europe that he encouraged President Roosevelt to develop atomic weapons for the USA.

Euclid (lived c.300 BC)

Greek mathematician who devised many of the basic principles of geometry.

Euclid also made important discoveries in the theory of numbers. He spent some time in Alexandria, Egypt, where he founded a school. Parts of his book, *Elements*, can be found in textbooks even today.

Faraday, Michael (1791–1867)

British scientist who discovered electromagnetic induction, which is the basis for both making electricity, and driving a motor with electricity.

The son of a blacksmith, Faraday had hardly any formal education. He first worked for a bookbinder, but developed his interest in science by reading and attending lectures. He built his first dynamo for making electricity in 1831.

Fleming, Sir Alexander (1881–1955)

British bacteriologist who discovered penicillin, the life-saving antibiotic, in 1928.

Fleming's find was an accident. He was researching influenza when he noticed that a mould had destroyed some influenza bacteria he was growing. Antibiotics made possible the effective treatment of infections.

Freud, Sigmund (1856–1929)

Austrian doctor who founded psychoanalysis – a way of studying how the mind works and how it influences us.

Freud was also the first person to explore the idea that what happens to us in our childhood affects the way we act later in life. Many of his ideas were rejected during his lifetime, but have since become very influential.

Galileo (1564–1642)

Italian astronomer who built one of the earliest telescopes and confirmed that the Earth revolves around the Sun, rather than the other way around.

The Catholic Church brought Galileo to trial and banned him for upholding this view – a judgment only set aside in 1992. Galileo also studied the Sun, and discovered four moons of the planet Jupiter.

Harvey, William (1578–1657)

English doctor who discovered that blood circulates around the body, pumped by the heart.

Harvey was considered the greatest doctor in England, yet his ideas were not fully accepted or confirmed until as late as 1827. Until he published his theory, the liver was seen as the body's most important organ.

Jenner, Edward (1749–1823)

English country doctor who discovered a way of preventing the disease smallpox. Jenner

▲ **Only a pinprick** Louis Pasteur supervises doctors giving vaccinations.

realised that patients who had been exposed to cowpox did not get smallpox, which was much more dangerous. He showed that if you give a person a tiny dose of cowpox, he or she will be safe from smallpox. This was the start of vaccinations.

Newton, Sir Isaac (1642–1727)

'Nature is very constant and conformable with herself.'

English physicist, who worked out that the force of gravity is governed by the same laws everywhere in the Universe. Newton's explanation of how the Universe works was not challenged until Einstein published his theories of relativity in the 20th century.

Newton also studied optics, discovering that white light, or sunlight, contains all the colours of the rainbow.

Pascal, Blaise (1623–62)

French philosopher, physicist and mathematician. When Pascal was growing up his father would not allow him to study a subject unless he believed the boy was ready for it, so Pascal studied in secret, learning difficult mathematical propositions by the age of 11. When he was 17, he published his first essay on mathematics, which was highly praised by experts.

Pascal's inventions include the hypodermic syringe, which was welcomed by doctors.

Pasteur, Louis (1822–95)

French chemist who developed the idea that germs are the cause of disease.

Pasteur also discovered a process for killing bacteria in milk and other food to make it safe to eat. This now bears his name: pasteurisation. The Pasteur Institute in Paris was founded by him in 1888, and remains a world centre for the study of microbiology and dangerous diseases.

Pythagoras (c.580– c.507 BC)

Greek philosopher and mathematician.

Little is known about Pythagoras himself, but the beliefs of his followers show us that he taught that numbers are the basis of all things. He played an important role in the development of mathematics and geometry.

Rutherford, Ernest (1871-1937)

New Zealand physicist who is often called 'the father of nuclear physics' because of his research into the atom.

Rutherford won the Nobel prize for chemistry in 1908. He later became the first person to split the atom, and his account of the structure of the atom is still accepted today.

 ## ● Technology and engineering

Arkwright, Sir Richard (1732-92)

British engineer and inventor of the water-powered spinning wheel, which changed the way cloth was made.

Arkwright began his working life as a barber in Bolton, but turned to engineering around 1767. His success allowed him to open huge cotton mills that used his machines. These were among the first factories of the Industrial Revolution.

Bell, Alexander Graham (1847-1922)

Inventor of the telephone and several other machines for transmitting the human voice.

Bell was born in Edinburgh but moved to North America in 1870. Much of his work was directed at helping deaf people to understand speech. In 1876 he demonstrated the first telephone, and in 1877 formed the Bell Telephone Company.

Brunel, Isambard Kingdom (1806-59)

Civil engineer and designer of ships and railways who built Bristol's Clifton Suspension Bridge.

His ships included the *Great Western*, the first steamship to cross the Atlantic regularly, the *Great Britain*, the first large iron ship to have a screw propeller, and the *Great Eastern* which laid the first transatlantic telegraph cable.

Cartwright, Edmund (1743-1823)

Inventor of the power loom and wool-combing machine.

Cartwright was a clergyman in Leicestershire. In 1784 he visited Richard Arkwright's cotton mill near Matlock, and was encouraged to build a weaving machine of his own. This was the power loom, which made it possible to weave wide cotton cloth for the first time.

Daguerre, Louis (1789-1851)

French pioneer in photography who invented the 'daguerrotype' method of producing an image on a silver-coated plate.

Daguerre and his partner Joseph Niepce are often cited as the inventors of photography, although others were experimenting with different processes at the same time.

Daimler, Gottlieb (1834-1900)

German inventor and engineer who made major improvements to the internal combustion engine, which he later used in building the first motor car.

Daimler's first vehicle was a motorcycle, made in 1885, and in 1889 he produced the first four-wheeled motorised car. A Daimler car won the first international car race from Paris to Rouen in 1894.

Edison, Thomas (1847-1931)

American inventor of the gramophone for recording and playing back sounds (1877), the electric light bulb (1879), and the first motion pictures with sound (1912).

Edison was almost deaf, and his school teachers thought that he was stupid, so he stayed at school for only a few months. He later established a laboratory at Menlo Park, New Jersey, where he invented more than a thousand different things, becoming known as 'the wizard of Menlo Park'.

Ford, Henry (1863-1947)

American motor manufacturer who in 1908 invented the assembly line for the Model T Ford car.

On the Ford assembly line each worker carried out the same task on a sequence of cars brought to him by conveyor belt. This made the cars much cheaper, so that even ordinary people could afford them.

Ford believed in paying workers a proper wage – so that they could buy his cars too. His workers earned $5 a day, twice the average rate at the time.

▶ **Mass production** Car workers assemble Model T Fords in an early factory.

Franklin, Benjamin (1706-1790)

American statesman, scientist, inventor and writer who proved that lightning and electricity are one and the same.

Franklin had a printing business, but from 1748 he spent most of his time studying science. He flew a kite during a thunderstorm to find out what lightning was. Fortunately, he was not killed, and invented the lightning rod as a result.

In 1787, Franklin became one of the 'Founding Fathers' of America by helping to draw up the American Constitution.

Gutenberg, Johann (c.1395-1468)

German printer credited with inventing the methods of modern printing.

Gutenberg built up a page of text from individual letters, called movable type. He then covered this with ink, laid a sheet of paper over it, and pressed the paper down in a device called, appropriately, a 'press'. Gutenberg's biggest project was a Bible, now

called the *Gutenberg Bible*, which was the first printed Bible.

Gutenberg himself did not finish printing the Bible; this was done by his partner, Johann Fust, who took over the business after Gutenberg failed to repay a large loan to Fust.

Marconi, Guglielmo (1874–1937)

Italian inventor who pioneered the development of radio.

In 1895 Marconi achieved radio communications over one mile. In 1898 he transmitted signals across the English Channel, and in 1901 he spoke to someone in Canada from England. His most distant radio communications were between England and Australia in 1918. Marconi won the Nobel Prize for Physics in 1909.

Stephenson, George (1781–1848)

British railway engineer who built the first steam locomotive.

As a young man, Stephenson worked in a coal mine, where he invented a safety lamp called the 'Geordie' in 1815. He also built locomotives for hauling coal, and in 1829 his *Rocket* proved itself faster than all other rivals, travelling at 48 km/h (30 mph).

Wright brothers

Orville (1871-1948) and Wilbur Wright (1867-1912) built and flew the world's first powered aircraft near Kitty Hawk, North Carolina, in December 1903. Orville flew for just 12 seconds, Wilbur for 59 seconds.

The Wright brothers owned a bicycle shop and were self-taught inventors who earned a living from selling bicycles.

Thinkers and philosophers

Aristotle (384–322 BC)

Greek philosopher whose ideas had a major influence on Western thought.

Aristotle was a pupil of Plato at his Academy in Athens. He later became a teacher himself, and one of his most famous pupils was Alexander the Great.

Aristotle wrote on a huge range of subjects, including morality, zoology, government, logic and the soul. His method was scientific, emphasising the importance of observation.

Confucius (551–479 BC)

Chinese philosopher whose moral teachings became the guiding principles for many

▲ **Paying respects** Chinese students celebrate Confucius's birthday.

aspects of Chinese society until the 20th century, when they were rejected by communists.

Confucius lived at a time when China was being torn apart by rival warlords, so he was concerned to find a way of creating stability in society. His sayings were collected by his followers into a book, called the *Analects*, which was published after his death.

Descartes, René (1596–1650)

French philosopher and mathematician who attempted to rethink all philosophy.

Descartes wanted to start from first principles, so he looked for the one thing that he could know without any doubt. This led him to his famous statement, *Cogito ergo sum*, or 'I think, therefore I am'. From here he built up an entirely new system of thought.

Machiavelli, Niccolò (1469–1527)

Italian author and political writer whose most famous work, *The Prince*, claimed to be a handbook for rulers on how to gain power and hold on to it.

Machiavelli advised rulers that the best way to ensure the loyalty of their subjects was to make themselves feared.

Marx, Karl (1818–83)

German social theorist who, with his lifelong friend Friedrich Engels, wrote the *Communist Manifesto* (1848) about class struggle. This influenced many thinkers,

including Lenin, who put its ideas into practice in the Russian Revolution of 1917.

Marx's other major work was *Das Kapital* (*Capital*), which he wrote in the British Library over many years.

Nietzsche, Friedrich (1844–1900)

German philosopher who rejected Christianity by saying 'God is dead'.

Nietzsche hated most people's ideas of right and wrong, and developed the idea of a 'superman', beyond good and evil, who would impose his will on the weak. This idea was later taken up by the Nazis, who used it for their own ends.

Plato (c.428–c.348 BC)

Greek philosopher who has had a profound influence on Western thought.

Plato founded his school, the Academy, in Athens, attracting students from all over Greece. His book *The Republic* sets out his thoughts on the ideal state, justice, morality and society. Many aspects of Plato's thought were later adopted by Christian thinkers.

Rousseau, Jean-Jacques (1712–78)

'Man was born free, and is everywhere in chains.'

French political philosopher. His book, *The Social Contract* (1762), declared that people should have rights over their government – an idea that was

People who changed the world

to be increasingly influential in the years leading up to the French Revolution of 1792.

Rousseau was also unusual for his time in that he called for the education of women.

Socrates (469–399 BC)

Greek philosopher who was one of the most important figures in Greek philosophy, although he never wrote anything.

Nearly everything we know about Socrates comes from Plato, who tells us that Socrates was a great teacher. He had no school, but would sit in the marketplace of Athens and speak to people about right and wrong. He was accused of being disrespectful to the gods, and was executed by being forced to drink a cup of poison.

Voltaire (1694–1778)

French writer and philosopher who was a central figure of the 18th-century Enlightenment – a philosophical movement that questioned all accepted ideas.

Voltaire wrote plays, books on philosophy and a satirical novel called *Candide*, about the dangers of optimism. He also experimented in chemistry.

 ## Writers

Austen, Jane (1775–1817)

Author of six novels about social life in 19th-century England. She was the sixth of seven children and started writing to amuse her family. Her most successful book was *Pride and Prejudice* (1813), though it was originally rejected by the publishers.

Cervantes, Miguel de (1547–1616)

Spanish soldier, novelist and poet whose most famous work is *Don Quixote*.

Cervantes was wounded at the Battle of Lepanto in 1571. On his way home he was kidnapped by pirates, who sold him as a slave in Algiers. He was ransomed in 1580 and returned to Spain, where he wrote many works, including the first part of *Don Quixote* (1605). Another writer published a sequel in 1614, but Cervantes published his own, much better, sequel in 1615.

Chaucer, Geoffrey (c.1340–1400)

English writer who is called the 'father of English poetry'.

Chaucer's most famous work is *The Canterbury Tales*, an extended poem recounting the lively stories told by a group of pilgrims on their way to the shrine of St Thomas Becket at Canterbury. Chaucer's writing has always been much admired; he was the first poet to be buried at Westminster Abbey.

Dante Alighieri (1265–1321)

'Abandon hope all ye who enter here!'

Italian poet and author of *The Divine Comedy*, which tells of an imaginary journey through Hell to Heaven.

Dante fell in love with a young woman called Beatrice, who died in 1290. She appears in many of his works, and is his

▲ **Underworld** Dickens's boy hero Oliver Twist meets a gang of thieves.

guide in part of *The Divine Comedy*. Dante was involved in the politics of Florence, and was forced to go into exile in 1302.

Dickens, Charles (1812–70)

English novelist. When Dickens was 12 his whole family was sent to a debtors' prison, while he had to work in a factory. This experience provided many episodes for his writings, especially *David Copperfield*.

His descriptions of poverty and injustice are so moving that they helped to change the law.

Dostoyevsky, Fyodor (1821–81)

Russian novelist whose works include *Crime and Punishment* (1866), about a murderer who is haunted by his crime, and *The Brothers Karamasov* (1879–80).

Dostoyevsky's other works are equally powerful, reflecting his lifelong concern with sin and forgiveness, and the need to live a meaningful life.

Eliot, George (1819–80)

English novelist whose real name was Mary Ann Evans. Her masterpiece is *Middlemarch*

(1871-2), which is considered to be one of the finest novels ever written in English.

Like many other women writers in the 19th century, she used a man's name instead of her own, so that she would be taken more seriously.

Flaubert, Gustave (1821–80)

French novelist whose first and best known novel, *Madame Bovary* (1857), caused a scandal.

The novel tells of the love affairs of a romantic young woman married to a country doctor, which led Flaubert and his publisher to be tried for offending public morals; both were found not guilty. Flaubert was a slow and careful writer, always searching for the exact word to express an idea.

Frank, Anne (1929–45)

German-Jewish diarist who fled to Holland with her family to escape the Nazis.

Anne and her family lived in a tiny sealed-off room in a warehouse in Amsterdam. They were betrayed in 1944, and Anne died in a concentration camp. Her father later found the diary that Anne had kept. It quickly became a best seller.

Goethe, Johann von (1749–1832)

German poet, novelist, scientist, playwright and scholar.

Goethe is considered to be the founder of modern German literature. His masterpiece, *Faust*, is a terrifying tale in which a man makes a pact with the Devil. Written as a dramatic poem, it took Goethe some 50 years to complete.

Homer (c.8th century BC)

Greek epic poet traditionally regarded as the author of *The Iliad* and *The Odyssey*. The first tells the story of the Trojan War, while the second tells of the travels of the hero Odysseus.

Both poems are from an ancient oral tradition, which means that they were recited long before being written down. It is likely that more than one poet contributed to their development.

Hugo, Victor (1802–85)

French poet and writer, and a leading figure of the French Romantic movement, which emphasised the emotions in art and literature.

Hugo's most famous novels were *The Hunchback of Notre Dame* (1831) and *Les Misérables* (1862). He spent many years living in the Channel Islands, and returned to Paris in 1870 as a national hero.

Milton, John (1608–74)

English poet, whose most famous work, *Paradise Lost* (1667), is one of the great epic works of English literature.

Milton dictated much of the poem after he had gone blind. It tells the story of Lucifer's rebellion against God, his temptation of Adam and Eve, and their expulsion from Eden.

Molière (1622–73)

French playwright who laid the foundations of modern French comedy. Molière did not try to

▲ **Young love** Shakespeare's *Romeo and Juliet* became a Hollywood hit.

make things look better than they really were, preferring to expose hypocrisy and evil around him. He made some bitter enemies, but had the protection of his employer, the French king, Louis XIV.

Shakespeare, William (1564–1616)

Shakespeare is known across the world as England's greatest poet and playwright.

He wrote more than 40 plays, including histories, such as *Richard III* and *Henry V*; comedies, such as *A Midsummer Night's Dream* and *Twelfth Night*; and tragedies, including *Hamlet* and *Romeo and Juliet*.

Little is known about Shakespeare's life, except that he was born at Stratford-upon-Avon, married Anne Hathaway and had three children. He travelled to London, where he was an actor and a playwright. His plays were first published after his death by two fellow actors who admired them.

Solzhenitsyn, Alexandr (1918–)

Russian author whose writings told the world about the cruelty of the Soviet Union.

His works include *One Day in the Life of Ivan Denisovich*

and *The Gulag Archipelago*. He was first imprisoned in 1945 for criticising the Soviet leader Joseph Stalin in letters to a friend. He was later banned, and in 1974 he was forced to leave Russia. He settled in the USA, where he lived quietly, away from publicity.

Sophocles (c.496 –406 BC)

Greek playwright who wrote over 120 plays, of which only seven survive.

His most famous play is the tragedy *Oedipus the King*, about a man who kills his father and marries his mother, without realising what he has done. Sophocles regularly won prizes in Athens for his plays.

Swift, Jonathan (1667–1745)

Anglo-Irish writer and clergyman. He is most often remembered for his satirical book, *Gulliver's Travels*. This appears to be no more than the story of Gulliver's journeys to four strange countries, but it exposes many ridiculous aspects of human behaviour.

This can be seen in the land of Lilliput, where the people are only 15 cm (6 in) tall, yet insist on great pomp and ceremony.

The Lilliputians' tiny size shows how their sense of their own importance is absurd.

Tolstoy, Count Leo (1828–1910)

Russian writer whose most famous novels are *War and Peace*, an epic story of Russia's struggle against Napoleon, and *Anna Karenina*, which describes the passion of a married woman for a young army officer.

For many years Tolstoy lived an aristocratic life of luxury, but he later rejected money as the root of all evil. He also became committed to nonviolence, and denounced both Church and state for supporting violence.

Twain, Mark (1835–1910)

American writer whose most famous novels, *The Adventures of Tom Sawyer* (1876) and *The Adventures of Huckleberry Finn* (1885), draw on his childhood on the Mississippi River.

Twain's real name was Samuel Clemens. He spent four years as a Mississippi river boat pilot before becoming a journalist and then a successful author.

Virgil (70–19BC)

Virgil, whose full name was Publius Vergilius Maro, is the greatest Roman poet.

Virgil's masterpiece was the *Aeneid*, written between 30 and 19 BC. It is an epic poem about the Trojan prince, Aeneas, who escapes from the destruction of Troy, has a passionate romance with Dido, Queen of Carthage, and goes on to become the founder of Rome.

Virgil wanted to burn the poem, which was unfinished, but it is now seen as the finest in Latin literature.

Arts and entertainment

Entertainment today is an industry worth billions of dollars each year, while TV, pop and movie stars are probably the most famous people on Earth. But there is nothing new about what they do. From the earliest prehistoric times, people have danced, played music and told each other tales.

Musical instruments

Drums and bone flutes
The first musical instruments were drums, probably starting as hunting tools struck against each other. By about 10 000 BC, people had discovered how to make flutes from hollow bones.

Horns and trumpets
The Hebrew *shofar* (ram's horn) is the oldest type of horn; it dates back to about 4000 BC and is still used in Jewish ceremonies. Trumpets date back to about 1200 BC, but the modern valve trumpet was invented only in 1813. Woodwind instruments are more recent. The clarinet was invented in Germany in about 1700.

Plucked instruments
The ancestor of the guitar was played in ancient Egypt about 3000 BC. Later, the Moors of North Africa introduced it to Spain.

Musicians in several parts of the ancient world played lyres and harps.

The lute was popular in medieval Europe. Violins and cellos were developed in Italy in the early 16th century from the earlier viols.

Keyboard instruments
More than 2200 years ago, a Greek engineer made an organ powered by water pressure. The first bellows organs were made 1800 years ago in Byzantium – present-day Istanbul, Turkey. The first electronic organ was patented by the American Laurens Hammond in 1934.

Harpsichords and clavichords date from the Middle Ages. The first piano was built in Italy by Bartolommeo Cristofori in 1709.

Musical notation
The first written music dates from about 2500 BC. The notation we use nowadays is based on a system worked out by an Italian monk, Guido of Arezzo, in about AD 1020.

Performing music

First opera
Most experts agree that the first opera was *Dafne* by Jacopo Peri. It was first performed in Florence, Italy, in 1597.

Longest opera
The Life and Times of Joseph Stalin (1973) by Robert Wilson was the longest opera ever performed. It lasted 13 hours and 25 minutes.

▼ **Made in Venice**
A harpsichord made in 1531.

Shortest opera
The Sands Of Time (1993) by Simon Rees and Peter Reynolds is the shortest published opera. Its first performance lasted four minutes and nine seconds.

Largest orchestras
Johann Strauss the younger conducted the largest orchestra ever assembled, at the World Peace Jubilee held in Boston, USA, in 1872. It had 987 instrumental musicians and a choir of 20 000.

The biggest orchestra without a choir was assembled for a charity concert in November 1998 in the National Indoor Arena in Birmingham, England. Its 3889 players were mostly schoolchildren. The conductor was Sir Simon Rattle.

Pop music

Early popular music
'Pop' music has existed for centuries. 'Greensleeves', which appeared in the early 16th century, is an example of a popular song.

Popular music in the 20th century was influenced by radio and electric recording. The first American singers to become 'stars' emerged in the 1920s and 1930s, and included Bing Crosby and, later, Frank Sinatra.

◄ **Pop superstar**
Madonna on tour in 1990. Madonna Louise Veronica Ciccone – to give the singer her real name – had her first hit, 'Like A Virgin', in 1984.

▲ **Jacko** The star himself, with creatures from the pop video of his album *Thriller*.

Biggest pop stars
The most successful rock-and-roll star was also one of the first: Elvis Presley. His first major success was his 1956 recording of 'Heartbreak Hotel'. Elvis had 18 No 1 'hit' records in the USA – the highest number for a solo artist since the beginning of the rock-and-roll era in 1955.

The most successful female pop star is Madonna. The American star has sold more than 100 million records worldwide.

Wealthiest entertainers
The 1960s group The Beatles became the wealthiest musical entertainers of all time. They sold around 1 billion records and had a record 18 US No 1 albums and 14 UK No 1 albums. The Liverpool-born quartet formed in 1960 and had their first hit, 'Love Me Do', in 1962.

Biggest selling album
Michael Jackson's *Thriller* has sold more than 45 million copies around the world since it appeared in 1982. Jackson was also the youngest singer to top the American singles chart. He was 11 when he and the rest of the Jackson Five sang 'I Want You Back' in 1970.

Dance and ballet

Cave people dancing
Prehistoric paintings found on cave walls in Europe and Africa suggest that people were already dancing over 20 000 years ago.

First ballets
Early forms of ballet were danced in Italy during the 15th century. In 1581 Catherine de Medici, widow of King Henry II of France, had a ballet specially composed for a royal wedding: the *Ballet Comique de la Reine*.

Professional ballet began in 1661, when Louis XIV of France founded the Royal Academy of Dancing in Paris. It was to train dancers who would perform at court.

Longest dance
The longest dance took place during the Depression of the 1930s, when many people competed in dance-hall marathons in order to win large cash prizes. Mike Ritof and Edith Boudreaux danced at the Merry Garden Ballroom in Chicago, USA, for 5148 hours and 28½ minutes, with strictly controlled brief rests. Their marathon started on August 29, 1930, and finished seven months later on April 1, 1931. They won $2000.

Books and writing

First books
These were short stories and tales written down in ancient Egypt nearly 5000 years ago. They were written on papyrus, made from the stems of a plant.

First printed book
The first known printed book, called the *Diamond Sutra*, was made in China in AD 868. Each page was printed from a separate hand-carved wooden block. The pages were then joined together to make a scroll.

Movable–type printing
The Chinese invented movable type, with separate, re-usable pieces of metal type for each character, about AD 1000.

The first books printed in Europe using this method appeared in about 1455 in Mainz, Germany. One of the first books printed there was a Bible in Latin, known as the Gutenberg Bible after the leading local printer. Twenty years later, William Caxton made the first English printed book.

▲ ▶ **The printed word** The *Diamond Sutra* (above), the oldest known printed book, was made in China. Right: Two of Dame Agatha Christie's 78 crime novels.

First encyclopedia
In the 4th century BC, the Greek philosopher Aristotle became the first writer to try to bring together all existing knowledge into one series of books – the first encyclopedia.

Bestselling book
Experts reckon that about 4 billion copies of the Bible have been sold over the centuries. It is also the most widely translated book of any kind.

Top-selling novelist
Agatha Christie is the top-selling fiction writer. Her 78 crime novels have sold an estimated 2 billion copies in 44 languages.

Oldest newspapers
The first newspapers were published in ancient Rome, where handwritten sheets called *Acta Diurna* (*Daily Events*) were stuck up for people to read from 59 BC.

When the printing press came to Europe in the 15th century, printed newssheets appeared in Germany, the Netherlands, England and other countries. They reported business and shipping news, and carried some advertisements.

The first newspaper as we know them today was the *Frankfurter Journal*, published in Germany from 1615. Austria's *Wiener Zeitung* is the oldest newspaper still in existence. It was first published in Vienna in 1703 and has appeared continuously, except during the Second World War, ever since.

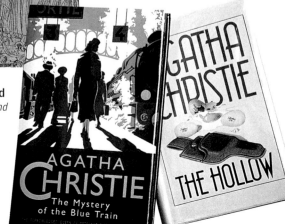

AGATHA CHRISTIE
The Mystery of the Blue Train

AGATHA CHRISTIE
THE HOLLOW

Biggest-selling newspapers

Japan's *Yomiuri Shimbun* has the highest circulation of any newspaper in the world: combined morning and evening sales of 14.5 million copies.

The biggest-selling English-language newspaper is the British *News of the World*. It sells more than 4 million copies every Sunday; its peak circulation was almost 8.5 million in 1951.

Theatre and circus

The London theatre

The first public theatre in England was called The Theatre. It was built near London in 1576. By 1642, nine more London theatres had been built, including the Curtain, Globe, Rose and Fortune. In that year the Puritan government closed all theatres. They reopened in 1660 with the Restoration of the monarchy.

Longest-running play

The Mousetrap by Agatha Christie is the world's longest-running play. It opened at the Ambassadors Theatre, London, on November 25, 1952. In 1974 it moved to

▲ **The Globe** Many of Shakespeare's plays had their early performances here.

St Martin's Theatre, where it continues. By the end of 1999 there had been about 19 600 performances.

Longest-running musical

Cats opened at the New London Theatre, London, on May 11, 1981. Since then the show has been seen by more than 50 million people in approximately 250 cities around the world.

Longest and shortest plays

The Non-Stop Connolly Play by John Arden took 26 hours and 30 minutes to perform in Dublin in 1975. *Breath*, written by Samuel Beckett in 1969, takes just 30 seconds to perform.

Biggest circus ever

The American P.T. Barnum set up his Greatest Show on Earth in 1871. It needed 100 railway carriages to transport it from place to place. Its 1890 tour had a record 263 performers and 175 animals.

Film and cinema

Pictures and movement

Eadweard Muybridge, a British photographer working in California, took the first successful photographs of movement in 1877 and 1878. Muybridge used a series of cameras to take photographs of both animals and people in motion.

Thomas Edison showed off the first commercial moving-picture machine at an exhibition in Chicago in 1893. It was called a kinetoscope and showed 35 mm black-and-white films viewed through a peephole. Each 'show' lasted about 90 seconds.

First screening

The French brothers Louis-Jean and Auguste Lumière held the first public movie screening on December 28, 1895. Their 'cinema', the place where

▶ ▲ **Longest runners** *Cats* (right), the hit musical based on poems by T.S. Eliot. Above: A 1950s advertisement for *The Mousetrap*.

PROUDLY PRESENTS ELIZABETH TAYLOR JOSEPH L. MANKIEWICZ'
CLEOPATRA

4 ACADEMY AWARDS

RICHARD BURTON / REX HARRISON

they projected their moving pictures, was a Parisian café.

First Hollywood movie
D.W. Griffith's *In Old California* was the first film made in Hollywood, in 1910.

First talkie
The Jazz Singer (1927) was the first successful Hollywood 'talkie' – a film with the actors speaking. Its first words were Al Jolson saying, 'You ain't heard nothin' yet.'

First full-colour movie
Becky Sharp (1935) was the first full-length full-colour feature film, using the Technicolor process.

First cartoons
Emile Cohl of France made more than 200 short animated films between 1908 and 1918.

Hollywood film studios started making animated films in 1915. Popeye the Sailor and Felix the Cat were some of the cartoon characters who first appeared around this time.

The first cartoon 'talkie' was Walt Disney's *Steamboat Willie* (1928). It starred Mickey Mouse.

▲ **A costly failure** Despite its star-studded cast, *Cleopatra* was a failure at the box office.

Most successful movie
Taking inflation into account, the 1939 film *Gone With The Wind* was the most successful film. At today's prices, it has taken more money at the box office than any other in film history. *Star Wars* (1977) is second and the 1997 hit *Titanic* third.

Most expensive movie
Cleopatra, in 1963, was the most expensive film ever made. Starring Elizabeth Taylor and Richard Burton, it cost $44 million (£15.7 million) – equal to more than $260 million (£158 million) today.

Most filmed author and story
Shakespeare is the most filmed author, and *Cinderella* the most filmed story. There have been at least 95 film productions of the fairy tale.

▼ **On the set** Hollywood pioneer D.W. Griffith in action with his megaphone.

The country that produces the most films
India is the world's biggest film producer. The first Indian film was *Raja Karischandra* (1912). The greatest output was in 1990, when 948 films were made. Films are made in 16 languages, mainly in the cities of Bombay ('Bollywood'), Calcutta and Madras.

Radio and television

First radio broadcasts
Experimental radio broadcasts began about 1909 – 14 years after Guglielmo Marconi transmitted the first radio signals. The first broadcasting station is generally agreed to be KCBS in San Francisco, built by Charles David Herrold in 1909. It broadcast music every Wednesday evening.

First public TV service
The BBC started the world's first public television service on November 2, 1936, from Alexandra Palace in London.

Longest-running TV show
The American station NBC has the world's longest-running television show: the political discussion programme *Meet the Press*, first transmitted on November 6, 1947. It was shown weekly from September 12, 1948, and is still running. Over 2700 episodes have been shown.

▲ **Ally Pally** An early TV camera and its operator in front of London's Alexandra Palace transmitting station.

First cable and satellite
Cable television began in Pennsylvania, USA, in 1948. It was used in areas where it was hard to receive normal TV signals. Cable developed into pay-TV (with viewers paying to watch particular programmes), begun by Home Box Office in 1972. Home Box Office was also the first to use a satellite to distribute its programmes.

Biggest audiences
The funeral of Diana, Princess of Wales, on September 6, 1997, drew the biggest global audience in the history of television. An estimated 2.5 billion people saw it. The most popular TV series worldwide is *Baywatch*, with a weekly audience of about 1.1 billion in 142 countries.

Sport

T he many different sports that people play were probably all originally games, invented for relaxation and, in many cases, exercise. They have also become a way of earning a living, as is the case with professional sportsmen and women, who can earn huge amounts of money for being 'the best'.

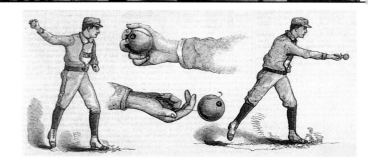

▲ **Applying spin** In baseball, the pitcher often makes the ball spin, as shown in these pictures from 1886.

How it began

American football
The first form of football played by American universities in the 19th century was a version of soccer, with no handling of the ball allowed. But the rules of rugby – which do permit ball-handling – crossed the Atlantic to Canada. In 1874, when a team from McGill University, in Montreal, was playing football against Harvard, the two sides agreed to play the second half under McGill's rules. This event turned out to be the beginning of the modern American game.

Athletics
The ancient Greeks invented many of the sports that occur in a modern athletics event, and every four years they held a competition – the Olympic Games – to find the best of all their athletes.

The games were holy to the Greeks, and making war was illegal while the athletes ran, wrestled, boxed and threw the discus. The games ended in the 4th century AD, but were revived by Baron Pierre de Coubertin centuries later. The first modern Olympics were held in Athens in 1896.

Baseball
An official commission set up in the USA to investigate the origins of baseball decided that the game was invented in 1839 at Cooperstown, New York, by Abner Doubleday, who became a general in America's Civil War. It is now believed that the commission was wrong about the time, the place and the man. Baseball developed from the English game of rounders, and was played in colonial America a century before Doubleday's time.

Cricket
The word 'cricket' probably comes from 'croc', an old-fashioned shepherd's staff. It seems that shepherds played a game in which one would try to hit a wicket gate (a small gate) with a stone, while another shepherd defended the gate with his croc.

The first record of a cricket match comes from 1744, when Kent beat All England by one wicket. Sailors and soldiers introduced the game to Australia, and Australia beat England in the first Test match, played in Melbourne in 1877.

In 1882, Australia defeated England in a Test match at the Oval in London. The following day, a newspaper notice announced the death of English cricket. It went on to say that the 'body' would be cremated, and its ashes taken to Australia.

England and Australia still play for the Ashes – a silver urn containing the ashes of a bail (a small stick which lies across two stumps) used during England's tour of Australia in 1882-3.

Cycling
The first cycle race was held in France in 1868, and was won by an Englishman, Dr James Moore. He covered the 123 km (76 mile) route from Paris to Rouen in 10 hours, 45 minutes.

All the participants in this race rode 'boneshaker' bicycles, with iron-rimmed wheels. The Tour de France – which covers about 4000 km (2500 miles) – was first held in 1903.

CYCLING
TOUR DE FRANCE WINNERS SINCE 1980

1980	Joop Zoetemelk – Netherlands
1981	Bernard Hinault – France
1982	Bernard Hinault – France
1983	Laurent Fignon – France
1984	Laurent Fignon – France
1985	Bernard Hinault – France
1986	Greg LeMond – USA
1987	Stephen Roche – Ireland
1988	Pedro Delgado – Spain
1989	Greg LeMond – USA
1990	Greg LeMond – USA
1991-5	Miguel Induráin – Spain
1996	Bjarne Riis – Denmark
1997	Jan Ullrich – Germany
1998	Marco Pantini – Italy

Golf
Modern golf originates from a game played in Scotland from the 15th century – by Mary, Queen of Scots, among others. The oldest club is the Royal and Ancient Golf Club of St Andrews, founded in 1754.

The first golf balls were probably made of wood. Then came leather balls, stuffed with goose feathers, followed in 1848 by the solid 'guttie', made of gutta-percha, the sap of a rubber tree. Dimples were added to the balls after it was discovered that used gutties, with cuts and scrapes, flew straighter than new ones.

GOLF
US MASTERS WINNERS SINCE 1980

1980	Severiano Ballesteros – Spain
1981	Tom Watson – USA
1982	Craig Stadler – USA
1983	Severiano Ballesteros – Spain
1984	Ben Crenshaw – USA
1985	Bernhard Langer – W Germany
1986	Jack Nicklaus – USA
1987	Larry Mize – USA
1988	Sandy Lyle – UK
1989	Nick Faldo – UK
1990	Nick Faldo – UK
1991	Ian Woosnam – UK
1992	Fred Couples – USA
1993	Bernhard Langer – Germany
1994	José Maria Olazábal – Spain
1995	Ben Crenshaw – USA
1996	Nick Faldo – UK
1997	Tiger Woods – USA
1998	Mark O'Meara – USA
1999	José Maria Olazábal – Spain

RYDER CUP RESULTS SINCE 1979

1979	USA 17, Europe 11
1981	USA 18.5, Europe 9.5
1983	USA 14.5, Europe 13.5
1985	Europe 16.5, USA 11.5
1987	Europe 15, USA 13
1989	Europe 14, USA 14
1991	USA 14.5, Europe 13.5
1993	USA 15, Europe 13
1995	Europe 14.5, USA 13.5
1997	Europe 14.5, USA 13.5

◀ **Concentration** Tiger Woods shows fine form during the 1997 US Masters.

ATHLETICS WORLD RECORDS

MEN

		Min/Sec	
100 m	Donovan Bailey – Canada	9.84	1996
200 m	Michael Johnson – USA	19.32	1996
400 m	Butch Reynolds – USA	43.29	1988
800 m	Wilson Kipketer – Denmark	1:41.11	1997
1500 m	Hicham El Guerrouj – Morocco	3:26.00	1998
Mile	Noureddine Morceli – Algeria	3:44.39	1993
5000 m	Haile Gebrselassie – Ethiopia	12:39.36	1998
10 000 m	Haile Gebrselassie – Ethiopia	26:22.75	1998

WOMEN

100 m	Florence Griffith-Joyner – USA	10.49	1988
200 m	Florence Griffith-Joyner – USA	21.34	1988
400 m	Marita Koch – East Germany	47.60	1985
800 m	Jarmila Kratochvilova – Czech	1:53.28	1983
1500 m	Qu Yunxia – China	3:50.46	1993
Mile	Svetlana Masterkova – Russia	4:12.56	1996
5000 m	Jiang Bo – China	14:28.09	1997
10 000 m	Wang Junxia – China	29:31.78	1993

HIGH JUMP

Men	Javier Sotomayor – Cuba	2.45 m (8 ft 1/2 in)	1993
Women	Stefka Kostadinova – Bulgaria	2.09 m (6 ft 10 1/4 in)	1987

LONG JUMP

Men	Mike Powell – USA	8.95 m (29 ft 4 1/2 in)	1991
Women	Galina Christyakova – USSR	7.52 m (24 ft 8 1/4 in)	1988

MARATHON – 42.195 km (26 miles, 385 yards)

Men	Belayneh Dimsamo – Ethiopia	2 hrs 6 min 50 sec	1988
Women	Tegla Loroupe – Kenya	2 hrs 20 min 47 sec	1998

OLYMPIC MARATHON

Men	Carlos Lopes – Portugal	2 hr 9 min 21 sec	1984
Women	Rosa Mota – Portugal	2 hr 25 min 40 sec	1988

Rugby Union

The most widely accepted account of the origin of rugby is that it began in 1823, when William Webb Ellis, a pupil at Rugby school, picked up the ball in a football match and ran with it. His captain apologised for this breach of the rules, and the school did not allow players to handle the ball until 1841.

When the new handling rule was accepted, it spread quickly. The English Rugby Union was formed in 1871, and the first international game was played between Scotland and England in 1872, with 20 players on each side. Scotland won.

Rugby League

The first rugby players, who came from public schools and universities, would never dream of accepting money for playing a game. But miners and millworkers from the poor industrial towns of northern England could not afford to lose wages for the sake of a match, even though they loved the game. In 1895, 22 northern clubs set up their own Rugby League, allowing payment for lost wages. This was limited to six shillings (30p) a day.

SOCCER

WORLD CUP RESULTS SINCE 1930

1930	Uruguay	4–2	Argentina
1934	Italy	2–1	Czechoslovakia
1938	Italy	4–2	Hungary
1950	Uruguay	2–1	Brazil
1954	W Germany	3–2	Hungary
1958	Brazil	5–2	Sweden
1962	Brazil	3–1	Czechoslovakia
1966	England	4–2	W Germany
1970	Brazil	4–1	Italy
1974	W Germany	2–1	Netherlands
1978	Argentina	3–1	Netherlands
1982	Italy	3–1	W Germany
1986	Argentina	3–2	W Germany
1990	W Germany	1–0	Argentina
1994	Brazil	0–0	Italy
	(Brazil won 3–2 on penalties)		
1998	France	3–0	Brazil

▲ **Ball game** Snooker grew out of the older game of billiards, seen here being played in the 17th century.

Soccer

Football in the Middle Ages was a brutal, hacking game, with no limit on the number of players. The modern game began to emerge in British public schools in the 19th century.

Different schools followed their own rules, causing arguments when the schoolboys reached university. The confusion was ended after Cambridge University issued rules for an 11-a-side game in 1863. The first FA Cup Final was held in London in 1872, with Wanderers beating the Royal Engineers 1-0.

Snooker

The rainy season meant hours of boredom for young British army officers stationed in India. They often played billiards, but became bored with this too. In about 1875, officers of the Devonshire Regiment came up with a solution: they added coloured balls to the table to make the game more difficult. There are only six coloured balls, and they are easily hidden by other balls on the table.

The new game got its name from army slang for a raw cadet – 'snooker' – because of the clumsy style of some players.

Tennis

The ancestor of modern tennis was a French game – now called 'real tennis' – played in a covered court. The cry *Tenez!* ('Get ready!') gave the game its name. Players hit the ball with the palm of the hand; gloves, then racquets, came later.

In 1875 the Englishman Walter Clopton Wingfield developed modern tennis. The first Wimbledon competition, with 22 participants and 200 spectators, was held in 1877.

TENNIS

WIMBLEDON SINGLES WINNERS SINCE 1980

	MEN'S SINGLES	LADIES' SINGLES
1980	Bjorn Borg – Sweden	Evonne Cawley – Australia
1981	John McEnroe – USA	Chris Evert Lloyd – USA
1982	Jimmy Connors – USA	Martina Navratilova – USA
1983	John McEnroe – USA	Martina Navratilova – USA
1984	John McEnroe – USA	Martina Navratilova – USA
1985	Boris Becker – W Germany	Martina Navratilova – USA
1986	Boris Becker – W Germany	Martina Navratilova – USA
1987	Pat Cash – Australia	Martina Navratilova – USA
1988	Stefan Edberg – Sweden	Steffi Graf – W Germany
1989	Boris Becker – W Germany	Steffi Graf – W Germany
1990	Stefan Edberg – Sweden	Martina Navratilova – USA
1991	Michael Stich – Germany	Steffi Graf – Germany
1992	Andre Agassi – USA	Steffi Graf – Germany
1993	Pete Sampras – USA	Steffi Graf – Germany
1994	Pete Sampras – USA	Conchita Martinez – Spain
1995	Pete Sampras – USA	Steffi Graf – Germany
1996	Richard Krajicek – Netherlands	Steffi Graf – Germany
1997	Pete Sampras – USA	Martina Hingis – Switzerland
1998	Pete Sampras – USA	Jana Novotná – Czech Republic

Youngest winners
MEN – Boris Becker (W Germany) in 1985, at 17 years, 227 days.
LADIES – Lottie Dod (Great Britain) in 1887, at 15 years, 285 days.

All-time sporting legends

Muhammad Ali (USA) – Boxing
See page 367.

George Best (Northern Ireland) – Soccer
When George Best was a boy, he would annoy the neighbours by endlessly kicking a tennis ball against garage doors. He practised dribbling with it too, so that by the time he came to play for Manchester United, at the age of 17, the football seemed to cling to his boots by magnetic attraction.

Best shot to the top with United, helping them to win the European Cup and being voted European Footballer of the Year in 1968. He also led a glamorous life, but found that nightclubs, drinking and gambling did not mix with football. Best was only 25 when he announced his retirement, and although he attempted several comebacks, he never again recovered the form that had dazzled the world.

Fanny Blankers-Koen (Netherlands) – Athletics
A 30-year-old Dutch housewife and mother, Fanny Blankers-Koen, was the sensation of the 1948 Olympics in London, when she won four gold medals – for the 100 m and 200 m sprints, the 80 m hurdles and the sprint relay. Many of her fans were disappointed that she didn't enter for the high jump or the long jump, though she held world records for both.

▲ **Applause** Don Bradman waves his cap in 1930 to acknowledge the crowds applause for a fine performance.

Don Bradman (Australia) – Cricket
As a boy in New South Wales, Don Bradman practised for hours, hitting a golf ball with a cricket stump. Such dedication helped to make him the greatest batsman in history. In 52 Test matches for Australia, he scored 6996 runs, at an average of 99.94 per match. The English team feared him so much that it invented 'bodyline' bowling in 1932 to stop him. A bodyline bowler tried to hit the batsman, rather than the wickets.

Ben Hogan (USA) – Golf
Doctors feared that Ben Hogan might never play golf again, after he was badly injured in a head-on car crash in 1949. But 'Bantam Ben' was a fighter. The following year he proved the doctors wrong by winning the US Open championship. Hogan won eight major titles, including the British Open in 1953.

Barry John (Wales) – Rugby Union
His balance, his swerves, his sidesteps, his dodging runs, the pinpoint accuracy of his kicking, and his confidence made Barry John the complete rugby fly half. Only 75 kg (165 lb) in weight, he tormented the mighty All Blacks during the 1971 Lions tour of New Zealand, twisting past would-be tacklers. Small wonder they called him 'the King'. His partnership with scrum-half Gareth Edwards was legendary, but Barry John was a star that shone briefly. He retired when he was only 27, leaving his many admirers full of regret that they would not see him play again.

Jean-Claude Killy (France) – Skiing
Jean-Claude Killy first strapped on a pair of skis at the age of five. He left school when he was 15 to concentrate on sport, and won a place in the French national team at 18. His most dazzling years were 1967-8, when his daredevil style brought victory in 18 World Cup races – six downhills, five slaloms and seven giant slaloms. Killy retired at 24 to try a new sport – motor racing – before deciding to become a ski instructor.

Rod Laver (Australia) – Tennis
The son of tennis-playing parents, Rod Laver was dubbed 'Rocket' by coach Harry Hopman as a schoolboy attending a coaching clinic in Brisbane. He was Australian Junior Champion in 1957, and won Wimbledon in 1961. In 1962 he won the Grand Slam (Wimbledon plus the US, French and Australian titles) along with the Italian and West German championships. In 1969 he again won the Grand Slam, the only player to have done so twice. His tally includes four Wimbledon titles, three Australian Opens and the US and French Opens twice each.

Carl Lewis (USA) – Athletics
Carl Lewis has been described as the greatest track athlete of all time. In the 1984 Olympics, he matched Jesse Owens's record by winning four gold medals. At the 1988 Olympics, he won two golds and a silver medal, followed by two more gold medals at the 1992 Olympics.

▲ **Approach run** Carl Lewis sprints towards the long jump in 1984.

◀ **Maximum effort** Fanny Blankers-Koen flies in the long jump in 1953.

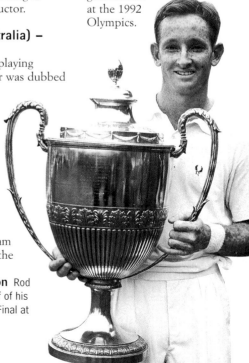

▶ **Proud champion** Rod Laver holds the proof of his victory in the Men's Final at Wimbledon in 1962.

Joe Louis (USA) – Boxing

Joe Louis was heavyweight boxing champion of the world from 1937 to 1949, a record of 11 years, 252 days that has never been beaten. He was known as the 'Brown Bomber', and was once described as 'a credit to his race – the human race'. He attempted a comeback after his retirement, to pay off heavy debts, but was knocked out. He lost only three fights – including the last one – out of 71 in his professional career.

Stanley Matthews (England) – Soccer

Few footballers have ever been more dedicated to fitness than Stanley Matthews, the 'wizard of dribble'. He first joined the England team as a 19-year-old, and was still playing on the right wing for England at the age of 41. His skills were displayed at their finest in 1953, when his team, Blackpool, won what has gone down in legend as the Matthews Cup Final. He continued to play League football after he had turned 50.

Colin Meads (New Zealand) – Rugby Union

By the standards of most rugby forwards, Colin Meads was not especially big at 193 cm (6 ft 4 in) and 104 kg (229 lb). However, he was so tough that team-mates and opponents alike called him 'Pinetree'. He won 55 caps as an All Black, and was a key member of the pack for a record 15 seasons. One achievement of which he was less proud came in 1967 when,

in a game against Scotland, he became the second player ever to be sent off the field for foul play in an international.

Eddy Merckx (Belgium) – Cycling

From boyhood, Eddy Merckx lived with a dream: to be the world's greatest cyclist. A punishing training schedule turned the dream into reality. He was the 'hard man' of the Tour de France – more than 4000 km (2500 miles) of winding roads, ferocious mountain climbs and hair-raising descents.

Eddy won the Tour five times, and the other riders were so impressed that they called him 'The Cannibal'.

Joe Montana (USA) – American football

Quarterback Joe Montana had an amazing ability to control a game. His team, Notre Dame, were trailing by 23 points in an important college match against Houston in 1979 when Montana led the fightback. He inspired, led and pushed his team to win 35-34.

As a professional, Montana led the San Francisco 49ers to four Superbowl victories – two of them after he had undergone major surgery for a back injury.

Martina Navratilova (Czechoslovakia and USA) – Tennis

See page 369.

Jesse Owens (USA) – Athletics

See page 369.

See page 369.

See page 369.

◄ **Acrobatic performance** Pelé delivers a powerful scissor kick during a soccer match in 1964.

Pelé (Brazil) – Soccer

In the 1950s, a brilliant new soccer star emerged in Brazil. Edson Arantes do Nascimento, the greatest player who ever kicked a football, won his nickname Pelé from his skill at pelada, the rough-and-tumble street football played by children in Brazil.

During his professional career, Pelé scored 1281 goals in 1363 matches – almost a goal a match. Two of them came in the final of the 1958 World Cup when Brazil, at their most majestic, beat Sweden 5-2. Pelé helped them to World Cup victory twice more: in 1962 and 1970.

Garfield Sobers (West Indies) – Cricket

Garfield Sobers won his first cap for the West Indies at the age of 17, and was 21 when he scored 365 runs, not out, against Pakistan, breaking a 20-year-old Test record.

In 1968, Sobers became the first batsman in first-class cricket to hit every ball in an over for six. Sobers was a great all-rounder, as well as a fine batsman: he was an excellent fast-medium bowler and a brilliant fielder. He took a total of 1043 wickets, at an average of 27.4, and made 407 catches.

Babe Ruth (USA) – Baseball

George Herman 'Babe' Ruth was baseball's most gifted all-rounder – a pitcher who won a total of 94 games and a hitter whose mighty swiping of the ball won

him the name 'the Sultan of Swat'. He joined the Boston Red Sox as a 19-year-old in 1914, and was sold after six years to the New York Yankees for $125 000, a small fortune at the time. During his career, he hit 714 home runs, 60 of them in one season alone (1927). This remained a record for the next 34 years.

Mark Spitz (USA) – Swimming

For 18-year-old Mark Spitz, the 1968 Olympic Games in Mexico City were a bitter disappointment. He had set his sights on six gold medals, but came away with 'only' two golds and one silver.

This 'failure' only made him more determined. In the next Olympics, at Munich in 1972, he took a record haul of seven golds, in the 100 m and 200 m freestyle, the 100 m and 200 m butterfly and three relay golds.

▲ **Water marvel** Mark Spitz powers to yet another victory in the 1982 World Swimming Championships.

Emil Zatopek (Czechoslovakia) – Athletics

With his head rolling from side to side, and his teeth clenched, Emil Zatopek looked in agony when he ran. But the real pain was felt by his rivals, who were left trailing behind. Zatopek set new standards for training, combining speed work with stamina runs. When he felt like dropping back, he forced himself to go faster. He once cycled from Prague to Berlin, to take part in a race, which he won. Zatopek was the star of the 1952 Olympics in Helsinki, winning the 5000 m, 10 000 m and the marathon.

◄ **The 'Sultan'** Babe Ruth could hit the ball exactly where he wanted. He is seen here in about 1920.

International organisations

International organisations help different countries to cooperate with each other on a range of important issues. Some aim to reduce the risk of wars, or to end them by settling disputes peacefully. Others work to improve living conditions, particularly for the world's poorer nations.

The United Nations (UN)

After the First World War, an international organisation called the League of Nations, based in Geneva, Switzerland, tried to resolve disputes between countries. But it did not have strong powers, and so could not prevent the outbreak of the Second World War.

In 1945, 50 countries set up the United Nations, with stronger powers to maintain world peace. In general, the UN has succeeded; it has prevented major conflicts from developing, though it could not stop a number of minor wars from taking place. Many more countries have joined the UN, which now has 185 members.

Switzerland is one of the few major independent countries that are not members of the UN. It has stayed out because it takes pride in being neutral –

▼ **Saving rhinos** Poachers kill rhinos for their horns, so the Worldwide Fund for Nature protects the rhinos by cutting off their horns. The animals feel nothing.

that is, it never takes sides in any dispute or war. In the UN it would have to take sides.

The main body of the UN is rather like a parliament: this is the General Assembly, which passes resolutions, although it cannot actually pass laws. It includes people representing all 185 member states, and decides all important UN policies. It meets from September to December, and at other times when there is an emergency.

The second main UN body is the Security Council, which has only 15 member countries. Five of them – Britain, China, France, Russia and the United States – are permanent members; the other ten are elected by the General Assembly for two years at a time. The Security Council is responsible for maintaining peace. If necessary, it can send peacekeeping forces (soldiers from UN member countries under a UN commander) to try to prevent or stop wars. But it usually tries to settle disputes by negotiations (discussions).

Another important UN body is the International Court of Justice, or World Court, which

▲ **Emergency aid** Red Cross workers deliver medicine and food to starving people in Eritrea.

settles legal disputes between UN members. All these bodies except the Court are based at UN headquarters in New York. The World Court is in The Hague, in the Netherlands.

There are also UN specialised agencies, which are devoted to particular subjects or problems, such as travel, trade, children, refugees and food-growing. Some of them were set up before the UN itself, but the UN coordinates their work. The main ones are listed below.

Food and Agriculture Organization (FAO)
Founded: 1945
Headquarters: Rome
Responsibilities: Agriculture, food and nutrition

International Atomic Energy Agency (IAEA)
Founded: 1957
Headquarters: Vienna
Responsibilities: Peaceful use of nuclear power

International Civil Aviation Organization (ICAO)
Founded: 1947
Headquarters: Montreal
Responsibilities: Air transport

International Labour Organization (ILO)
Founded: 1919
Headquarters: Geneva
Responsibilities: Employment and working conditions

International Maritime Organization (IMO)
Founded: 1958
Headquarters: London
Responsibilities: Sea transport

International Monetary Fund (IMF)
Founded: 1945
Headquarters: Washington DC
Responsibilities: Financial cooperation and support

UN Children's Fund (UNICEF)
Founded: 1946
Headquarters: New York
Responsibilities: Children's health, nutrition and education

UN Educational, Scientific and Cultural Organization (UNESCO)
Founded: 1946
Headquarters: Paris
Responsibilities: Education, science, literature and the arts

UN Environmental Programme (UNEP)
Founded: 1972
Headquarters: Nairobi
Responsibilities: Environment, pollution and resources

UN High Commissioner for Refugees (UNHCR)
Founded: 1951
Headquarters: Geneva
Responsibilities: Homeless people escaping wars and disasters

World Bank
Founded: 1945
Headquarters: Washington DC
Loans for developing countries

World Food Programme (WFP)
Founded: 1974
Headquarters: Rome
Responsibilities: Famine relief

World Health Organization (WHO)
Founded: 1948
Headquarters: Geneva
Responsibilities: Health and medicine across the world

World Meteorological Organization (WMO)
Founded: 1951
Headquarters: Geneva
Responsibilities: Weather research and observation

World Trade Organization (WTO)
Founded: 1995
Headquarters: Geneva
Responsibilities: International trade and tariffs

Other global and regional bodies

Several major international organisations exist outside the UN system. They include the International Air Transport Association (IATA), whose members are all the world's major airlines; the Organisation for Economic Cooperation and Development (OECD), an association of 29 developed countries that assists further development in those countries and coordinates their aid to others; and the Organisation of Petroleum Exporting Countries (OPEC), an association of 11 countries that depend largely on the sale of oil for their income.

There are also many organisations that link countries in just one region of the world, or countries that have similar political aims or historical links. An example of the last is the Commonwealth. This grew out of the British Empire – countries and territories that were once ruled by Britain. Now almost all these countries are completely independent, but most of them continue to have links by being members of the Commonwealth. The Queen is head of the Commonwealth, but many member countries are republics with their own president; some have their own king or queen.

Other important organisations include those listed below.

ANZUS Treaty
Australia, New Zealand and the United States are members of this defence pact, which was signed in 1951.

League of Arab States (Arab League)
Since 1945, the Arab League has promoted the political concerns of Arab countries.

Association of South–East Asian Nations (ASEAN)
ASEAN promotes the economic concerns of the region. Its members include Indonesia, Malaysia, the Philippines, Singapore and Thailand.

Commonwealth of Independent States (CIS)
The CIS was formed in 1991 by Russia and ten other countries that used to be part of the Soviet Union (USSR). Its aim is to coordinate economic policy and prevent wars between its member nations.

Conference on Security and Cooperation in Europe (CSCE)
About 50 countries in North America, Eastern and Western Europe and the former Soviet Union belong to the CSCE. The organisation exists to promote economic development, peace and human rights.

Council of Europe
Some 40 European countries belong to the Council of Europe, which was formed in 1949, and is mainly concerned with political and cultural matters. In 1958, the Council established the European Court of Human Rights to protect the rights of individuals.

European Union (EU)
Formerly known as the European Community (EC), the Union is an economic and political association of 15 countries. Formed in 1967, it has grown steadily, and several countries are waiting to join. In 1999, 11 member countries started using the Euro, a single currency, which will eventually replace the money used by each individual nation.

International Criminal Police Commission (Interpol)
Criminals who run away from the police in one country may be tracked down by Interpol. Formed in 1923, it allows police forces of 177 countries to exchange information about suspected criminals. Interpol works with local police; it cannot arrest anyone itself.

North Atlantic Treaty Organization (NATO)
Established in 1949, NATO was originally a defence pact between the United States, Canada and 14 Western European countries. In 1994, several Eastern European countries that used to be part of the Soviet-dominated Warsaw Pact joined with NATO in a 'partnership for peace'. In 1999, the Czech Republic, Hungary and Poland became full members of the alliance. In March 1999, NATO forces began a war against Yugoslavia, although no member country was directly threatened. This action opened up a new era in NATO's history.

Organization of African Unity (OAU)
Almost all African countries belong to the OAU, formed in 1963 to promote political and economic cooperation between member states.

Red Cross
Many people throughout the world owe their lives to the Red Cross. It was founded in 1864 to protect anyone wounded in war. Today, the organisation also assists people who have suffered from natural disasters, such as earthquakes and famines.

Worldwide Fund for Nature (WWF)
The WWF is a conservation organisation, which works to protect wildlife and wild places throughout the world. Formed in 1961, it used to be called the World Wildlife Fund.

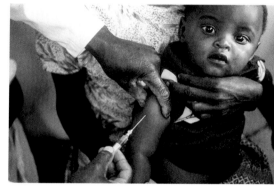

▼ **Safe** Thanks to the World Health Organization, many children are inoculated against common diseases.

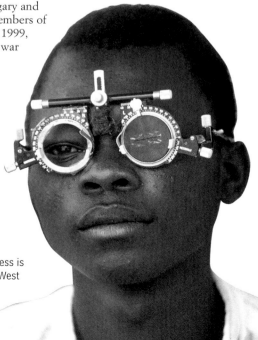

▶ **Eye test** River Blindness is an unpleasant disease in West Africa. This girl is being tested for signs of the illness.

Measurements

In everyday life, measurements play a vital part. Without them, it would be impossible to make machines, because the parts have to be exactly the right size; and it would be impossible to tell the time or take a temperature. Measuring instruments allow us to do all this – with an amazing level of accuracy.

The metric system

To work, measurements use fixed amounts called units. Ever since people first started measuring things, many systems of units have been devised, but today only one system is used worldwide. Officially, it is called the Système International (SI). In English-speaking countries, it is commonly known as the metric system. This system is easy to use because its units are based on the number ten and multiples of ten.

Basic metric units

The metric system has seven basic units. Each one of them is defined very precisely:

Quantity	Unit	Symbol
Length	metre	m
Mass	kilogram	kg
Time	second	s
Electric current	ampere	A
Temperature	kelvin	K
Brightness	candela	cd
Amount of a substance	mole	mol

Derived metric units

The metric system has many other units as well. These are called 'derived units' because they can be made up by combining different basic units. These are some examples of derived units:

Quantity	Unit	Symbol
Force	newton	N
Energy	joule	J
Power	watt	W
Area	square metre	m^2
Volume	cubic metre	m^3

The imperial system

Scientists nearly always use the metric system, but for everyday measurements, some English-speaking countries still use a much older system. It is called the imperial system in Britain, and the United States Customary System in the USA. Unlike metric units, imperial units do not fit together easily, which makes it more difficult to use them in calculations. Here are some examples of common imperial units:

Length
12 inches = 1 foot
3 feet = 1 yard
1760 yards = 1 mile

Mass
16 ounces = 1 pound
14 pounds = 1 stone
8 stones = 1 hundredweight
20 hundredweight = 1 ton

Volume of liquid
20 fluid ounces = 1 pint
8 pints = 1 gallon

Big and small measurements

In the metric system, units can be scaled up to measure things that are very big, or scaled down to measure things that are very small. This is done by adding a prefix to the beginning of the unit. As you can see here, these prefixes are very useful, because they save people having to write out very long numbers:

1 terawatt (TW) = 1 000 000 000 000 watt
1 gigawatt (GW) = 1 000 000 000 watt
1 megawatt (MW) = 1 000 000 watt
1 kilowatt (kW) = 1000 watt

1 millisecond (ms) = 0.001 second
1 microsecond (µ) = 0.000001 second
1 nanosecond (ns) = 0.000000001 second
1 picosecond (ps) = 0.000000000001 second

Conversion factors

You can convert an imperial measurement to a metric one – or the other way around – by using 'conversion factors'. Here are some examples:

To turn these...	into these...	multiply by	To turn these...	into these...	multiply by
inches	centimetres	2.54	centimetres	inches	0.40
miles	kilometres	1.61	kilometres	miles	0.62
acres	hectares	0.40	hectares	acres	2.47
ounces	grams	28.35	grams	ounces	0.035
pounds	kilograms	0.45	kilograms	pounds	2.20
gallons	litres	4.55	litres	gallons	0.22

Sizes and distances

All measurements shown are in metres

Width of a single atom	0.0000000001
Length of a bacterium	0.000003
Smallest object visible by naked eye	0.0003
Height of average man	1.8
World's longest snake	8.5
World's tallest tree	112
Tallest radio mast	620
Width of the Earth	13 000 000
Distance to the Moon	385 000 000
Distance to the Sun	150 000 000 000
Distance to the nearest star	40 000 000 000 000 000
Distance across our galaxy	760 000 000 000 000 000 000
Distance to nearest galaxy	21 000 000 000 000 000 000 000
Farthest ever seen	100 000 000 000 000 000 000 000 000

Times

Some time-spans: from fractions of a second to billions of years

Lifespan of a typical subatomic particle	0.0000000001 seconds
Single wingbeat of a midge	0.001 seconds
Fastest standard camera shutter speed	0.004 seconds
Single human heartbeat	1 second
Time for light to reach Earth from Moon	1.3 seconds
Time for light to reach Earth from Sun	8.3 minutes
Time between high tides	13 hours
Average lifespan of a housefly	40½ days
Time since computer was invented	54 years
Average human lifespan	72 years
Time since wheel was invented	5200 years
Time since people first began farming	12 000 years
Time since humans first appeared	500 000 years
Age of the Solar System	5 000 000 000 years
Age of Universe	15 000 000 000 years

Speeds

From the tiny movements of continents to the speed of light.

Continent drifting across Earth	0.000095 km/year
Hair growing	0.00063 km/year
Ice movement in glacier	0.032 km/year
Fastest growing plant (giant bamboo)	0.32 km/year
Crawling snail	0.011 km/hour
Fastest centipede	1.8 km/hour
Person walking	4.3 km/hour
Athlete sprinting	36 km/hour
Cheetah running	100 km/hour
Sound travelling through air	1238 km/hour
Rifle bullet	2520 km/hour
World's fastest plane	3528 km/hour
Sound travelling through seawater	5508 km/hour
Fastest manned spacecraft	39 600 km/hour
Earth orbiting Sun	108 000 km/hour
Light travelling through space	1 079 252 849 km/hour

Time zones

Because the Sun moves across the sky from East to West, the time of day depends on where you are. For example, when it is early morning in New York, it is already midday in London. To simplify time-keeping, the world is split up into 24 separate time zones. Within each zone, clocks all show the same times.

● am ● pm

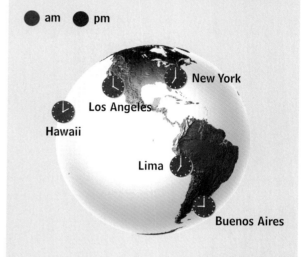

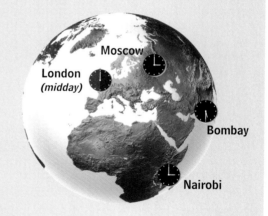

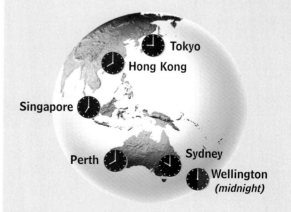

Acknowledgments

Abbreviations:
T=top; M=middle; B=bottom; L=left; R=right
BAL=The Bridgeman Art Library
B&W=Bradbury & Williams
IA=International Art
SPL=Science Photo Library
WLA=Wildlife Art

2 Top to bottom: IA/Lee Peters; IA/Paval Kostal; SPL/Rosenfeld Images; OSF/Peter Gould; Kevin Jones Associates; Popperfoto; Gerald Cubitt. **3** NHPA/Stephen Dalton. **10** OSF/Matthias Breiter, TL; Tony Stone Images/John Warden, TM; Tony Stone Images/Tack Dykingo, TR. **10-11** Kevin Jones Associates. **12** SPL/NASA/GSFC, BL. **12-13** IA/Lee Peters. **14** B&W, ML; SPL/Space Telescope Science Institute/NASA, TR. **14-15** Kevin Jones Associates. **15** Natural History Museum, London ML; SPL/Space Telescope Institute/NASA, T. **16** IA/Pavel Kostal, TR. **16-17** Kevin Jones Associates. **17** Mary Evans Picture Library, TL; JPL, TR. **18** IA/Pavel Kostal, ML; B&W, B. **18-19** Kevin Jones Associates. **19** NASA, TL. **20** Michael Robinson, ML; SPL/NASA, TM. **20-21** Kevin Jones Associates. **21** Colour Images Library, TL; Michael Robinson, TR; B&W, BR. **22** Michael Robinson, B. **22-23** Kevin Jones Associates. **23** Michael Robinson, T; DRK/Stephen J. Krasemann, BR. **24** Michael Robinson, BL; Magnum Photos/Rene Burri, TR. **24-25** IA/Pavel Kostal. **25** Natural History Museum, London, BR. **26** C.M. Dixon, T; IA/Pavel Kostal, ML, MR; Frank Spooner Picture Library/Naoto Hosaka, BL. **27** Kevin Jones Associates. **28** Michael Robinson, L. **28-29** IA/Ed Stuart. **29** Michael Robinson, TR; Tony Stone Images/John Warden, M; SPL/NOAA, BR. **30** Magnum Photos/Steve McCurry, ML. **30-31** IA/Pavel Kostal, B; Michael Robinson, TR, TL, TR. **32** Tony Stone Images/Jack Dykinga, TR. **32-33** IA/Pavel Kostal. **34** Magnum Photos/Hiroji Kubota, TL; OSF/Matthias Breiter, B. **34-35** IA/Mick Saunders. **35** Still Pictures/Gil Noti, TL; OSF/Terry Heathcote, TR. **36** DRK/Doug Perrine, T; SPL/Manfred Kage, M. **36-37** WLA/Mark Stewart. **37** Colin Woodman, TR. **38** B&W, TL; View/Dennis Gilbert, TR. **38-39** IA/Pavel Kostal. **39** Martin Woodward, TL; Planet Earth Pictures/Ashley J. Boyd, TR. **40-41** WLA/Chris Shields. **41** ARDEA/Jean-Paul Ferrero, TL; Gerald Cubitt, TR. **42** OSF/Martin Chillmaid, BL. **42-43** WLA/Richard Bonson. **43** DRK/Peter French, TR; Michael & Patricia Fogden, TR. **44** OSF/Survival Anglia/Joel Bennett, M. **44-45** WLA/Mike Rowe. **45** Bruce Coleman Ltd/Bo & Clara Calhoun, TR; NHPA/Daryl Balfour, M. **46** Planet Earth/Roger Mear, TM. **46-47** WLA/Mark Dando. **47** B&W, TL; ARDEA, TM; Tom Stack & Associates/Thomas Kitchin, TR. **48** OSF/Bob Goodale, BL; Tom Stack & Associates/Peter & Ann Bosted, BR. **48-49** IA/Pavel Kostal. **49** Natural History Museum, London, MR. **50** National Gallery, London, MM. **50-51** Photography Norman Brand. **51** Corbis/Bettmann, TR; Natural History Museum, London, BM. **52** DRK/T.A. Wiewandt, ML; Brown Brothers, BM; DRK/Steven C. Kaufman, BR. **52-53** IA/Lee Peters. **53** DRK/Don & Pat Valenti, T. 54 OSF/Mantis Wildlife Films, TL; Bruce Coleman Ltd/Peter Davey, TR; OSF/G.A. Maclean, ML. **54-55** WLA/Ray Grinaway. **56-57** Kevin Jones Associates. **57** OSF/Kathie Atkinson, TM. **58** SPL/Adam Hart-Davis, B. **58-59** IA/Jim Robins. **59** NHPA/Daryl Balfour, TM; DRK/Wayne Lynch, MM; Natural History Museum, London, BL. **60** Colorific/Louis Psihoyos/Matrix, BL. **60-61** IA/Lee Peters. **61** Planet Earth Pictures/Mark Schumann, TL; WLA/Cy Baker, TR. **62** SPL/CNRI, BL; Natural History Museum, London, BR. **62-63** IA/Sarah Smith. **63** SPL/NIBSC, TL; Auscape/Jean-Paul Ferrero, MR. **64** SPL/Vaughan Fleming, ML; DRK/S. Neilson, TR. **64-65** WLA/Ray Grinaway. **65** Auscape/Jean-Michel Labat, Tl; WLA/Robin Carter, TR. **66** Bruce Coleman Ltd, TL, TR; WLA/Cy Baker, BL, BR. **67** Martin Woodward, T; IA/Sharon McAusland, B. **68** OSF/G.A. Maclean, ML; WLA/Wayne Ford, BL. **68-69** WLA/Richard Bonson. **69** WLA/Wayne Ford, TL, TR. **70** Bruce Coleman Ltd/John Shaw, BL; DRK/John Cancalosi, BR. **70-71** WLA/Richard Bonson. **71** WLA/Cy Baker, TL; NHPA/Eric Soder, MR. **72** Tom Stack & Associates/David M. Dennis, M. **72-73** Kevin Jones Associates. **73** NHPA/Daniel Heuclin, TL; WLA/Philip Hood, TR. **74** Natural History Museum, London, ML; **74-75** Kevin Jones Associates; WLA/Philip Hood, B. **75** Natural History Museum, London, MR. **76** NHPA/Anthony Bannister, T; NHPA/Norbert Wu, BL. **76-77** WLA/Ian Jackson. **77** OSF/Peter Gould, TL; DRK/Norbert Wu, TR. **78** NHPA/Laurie Campbell, ML. **78-79** WLA/Robin Carter. **79** Bruce Coleman Ltd, MM. **80** IA/Sean Milne, TL; SPL/Claude Nuridsany & Marie Perennou, BL; NHPA/Martin Harvey, BR. **80-81** IA/Sean Milne. **81** B&W, TR; NHPA/Anthony Bannister, BR. **82** Robert Harding/Minden Pictures/Jim Bradenburg, ML. **82-83** WLA/Ray Grinaway. **83** WLA/Ray Grinaway, TR; OSF/Doug Allan, B. **84** DRK/Fred Bruemer, ML; **84-85** WLA/Ian Jackson. **85** NHPA/Anthony Bannister, T; DRK/Stephen J. Krasemann, BR. **86** DRK/Joe McDonald, ML. **86-87** WLA/Ray Grinaway. **87** OSF/Konrad Wothe, ML; FLPA/Joan Hutchings, BL; Tom Stack & Associates/Larry Lipsky, MR. **88** WLA Chris Shields, TL; DRK/Stephen J. Krasemann, TR; DRK/Johnny Johnson, BR. **88-89** IA/Ron Hayward. **89** NHPA/Kevin Schafer, TR; NHPA/A.N.T., B. **90** Bruce Coleman Ltd/Jane Burton, TL. **90-91** WLA/Sean Milne. **91** WLA/Sean Milne, TM; Tom Stack & Associates/W. Perry Conway, ML; Bruce Coleman Ltd/Peter Davey, MR. **92** DRK/Stephen J. Krasemann, ML; DRK/Norbert Wu, MR. **92-93** WLA/Ray Grinaway. **93** Tony Stone Images/Chris Noble, TL; FLPA/Weiss/Sunset, TR. **94** B&W/Martin Woodward, BL; B&W, BR. **94-95** WLA/Chris Turnbull. **95** Bruce Coleman Ltd/Dr Scott Nielson, TR; DRK/Anup & Manos Shau, BL. **96** OSF/Avril Ramage, TL; OSF/Mantis Wildlife Films, TR. **96-97** WLA/Brin Edwards. **97** WLA/Una Fricker-Bees, NHPA/Daniel Heuclin, BL. **98** DRK/John Cancalosi, BL; OSF/David Tipling, BR. **98-99** IA/Lee Peters. **99** Martin Woodward, TL. **100** NHPA/Rich Kirchner, ML. **100-1** IA/Sharon McAusland. **101** OSF/Peter Cook, TR. **102** Bruce Coleman Ltd/Gerald Cubitt, M; B&W, BL. **102-3** WLA/Jonathon Potter. **103** OSF/David Tipling, MR; NHPA/Martine Wendler, BR. **104** SPL/Petit Format Nestle, TL; SPL/J.C. Revy, TM; SPL/David Scharf, TR. **104-5** John Temperton. **106** Biophoto Associates, B. **106-7** John Temperton. **107** SPL/Salisbury District Hospital, TL; IA/Sharon McAusland, MR, BL. **108** IA/Sharon McAusland, BL. **108-9** John Temperton. **109** Roy Williams, TR; Allsport/Bob Martin, BR. **110** SPL/Ken Eward, ML; B&W, R. **111** SPL/Klaus Guldbrandsen, TL; IA/Sharon McAusland, TR; WLA/Sean Milne, BL. **112-13** IA/Lee Peters. **113** Martin Woodward, TR; SPL/Matt Meadows, BR. **114** SPL/David Scharf, ML; Liz Mundle, B. **114-15** IA/Sharon McAusland. **115** B&W, TR. **116** IA/Sharon McAusland, ML; B&W, TM, TR; Roy Williams, MR, BR. **116-17** John Temperton. **117** Roy Williams, TM, MM, BL, BM; IA/Sharon McAusland, M, BR, **118** Martin Woodward, TL; Ishihara Plates/Kanehara Shuppan Co Ltd, TR. **118-19** John Temperton. **119** IA/Jim Robins, TL; B&W, TR. **120** Debra Woodward, M; Martin Woodward, BL; Halli Verrinder, R. **121** Debra Woodward, ML; John Temperton, R. **122** SPL/Dr P. Marazzi, ML; SPL, BM. **122-3** John Temperton. **123** IA/Jim Robins, TR; SPL/Mark Clarke, BR. **124** IA/Halli Verrinder, ML. **124-5** John Temperton. **125** John Temperton, TL, TM; SPL/Astrid & Hans-Frieder, TR; Corbis, BL. **126-7** IA/Lee Peters. **127** Debra Woodward, TL; John Walmsley, ML; SPL/Richard Wher, BM; SPL/Geoff Tompkinson, MR. **128** Corbis, BL; Debra Woodward, TR. **128-9** Kevin Jones Associates. **129** Martin Woodward, TL; Dave Young, TR. **130-1** IA/Sharon McAusland. **131** SPL/CC Studio, TR; SPL/Petit Format/Nestle, MR. **132-3** Debra Woodward. **133** SPL/J.C. Revy, TR. **134** Panos Pictures/Eric Miller, BL; Bubbles Photo Library/Frans Rombout, TR. **134-5** Kevin Jones Associates. **135** Bubbles Picture Library. Jennie Woodcock, T. **136** Debra Woodward, BL; SPL/CNRI, BR. **136-7** IA/Lee Peters. **137** SPL/David Scharf, TL; Martin Woodward, TR. **138** Martin Woodward, BL. **138-9** Kevin Jones Associates. **139** SPL/Biophoto, TL; B&W, TR. **140** SPL/Garry Watson, TL; SPL/J.C. Revy, TR; B&W, ML; SPL/Maximilian Stock, BL. **141** Kevin Jones Associates, B; Roy Williams, T. **142** SPL/CNRI, TL; SPL/Oscar Burriel, TR; Debra Woodward, BL. **142-3** IA/Lee Peters. **143** SPL/Dr P. Marazzi, TR. **144** Debra Woodward, ML; SPL, TR. **144-5** IA/Jim Robins. **146** SPL/Rosenfeld Images, TL; Science & Society Picture Library, TM; SPL/Eye Of Science, TR. **146-7** Matthew White. **148-9** Michael Robinson. **149** SPL/Astrid & Hans-Frieder, TR. **150** Martin Woodward, ML; SPL/Peter Menzel, BM. **150-1** WLA/Jonathon Potter. **151** Allsport/Mike Dowell, TL; Rex Features/John Massis, TR. **152** Tony Stone Images/Paul Chesley, BL, B&W, BR. **152-3** Richard Rockwood. **153** SPL, BM. **154** Popperfoto, BL, Martin Woodward, TM. **154-5** Simon Jarret. **155** Martin Woodward, MR. **156** Graham White, ML, Martin Woodward, TR. **156-7** Richard Burgess. **157** Martin Woodward, BM; SPL/L. Weinstein, BR. **158** Graham White, TL, BL. **158-9** Science & Society Picture Library. **159** Michael Robinson, TL; Martin Woodward, MR; SPL/Alex Bartel, BR. **160** B&W, MM. **160-1** IA/Lee Peters. **161** Spycatcher of Knightsbridge, TL; Science & Society Picture Library, ML; MR; SPL/Laguna Design, R; SPL/Geoff Tompkinson, BL. **162** Michael Robinson, ML; Rex Features, BL. **162-3** WLA/Luigi Gallante. **163** Topham Picture Point, TL; Sygma, TM; Frank Spooner Picture Library/Alain Benainous/Gamma, TR; ARDEA/Jean Paul Ferrero, B. **164-5** Richard Burgess. **166** WLA/Jonathon Potter, TR; SPL/Eye Of Science, ML; SPL/John Burbridge, MM; Matthew White, MR. **167** SPL/David Parker, TL; SPL/John Sanford, MM; Genesis Space Library, MR; Matthew White, BL; WLA/Jonathon Potter, BR. **168** Martin Woodward, T, BR; Matthew White, BL. **169** Matthew White, T; Martin Woodward, BL; B&W, BR. **170** Autoscript Ltd, TL; WLA/Marc Dando, B. **171** WLA/Marc Dando, T; Michael Robinson, MM; Delphi Information, BL; Martin Uren, BR. **172** SPL/Rosenfeld Images, TR; B&W, BL. **172-3** Martin Woodward. **173** Michael Robinson, MR; B&W, BR. **174** Katz Pictures/George Steinmetz, BL. **174-5** Matthew White. **175** Rex Features/Trippett, TL; Kobal Collection, TM; Rehab Robotics – Staffordshire, MR. **176** Graham White. **176-7** Rex Features/Jackson. **177** Graham White, TL, BL; B&W, TR; Rex Features, ML; Colorific/Bob Sacha, BR. **178** Corbis, ML; B&W, BL. **178-9** Richard Rockwood. **179** British Library, London, TR; B&W, MR. **180** SPL/NASA, ML; Rex Features/EOSAT/Sipa, TR. **180-1** Kevin Jones Associates. **182** Martin Woodward, ML; Popperfoto, BM. **182-3** Martin Woodward. **183** Martin Woodward, TM; Sygma/Bill Natton,TR. **184** Science & Society Picture Library, ML. **184-5** Matthew White, T; B&W, B. **185** Rex Features, ML; Magnetschnellbahn-Planungsgesellschaft MBH, MR. **186** B&W, TR. **186-7** Graham White. **187** Corbis/Chris Ranier, TL; Corbis/Ralph White, TR. **188** Image Bank/Alan Becker, BR. **188-9** Graham White. **189** Hulton-Getty, MR. **190-1** Peter Sarsen. **191** Science & Society Picture Library, TR. **192-3** Kevin Jones Associates. **193** Genesis Space Photo Library/NASA, MM, BL; NASA, BR. **194-5** IA/Ron Hayward. **195** Royal Geographical Society, TM; Michael Freeman, MR. **196** SPL/US Department of Energy, ML. **196-7** Environmental Images, T; IA/Ed Stuart, B. **197** Martin Woodward, TL; IA/Jim Robins, MR; Graham White, BM. **198** Environmental Images/Phil Harris, ML; Ove Arup & Partners/Commerzbank, Frankfurt, MR; Corbis/Eye Ubiquitous, BL; Environmental Images/Martin Bond, BM. **198-9** Roger Hutchins. **200** SPL/David Parker, BL. **200-1** Roger Hutchins. **201** Martin Woodward, TR; Roger Hutchins, MR. **202-3** IA/Lee Peters. **203** B&W, TR. **204** Frank Spooner Pictures/A. Duclos M. Salaber, TL; Frank Spooner Pictures, TR; G. Dagli Orti/Egyptian Museum, Turin, BL. **204-5** Judy White. **206** Photo Researchers Inc/Renee Lynn, ML. **206-7** David McAllister. **207** Michael Holford Photographs, TR; National Museum, Copenhagen, MR. **208** Magnum Photos, TR. **208-9** Roger Hutchins. **209** Roger Hutchins, TR; Michael Holford Photographs, ML; Mick Sharp, MR. **210** Egyptian Museum, Turin/G. Dagli Orti, T; Martin Woodward, ML; British Library, BM. **210-11** WLA/Sally Launder. **211** B&W, T. **212** Royal Geographical Society, T; Michael Holford Photographs, BL, BR. **212-13** Matthew White. **213** B&W, TL; Popperfoto, TR; Royal Geographical Society, BR. **214** B&W, ML; Brown Brothers, BL; Fotomas Index, BR. **214-15** Roger Hutchins. **215** Brown Brothers, TM. **216** Science & Society Picture Library, TL, BL, BR. **216-17** WLA/Sally Launder. **217** Brown Brothers, T. **218** Michael Holford Photographs, TL; Sonia Halliday Photographs, BL. **218-19** Roger Stewart. **219** Aviation Photographs International, TR; Graham White, BR. **220** B. & C. Alexander, ML; Martin Woodward, MM; SPL, BM. **220-1** B&W. **221** Magnum Photos/George Rodger, TL; B. & C. Alexander, TR; Still Pictures/Jorgen Schytte, ML; Still Pictures/Mikkel Ostergaard, MR; Still Pictures/Ron Giling, BL; Trip/B. Adams, BM; **220-1** Sally & Richard Greenhill, background. **222** Sally & Richard

Greenhill, ML. **222-3** Rex Features. **223** B&W, TM, BR; Debra Woodward, TR, MR. **224** Michael Holford, TL; Impact/Mohamed Ansar, BL. **224-5** Impact/ Piers Cavendish, T; Collections/Brian Shuel, TL; Network/Nikolai Ignatiev, TL; Michael Holford Photographs, TR; Sygma, ML; Trip/H. Rogers, BL; Sonia Halliday Photographs, BR. **226** Fortean Picture Library, BL; Michael Holford Photographs, BR. **226-7** Roger Stewart. **227** B&W, TL, BR; British Library/ Oriental Collection, BL. **228** Martin Woodward, BM. **228-9** Ann Winterbotham **229** Magnum Photos/Richard Kalvar, TL; Michael Holford Photographs, TR, MR. **230** Kevin Jones Associates. **231** *Peasant Wedding*, detail, Pieter Breugel the Elder, Kunsthistorisches Museum, Vienna, TL; Michael Holford Photographs, TM; Debra Woodward, TR; Sally & Richard Greenhill, BL; Magnum/Abbas, BR. **232** Corbis/Bettmann, ML. **232-3** Judy White. **233** G. Dagli Orti, M; Corbis/ Catherine Karnow, MR. **234** Michael Holford Photographs, TL; Richard Bonson, BL. **234-5** WLA/Robin Carter. **235** Still Pictures/Peter Frischmuth, BL; Magnum Photos/Harry Gruyaert, BR. **236** *An Experiment on a Bird in the Air Pump*, Joseph Wright of Derby 1734-97, The National Gallery, London, T; Wall painting from Tomb of Nebamun, Thebes 1400 BC, British Museum/Michael Holford Photographs, BL; *Madonna and Child with St Andrew, and St Ursula*, detail, Bartolomeo Montagna, Pinacoteca di Brera, Milan/Michael Holford Photographs, BR. **236-7** Richard Rockwood. **237** Graham White, TM; Sygma/R. Bossu, TR; British Museum, ML; Photography John Meek, MM; *The Daughters of Catulle Mendes at the Piano*, 1888, Pierre Auguste Renoir, Private Collection/BAL/Peter Willi, BL; *Man with a Guitar*, 1914, Georges Braque, Musée National D'Art Moderne, Paris/DACS/ BAL, BR. **238** Frank Spooner Pictures/ Kaku Kurita, ML. **238-9** Roger Hutchins. **239** View/Frank Gehry, MR; Angelo Hornak, BR. **240** Graham White, ML; Russell Hobbs/Topham Picture Point, BL. **240-1** Matthew White. **241** Bizarre, series, Newport pottery, coffee set by Clarice Cliff, Private Collection/BAL, TM; Alessi, TR; Allsport, BR. **242** Sygma, TL; From, *Textile and Weaving Structures*, Peter Collingwood, B.T. Batsford Ltd, London/ Photography David Cripps/Bellew Publishing Co Ltd, 1987, TR; Frank Spooner Pictures/A.Duclos/M. Salaber, BL; Blown Beaker 'Nuppenglas', Cologne, 1886, R.G. Ehrenfeld, Corning Museum of Glass, New York/BAL, BM; Topham Picture Point, BR. **243** Topham Picture Point, TR; Debra Woodward, BL; Pond and Giles/Robin Carter, R. **244** Manuscripts Collection, The University Library, University of Sussex/The National Trust, TL; Kobal Collection, TR; *Apple*, pattern poem, 1965, Reinhard Dohl from *An Anthology of Concrete Poetry*, edited by Emmett Williams, published by Something Else Pess Inc, New York, BL. **244-5** WLA/ Sally Launder. **245** *The Inventing Room – Ever Lasting Gobstoppers and Hair Toffee*, illustrations by Quentin Blake from *Charlie and The Chocolate Factory*, Roald Dahl, Puffin Books, 1998/A.P. Watt Ltd, TL; Drawing by John Tenniel, from *Through The Looking Glass, And What Alice Found There*, by Lewis Carroll, Macmillan & Co Ltd, 1927, TR. **246** Topham Picture Point, TL; Sygma/S. Touhig, BL. **246-7** Denis Ryan. **247** Redferns/Geoff Dann, TL; The Warwick Gitterne, British Museum/BAL, TM; B&W, TR. **248** Magnum Photos/Ian Berry, TM. **248-9** Judy White. **249** Sygma, TM; *Peasant Wedding*, detail, Pieter Breugel the Younger, Museum voor

Schone Kunsten, MR; *Planted Seeds*, work by Darshan Singh Bhuller/Photographer Chris Nash, BM. **250** Popperfoto, TL; Performing Arts Library/Clive Barda, ML; Topham Picture Point, B. **250-1** Roger Hutchins. **251** Frank Spooner Pictures/ Guy Hobbs, TR. **252** Joel Finler Collection, Ml, MM; Kobal Collection, TR. **252-3** Jeff Anderson. **253** B&W, TL; Jim Henson Pictures/Peter Elliott as Buddy/ Photography Nick Wall, TR. **254** Frank Spooner Pictures, ML; Rex Features/Steve McFadden, B. **254-5** WLA/Luigi Gallante. **255** Rex Features/Peter Brooker, BR. **256** Colorsport/J. Langeuin, Tl; Sygma/Joe McNally, BM. **256-7** Allsport/Steve Smith. **257** Allsport/Nathan Bilow, T; B&W, B. **258** Michael Holford Photographs/British Museum, ML, BM; ET Archive, MR. **258-9** Martin Woodward. **259** ET Archive, TM; AKG, TR. **260** Mary Evans Picture Library, T; Corbis/Bettmann, B. **260-1** Jeff Anderson. **261** Frank Spooner Pictures/Andrew Reid, TR. **262** E.T. Archive, TL; SPL/Dr Yorgos Nikas, TM; Michael Holford, TR; SPL, ML; NHPA/ Stephen Dalton, MM; AKG, MR; Siemens, BL; Photography John Meek, BM; ET Archive, BR. **263** NASA, TL; Auscape/ D. Parer & E. Parer-Cook, TR; WLA/ Jonathon Potter, ML; DRK/S.Nielson, MM; Still Pictures/Frederic Diuillon, MR; SPL/NIBSC, BL; Jeff Anderson, BM; BAL/Walters Art Gallery, Baltimore, USA, BR. **264** SPL/Celestial Image Picture Company, BL; B&W, TR. **265** SPL/Rev. Ronald Rover, TL; SPL, TR; B&W, B. **266** SPL/NAO, TL; Associated Press/ Yomiuri Shimbun, TR; SPL/Royal Observatory Edinburgh, ML; SPL/Dr Fred Espenak, B. **267** SPL/David Nunuk, TL, TR; SPL/Steven Jay, BL; SPL/Pekka Parviainen, BR. **268** SPL/US Geological Survey, L; JPL, LM, RM; USGS, R. **269** Genesis Space Photo Library, T; JPL, L, LM, RM; SPL/NASA, R. **270** JPL, TL, TR, BM; SPL/NASA, BL; Novosti, MR; SPL/Novosti, BR. **271** Novosti, TL, BR; NASA, TR, BL. **272** NASA. **273** NASA, TL, MR; Novosti, BL; Genesis Space Photo Library, BR. **274-5** WLA/Jonathon Potter. **276** Tony Waltham, BL; Rex Features/ Jorge Nunez/Sipa Press, TR. **277** Still Pictures/Frederic Didillon, TL; SPL/Tom Van Sant/Planetary Visions, MM; NHPA/ Kevin Schafer, B. **278** Planet Earth Pictures/William M. Smithey, TR; B. & C. Alexander, BM. **278-9** Courtesy David T. Sandwell and Walter H.F. Smith. **279** Topham Picture Point, BL. **280** DRK/ Stephen J. Krasemann, TR. **280-1** Kevin Jones Associates. **281** OSF/Niall Bevie, TL; ARDEA/D. Parer & E. Parer-Cook, MR; Tom Stack & Associates, B. **282** Magnum Photos/T. Hoepker, ML. **282-3** B&W. **283** NHPA/B. & C. Alexander, BL. **284** Magnum Photos/Bruno Barbey, TL; Mary Evans Picture Library, TR; Colorific/Boccon-Gibod/Black Star, BL. **284-5** Dr Robin Adams/ International Seismological Centre. **285** Still Pictures/ Shehzad Noorani, ML. **286** SPL/Alfred Pasieka, ML, BR; DRK/S. Nielson, MR. **287** OSF/Niall Bevie, TR; OSF/Richard Packwood, ML, BL; OSF/Martyn Chillmaid, BR. **288** OSF, TR; OSF/Karen Gowlett-Holmes, ML; OSF/Barrie E. Watts, BR. **289** Gerald Cubitt, ML; NHPA/Stephen Dalton, BL; copyright 1997 Digital Vision Ltd, BR. **290** DRK/ Larry Ulrich, TL; Auscape/Jeff Foott, TR; Gerald Cubitt, BM. **291** SPL/David Scharf, T; Tom Stack & Associates/Rod Planck, BL; Bruce Coleman Ltd, BR. **292** OSF, TR; Auscape/Ben & Lynn Cropp, BL; SPL/Juergen Berger, Max Planck Institute, BR. **293** Bruce Coleman/ Jane Burton, T; Gerald Cubitt, B. **294** Gerald Cubitt, T; NHPA/Daniel Heuclin, B. **295** NHPA/Daniel Heuclin,

TR; Gallo Images/Anthony Bannister, MR; SPL/David Scharf, BL. **296** DRK, TR; NHPA/Gerard Lacz, ML; ENP Images/ Jeremy Stafford-Deitsch, BL. **297** ENP Images/Jeremy Stafford-Deitsch, TL; ARDEA/J-M Labat, ML; DRK/Norbert Wu, BR. **298** NHPA/Daniel Heuclin, TL; DRK/Doug Perrine, TR; Gerald Cubitt, B. **299** Hedgehog House/Barbara Todd, TL; DRK/Belinda Wright, BR. **300** DRK. Fred Bruemmer, TL; Bruce Coleman Ltd/ Staffan Widstrand, TR; DRK/M.P. Kahl, B. **301** NHPA/Dave Watts, T; Gerald Cubitt, B. **302** Auscape/François Gohler,TL; DRK/Wayne Lynch, BL; Gallo Images/ ABPL/Daryl Balfour, BR. **302-3** Gerald Cubitt, T. **303** NHPA/Christopher Ratier, B. **304** ARDEA/François Gohier, TR; Bruce Coleman Ltd/Rod Williams, BL; Auscape/D. Parer & E. Parer-Cook, BR. **305** DRK/Peter Vett, TL; Gerald Cubitt, BR. **306** SPL/D. Roberts, TR; SPL/Eric Grave, MM; SPL/Dr Yorgos Nikas, BL; SPL/Prof P. Motta, BR. **307** Siemens Medical Engineering, L; SPL/CNRI, MM; SPL/Prof P. Motta, BR. **308-9** Photography John Meek. **310** SPL/Sinclair Stammers, T; SPL/Dr P. Marazzi, ML; SPL/Eye Of Science, MM. **311** SPL/NIBSC, TL; SPL/ Clinical Radiology Department Salisbury Hospital, MR; SPL/Mark Clarke, B. **312** SPL/Manfred Kage, T; Sygma, MR; Audi, BL. **313** Magnum Photos/Abbas, T; SPL/Eye Of Science, ML; SPL/Alex Bartel, MR; Wilson/Hammer 6.2/ Photography John Meek, B. **314** Science & Society Picture Library, TR; B&W, BL; Katz Pictures/Visum/Gerd Ludwig, BM. **315** Science & Society Picture Library, TL, BL; Hulton-Getty, TR; Colorific/Kevin Horan, BR. **316** Tony Stone Images, T; Popperfoto, B. **317** SPL/David Parker, RT; View, TL; Arcaid/Richard Bryant, B. **318** Michael Holford Photos, T; ET Archive, BL; AKG, BR. **319** Scala/Museo della Scienza, Florence, TL; Ann Ronan Picture Library, TR; AKG, BL; SPL/Jean-Loup Charmet, BR. **320** Science & Society Picture Library, TL, BR; AKG, TR, BL. **321** ET Archive, TL; Ann Ronan Picture Library, BL; Science & Society Picture Library, BR. **322** Michael Holford Photographs, TL; Science & Society Picture Library, TR, B. **323** Science & Society Picture Library, TL; AKG, BL; SPL/Hank Morgan, BR. **324** Angelo Hornak Library, TR. **325** Mountain Camera/John Cleare, T; Angelo Hornak Library, B. **326** Sygma/D. Nicholas, TL; Roy Williams, TR. **327** Angelo Hornak Library, BL; Robert Harding Picture Library, BR. **328** Michael Freeman. **329** Magnum Photos/Bruno Barbey. **330** Michael Freeman. **331** Sonia Halliday Photographs/Jane Taylor. **332** ET Archive, ML; Magnum/Hiroji Kubota, B. **333** ARDEA. **334** Michael Freeman, BL. **335** Magnum Photos/Thomas Hoepker, BR. **336** Michael Freeman, ML, TR. **337** Sygma/M. Setboun, BR. **338** Roy Williams, MR. **339** Magnum Photos/ Abbas, BR. **340** Magnum Photos/Bruno Barbey, B. **341** Michael Freeman, T. **342** ARDEA, BL. **343** ARDEA/D. Parer & E. Parer-Cook, MR. **344** Michael Holford Photographs, TR; Sonia Halliday Photographs/James Wellard, BL; ET Archive, BR. **345** Michael Holford Photographs, TL; AKG, BR. **346** ET Archive, T; Michael Holford Photographs, B. **347** Michael Holford Photographs, TL; AKG, TR; ET Archive, BL; Sonia Halliday Photographs, BR. **348** Sonia Halliday Photographs, TL, BL; BAL/ Walters Art Gallery, Baltimore, USA, BR. **349** ET Archive, TL, BR; Sonia Halliday Photographs, M. **350** ET Archive, T, B. **351** BAL/National Library of Scotland, Edinburgh, TL; AKG, TM; Michael Holford Photographs, B. **352** Sonia

Halliday Photographs, T; BAL/Museo de America, Madrid, BL; ET Archive, BR. **353** Sonia Halliday Photographs/Jane Taylor, TL; ET Archive MR; Michael Holford Photographs, BR. **354** BAL, TL; ET Archive, TR; BAL/V&A Museum, London, B. **355** BAL/Louvre, Paris, TL; *The Iron Forge*, 1772, Joseph Wright Of Derby, Broadlands Trust, Hants/BAL, TR; BAL, M; *The Execution of King Charles I of England*, 1649, Weesop, Private Collection/BAL, B. **356** BAL, T; *Washington Crossing The Delaware River*, Emanuel Gottlieb Leutze, Metropolitan Museum of Art, New York, BL; AKG, BR. **357** ET Archive, TL; *The Events of February*, 1848, engraving, Musée De La Ville De Paris/Musée Carnavalet/BAL, TR; National Maritime Museum, London/ BAL, B. **358** ET Archive, T, B. **359** ET Archive, TL, BM; AKG, TR, BR. **360** ET Archive, TL. **361** Magnum Photos/Rene Burri, TL; AKG, TR; Magnum Photos/ Robert Capa, B. **362** ET Archive, T, B. **363** AKG, TL; Sygma, TR; Magnum/ Majoli Alex, BR. **364-79** Jeff Anderson, **364** *Salisbury Cathedral*, John Constable, Private Collection/BAL. **365** *The Houses of Parliament, Orange Sky*, 1904, Claude Monet, Musée des Beaux-Arts, Lille/BAL. **366** Arcaid/Scott Frances. **367** Theatre Museum/ET Archive. **368** The Kobal Collection. **369** Popperfoto. **370** *The Resolution and Adventure at Tahiti*, detail, Hodges, National Maritime Museum, London/BAL, T; Bibliotheque Nationale, Paris/BAL, B. **371** V&A Museum, London/ET Archive. **372** ET Archive. **373** Archive Nationales, Paris/BAL. **374** SPL/Mehau Kulyk. **375** ET Archive. **376** ET Archive. **377** Trip. **378** Mary Evans Picture Library. **379** Kobal Collection. **380** Harpsichord by Alessandro Trasuntino, Venice, 1531 (RCM 2), Royal College of Music, T; Pictorial Press/J. Mayer, B. **381** Rex Features. T; British Library/ET Archive, BM; Photography John Meek, BR. **382** British Museum, ET Archive, TL; Mander & Mitchenson Collection, BL; Rex Features/M. Le Poer Trench, BR. **383** Kobal Collection, TL, B; Hulton-Getty, TR. **384** Mary Evans Picture Library, T; Allsport/David Cannon, B. **385** Mary Evans Picture Library. **386** Popperfoto, TL, BL, BR; Allsport/ David Cannon, TR. **387** Popperfoto, T, B; Allsport, M. **388** Still Pictures/Jorgen Schytte, T; Still Pictures/Michel Gunther, B. **389** Still Pictures/Jorgen Schytte, T; Still Pictures/Mark Edwards, B. **390-1** B&W.

Toucan Books would like to thank the following for their help:
Sarah Ameyaw; Sarah Angliss; Jennifer Birch; Roy Brown; Leon Eversfield and Virgin Global Challenger; Norman Garwood; Sushmita Ghosh; Nigel Gooby; Richard Greatrex; Nicholas, Jane, Matthew and Joshua Henshaw; Geoff C. Hines, ABB; R. Holt & Co Ltd; John Keery and Clarks International; Marina Misaljevic; Sameer Naseen; Cait Penny; Pilkington Automotive; Piper, The New Piper Aircraft Inc; Railway Gazette; Eren Sarigul; Chris Smith and Ove Arup & Partners; Martin Uren; Colin Uttley; V&A Education Department; Stevie Williams; Jimmy Xu; pupils at St Michael's School, Otford, Kent.

Printing and binding: Brepols Fabrieken N.V. Belgium
Separations: Litho Origination, London
Paper: Smurfitt Townsend Hook Limited, Snodland, Kent
Front cover: Copyright 1997 Digital Vision Ltd, TL, TR, BR, BM; TRH Pictures MM; Arcaid/Richard Bryant BR.
Back cover: John Temperton, T; IA/Lee Peters, M; Lloyd's Building, B.
Spine: Copyright 1997 Digital Vision Ltd.

040-884-01